MY CENTURY

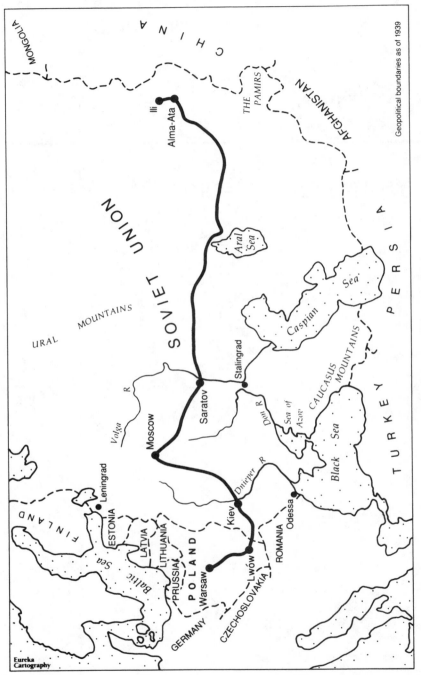

The Principal Points on Wat's Odyssey

Geopolitical boundaries as of 1939

ALEKSANDER WAT

MY CENTURY

THE ODYSSEY OF A POLISH INTELLECTUAL

EDITED AND TRANSLATED BY RICHARD LOURIE

WITH A FOREWORD BY CZESLAW MILOSZ

W. W. NORTON & COMPANY

NEW YORK • LONDON

Library of Congress Cataloging-in-Publication Data

Wat, Aleksander.
    [Mój wiek. English]
    My century: the odyssey of a Polish intellectual / Aleksander Wat;
edited and translated by Richard Lourie; with a foreword by Czeslaw Milosz.
    p.   cm.
    Translation of: Mój wiek.
    Includes index.
    ISBN 0-520-04425-8 (alk. paper)
    1. Wat, Aleksander—Biography.   2. Poets, Polish—20th century—
Biography.   I. Lourie, Richard, 1940–   . II. Title.
PG7158. W282A3613   1988
89.18'517—dc19   87–18457
[B]

First published as a Norton paperback 1990 by arrangement with the
University of California Press

The University of California Press wishes to acknowledge the generous
assistance of the Alfred Jurzykowski Foundation, Inc., and the Ludwig
Vogelstein Foundation, Inc., in the publication of this book.

ISBN 0-393-30685-2

W. W. Norton & Company, Inc.
500 Fifth Avenue, New York, N. Y. 10110
W. W. Norton & Company Ltd.
37 Great Russell Street, London WC1B 3NU

Printed in the United States of America
1   2   3   4   5   6   7   8   9

JAPANESE ARCHERY

1.
The hand tells the bowstring:
    Obey me.

The bowstring answers the hand:
    Draw Valiantly.

The bowstring tells the arrow:
    O arrow, fly.

The arrow answers the bowstring:
    Speed my flight.

The arrow tells the target:
    Be my light.

The target answers the arrow:
    Love me.

2.
The target tells arrow, bowstring, hand and eye:
    Ta twam asi.

Which means in a sacred tongue:
    I am Thou.

3.
(Footnote of a Christian:
    O Mother of God,

watch over the target, the bow, the arrow
    and the archer).

ALEKSANDER WAT

Translated by Richard Lourie

CONTENTS

CHRONOLOGY

1900   Aleksander Wat is born in Warsaw, May 1, to a family of Polish-Jewish intelligentsia.

1918   Poland regains its independence.

1919   Wat studies philosophy at the University of Warsaw. He is a co-founder of the Polish futurist movement.

1920   Polish-Soviet war. Soviet army retreats in disarray after the Battle of Warsaw on August 16. Poland is ceded western Byelorussia and eastern Galicia by Treaty of Riga in 1921. Wat publishes *Me from One Side and Me from the Other Side of My Pug Iron Stove*, a collection of futurist poetry.

1926   Wat's first trip to Paris. Piłsudski assumes power through a coup.

1927   Wat marries Paulina (Ola). He publishes *Lucifer Unemployed*, a collection of experimental stories. Vladimir Mayakovsky's first trip to Warsaw.

1928   With the idea of starting a magazine, Wat travels to Germany and France to make contacts.

1929   Wat begins as editor of *The Literary Monthly*, the most important communist magazine in Poland between the wars.

1930   Vladimir Mayakovsky commits suicide in Moscow.

1931   Andrzej Wat is born, son of Aleksander and Ola.

1932   *The Literary Monthly* is closed down by the authorities. Wat is imprisoned briefly, his first arrest.

1933   Hitler comes to power in Germany.

1933–1939   Wat works for Gebethner and Wolff publishing company.

1938   The Polish Communist party is dissolved.

1939   Molotov-Ribbentrop Pact, August 23.

1939   Germany attacks Poland on September 1. On September 6, Aleksander, Ola, and Andrzej Wat flee Warsaw. Traveling with relatives in two cars, the family is separated. As part of a secret understanding with Germany, the Soviet Union attacks Poland on September 17. Wat goes to Lwów, works briefly for the *Red Banner* newspaper, continues to search for his wife and son.

1940   Wat is arrested by Soviet authorities in Lwów, January 24. Ola and Andrzej are deported to Kazakhstan in Soviet Asia, April 13. In October, Wat is transferred to a prison in Kiev and then in late fall to Lubyanka in Moscow.

1941   Germany invades Russia, June 22. Lubyanka is evacuated. Wat is transferred to a prison in Saratov, where he undergoes a religious conversion to Christianity. In late 1941, Wat is released from prison. Polish government in London is now allied with the USSR. Wat travels to Alma-Ata, where he works for the Polish delegation as a school inspector.

1942   Wat is reunited with Ola and Andrzej in April.

1943   Stalin severs relations with the Polish government in April. Wat is deported with his family to Ili in Kazakhstan. In March, the NKVD attempts to force Poles to accept Soviet citizenship in the "passportization" campaign. Wat organizes resistance. Both he and Ola are imprisoned and eventually released. They retain Polish citizenship.

1943–1946   In Ili.

1946   The Wats return to Poland.

1946–1949   Wat is active in the literary world.

1949–1956   Wat is persecuted during the Stalinist era.

1953   Stalin dies.

1956   Khrushchev's secret speech. Gomułka comes to power in Poland.

1957   Wat publishes *Poems,* wins *Nowa Kultura* prize, is acclaimed by the young generation.

1959   The Wats assume permanent residence in Paris.

1962   Wat publishes *Mediterranean Poems* in Poland. He falls out of favor soon thereafter and is banned.

1964–1965   Wat in Berkeley. With Czeslaw Milosz, he tapes memoirs, published in 1977 in London under the title *My Century*.

1967   Aleksander Wat dies in Paris.

1968   *Dark Trinket*, poems 1963–1967, published in Polish in Paris.

FOREWORD

My Century differs greatly from those books that usually bear the name "Recollections" or "Memoirs." Because this book belongs to a separate literary genre—the tape-recorded conversation—its value as a source of information about this century is arguably greater. Although the syntax has been smoothed and repetitions eliminated, the features of direct speech to a particular listener have been preserved. The speaker here emerges more actively and vigorously than do the authors of written memoirs, and he freely reveals the movement of his thought with its attendant multitude of associations.

Aleksander Wat, who died in Paris in 1967, was for a shade under half a century a well-known figure in the Warsaw literary world, although his activities were variously assessed at different periods. At the very beginning of Independent Poland after World War I, Wat had a scandalous reputation as one of the Polish futurists. Later on, at the end of the twenties, he joined what was euphemistically known as the left wing, which included his friends, the critic Andrzej Stawar, the poet Władysław Broniewski, the director Leon Schiller, and the set designer Władysław Daszewski. Wat's absence from Warsaw during World War II did not mean that he was forgotten; by various routes word reached us of his imprisonment in Lwów and his deportation to Soviet Asia, and copies of his poem "The Willows of Alma-Ata" were also in circulation. After 1946, when he returned to Poland, he engaged in some literary activity in the period of initial "liberalism." Then between 1949 and 1954, he was forced into silence as a heretic. But finally, at the end of his life, he had a sudden turnabout in his luck: he was valued highly as a poet and considered a contemporary by the "young."

Were this book a memoir or an autobiography, it would have begun at the beginning, systematically providing all the information about the author. This book does indeed contain a great deal of biographical information, but since it is usually cast as digressions, it is advisable to provide readers with the basic facts so that they will know in advance whose story they are reading.

Aleksander Wat (pronounced Vaht) was the name under which he first appeared in literature. His real name was Chwat. He was born on

May 1, 1900, in Warsaw to a Jewish family with a deep sense of both Jewish and Polish history. Among his ancestors he counted the eleventh-century philosopher of Troyes, Rashi, who wrote commentaries on the Bible that are reprinted to this day; Isaac Luria, the famous sixteenth-century Cabalist; and Gaon, the great rabbi of Kutno, Wat's great-great-grandfather on his mother's side. Wat's grandfather, the owner of an estate and steel works, manufactured weapons for the uprising of 1863, in which his brother, Berek Chwat, was killed. Wat's father was a highly educated man, an expert on both the Cabala and modern philosophy. The house was full of books in various languages. The children were taught to revere Polish literature but also learned French and German early on, not to mention Russian, the official language in school. An upbringing of that sort led one toward art and philosophy and, in politics, toward socialism. Wat's older brother was a Social Democrat; he was to perish in Treblinka. Another brother, a member of the PPS (Polish Socialist party), emigrated and settled in Belgium. One of his sisters became a leading actress on the Warsaw stage under the name Seweryna Broniszówna. His younger brother, a painter, perished in Auschwitz.

Since religious issues are constantly present in Wat's poetry and may well constitute the essence of this book, a few words should be said about childhood influences here. Wat grew up at the borderline of Judaism, Catholicism, and atheism. His father was faithful to the religion of his ancestors but kept that religion to himself. Wat's uncle, a pious Jew, an ascetic, emigrated to Palestine. But there was no lack of Catholics in the family either, for one of his mother's relatives was a priest, the canon Luria who lived in Vienna. The most enduring influence was probably that of the peasant Catholicism of Anna Mikulak, a beloved servant for many years and almost a member of the family, whom Wat recalls with love and gratitude. As a child, he was sensitive to ritual and may have remained throughout his life what he was by birth, that is, an heir to the priestly caste. The Jewish holidays, with the exception of the Seder, were not observed in his home. Anna Mikulak often took the boy to church, however, and the Catholic liturgy, in particular the vespers, appealed to his youthful imagination. He said he owed his "first initiation into the thrill of metaphysics and into poetry" to Anna Mikulak's lullabies, and he learned folk songs and sayings from her as well.

This book treats the author's spiritual history, his literary and political adventures in Poland's twenty years of independence between the wars, and his fate after 1939. A general characterization of Wat's literary achievements, however, is appropriate here, for they are not touched on in *My Century*. An impartial assessment of his work is not, of course, attainable from people like myself who were his friends. Wat had extraordinary intelligence, was unusually well read, and had a refined mind; he was part of the Central European intellectual elite that was to be destroyed by totalitarian systems. In keeping with the customs of that elite, Wat adored intellectual debate to the extent that what he wrote always seemed a fraction of what he would say. Paradoxically, and contrary to his intention, his longest book was not the product of writing but this collection of tape recordings.

In 1918–1919, as a student of philosophy at Warsaw University, Wat's thorough knowledge of Schopenhauer attracted the attention of Professor Tadeusz Kotarbiński. At the same time, Wat was writing futuristic poetry, which horrified many people, including his mother's sister, who wrote and said that Wat was "mutilating the beautiful Polish language." Later Wat would always contend that he had not been a futurist but a dadaist, that a confusion of terms had occurred. Vladimir Mayakovsky, however, who visited Aleksander and Ola Wat frequently during his two trips to Warsaw, wrote in his recently published notebook, "*Wat—urozhdyonny futurist*" ("Wat is a born futurist"). Polish futurism is now being given ample study by historians of literature, and Wat's testimony will be especially valuable for them.

Without, however, deprecating the significance of the first revolt against syntax in Poland, it would be unfair to freeze Wat in his youthful phase—that is, futurism, or, as he preferred, dadaism—as seemed likely to occur. His first book of poetry, *Me from One Side and Me from the Other Side of My Pug Iron Stove*, appeared in the fall of 1919 (the volume is dated 1920). His next book, *Poems*, appeared only in 1957, and his third and last, *Mediterranean Poems*, in 1962. His poems in manuscript were incorporated into the posthumously published collection, *Dark Trinket* (Paris, 1968).

What caused that decades-long fallow period? *My Century* explains what Wat was doing in the meantime, and the more basic reasons for his silence can be reconstructed from this book, especially where he passes judgment on his one collection of short stories, *Lucifer Unemployed*, 1927. Europe had no shortage of people who suspected that Europe had destroyed its own foundations. Few writers, however, have achieved a level of derision as furious as Wat's in his perverse tales, which are akin to Karel Capek's anti-utopia and, in Poland, to Witkacy's work. Wat had arrived at a junction past which creative literature no longer had meaning.

How and why did that absolute mocker suddenly become an admirer of the Russian Revolution? This is a vast subject, and when dealing with it, the author is diagnosing not only himself as he once had been but thousands of other twentieth-century intellectuals as well. In any case, if revolutionary commitment stimulated many people to literary propaganda, Wat, after making his pact with history, ceased publishing his poetry and short stories, in which his muse may have proved wiser than Wat himself. As the editor of *The Literary Monthly*, the only communist magazine that had a genuinely broad range and influence in Poland between the wars, Wat engaged primarily in journalism; later on, when he had abandoned political action and was working as the literary director in the firm of Gebethner and Wolff, the mounting political menace of the thirties so depleted his creativity that his name scarcely ever appeared in print.

Only when his pact with history was dissolved did Wat the poet regain his voice. How was the pact dissolved? By everything this book contains—by everything that the author lived and thought through in Lwów in 1939 and in numerous Soviet prisons and in the desert lands of Asia—and by his illness, which began in Warsaw after the war, when doctrinal fervor was obligatory and Wat was one of the plague-stricken (the sight of him caused people to cross to the other side of the street). Wat suffered a stroke then, which should have killed him but from which he recovered except for the burst blood vessel in his brain that would for many years make itself felt in attacks of severe pain, a condition triggered psychosomatically and one for which the doctors found no effective remedy. Wat's true poetry was born of illness and old age and is a meditation on life, time, and death by a man who had been through too much. At the same time, the "futurist" of 1919 is constantly present in that poetry, as if he had been preparing himself to reemerge on this higher level of knowledge. Futurism is also the source of the mixture of circus clowning, dreams about his own life and about history jotted down with fresh, sarcastic exclamations, and philosophical maxims that makes it impossible to link Wat with any sort of esthetically oriented avant-garde.

Wat's primary place is with the people of the twenties, like his friend from Warsaw and Zakopane, Stanisław Ignacy Witkiewicz; in fact, Wat could have been a figure in Witkiewicz's gallery of "psychological portraits" or a character in one of his novels—but not one of the unrealized geniuses. Of the poets who emerged around 1918 with the program of "liberated words," only Wat—not Anatol Stern, Stanisław Młodożeniec, or Bruno Jasieński—was to achieve maturity and to leave behind poetic works of high quality.

After 1956, Wat began to receive fame and support. The name of the former editor of *The Literary Monthly* meant a great deal to those who had survived Stalin's destruction of Polish communism, and Wat had suffered greatly both in Russia and in Poland. In 1957 he was awarded *Nowa Kultura*'s prize for his book *Poems* and was now able to travel as well. Since the severe winters caused his illness to worsen, Aleksander and Ola (Paulina) Wat lived mostly in the South of France and, after 1958, in Italy. Somehow their passports were extended, and they enjoyed the status of semi-émigrés or, some might say, convalescents.

I had not known Wat personally before the war. Our friendship dated from a mournful New Year's Eve in postwar Warsaw and grew stronger during my visits to the Wats while they were abroad. I realized then that Aleksander's poetry was only a small fraction of a great whole that was constantly forming in him, demanding to be voiced; another part of that whole was his stories—the stories of a witness and a participant that charmed his listeners. If put to writing, that whole would have been a philosophical interpretation of the essence of the phenomenon that for Wat encapsulated all the degradation of the twentieth century—Soviet communism. Wat felt burdened with a moral responsibility for the sufferings of millions of people, whatever their nationality—the suffering he had encountered in one prison after another. This was before Solzhenitsyn, who was later to serve as an example of how strong an impulse the sense of moral obligation can be.

It is worth noting that Wat had no intention of inquiring into the offshoots of the principal phenomenon, such as the "people's democracies"; his concern was the "how and why" of the system that had arisen in Russia. His own reflections on that subject were based in part on his many conversations with Russian writers such as Victor Shklovsky, Mikhail Zoshchenko, and Wat's close friend Konstantin Paustovsky. After an unknown author writing under the pseudonym Abram Tertz began to send his work to *Kultura* magazine in Paris, thereby becoming famous in the West (for a long while afterwards it was an open secret that Tertz was the young critic Andrei Sinyavsky), Wat wrote, also under a pseudonym, Stefan Bergholc, the introduction to Tertz's *Fantastic Stories*. It is an excellent effort, both in its penetrating analysis and in its breathless, telegraphic style.

Would Wat have written his great summa if he had not suffered the severe recurrence of his illness? One suspects that the obstacle was not only his illness—pains in half his face and often his entire face and in his head made work impossible—but also the very surfeit of what he had to say which is evident both in his poetry and in the introduction to Tertz's book. As K. A. Jeleński justly remarks (Lumen Obscurum, *Wiadomosci*, London, Nov. 10, 1968, a review of Wat's volume *Dark Trinket*), Wat would have been satisfied only by the "secret of the universe," by a work titled *Everything About Everything* that not only would have included politics but would have gone far beyond it. It was not Wat's intention to be a chronicler of his century; what he sought was the secret, hidden meaning of events. For him, the form given Marx's thought in Russia was a tangible sign of verdicts that had to be deciphered and of the plagues that all humanity had called down upon itself.

Something should also be said of how this book came to be. In 1963 the Center for Slavic and East European Studies at the University of California at Berkeley invited Wat, who was living in France at the time, for a year in Berkeley. That sort of invitation is rare for the Center, whose range of activities does not include teaching and is, for the most part, limited to giving technical aid to professors and arranging lectures. Just at that time, however, the Center had a little more money than usual. Those who extended Wat the invitation did so out of the desire to aid him, that is, to assure him time free of financial care and to enable him to write. It was no secret that Wat was constantly in straitened circumstances. For a year and a half he had lived in Nervi, outside Genoa, where he worked as a literary consultant to an Italian publisher; then he revisited La Messuguière, the writers' colony near Grasse in Provence. There he wrote *The Songs of a Wanderer*—and he was indeed a wanderer, tossed one way, then the other. Wat was invited to Berkeley in the hope that California's climate would be more beneficial to him than that of the Mediterranean and would allow him to liberate himself from his illness. I would not wish to exaggerate my own role in Wat's invitation; the decision was made by Professor Gregory Grossman, then the director of the Center, and primarily by Professor Gleb Petrovich Struve who had recently met Wat at a seminar in Oxford and had been taken with him. Struve's opinion counted for more than mine; he had been at Berkeley for many years, and at that time I was still something of a newcomer.

The image of America that Wat brought with him to Berkeley at the beginning of 1964 did not correspond to reality—to that tone of daily life that cannot be put into words and of which books provide no idea. The excitement of travel benefited Wat's health, the pains subsided, and, for a few weeks, he was euphoric. The crash, however, came soon, and one may suspect that Wat's illness reemerged because of the alienness of his new environment.

As of now at least, more good people are to be encountered in America than in Europe. Theirs is, however, a somewhat coarse and seemingly careless goodness because there is a low level of psychological intensity in human exchanges here, both of the good and the bad. If

Wat, a typical Central European intellectual, had expected debate, deference, an attentive and devoted audience, he was sadly mistaken. He soon realized that no one had the time for long conversations here, that everyone was on his own. You want to give a lecture, fine, give it. You want to write, write; you don't want to, so don't. All this creates an impression of indifference, of the individual vanishing into a landscape and masses of people, both of which dwarf him. This impression may often be mistaken, but it can be depressing. Moreover, Wat knew enough English to read but not to speak, which meant that he had to seek companions among the small number of people who knew Polish or Russian. And then the question arose of how many of them would understand what he had to say. In the end, Wat's knowledge was nearly hermetic here in America.

Despite the rumors circulated in Poland by his enemies, Wat's was not an imaginary illness. But it was also never possible to predict when the physical pain would attack him. Wat ascribed demonic qualities to the Pacific Ocean, of which he had little notion when coming to California. The Pacific is, indeed, violent and cold here, and the extensive local mists are, in their predominant gray, reminiscent of some northern sea. The Pacific has a more elemental presence than the Mediterranean. Whatever the complex of factors, Wat began to suffer more than ever before; he grew thin, was at best able to go from his bed to his chair, and demanded that his doctor give him increasingly strong painkillers (Percodan). The drugs did relieve his pain for short periods but kept him in something of a stupor. How could he write under those conditions?

Could his unwritten summa have opened the door to the pain just at the moment when there were no obstacles to beginning that work? During his first euphoric weeks in Berkeley, Wat made plans, disturbing because of how much he expected from himself, both in the reading required and the number of pages to write. If he was unconsciously protecting himself from a journey into the depths of his being, he was also an excessively scrupulous man, and after a few days of idleness, he began to reproach himself. Professor Grossman attempted in vain to assure Wat that no one expected him to "produce," saying he would be better off relaxing, forgetting any obligations and doing some writing— for example, his memoirs. But months passed, the illness did not abate, and there was no question of any relaxation. This ate away at Wat, worsening his condition still further. Finally, one day Professor Grossman invited me to his office and said that Wat was falling apart and that we ought to search for a way to help him. But what? If, said Grossman, Wat complains that he's completely blocked and comes to life only when he starts telling stories that make him forget the pain, maybe talking with him and tape-recording the conversations could somehow unblock him. Would I take on the task?

I took it on. It must have been the beginning of 1965 by then—the Wats were in Berkeley until June 1965 and then returned to France. I would drive to the Wats' apartment on Benvenue Street a few times a week for taping sessions, and when they left for Europe, we had a substantial pile of recordings. Wat considered this no more than half or even a quarter of what he wanted to say. In July of that year, having followed Wat to Paris, I rambled through the small familiar streets of the Latin Quarter every other day to make further recordings, until the sessions that compose this book were done.

Initially, thus, the aim was therapeutic. We should not, however, exaggerate our love for friends—had Wat been boring, no doubt my good intentions would have proved insufficient. Something remarkable occurred, even during the initial sessions: I listened as if enchanted, and the greater the attention Wat saw in my eyes, the higher he would soar. It is worth stressing that the subject itself did not seem particularly attractive to me. I had long since settled accounts with the whole field of what is called political science, and my profession, teaching literature, had been the result of conscious choice. Moreover, if Wat's obsessions concerned his previous political involvement, my own sensitivity to such matters, considerable itself, had a different background; that is, I was less emotional on the subject. I agreed with Wat that communism lent the twentieth century its specific character, but, to be frank, I was also apprehensive that this book would turn out to be yet another confession of a disillusioned ex-communist. So then how was it that Wat was so stimulated by my presence that he called me his "ideal listener"?

I quickly realized that something unique was transpiring between us. There was not a single other person on the face of the earth who had experienced this century as Wat had and who had the same sense of it as he. This has nothing to do with the cruelty of fate or history, for an enormous number of people were more grievously afflicted by it than he was. No, what matters here is a cast of mind, a culture typical of a single geographical area and social class, not to be found among the Russians, French, or Americans—specifically, the culture of the Polish intelligentsia. But is that such a rare thing?

Let's put a finer point on it, then: not only was Wat a member of the intelligentsia, but he was also an intellectual, educated in philosophy, and his Jewish origins made for a valuable shading, one that provided him with a certain distance on Polish ways; moreover, he was a member of the Writers' Union for many years, and, further, he was a poet. These are the grounds that make Aleksander Wat unique. No one in his generation, I thought, was leaving historians a gift of this sort, in this field. That Wat had survived bordered on the miraculous, and so I thought it an honor to serve as a medium in those odd séances.

It was, after all, an unusual arrangement; it was not in Warsaw, where a multitude of involuntary constraints would have diminished the substance of what was said, but in America and Paris that a Polish poet spoke of his life to another Polish poet, younger by a generation. It was important that we belonged to the same fraternity, though he had emerged in the twenties and been formed by them, and I had been formed by the thirties. We shared a knowledge of the writers, the titles of the works, the literary gossip, the legends, and we were even equal in our ease with French and Russian literature. And so Wat did not have to popularize or explain, which would immediately have broken the flow of the narrative. I kept my questions to a minimum, asking them only when there were indications that Wat needed encourage-ment to launch a new monologue. I had the feeling that a record of twofold significance was being created; it was both a report on the be-havior of twentieth-century intellectuals petrified at the sight of com-munism—their Medusa head—and an indispensable supplement to any textbook on the Polish literature of our century. And, in fact, who would now dare to discuss Broniewski, Jasieński, Leon Schiller, Stawar, and a host of other figures from the boundary of literature and politics without first looking into this book?

Wat had such sensitive antennae that he could catch the slightest sign of boredom, but in me he found only interest. The taping sessions did not cure him, but they did replace paper and pen to a considerable extent. The responsibility for this book's not being twice as long falls on me because after I left Paris, Wat attempted to continue recording with someone else, and it turned out that the absence of a certain current, difficult to name, that flowed between us in conversation doomed those efforts to failure.

My relation with Wat should be described clearly here to allay in advance any suspicion of bias in my judgments. Our friendship was not particularly ardent and deserves rather to be called a relationship of colleagues, I the younger, he the senior (the difference between us was eleven years, a literary generation). My sense of stature was of funda-mental significance. Stature is not easy to explain. It is not measured by what is called talent, because the talented are not always deserving of respect. Neither is it measured by intelligence itself, for various uses can be made of that faculty. Stature is like authority, and when granting it to someone, we do not doubt that we are giving that person any more than is deserved by nature. At one time regalia, mitres, the ceremony of investiture answered our need for a hierarchy of value even though neither social position nor any other outward sign reveals true stature. Wat and I needed few words to understand each other and perhaps our common ground was our sense of how hierarchical the human world is.

In this book Wat pays homage to various people in keeping with their stature, including illiterate Ukrainian peasants, Polish workers from the Polish Socialist party, Jewish shoemakers from little Galician towns, and even Russian bandits. A certain personal magic seemed at times to save Wat from various difficult straits, and who knows if the people who felt that magic were not prompted, albeit unconsciously, by the same considerations that prompted me when, not closing my eyes in the least to his comical traits and faults, I paid him my respect.

Wat had no luck in his literary career. His book *Mediterranean Poems* had scarcely appeared in Poland in 1962 when his name was back on the index, though not as a punishment for public statements; exasperated by the well-known bureaucratic game of cat and mouse each time he extended his passport, Wat had finally opted for émigré status. Unfortunately, the Polish émigrés had very little idea of who Wat was. And when it came time to attempt to publish *My Century*, an incurable Polish defect once again made itself felt—poor discrimination of value, so that the higher and the lower, the wise and the unwise are placed on the same level, causing numerous works of value to vanish amid a universal babble.

To prepare this book for print required long and arduous labor, the greatest credit for which belongs to a person who herself appears in the pages of this book: Ola Wat. She transferred the entire book, sentence by sentence, from tapes to typescript, which she retyped after I had done the initial editing. That was not the end of it, however, for the results of those endeavors were only partially satisfactory. In my close editing of the text, I was guided by my concern for future historians; that is, I assumed that it was not for us to prejudge what would be most useful to them. Thus, the language spoken in the Warsaw intellectual world has been carefully preserved along with the numerous repetitions of words, sentences, and situations (the same incident presented a bit differently each time and thus with new shades of meaning). Out of reverence for the taped original I did not, however, make sufficient allowance for the needs of the nonscholarly reader who after a certain time would grow weary from too many departures from stylistic norms. I recognized the need for a compromise. The final editing and copyediting were done by Lidia Ciołkosz, after which the manuscript had to be retyped once again. I mention this to show that the path from tapes to the printed page is not as straight as might be assumed.

There is no question that *My Century*, the name we gave this book after due deliberation, will most interest readers who know "who was who," that is, those for whom the multitude of names appearing on these pages will be more than mere sound. As we know, time is unkind to most of those famous at one point and even if, in the desire to avoid any malice, we omit Polish examples here, a great many of those whom Wat mentions are known only to specialists today. One may well doubt that French writers like Henri Barbusse exist outside the encyclopedias now or that the name of Friedrich Wolff, the author of the play *Cyanide*, famous before World War II, has any associations for the contemporary reader. Yet *My Century* is capable of seizing even readers who know little of the times. The book is a shifting panorama whose action takes place in a variety of geographical settings, from Paris and America (if we count the stay in Berkeley) to the feet of the Pamirs, where, as Wat says in "Songs of a Wanderer,"

> in the whiteness of snow—violet mountains
> violet peach trees by violet rocks and the violet
> tenderly washed by the greens of a stream,
> a philosopher on horseback, a ragged knight
> in a scarlet sash from Kashmir, gallops wildly past us,
> la ilah ill Allah, us, bent to the dust
> by gray labor-camp sacks.

The book has many heroes, though it might seem to have but one: the consciousness of the narrator. As things now stand, it is no longer possible in the twentieth century to remove consciousness from the foreground, and we must always remember how much depends on its quality—whether the people described are distinct or cast into shadow. Wat had an uncommon ability to observe people—hence that multitude of characters who "seem alive," their gestures and even their moral essence caught, and that great variety of people representing various social elements and nations of Europe.

When Wat still hoped to write his great summa himself, he sketched out an introduction, which was found posthumously among his papers. The tape recordings, as we have said, arose in place of that work; nevertheless, Wat's introduction could also serve *My Century* to a considerable extent. In that text, he says:

The author is not a politician, meaning a person who makes history. Neither is he a historian, meaning a person who describes historical acts. He is a poet and, in so saying, does not have in mind the no-doubt-meaningless fact of writing verse but rather a certain specific way of experiencing all experience, which also includes the workings of history: he connects phenomena, facts, and events and expresses them in a certain specific way. . . .

And although the author is not involved in politics, politics has been his fate. "Politics is destiny," said Napoleon more than 150 years ago, at the threshold of our era, no doubt while looking off from the balcony of a small rococo palace in Erfurt that still reminds Ulbricht's subjects of the times when their rulers' world was a stage for games, malicious or pleasant. Napoleon had made the remark in admonition to Goethe, who was going on about Voltaire's "tragedies of fate."

Politics is our destiny, a cyclone in whose eye we constantly are even though we take shelter in the frail craft of poetry. . . .

This book is not to be an autobiography, a confession, or a literary-political tract but a recapitulation of personal experience in more than half a century of "coexisting" with communism. *Sine ira et studio.* In form it is close, *toute proportion gardée* to Herzen's *My Past and Thought.*

It remains only to thank all those who contributed to the creation of this book, albeit not as the author originally intended, and to its publication. I am grateful to the Center for Slavic and East European Studies of the University of California at Berkeley, which owns the rights to the tapes and which, free of charge, granted permission for a Polish edition; to Professor Gregory Grossman; to Eileen Grampp, the Center secretary, who always took efficient care of the recordings; to Roma and Simon Hersovici, who cared for Ola Wat after her husband's death; to Leopold Łabędź, the editor of the London magazine *Survey*, a true friend of Wat's and one who made efforts over a long period to find a publisher for this book; to Lidia Ciołkosz, not only the book's painstaking editor but a reader conscious of its value as a document. For Ola Wat, the executor of her husband's literary estate, the publication of this book is in itself recompense for her great labor on its behalf.

Czeslaw Milosz

*Translated from Polish
by Richard Lourie*

INTRODUCTION

Editing this book was more exacting a task than translating it. *My Century's* original two volumes had to be reduced by something like half. It quickly became apparent, however, that an obvious principle—retain the best, reject the worst—was not going to work here. The result would have been a march of brilliant disquisitions whose very dazzlement would have been treason to the original. After all, with the exception of a few chapters reworked in writing by Wat, this book first existed on tape, spoken aloud, proceeding by association. When I found myself sprinkling a little boredom back into the narrative, I realized that the translation would have to match the original not only in substance and tone but in pace and contour as well. It would have to reproduce the meanderings of actual speech and, at times at least, stay close to its original texture, which bristles with famous and forgotten names, political abbreviations, and details both global and local.

Many fascinating fragments also had to be sacrificed because of problems with context or transition. For example, too many difficulties of chronology were created by Wat's remarks on the infamous pogrom in Kielce, Poland, in 1946. Those remarks appear well before the reader knows that the Union of Polish Patriots worked with the NKVD or that the "delegation" was that of the Polish government in exile. Quoted here, it can both hint at the riches lost in editing and illustrate the historical acumen of Wat's mind.

WAT: In Ili, the head of the Union of Polish Patriots was an old prewar communist, a woman teacher, terribly doctrinaire. It must be said that she had a high sense of honor because in the period when the delegation existed and provided a lot of help to the Poles, she lived in poverty but never turned to the delegation for help. Never even registered with it. She was consistent in her communism. Later on, when she became the head of the Union of Polish Patriots, she was very firm in destroying her enemies. During the repatriation effort, she was in close contact with an old communist who had gotten through all the purges without a scratch because he was high up in the NKVD. This was a Pole named Spychaj, a worker, a Chekist. Spychaj was one of the founders of the Union of Polish Patriots and had been in Russia for many years. His younger brother was in charge of the People's Army in the Kielce area, his name was

Spychaj too. He was in charge of Kielce in 1946 when the pogrom took place there. He almost went to prison for that, but he was just transferred elsewhere, to another post.

MILOSZ: What do you think about that pogrom?

WAT: On the basis of what I've heard from many quarters, the pogrom was launched—launched isn't the word, more like provoked—by the Kielce security forces (there wasn't a policeman in sight that day). Spychaj was in charge of those forces. It should be remembered that Spychaj had that older brother in the NKVD who hadn't returned to Poland. This is all conjecture of course but the instructions must have come from the Soviets. In other words, the younger Spychaj was acting on orders.

MILOSZ: Yes, that's the same version I heard too. The point was to exploit Polish anti-Semitism in the international arena.

WAT: Yes, that was the point. Spychaj was supposed to stand trial but was transferred instead. And sometime in 1956 or 1957 when Poland started letting the first Jews emigrate to Israel, that same Spychaj was in charge of the security department that issued visas to the Jews. As an expert in such matters.

Like all intellectuals in a closed society, Wat had to rely on rumor, guesswork, intuition. His sense of German communism's being doomed because Stalin didn't want a Communist Germany was validated by Friedrich Wolff, a German playwright. Wat had met him in Berlin in 1928 and saw him again in Warsaw in 1934 or 1935 when Wolff was on his way to Moscow. Wat retells what Wolff divulged to him when they went out to a bar: "It was a tragic story. Wolff had been the head of a section, a communist cell. After the Reichstag fire, everything was put in place for a communist revolt, resistance. They knew where their weapons had been buried, in a woods outside Berlin. With German precision, everyone had been assigned a role. Wolff's group had assembled and they were only waiting for a messenger to bring them the word. But the messenger never came. Not just to his cell, not to any."

A sudden line now connects Wat's impressions of 1928, the burning of the Reichstag in 1933, and a quick drink in Warsaw a year or two later. The "ideal listener" did not require any segue or explanation and, for that reason, Wat could make great leaps of mind that kept stimulating them both. The printed Polish text, however, contained only what the tape recorder had taken down.

I was present at some of those taping sessions in Berkeley, listening with a mix of reverence and bewilderment as Milosz asked the questions that released the genii of Wat's monologues. Fifteen years after the fact, it seemed so fitting that I prepare the English-language version of *My Century* that I barely considered how many hundreds of hours it would take. It was to be a labor of love, and, happily, that labor is now done and the love has outlasted it, which is not always the case. For some reason, Wat, the sixty-five-year-old survivor, and I, the twenty-five-year-old American innocent, hit it off quite well right from the start. I dedicated a poem to him, for which he thanked me warmly in his inscription to a copy of *Mediterranean Poems* he presented to me. It even turned out that we were related; there were Louries (Lorias, Lurias) in his family as well. It was Wat who encouraged me to take pride in our common ancestor, the sixteenth-century mystic Isaac Luria. In that and many other ways, he exposed me to the real weight and range of time; that is, he taught me history.

Because Wat's primary interest was in discussing history as he had experienced it and reflected on it, because the life of his generation was so branded by the objective, and because he was reticent about speaking openly of the intimate, some of his best personal qualities do not stand in clear relief here. For example, the zany humor that plays over his poetry is largely absent, though a glimpse of that brio can be seen in the last photograph taken of him, in which he cavorted with his grandson. A month later, Wat's physical pain reached a limit beyond even his heroic ability to endure, and he put an end to his own life.

The great human beauty of his marriage to Ola Wat is more apparent in her book, *All That Is Most Important*, than it is here. Her account of those years rises to poetry, for even when separated from her husband in Soviet Asia in wartime, she and her son on the brink of starvation, she never lost her keen intelligence, her ability to observe, her capacity for awe. It is fitting that the epilogue to *My Century* be a section of Ola Wat's book, especially since Wat did not speak at any length of the rebellion he led against the NKVD attempt to force Soviet passports onto Polish citizens. His own book would be incomplete without a description of that battle, which was the ethical crystallization of all that he had suffered and discovered in Stalin's prisons.

Wat's transformation from a lost twentieth-century intellectual to an ethical being was amply demonstrated by the actions he took in Ili. The exact nature of the religious transformation he had experienced in Saratov, was, however, never as clear and definite as the consequences in which it resulted. The exigencies of editing material that was fragmentary to begin with might lead to the erroneous conclusion that Wat simply converted to Christianity. The reality was far more complex than that. Wat continued to move among various senses of self, various religious orientations, sometimes a Jew, sometimes a Christian, sometimes viewing Christianity as the culmination of Judaism or as a synonym for the West. Perhaps he is best understood as a man whose life was coterminous with this century and who had experienced all the beliefs, temptations, and despairs peculiar to our civilization.

One spring day in the middle sixties I saw Wat strolling across a plaza formed by UC Berkeley's white stone buildings with their Spanish red-tile roofs, the air smelling of eucalyptus and yesterday's tear gas. I almost called out to him but decided just to watch him walk by. He was utterly dapper—his moustache silvery, his dark fedora cocked at an alert, amused angle, the umbrella nonchalant on his forearm. At that time, I did not know that during the war, after months in Lubyanka, Wat had paraded through the streets of Alma-Ata in an excellent cheviot suit, a gift of American aid. Though clothing is always magical, no suit was ever charged with more significance than Wat's: "I was the embodiment of the West and Christianity. I walked about that barbarous land, that land of age-old poverty and Eastern barbarity, and I was an embodiment, an image, an imago. The imago of the West." And he still was as he strolled the campus that day. And he still is, in the pages of this book.

RICHARD LOURIE

1 THE EARLY TWENTIES. STRUCTURE OF POLISH SOCIETY. FUTURISM. JAN HEMPEL. WŁADYSŁAW BRONIEWSKI. BRUNO JASIEŃSKI.

MILOSZ: My first glimmerings of political consciousness came, as you might imagine, in 1926, during Piłsudski's revolution. And so I'm especially interested in that period, the twenties, a very important period after all in the history of Europe. It was right after the revolution in Russia, there were various leftist sympathies, Poland was finally independent again, and so there was a sort of euphoria that blurred all that. Do you remember what you were like in the twenties? Right now I'm interested in the emergence of ideological and political problems in the intellectual, literary world, that is, the connections between politics, Marxism (as it was loosely understood then), and the literary left in the twenties.

WAT: I use the word "revolutionism" because until about 1926 or so, it is practically impossible to speak of any Marxism in the literary world. The Polish Marxists in the twenties were a small sect and there was nothing new about them either; they were more like the remains, or rather the survivors, of the old orthodox socialism. In fact there was no body of doctrine at work.

What had happened? An enormous revolution had taken place in Russia, the contagious example of a country that had set to rebuilding itself from the foundations up. Whether that rebuilding would occur in accordance with Marxism or some other ideology was of no importance. What was important was that the rebuilding was being done by the plebeians, and from the very foundations up. But since that was a plebeian effort, not only in social origin but somehow in its *modus vivendi*, in its very style, a plebeian civilization, Russia was an extremely limited example for Poland; that is, it was rather limited to being a catalyst. So in 1918 and 1919, there were strikes by agricultural workers; the lower classes were revolting. Obviously, communist ideology was at work there, that is, the communist *praxis:* There were Russian-style workers' councils. But this was more of a catalyst that, though it had an effect, had no chance of success in Poland, because, in my opinion, Poland is not a plebeian nation in the sense that Poland was not attracted to any plebeian model, any ideal of plebeian life. And not only for the enormous group that had just emerged and taken possession of Poland, that is, the group that did not necessarily work for the state but who were officials nonetheless. Poland had become a land of white-collar intelligentsia very quickly and the liberal professions adopted their style. The intelligentsia's mentality was connected with a certain ideal way of life, the life of the gentry. *Pan Tadeusz*—was the Polish bible as well as the Polish *Iliad*.* So what appeal could that plebeian ideal have not only for the intelligentsia but for the middle classes, to which the intelligentsia, the most active group of the period, were at that time related?

Then there were the peasants. The Polish peasants were always very taken by the culture of the gentry. Always! And so who were those peasants? Poor country people, poor villagers. The farm hands had rebelled, but in the mass they really had no hope of having land of their own. They were unsettled people, though they did have their own workplaces, their unions, but they were unsettled in the medieval sense, that is, subject to all the currents of revolutionary change. But all those farm-hand revolts found no support in the countryside—not among the rich peasants, the so-called kulaks, and not among the poor villagers and poor country people either. Because, finally, the poor Polish peasant's ideal was the well-to-do peasant, and that brings us back to *Pan Tadeusz* and the ideal of the yeoman. Great and small landowners were often related, as they were where you come from in Lithuania.

And so, the workers. The workers in Poland were a fresh phenomenon. What is called the proletariat, that class with the romance of revolution about it; you may remember that very fin de siècle image, the classic Greek profile of a worker, his chest bared, wonderful biceps, a hammer in his hand, and in the background a sun with large rays rising above the horizon. That really says everything about that myth of the victorious proletariat. The same mythology is in the song "The Red Banner." That was the sphere of influence of the PPS [Polish Socialist Party], the better-paid workers, from a generation or two of skilled

* *Pan Tadeusz*, by Adam Mickiewicz (1798–1855). A long poem, something between a novel in verse and an epic, its place in Polish literature is like that of *Don Quixote* in Spanish literature and *Eugene Onegin* in Russian. Czeslaw Milosz has called *Pan Tadeusz* "a vast panorama of a gentry society at the moment it is living through its last days" (*The History of Polish Literature*, 2d ed. [Berkeley: University of California Press, 1983], p. 228).

2

workers. All the rest of the workers were connected to the peasant proletariat, from the country; in large measure we're seeing the same process today except on a significantly larger scale.

And then there were the Jews. There was practically no Jewish proletariat; even the big Jewish factory owners did not allow Jews to work
in the big factories. They were cottage-industry workers and small
tradesmen, tailors, needleworkers. For example, one of the most active revolutionary unions was the needleworkers' union. Many of the
wives of today's ministers, many of the egerias of the communist poets,
today's high-ranking women officials in the UB [Polish equivalent of the
KGB] were either from the needleworkers' union or the Jewish nurses'
union. They were the most active, the most revolutionary, the most
heroic element. The women communists who spent time in prison,
who were always raising money, were mainly nurses and needleworkers. It must be admitted, though, that there weren't many of them, but
they were an enormously dynamic element. Today, communist publications exaggerate the influence of the Communist party in Poland.
Quantitatively the Communist party was not large, but one communist
was worth several people, especially since the women in those unions
were a very intelligent element, eager for self-education.

But let's return to your question. One cannot speak of any ideology
radiating outside those circles in the beginning of the twenties. You
spoke of the contact between ideology and literature—there wasn't
any. Around 1924 when our group of futurists and dadaists got fed up
with futurism, that is, when we came to the conclusion that things
couldn't go on like that, Stefan Kordian Gacki founded the magazine
F 24, the first avant-garde magazine, which, among other things, published Ważyk's *Semaphores*. But all of us, meaning a few young people,
were undoubtedly under the influence of futurism and the Russian
Revolution. Jasieński arrived back from Russia in 1919 or 1920; he had
seen it all. He had gone through the revolution in Russia, and he began
writing by imitating the futurists and all that, just as Skamander had
begun by imitating.*

In any case, ours was a group of young people who had neither Skamander's influence nor its skill. We were very clumsy, a far cry from
their fantastic formal skill. We weren't rooted in the tradition of Polish
poetry; we were rather under foreign influence, reading foreign poetry. In that respect, Skamander had the advantage. Our group defi-

---

* Skamander. A literary journal and the group of poets around it. The first movement of
  poets in independent Poland, it was lyrical in tone and liberal politically.

3

nitely had less panache and was less rich in talent. The group of young people who had formed Skamander was truly talented. The difference between us, however, was that the Skamander people occupied an excellent position in the official intelligentsia, a bourgeois realm, Polish provincialism really, while we young people in those turbulent little groups on the margins of Skamander had something over them. I don't know if it was an advantage or a disadvantage, but we had begun to realize that the old had come to an end. Some absolute change had occurred and you had to make changes; it didn't matter how, what, or where, but you had to break things, change.

At that time, social issues were not of much concern to me. I had been fired up by a completely different sort of reading, starting with Nietzsche, Kierkegaard, Stirner, and God knows what else, and all that led me away from any communism or socialism. But naturally there was some *feeling*, some emotional pull. First and foremost, there was a need, intellectual but emotional as well, for a total renewal, a feeling that some sort of earthquake had occurred, an absolute earthquake, a feeling that none of the elite in Skamander had experienced. In my case, this had nothing to do with the Russian Revolution; rather, it might have been the influence of the books I'd read that anticipated a catastrophe, the decadence of Europe, Spenglerism before there was a Spengler—moods that were, after all, intense in the Europe of those years. There was dadaism, which might of course also be called nihilism, a loss of faith in the possibility of any future for European civilization, a questioning of European civilization. So, even though we were still kids, Poland's new independence was for us considerably less important than the overall catastrophe of the age, the great unknown that lay ahead of us. Besides, since we were young and devil-may-care, all that seemed terrifically promising to us. It's my impression that this is the difference between the catastrophism of my generation and yours.

The catastrophism of your generation coincided with Stalinism on one side and Hitlerism on the other. You were caught in that scissors, especially in Poland. You too had a feeling, perhaps a deeper one, that an era had ended, that the world had ended, that civilization was impossible, but at the same time you were caught between two enormously powerful, dynamic monsters. In your day, Poland's situation really did make that communist adagio seem credible: either fascism or communism. That sounded credible given the Polish situation in the thirties. My generation, that is, people like myself had the same feeling of catastrophism. But we didn't have those monsters in front of us; just the reverse, we had a chasm in front of us, ruins, *à la longue* cheerful ruins, you see, a cause for spiritual joy because here, precisely, something new could be built, the great unknown, the journey into the unknown, the great hope that from this, these ruins . . .

MILOSZ: I'd like to remind you that that joy was also evident in the poetry of Skamander, more or less before 1930.

WAT: That's true, to some degree. That was a different joy, however. That was a patriotic joy that a normal society had come into being, Poland as a normal society where poets could exist and write normally, fulfill the normal function of the poet. That was their great joy.

But for us the joy came from the fundamental collapse, that there was now room for everything, that everything was doable. The joy that everything was doable. And in that regard perhaps even the word "futurism" makes a certain sense. When Marinetti went to Russia, the futurists there gave him a chilly reception. Their ideologies were at odds; they were for a socialist revolution, then a communist one, and Marinetti was for the war, for fascism, militarism, and so on. Marinetti wrote very little, in fact, no real work at all, but that's not what matters here.

We didn't know a single futurist work when we launched our own futurism. One slogan was enough, one little discovery, one phrase composed of two words: "liberated words." You see, that slogan, the idea of words being liberated, that words were things and you could do whatever you liked with them, that was an enormous revolution in literature; that was a revolution like, let's say, Nietzsche's "God is dead." Suddenly, words were liberated; you could do what you wanted with them. And that provided us with an incredible dynamism. Had there been no Marinetti, either there would have been no Joyce, not to mention Khlebnikov or Mayakovsky, or else Joyce or Khlebnikov and Mayakovsky would have had to create Marinettism. Because that's where you had to begin—establishing the freedom of words.

Socially, politically, we were cynical. At bottom we conceived of socialism as the socialist doctrine, the socialist ideal. We fancied ourselves enemies of collectivism, precisely that, collectivism. We were against all rules and regulations. By analogy we saw the Russian Revolution, what we knew of it, as a hundred and fifty million people on an enormous territory who were destroying absolutely everything that had existed until then, as Mayakovsky had written even before the Revolution; that everything could be made anew, the way you wanted it, that was fascinating, of course, to the imagination of intellectuals. And again, by analogy, we thought a revolution in literature is, in fact, a social revolution. No one knew what communism would be like. For the time we thought of it as a great nihilism, the masses in a great convulsion, a bloody one, it's true, but as Pilnyak portrayed it—that village Russia, that savagery, those archaic forces that had erupted, that was no longer *demos* but really the most archaic layers of the population. The dark sectarian layers, Russia inundated by sectarianism—all that was very attractive to us in our esthetic, literary revolution.

Well, at a certain moment we took a step and joined Hempel's *New Culture (Nowa Kultura)*. That was a monthly. I remember that I contributed some crazy short story about Azef, the double agent. Then I contributed a poem about God the policeman, very atheistic. I was there and Stern, Jasieński, Brucz, and Broniewski as well.

How did Broniewski get mixed up in this? I met Broniewski at the university, in the philosophy department. He was an officer, just demobilized after seven years of combat, a God-seeker, undergoing some crisis in his worldview, which he took with incredible seriousness. He lived with his mother and sisters on Danilowiczowska Street; his uncle, maternal or paternal, was General Konarzewski. He had an archetypal nobleman's room, with a Persian rug, crossed swords, daggers from his ancestors. There was an upright piano there, too, and he used to torture us with it: the way he played Chopin was godawful, but you had to listen because he was very despotic about that. At the same time he had a certain, let us say, intellectual coarseness, which he retained till the end. For he was not an intellectual. Let's not overdo that either, for sometimes between his third and his fifth drink, he would display an excellent intellectual wit, a very fine wit, but only then. It was different at different times, sometimes between the second and fourth drink, sometimes between the third and the fifth.

Formally, Broniewski was a Skamandrite. It was the poetic tradition that made him reject us; he saw us as barbarians—and that was true—and as anti-Polish because our poetry was absolutely un-Polish. But, on the other hand, Lenin, and Mayakovsky, who also repelled him formally at that time—Mayakovsky the bard of the Revolution—propelled Broniewski toward us, the futurists who wanted to make a revolution in literature. Besides, we were under the influence of Mayakovsky, which, spiritually, ideologically, made us closest to Broniewski. And so he hung around with us and could not bring himself to go over to Skamander. And so he wound up with Hempel. As far as I recall, it was he who initiated that alliance, that contact between us and Hempel. That Ark of the Covenant.

Hempel was already with the communists. Hempel was a very curious Polish phenomenon. His family—one nephew was ambassador to Japan, and he himself had been connected with the Piłsudski-ites way back, at one point in his early youth. He had been a God-seeker, a

6

theosophist; he began by writing theosophical poetry, and he founded the Theosophical Society, a circle of people who lived in Zakopane and prayed to the sun from a mountain every day at sunrise. There were little groups like that back then in Poland. It's not generally known how many such eccentric little groups there were at the beginning of the twentieth century.

In the period I'm talking about, Hempel was already committed, every inch of the way, to communism. He had married a worker, a simple working woman; he had taken courses in Russia and by that time was already a paid party functionary. There was such a category; they were paid very poorly; in fact, they lived in poverty, but they were already officials, already apparatchiks. Hempel was the first apparatchik I had ever known. And it was in his capacity as an apparatchik that I made his acquaintance. He was a very noble, good person, with very noble intentions, but I saw him as browbeaten and frightened of his superiors. The man I came to know was an exhausted errand boy, tied hand and foot. Back then, at *New Culture*, he still seemed the master of the magazine, an editor, an ideologue. But back then—this was 1923, 1924—the party organization was quite loose; the party was not a monolith yet. After the third issue, which contained our futurist poetry, a terrible scandal erupted in the heart of the party. Hempel was given an incredible tongue-lashing, which was followed by our dismissal. He just threw us out, broke with us. But he kept Broniewski on as secretary of *New Culture*. And so that was the first contact between the literary avant-garde and the party, based on mutual misunderstandings. The illusions on both sides were dispelled quite quickly.

MILOSZ: Excuse me, but now a little chronology. I don't remember if, for example, we've spoken about Bruno Jasieński. He published *Boot in the Buttonhole* in 1921. When did he write *The Tale of Jakub Szela?*

WAT: Oh, that was much later, much later. In 1926. He was in his communist period by then. And when did Jasieński's communism begin? Jasieński left for Paris with his wife in 1925. His father-in-law, a wealthy merchant in Lwów, had given them some money. But still they had to rough it in Paris. I arrived in Paris in 1926, at the end of May. He was in very bad straits, and because we saw each other every day, I knew that it was poverty that turned him into a communist.

He had, however, already gone through a certain evolution, for not very much remained of the arch-snob with the monocle and the curl on his forehead, always on the prowl and surrounded by young women as he had been in Warsaw and Kraków. In Lwów he became friendly with a theatrical troupe that was leaning toward communism, and he was

7

already transformed; you could already see what Russians call *zakalka*, the "tempering," the traces of ideological ferment. At least it was there when I talked with him in Paris. But his conversion to communism was sealed in connection with the scandal over *I Burn Paris* when the French authorities expelled him for that book, which caused a great outcry. I was there when he got the idea for *I Burn Paris*—which came from his insufficient knowledge of French. This is exactly what happened. One day Jasieński came home—I was there for lunch—and he said with incredible passion and fury that he had seen Morand's new book, *Je brûle Moscou*, on display in a bookstore. He was enraged and kept striding around the apartment, swearing, unable to get a hold of himself . . .

MILOSZ: He didn't know that *brûler* had another meaning, to pass through a place quickly?

WAT: Three or four days later he told me the plot of the novel he was going to write, *Je brûle Paris*. That's how great works of literature come about sometimes. He was expelled from France in 1929 for *Je brûle Paris*. From Paris he went straight to Leningrad by ship. I've seen a photograph: a great triumphal arch in Leningrad, enormous crowds.

Jasieński's *Song of Hunger* had been written very early, in 1922, in Poland. He had come as a young man from Russia, very full of himself yet at the same time terribly cynical, and that cannot be called communism. In any case that wasn't communism, that was bolshevism, and it certainly wasn't Marxism. He hadn't had any organizational connections before. He became connected only in Russia, and there he at once began a great career as a communist: unfortunately, he behaved very badly in Russia. He was very active in organizing the International Writers' Congress; he was in the Literary International, in the administration. In 1934 there was that big congress that Malraux attended. Jasieński organized that one. Jasieński initiated the campaign against Babel; yes, he was one of those who attacked Babel the hardest. Jasieński was extremely active then, horribly sectarian; he was among the most repressive, even against Mayakovsky.

Moreover, he was part of Yagoda's court [Yagoda headed the NKVD under Stalin]. He was the pride of Yagoda's salon. Stande, Hempel, and Wandurski died as Poles during the liquidation of the Polish communists, but as far as I know—this isn't certain—there were rumors that Jasieński had fallen along with Yagoda. After all, he had become a delegate to the Supreme Soviet of Tadzhikistan, an honorary citizen of Tadzhikistan, and some sort of honorary vice president of Tadzhikistan's council of ministers. He had a palace there and two Arabian horses.

He'd go out there for vacation, for a month, two months. And so he had quite a checkered career. Then he came to his end, died, near Vladivostok, on his way to a labor camp in Kolyma.

2 THE PROBLEMS OF AUTOBIOGRAPHY. THE GGA MANIFESTO AND ANTIPOETRY.

WAT: Today we ask ourselves if the novel is possible, but we'd be much more justified in asking ourselves the general question whether autobiography is possible, as pure autobiography, memoirs, or confessions. By analogy with what is happening in physics, just as the atom has ceased to be the simplest unit, subject to no further reduction, so has the event, the fact, become incredibly complex. In this era, in this generation, we are entirely convinced that facts are not simple; quite the contrary. And what's more, in things that touch on the human condition, the individual, humanity in some way, opinions about facts are completely and inextricably enmeshed in value judgments, attitudes, stances. And so an autobiography, which is supposed to present the history of a soul or the fate of a person, encounters at every step (of course, blessed are those who are not aware of this) the multidimensionality of facts that contain their own contradiction. Even worse, various opinions about a given fact are equally justified even if they are mutually contradictory. And so that makes it difficult to write or speak about things autobiographical. Obviously we ought to return to that state of naïveté, that former state of grace, when these things were not questioned.

MILOSZ: In the past, biography held to certain conventions. And authors did not attempt to tell absolutely everything; they simply accepted the conventions and they made a selection. They knew that selection was inevitable and did not reflect badly on us. Today there is a desire to tell absolutely everything.

WAT: There's simply no faith in any definite principle of selection.

MILOSZ: Fine, but as you know, selection is the measure of form. There is no form without selection. Only silence remains. Or pure gibberish. And so I think one shouldn't have too many scruples on that account.

9

One other question. Constructivist tendencies had a counterpart in literature. I'm thinking of the First Kraków Avant-garde, Peiper and Przyboś. That was precisely what they were doing, glorifying civilization. "The metropolis, the masses, the machine." In fact, that too had certain leanings toward socialism. Peiper even wrote about socialist rhyme.

WAT: In practical terms, we really were *outsiders*, with our scandals, our protests against society, our deliberate provocation of society; we were antiliterature. Those manifestoes of ours, that introduction to GGA, that was antipoetry. You don't know our almanac GGA? It would be worth it to reread the introduction because very few people know about it. In 1920 Stern and I published the GGA almanac. The poetry doesn't matter because, at least in my case, we tried to publish the worst poetry imaginable. And we really did that, deliberately. The most incompetent, clumsy, eccentric, nonsensical poetry—but not the sort of nonsense that came around later on. Programmatically clumsy, incompetent poetry, hideously clumsy. But what is interesting here, perhaps the most interesting thing from that period, is a long introduction the two of us wrote. Obviously, I won't quote it in full. I'm quoting from my memoirs of futurism, which I published in *The Literary Monthly* in 1929.

From the primitivists to the nations of the world and to Poland. The great iridescent monkey known as Dionysus has long since bit the dust. We are throwing his rotten legacy out. We proclaim:

(1) Civilization and culture with its justice—to the trash heap. We choose simplicity, vulgarity, gaiety, health, triviality, laughter.
(2) We abolish history and posterity—also Rome, Tolstoy, criticism, hats, India, Bavaria, and Kraków. Poland should renounce tradition, mummies, Prince Joseph, and the theater. We will destroy the cities. Instead of all those mechanisms—airplanes, tram cars, inventions, the telephone—the primordial means of knowledge. The apotheosis of the horse, only homes that are collapsible and mobile, a language of shouts and rhymes.
(3) We see a social system dominated by genuine idiots, capitalists. That is the most fertile ground for laughter and for revolution.
(4) Wars should be fought with fists; murder is unhygienic; women should be changed often; a woman's value is in her fertility.
(5) Art is only that which produces health and laughter. Art's essence is to be found in circuslike spectacle for great crowds. Its outer characteristics are publicness, overt pornography. From the smoky pub of the infinite we throw out the wretched and reactionary creatures known as poets who are crushed by unsatisfied needs, joie de vivre, ecstasy, inspiration, eternity. Instead of esthetics—antigrace; instead of ecstasy—intellect,

conscious and deliberate creation. Poetry: we allow rhyme and rhythm to remain, since they are prime and fertile. Destruction of constrictive creative regulations; clumsiness is a virtue. Freedom of grammatical form, spelling, and punctuation for the creator. Mickiewicz is limited. Słowacki is incomprehensible mumbling. We glorify reason and therefore reject logic as a limitation, the cowardice of the mind. Nonsense is magnificent because of its untranslatable contents, which throw our creative breadth and power into relief just as our art reveals our love for people and all things. We emanate love. Let us open our eyes. Then a pig will seem even more enchanting than a nightingale, and a GGA gander will dazzle us more than a swan's song. GGA, GGA, gentlemen, has come out into the world arena, brandishing its two G's and shouting its A!

Interesting, as you see, but obviously quite eclectic; a lot of Marinettism, though it's against Marinettism . . .

MILOSZ: But that early anticivilization movement was subdued by constructivism in its various forms.

WAT: It was, and we ourselves moved on to different positions. We just began with antipoetry and antiliterature, but, as we began to write, we acquired a taste for poetry and so imperceptibly our positions, our literary practice, began to verge on the civilized, the constructivist. A perfect example of that civilizing trend, the search for a new alphabet, a new language for the metropolis, the masses, the machine . . .

3 DEMONISM AND EXORCISM. *THE LITERARY MONTHLY.* FRATERNITÉ OU LA MORT.

MILOSZ: In this session let's speak about the period when you were close to the idea of starting the journal, *The Literary Monthly.*

WAT: Now, so soon? Couldn't we put it off for a while? All that, my coming to the idea of communism, my intimacy with that idea, was really a demonic bond whose fruits are being felt only now, in my illness. And, you know, when we sit down with this machine, I feel that you are performing an act of exorcism on me. My illness is essentially demonic; I have always had that feeling about it. Because, in fact, there is no illness; in fact, all my organs are in good shape. Perhaps we should talk about my illness.

MILOSZ: No, no.

WAT: But the devil behind my illness is the devil of communism.

MILOSZ: Really?

WAT: Yes, yes, obviously. I was always healthy though I may have had a certain philosophy of pain right from the start. The philosophy of pain—that's an old story in literature; beginning with the romantics, if not Pascal, the greater part of literature is dominated by it, right up to the present day. Pain or despair. Only the costumes change.

MILOSZ: And you had that philosophy of pain as a young man?

WAT: Very much so. Actually, when I began to write—I mean, to publish, instead of studying philosophy and mathematics at the university (for which I felt the greatest calling and for which I had talent), for all my dadaism, I wrote *My Pug Iron Stove*, which truly contains an authentic despair, an entirely ungrounded horrible despair, ungrounded suffering, but one that nevertheless was entirely genuine, authentic. . .

MILOSZ: But then in your case, when you speak of the philosophy of pain, how do you view the leap you made to openly revolutionary concerns, social transformation?

WAT: You see, that entire ballast of weltschmerz, all the despair we discussed in our first session came from a sense that things could not go on like that, that this was it; we had to start over from the very beginning. Futurism, Polish dadaism, was connected to the philosophy of despair, to the impossibility of going on, that entire mal de vivre. I was truly sincere; I did suffer a great deal. Today I can laugh at it, but I did suffer. And I went through a revolt against that suffering, that pain . . . The lapses in our conversations are mostly the result of the pain killers I have to take to be able to talk with you at all. And I'm afraid there's yet another danger here: I could easily slip into confessions. Confessions of an ex! I'll probably have that tendency, not only because it's the path of least resistance but because, as I told you, for me communism is pathogenic, a demonic, pathogenic factor.

MILOSZ: But that makes for a very good point of departure.

WAT: Of course, if I were a religious person or if we lived in other times . . . Doctors can't cure me, but a good exorcist probably could. Because my main demon is communism, and as soon as we approach the subject of communism, I'm afraid I'll start slipping into confessions, which is not a good thing to do. A certain distance must be kept.

In the end, to speak of one's times means to be like Livy, not St. Augustine.

MILOSZ: Well, we probably won't return to Livy's style, so say a little more on that.

WAT: The sin, the error of historiography today (I mean the best historiography, the one produced by writers) is that it confuses those two basic styles of speaking about one's times. It mixes St. Augustine with Livy. If we take Machiavelli, for example, his meditations on Livy provide tremendous intellectual pleasure. Their line of reasoning and thought is exceptionally pure—not the least like St. Augustine's. But from Rousseau on we again see history confused with autobiography. And isn't that one of the signs of our illness? The muddying of history with biography. Isn't that a sin?

MILOSZ: A while back we were discussing recurrence, and you spoke of your own history as an individual being the same as that of the twentieth century.

WAT: You're right. There's no going back to Livy and Machiavelli. *The Literary Monthly* is the corpus delicti of my degradation, the history of my degradation in communism, by communism. It was in a communist prison that I came fully to my senses and from then on, in prison, in exile, and in communist Poland, I never allowed myself to forget my basic duty—to pay, to pay for those two or three years of moral insanity. And I paid, and paid.

MILOSZ: You should be aware that you're sitting with someone who once was a passionate reader of your magazine.

WAT: *The Literary Monthly?*

MILOSZ: Of course. As a very young man.

WAT: When I returned to Poland, a great many government ministers told me that they had grown up on *The Literary Monthly,* which had enjoyed enormous authority. It was published in editions of three thousand to five thousand but had at least twenty times that in readers. To a considerable degree, it was my creation, mine and Stawar's, but I was the organizing force behind it; I made the magazine as a whole, set the tone, introduced all that propaganda. And so for a good many years, in Russia and later on in Poland, I was aware that I would have to pay for that.

The Literary Monthly came out of a group of Polish intellectuals, from the Marxist circle that was formed in 1928. The group included

Broniewski, Stawar, Daszewski, Leon Schiller, me, Stande . . . There were eight of us. Of those, five perished in Russia: Drzewiecki, Hempel, Stande, Wandurski, Jasieński. Jasieński didn't take part in our meetings—he was in Paris at the time—but there was a connection with him. In any case we felt like a group . . . And of all of them I'm the last survivor.

The only one who died *in odore sanctitatis* was Broniewski. But what an *odore!* He'd make scenes when he was drunk. After the first act of the premiere of Leon Kruczkowski's play *The Rosenbergs*, Broniewski was plastered and shouting for the entire lobby to hear: "Now they're turning spies into heroes, but I was in Lubyanka and nobody's making a hero out of me." Every once in a while when he got good and drunk, he would show his true colors. Everyone knew that this prodigal son had returned to worship the golden calf for the vodka, to satisfy his vanity as a writer. Broniewski was ruined, an alcoholic, destroyed morally. Obviously, it would be an oversimplification to speak only of cushy jobs and vanity, though his vanity as a poet was something terrible. You could always get on his good side by praising his poetry.

But it was more than that which kept many communists in the party. Back in 1937, the time of the Moscow trials, when I spoke with some quite important communists, friends of mine, I would ask them, "So is everything clear to you now?" And they would answer, "Yes, it is, but we can't walk away from it. That's our entire youth." Communism proved how incredibly hard it is to walk away from one's youth when that youth was some sort of high point, a period of unselfishness, a beautiful way of life. All those old communists had come to communism by different routes but they all had come to it through idealism, great unselfishness.

There were many reasons for the liquidation of the Polish Communist party. One reason was that the Polish communists, the intelligent ones, the most intelligent ones, knew, well before the war and even before the trials, what the so-called crimes of Stalin were. But they didn't have the strength to walk away from their youth, their idealistic youth.

Even today, one strength of the Communist party in Africa or in the West, in France, comes as a result of the atomization of modern societies and communism's offer of a fraternal sect, the brotherhood of the sect and *la deliquenca settaria*.

MILOSZ: They live in that world, they fall in love there, marry, and spend all their time there.

WAT: The warmth of brotherhood. *Fraternité.* Obviously, it took the genius of Dostoevsky to understand that this was *fraternité ou la mort.* Dostoevsky foresaw what that *fraternité* was capable of turning into. In materials on Auschwitz I came across a little verse from an SS song: "Und willst du nicht mein Bruder sein, so schlag ich dir dein Schädel ein" (And if you don't want my brotherhood, I'll smash your skull, and smash it good) . . . *Fraternité ou la mort*—it all starts with *fraternité.* But it was clear that no other party, no church was providing it. The church was too large, too cold, ritualistic, ornamental. The magic of the church had actually been externalized. And that is why the Catholic liturgy held such attraction for French esthetes, starting with Barbey d'Aurevilly. It had already been so externalized that the magic had become an element of style, decoration. The communist church had the wisdom, like the early Christian communities (though I greatly dislike comparisons with early Christianity; those analogies are nearly always misleading), to base itself on the cell where everyone knew each other and where everyone loved each other. And the warmth, the mutual love found in that little cell surrounded by a hostile world made for a powerful bond.

I never actually was a communist, I was never a Marxist. I was a mad fanatic, a sectarian. I did the work of ten men at *The Literary Monthly.* I was incredibly active and dynamic. All I wrote was a bunch of articles. I didn't write a single literary work—not one poem, not one short story. I did write some short stories at that time, but I destroyed them. I knew that I was not impregnated with that holy spirit. My relation to communism was a little like Simone Weil's to Catholicism. I was afraid of infecting it. I could feel the burden I carried within myself as a literary man, a poet—the burden of the old capitalist bourgeois decadent Adam. Bourgeois decadence. And I was afraid of causing infection. Just as they're afraid to send satellites to Mars so as not to cause any viral infection there. Just as Simone Weil was afraid of converting, so as not to bring her Jewishness into the church.

Just before *The Literary Monthly* was founded, elections to the parliament were held. A little while before, my *Lucifer Unemployed* had been a literary success.

MILOSZ: What year did that appear?

WAT: In December or November 1926, but it was dated 1927. And so I was a very good catch for the communists. At one point Stawar approached me with a proposition; they wanted to nominate me for election to the parliament (Sejm). The party had been outlawed, but there was a communist faction in the parliament and a pretty good-sized one too. But for that I would have had to join the party. I didn't join the party. And then I founded *The Literary Monthly*. I committed the most motley acts, but I didn't join the party. To some degree that was a question of my character, inborn or developed: I knew that if I were a member of the party, I would be surrendering my mind. When the majority outvoted me, I would have to accept the majority opinion. And I didn't want that. Voluntarily, all the way but not . . .

But now take your generation from Wilno, the generation of left-wing writers in the mid-thirties. It produced one Politburo member, ten ambassadors, thirty ministers, Central Committee members. That group came not out of the twenties but the mid-thirties. And that was no accident either. Obviously, this touches on some of the essential sociopolitical features of the time—the motivation for going over to communism, for your group's joining the communists, a difference in motivation and in the entire social and psychological context in the country and the world in the twenties. The psychological motivations of the first group are absolutely different from both the situation and the motivation of the second group.

That's an interesting subject. Why was our group so much destroyed by history and communism? Why did communism destroy the lives of those people, and why did the people who joined the communists in the mid-thirties make such careers for themselves? Eating crow all the while as they made those careers, of course.

MILOSZ: Some people couldn't.

WAT: Some couldn't, yes. We're not talking about you and me. And so perhaps we can try to confront that question together. Why did it happen that way? What are the reasons behind the pronounced difference, which is almost the stuff of tragedy? . . . As if it were still possible to write tragedies in the twentieth century . . . Maybe we'll put that off till next time. I'm in a lot of pain right now.

4   GOING OVER TO COMMUNISM.

WAT: Last time, as I recall, we ended up on the difference in the fates of those two groups that went over to communism, one at the beginning of the twenties and the other in the thirties—the ultimately tragic fate of the first group and the splendid careers of the second. What caused that difference? The whole context of the times, obviously. But I have the impression that there was an essential difference not only between the generations but between the motivations that inclined young intellectuals toward communism.

Specifically, the motivations that inclined us to socialism were markedly social: questions of worldview, ideology, conscience, the cause of social justice. There were few political motivations, little politics in the strict sense of the word—little manipulation of reality. We lacked political passion. That was one of the features of the pre-Stalin Communist guard, especially the Polish one: the unmistakable predominance of ideological, philosophical, and social motives over the political. There is a significant statement in Togliatti's testament. He speaks of the Italian Communist party: we had great successes when we ceased to be concerned with general problems—the nature of the state, the nature of imperialism—and instead favored the particular tasks of the moment, like the struggle against the government, trade unions, pointing out the weak sides of social democracy, and so forth. But all ideology, the entire ideological superstructure, is only a tool and an essentially unwieldy one, as Togliatti said. In Russia, of course, after the victory of the Revolution, the situation took that form at once. The day after taking power, the Bolsheviks were confronted with specific policy questions *hic et nunc*. But the old guard of the Bolsheviks, particularly those in the Comintern, and especially the Poles on the Comintern, were people primarily interested in those general questions—philosophical problems, not strictly political ones. What Togliatti said about the empty, sterile problems, like the nature of imperialism, the nature of the state, and so on—those all were problems that were thoroughly discussed in our own little way in our Marxist club. We were led there by those problems.

. . . Hitler's coming to power. That was a determining factor in Russia too, very important for Stalinism. For all of communism. Hitler's coming to power doomed the Polish party to liquidation later on, the old Comintern members too—the ones with the worldviews, not the pragmatists. I have the impression that the generation that came up through the universities and in the battles that took place there— very concrete political battles, political maneuvers against the fascist groups—was a generation that had already gotten used to eating frogs, for that's what brass-tacks politics is all about: every day you eat your portion of crow. They simply were already a generation of pragmatists. Thus that madcap ease with which a great many of them, almost the majority, with only a few individual exceptions, merged with Stalinism after the war and advanced far in Poland in the wake of Stalinism. There were hints of this in their very beginnings, in that generation's motivations for joining the movement.

We used to meet at my place, or at Leon Schiller's. He was a fine specimen of the salon communist, a type that could be found at that time in other countries too—England, France. He was on very friendly terms with the minister of internal affairs and was close with Beck and Pieracki. But that's Poland. And when left-wing writers came from the West, from Germany or France, like Priacel, Barbusse's secretary, they couldn't get over our sitting in the Café Ziemiańska with the colonels, with Wieniawa-Długoszowski.

One time the vice-minister of internal affairs, Korsak, sat down with us. Korsak was tremendously fond of Władysław Daszewski. The Ministry of Internal Affairs was near the Polish Theater; Korsak would pick up Daszewski and give him a lift home because they lived near each other. And so things were idyllic with the people on top, which infuriated the smaller fry. But there was also a question of infiltration here.

When we were arrested after *The Literary Monthly* was shut down, and we were still in the cellars of the Security Prison, the cell door suddenly opened and the warden, a very elegant man in civilian clothes, called us out. It was Passover and the Jewish bakers had been arrested. We were in a large cell with those bakers. He called us out and said to us in the corridor, "Colonel Wieniawa-Długoszowski has sent you gentlemen a few provisions." Two gigantic bags from Hirszfeld's delicatessen, the best in Warsaw, two liters of the finest vodka, caviar, and so on. "But where can I put you with all this?" He took us to a cell where a famous bandit, who had murdered a family, was chained to the wall. "I'll give you gentlemen this food on condition that you don't share with him. He's not allowed any. He's a criminal, a bandit." We refused. He scratched his head and then somehow found an empty cell for us.

Anyway, what were those meetings of ours like? Someone from the party always came, sometimes some anonymous person, probably from the Central Committee, sometimes somebody who was in hiding. There was a lecture, followed by a fierce debate. Then Schiller would sit at the piano and play. Sometimes he would play "My girlfriend's so ugly her teeth fall out" or "The wind is laughing at the window, dammit, life is vile . . ." A beautifully furnished apartment and so on. Sometimes the meetings were at my place; I had a decent apartment on the fifth floor, in a courtyard. And in the windows right across from ours there were always, almost to the very end, for something like three years, two police spies observing the goings-on.

Conditions were really quite idyllic and were based on a certain snobbery and on certain calculations by the ruling circles and even the police. No doubt about that. It was just a matter of keeping things out in the open. If something's in the open, you can detect its intentions. When they closed down *The Literary Monthly*, Mackiewicz wrote a long defense of the journal in *The Word*. He was very upset and said, "We knew what they were going after as long as *The Literary Monthly* was being published—what they wanted, how they were thinking, what methods they were using; but this way we're groping around in the dark."

There was another factor that to some degree protected us. When they confiscated I think it was the second issue of *The Literary Monthly*, or maybe it was the first, the prosecutor, Kawczak, from the section that dealt with communist press affairs, summoned Breiter, a lawyer. He knew that Breiter was on friendly terms with us. He told him, we're not going to arrest them; we don't want to create any martyrs. Just point out to them that there are Warsaw area regulations that specify that a periodical is closed down after the second confiscation. Obviously, as soon as I heard this, I left immediately to have the next issue published in Kraków. And then later in Bydgoszcz when things got too difficult in Kraków. It reached a point where I had juggled things so that the issue was put together in Warsaw, and I had an editor-in-chief in Lwów, a Ukrainian who was paid for this, a left-wing Ukrainian, our so-called assistant editor. But I had the magazine printed in Poznań. It turned out that Poznań was the best place. I'd hit on a print shop whose owner was the local censor's lover. What's more, the censor's office in Poznań was very understaffed, and so that woman censor read the daily papers, looked through the weeklies, and only glanced at the titles in *The Literary Monthly* because she didn't have enough time. And that was how we could keep the magazine going: it was subject to the prosecutor in Lwów and would have to be confiscated by authorities in Poznań, but we were nearly always in Warsaw.

Right from the start the editorial board consisted of Stawar, Broniewski, Hempel, Daszewski, and Stande. Deutscher joined later on. At that time he was working for the Zionist *Our View*, but he had been a communist for a long time and wrote feuilletons that were half literary, half political, very passionate, very furious, frothing.

But it seems to me that we've started talking about *The Literary Monthly* too soon. I think we need to treat the background more fully, the motivations. *The Literary Monthly* was the phase of the greatest fanticism, and so we should approach the subject gradually. It was blindness, a total spell, at least as far as I was concerned.

MILOSZ: Let's return to the period before *The Literary Monthly* was founded. What interests me is that by then you had already written *Lucifer Unemployed*. That's an incredibly paradoxical, ironic book. A mind playing with all the possibilities. And besides, that book is like your poetry, that poetry that was so highly valued by the younger generation in Poland in the period after October 1956. For that is a mind incredibly perverse, playful, paradoxical, perfectly suited to people who had experienced a good deal and who after 1956 had achieved a certain freedom, at least to talk and to write.

WAT: When Herling-Grudziński received a copy of the second postwar edition of *Lucifer Unemployed* in 1959, he wrote me a letter: "Aleksander, did you write this after you became disenchanted with communism?" And really I thought that was an entirely logical supposition because that little collection of stories contains some utterly sober judgments about communism—communism that had shattered on the atom of the soul. There are many such observations, objective, sober, that today can be accepted as accurate and fair. But as I said, I wrote those short stories in 1924 and 1925. I published them in book form in 1926, but my communism began only in 1928. So what happened then? I became stupid.

A very simple story. I couldn't bear nihilism, or let's say, atheism. If you go through those short stories systematically, one after the other, you'll see that what I put together in *Lucifer* was a confrontation of all humanity's basic ideas—morality, religion, even love. It's especially paradoxical and interesting that just then I was going through the second year of a great love. But that cerebral questioning and discrediting of love was thorough, taken right to the end. The discrediting of the very idea of personality . . . everything in general brought into question. Nothing. Period. Finished. *Nihil.*

MILOSZ: May I interrupt here? I don't know much about these things, but it seems to me that something similar happened in Weimar Germany, where people began with nihilism, sarcasm, and later on went over to the Communist party, drew closer to communism. Brecht, for example.

WAT: And Aragon? I was actually speaking about myself, but it was very typical. Mine was a flagrant case because in 1928 I published a book that was incredibly mocking, absolutely negative and nihilistic.

There's a short story by Graham Greene, one of his best. A man goes away from home on vacation and some young hoodlums take over his house. They take out everything in the house, they dismantle the staircases, they remove everything; only the walls are left. Later, the

20

man comes back, sees his house from a distance. Everything looks entirely normal, the way it was before. But he finds the interior consumed, an empty space. And my malice of that time, that terrible obstinate malice, came from a sort of intellectual hoodlumism. From a feeling that though the outward forms had been preserved, inside everything had been eroded, removed, cleaned out. It turned out that this was more than I could bear. I closed my eyes to it. I locked up all my ideas, everything. I threw the key into the abyss, the sea, the Vistula, and I threw myself into the only faith that existed then.

There was only one alternative, only one global answer to negation. The entire illness stemmed from that need, that hunger for something all-embracing. In fact, communism arose to satisfy certain hungers. The phenomenon was inevitable insofar as powerful hungers had arisen in modern societies, even in those of the nineteenth century. One of those hungers was the hunger for a catechism, a simple catechism. That sort of hunger burns in refined intellectuals much more than it does in the man on the street. The man on the street always had a catechism; he replaced one catechism with another.

It was a very simple matter, a matter of mathematics. There was too much of everything. Too many people, too many ideas, too many books, too many systems. Too much of everything . . . absolutely awful multiplicity. It had become so vast that a refined intellect was unable to deal with it.

MILOSZ: I'd be very interested to know to what degree your group was familiar with Russian literature, with what was happening in Russian literature at that time, at the end of the twenties. There was Pilnyak, Seifullin, other writers. Ehrenburg was one of the more popular writers.

WAT: Yes, I translated two of Ehrenburg's books.

MILOSZ: So the question is to what degree your group knew those works and how certain of those works of Russian literature might have affected you. Many of the works of Russian literature of the twenties contained the horror and the fascination of what was happening there.

WAT: We were very *à la page*, we knew everything . . . But the question was what effect it had on us. You hit the nail on the head: horror and fascination at the same time. And there's another very important point here, one that on the surface would seem to make communism repellent but that fascinated and attracted intellectuals (me in this case, but I'm speaking in the plural because I could quote many analogous examples, right up to the present day). Specifically, it was all that cruelty. All that blood spilled for the Revolution. That terrible Pilnyak, that book of his, *Naked Year*. All the savagery that had surfaced worked in favor of communism. For since such a terrible price had to be paid . . . I am really not a cruel person, I have no cruelty in me. In prison I may have killed some lice and bedbugs, and I might have killed some flies when I was five or six, but afterwards I felt very disgusted by it.

MILOSZ: In one of your poems you say you killed a turtle.

WAT: The poem is not accurate. I was there when it was being killed, but I didn't do the killing. I never killed a single turtle. I accused myself injustly. Ola is my witness. No, on the contrary, I'm terrified by blood.

But blood in the abstract, blood you don't see, blood on the other side of the wall—as Pascal wrote about that other side of the river—blood spilled on the other side of the river. How pure and great must be the cause for which so much blood is spilled, innocent blood. That was terribly attractive . . . There's another thing here, an unspoken question: who was spilling the blood? The hope of the world, the people in whom the greatest and most unquestioning trust had been placed. Da ist der Hund begraben. The intellectual who has lost confidence in everything and everyone cannot live like that. Isn't that so? That was my point of departure. That was behind my *Lucifer*. But I couldn't live like that! And then I took Lenin as my idol.

Besides, experts in religion know that when great religions are dying, warped religions—sects—emerge. It's always like that. Then the demigod emerges, the charismatic leader. An old story. It goes back at least as far as the romantics. Kireevsky, a post-romantic and one of the Slavophiles, wrote that politics was such a crime and a disgrace that it was better for one person to take all that disgrace upon himself. In that way the nation is spared the disgrace. That was the theoretical justification for Russian autocracy: the tsar sacrifices himself, he takes on the disgrace for the entire nation, the disgrace of leading the state. Blood is spilled, horrible crimes are committed, but now there is a sanctified person, an idol, the tsar or Lenin, the charismatic person who redeems everything in which the highest hopes had been placed. He takes the entire sin upon himself . . . My savior, Lenin, has taken on the sin.

. . . Well, but the question was about us. We knew that terrible things were happening there—but what's interesting is which side of the river you're on intellectually. I'd like to give you an example. We were collecting signatures to protest Minister Michałowski's prison regulations. I was involved in a lot of campaigns like that; I collected signatures from professors and writers. Political prisoners were to be treated the same as criminals. Among others I appealed to Słonimski. Słonimski said to me, "Of course, I'd be glad to sign, but on condition that there's some mention of Soviet prisons." In the end I wasn't stupid—I was intelligent; at least it appears that way from my short stories—but I remember clearly my amazement, my pain, even my contempt for that Słonimski, who would combine such things. Why couldn't he understand that it is one thing to imprison the enemies of freedom and another to put the defenders of freedom in prison? One thing to imprison people who were in principle in favor of prisons and another thing to imprison those who were against prisons in principle? After all, I wasn't a prevaricator, and I wasn't a fool. But I truly thought that there was some sort of fundamental difference. My mentality at that time was a model of the mentality that gets involved with communism and then just goes along. I consider that distinction as one of my intellectual low points. A distinction that the progressives are making to this day. A terrible distinction. To make it one has to be completely blind, intellectually and morally.

5 MAYAKOVSKY IN WARSAW. PAUL ELUARD. A THEATRICAL MONTAGE FOR THE NATIONAL EXHIBITION IN POZNAŃ. BERLIN IN 1928.

MILOSZ: When was Mayakovsky in Warsaw, what year?

WAT: He was there twice. I can't give you the exact date, but he was there in 1927 for the first time, and he wrote about it. The second time was on his way back from Paris, not long before his suicide—on his way back from Paris where he'd had that unsuccessful love affair. Mayakovsky had been an influence in Poland even before that; he'd been an influence right from the beginning. What Bryusov, Balmont, and Blok were for the Skamandrites, especially Tuwim, Mayakovsky was for the futurists. He had come as a revelation. Mayakovsky in his early anarchist phase—"A Cloud in Trousers," "Simple as Mooing," and the tragedy *Vladimir Mayakovsky*—that's the completely decadent Mayakovsky.

Merezhkovsky wrote something called *The Coming Lout* (*Griadushchii Cham*)—I don't remember if that was a book or a long essay. It was a familiar expression, but he applied it to Mayakovsky. Well, what affected us—me, Stern, Jasieński—though we didn't call it loutishness, was that aspect of his loutishness that was expressed in an enormous aggrandizement of everything: the mental despair, the trivialization of lofty feelings. "Tongueless the street writhes with nothing to sing of its pain." The gigantic voices of the street. For us it was a genuine revelation that poetry could, and could even want to try to, express the street. That really was "the coming lout"; we just didn't realize it. Furthermore, Mayakovsky was such a powerful influence because we were young. Those brutal words and all that hugeness and his yellow jacket, but he had a sensitive, sentimental heart. For example, "Mama, tell Lyuda, Olya, there's no place for him and his heart is on fire." That proletarian sentimentality.

I have to say there was no Mayakovsky in my *Pug Iron Stove*, in the little I had written, though he had a very great influence on Stern's and Jasieński's poetry. But he fascinated me. Still there's that dichotomy: you can be greatly fascinated by the personality, the poetry, but *imperméable* in your practice as a poet and not submit to that influence. You see, this is rather important as it relates to our fascination with Mayakovsky. Mayakovsky's influence was like an inclined plane, a gangplank that conveniently led from the avant-garde position, formal innovation, to communist, revolutionary writing.

MILOSZ: The same thing recurred in the thirties, the same story with Mayakovsky.

WAT: Yes, it even happened again in Poland after the war. Mayakovsky is the model, the archetype, the prototype for the mixing of those two elements. There's another semantic confusion here. For obviously those things are connected emotionally; they have a common root. An emotional hunger, a revolt that is as real in the arena of form, poetry, esthetics as it is in life. Mayakovsky was an example of how that equation is made, that false identification of what is unjustly called revolutionism in art with social revolution.

Here's something interesting: it is precisely we who are called intellectuals who have that terrible need for monotheism. Whether we are left-wing or right-wing or in some field like poetry, we feel a violent and unconscious but powerful need to have our views on politics and on life, and even on our art, conform to each other, belong to the same world. The real communists—the Leninists, the Stalinists—had none of that in them. In spite of their doctrines being absolutely the most monotheistic and monolithic ever devised, they excelled at making distinctions in practice. The *Appassionata* would make Lenin weep. He couldn't stand Mayakovsky's poetry; he had a high opinion of Gorky's prose. Stalin called Mayakovsky the most important poet of the era of

24

building socialism, but that was political. Basically, as we know, Stalin could not abide Mayakovsky and his innovations. That was a great misunderstanding on the part of the innovators, the intellectuals in the twenties, and one that is still in operation to this day. That was Mayakovsky's tragedy; that was the tragedy behind his suicide. Along with the whole New LEF group,* the constructivists, he learned of that breach, that fundamental error, right on the spot, right in the test tube. They learned that the road to the party absolutely did not lead through a revolution in art; on the contrary, only traditional art, the most retrograde art, not innovation, could be the instrument of the party.

Mayakovsky's influence came early, by the very beginning of the twenties. It reached Poland in 1918. I was reading Mayakovsky in 1919, 1920. There were plenty of esthetes coming back from Russia with all that futurist literature. So obviously Mayakovsky's direct influence came in the early twenties. And the journal *New LEF* was an influence. Those were super-communists who didn't understand what the game was about. They took Marxist theory seriously in that they considered one of communism's principal values to be the destruction of petit-bourgeois values, petit-bourgeois beauty. But it was just the other way around: the point was to petit-bourgeoisify the great masses. Later on they thought that communism aspired to create an industrial society. They seriously thought that it was a question of creating an urban society, that is, the metropolis, the masses, the machine. And that works of literature or painting ought to be made like a machine. Rationalism was to be de-emotionalized; it had to be pure rationalism taken to its end, a functional rationalism serving certain circles, forces, propaganda.

MILOSZ: Functionalism, like the Bauhaus.

WAT: Yes, of course . . . They didn't understand that Soviet rationalism, especially in the period when it was full-blown, in its full-blown realized form, meaning Stalinism, had to be limited to a little catechism that could be learned by heart. It boils down to the Soviet astronaut who said that he had been in heaven and hadn't seen God. Voila! That's communism's rationalism in full flower. You can't go any further than that. But in fact what was at issue was the creation of powerful symbols, the crystallization of forces—specifically, nonrational forces: the leader, the party, and so forth. And not only was dryness not desirable, but, on the contrary, the demand was for the highest exaltation,

---

* LEF (Left Front of the Arts). A movement founded by Mayakovsky and others, favoring a genuinely revolutionary literature.

the entire emotional charge that Tolstoy or Chekhov or Pushkin had invested in their great works. Obviously, LEF did not understand that. We didn't understand that either at the time.

I have the impression that the French avoided this. There's a certain difference here. The transition of the French—Aragon, Eluard—from surrealism to communism did not occur according to any constructivist model like the metropolis, the masses, the machine. They didn't know about LEF; they didn't know Russian. Constructivism was alien to them. You have to distinguish between Picasso's cubism and constructivism.

When Eluard and I spoke—I became friends with him after a while—I asked how their transition to communism had taken place. Eluard was in Poland a couple of times. At first he spent nearly all his time at our place. When he first came, I was on the board of the Writers' Union and I did the honors. He somehow took a liking to us. I have books with dedications from him. This was at the beginning of Stalinization. He was especially open with Ola. He would lie on the couch; he'd come back exhausted after all those receptions, all the various visits; he'd lie down on the couch and cry. It really was a tragic sight. His wife had died the year before and Eluard had a single terrible obsession: he could see her disintegrating in the ground. He couldn't rid himself of that vision; he lived with that vision constantly. We felt sorry for him, very sorry. We tried to console him. A year later—it must have been 1949—he arrived for the unveiling of the Mickiewicz monument. Now he was with his new wife, whom he'd met in Mexico. A French woman, very brave, and no doubt a communist. On the whole the wives played an enormous role in all that. The wives, especially the Jewish ones, played an enormous role in pushing writers toward communism.

MILOSZ: It's no secret that women have no sense of measure.

WAT: Yes . . . And so Eluard arrived, and an interview with him appeared in the press. This is what he said: when my wife died, I wrote many sad, tragic poems, poems full of despair. But Comrade Thorez told me one cannot poison the soul of the proletariat with sadness. And he was right. Now I have reworked the endings of those poems. Ola asked him if that were an authorized interview, and he confirmed that it had been. We almost broke off relations with him. Broniewski, for example—I'm not talking about Broniewski at the end when he was already a ruined man—Broniewski would not have been capable of acting like that. Nor would any of us have been.

I made my first trip to Western Europe in 1926, but I still wasn't politically involved then. The second trip was in 1928. That happened

26

to coincide with the idea of publishing a magazine, and so I combined the useful with the beautiful. I very much wanted to make some personal connections so that the magazine would have a wider scope. I stayed in Germany and France, looking for connections. Should I tell the story of how I got to go abroad? It could shed a little light on the Poland of that time.

The year 1928, as you know, was the tenth anniversary of the rebirth of an independent Poland, and an exhibition was to be held in Poznań. Things still weren't going too badly at that time, and so every ministry had sums, enormous in Polish terms, to be spent on mounting that exhibition. One day I was visited by Dr. Alfred Krygier, an old PPS member and a man of great integrity, nobility. (After World War II he was the director of the Social Insurance Institution, and he provided me with an apartment in Warsaw after my return from Russia—out of old friendship.) He was in the right wing of the PPS. In 1928 he was the head of the National Health Insurance Union and had an enormous budget to work with. That was one of the richest institutions and was the domain of the PPS. Krygier was interested in all the avant-garde movements, and so he made me a very odd proposition, namely, to stage a dramatic montage entitled *Social Policy* at the Poznań exhibition, a theatrical piece that would illustrate the social legislation of the last decade. He also invited Schiller to direct and Daszewski to do the sets. It seemed odd and rather daft to me. At that time there were still no written models for staged montages of that sort. But I was intrigued and set to work. Krygier gave me a great deal of material, including some large volumes of questionnaires from the Central Labor Inspection Bureau, really first-rate literature, unusually straightforward material on the social policy conditions prevailing in the factories and in industry in general.

MILOSZ: Do you view those achievements as positive today?

WAT: The achievements made in the first ten years were enormous. Poland's social legislation was very progressive, second only to Germany's. And, besides, there was that generation of socially committed people who'd been brought up before 1918, a very good generation, a bit on the romantic side. A great many of them were of the intelligentsia. They were appointed to positions in the social legislation system—in labor inspection, juvenile care. They were socially committed workers in the true sense of the word. People's Poland had no people of that sort.

MILOSZ: How did those bills get passed in the parliament?

WAT: They were passed very early, when the PPS still had a lot of power. The PPS was very strong in social legislation right up to the May '26 coup . . . no, even later, until the rigged elections to parliament. By then I was, as you know, already half a Marxist, on my way to becoming a communist.

And so what did I do? Naturally, I did a montage—the first montage à la Piscator and Meyerhold in Poland—film, telephone, announcers. The script was abominable because I had to get everything done in four or five weeks. I read the material that Krygier had given me for nights on end; it was interesting as hell, and it was only then that I got a realistic picture of things. The things that I learned about the fate of workers in various parts of Poland! Those accounts really went straight to the point. I immersed myself in those materials, but I just didn't have the time to recast them, to digest them. It was all raw and superficial, and so the script was abominable. It included songs, choruses and marches, monologues, telephone conversations, and, on the screen, an eight-hour workday. The announcer would read a short paragraph from the labor laws, and then the telephone would ring. He'd answer the phone and receive information from various large factories as to how many violations of the laws had been recorded there in the course of the year. In a word, I showed that all the laws had been broken. And naturally, to top it off, there was a chorus of unemployed workers because people were out of work by then.

MILOSZ: Was it true that the laws were broken?

WAT: They were being broken. Of course they were broken. But the trade unions were quite powerful. And the factory owners paid fines for breaking the law. And they paid extra for overtime. Let's not exaggerate—it was a struggle, but there's no question that basically the government was very pro-worker. Then came the depression. It wasn't only the Piłsudski-ites who smashed those progressive domains, the power of the trade unions; they had already been broken by something else, namely, the depression and unemployment. But at that time unemployment was only just gathering momentum.

To make a long story short, it was pure communist theater. We were supposed to get a good-sized hall, but when Krygier read the script, his hair stood on end. First, there was a meeting of their three-man committee to determine whether it could be staged at all. Krygier did not demand any changes or cuts. The committee decided to allow it, imagine that, but without giving it any publicity. Krygier liked it very much and thought it would make a wonderful show. He had been in Berlin and had seen Piscator's plays, and—to put it as crudely as possible—there was a certain artistic snobbery at work here. Schiller and

Daszewski were both very taken with it all. And finally, since it was too late to begin anything new, he'd be left with nothing. There were some personal factors, too—it had been his project, his baby. So a theater was constructed especially for us in the basement of the Ministry of Labor building. But there was no publicity. Just the performance.

I went to Poznań for the premiere. Only certain people were privy to the existence of the theater. But anyone who visited the building came upon the theater, and so the little house was always full. One day a group of industrialists from Upper Silesia was at the exhibition, and they too happened on the play. Prystor, a minister, and Piłsudski's wife were in Poznań at the time and were taken to the performance. Naturally, they shut down that little theater immediately.

Krygier had a lot of trouble from all this, but he was an unusually considerate and tactful man, and whenever he was asked about those problems, he always denied they existed. His friendship for me remained intact despite all that trouble and his close call with being sacked. But you see the paradoxes in Poland then! And Poland is still full of paradoxes, to this day! An encomium was required for the tenth anniversary of Independent Poland. Besides, that social legislation was really the best thing the country had produced. And so I had treated those people abominably.

We earned very good money from it. Schiller and Daszewski could not forgive me for causing them to earn less than they could have. Funds had been allocated for the exhibition and had to be spent. And so the performers and the painters, anyone who did anything, were paid enormous sums. Later on I was told that we were suckers and that I had done my colleagues a bad turn, because we could have gotten fifteen thousand złotys each. Krygier had asked me right at the start how much money I wanted. I said, "I have to have everything ready for you in five weeks, so let's say twelve hundred, fifteen hundred złotys." He burst into laughter and said: "You're miscalculating, there's certainly more work than that. I'll give you three thousand." Later on he slipped me five thousand. And that was a great deal of money then, as you remember.

And with that money I went abroad with Ola and the Daszewskis. *The Literary Monthly* already existed as a project, and I wanted to make contact with pro-communists and the German progressives and then with the French. Which I did. They made a colossal impression on me. Berlin provided yet another important component in my fascination with communism. By nature I was skeptical. Berlin gave me a vision that it would come to be not today but tomorrow, the day after tomorrow—communism was just around the corner.

Berlin in 1928. To be brief about what I saw in the Berlin of 1928:

obviously, the same thing the Nazis saw. Decadence, decadence, a Babylon of debauchery. On Friedrichstrasse, a main street, in broad daylight, in the afternoon, there'd be prostitutes walking side by side, taking up the entire sidewalk. That was very striking, impressive. But they were all very maternal, fair-haired German women proudly walking the streets. Three, four, side by side, so that sometimes the other pedestrians had to step off the sidewalk for them. In broad daylight. On Kurfürstendamm, an amazing number of faces straight out of Grosz, Otto Dix, the hideous snouts of speculators.

Once I was taken to a side street off Kurfürstendamm, to some sort of nightclub for homosexuals. That was the first time I had ever seen that. Some of them were wearing women's clothes, their faces made up. The way they danced was monotonous; they danced like automatons. The cheap glare of the Chinese lanterns, the incredible sadness, the theatricality—that sadness got to me . . .

There were naked women in the Parisian brothels, on the Rue Blondel. Bruno Jasieński loved to go there, but only for a bock, a beer. He and I and Brucz used to visit the Rue Blondel very often. Only for a bock, which cost two francs. An abridged view of a society. There were a lot of Frenchmen among the clientele. They came by only for a beer, and they didn't find it exciting. In Italy this sort of thing drove some people wild, but there was nothing of that sort in Paris. For the Parisians it was *drôle*. A sort of folk amusement, folklore. In the evenings, workers, intellectuals, patresfamilias would come there. Nothing debauched about it . . . and so there was no sadness on the Rue Blondel. Naked prostitutes dancing together—that was very *drôle*, nothing melancholy about it. In Berlin, those male prostitutes—that had the sadness of all this about it, *la tristesse de tout cela*. Heartbreaking.

So were we talking about decadence. Unemployment was horrible by then. Once, around eleven in the evening, an older prostitute, decently dressed, elegant, stopped me on the street. I gave her a very cold look. She said, all right, but I have a fifteen-year-old daughter; I can take you to her; the price is such and such. Selling daughters. Terrible poverty, you see. I ventured into that district—people were dying of hunger, starving to death. Side by side with all that luxury. Another thing: that was the beginning of talking pictures. *Sonny Boy* was showing then. It was the first time I'd seen one.

Most of my contacts were with *Linkskurve*. That was the most communist periodical. There was *Weltbühne*. But they were *poputchiki*, fellow travelers. *Weltbühne* was Ossietzky, Tucholsky. I became close with Tucholsky. He was a fellow traveler too.

Practically no one was talking about Hitler. That was 1928. Somehow people weren't interested. But there was a terrible tension produced by Hitlerite sentiments. It was in the air, in people, the middle class in particular. I had a foretaste of it when I was traveling by train across Germany. I met someone I knew on that train—Weinberg, a philologist, who looked very Jewish. A fat German got on and tried to push him off the seat. The German made a scene: "Polnische Juden, polnische Schweine." One of those lower-middle-class people, an ice cream vendor, said: "Ich kummere mich nicht in der Politik." (I'm not interested in politics).

I went to *Linkskurve*. The magazine's office was in the party building, the Liebknecht party building on Alexanderplatz. The proletarian district began there. A great, splendid fortress. And it so happened that on the way there I came within 100 or 150 meters of the police barracks. The gate was open and the police were doing calisthenics in the courtyard, out in the open. They were all boney and their faces had the same hemorrhoidal color as Gogol's Akaky Akakevich. They looked as if they'd fall over if you touched them. Prussia had a social democratic government at that time.

When I went into the party building, the people there looked like big-bellied bulldogs. In the doorkeeper's lodge—he looked like a German bulldog himself—I said that I had an appointment with Kurt Kleber, the editor of *Linkskurve*. "He's not here! He won't be here for an hour; he's at a meeting." And so I answered: "All right, I'll do a few things in town and come back in an hour." But no! Out comes that bulldog of a German, takes me by the arm, brings me to a side room, and locks me in. They weren't going to let me out until they were sure who I was. As soon as Kurt Kleber arrived, they set me free.

But all that made an impression of muscle, power, dynamic force—a triumphant future, a singing future—against the background of Hitlerism, rising unemployment, crisis, social decadence. At that point we still did not believe that Hitler would succeed. After all, there was a powerful communist army, an army of committed communists, and they had weapons. My hypothesis is that at a given moment, Stalin deliberately paralyzed the German Communist party. The party was, after all, paralyzed . . . I have my own views on Stalin. I consider the guy a genius. Obviously, a lot of things happened by chance, but he knew how to turn chance to his advantage. In my opinion, Stalin did not want communism in China, just as he didn't want it in Germany. In my opinion, it was absolutely clear to Stalin what would happen if a great powerful nation with a great future went communist. Stalin knew that communism had to be kept within boundaries controlled by the NKVD and the army, primarily the Chekists. It couldn't go any further than that. If it spread further, not in little countries like Poland but in countries like Germany with its eighty million people, then Moscow's role would have fallen immediately and become secondary.

. . . So there I was, Aleksander Wat, roaming Berlin, seeking contact with communist or pro-communist writers, and what I had seen was a great communist army standing with weapons ready and waiting. I could see that things were different in Germany. These weren't decadent Frenchmen, surrealists, nihilists—these people meant business.

**6   PARIS IN 1928. JAN HEMPEL. POWER STRUGGLES
IN THE SOVIET UNION. WITKACY'S NOVELS. POLAND
AFTER PIŁSUDSKI'S COUP.**

WAT: I was talking about the impression Berlin made on me: a Babylon but, at the same time, the city of the true Armageddon. Everything indicated that it was going to be the battlefield for some gigantic demonic forces of history, that some ultimate battle would be played out there. That was a strong impression. It all came to me at once, and I would bring up the subject in conversation. I received a great variety of answers, wildly different. It was 1928; Prussia had a social-democrat government, but Hindenburg was the head of state. By then Hitler constituted a certain force, but for some reason no one talked about Hitler with me. The only person who mentioned Hitler and who somehow foresaw Hitlerism—Hitler had a large party at the time—was Tucholsky, the editor of *Weltbühne*. In conversation I would say that I had the feeling that any day now the battle of Gog and Magog was going to occur, that the aborted revolution in Germany was finally going to take place. For the most part the communist writers corroborated this and were themselves in a state of anticipation, tension.

From Berlin I went to Paris to meet up with Ola. I had stayed on in Berlin while she went on to Paris with the Daszewskis. I arrived on July 14 to go out dancing. We stayed in a hotel right by the Café du Dôme . . . What was the name of that little street?

MILOSZ: That was right when Montparnasse was at its peak.

WAT: No, it wasn't. The peak was in 1926, when I was in Paris for the first time. When I arrived, I immediately found myself in a completely different world, where politics played no fundamental role, where politics were local. Poincaré—Poincaré *la guerre,* as they called him—was still prime minister, I think. When I had left Paris in 1926, after staying there a few months—when I had been there with Jasieński—it was just at the time of that terrible inflation in France. Poincaré became prime minister and stabilized the franc. Paris exists outside of time, you see. Obviously there are political struggles, but every time I have been in France, I have been left with the impression that political struggles there are something for professionals. A class of professional politicians had been created, and they did the most varied *contredanses* according to constantly changing rules. But France is basically stable; it has a Chinese side to it—the Chineseness of France, the rituals of daily life, mealtimes. Every time I returned to France, it felt as if I had just left, in spite of very great changes having occurred there.

Perhaps I should speak of my surface impressions. France's political life seemed to have ended in 1870. From then on there had only been those professionals; politics had been divorced from the life of the nation. I had a similar impression when I went to France after the war. A certain stabilization . . . France's provincialism in relation to Europe, but the provincialism of a country magnificently situated in Europe, warmed by the Gulf Stream, stable in the richness of its culture, its creative forces.

I found that stability rather repellent, for I wanted a revolution; I was searching for a revolution. I had a good time in France though— Montparnasse, you know. But I also had a great disillusionment. As I said, I was looking for contacts for our forthcoming magazine. I can't say that I was looking all that hard. I don't know if you know this, but the French Communist party was held in low esteem in Poland. French Marxists were just laughed at.

After France I returned to Poland and our Marxist circle. The more intelligent communists dismissed me in the belief that I would never be a communist or a Marxist. A flabby intellectual, a humanitarian, a petit-bourgeois or bourgeois intellectual. Hempel wrote about this later on, in the Soviet Union.

MILOSZ: What year did Hempel die?

WAT: During the purges. If we're going to bring in Hempel here, there are a couple of things I could tell you about him. As I said, Hempel began as a theosophist. His family was well connected; his nephew was ambassador to Japan; in general they were very close to Piłsudski. But Hempel was a God-seeker. His sister published a book after the war, her reminiscences of Hempel. As I told you, he married a worker. He lived in terrible poverty, and he worked with incredible enthusiasm. One of Broniewski's most successful poems—maybe you remember it—is that poem about Hempel . . .

MILOSZ: Yes, they're in the cell . . .

WAT: We were all in that cell together, and, you know, that poem is extremely accurate and true, because Hempel really did conduct himself splendidly in prison. We didn't know how to behave in prison; we hadn't had any practice yet. That bothered us terribly, even though the prison was a soft one, no comparison to Soviet prisons. Hempel was very fatherly to us. He'd had practice; he'd been arrested time after time, but since his family had excellent connections, they kept getting him released. But the authorities, the police, intelligence, kept demanding that he leave and go to Russia.

Under Piłsudski the various government departments were baronies. Intelligence was one barony, and often its interests collided with those of the police; they were in competition. Sometimes the police would arrest some leading communist, and Section Two would release him, or vice versa. They often played tricks on each other. I don't know which agency was concerned with getting rid of communists by sending them to Russia.

There were two ways, two possibilities. One was through Sempołowska, who was responsible for taking care of the graves of Soviet soldiers and dealing with the cases of communists who were in prison. Gorky's wife was supposed to deal with Polish prisoners in Moscow; there might have been some sort of unwritten agreement to that effect. But where people with especially close ties to literature were concerned, the authorities encouraged them to get out, leave the country. But the party rarely allowed that, you see; as a rule it did not allow that. No one in that position would try to obtain the party's permission to leave the country. That would look as if you were running away, a serious transgression. The principle was that you had to stay in the country.

Hempel was arrested frequently, but he did not leave for Russia. He went there, of course, but those were short trips. People also went there secretly for training. But he did not emigrate. Hempel was seriously ill when *The Literary Monthly* was shut down and we were put in jail, and finally the party agreed or ordered him to leave the country for Russia. An understanding was reached through an attorney that he would be released from prison on condition that he leave the country. The party had given its permission.

What happened to him in Russia? There's his sister's book, his letters. That was a pitiable existence, incredibly pitiable, first in the

Hotel Lux, or whatever it was called, where the Poles lived, and then somewhere outside of Moscow. Cut off from everything, he somehow got a little work to do. Moscow was starving, the fuel situation was difficult—and he describes that incredibly hard day-to-day existence. He had lost all influence, and besides we know now that at that time— 1933, 1934, 1935—people were already trembling. Anyway, Hempel was dedicated person, a man of great goodness, a saint really, in the Christian sense of the word. But he was a party functionary—that simply means he lived off the party's money. Those were small, paltry sums. That was still the time of party asceticism. In Russia, for example, there was *part-maksimum;* that means if some high official earned more than a certain maximum, he would have to give the excess to the party. A time of asceticism, not dolce vita. That only came later, in Stalinist times—though there had already been Yagoda, you know. There were certain dolce vita circles, but as a rule those were severe times.

For a long time Hempel was *The Literary Monthly's* link with the party. It was sad to see him running back and forth between me and the party. I was quite tough—he would bring me a whole series of things to print—party material, various articles—and I wouldn't print them. I had reserved the right to veto. So he was constantly running back and forth between me, the editorial board of *The Literary Monthly,* and the party to straighten things out, to reach some compromise because it was important for them to support *The Literary Monthly.*

Afterward, things happened; for example, they didn't want to approve Broniewski's poem "Bakunin." How could we print a poem glorifying Bakunin, whom Marx had kicked out of the International? But I insisted on printing it. Then there was another poem of his, Esenin-like, very pessimistic. We're building socialism, and he poisons us with pessimism. I was never a fan of Broniewski's poetics, never, but he was a poet . . . and I held my ground.

Hempel was pitiful, terribly cowardly in relation to the party. He had incredible courage; he was absolutely lionlike in relation to the government authorities and the police; in prison, for example, he was truly a man of steel. But he trembled before the party to exactly that same degree. He really trembled about what the editorial board or the Polish Central Committee or Moscow would say.

There was another organization too, for all those organizations were quite independent of one another. One organization was the Comintern; the Polish party constituted a section of the Comintern, but the Russian party had already turned the Comintern into its own tool. There was another agency, the Soviet embassy. It was a channel for the

Soviet Ministry of Foreign Affairs, which conducted its own independent policy, often in sharp conflict with the Polish Central Committee's, and we could feel that at *The Literary Monthly.*

Anyway, I want to finish up with Hempel. He led a horrible life in Moscow; it was obvious that he was completely disillusioned, quaking in his boots, afraid of arrest. I don't know how Hempel died, but the epilogue to the story is tragic and, once again, typical.

At some point in 1950 we ran into Hempel's wife in Krynica. After all those years! We both knew her from the days of *The Literary Monthly.* Ola had become close with her; we used to go to their place in Żoliborz, and they'd come to see us. She was a true, brave working-class woman; she had five or six years of public school. Politics was not a special concern of hers, but she was a good loyal Bolshevik wife. A Bolshevik's wife, but a true Polish proletarian. They had two children, two sons. We were in prison in Poland after *The Literary Monthly* was shut down—that was in 1932—and then suddenly in 1950 or maybe 1951 we run into Hempel's wife on the promenade. Well, terrific joy at meeting, fond memories.

She told us her story. When they put her husband in prison [in the USSR], they imprisoned her as well. As usual, their two little underage sons were put in an orphanage. The orphanages were hotbeds for *urks* [criminals]; it was almost a rule that a boy put into an orphanage, especially if he had such political parents, would become an *urk*, a *bezprizorny* [a homeless runaway]. They always ran away from the orphanages; there were some exceptions, but most of them ran away. She was put in prison and then a camp. She was utterly exhausted, one foot in the grave, and one day she simply, well, died. So they brought her to the mortuary. She came to in the mortuary and started moaning. There were a lot of corpses there. She crawled out of the mortuary on her hands and knees just as a Polish doctor, also a prisoner who knew her, was passing by. Well, somehow or other, he took care of her.

MILOSZ: Was that before the war?

WAT: That was before the war. He took care of her and saved her life. The one son she managed to find perished later at the front; she couldn't find the other one. She looked very hard; the Polish embassy and the party looked for him, very hard because Bierut [head of the Polish government, 1947–1956] had been a pupil of Hempel's. In fact, Hempel was his mentor; Hempel had done a terrific amount for him, and so Bierut took a strong interest.

Hempel probably died rather quickly. He was a sick man, fragile; he probably couldn't hold out long in prison. So I asked his wife what she was doing now, where she was working. In the House of the Party, at an advanced party school; she ran the cafeteria or something like that. Well, but that was an episode, a tragic episode. She's probably still alive, and she may still be working there in the House of the Party.

MILOSZ: Here, it's in the encyclopedia: Hempel, Jan, 1877–1936, activist in the Polish workers' movement, co-op worker, publicist. A member of the Communist party of Poland since 1921, frequently jailed; after 1932 in the USSR, where in 1936 he was imprisoned and sentenced on the basis of a false accusation. Rehabilitated.

WAT: Yes, the usual story . . . Well, but now I'll return to me. You see, I was, as it were, walled in by the party's mythology. The quarrels reached me; I knew there were enormous quarrels in Russia. That was a crucial time, 1928: the Fifteenth Party Congress, when Stalin was already writing that no fortresses could halt communism, we would seize every fortress, no law bound us. Stalin started that slogan then: We will seize all the fortresses; the communists will seize all fortresses! We are not bound by laws; everything depends on us, on our will to fight. Accelerate industrialization—then bring socialism to the villages. I wasn't much aware what would come of this, but I was terribly taken by it. The end of NEP [New Economic Policy]. Although NEP was theoretically considered only a step back—a new formation historically conditioned by the dictatorship of the proletariat and thus in fact a step forward—NEP was still something that made every sincere communist ashamed. Like a disgrace in the family, a daughter going bad, shameful no matter what. And 1928, that was the time of the new general line.

I knew that enormous battles were going on there. Those battles were entrancing; it was the battle for humanity, a battle between the enormous masses and that avant-garde, that handful of people who wanted to change not only Russia but the entire history of humanity. Aside from that, I also knew those were personal battles, but I closed my eyes and stopped up my ears to everything that posed an obstacle to my faith. I interpreted everything so as to strengthen my faith as much as possible. For me those personal battles, all those various configurations, that *contredanse*, Kamenev, Zinoviev, Stalin, Trotsky, Bukharin, Tomsky—as you know, Stalin was constantly changing partners to force the others out; the alliances kept changing—for me those were not personal struggles. For me those were battles for a correct interpretation, battles on which the fate of humanity depended. The individuals were only representatives of certain historical forces and policies; the individuals were hypostases. The reactionaries could say that this was a power struggle, but we could not—God forbid! But meanwhile that power struggle in Russia was incredibly fierce, not bloody yet, but already fierce and rough, very rough. That struggle had repercussions in Poland, but the Polish party still had its internal problems, its own internal struggles. And so I was living like a drunken child in a fog. I knew nothing; that is, I knew and I didn't know, like all the rest of our circle. Only in prison did I see what political struggle in the communist camp meant, between communists, what mighty hatreds, what fanaticism, what ruthlessness that struggle could assume . . .

MILOSZ: I'd like to give the conversation a more literary turn here. You know Witkacy's novels [Stanisław Ignacy Witkiewicz published under the pseudonym Witkacy]; you know when they were published: *Farewell to Autumn* in 1927, *Insatiability* in 1930. They give a picture of that Poland . . .

WAT: You should realize that Witkacy is not a mirror; he might reflect something, but he was not a mirror on a highway. Conscious deformation is such an enormous factor in his work that it is impossible to decipher an image of Poland from Witkacy's books. In fact, they are all images of Witkacy himself. All sorts of things had been thrown into that pot, things taken not only from Poland but from the European situation in general. He mixed them all together but lent them his own likeness. Witkacy's books are Witkacy himself; they're portraits. Each one is a portrait of Witkacy, one of the many Witkacys. But Witkacy is himself such a reflection of his times that his writings can provide a lot of information about Poland and the world, of course, if he's taken indirectly. But as a direct source, a reference, Witkacy is not authoritative.

MILOSZ: You spoke of Berlin as Armageddon. How did Berlin contrast with the Poland of that time, in the first years after Piłsudski's coup?

WAT: My dear Czeslaw, the main thing after Piłsudski's coup was the economic situation. The miners' strike in England and the excellent market for Polish coal corrected the situation, stabilized the złoty. The Piłsudski-ites took full advantage of that.

MILOSZ: In the circles you moved in, weren't Piłsudski and the coup viewed as fascistic?

WAT: In strictly communist circles, meaning those on top in the opinion of the minorityites, this was of course pure unadulterated fascism. They considered that this was already fascism. That was the fundamental difference between Warski's faction, the majorityites, and the minorityites who defined Poland as a fascist country. In my circle it was half and half. There already was pressure to term this fascism, but you could still defend yourself against that nonsense—calling the Poland of the time fascist. And, don't forget, there were elections to the Sejm in 1928.

You asked me how things looked in comparison to Germany. A communist coup was expected in Germany. In Poland, however, there was a radicalizing of the masses. It shouldn't be forgotten that in the parliamentary elections of 1928 the Communist party, which never numbered more than some thirty thousand or so, along with the Western Ukrainian and Western Byelorussian parties and various other little groups, garnered over eight hundred thousand votes.

MILOSZ: Were they on the ballots?

WAT: They were on a few ballots under various names. All told, nineteen Communist party members were elected to parliament.

MILOSZ: Under Piłsudski?

WAT: Yes, under Piłsudski.

7 WITKACY. THE SOVIET EMBASSY. MAYAKOVSKY.

WAT: Every time after we tape, I have a strong desire to add a great many postscripts, and postscripts to the postscripts. But are you interested in Witkacy? . . . You asked me about the image of Poland in Witkacy's works. I said there wasn't any, that it was oblique, but that isn't entirely correct. Everything requires certain *distinguo*, and here too . . . Witkacy went through the Revolution in Russia. He was an officer in one of the most glamorous, elegant, and aristocratic regiments. We've both seen the photograph of him in uniform; he looked like a young god, exceptionally handsome. Besides, that photograph was especially successful because it was done with mirrors, a system of mirrors, so that there were eight Witkacys sitting around the table. How was he able to live in that regiment with no means of his own, without being rich? Those regiments required a lot of money; they were very expensive. But I suppose he must have been incredibly fascinating . . .

MILOSZ: When Witkacy arrived in Petersburg from Australia during the war, I think he found some relatives there, very well-connected people. He couldn't have spoken Russian, could he? He grew up in Zakopane.

WAT: He had a fantastic talent for imitating people and the way they spoke. A fantastic acoustic memory, so he could have learned it very quickly. Apropos—do you know why he went to Australia [as the secretary of Bronisław Malinowski, the anthropologist]? His fiancée committed suicide, and there was every sort of circumstantial evidence that he had been "experimenting" with her and had pushed her into it. And then he was sent off to Australia posthaste because it looked as if the attorney general's office was going to enter the case. As a very young man he had apparently started performing experiments on people.

Well, and he was in the Revolution. He greatly disliked talking about it. That is, from time to time he would tell me something, but I learned a great deal from his friend, Cavalry Captain Langner, who had inside information about Witkacy's life. Witkacy was tremendously popular with the soldiers, and so they didn't do anything to him. There must have been some drama, some drama of conscience. I don't know anything; I'm only guessing. His friends, his fellow officers, must have been massacred. He didn't like to talk about Russia, the Russian Revolution, and he was terribly afraid of communism. He used the idea of communism in his novels, but that was more of a game. But when he was serious, he was terribly afraid of it.

We were close. But when I became a neophyte communist, I ceased to be what's known as *salonfähig* because I couldn't keep from making propaganda. I did it with everyone. I even remember a dinner at our place when Witkacy was there, and Zarembina and Zahorska, I think. The dinner ended awfully because I was a disgusting host; I bored them stiff trying to convince them about communism, and he didn't like to talk about it at all. I have the impression that there were some traumas there, maybe some act of cowardice, because he had an unusual dislike for talking about it. While we were friends, I asked him a lot about his Russia and either he wouldn't answer or he would give answers that sounded like fantasies.

MILOSZ: Wasn't he a man of enormous courage?

WAT: Courage in battle is one thing and courage in dealing with a mob, mutinying soldiers, and so on is another. That's not a question of physical courage . . . It must have been something like that scene in Pasternak when Zhivago is with the partisans and fights along with them despite his own convictions. So, I have the impression that something of that sort happened with Witkacy. There are always many factors that go into a suicide, but the final impetus, what pushed him into it, may have been, as I said, his fear of prison, especially of Soviet prisons. He might have already been through something of that sort. When I was released after being arrested in connection with *The Literary Monthly*, we were in a bar and he kept looking at me, and later, in Zakopane, he kept grabbing his head and saying, "Aleksander, how could you stand it? Eight weeks!" We talked about a hundred different things, but he kept interrupting: "How can a person stand eight weeks in prison?"

. . . One other thing to finish up with Witkacy. I think that Witkacy modeled himself on the hero of *The Possessed*. The one who grabs the governor by the nose. An empty man, a completely burned-out man. A man who experiments on himself and on other people. All the most risky experiments pushed to the very limit. And a person who fascinated those around him. After all, that was the Witkacy I knew— sprees, slumming, exactly like Stavrogin. I absolutely felt that I was with Stavrogin when one time in Warsaw Witkacy took me to see a painter named Jeżewski. He was a better-than-average painter, and the woman he lived with was a painter, too, terribly ugly, fat, a real shrew, and a little demented. They lived by making color postcards; they just colored postcards. Three-day drunks used to take place there . . . incredible filth, a terrible stink. Bedding all over the floor, feather beds of some sort. The sheets probably hadn't seen the inside of a laundry for a year. They both reeked of filth. They would shut themselves up for a three-day spree: bread, sausage, and vodka for three days. Everybody brought vodka. I was once there for almost two days, but I couldn't take any more than that. Witkacy said that the *obshchaya skhvatka* [orgy] would take place on the third day. That was his favorite expression. An orgy. He was always talking about those orgies. Arms and legs all mixed up, you couldn't tell what was whose . . . So, a real Stavrogin!

I think we were talking about my circle before *The Literary Monthly*. I would like to define one circle that played a rather large role among left-wing writers, in their life, the covenants of the literary left—the Soviet embassy. But before that, I'd like to make some general sociological remarks about the Polish communist milieu, specifically the intelligentsia. There were some rather contradictory things there.

At one point we spoke about the feeling of brotherhood. No other milieu provided it to that degree. Obviously, the army, combat, provides that feeling in wartime. Well, in the end, to some degree, fascism does too. From a certain point of view fascism and communism can be seen as veterans' movements, movements made up of people just returned from war. Lenin had not returned from war, but he relied on veterans—revolutionary soldiers. To a great degree that mass of veterans lent the Revolution its style; Lenin owed as much to Clausewitz as to Marx. Lenin immediately conceived of the party in military terms, the military hierarchy, military discipline. Yes, there was some concordance there, precisely that sense of brotherhood in communist circles, human warmth, ridding oneself of what is called alienation today. But it's not that simple. Primo, that was always a brotherhood in opposition to . . . although one can ask oneself if there ever exists any brotherhood that is not a brotherhood "in opposition to." But in this case the very fact that this was a brotherhood "in opposition to"—the discipline, the theory, the militant practice—had enormous significance. So, it was a brotherhood among a group of people, conspirators, whose entire environment was against them. A hostile environment.

But one thing runs through that brotherhood like a red thread, namely, the brotherhood could be retracted. It was like that at the very beginning of bolshevism, even before the Revolution, before the war—and besides, that was fair, because in Russia bolshevism was riddled with provocateurs. Malinovsky, one of Lenin's closest people, was an Okhrana police spy. Lenin even defended him after it was disclosed. So by then the mystique of suspicion had already been created. The brotherhood could exclude someone as soon as he did not meet the demands made on him 100 percent, that is, when he was not entirely in agreement. Any heterodoxy went right out the window in the brotherhood. It is important that the brotherhood of X and Y contained, in potential, the possibility that brotherhood could turn into hostility. *Fraternité ou la mort.*

There is another feature I'd like to discuss while we're on the subject of those milieus. There is some analogy with the Hassidic milieu here, the psychology of the sect. The master, the chief, the leader. The cult of the master, like the cult of a rabbi or a *Tsadik*—really more that of the *Tsadik*. Naturally when Warski was discredited and removed, he was cursed and spat on, and some people were fanatical about it. But still he had been a *Tsadik* for many long years. And in spite of all the fanaticism and factional battles, there was some sort of profound reverence, sometimes buried deep in the soul. The need for a spiritual leader. Which is what communism has in common with sects like the Taborites, the medieval sects, isn't that so? Here the analogies are very pronounced, as far as cults are concerned. The cult of Stalin as leader did not arise out of nothing; it was neither just Stalin's megalomania nor his reign of terror.

And besides, this is an aspect of communism's essential retrograde nature. For as you know, one of my visions of communism is a fanatic progressiveness that automatically excites and unleashes all of history's retrograde forces. A sort of reaching back to the oldest archetypes of social life. There's no question that the cult of the leader is in fact the cult of the monarch. For example, I've been reading some political and philosophical fragments from a text by Novalis in which today's social system in China is foreseen as something desirable, beautiful—so much so that it must be headed by a monarch or a king, the ideal of a medieval king.

It seems to me that one of the essential causes of the Polish October [in 1956], that revolt by the old Polish Communists, those KPP [Communist Party of Poland] members, that sudden revolt against the Soviets (they were willing to go against tanks, and they had armed the workers), was that the hatred caused by the murder of the leaders, the old leaders, which had been buried in the unconscious, was at last able to come to the surface. Every Polish Communist party member had retained in memory a profound affection for those leaders. So in that milieu there was something of a model for relations between comrades that was reminiscent of a more classical, patriarchal type, and at the same time there was that infernal dialectic between heterodoxy and orthodoxy. Between enemy and friend.

But now I'd like to say a few words about the Soviet circles with which I was in contact. My first encounter with Bolsheviks occurred in Zakopane, very early on, right after the First World War. An old friend of Lenin's lived there, Boris Vigilev, a Bolshevik. He was suffering from tuberculosis. He had not returned to Russia because his tuberculosis was of the sort that made it dangerous to move him. He was a friend of Strug's—it was Strug who introduced me to him—a friend of Gorky's. The first Bolshevik I ever met. One of those incredibly noble consumptives, living in some utopian, abstract world. Christian souls. I spoke with him a great deal, and he really did have a gentle Christian soul; he would seem to be saying, "I saw a beautiful woman today," when he was talking about how many sailors had been executed. He spoke of that with enormous gentleness. Humanitarianism butting up against cruelty. One of the most enigmatic aspects of the communist mentality . . .

MILOSZ: Didn't the meetings with circles around the Soviet embassy expose you to danger? There must have been surveillance, wasn't there?

WAT: There was total surveillance, but we paid it absolutely no attention. And we started spending a lot of time at the embassy. In the beginning we'd go there when Soviet writers came. And later on we started attending parties and film screenings. Obviously, Mayakovsky was the big hit, the center of things. Mayakovsky's arrival galvanized us. That was before *The Literary Monthly*. Mayakovsky came to Warsaw twice. He described the first trip himself in his sketches, where among other things he said that I was a born futurist, *urozhdyonny futurist*. His second trip was after his return from Paris, not long before his suicide. During his first visit our acquaintance was on the official side, just that, an acquaintance—though we did get together quite frequently. But during his second stay—I don't remember how long he was there, ten days, I think, or two weeks—we were already very close, seeing each other every day in fact.

MILOSZ: Isn't there a photograph of you and Ola in Mayakovsky's published diaries?

WAT: Yes, it was taken at the embassy, but during his second trip. I'm speaking of his first trip.

He was very handsome and a bit on the superhumanly tall side. A type of good looks that were very reminiscent of Witkiewicz's, only bigger boned, everything in proportion but on a scale that exceeded the normal measure. One of the biggest Russians we had ever seen. A picture of manhood, Russian manhood. His eyes were very gentle. With all the strength one felt in him, it was his gaze that was striking. And I think that's another strong similarity with the young Witkacy. Mayakovsky had a gentleness that smacked a little of cosmic melancholy, however. Someone from the embassy said that officially Mayakovsky would, unfortunately, not be able to speak because of the ban. Mayakovsky rose and leaned against something—an upright piano, I think. He was asked to recite a poem. He recited "My Soviet Passport." As you recall, that's a poem of pride in being a Soviet citizen. That was his response to the ban. A voice like Chaliapin's, a powerful voice, an imperious voice and words. I assume that chills went up the spines of quite a few of the people there, for that truly was imperious power. That wasn't a man, that wasn't a poet; that was an empire, the coming world empire. Incredibly haughty. But can that really be called haughtiness? No, that was the pride of the victor. All that somehow made other people pale by comparison.

During Mayakovsky's second visit, Ola took him around to the stores. He bought a tremendous amount of stuff to bring back to Moscow. Twenty pairs of scissors, two hundred razors, and so forth. He ordered everything sent to the embassy. He was wildly enthusiastic about everything that was exquisite and fanciful. Years later we learned that he had given all those things to his friends. But that was the first time I had encountered that. I didn't understand it at the time; only later in Russia did I understand what the hunger for things meant in the Soviet Union. An almost metaphysical need. It's not the instinct for ownership. Absolutely not. It must be said that if there is a positive side to that system, it's that there's no cult of the golden calf there, no doubt because of that communist upbringing. A mad greed for money, but not to amass it. Mayakovsky had a fantastic hunger for things.

During his first visit he was jolly, cheerful, larger than life. But during his second visit when he was on his way back to Moscow from Paris, after his unhappy love affair with that émigré, he was already completely ruined, completely played out. Incredibly depressed, he didn't want to talk politics, and he didn't want to talk about his own troubles: RAPP's attacks on him, * the dissolution of LEF. But that was precisely what interested us greatly because we were LEFists. He had absolutely no desire to talk about things Soviet. He spent most of his time in the embassy playing billiards, and he drank a great deal at that time. He had grown terribly melancholy.

Our conversations were usually interesting, but I don't remember them. I remember only that on one or two nights he kept returning, a bit obsessively, to three writers, Blok in particular. He talked a lot about Esenin—that was about half a year or a few months before his own suicide. And he told me a lot about Shklovsky at that time. Those three people—I had the impression that they were some sort of nightmare for him, some sort of trauma, something that put him out of joint. I do remember that he said explicitly that he had not understood Blok, that only now had he really understood him. He told me of Blok's tragic death in hunger and neglect. I think he said that Blok had been right and he had been wrong—something to that effect. I could not accept that idea because I was a neophyte, full of enthusiasm, but it left some trace because something of it was there even in the obituary I wrote on Mayakovsky.

You had the impression that not only did he have problems in Russia but that he was in despair over the path that Russia had taken. Some sort of premonition. Besides, he was very superstitious. And he also had the habit of constantly washing his hands. Well, the Freudians would classify that as anal eroticism, onanism, and so forth, but I don't

---

* RAPP (Russian Association of Proletarian Writers). From 1928 until 1932, when the Writers' Union was formed, RAPP had near-dictatorial power over Soviet literature.

think that was the case. He offered an explanation of it himself: his father had died from blood poisoning, quite by accident. That was the source of his need for hygiene.

You see, I had an image of Mayakovsky, but that entire period is fading away from me because I consider any aid I render to communism a mortal sin. So evidently there's some sort of antimemory at work here. We simply fell in love with him as a poet. The image of him— with all that strength and size and a certain great inner tenderness. Tenderness—he was very tender. But when news of his suicide arrived, I was not surprised in the least. At that time—*ex post*, of course— I saw the Mayakovsky of the second visit as a candidate for suicide.

OLA WAT: He was in great despair . . . like a man in a trap.

WAT: The suicide of communists. No doubt even communists sometimes commit suicide out of disappointment in love. But that's rather rare. Remember that before his death Mayakovsky wrote that poem about Esenin in which he condemned him fiercely: that is not permitted. A communist has no right; he is not his own master. Mayakovsky was very strong and self-disciplined. I think there was a double despair at work, even a triple despair, or perhaps a quadruple one. The love factor was very important because he was unquestionably in love. But he had terrible problems; he had come under heavy attack. He had incredible difficulties being accepted into RAPP. There was a question of whether to accept him or not. He was attacked, denounced in writing. He had a very hard life. Probably he was not in danger officially. They had sent him abroad; his wallet was stuffed with dollars; they furnished him with enormous sums of money for those trips. And so I think that officially nothing would have been done to him. But he was hounded by the press. And another thing: he had liquidated his own child—LEF—and in none too pretty a manner, in an absolutely conformist manner. He was forced into that conformism, and so he was dissatisfied with himself.

I have no basis for saying this because I don't remember our conversations; I remember only their flavor. But it did occur to me to wonder if he weren't disenchanted with communism. I'm not sure if that was not also a despair due to ideological disappointment. He saw where they were going; even then the more intelligent people could see that. But all factions had long since been banned; Stalin had already emerged. And maybe that conversation about Blok had been on that subject as well, for he was constantly repeating that Blok had been right. I don't think he remained a Bolshevik to the end. During his second visit

Mayakovsky had no desire to talk about ideology. During his second visit he didn't even like to answer questions.

Borowski's suicide was similar to Mayakovsky's [Tadeusz Borowski, author of *This Way to the Gas, Ladies and Gentlemen*]. Borowski would come to see me when Stalinism was at its height to talk about his own schizophrenia, his profound disenchantment, his excessive zeal as a communist, his fanaticism as a means of destroying himself.

Mayakovsky had nothing of that in him. In the last years, especially around 1928, his public statements were not very pretty. In one of them, for example, he spoke recklessly about his closest friend, Shklovsky, the theorist. He denounced him. "Of course, we know that Shklovsky was a reactionary" . . . one thing and another. All his various declarations of loyalty. That was no longer a rebel—Mayakovsky the rebellious nonconformist. By then he was already very much a conformist, joining RAPP, which he hated. RAPP's entire mentality disgusted him.

8 RUSSIA. COMMUNISM. PATRIOTISM.

WAT: I've spoken about the people from the embassy. It might seem unimportant, but in our case it was of enormous importance because to us those were people from "over there"—Russia, a gigantic country, savage, neglected for hundreds of years, where a new life for humanity was to be built, where humanity would be organized on ideal foundations. A hundred and thirty million or so people who were disadvantaged, unfortunate, but also half savage. That was the impression every Pole had. And there was a handful of people who would organize that great mass, bring it to life, and make it into a leaven for the future, for mankind. But for us those people were phantasms. We wanted confirmation and we sought it in those people. Books were books, but you had to see how it looked in human form, in its human incarnation. When we attended receptions at the embassy, we'd see all sorts of faces. They weren't difficult to decipher. Some were Chekists, some weren't; there was even a hero of the Revolution, Ovseenko, but he was the first Soviet man to disappoint us. The others didn't have to set any standard, but he ought to have. He emanated the extreme dryness and style of a tsarist privy councillor—he, the new dignitary.

I don't recall Stalin's name ever coming up. It's a very strange thing—*The Literary Monthly* existed until 1932, and despite all the propaganda I did for the Soviet Union, I don't think Stalin's name was ever mentioned once during that entire time. What did I know about Stalin? I knew a little something. When I look back on all that, I'm amazed at what a muddle it all was. It seems that terrible ignorance is typical of all progressives. The mental map of a progressive who needs a sanctuary that has an actual geographical location is full of areas that should be marked *hic leones*, blank spots—ignorance about a great many essential things mixed with a certain detailed knowledge.

MILOSZ: What you're saying is really, in a certain sense, the classic image of the way Western intellectuals relate to the new world in the East. It's odd that this also happened in Poland, which had abundant historical experience and ought to have understood something about Russia. Probably people like you—now I'm speaking *post mortem*—people like you reacted violently against the Polish national clichés, which sounded like utter nonsense, and we can agree that when it comes to judgments about Russia, those clichés do contain a lot of nonsense. But they also had some understanding of the phenomenon in terms of size, area, the wild dynamic forces latent there. Perhaps you could say something about that.

WAT: You're right on target with that. In Poland more than anywhere else young people like us, and even older people too, rejected en bloc, in advance, a priori, all the knowledge about Russia that had accumulated over generations—precisely because those were clichés, the stereotypes of a society we had rejected. As a matter of fact, some of the most simpleminded, stupid Polish notions about communism were right on target. The only problem was that they were shot from the wrong side of the fence.

I'll give you an example. I have a clear memory of a conversation, from more or less that time, with Jan Nepomucen Miller, a rather unintelligent man. Miller said that he could actually think of himself as a communist if it weren't for Russia's geographic proximity. The Russians are a tremendously dynamic and gifted people, and if Poland went communist, the Poles would immediately be Russianized because the Russians were a much stronger ethnic group than we were. And it turned out that Miller was right to a certain degree: even though the Poles were Russianized, they resisted it. Poles can be very tough. The communists in Poland did everything possible to Russianize the country. Russia exerts tremendous pressure to force assimilation. To us, all that was drivel, stupid empty talk. Our eyes were focused on internationalism.

Not only that, to maintain close, friendly relations with diplomats from the Soviet embassy—in Poland that was treason. But that's part of a very complex problem: if a person is a communist, isn't he immediately what would be called a traitor to Poland? I'm not a good example here; I had a cosmopolitan upbringing. But take Broniewski, an extreme case. As a sixteen-year-old high-school student, he ran away from Płock, joined Piłsudski's Legions, and spent seven years at the front. One war had scarcely ended when he went off to another: Broniewski took part in the uprising in Upper Silesia. He left the army only when there were no more wars to fight. He could recite *Beniowski* by heart. He had everything necessary, all the ABCs of Polishness. He was brought up in that spirit. And his patriotism was always beyond question. In Lwów [in 1939] he acted as a Pole, and with the greatest dignity. He was told straight out that he did not have the right to read his poem "Goes the Soldier Out of Bondage" (one of his best poems) in public, and he didn't comply. He recited that poem every chance he got.

But I'm speaking about Broniewski's patriotism. That wasn't true for everyone. Our group didn't question Poland's borders, but as I've told you, before Nazism the party's official policy was to give Silesia and Gdańsk back to Germany. The core of the party was anti-Polish in outlook. Broniewski was a Polish nationalist, and Wanda Wasilewska was a nationalist too. But those were people who really did think and talk about a Soviet Poland. The myth was that this Soviet Poland would be entirely Polish and at the same time the seventeenth republic in the union of all nations. Utopian, obviously. The people who ran the party conducted a decidedly anti-Polish policy; there was even a certain passion to their anti-Polishness. And those weren't only the Jews in high party positions. That outlook was to be found even more often among certain Poles.

Given Poland's situation, the question of patriotism, treason, and communism was a tangled one. And so as far as our group is concerned, we didn't feel that we were committing treason because we thought that we represented the aspirations of the Polish masses, the workers and peasants.

MILOSZ: Well, we went off on quite a digression about nationalism, patriotism, and other such tendencies. That was valuable. Now we can go back to that other period—was it 1928?

WAT: I was telling you about 1928 and 1929. *The Literary Monthly* was a going concern by 1929. Quite a strange institution. It wasn't an altar, but not that far from one either. The magazine was important to the leaders of the party. I was not a member of the party. Within the party there were various views about my status. Some people approved of it because it helped protect *The Literary Monthly*. Other people thought I was a hopelessly middle-class intellectual who if he were in the party would quickly grow disillusioned with it. Quite recently, an old friend of mine, an excommunist, told me that many people in the party maintained that I was very useful, meaning that I was a decent person but of a hopelessly different mentality. Other people resented my status and brought a lot of pressure to bear, saying that I should be in the party. I didn't want to be in the party, maybe because I thought that I was unworthy, that I would infect the party with my intellectuality. And so it was quite an odd situation. And it was because I wasn't in the party that I didn't ask any questions. Basically, the party is a secret organization and you don't ask questions. Maximum discretion was required from anyone in the party, and even more from me.

I was seeking warmth and brotherhood in the party, in my affiliation with it. But at that time, 1929, 1930, the party was a snake pit. No mass executions had occurred yet, but it was a snake pit. Obviously, the conflict between the minorityites and the majorityites had been a bitter one. And then there were the Trotskyites, the Bukharinites, the Stalinists—you had to grapple with all that. But after working on *The Literary Monthly* for quite some time, I took a narrow view and didn't see any of that. Those disputes seemed purely theoretical, a difference in views. None of it seemed important. I believed in the monolith, and I saw a monolith. In that period, the greater my disenchantment, the more I closed my eyes and turned a deaf ear. I still wanted to keep the faith.

As a matter of fact, communism has assumed paradoxical forms throughout its history. Stawar, Broniewski, and I—that was one group. We represented the imponderabilia of literature; we were the liberals of poetry, humanism, culture, and so forth, as opposed to the political people. But here's the paradox: Hempel, Stande—they were the liberals. We were rabidly sectarian in our views. The party was both delighted and disappointed by *The Literary Monthly*. It was delighted that the magazine had met with such a strong response from young people, workers, and so on, even though it was difficult reading. But the party was also disappointed because it actually wanted a more camouflaged magazine; it wanted *The Literary Monthly* to win over the uncommitted, the more progressive writers, the young writers, and so on. But we were sectarians. For us, anyone who wasn't a committed communist was in the enemy camp. There was a lot of pressure on us all the time—and from our Soviet friends too, who asked why we were making the magazine so openly communist.

Even then I was doing some writing, but I didn't want to publish anything because my entire so-called poetics was anti-Marxist, steeped in the irrational. I also tried my hand at fiction, but I wanted to write fiction that conformed to my views, and what came out was terrible. And so I didn't publish anything. And my communist conscience wouldn't allow me to print anything I thought was good. All I printed of mine were my articles; I didn't contribute anything else, even though I was writing a lot at the time. But I destroyed it all because it was all either no good or un-Marxist.

What were my views on literature, what literature was supposed to be like? Well, the reportage we printed was not only a matter of necessity. I truly thought that there would be no literature in a happy communist society, just as there would be no philosophy. I felt, I realized, that literature was connected to what is least social in man, the antisocial and the irrational. I thought that this was tragic, but that's what literature was at its core. Humanity had to be built rationally. I could see the ugliness of socialist realism, and I thought there could be no communist literature but social realism, meaning no literature. I chose what Shklovsky and the LEF group had chosen: not literature but facts, propaganda.

9 *THE LITERARY MONTHLY:* ARTICLES AND ATTACKS.

WAT: Let's go back to the first issue of *The Literary Monthly*. The first issue immediately took a stringent tack. For example, in the first issue, I attacked Remarque, saying that his was obviously a case of camouflage, that his pacifism channeled antiwar sentiment and reconciled people to the possibility of war, and so on. In a word, the entire Stalinist arsenal (without Stalin) with which I had already been infected. In the second issue I began to denigrate futurism. In the second and third issues I had a long essay, "Memories of a Futurist," or "On Futurism," where, as they say, I put everything in its place, all the avant-garde movements.

Well, as soon as *The Literary Monthly* appeared, it was followed by Słonimski's incredibly acrimonious, malicious, and witty attack on it. Słonimski wrote a feuilleton in which he abused me in particular, my article on Remarque. He was indignant that I had so reviled the noble Remarque and nearly made him into an apostle of the Second World War, which was obviously an exaggeration; that I hadn't done. When *The Literary Monthly* was in the preparatory stage, it seemed that relations would be good with Słonimski, at least in the cafés, and a certain minimal contact even seemed a possibility. But Słonimski's feuilleton was a real hatchet job; he had treated us badly.

Our own reactions were very much out of proportion, furious in the Stalinist style, using invective, abominations. Terrible names: "a vulgar comedian," and so on. I acted as the figurehead in that sorry affair; that means that even though the article wasn't signed, I was speaking on my own behalf. But Słonimski's feuilleton had infuriated *The Literary Monthly*'s entire editorial board and ours was an open article; everyone wrote something, and the result was horrible.

After that, Słonimski went all out. Such mudslinging—instead of a polemic, the most repugnant sort of name-calling. We wouldn't shake hands for a couple of years. But then we forgot about it, and our relations were, on the contrary, very good. But that reaction had been merited because right from the start we had presented ourselves as Bolsheviks with knives in our teeth, fanatics. And so the radical intelligentsia all cut themselves off from us. This clarified the situation. The classic situation of communists in a country like Poland. Guerrillas. Daggers drawn! A knife fight!

If you look through *The Literary Monthly*, you'll be surprised at how easily communist thinking degenerates. Before *The Literary Monthly* was founded, our meetings were marked by subtle analyses of the international and economic situation, with *distinguo* for different capitalist groups and ruling powers. At our conferences, the reports were very intellectual and we knew how to discuss things like grown-up, intelligent people. At bottom, I don't know if any of us had read through all of *Das Kapital*—I tried, but it bored me, and I have the feeling that I wasn't alone in that. That's universal among communists; it happened again and again. Who had read *Das Kapital* in Russia? But we were incredibly taken by *18 Brumaire* and *The Poverty of Philosophy*. Particularly *18 Brumaire* and *The Civil War in France*, where Marx forgets about the Marxist method, where he does not use economics as the basis to explain everything and instead analyzes the political struggle.

And so *The Literary Monthly* found itself in a certain isolation. Reportage was also supposed to have been a way of breaking through to the people, and it had an immediate magnetic effect on the workers who were moving toward communism. I don't even know how to explain how that happened. The communist intelligentsia reproached *The Literary Monthly* for articles that were too difficult and contained too many foreign words. Many of the articles really were quite intellectual. Workers and tradesmen, however, were constantly coming to see me; on the whole a great many people came. The workers didn't complain. They'd say, yes, it's difficult; you have to take some trouble and keep on reading, but that's how you learn. I could see that there were many things they didn't understand. They didn't understand Stawar's articles, but they would find some sentences they could understand. And it was miraculous that in such an intellectual and baffling context there were those sentences that they could understand and that corresponded to their own thoughts. For them this provided some higher sanction of the mind, the higher mind, the intelligence. And they could rest assured in their faith in communism because such intelligent people, people they couldn't understand, sanctioned it . . . When I talk about *The Literary Monthly* and those times, I have the feeling that I'm in some sort of large dark redwood forest with monstrous bushes. I don't know which way is in and which way is out.

MILOSZ: I'm amazed that in a certain sense this is all still current for you, I mean, still painful for you. Why don't you look at it purely historically?

WAT: But, you know, that was a certain central moment in my life, the moment of choice that created all the consequences. And another thing, it involved a great many other people; a great many people were influenced by my choice. And my later disenchantment with communism resulted from that too, was absolutely determined by it. If you come to communism, say, out of class motives or out of political struggle like Silone and others, like your generation in Wilno at the university, out of battles with the ONR,* that might be another story. But mine was a pure choice, subjective, not especially conditioned by anything outside my own will, my own outlook, my own sense of the world, my own spiritual needs. Do you understand? It was a free, pure

---

* ONR (Nationalist-Radical Camp). A right-wing political party in Poland between the wars.

choice! If one makes a pure choice of that sort for communism, that means a certain enchantment is chosen, and it has to result in disenchantment. That process of disenchantment takes a few different forms, which, for the most part, keep repeating themselves.

MILOSZ: In view of the events in 1939 and later on when Poland was conquered by Hitler, and still later by Stalin, were there many choices?

WAT: There weren't a lot of choices. There could be no choice. If you're talking about the situation, about choice in Poland, about the movement of individuals in a history whose balance was tipping then— the history of the world truly was tipping then—then any action, yours, mine, could make no difference. After all, what's going on now is a continuation of that; it is still a thirty years' war. The whole is determined, just as the entirety of the macrophysical world is determined. But if you descend to the level of the individual, you're descending to the level of the electron. The electron has free will and makes its own choices. I don't think it would be right to relate the electron's choice to a situation as specific as the politics of Poland and so on. The electron's choice, which is not determined, has to be related to the greatest whole, which is determined. And the greatest whole, that's two worlds that are in constant conflict. Among the communists I knew were some of the most attractive people I have ever met, people whose motives were incredibly pure. They made their choice with intentions that were pure—I would use that monstrous distinction—subjectively pure. Objectively, they made a choice for Stalin. In relation to the great determined whole, they made a choice for Stalin and what he was. It seems to me that I have cause for not treating this as an episode that is limited geographically.

It is difficult for me to remember what I was like in that period, though on the whole I have a good memory. For example, I remember a series of later events quite well. But I have to wrest this period from memory because that was the central moment of choice. And yet there's another paradox. Those few years were very happy ones, perhaps the happiest time of my life. Ola and I were very much in love. I had extricated myself from desperation, hopelessness, and the sense of absolute absurdity. That's nothing new. Beckett's nothing new. All this had become prevalent before dadaism, after all. But let's take dadaism itself. Those weren't only cynics; those were people driven to despair. That's an old story in Europe. I had extricated myself through a conscious effort, a decision deriving precisely from that existential choice. I had a cause, I had a goal, and once again I had what we were talking about, what intellectuals in our time dream of: a *vita activa*.

Not only to interpret, but to change the world with your own hands. And I had my brothers in the jungle, bombarded and surrounded in a wild jungle.

And one more thing: the game was fundamentally honest. For after all there could be no doubt that it would end with prison. Only the idyllic conditions in Poland kept people out of prison or limited their stays to a few weeks when the district attorney, the investigating magistrate, the secret police of the time had enough material on all of us, and on me in particular, to send us to prison for at least five to ten years. After all, apart from *The Literary Monthly*, I was involved in a lot of other things. So that was an honest game; you accepted that sooner or later you'd have to pay. There was a lot of recklessness in this. Besides, Kawczak, the district attorney, had said, "We don't want to make martyrs out of them." But finally it had to come to an end; it was supposed to.

I'm not speaking of another motivation that was at work in our good-sized group—solidarity with the oppressed. I did not find brotherly warmth among my colleagues and among the communists at *The Literary Monthly*. On the contrary, when I entered the game, it turned out that the same dogged struggles, hatreds, suspicions were there, certain factions, certain echoes of distant battles that were occurring in Russia. But it was only then that I had contact with unemployed intellectuals and workers. For example, a terribly nice person came to see us at the editorial office. He lived on Krucza Street—he had two or three children—an unemployed upholsterer. I helped him out; I had some armchairs made, and I encouraged anyone I could to give him some orders. He was an excellent craftsman. A month didn't pass without his coming by. A nice modest person. He never complained. One day he cut his children's throats and his wife's and then committed suicide. That was a notorious case.

When running *The Literary Monthly*, I had my finger on those wounds, those sufferings. There was a certain double action here, however, a movement in opposite directions. To the degree that I was creating *The Literary Monthly* and entering into working relations with the communists, with the leading communists or my colleagues on the editorial board or people outside the board, I was increasingly struck by various suspicious things and found it increasingly less to my liking. But I was also increasingly in touch with people's wounds, their suffering, their endless suffering. For some of them there seemed to be no remedy apart from a revolution. Only later did I learn that a revolution would bring those people nothing except new sufferings. But I didn't know that then.

We printed various poets. Well, those weren't good poets. I was young then and quite shameless—I corrected their poetry. The first issue came out in December 1929. I open the issue and here's Stawar's article "Red Wings," where he deftly points out a certain camouflage technique. For example:

When a country goes radical, there's trouble. Social relations are laid bare. Foreign capital is cynically exploiting the Polish worker. And the regime writer catches hold of these moods, directing everything, all the hatred and all the blame, the sin, onto foreign capitalists.

Stawar used to do that very intelligently, but on a vulgar Marxist-Leninist base.

. . . The third issue. An article in praise of Russian formalism. We were entirely in favor of formalism, Shklovsky, LEF. Mayakovsky and Shklovsky were against socialist realism, the Proletcultists, and so on and in favor of a progressive, avant-garde, revolutionary art. There was another article against pacifism. The things we attacked! Stawar's polemic with the Piłsudski-ite left. We were always attacking the radical left. Madness, my dears, madness! It was already 1930; Hitler was already in view, coming to the fore; the ONR was already emerging in Poland. But *The Literary Monthly* was playing around unmasking radicals, the radical intelligentsia.

. . . I wrote Mayakovsky's obituary. A year ago I looked through that obituary. I picked up a copy of *The Literary Monthly* and wondered what I had written in it. But, thank God, I was tactful; I didn't reproach him for committing suicide. A photograph of him on his deathbed. A poem about him by Stande. A translation of him by Wygodzki. The whole issue dedicated to Mayakovsky . . . It was then that the confiscations started. They hadn't confiscated anything for a very long time.

In the seventh issue I published some reportage. The workers didn't know what reportage was supposed to be, and so I wrote a short article on reportage and provided some examples, very carefully chosen ones. From Larisa Reisner, a Soviet communist and a beautiful woman; one about Ulstein, the baronial exploitive press consortium; about Ford in Detroit, people turned into machines, assembly lines. On the other hand, a new world in the Soviet Union, shockworkers, and so on.

In the eleventh issue, I had reportage about Wilno, a factory there. I had reportage by Stanisław Wygodzki from a prison in Piotrków. I was corresponding with *New Masses*, the American communists. One of them wrote me that their magazine was beginning its twenty-first year of publication. A Pole, Edward Falkowski, a cook in the socialist school's restaurant, had founded the *New Masses* in 1910.

The twelfth issue was confiscated in its entirety. A financial blow. That was in 1930, October–November. Why was it confiscated? It was still being printed in Warsaw. And it was precisely then that we were warned by the district attorney, Kawczak, that if there was one more confiscation, the magazine would be shut down.

10 *THE LITERARY MONTHLY.* ISAAC DEUTSCHER. FIRST ARREST. POLITICS AND BEDROOM FARCE.

WAT: One remark: I have a tendency to denigrate and slight certain things, to paint things blacker than they were in reality. Obviously, I have my reasons now for taking such a bleak view and denigrating my past. But there are also reasons that predate these, which have been operating for a long time.

As for the journalism in *The Literary Monthly*, it was on a fairly high level. And it may have been more sensible than what the Marxist and communist writers wrote in Poland during the time of Stalinism. Many of those people of course had been inspired by *The Literary Monthly*. Whether they had been inspired by it or not, they discovered it anew and used it as a model. Now their work strikes me as more simplistic than *The Literary Monthly*'s. It would be difficult to say that *The Literary Monthly*'s main articles were simplistic; if they were, the magazine would not have exerted such influence on its proselytes and its opponents. It would have been taken less seriously if it had been simplistic . . . Now I cannot even force myself to read those articles. But certainly I paint too black a picture now . . . And the reportage illuminated life at the bottom, the life of the masses, the lower classes, and the national minorities like no other magazine, no other publication at that time.

So issue after issue came out. The fifteenth issue again had reportage and bellicose poetry. Another long-winded polemic, Stande's Talmudic polemic on the subject of the Marxist critic, full of quotations from Plekhanov and Lenin. But Stalin's name didn't come up. It was only 1930. And obviously we were very polemical about current literature. Deutscher's article on Sholem Asch—another unmasking:

Our role on Polish soil is especially important in view of the Jewish masses' turning fascist, a process that encounters special difficulties because of the combination of social and national oppression. And hence the cult the Jewish bourgeoisie is building up around Asch. The exceptionally gracious relationship on the part of Polish literature's official circles—banquets, receptions, the welcome given Asch—circles that in general repudiate contact with Jewish writers—is to be explained not only by the fascist values in his fiction but also by the specific political actions that Asch is undertaking in the arena of so-called Polish-Jewish relations. Asch has truly shown great initiative and activity in the effort to harmonize the policies of the Jewish political parties with and to subordinate them to the postulates of the fascism now prevailing.

It was precisely that reportage that offered me great opportunities . . . I told you about the people I encountered, like that upholsterer who killed his children and committed suicide. I was touching the wounds and so I became more involved. But by that time the entire intellectual superstructure had already begun to bore me to death. I had already realized how bankrupt it was. As *The Literary Monthly* was becoming increasingly effective politically, its literary bankruptcy became apparent—the whole group's, and mine personally. That was 1931.

I went back to what had interested me very much before I went over to communism, namely, Proust and Joyce. I wrote an essay about them. I started to return to intellectual health, but I could see the catastrophic elements in their work—I mean, the extent of their decadence. As I remember it, my interest was simply in the problem of the human personality, the disintegration of the personality. The ego. The "I." So it was rather personalistic criticism. The Western world had brought things to a pass where the very essence of that world—namely, the personality from which it drew its strength and beauty—had been called into question. The personality was called into question by Proust, by those skeins that only memory can join together. And in Joyce too. Writing about those authors indicates how tired I was of the subjects Stande wrote on. Again Deutscher unmasks Pan-Europe and Romain Rolland!

In his creative work Romain Rolland is a classic representative of petit-bourgeois humanitarianism. He is a spokesman for those elements of the intelligentsia who have blended in with the machinery of bourgeois culture and imbibed its best, earliest traditions along with its most harmful reactionary fetishes.

The Literary Monthly was a sizeable venture politically and exerted enormous influence. That's difficult to fathom today. We put out editions of five thousand, but every copy was read until there was nothing left of it. Twenty people would chip in to buy a copy. There were copies in all the prisons. The magazine was read by everyone leaning toward communism, and it had uncommon authority. It's hard for me to say how it achieved that authority. But it might have been the most intelligent of the open, legal communist periodicals.

Literarily, it was a flop. We were closed up in our little ghetto of just a few people. We had brutally separated ourselves from the entire literary world, and so there was no question of influencing that world. There was rather a direct influence on the youth who were still in high school or in the first or second year at the university and who hadn't entered literature yet.

Thus, for example, in his memoirs Putrament writes that he dedicated a poem to me, entitled "Aleksander Wat." Which shows, as he once told me himself, that *The Literary Monthly* was the stuff of legend for him, and I, as the founder of *The Literary Monthly*, was a legendary figure. And that's the source of that terrible ferocity with which he persecuted me as a renegade in the Bierut years. That was probably a case of disappointed love; after all, he had written a poem about me.

I had constant proof of *The Literary Monthly*'s effect and influence. I must, however, point out that never—neither in Russia when under interrogation nor in Poland after the war—did I make any reference to my so-called services in connection with *The Literary Monthly*. Not even at the times when I was completely beaten, during the first year of my illness when I simply could not live with my pain and made efforts to be sent out of the country for treatment. In those applications to be sent abroad or in the autobiographies I attached to them, however, I never traded on those services with so much as a single word. Besides, my God, I couldn't do that, after all, even if only because in Russia, in prison there, I had acknowledged *The Literary Monthly* as my greatest sin. And so I didn't bring it up.

But like that mysterious brother in Pasternak who keeps getting Doctor Zhivago out of trouble, *The Literary Monthly* kept getting me out of tight spots too—that is, people's memory of *The Literary Monthly*. Because it really was a legend—for the old KPP members especially. After the war, when I returned to Poland from Russia, they couldn't make an anthology of *The Literary Monthly* because I was a renegade. Stawar was a renegade, and none of the others had been rehabilitated in Russia yet. But still they were constantly stressing the magazine's importance privately, in conversation.

At one point in 1948 I was still going to receptions. At the last reception I attended in the beautiful palace and park of the Council of Ministers, a man walked over to me and said, "What, don't you recognize me? But I was in the editorial offices of *The Literary Monthly* so many times. That was an incredibly memorable period for me! Those were my beginnings. *The Literary Monthly* introduced me to the world of communism." And he looked into my eyes with such affection that it would have felt stupid to say that I didn't recognize him. I muttered: "Yes, yes, now I recognize you!" And then like a fool I asked, "And what are you doing here?" "Here? I'm the deputy prime minister!" he said, but with utter modesty. That was Korzycki from the Peasant party. So, there was plenty of that. . . .

Well, 1931. As a literary group we were completely lost. Not only had we not extended our influence, but I was completely at a standstill literarily. In reality, Broniewski was the only one left. At the same time a definite split had occurred within the editorial board. Hempel had taken something of a fall in the party. He was still on the editorial board, but he was no longer the trusted link with the party. There were fights with Stawar, and something happened with Deutscher too at that time. Hitler was already casting a shadow. It was then that they finally shut us down. We were arrested at the beginning of September, if I'm not mistaken. How did it happen, why? Perhaps there is some explanation in the party archives in Warsaw as to why they didn't shut us down earlier, and why they chose to then. But it's not out of the question that it was simply a matter of chance.

Ola had just given birth to Andrzej. The delivery had not gone well. She had a puerperal infection and fought with death for a month. That was not a good time for me. She was saved by a miracle, for there were no antibiotics, no penicillin then. When Ola was out of the clinic, we moved into my in-laws' apartment on Żórawia Street, much larger and more comfortable than ours. Only the maid stayed on at Hoża Street at the editorial offices and our apartment. My in-laws were not in Warsaw—they had gone away for the summer—and I called an editorial meeting there, and not on Hoża Street.

Apparently—this is how I reconstruct it—police spies were following Hempel or Nowogródzki and saw one or the other in a place where there hadn't been any communists before. Broniewski came later on. They were all people known to the police spies. The police spies probably didn't know what was going on. Nowogródzki was an important communist, and so they might have suspected that some important communist meeting was being held in a new place. All Żórawia Street was full of police, police all over the place. Around ten of them with revolvers came into the apartment. They were led by the assistant commissioner, Pogorzelski. They came into the living room where we were holding our meeting; there were stacks of manuscripts on the table. I remember how Pogorzelski's eyes began to gleam. I may be mistaken, but he probably thought that this was a meeting of the party central editorial board or something of that sort because as soon as he had looked more closely and seen *The Literary Monthly* material, his face fell. I could see a certain boredom come over it. Disappointment!

Of course there was a search. Ola was still weak then. Well, for some reason they didn't touch Ola, but they did take her brother, a medical student, a sickly boy who died of tuberculosis a couple of years later. Later on I had some pangs of conscience. They took him even though he had no leanings toward communism, had nothing in common with it. They released him after four or five weeks, but in the meantime he had taken part in a nearly four-day-long hunger strike with us.

Should I tell a funny story here? They took each one of us individually. I was taken to a car and brought to Hoża Street, where they were planning to search my apartment. We rang the bell. A commotion. Our maid was named Genia, a very pretty girl who was promiscuous. She had a fiancé who worked at Borman's as an electrical engineer; he was her fiancé in the evening hours. She was a very intelligent girl, very charming. It was the police, so she had to open the door. It was midnight. Some guy was in our bed, very good-looking. A dress coat and dress shirt were hanging on the chair. It turned out that he was a footman from the Italian fascist embassy, a Pole, her sister's fiancé apparently. He was in despair of losing his job. The plainclothesman wanted to take him in along with me. He explained that he worked in the embassy, but the plainclothesman didn't believe him. Finally, we all started laughing because the situation was laughable. The plainclothesman called the embassy to find out if he worked there and then handed him the receiver. He took it and explained that he had dropped by an apartment and the communist who lived there was being arrested. And clearly the people on the other end asked him, "Who is this guy?" to which he answered, "How should I know who the guy is?" That I found irritating. He sleeps with my maid in my marriage bed and, to top it off, he speaks like that of me. And so I said to the plainclothesman in jest, "You know, maybe we should be brought in together." But of course they let him go.

That's not the end of the story, though. After the war, Buczkowski—not Leopold, but his brother Marian, who was also a writer—told me, "Picture this. You were living on Hoża Street and you had a maid named Genia. My brother—not the writer, the bank teller—was strolling down Aleje Jerozolimskie with his friend. Two chic-looking girls came walking by. One word led to another, and one of the girls brought them back to her place. They bought vodka and a little something to eat on the way. The one who had brought them home said that she worked as a secretary at *The Literary Monthly*. My brother's friend had already gotten into bed with one of them, so that left Genia for my brother. But then suddenly he was overcome by some terrible attack of anxiety. He couldn't understand it himself. He left Genia, ran into the bedroom, dragged out his friend and said, "Get dressed right this minute. We're getting out of here." It was 11:15 at night. The next morning he read that I had been arrested. Out of simple disappointment Genia had apparently called up that footman and had him come over. And that's how comic incidents get mixed up with things of political importance. Sex and politics in this case.

Of the material on the table there was one thing that was very dangerous to me personally and had me frightened. Specifically, I had organized a protest against Michałowski's new prison regulations. All that material had already been prepared to be sent out: the text of the protest, the original with the signatures I had collected. A great many copies had already been placed in addressed envelopes, including those addressed to correspondents from the foreign newspapers, which were never looked on favorably in Poland. If my case promised to be particularly bad, it was apparently, as I later learned in detail, on account of Michałowski's fury; he said he would not release me.

Another thing I was worried about was that they would ask about our friendly relations with the Soviet embassy. While *The Literary Monthly* was being published, however, those relations had fallen off considerably, precisely because of the question of safety. I avoided contacts so as not to place the magazine in greater jeopardy. But we went to all the receptions, especially when Soviet writers were in town. Moreover, I had gotten material from the embassy, all the literary periodicals. I had an enormous collection of periodicals. They gave me all the latest publications, books. And so I was afraid that they would pressure me on that point during the investigation. Aside from that, I did not, in the end, belong to the party and so I couldn't expect a long sentence. But those things were beyond question: the campaign against Minister Michałowski, slandering Poland abroad via the foreign correspondents, and the matter of the Soviet embassy.

Strangely, there was never the slightest mention of the Soviet embassy during the investigation. And not only during the investigation, which is also interesting. In Poland in 1931 there was absolutely no mention, not once, of our contacts with the embassy and with Soviet writers. All in all, I doubt whether the word "Soviets" was even uttered. But when I was arrested in Lwów and investigated by the Soviets, I was afraid of all this again, because the greater part of *The Literary Monthly*'s staff had been liquidated by the Soviets as agents—Hempel,

Stande. I was afraid that they would rebuke me for my contacts with the members of the Soviet embassy who had also been liquidated by them. And they were fully informed about all that. When they finished the investigation, they read me the depositions. Borejsza's deposition really qualified me for the death penalty. Among other things I remember verbatim:

He founded and edited the magazine with the cooperation of Jan Hempel, Stande, Wandurski (which wasn't true; Wandurski had already left Poland) and Jasieński who, as substantiated by investigation in the Soviet Union, were agents of Polish intelligence and were executed.

So, as you can see, Borejsza gave me quite a lovely recommendation.

Nevertheless, there was never a single word on that subject, neither in Lwów nor in Lubyanka. I explain the silence of the Soviet authorities, the NKVD, on the subject of *The Literary Monthly* as the NKVD's reluctance to bring up issues that had long since been entirely liquidated and closed, sent to the archives for eternal storage. There was no trace left of the people I had been in contact with; they had all lost their lives already. A bureaucracy's normal sense of purpose requires that certain material be considered dead and not returned to. So I assume that they no longer had any interest in that. Why didn't the Polish investigating authorities say anything on the subject? That was the period when the flirtation with the USSR had begun; Radek came to Warsaw soon after that. Miedziński had gone to Moscow as Piłsudski's emissary and had had talks with Radek. There was talk about a nonaggression pact to establish closer ties with the Soviets, to set up a Polish-Soviet friendship society or some sort of Polish-Soviet society. These are just guesses—I don't know how correct they are.

But the fact is that when they took us and brought us to the security division, I was in front of an investigating magistrate right away, that same night. Later there was an NKVD man who reminded me of that policeman. They're all alike, at least certain types. There is a type of policeman, in the secret police, to be found in all countries, all social systems. The magistrate was incredibly crude but not brutal, and incredibly gloomy. His first statement was, "As you know, sir, today (or yesterday) the Sejm declared a state of martial law (or something to that effect). Your crime now carries the death penalty." That was a little too crude to frighten me. Any such state of martial law aside, I knew perfectly well that there was no question of the death penalty for me; he had overshot the mark, and in this case the attempt at intimidation had failed. After that interrogation—it lasted about an hour, an hour and a half—all my personal data were taken down. Obviously, they began by ascribing some demonic role to me, a high place in the upper party hierarchy, some sort of secret activity. Very trite stuff, and there was nothing else besides that trite stuff.

Did I behave like a coward? Probably not too much. I can't reproduce the state I was in then. As I've already told you, I knew that this would happen in the end. That was just a bad period for me because Ola had just come through a serious illness, and Andrzej too was on the weak side, and then there was my brother-in-law. All in all, none too good. I had a sort of inborn sense of fatalism that was of great help to me. In those ultimate situations, in Russia too, some sort of Oriental soul would immediately emerge: happiness is over, fate is unavoidable, fate is knocking. And so, inasmuch as I can recall what I felt then, it was just that—happiness was over. I imagined that I'd be given four years, five years maximum. That was very hard for me to think about in relation to Ola, for we really had never been apart; we were inseparable.

But this was also a certain baptism, a knighting. I imagined that it was only in prison that I would be elevated and become worthy of the church, the heart of the fighting proletariat. That would be my university, my school, my holy communion. I consoled myself that I would come out of it not as a broken, flabby intellectual but as a manly, courageous revolutionary—as a person who had begun to believe in the church but who is still not a member of the church believes that when he is baptized, sprinkled with holy water, all his doubts, all his uncertainties will immediately fall away from him. And then, you see, I would find myself in the light of revelation, the pure light. But already by that time intellectual doubts were eating away at me. I could see the vulgarity of *The Literary Monthly*, the intellectual vulgarity in it—the worst vulgarity of all: cerebral vulgarity. And so I thought that I would rid myself of that, that I would enter some other body.

How did I behave afterwards during the investigation? I suppose I passed the test. I may have talked too much—I'm a blabbermouth. So sometimes after those talks with the investigating magistrate I rebuked myself for blabbing too much. But I think I rather behaved with dignity. In any case I behaved properly in the cell. I took part in the hunger strike, for four days. On May 1 when they took us out for our walk, we knew there'd be a massacre if we demonstrated. And in fact when we came out into the yard and each of us was wearing something red in his lapel, we could see armed guards, plainclothesmen in all the windows. Nevertheless, we walked about that small yard with a brave, soldierly step. Soldiers of the revolution. And we sang "Higher and higher and higher" in Russian—not too loud, it's true, but loud enough, and there were those menacing faces, those revolvers. They were probably supposed to give us a beating, but they didn't. And so I adapted to all that.

They arrested us in September during Jewish New Year. They packed us into the cellars of the Security Division, which was housed in the cellars of Central Prison on Danilowiczowska Street, where we were imprisoned later. The investigating offices were upstairs, and the Security Division was down below in the cellars. The cells were quite clean but covered with graffiti. Plank beds. And they pushed us into a large cell, which at the time was occupied by Jewish bakers. That was a very communist union. I don't know if they had been preparing a strike, but they had all been picked up during the holidays and jailed in the Security Division. There was plenty of food in those cells. Jewish bakers arrested during the holiday, and so of course they had all their holiday treats with them. Broniewski was there; Stawar and I and Hempel and Nowogródzki, who had come to an editorial board meeting for the first or second time. Spirits were high in the cell; those were communists who were used to the Security Division. They had been arrested frequently and released. We found prison so interesting that there really was no time to think about ourselves. Those were lively days.

11 CENTRAL PRISON. BRONIEWSKI THE EGOTIST. CONTACT WITH THE WORKING CLASS AS EDITOR AND CELL MATE.

WAT: It was cell number thirteen as I remember. In the beginning we were in with the bakers, and later on we were put in a separate cell. I don't remember exactly how long we were in the cellars at Security. I think it was rather a long time, but your sense of time becomes confused in prison; you can't rely on it. We were in cell thirteen while the initial, basic investigation was going on; only later were we taken to prison. What's more, everyone involved in that case was in the same cell, which is in obvious contradiction to all principles of investigation. That could never happen in Soviet Russia.

The main thing is how a person stands up to prison. I learned right away that I could not take being in prison, much as I had thought about it before. It had been easy to visualize myself as a prisoner—there was even a certain piquancy to that—and then suddenly it turns out that it makes you want to howl. What was it that bothered me? Obviously, it was personal: separation from my family, especially with Ola being ill. She had just come out of the clinic with Andrzej. It was then that I felt the true hardship of prison, which I was able to understand in its pure form only in Lubyanka. Really, as the communists say, the first ten years are the hardest. But that isn't true. At some point toward the end of my time in Lubyanka, I learned how to be in prison. And it was only there that I could see what makes prison so terribly difficult for a certain class of people: not everyone bears up to it in the same way. Well, it's what I said: it's only in prison that you learn that the individual is not autonomous, that you're part of the symbiosis in which you live, and so there is a feeling of separation, of being crippled, cut off.

Another thing that became real for me, particularly in Lubyanka, was the feeling of being walled in. Obviously, it would be difficult to say the same about Warsaw prison where there was constant communication, both between prisoners from different cells and with the outside world. There was a well-organized system for smuggling notes out to the city, and not only that, but notes were received from the city as well. So, for example, I received quite large food packages every day and they always contained herrings. There was always a letter from Ola in the head of the herring. So, the most elementary precautions were not taken by the prison guards and the Warsaw police. I felt even less walled in than Broniewski, who was like an animal, a caged lion. He was constantly pacing in circles; the bars were constantly before his eyes, the feeling of the bars.

A third thing that is particularly hard to bear and that is experienced to perfection in Lubyanka in cells that are absolutely walled off from the world are those paradoxes of time when the present becomes incredibly distended, expanded like an accordion, while the time behind you, the past, contracts. It seems that the days you have behind you, the past, are only a single day, that time contracts, has little content, whereas the time you have ahead of you is a wasteland, totally terrifying. I'm describing this very briefly here because the experience of time in prison can be described only in connection with Lubyanka, but even in such decent, homey prisons as the one in Warsaw, those phenomena also occurred, though to a lesser degree.

It was there that I learned to value Jan Hempel highly. As the co-editor of *The Literary Monthly*, he had always been in a panic; he was always a worn-out party functionary, always saying, "Oi, what are the leaders going to say about this? Oi, oi, what are they going to say about this in the party?" He was always looking around; his hands were al-

66

ways trembling. And then suddenly in prison, an enormous contrast—
the calm, the majesty, the goodness that he radiated, the calm concentration that was the source of the goodness he radiated. He taught us
not only how one should talk and act during an investigation but also
how to behave in prison. He reconciled all conflicts, particularly the
conflicts that erupted between me and Broniewski. Some sort of prison
hatred, prison poison, flows between people locked up in the same
cell. He was always reconciling people, talking them around. He was
the father of the cell.

Once during the night Hempel woke up—he suffered terrible stomach pains; he had a stomach ulcer—and he said, "Two blast furnaces
have just been fired in Magnitogorsk." He really would sit in that stinking cell and talk about Magnitogorsk with a sort of quiet passion. A
dreamer. That was a point of connection with the former sun worshipper who used to pray to the sun in the morning; now he worshipped
the glow that rose above Magnitogorsk—an easy transition, isn't that
so? Since we're talking about Magnitogorsk: we really did dream of
the blast furnaces there. At that time we did not know—a little later
on the party found out, especially the higher spheres of the intelligentsia—but we didn't know then that Magnitogorsk had been built
on the corpses of peasants herded there from the Ukraine, from all
over Russia. We didn't know about that but, even had we known, I
don't believe that would have changed things much in that period. We
had our answer ready: the price of revolution. We had entered that
circle; I at least was already in that terrible circle where people are
human material, an abstraction. People are ideas, they serve the idea,
are part of the idea, are the instrument of the idea—and I suppose that
would not have shocked us.

But we're talking about specifics here. Broniewski acted like a horrible egotist in the cell. At the same time there was something attractive about him. *Indomptable*, totally undaunted, he was constantly
pacing the cell, marching around, smoking one cigarette after another,
and he had a mania about escaping. That was a rather common mania,
but he took it seriously. He had a great variety of childish, fantastical
ideas of how to escape, tunnel out, file through the bars. Sometimes
the scenario was very complicated, supercomplicated, but he didn't
take this as a flight of fantasy that somehow or another had to feed itself
in the cell; he really took it seriously. Besides, you read in all the memoirs of officers who were prisoners of war about those types who lived
by that mania even when it made no sense or when it could have ended
with the massacre of their colleagues.

Broniewski could not sleep at night; I mean, he'd fall asleep and then wake up rather soon. It would start with his blowing his nose, clearing his throat, coughing, sudden movements, but we wouldn't react. You know, in prison sleep comes as a great relief. Even when you're not asleep you have to somehow become immersed in yourself, close your eyes. You can return home—those are the best hours. And then at one or two in the morning he'd start clearing his throat, tossing and turning, and finally, when there was no reaction he would jump out of bed, furious, start singing and smoking cigarettes, and, if that didn't work, he'd grab you by the hand and either recite his poetry or launch into a philosophical conversation. He would recite from memory either his own poetry or else, usually, Słowacki's. He had an excellent memory; he knew a great many of Słowacki's poems by heart. Of the poets I've known, only Broniewski, and perhaps Gałczyński, were poets who never forgot that they were poets in the good sense of the word, who absolutely refused to descend from that *mode d'exister* that is the poet: poetry in any circumstance. (Obviously, nowadays a certain lack of judgment is required to believe in the mission and calling of the poet as bard.) He recited his own poems very well. There was a certain theatricality to it; you always knew at what point his face would suddenly go pale with rage, when his voice would become muffled and he would begin to draw out his words, and at what point it would again become pure, idyllic, pastoral. And so you had to listen to poetry, sometimes for whole nights on end. He was robbing me of sleep, which made our relations very bad, tense, but, thanks to Hempel, it never ended in a fight.

Stawar was there too, a very closed person, very straightforward and wise, but always a terrible purveyor of gloom. He was even gloomier in jail than in regular life and predicted the worst possible sentences. Nowogródzki was with us too. He was the most intelligent politician when it came to Marxism. Later on there were fewer such people, but the old KPP people, Marxists like him, really knew Marx's *Kapital*.

They had phenomenal memories for quotation, encyclopedic when it came to statistics. How much bread was produced in Russia in 1913 and how much in 1928, how much sugar was consumed per capita. They knew all that, absolutely everything; that was a peculiar ability of theirs. I don't know, perhaps they were people who had had some higher Talmudic education in their childhoods. In religious Jewish homes children at five or six begin memorizing whole pages not of the Bible but of the Talmud with all its casuistry. I knew a person who was learning the Soviet encyclopedia that way. At that time the encyclopedia had only reached the letter K, and so he was incredibly well educated up to the letter K, knew everything up to K.

I remember well that I used to have philosophical debates with Nowogródzki. I recall a debate over principles, a philosophical-esthetic debate, naturally. I don't remember the details, but I have excellent recall of the boundaries of the discussion, its themes. The theme was that the ultimate end was good. That we knew. We agreed that the means currently being used were bad; that was in accord with our standards as communists. At that time it wasn't said that the means being used were good; that was for the common people. The esoteric truth, however, was that the means were bad but the goal, great, splendid, and singular, justified them. So the entire discussion and my own doubts revolved around that good end.

That was a fundamental question, the most basic question that was disturbing me during *The Literary Monthly* period. Everyone who went over to communism had to accept the Leninist principle that you couldn't make omelettes without breaking eggs. That was the first thing. But a basic question arose here, and I asked myself that question: what certainty is there; where are the criteria for that certainty? I was defenseless in my debate with Nowogródzki because he showered me with numbers, and it's difficult to argue with numbers—if numbers are accepted as an argument. One could use as a counter-argument Ivan Karamazov's position that all the harmony of the universe is not worth the single tear of a child who has been wronged. Obviously, a certain gradation could be introduced here as God did with Abraham and with Sodom. Not one tear but ten, or ten children. But as soon as one enters Marxism, several unspoken assumptions are accepted. The omelette is the first assumption, and the second is that numbers are an argument, that one can have a certain faith in determination, not only qualitative but quantitative. Qualitative determination is typical not only of Marxism and communism but also of many religions. But the quantitative (Abraham and Sodom: ten yes, but eleven no) is the contribution of French scientism: quantity as an ethical argument, the majority, the minority, what constitutes the majority. It all follows from that. It follows that fractions cannot exist, that the minority must without further discussion submit to the decrees, worldview, and theories of the party majority.

I don't recall the details of the investigation. It was dull, boring, and, at bottom, unthreatening. The investigator—I remember his face but not his name—was a type common in Russia, and later on in Poland too. Not a policeman by temperament or conviction, but a policeman-clerk, a policeman-bureaucrat. His behavior had its contrasts. On the one hand, he made terrible threats to us; as I told you, the death penalty (which was ridiculous), very heavy sentences. And, on the other hand, though he had a lot of material that would have been entirely sufficient to slap us with long sentences, he did not extract the dangerous elements from that material—elements that would have been difficult for us to explain away. I assume those were his instructions. It was possible that in the main the incident had been caused by our changing the place of the meeting, and they might have wanted to extricate themselves from the whole thing after a certain time.

One point argues against that: the absolutely fantastic publicity our arrest was given by the entire press—not just the gutter press, but the Catholic press too. The day after our arrest there were enormous front-page stories and for two or three days our pictures were in the paper, with our numbers, of course. People always look like criminals in mug shots. I think they turned everyone, with the exception of Broniewski, into Jews. So Hempel was turned into Szloma—I don't remember what it was—Grynhorn or Grynwasser. They went wild with the story, writing that some incredibly big fish had been caught, and material evidence of an international Comintern conspiracy had been found and an enormous sum of money, dollars. God only knows . . . To make a long story short, it was a great sensation. It should be said that the well-educated press behaved decently, the people with *Kinderstube*, that is, the conservatives. The *Warsaw Courier* wrote very discreetly about it, and so, I think, did the Wilno *Word* and Krakow *Time*.

I must have been a month there in Security, in cell number thirteen. One day we were simply escorted upstairs to Central Prison, where our group was broken up and sent to different cells. And that was when my great experience of life began, for I found myself in a cell that was almost all proletarians—in any case, pure communists. It was a school I had not expected and was unprepared for. What was my previous contact with the proletariat, with the Warsaw working class? For a long time I had known some former workmen, old communists and PPS members, one a beautiful specimen of the Polish worker who had participated in the events of 1905. Those were people with life wisdom.

In nineteen fifty something, I said half in jest to Stawar, "Listen, I really owe all this to you. You're to blame; you got me into communism." Stawar was a straightforward and basically good person, but, as often happens with self-educated people from the working class, he had great intellectual contempt for people, a certain grimace of contempt. Sometimes that itself would serve him as sufficient argument. When he made that grimace, the corners of his mouth turning down, that often meant that the discussion was over for him. And so he answered me with a grimace of contempt like that: "You would have ended up there anyway."

At the time I told myself that he was probably right. No Freudianism is needed here, for this isn't sex; I don't think any father or mother image was at work here, at least in my case. I had a lot of brothers and sisters, and they were engagé; one was in the PPS. In 1905, when I was five years old, my father and sisters returned home bloody from the massacre on Theater Square, and I used to sing and lead my playmates around the courtyard with a little red flag. So, you see, that flag "will flutter above thrones; it bears the thunder of vengeance, for the blood of the workers is on it"—those are things that truly lodge in your heart. Those little demons or angels that enter you along with a song. And it comes as no surprise that the communists fought against jazz for as long as they could.

A little more about my contact with the working class. Roughly before the time of *The Literary Monthly*, I was friendly with various people who brought me to the People's University, where I gave lectures for workers. But I felt embarrassed, a member of the foolish, contemptible intelligentsia with their sense of guilt toward the proletariat. I spoke quite frequently at meetings of the Writers' Union and I was nervy there, extremely nervy, but I blushed at those meetings of workers. The workers' auditorium always made me feel embarrassed. Later on, during the *Literary Monthly* period, workers would come to see me, but something made those relations false; they were coming to see me as the great editor, with a whole mythology. I told you there was a certain mythology around *The Literary Monthly*, which was expressed in Putrament's poem about me; he didn't know me then.

Aha, perhaps another incident to show the extent of that mythology. As far as intellectual circles were concerned, *The Literary Monthly* had more effect on high school students than on those at the university. In the early sixties, at a reception at the Bondys in Paris, Romain Gary walked over to me. Bondy had brought him over and said, "C'est un poète polonais, Aleksander Wat." And then Gary replied in Polish, "Aleksander Wat, the editor of *The Literary Monthly*?" And it turned out that from his youth in Poland (he had attended the Kreczmar high school), he remembered only two things—Antoni Słonimski, who wrote *The Weekly Chronicle*, and Aleksander Wat, *The Literary Monthly*. And that was it.

The workers came to us as if to some sort of sanctuary, and that made our relations quite false. They were somehow intimidated; they were trying to be intellectuals, to speak like intellectuals. Sometimes I would sound out their opinions to see how to edit the magazine, but I couldn't get a straight answer. If I asked some workers whether, for example, they had understood some very difficult article by Stawar, they would always answer that they had. And so, basically, my knowledge of the working class came via a mythology and via a superficial vision, more of an optical illusion. An optical illusion about a certain category of workers.

And now the cell. I don't remember how many of us there were— maybe fifteen, a very large cell. It looked out on Danilowiczowska Street. Later on Ola would stroll down the other side of that street and I would climb up to the window at the appointed hour and watch her— I forget how we arranged that. It was a jolly, high-spirited cell. In intellectual cell thirteen things had been a little on the sour side, and, what's more, there was violence, Broniewski's outbursts, always tension, in spite of Hempel's elixir of gentleness. The communists had been in jail before. They had worked out a certain routine and it was really a rest period for them. They were fed; they weren't doing anything. Those were people who worked hard.

One of them was a very young Jew, who worked in some large tailor shop. Mercurial, he didn't pace like a caged lion but bustled around from one person to another, nonstop. He had an incredibly cheerful disposition. He had often taken part in strikes; he was constantly talking about strikes. He worked in a Jewish tailor shop and the Jewish tradesmen were constantly on strike then. There was also a Pole with a face like a half-baked loaf of bread, a broad country face, an entire expanse of face, and very friendly light blue eyes. But the hands of a murderer, a boxer, fantastically strong; he really was a man who could bend steel. But he was a baker. I'm talking about the two people who left me with the fondest memories, but as you know, the basic makeup of the cell was low-level communists. There was not a single prominent communist there, not a single big fish—no big shots in my cell. They were rather less than middling, mostly from the unions, trade union functionaries.

In the communist hierarchy that class of people was held in some contempt. "The union people." It's the same in Russia with the people who deal with the economy, the factories, trade, and so on. A very strong contempt, almost aristocratic. That's very strange because the workers were the highest aristocracy in the iconography, the mythology. The way Stande, an old communist, treated the workers was typical. He treated them with extreme respect but it was the respect that real aristocrats, good aristocrats, show commoners, the plebs: incredible courtesy, great respect, but still very paternalistic. Contempt was shown, however, to low-level party functionaries who dealt directly with the concerns of the working class, the people from the union movement—a sort of lower class at the time.

So, that's who was there in the cell. There was one leather worker, a fanatic who said, "The Kremlin knows best." There was also a very nice person from the metalworkers' union who was later to hold a prominent position in People's Poland. A few of them made major careers in postwar Poland. I saw a couple of them again, or at least I heard about them. The rest perished.

I was struck by many things, a great education. One thing was especially touching. When we were escorted down the prison corridor—I can't remember what floor that was then—some cell would just be going out for a walk, and immediately a whisper would start up: *"The Literary Monthly."* The whole prison already knew that *The Literary Monthly* was in prison. Of course, as the intellectual, the editor, I gave lectures. There were always lectures going on. We had books—one book by Lenin, a primer on philosophy by Bukharin, a popular book among communists. And I was supposed to teach them the basics of philosophy according to Bukharin's book.

I knew that book by Bukharin very well from before, and obviously, after my study of philosophy, it struck me as tremendously naïve. The book begins by immediately singling out teleological, idealist systems, which are always teleological. [He says that] teleology is basically the same thing as theology. Right away, on page one. And so the naïveté and falseness of this were always obvious to me. But it had never occurred to me before to question this book, because a whole series of transformational formulas was at play there. Obviously, philosophy is not a simple matter, and Marxist philosophy is hellishly complicated. But like every modern discipline, it is accessible in its deep, dialectical, subtle sense to people who steep themselves in it precisely because it is complicated. A very simple thing. Since this is a philosophy that is not only to explain the world but to remake it, to act on the broadest masses and specifically on the uneducated masses, it must therefore be reduced to a certain catechism. But a catechism has to have a goal. Of course, not all idealist systems are teleological, and, of course, not all teleological systems are theological, but a catechism has to use equations. And it is here that the false equations come into play in a much more important area. The false equations are that humanity, the vanguard of humanity = the working class = the vanguard of the working class = the party = the leadership of the party = the leader.

I could read Bukharin condescendingly and still consider him a saint because his was a useful handbook of philosophy for the masses. That's how I read it for myself, but now I was supposed to teach it. Many of our intellectual civilization's problems, our intellectual problems, arise because people do not read aloud. An enormous percentage of literature would simply vanish if the authors had to read their works aloud, only aloud. They would be ashamed; the falsehood would be obvious. When people read only with their eyes, all the falsehood can enter imperceptibly even the most critical eye. The mouth is for speaking the truth or lies, whereas the eyes are really esthetic. The eyes see whether something is beautiful or ugly, useful or useless. And suddenly there was I, who had always imbibed Marxism, Marxist philosophy, only with my eyes, in prison with those people avid for knowledge. *The Literary Monthly* gave me an insight into something that is never sufficiently appreciated—the mad hunger for truth and knowledge among those elements of the masses who have been awakened. Obviously, this applies to those who go after the light, who have the energy to go after the light. But that was a formidable force in that cell.

And so my estheticizing eyes could see that they were waiting for a revelation; they were listening to Bukharin as if to a revelation and they took what he said for the truth. But my own voice told me that it was false; my ears could hear that it was false, that it all was deficient, untrue, unproved, and so on. And that was a great torture for me. After a while—I think after three or four lectures—I could see that something had to change. And so quite naïvely I began to polemicize with the text. Still a believer, I was trying to find a paraphrase that would be truer and would be accessible to that audience. They noticed that I was polemicizing with a sacred text. After three or four sessions either I quit or they let me understand that I should quit. Every cell had its own leaders, its own party cell, and it was known that I was not in the party. A sympathizer. By that time the leaders were treating the real comrades, the functionaries, with enormous suspicion, and there was already a stink of heresy in the air. So that was one experience.

Another experience concerns the motivation for the transition to communism. Theoretically, I knew that an intellectual, a repentant intellectual, goes over to communism out of a sense of guilt, in defiance of his own vital interests; he's impelled by a need for truth or justice; his motives are unselfish. Theoretically, I knew that with the proletariat—and this is as it should be—their vital interests came into play, not individual but class interests. But dedication, disinterestedness were also present in the sense that they were in jeopardy of prison, persecution, unemployment, being thrown off the job or out of school. Theoretically, I knew of the existence of resentment; it had already been described definitively long before this. But there I saw for myself how a twofold social resentment was an enormous force impelling people to communism. Of all the feelings that go into the making of social resentment, two stand out. One is social envy. That very nice young man once said something of this sort: "I was born the son of a shoemaker; why wasn't I born the son of a general?" And so, envy is not being born the son of a general . . .

MILOSZ: Is that class hatred? Maybe they're the same thing?

WAT: No, no, they're not the same. Let's make the distinction a little finer here. They're not the same thing; that wasn't class hatred. It was also expressed in what someone else said plainly at the same time: "After the revolution, I'll try and become the warden of this prison, and then I'll show those sons of bitches," meaning the prison administration. That's not only hatred but resentment—those on the bottom want to be on top. None of that was any secret; that was no discovery of America. Theoretically, I knew that. I just hadn't realized the temperature that feeling had reached, its actual power. Of those fifteen or so young people (one was somewhat older; he may have been a little over forty), the great majority had probably come to communism with precisely that question: why aren't I a general's son? If I were a general's son, then of course everything would be all right.

Another thing I also knew but which had to be experienced first-hand was the thunder, the wrath of vengeance, the need for revenge, its nightmarish dynamism.

My third important prison experience with the communist working class was of fanaticism and interparty hatred. The cause, at least the apparent cause, for the split into minorityites and majorityites had long since ceased to be current. There were a couple of majorityites in the cell; no one talked to them. I don't remember why the prisoners called the hunger strike—even water was refused—it lasted almost four days. Very strange sensations occurred; on the third day there was a kind of spiritualization. The minorityites protested that the two majorityites were on the hunger strike with them. The majorityites were the same type that today are revisionists, that is, people with wide horizons, not Muscovites, not fanatics, assimilated if they were Jews. The Jewish street name for them was the *rojte asymilacje*, the red assimilation, and the street disliked them very much. And so I saw that incredible hatred for heresy, for those who thought a little differently—but the temperature, the power of that hatred was surprising.

MILOSZ: But Stalinism had deep roots in the masses' reactions.

WAT: Stalinism had incredibly deep roots in the reactions of the communist masses, that is, those who had taken the communist road. I have always maintained that Stalinism was in fact the sole perfect, the sole pure manifestation of Marxism and communism—in particular the

Stalinism of the years 1937 and 1941, Stalinism with its grandiose terror. Those are old truths; the old historians stated them. The Greek historians knew that the plebs always choose a dictator. The plebs want to have a leader, they want a dictator, and they want terror, and so this is not only a matter of Marxism and Leninism.

How did we communicate with the outside world? Through the guards and also through the trustees, thieves who cleaned the cells in the prison. There was one trustee, Josek, who cleaned our cell. A nice person, an old Warsaw thief. A funny thing happened. I was receiving enormous food packages (both from my mother and from my mother-in-law), and so of course there was enough not only for the whole cell but for Josek as well. And he said to me, "Mr. Wat, remember, if somebody ever robs you, come to the bar at the corner of Niska and Pokorna streets and ask for me, Josek. I guarantee that in two or three days you'll have everything back." Well, to finish this up: one day after my release I went home—I was living at 13 Hoża Street—and out of the gateway comes Josek, a house painter with a ladder and paint buckets. We see each other and rush to give each other a hug. Suddenly Josek gets scared and says, "But what are you doing here?"

I say, "I live here."

"You do? Which apartment?" It turned out that he and his partner had been hired to paint one apartment, and he was afraid that it had been mine. They'd been operating there for two days already.

It turned out that the minister of the interior, Michałowski, had it in for me. I knew that people were making efforts for us, but I couldn't be certain those efforts would meet with success. It was all very uncertain. Somewhat later a rumor spread that Broniewski had been released. He was the first to be released, after six weeks. They promised to release us all, adding that I'd be in longer. No one knew how long—it was a difficult case. Besides, I was the editor. Meanwhile, instead of releasing me, they brought me to Mokotów Prison.

12 COMMUNISTS IN PRISON: WORKERS AND FUTURE
STATESMEN. RELEASE FROM PRISON. HITLER TAKES
POWER. FASCISM OR COMMUNISM.

WAT: Perhaps I'll return for a moment to what I was saying about my experiences in Warsaw prison. Ampler formulation is needed here.

I spoke of those prisoners who were of the common people. This was the first time I had entered the world of communists—the communist plebs, not the intellectuals—the first time I had been with them. I found strong traces of social resentment among them, social envy, a need for revenge, and so forth. I would not want this to create a negative image of them. Obviously not all of them, but many of them were very beautiful people, absolutely self-sacrificing, with a certain great moral purity. Their resentment and their need for revenge had an entirely different background than does that of middle-class people or intellectuals, writers for example. But for one charming birdlike communist from the lower levels of the party, that feeling of resentment was natural, that *libido* in him, some future *libido dominandi* (you could imagine that he too would have liked to be the warden of that prison). This resentment did not diminish their minds or their moral values. Those feelings were natural for them, even esthetic to a certain degree, if one uses the word in a broader sense, to mean a sort of *modus* for reacting to the world. That was a natural reaction. That was perfectly clear to me, despite my being very much struck by it and its making a very negative impression. But that never caused me to lose either my respect or my very warm affection for them for a single second.

Unfortunately, they did not reciprocate that affection, though on the whole relations were good. Overall, my relations with people in prison were good, sometimes even very good, right from the start. There is a sort of prison charisma that is independent of the prisoner's character—you either have it or you don't. I saw worthy people who aroused immediate antipathy in a cell, and the reverse held true as well. So, people rather liked me throughout my career in Soviet prisons, but perhaps least of all in Warsaw, because there I alienated them with my unorthodoxy, my lack of understanding, my otherness. And that was important to me. So, on the one hand, they did not disenchant me; on the contrary, I had a sort of nostalgic feeling for them, a longing to be part of them; I saw a beautiful noble warmth in them, a fire, a good fire. On the other hand—here a distinction must be made—I acquired even more suspicion than I had had at *The Literary Monthly* for the doctrine that was their doctrine and in which they felt like fish in water. And so those small differences between us were very much to the point. The sad lesson I learned was that they weren't for me, nor was I for them.

I was taken to the investigating magistrate, relatively nearby. I was not an important prisoner; only one policeman escorted me, on foot. You know, there are rare situations that remain with you for your entire life, as if they had just occurred. Leaving prison after seven or eight weeks, being among free people, was one such experience, of the same stuff of which poems are made. I don't mean the strangeness of life, but rather the feeling that either I'm two-dimensional and the people I'm rubbing shoulders with are three-dimensional, or it's the other way around and I'm three-dimensional and they're two-dimensional. I had the feeling that I could pass through them, that I was weightless, that they could pass through me, that I was a walking shadow. But all that mattered was that for the first time in eight weeks I was out among free people—very strange at the time—people who moved in various directions like atoms, like the electrons in an atom, in various uncoordinated and undetermined directions.

One other factor was important here too: not only had I been locked up for a long time, but I knew I would return to being locked up. You have an entirely different feeling when you are leaving a prison for good. When I left other prisons, Soviet prisons especially, the moment of walking out was more one of fearing the world, a rather dark and heavy experience. But not that time. I had the melancholy of a creature who is two-dimensional, but there was a certain joy as well—that it was autumn, the golden Polish autumn. It was a very beautiful day on Krakowskie Przedmieście; there were a great many women, lightly dressed that day, wearing nothing over their dresses. The street was like a garden. The policeman escorting me was very friendly. I met with my sister, and she gave me some money and a couple of packs of cigarettes, which I, of course, gave to him. He was a peasant lad, entirely without malice, and he even went into a bar with me on the way back. We drank a beer—he didn't want any more than that; he was afraid of being seen. Those were idyllic times.

That's the situation of poetry. Now, it occurs to me to turn that sentence around, to say that the situation of the poet—but this sounds affected—is precisely like that of the prisoner who leaves prison for a short spell of writing. Perhaps this is the process we call inspiration.

When I was transferred to Mokotów Prison, I went directly to the shower room, and there I met the entire floor at once. An entirely different crowd of communists, the cream. They could even be called the gilded communist youth. The gilded youth, in doctrine and in culture. Tadeusz Zabłudowski, whom I recognized, was there, and a few other important communists, including Ortwein, the son of a very rich furniture manufacturer. In a word, people from good families, not only Jews but, if they were Jews, then Jews of the *rojte asymilacje*, educated, always well-dressed and aspiring to top government positions—you could see that they'd be the future ministers, ambassadors. Everything was already in place, a very odd setup.

And, can you imagine, I committed two blunders there in Mokotów, one coming in and one leaving. But the blunder I made coming in was terrible because it immediately lowered me in people's eyes. They greeted me quite enthusiastically in the shower room. Later on Zabłudowski told me what a terrible blunder I had made. The first thing I had said to them was that I was only passing through; I was sure to be released any week now because Goetel was interceding for me with Pieracki, this one with that one. Absolute asinine naïveté. I knew that everyone in prison had family or friends who were using every connection they had. For example, Colonel Nagler got the poet Szenwald out, and Hempel's Sanacja family was always getting him out;* they used to stand on their heads for him. All that went on, but you weren't supposed to mention it. And so that blunder weighed heavily on me. I wasn't at Mokotów long, probably two or three weeks, but relations were already chilly, except with Zabłudowski, who was friendly and always talked with me on our walks. The others no longer paid much attention to me. I had compromised myself.

Mokotów Prison was pleasant, nice. I was in solitary. At an earlier time, the doors to the solitary confinement cells had been open; there were discussion clubs. But when I arrived, there was only an hour's walk, and you were not supposed to be able to talk. But somebody was always delivering a report, especially on the international situation, which was very interesting at the time. There were even discussions. They all took place on the move, like President Johnson's meetings with reporters in the Rose Garden. The cells were very clean, very ascetic, like monks' cells. The bunks went up flat against the wall and were pulled down at night; a stool was attached to the floor. I had a lot of books; I had paper and ink. I received books from home and, besides, we circulated the books, swapped them with one another—the books circulated absolutely freely.

I was in Mokotów three weeks. How did they get me out? It was rather difficult. Hempel's release was arranged on condition that he agree to leave for Russia. The party agreed because he was seriously ill, and besides, he was used up as far as the party went; he could no longer be of any use. In fact he left not long after his release. He got out a week or ten days ahead of me. Stawar was, I think, released from Central Prison, and I was released right before Nowogródzki, or at the same time.

How was it done? In fact not so much through Goetel as through Stefania Sempołowska. Ola went to her office on Smolna Street, and she sent Dr. Stefanowski to see me in my cell. He was Piłsudski's personal physician, a Legionnaire, a person of unusual purity, tender

---

* Sanacja (purification, in Polish). The name given to Piłsudski's government and its followers after his coup in 1926.

goodness, and unselfishness. He had to be reckoned with because Piłsudski was very fond of him; it was hard not to like him. On the day before Dr. Stefanowski came to see me, my friend Mieczysław Erlich brought me some harmless powders from the prison medic that caused my heartbeat to accelerate to almost twice the normal rate. I took the powders, and the next day Dr. Stefanowski examined me. There was also a prison doctor who had great respect for Stefanowski and so didn't interfere. Stefanowski drew up a certificate saying that my heart was enlarged and that my condition required treatment. On that basis I was released. Ola's parents paid my bail.

And then I made a dramatic exit, as dramatic as my entrance. Erlich told me about it afterwards (he was also released at that time). He said, "Aleksander, didn't you know anything? When a person leaves prison, he leaves all his things there." I had a plaid blanket, some books, and various other things; they should have been left there for communal use. But I was brand new to prison; I had no experience, and I didn't know anything about all that. They told me to get ready with my belongings, and when I left late that evening, I only shouted out as I went down the corridor, "Good-bye, see you later!" But I took my things though I didn't need them—what did they amount to anyway!

I went to Ola's parents' (Ola was living with her parents). A huge dinner—they knew beforehand I was coming. One of my sisters was there too. She told me that my other sister, the one I'd been closest to all my life—the age difference wasn't much—and who had been killing herself to get me released, was in the hospital with typhus, but everything was all right now. And with me there they called the hospital to tell my sister Ewa that I had been released. The next day the news came that she had died that very night. That was a terrible blow to me, the more so because I reproached myself, unfairly, of course, that my being in prison might have played some part in it.

I left with another experience under my belt. I had discovered another milieu, that of all those future ministers who had already rejected me outright. Again, some of them were wonderful, like Kasman, a wonderful person, or Zabłudowski, who later on in People's Poland proved to be a good and exceptional person. Communism in its perversity worked it so that Berman, who knew Zabłudowski's nobility and honesty, put him in charge of the office of the general censorship. The perversities of communism. But Dzierżyński's legend had some influence here; he was supposedly made the chief of the Cheka because of his tender heart; he loved children.

That milieu could already be glimpsed in embryo through the uterine walls; the embryo could already be seen developing. Many of its features had already appeared: that haughtiness of people admitted into the highest light; they were a bit like missionaries, or, say, Baptists or Adventists. The haughtiness of people who are on the side of the good, and betting on a good horse, a just one, a horse that would win the race. That terrible haughtiness and their dandyism were particularly striking. It is impossible to overestimate dandyism as a motive for embracing communism, and not only in countries that became communist recently. It wasn't Russia but People's Poland that came under the influence of dandyism—dandyism in an almost Baudelairean sense, along with a certain asceticism. Provocation is chosen. I chose Satan because he is beautiful; he provokes and irritates the Philistines. He is severe and cruel and strikes fear in the profane.

I was out. What was my situation? Financially, quite deplorable but not drastic. Ola's father was a wealthy man, though a very miserly one. I wasn't up against the wall. On the contrary, my mother-in-law thought that Andrzej needed a nurse, and so on. I began translating for Rój publishers.

When I began moving toward communism, my literary position was quite good, though I didn't make any efforts in that direction. After *Lucifer* my literary position was excellent; my stock, so to speak, was high. Three books had received good reviews at the time, and mine might have been the best of them. But *The Literary Monthly*, which denounced everybody, had established the image of Wat the anti-Polish Bolshevik with a knife in his teeth. There's something I should emphasize here: what Poland between the wars was like, compared with conditions today. Despite my image as a rabid anti-Polish communist, everyone there—Wierzyński, Goetel the fascist, Tuwim, and others—tried to get me released from prison. Anything like that would be out of the question in People's Poland.

Though I wasn't in a good situation after prison, I was young and strong and didn't take my situation to heart. After my release it was obvious that I had to be very careful; I'd been burned. It was also in the party's interest for a person who, whatever else he might be, was still a sympathizer—though one unfit for conspiracy (for it was clear that I wasn't cut out for conspiracy)—to be careful. Besides, when I was editing *The Literary Monthly*, I was always straining at the leash and they'd curb me, make me more cautious.

But I had a secret meeting a month after being released from prison. I don't remember his name—a communist who later came to a terrible end, a man who could not stand up to prison. He was released after a very short time, but he must have been a little unbalanced, because he committed suicide; he jumped out of a window after he was released.

He was the liaison. He immediately proposed that I start a new magazine. I'd be kept in the background; front people would be found, people who hadn't been compromised. Stawar and I would be in charge. They found some young lawyer for us. We were very careful about our meetings with him; we took taxis to cover our trail; we met in a wealthy bourgeois home that was under no suspicion. But clearly we had been tracked down, because when he submitted his application for a license (you had to have a license), it was turned down and no reasons were given.

I kept asking myself how much of my loosening connection with the party was cowardice prompted by the ordeal of prison and how much was the disenchantment that had started to become clear when I was at *The Literary Monthly*—I even know exactly when. I remember that by the time I was writing about Proust and Joyce, I was deeply troubled. But there's no question that my first stretch in prison was very hard on me, and I assume that the fear of going back to prison was also a factor here. It's very oppressive to think about going back to prison.

By the time I was imprisoned, I had become mistrustful of the doctrine and the practice; I had replaced the exclamation points with question marks. Stalin was not one of my concerns in *The Literary Monthly* period; I wasn't aware of him yet, though I knew of his existence. But by 1931 Stalin's shadow was on the screen; he was the leader by then; there was talk of him.

And then terrible things began happening in Germany—joint action by communists and Nazis, the overthrow of the Prussian social-democratic government, the slogan "The enemy is on the left," the joint strike by the Nazi and communist truck drivers, and then the *Macht ergreifen*. Hitler was in power. I usually read *Inprekor;* it was a source of political wisdom for me, my initiation into the world situation—mostly facts and figures, but what facts and figures! And it really had fantastic analyses too, irrefutable figures, like reinforced concrete. They made dealing with figures into an art form. And so, I got a copy of *Inprekor* right after Hitler took power, and on the front page was a joyful article by Leński-Leszczyński, the leader of Polish communism. The dilemma in all its intensity: either communism or fascism. Obviously, Hitler's day will come and go; the masses will rise up; victory is already in sight! His tone was joyful! I felt as if I'd been struck by lightning. I'd been listening to the radio, following Hitler's rise to power, and then . . . joy?

Then another process began. I became very interested in Hitler's Germany. Of course I could see that the communist policy was wrong, an absolutely ruinous strategy. Fine. In the thirties I showed a certain contrary side. When Hitler took power, other people accepted the dilemma and moved toward communism. They accepted that there really was no other choice but communism or fascism. In Poland people chose either the ONR's rightist nationalism or communism, or at least something close to communism—the united front and so forth. On the whole, the reactions were typical, for the times, for Poland, and for the French progressive intelligentsia. I wasn't typical. I had been through that ten or fifteen years before. This time I took another path, one that went in the opposite direction: it was precisely Nazism that repelled me from communism because I had begun to see similarities, analogies. And so day after day I read eagerly about what was happening in Germany, but also about what was happening in Russia. Similar gestalts, beginning with the cult of the leader, *ein Volk, ein Führer*, then the massacring of the opposition. While it's true that Stalin hadn't yet begun massacring people, like Hitler he was removing his opponents; they learned a lot from each other, you know.

MILOSZ: Did Stawar write about that?

WAT: No, Stawar . . . that's another matter. We were friends to the end, but there was a great difference in our positions. Stawar took a different view—Stawar and especially Deutscher. Deutscher was first. The anti-Stalin currents in the party were extremely strong at that time, but they were moving in the direction of Trotskyism. That was the difference, you see. They kept on in a Marxist-Leninist direction, shifting toward Trotskyism. Though Stawar had many reservations about Trotsky, in the end he stayed with a Marxist-Leninist foundation. Something else had happened with me. I had simply gone on ahead. Life has refuted a great many of my ideas, but in this case it acknowledged that I was right. At least I continue to think that Stalinism is Marxism-Leninism as it works out in practice, its culmination. And that was what was gnawing away at me at that time.

13 THE THIRTIES. LIGHTNING BOLTS FROM RUSSIA. SPLITS IN THE PARTY. ANTI-SEMITISM.

WAT: After *The Literary Monthly* was shut down, there were attempts to found a new magazine in 1932, 1933, 1934, up through 1936. I took a very active part in all that. Perhaps I should reminisce some more about that because it reflects the ferment, the enormous internal problems that were wrenching the Polish party at that time. It would not be easy to find common denominators for those divisions. But there was only one very strong current: Trotskyism. It should be remembered that in 1925 the Polish Communist Party Congress took a pro-Trotsky, anti-Stalin position, and Stalin did not forget that.

In all those splits you have to distinguish between the upper strata of the party—the party intelligentsia, including the higher sphere of the intelligentsia like students, doctors, and lawyers—and the lower strata of the party. That division grew much sharper in the thirties. Somehow the communist peak broke off from the great masses, which were composed of activists, sometimes even outstanding ones, but worker activists, union activists. Anyway, it was natural that all those philosophical debates on the Soviet Union and all the factional struggles took place among the higher strata of communism. They had good detailed knowledge of what was happening in Russia and were very disturbed by it. And all those factional struggles in Russia found an immediate reflection among the higher strata of the Polish communists in a way that proved disastrous for the Polish Communist party leaders. There's no question that by 1932, 1933, 1934, even before the Moscow trials, a fundamental anxiety prevailed about Soviet domestic and foreign policy. It was there when you spoke with people intimately, when you were trusted—and I had many such conversations. And I was filled with doubt myself, indecision, uncertainty. At times people would express open opposition. As far as the believers among the communist masses were concerned, they weren't too interested in all that; they took Soviet propaganda on faith and had no desire to check how truthful that propaganda really was.

The twists and turns in Stalin's foreign and domestic policies were explained in various ways. Perhaps the most intelligent remark I heard was made by a woman who was rather a Stalinist. That was Estera Stróżecka, who spent most of her time in France and came to Poland legally, for short visits to her family. She justified Stalin's policy in a most convincing manner. She simply said that Stalin was, correctly, foreseeing the outbreak of a world war in that decade and that all the twists and turns in his policy were to be explained by his desire to avoid war, to influence things so that it became a war among capitalist states, war among themselves. She even went as far as saying—and the war in Spain must have already started by then—that this was the reason behind Stalin's policy toward Spain. And so that seemed the most rational explanation. Later on I became convinced that this really had played a major part in the moves Stalin made and, specifically, in the war in Spain. Those were pre-atomic times, and Stalin couldn't have been concerned with establishing a foothold in Spain—he wasn't counting on there being a communist state in Spain. All his actions, meaning the support he gave quite openly, sending advisors, troops, generals and executing anarchists—in all that he was probably interested in deceiving the Western capitalist countries, to draw France and England into war with Germany and Italy, although he may not have been counting on that. And even without counting on it, he had no trouble in compromising the democratic countries; their own nonintervention compromised them. Had the situation been different, he would have camouflaged his aid to Spain more; he wouldn't have flaunted the aid the communists were providing.

MILOSZ: But don't you think that in general Stalin made the error of operating by analogy with World War I, chiefly in overrating France's strength?

WAT: He overrated France, no doubt of that; but still there was a certain constant in his policy. Right before his death, at the Nineteenth Congress, it was Stalin, after all, who formulated the policy of coexistence and the possibility of peace, specifically the policy that assumed that war between the capitalist states, the imperialists, and the Soviet Union was not in the least inevitable—it could easily be avoided—though war was inevitable among the imperialists themselves. That was the Stalin doctrine, and the basis of his alliance with Hitler.

I have to say something about Władzio Broniewski's trip. I don't remember what year it was—1934, 1935. Władzio had a very special standing as a communist. He was probably the only communist in Poland who was not only tolerated but, how to put it, had the stamp of total approval on him, both as a poet and a former Piłsudski-ite. Even policemen valued him highly as a poet; he had an effect on them as a poet. He was recognized; an exception was made for him; he was allowed to be a communist. So, Broniewski traveled to Russia on a regular passport. When he came back, I asked him about various things, including the famine in the Ukraine and collectivization, mentioning that the press had reported that five million peasants had lost their lives. And he said, "Yes, that's right; it's being talked about a lot." Tretyakov, the author of the play *Cry China*, had told him that something like four or five million had been annihilated, wiped out. And so I said to Władzio—I remember this exactly; there are moments in life you don't forget—"So, is that the truth?" He whisked his hand disparagingly, dismissing the subject; what did those five million muzhiks mean to him. He didn't say it, but that gesture!

All the thunder and lightning in Russia cut zigzags through the Polish party in a way that was hard to explain. Those zigzags were to a large degree a function of class origin, education, general intellectual formation, and temperament too. Lightning bolts one after the other. Collectivization, those five million peasants—that was a bolt of lightning—and even before that the first trial, which in fact began Stalin's reign of terror, so different from the Revolution's terror: the trial of the technical intelligentsia. Then immediately came those millions of martyred peasants; clearly that was the foundation for creating the ideal terror, Stalin's terror, meaning one that was perpetual, ubiquitous, educational, and so forth.

Those lightning bolts from Russia also struck the lower strata of communists, the communist masses, the worker activists, but there was less hesitation among them, unlike the intelligentsia, who are Hamlets by nature. In the lower strata, the division into Trotskyites and Stalinists was much more clear-cut. Someone who was a Trotskyite was a Trotskyite without hesitation, with an entire Trotskyite bible, holy writ, and catechism, just like the Stalinists. They had a fierce hatred for each other. Don't forget about the situation in Poland at that time. Piłsudski had died in 1935. But toward the end of his life a clear drift toward fascism had already begun. Communists were still walking the streets freely in 1935, 1936, but still the drift toward fascism was becoming stronger and stronger. There had been a surplus production of young intellectuals, there was unemployment, things were very bad; society was utterly disoriented politically, anti-Semitism was on the rise, there was a cruel policy applied to the Ukrainians—horrible persecutions; and the provincial authorities acted like petty tyrants.

One day, Kwiatkowski, a funny man who always knew the latest gossip, came running up to me and said that he had in hand a leaflet from

Moscow that named the double agents and police provocateurs in the [Polish] party. He read off quite a few of the names to me. I don't remember most of them—I prefer not to remember—but two names I remember perfectly, because there were bound to be further consequences with them: they were Halina Krahelska and Władysław Daszewski, which was utterly shattering.

Daszewski, you should know, was a hard-nosed communist, very hard-nosed. But at the same time he was an elegant, witty man, extremely successful with women. He was very sexy, and he had a lot of girlfriends in the literary world and elsewhere. Korsak, the vice minister of internal affairs, was very fond of him. Daszewski also maintained close ties with the communists and was very much a communist by conviction. He came from the so-called lower classes, from a very poor family, and was self-made. He had the obstinacy of those who hadn't had it easy, hadn't gotten off to a good start in life. He became very friendly with the Skamandrites, but he had a tremendous reserve of hatred for the well-born. He frequented the salons, an intelligent, witty, pleasant, likable ladies' man. But he was morally insane (his relationships with his two wives were highly amoral)—a person of enormous charm, graceful gestures, graceful speech, but with enormous hidden hatred. One day, right before the war, I ran into him at the Café Ziemiańska. We always began by talking utter nonsense, and so I said some utter nonsense to him, and he replied, "I'm just coming back from my mother's funeral, and now I'm going to drink some vodka." And I thought that was his contribution of nonsense. It turned out that he wasn't joking; he really had been on the way back from his mother's funeral. A cold person—nothing mattered to him. That was the day when mobilization announcements were posted and then canceled later; it was close to September 1. He was rubbing his hands; you had to see it, that expression, that satisfaction: "They'll shit their pants, you'll see. Słonimski, Tuwim—they'll shit their pants in fear."

Such terrific hatred for his friends who were enormously fond of him I found very revealing at the time. I mention this because of the sinister role Daszewski was later to play in Lwów.

You should know one thing: the disbanding of the Polish party had been in the air for many months before it happened. But obviously the disbanding of the Polish party remains an enormous nightmare to this day, the so-called disgrace of every Polish communist. It consisted of the liquidation of the Poles in Russia, especially all the leaders. Most of the people liquidated had some sort of name—beginning with Warski. First they were accused of being agents of Polish intelligence, police plants, provocateurs; and they were also accused of being Trotskyist influences. Undoubtedly, those were valid charges, though they were blown incredibly out of proportion. One may assume that Polish intelligence even had a man among the party leaders, though that's not definite; but still there were many people who had been in the Legions or Piłsudski-ite organizations before. There were a great many provocateurs among the lower echelons. One provocateur—I forget his name—had blown the cover of something like one hundred people; he came to light in a famous trial. There were many provocateurs, but, again, things were exaggerated; there weren't as many as Moscow charged. And undoubtedly there were Trotskyite sympathies; they divided the lower echelons in two but ran rampant at the top. But the disbanding of the party did not mean an end to communist activity in Poland. The Polish party leaders, the links between the Russian party, the NKVD, counterintelligence, Stalin, and the Polish communists had simply been eliminated. The Polish communists in prison were still communists, however, as were those at liberty; they found themselves without a party and were directed by people who enjoyed Moscow's confidence. Obviously, the range is great here, from people known by the embassy or Moscow, who were trusted, to direct agents of counterintelligence or of the NKVD, of which there were many. There was no way of telling who was simply a so-called decent communist, *tout court*, and who was an agent. Who could know that?

One of those trusted people was Jerzy Borejsza, who became known at the time of the Spanish Civil War because he published a series of well-written articles about the war. I had known Borejsza for quite a long while, but casually. And then, to my absolute surprise, when I was no longer accepted by the more important people in the party—they weren't keeping up relations with me, in any case were very cold to me—Borejsza came to see me, and, as it turned out, not only me, but even Stawar, the excommunicated—people wouldn't even shake his hand. He invited us to a meeting at the home of Romuald Miller, an architect; I went there with Stawar. Borejsza was there, Romuald Miller, Jan Nepomucen Miller, Daszewski, and Barcikowski, a lawyer from the League of Human Rights. There were a couple of other people, too. Borejsza spoke for the first time of the project to found the Democratic Club to be headed by old Professor Michałowicz, who hadn't come to the meeting but had already agreed. He also mentioned a number of other people [who would be involved], including Krahelska and Rzymowski. But I had been informed beforehand that Moscow had branded Krahelska and Rzymowski as agents of Polish intelligence. And so Stawar and I did not agree to take part, if only because how could one start a club with Krahelska when Moscow considered her a provocateur? Those weren't the words I used, but I said something to that effect; I voiced opposition. I think that was my last negative contribution to the communist enterprise. Of course, friends who were communists visited me privately right up till the war. We would argue. They would wring their hands and say, "We know it's the truth. There's nothing we can do about it, our entire beautiful youth . . ."

And how about me? I was terribly sad in those days. Before that, I had a rather jolly disposition, very much the extrovert, at least starting with the futurist period. Before that I had been introverted, but then I became tremendously extroverted and very jolly. We ran an open house, plenty of guests, drinking. But now I was dominated by melancholy and an absolute premonition that Ola, Andrzej, and I would die horrible deaths, that Poland would go under. And that lasted for years; the premonitions became more intense—I can't forget this—they became more intense in the two or three years before the war, because of the anti-Semitism. I actually had fantasies of emigrating, leaving the country. It was a dismal time, incredibly dismal for me; no faith, no solutions.

I must say that I never personally experienced any anti-Semitism, not even at Gebethner's, even though the company was seventy-five years old at that time and I was the first Jew to work there. My relations there were very good even though every once in a while I would be unable to restrain myself and would speak out publicly. For example, there was a peace rally organized by the League of Human and Civil Rights at which Czapiński, Słonimski, I, and I don't remember who else spoke. I didn't speak very long. I was supposed to say something about the "brave new world," but I had a cold, a fever, and a sore throat, and my voice couldn't hold out. When they shut down the League, they came at night and arrested me even though I was only very loosely connected to the League since I knew it was a communist front and had spoken only that one time and attended a couple of meetings.

I was happy to be released [after one night] and not to have to spend time in prison. I didn't know why they had arrested me; they had to know I wasn't active; I had so many restrictions on me. So why did they grab me again? But evidently my name was on file. I couldn't see the point of being held for one night. It was still early in the day, and I went to a café for breakfast. There I saw a copy of *Maly Dziennik* and some of the other papers. And I read that a leading "commie Jew" had been arrested the previous night. And *Maly Dziennik*, or one of the other Catholic papers, wrote that the respectable Catholic firm of Gebethner and Wolff employed a dangerous communist as a director. Nothing was said about my release.

Later on I learned that a few weeks before all this Councillor Bahr from the Ministry of Internal Affairs had gone to see Jan Gebethner, who was a progovernment deputy to parliament, and told him that he had to dismiss me. That infuriated Jan, who said that neither the state nor the Ministry of Internal Affairs was aiding his house financially, and they had no right to meddle. And it was because Jan Gebethner refused to dismiss me that they had me arrested that night.

I called Ola and then went to Gebethner's. I went to Jan's office right away and told him what had happened. The newspapers were already on his desk—and, I forgot to mention, one of the most important Catholic periodicals had made no bones about threatening that the priests would boycott his publishing house if I continued to work there. And so I said, "Jan, we're in a tough spot. You can't break glass with your dick." I told him that I was resigning.

He turned red, flew into a rage, leaned across his desk, and said, "Do you know what I have to say to you, sir. You can kiss my ass!" And so we both burst into laughter and went out for a vodka. As you can see, he was tremendously decent. But still things weren't going well, and I felt so threatened by that boycott that I asked Jan to find a cover for me, and he used Giergielewicz as a front for me. Giergielewicz was the very personification of tact in the way he acted toward me. I worked at Gebethner's until the very end, until I fled Warsaw. I made no secret of working there, but officially it was Giergielewicz who was the director, not me.

And so personally I never felt any anti-Semitism on my own hide— but what does that prove? I had good relations with a great many NDs,* old NDs. A few of them looked askance at me, but those were rather the young ones.

But, for example, Andrzej, who was six years old at that time, experienced anti-Semitism. I was bent on his going to an ordinary public school, not some exclusive school. I knew the principal of a school on Nowy Świat, and so I sent Andrzej there. Ola went with him the first day. Andrzej didn't look Jewish except for his frizzy hair. The teacher wasn't in the classroom yet when the door closed behind Andrzej. But Ola had an inkling of trouble. She opened the door halfway and saw Andrzej up against the wall. He was surrounded by a bunch of rough

---

* ND (National Democratic Party). A right-wing movement, one of whose principal goals was an ethnically homogeneous Poland.

kids who were shouting "You kike!" at him and about to beat him up! And so of course Ola grabbed him and took him away from there at once. There was plenty of anti-Semitism like that, and I had the same feeling that every Jew, even the most assimilated, had: the absolute certainty that as soon as you turned around, your friends would say, "That Jew!"

14 DISBANDING OF THE POLISH PARTY. THE ESSENCE OF STALINISM. GEBETHNER'S PUBLISHING HOUSE. DEATH OF MY MOTHER. OMENS.

WAT: The disbanding of the [Polish] Communist party by Moscow made no impression on me, whereas the deaths and camp sentences of many of my friends and people I knew well made an enormous impression on me. All those people had been liquidated, and so of course that made a horrible impression on me. It was known right away that they were in jail, that they were being tried, accused of working for Polish intelligence and so on. That had already started by 1937. The first arrests of Poles in Russia took place in 1936, 1937. The others were summoned there only in 1938, but the majority of those people had already been imprisoned for a long time. Warski had been in prison for years, practically all the more important [communists] had too. A few had been in Paris and were summoned to Moscow from there. The process of liquidating these people began before the party was disbanded. Part of the wave of Stalin's great purge, the trials, and so on.

As I've told you, my attitude toward the Moscow trials was this: I didn't have a second's hesitation, a second's doubt that it was all a provocation by Stalin. Not a second's. Besides, I thought that Trotsky would have done the same as Stalin, and he might have been even worse, and that conviction inoculated me against the Trotskyites' exaggerations of those crimes. So I buttonholed my friends and acquaintances who were communists, grabbing them by the lapels to talk with them. Mostly they tried to slip away; few of them had any nerve. And, of course, simple people said, "They see things better." I told you what the more intelligent ones would say: "It's war! You have to clean house before a war; it's tough; there are victims." Those broken eggs, that omelette again. But most of them didn't even have the nerve to say that; they squirmed out of it. Some of them simply said that they couldn't walk away, couldn't quit, couldn't repudiate themselves, their youth, the best years of their lives, their ideals, and so on.

I had been through my reassessment earlier, the moment when I learned about collectivization had been absolutely decisive for me, and I had no need for the trials; by then the trials were a sort of by-product. The trials were mostly within the party, and I knew that the people being persecuted had themselves persecuted others. For me the news about collectivization had been the turning point and, apart from that, the similarities between communism and Nazism. And perhaps precisely because I was never, not even when I was enthusiastic, an *anima naturaliter* communist, I had gone further in my reassessment, gone right to the very heart of the matter: Marxism and materialism. I was unable to counter it with anything positive; the alternative—communism or fascism—was false, but it fitted the reality. What could I do! I wasn't going to stand in the middle like Buridan's ass. I had no hesitation in choosing between the two, but I felt somehow will-less.

I had written quite a lot up to 1935, publishing practically nothing that was literary. It's all been lost. It would have made for a couple of volumes of short stories, something between short stories and essays. As I told you, I didn't publish because that wouldn't have been at all in keeping with my Marxism.

Moreover, I had realized—this is one of the many points of view possible on communism—that communism is, in fact, exteriorization. Communism is the enemy of interiorization, of the inner man. If we had leftist sympathies, fantasies, fascinations and were spellbound by communism, it was because we had seen both the treachery and the danger of interiorization. But today we know what exteriorization leads to: the killing of the inner man, and that is the essence of Stalinism. The essence of Stalinism is the poisoning of the inner man so that it becomes shrunken the way headhunters shrink heads—those shriveled little heads—and then disappears entirely. It doesn't even decay away inside, because the communists are afraid of inner decay. No, it should turn to dust. That's one point of view, and obviously you can have a hundred points of view on this subject, but one of them seems right to me: that Stalinism means the killing of the inner man. And no matter what the sophists say, no matter what lies the communist intellectuals tell, that's what it all comes down to. The inner man must be killed for the communist decalogue to be lodged in the soul. Of course this does not mean that Western civilization is a civilization of interiorization, and perhaps it even brings out all the treachery, all the evils of interiorization. But interiorization is possible in Western civilization, it is tolerated: one can live the inner life.

It turns out that I was not good material; at bottom, one of the laws of my destiny was the interiorization of everything. I began very early. *My Pug Iron Stove* was an inept attempt, but I had a certain dynamic for living within myself. Especially since I knew both how dangerous that was and how easy it is to decay. I knew about rot and was impelled away from it, which made communism all the more attractive.

Well, as for my reassessment: I had been through it early on and, for the most part, had walked away from all Marxism and wanted nothing to do with it. That was a terrible situation. My anticommunism, my leaving communism, did not allow me to be an anticommunist in the Poland of that time, where everything was moving toward fascism. I had no certainty about leaving communism. I knocked, I asked. But the situation was hopeless because I received no answers from all those full-blooded communists, those *anima naturaliter* communists, all those who were connected with the party. Always slogans, always clichés. Oh yes, I did get a live response from one man: "You're right; you're right, but what can I do. I can't do anything now."

I had come to such a standstill that I decided not to write. The end of writing. That was a healthy decision because I didn't know anything, because there was a complete philosophical void in me. I was completely lost. And I really didn't do any writing after 1935 or 1936. I worked in Gebethner's publishing house until 1939. I read, criticized, corrected, gave other people advice. Besides, I liked doing that very much, analyzing manuscripts.

My duties were very limited when I first began working at Gebethner's. The job itself came through connections. They published a wholesale list, for they had a wholesale house too. I was put in charge of that list. The company was flat on its back when I began working there; it was five million in debt to the banks, if I'm not mistaken.

Jan Gebethner was a lively man, the liveliest of the brothers, brimming with initiative, an excellent businessman, but a businessman-intellectual. He had a knack for getting the company into incredible trouble from which no one else would have been able to extricate it, but he was brilliant at getting it out of trouble and did it all the time. He was from a family of NDs, a very jingoistic, religious family. Jan himself was extremely religious, but I found out about that only by chance. He was always in the office before eight, very conscientious. I used to come in at ten o'clock—that was something I allowed myself. I found out that he went to church every morning for the early mass.

Apart from family and friends, no one knew about this; he practically kept it a secret. And so he was really a believer, not a pious fraud. He was known as cynical and crafty in business, but with all of that—and this combination is typical of Warsaw—he had certain moral principles that were like reinforced concrete! When he was a deputy to parliament from the OZN, he threw a department director from the Ministry of Internal Affairs out the door—the director had come to intervene in my case and have me removed from work.

Those were such terribly sad times, but that work was a blessing. For the first time in my life work was a blessing; there was one other time later on . . . Anyway, the sadness of those years. We were living fairly close to Aleje Ujazdowskie, and on my evening walks with Ola I would walk that street with a sense of personal disaster, one indissolubly bound to the general disaster. (You must have felt the same thing.) And so on those unforgettable evenings we said very little to each other, and when we did speak, it would be about the future, the unknown. We had a lovely apartment, but life was sad in that lovely apartment. Never in my life have I had such intense premonitions as I had then. Premonitions of terrible things in store for me and for the country. I am not speaking *ex post* here; this lasted for at least three years before the war. In those days that was the dominant motif in all my feelings, absolutely the dominant motif, a feeling that there was absolutely no way out. I had signs, omens with birds, really some very strange signs.

My mother died of cancer, in Otwock. She had been ill for a few months. We brought her out to Otwock, and I was with her at the end. My mother died fully conscious; that too became part of the sadness. My conscience was bothering me a lot; I had never been good to my mother; I hadn't treated her well. I had always venerated my father, but I was not a good son to my mother. I really wasn't a good son, and very often I treated her with utter indifference. And my mother was the perfection of what is called the Jewish mother.

There were seven of us at home; my oldest brother must have been eighteen or twenty years older than I. They were all night owls; I was still very young and so I didn't stay out, but the rest of them would come home at three or four o'clock in the morning. My mother would never go to bed; she was always out on the balcony or waiting in the living room until the last one came back.

She really was an incredibly loving mother, but I was not a good son. And so I felt both sorrow and pangs of conscience. My mother was dying in full consciousness; she had terrible swellings, she couldn't move around at all. She was dying in circumstances that might even be called good: her windows were always open and looked out on a forest of fir trees; it was summer, right before the war—six or seven weeks before. The only thing was that her eyes seemed covered by a film—bulging eyes, eyes that were already dead.

She told a great many stories. We had a maid name Anusia, who had raised all of us children. A peasant woman, but she didn't speak like a peasant though she did know a lot of peasant sayings. In fact, a little bit of my dadaism was influenced by some of her nonsense rhymes. She didn't have the peasant way of speaking; she spoke like a member of the intelligentsia, completely urban, except that she knew all those regional rhymes and sayings. She had sinned when she was sixteen, or else someone seduced her; anyway, she had to run away from her village. My parents took her on as a wet nurse, and, apparently, at some point during her first year with them she felt such a strong need for repentance that she went outside in her night shirt one winter night and lay down in the courtyard with her arms outstretched. Maybe those are fables, myths, stories, but I do know that, sick or not, right up to the end, until 1939, she never missed the annual pilgrimage to Częstochowa. She was in church at least twice a day. Not only that, but when I was a child she would take me to church on the sly every once in a while, to vespers, which made a great impression on me.

The liturgy has remained with me my entire life. I did not go to synagogue. My father was religious, a distinguished Cabalist; rabbis consulted him on various matters. But my father was not only a man of tolerance; he had a general principle of not interfering in anyone's life, particularly his children's. And so I really grew up in an atmosphere of atheism, because my brothers and sisters were older than I and were socialists, or atheists in any case. I lived near a synagogue but I didn't go to it. I went a few times on the High Holidays, but it really was something between a synagogue and a church.

Anusia worked for my sister after my mother died. Then the Germans came and took her, no one knew where. My parents and my older brothers and sisters had always promised Anusia that she would have a Catholic funeral with six priests. That was what she wanted, but that couldn't be done because no one knew where she died. She raised all of us. My mother talked with her more than anyone else; they reminisced endlessly, especially about the old days, before I was born.

I was there when my mother died. She suddenly stopped talking and died very peacefully. Then, feeling very sad and guilty, I went out for a long walk in Otwock, outside the town actually. There were some woods where the moss grew high on the tree trunks. I must have been in a very strange state because twice rabbits ran right past my feet so close I could have reached out and touched them. I could see that animals weren't afraid of me.

But there was something I wanted to say. There were five birds. I'm no expert on large birds, and so I don't know whether they were partridges or something else, but anyway I had never seen birds like that in those parts. And I knew the area outside of Otwock. As I walked, they kept circling above me—I swear it—they kept circling and then they sped off to the west. I was walking east. They went off to the west and then came back and circled over me again. Then they flew off again. It happened three times. Then, finally, after the third time, they disappeared. The war began very soon after that and I fled to the east. And when I found myself there in the east, that first day in Lwów, there was a hawk circling, circling quite low over the crowded street. And I was arrested not long after that.

I had one other sign; then the signs stopped.

The Molotov-Ribbentrop Pact. I don't want to brag, but I was absolutely certain that Poland would be divided and that war would break out. Before that I had thought Poland would give in, that something would be worked out over Gdańsk. But as soon as the news of the pact arrived—I think it was August 23—I knew that Hitler and Stalin would be coming into Poland.

Then later, *ex post*, even in Lwów, I thought, Either the Russians will arrest me and I'll go to some camp or to Lubyanka, or the Germans will send me to Dachau or some other camp—or somehow I would escape. But once again the infernal machine was much more precise. In the sixties, in Poland, *Polityka* published a list of people whom the police had designated in May 1939 to be sent to the concentration camp at Bereza Kartuska—two hundred members of the intelligentsia, six or seven writers, including me. And so it turned out that there weren't two nooses to be slipped over me, but three.

Was that my fault? I had gotten myself involved in history. Unfortunately, one of the sad laws of my fate is to be an anachronism. I was political when it was time to be a poet and a poet when it was time to be political. I was a communist when decent people were anticommunist, and anticommunist when intelligent people were going over to communism. I was avant-garde, an innovator, when there was no such movement, no ear for innovation, especially among the young people in Poland, and some years later I became syncretic just as the new youth wanted innovation. Nothing ever at the right time. I didn't choose freedom, so-called freedom, at the right time either. My illness is a result, an expression, of my anachronism. Yes, I was everything you had to be, but not at the time you were supposed to. I am not speaking like this because I consider my fate exceptional. On the contrary—how to put it—it's an exemplification of millions of other, similar, fates. I just moved around too much, you see. I was too active. When a person who can't swim is in the water, the worst thing for him to do is to flail around. And I kept moving. Enormous History, a mighty machine, and I had stuck my little foot in.

I found myself in Lwów in October. But that's another story. Lwów is *ein Kapitel für sich*, a very sad *Kapitel* in my life. I was arrested on January 24, 1940. Those three months in Lwów, three sad months to remember, three months of fear, play-acting, clumsy lies. Clumsy because I was betraying myself, because I couldn't stand up to it all. I had fled Warsaw with my brother-in-law and my sister. I was alone in Lwów because Ola and Andrzej were in another car and had gotten lost. I was afraid. I knew that everyone connected to *The Literary Monthly* had been killed in Russia, so I didn't have the slightest doubt that the same thing was in store for me. I could imagine what Soviet prisons and camps were like—I knew—and I knew what Ola's and Andrzej's fate would be. I was in the town of Łuck, and they were in some other small town. We were looking for each other, and so I had to show my face. I went around to the cafés; I handed out cards saying that Aleksander Wat was searching for his wife and so on. I handed out a thousand, maybe five thousand cards, and that's how I found them in the end. And Ola came to Lwów.

15 WAR. FLIGHT TO LWÓW. THE RED ARMY. A NEW WRITERS' UNION. *THE RED BANNER*. SELF-CRITICISM.

WAT: Maybe I'll backtrack a little. Maybe all this will be clearer if I say something about my first impressions, my first encounter with the Soviets. I'll skip the details about fleeing; practically every other Pole has written about that. My flight was very picturesque, one variation on a thousand. There's just one thing I'd like to say. I had left a period of terrible sadness behind in Warsaw. Sadness and the certainty that terrible things were going to happen. In general, and to me. Not death, but horrendous experiences that would make the living envy the dead. I spent at least three years in that hermitage of a life. But when the war broke out, all that somehow seemed swept aside. It would be exaggerating to say that I was euphoric, but some knot was cut that first day when the bombs started falling. It was a sense of relief, but I had ceased to exist on the cerebral, spiritual, moral level; I was on a level where I submitted to reflexes and impulses. And so, on the sixth day of the war, I had a mad impulse, an impulse to flee; I had to flee with Ola and Andrzej. I flew into action, grabbed Ola and Andrzej, and took them to Warsaw on the last train. I did not even say good-bye to my father, who was living not far from us in Otwock. I existed only on the level of impulse.

My sister called me and said there was room in their car. Did we want to go with them? Without baggage or anything, of course. We ran to their place and were bombed on the way. There was no question of heading for Rumania because my brother-in-law, who was of the Kiev gentry, was an absolute optimist and believed that our troops would be in Berlin in two weeks. We traveled by night, but if we came to a nice village and there was food to be had, we'd buy up all the chickens and eggs and spend a day or two by a lake, swimming and so on.

On the way we lost each other; the two cars just lost track of each other. Ola and Andrzej were in the other car with my sister and brother-in-law. I think it happened around Janow Podlaski. It was daytime; we weren't driving. I was lying on the grass by the road. I didn't know where Ola was, whether they were in Janow or had passed us. Suddenly, bombs began raining down. I was terribly afraid that those bombs might hit them. And there I was on the grass, surrounded by herbs, the smell of honey, rosemary, the bushes warmed by the sun. I took a crap in those bushes. And I was flooded with the joy of life, one of the greatest moments of joy in my life. I was at one with nature. I bring this up because there's a funny side to it. In my book *My Pug Iron Stove*, which I wrote at nineteen, there are sentences and situations that came true later on in my life. And so there's one story in *My Pug Iron Stove* (Witkiewicz wrote a piece about it): "Consolation flowed through Benvenuto Cellini's friend when he took a crap in the ripe berry bush." And a sense of consolation really did flow through me. But that's just a minor episode.

The first Russians I saw were in Łuck, a garrison town in the borderlands. Tanks, a terrible racket. Tanks, Russians, mass meetings. I want to give only my impressions here. You know, those Mongol-like faces, those shoddy uniforms, those raggedy Mongolian peaked caps. It was Asia but in such mass amounts, Asia at its most Asian.

I met a friend there, and we went to the movies to see *Ivan the Terrible*. We had to run out of the theater—the stench was unbearable. Boots and more boots and that smell of birch tar and sweaty feet and cheap rolling tobacco. When I had been moving toward communism, I had accepted those Asiatic faces as a fact of life, and I didn't think about them when I was moving away from communism either. I thought that to oppose the European and Asian was merely empty anti-Soviet propaganda, a nineteenth-century issue. Very superficial stuff. But there it was—pure Asia.

I had one other experience, not so much an experience as an observation that later on became part of an experience. I was in Łuck and I couldn't get out of there. I wanted to find Ola; it was the first time I had ever been separated from her (no, it was the second time). I wanted to find Ola and leave Łuck, and so I went to the military command. It was mobbed. The commanding officer, a Bolshevik—I forget his rank— was standing in the middle of a hall, and people were going up to him with their petitions, one after the other. A Polish peasant went up and said that his horse had been taken away from him and that was the only horse he had. And the thing is, that officer, without asking all sorts of questions (this was the first time I had seen any of them act on their own initiative like that) summoned a soldier then and there and ordered him to take the Pole to the stable or the courtyard and give him any horse he chose. I mention this in passing because certain elements here come up later.

And so, as I told you, Lwów was mobbed with refugees, fugitives from Warsaw, colleagues of mine. Literary people were petrified. There were no important people there yet; neither Wasilewska nor Borejsza were in Lwów yet. But Dan was there, among others. For some reason Dan was very concerned about me, and quite sincerely too. He was very friendly to me even though we hadn't known each other before. Then, out of nowhere—a meeting. I don't remember who called it. A meeting of the literary left in the broadest sense of the word. Well, they really didn't have their bearings yet: they saw me as an old Bolshevik, me and Władzio Broniewski. And so they elected me to chair the meeting, saying that we had to join forces, and so on, elect a board. And even though my principal intention was to hide in the provinces, I made an appearance there to help find Ola. The wave had already caught me. Dan told me that Korneichuk was in charge of organizing literary life there and that he had spoken to Korneichuk about me.

My second conversation with Dan was of a different sort; he talked about himself. He said that he had been in very difficult straits, but thanks to Korneichuk, he was now in a better position and not afraid anymore. And he said that my situation was really entirely analogous to his. He also said that he was well aware how dangerous my situation was and that of course I should go with him to see Korneichuk.

Korneichuk was at the Hotel George. We waited for a long time in front of his room, his suite; then out came two very good-looking, ample-bottomed girls, and a little while later he invited us in. He was wearing silk pajamas, acquired in Lwów of course, and a lot of cologne. He had the charm of a waiter. There was really no conversation. He was obviously tired, but very cordial. He said that comrade Dan had told him about me, that elections would be held soon, there would be a large meeting, and that he would be very happy if I were on the board and so forth. Small talk, very brief.

Then came that large meeting of writers that has been distorted greatly in some accounts. For example, it's been said that there were Russians among the presiding officers. That's an error, because the Soviets carefully observed the rules against there being any Russians on any presidium. That incredible Stalinist scrupulousness about preserving the forms. The officers were Ukrainians because that was the Western Ukraine. There were plenty of Russian writers there—they were constantly arriving—but no one interfered in anything, no Russian held any post. Meanwhile, there was one very interesting thing. The Ukrainians were taking it all very seriously, even the Soviet Ukrainians; they weren't letting the Russians do anything. If a high-ranking Russian writer wanted to intervene in some case, defend someone, they would protest and kick up a fuss: it's none of your business; the Ukraine is ours.

Who was on the presidium? Korneichuk, of course, and Dovzhenko, one of the great film directors, and Tychyna, the Ukrainian Mayakovsky. Korneichuk made a speech. A real diplomat. The hall was full. They had dragged in everyone with any connection to literature, too many people. [Korneichuk said:] "You don't trust us, I know that, and I don't require any trust from you in advance. Have a good look at us. We have time; take a year or two. If you like it, wonderful; if not, tough. It's up to you. But meanwhile, we'll give you conditions in which you can live, work, and observe us in action. We won't put any pressure on any of you; we won't use any propaganda on you. You'll judge for yourselves. You should take your time. Why rush? There shouldn't be any rush."

I remember his speech exactly, and that was the tenor of it.

The Germans were in Poland bombing and destroying, and there we were being invited to just live and take a good look at things and not a hair on our heads would be touched.

The elections to the board. Dan and Korneichuk drew up the list of course. Dan was elected to the organizational committee, Broniewski, a few Ukrainians, including two or three Ukrainian nationalists, two Jewish writers. The other Poles were Boy Żeleński and myself. And later on when Wanda Wasilewska arrived, she was co-opted as well. The general secretary was Korneichuk's factotum, a Ukrainian, Churkovsky, who supplied him with girls and silk pajamas and God knows what else. An incredibly low person. Later on, when Korneichuk left, that Churkovsky remained the general secretary with all the power in his hands until the end. When the Germans came, it turned out that he had been a German agent. He deceived the Russians for two years.

There was a multitude of refugees. People had nowhere to live, nothing to live on, terrible hardship. The Ukrainian and Jewish writers were mostly local people, and so they were in a good position. But the struggle for existence came before everything, and they wouldn't allow the others any room at the trough.

And moreover there was a political struggle going on. There were two currents, which were a mystery to me at the time though they're clear enough to me now. Korneichuk left quite soon. His place as *chef gauleiter* of literature was taken by Petro Panch, an author of children's books. A very non-Slavic type, Anglo-Saxon, very dry, extraordinarily self-possessed and cold. He had apparently been an officer in the White Guard, which was quite possible, and there was no doubt that he was now with the NKVD; that came with the position he held. The board met in session twice a week. What did the board do? Its principal concerns were food and housing. Those were the only things I wanted to deal with. Looking for apartments, supplying people with money. That was a great boon to people. Winter had started, and they had no clothes, food, or fuel. Of the people on the board, there was Dan, a party member or former party member—he was probably out of the party by that time. Wanda Wasilewska was apparently not in the party either, but she had been connected with the Soviets for a long time. And me, a renegade for many years, a sympathizer. And Broniewski, a sympathizer.

I would say that those few weeks in Lwów were the most disgusting period of my life. I acted like a coward. I lied. I knew that they would arrest me, that Ola and Andrzej would go under. I was trembling in my boots. I pretended that, yes, I had regained my faith in communism. I didn't harm anyone. On the contrary. And I wrote no poetry about Stalin. I had been out of literary life for the last three or four years, and that was the perfect pretext for me to say that I was washed up as a writer. I played that up. I dealt only with food, housing, money, arranging things for everyone.

But of course I told lies. I pretended that I had regained my faith. I performed no acts of self-criticism because no one asked me to; had they told me to, I would have. I was trembling in fear for Ola and for myself.

I knew what lay in store for us, but no one told me to engage in self-criticism. A smart person would have figured that out himself. And Dan kept urging me to. The thing to do was to report to Panch for a talk, just go see him and say, I was with you, then I strayed, but now I see I was wrong. But I never had that conversation. I dealt with matters of daily life, and I told lies, in cafés, conversations, union meetings, saying that I was a communist 100 percent, that now I understood everything, that Stalin was a wise man.

Dan, who was looking out for me and who kept promising to extricate me somehow from it all, began urging me to join *The Red Banner*, which had been publishing for quite a while. He said that it would be the safest place for me. During the six or seven weeks that I worked on *The Red Banner*, I published three or four, maybe five, small stories about meetings in factories. I really did not write anything bad, just reports of meetings in factories. What was bad about those reports was that I did not write what I had seen. I wrote that so and so spoke and that so and so was elected to the board. But I had walked around the factories, and I had seen the poverty of the workers, the terrible hardship in Lwów. Workers were fainting from hunger in the chocolate factory.

There was a double standard operating there, because all the big shots were living very well, under the circumstances—the big shots and the speculators. Another image of Lwów: the incredible blossoming of speculation. There were two streets in Lwów popularly known as "Whoresdale" before the war because the little prostitute hotels were there. It was the center of economic life. Day and night the area was full of Soviets, hard currency, gold, diamonds, anything you wanted. Prostitutes. The deportations hadn't started yet. At one point in November the speculators on the black market began circulating between Warsaw and Lwów especially since one night the Russians had invalidated Polish currency. I was working on *The Red Banner* at the time. They simply detained the entire printing and editorial staff because the next day's paper would carry the decree about the switch to Soviet currency, the ruble and the chervonets. The idea was to keep the city from learning about it during the night. But then, not long after that, Polish money became the object of such fantastic speculation that hundreds of people from Warsaw, especially Jews, began making their way to Lwów, buying up all those złotys dirt cheap, and bringing them back to Warsaw. And the other way around. Nightmarish.

But I forgot to tell you about the worst of it at *The Red Banner*. There was a purge of the staff. There were a bunch of ex-Trotskyites there, not to mention Dan. They didn't touch a hair on his head because, and I have certain reasons for thinking this, he had sold out; that is, he was protecting himself; he had an agreement with the NKVD that he would report to them. He probably said the best possible things about everyone. I'm even sure of that. But one day a group came to the editorial offices—two or three people, one of them a good-looking redhead but a forbidding girl. They were professionals who had come to question the staff. Everyone was there. They asked the questions, and everyone had to speak about himself, tell his life story. Everyone was seated; the room full of inquisitors and eyes. That was the only time that I engaged in any self-criticism. I played it like an actor, knowing that I was playing for my life and Ola's. There had already been a purge. One ex-Trotskyite had been thrown off the editorial board and had been immediately arrested afterwards. I played it like an actor, splitting myself in two. You're there, it's your turn in five minutes, and during those five minutes you have to split yourself into two distinct entities. Like a guillotine. You have to sever one part from the other. And you have to feel that split within yourself because otherwise it doesn't work and you foul up. The inquisitors have excellent eyes and sharp ears. I remember glancing at my watch and saying to myself: I'm going to have to talk in five minutes. And during those five minutes I had to perform inner surgery. I really could feel something tearing apart inside me. The actor, Aleksander Wat, was there, and I was also there in the wings, an eye that watched that actor move, speak—his gestures, intonations, everything. Later, when I went back home to Ola, I was covered in sweat; the sweat was still pouring off me. Apparently, I had played the part brilliantly. I admitted that I had said that there was a dictatorship, terror, and fear in the Soviet Union, that everyone lived in fear, but now I had come to see the error of my ways. Terror—why the very idea! And I said that now I understood the wisdom of the policy that had anticipated the current situation with scientific accuracy. For the love of God, I said, how can any of you have any doubts; after all, this city is full of Soviet people and we're in daily contact with them and I've seen for myself (of course I used more sophistry here) that there's not even a hint of fear in Soviet people. It's just the reverse; what's striking about them is their independence, their spontaneity, their initiative. And it was then that I brought in that scene in the courtyard when the officer had made his decision without the slightest hesitation. "You want a horse? You'll get one!" I played on them, I blackmailed them, I let them know that if they doubted my sincerity, that would mean that they weren't sincere themselves. No, they didn't throw me out. But one of the main communists on the editorial board did nod his head and say: "Yes, yes, your self-criticism was convincing, but you left out one thing you shouldn't have—your friendship with Stawar." But I still felt that I was out of trouble, that I had saved myself for the while.

16 LWÓW. WANDA WASILEWSKA. BRONIEWSKI. SOVIET WRITERS. SIGNS THAT I WILL BE ARRESTED.

WAT: The atmosphere in Lwów, in November, December . . . A city that had lost its beauty, a city besieged by fear. Did you know Lwów before the war? Lwów was one of the loveliest Polish cities in the sense that it was a merry city. Not so much the people, but the city itself. Very colorful, very exotic, it had none of the grayness of Warsaw, or even Kraków or Poznań. Its exoticism made it a very European city. Vienna, of course, had influenced Kraków, but its influence made Kraków an Austrian bureaucratic city, a city with an Austrian bureaucracy and an Austrian bureaucratic university. Lwów was a bit more like the Vienna of operetta, the Vienna of joie de vivre. Like some of the Italian cities. Not all of them though—some Italian cities are dismal as hell. Lwów was like Marseilles. Well, the Soviets had barely arrived, and all at once everything was covered in mud (of course it was fall), dirty, gray, shabby. People began cringing and slinking down the streets. Right away people started wearing ragged clothes; obviously they were afraid to be seen in their better clothes.

Who was in the Writers' Union? A lot of conformists, and so on— there were a great many people like that hovering around the union. The refugees had nothing to live on; they wanted to warm themselves at that fire—everyone who had any contact with communism before the war, close or not so close. Those who had been close to communism could be divided into people like me—meaning those who were lying—and the faithful, the ones who had remained faithful despite the purges, the disbanding of the party, and the trials. Their day hadn't come yet; they were still waiting for the iron broom. The iron broom was the symbolic name for the Cheka and the NKVD. At the beginning of the purges Stalin had been given a gift by the presidium of the Russian party: a miniature dog's head and a miniature iron broom, the emblem of the *oprichniks*.* And so they were marginal people, waiting

---

* Oprichniks. Ivan the Terrible's secret police.

for their day to come, and it was coming closer all the time. And there were other people, people who were ill at ease and who had various sins against the party on their conscience—people like me and Ważyk. To make a long story short, everyone was scared to death. Some people were exulting, and others were scared and lying. It wasn't only the writers who weren't absolutely confident, absolutely sure—the old communists who had committed some sins felt the same. There was a multitude of liars in Lwów in those days.

Events? The main thing was the elections to the National Assembly of the Western Ukraine in October. Wanda Wasilewska wasn't there yet. She was not a delegate; she arrived in Lwów after all the candidates had already been announced but before the actual voting; she gave a speech at a preelection meeting. It was only later on that she was elected a deputy to the Supreme Soviet in Moscow. Of the writers, Halina Górska and Adam Polewka [were candidates].

Halina Górska was a sentimental socialist, a pure soul, terribly elegiac; everything pained her, every act of injustice in the world. Ola and I became friendly with her in Lwów and we were at her house fairly often. A very pure home, pure people. And that was her misfortune because, since she had the reputation of being a pure, highly moral, and decent person, she was, of course, chosen to be a candidate. And I remember perfectly—Ola and I were there at the time—she did not want to accept the candidacy. Her husband, who had no connection to communism, a very decent man—he and everyone else begged her not to refuse. It would have been madness; a great wave of arrests had already begun. So we tried to influence her not to be headstrong, not to make any quixotic gestures. That this was bad advice is another story. Had she refused, they probably wouldn't have done anything to her, especially since she was in a situation like the ones I was often in: you yield once and then you're on a slippery path, an inclined plane. And then you make a countermove, a move much more dangerous than the original situation would have been, if you hadn't taken that first step. Because it was at that meeting of the National Assembly (the sessions were held in the Great Theater's large hall)—I was in the gallery, I had a ticket—that Górska was the only person who abstained from voting on the incorporation of the Western Ukraine [into the Soviet Union], and that was undoubtedly a much riskier step than accepting the candidacy in the first place.

As secretary of the Communisty party of the Ukraine, Khrushchev was present during the voting. Tudor, an old Ukrainian communist, the editor of a literary magazine, *Windows*, a philosopher by training and a poet, was also a delegate, and he spoke out in defense of the Poles. He just said straight out that they had to put a stop to the murdering of the Poles in the provinces, in the countryside, and so on. He argued his case in a rational, calm manner, even with a bit of sophistry, not taking a humanitarian tack but a political one, though it was humanitarian as well. Khrushchev cut him off. Foaming at the mouth, Khrushchev began shouting at him that he had absolutely no understanding of dialectics, that the masses were acting justly, that this was justice meted out by the masses; no one should dare stand in the way of the masses, the wrathful masses who had suffered so much. Afterward, everyone was afraid that Tudor would disappear. He didn't, but I don't know what happened to him in the end, how he died.

A great many Soviet writers came to Lwów, almost all in uniform, as war correspondents. At that time it was officially called the "Polish war." They didn't say that in *Pravda* and *Izvestiya*, but in the local papers, the Ukrainian papers, this was the Polish war. Probably the point was to expunge the shame of the Soviet defeat in 1920. A war against the Poles. That was forgotten about later on, and then it was just called "the liberation of the Western Ukraine." Their military rank depended on their literary standing. Demyan Bedny was a general— that, I remember perfectly—and Shklovsky was, I think, only a captain or a major.

And all of them, absolutely all of them (I knew a few of them from before the war) kept asking, "Where is your Wanda Wasilewska?" A couple of them said that Stalin had demanded that Wanda Wasilewska be found. There are two possible explanations here. Stalin read a great many novels. He read everything; he had no taste. Apparently he considered Wanda Wasilewska a great writer. Her novel about Polesia had an influence on him. I even have a few facts to back this up.

When I was in Łuck, at the very beginning, trains kept arriving there from Russia loaded with kerosene, matches, and salt. And they'd take machines and wool back to Russia. That was baffling. Why were they bringing those items to Łuck, a provincial capital; why were they constantly talking about those items at the mass meetings? After all, the Soviets surely had good intelligence; they had to know that there was no shortage of matches, salt, or kerosene in Łuck or Lwów. But those three items were in short supply in the Polesian villages, in those God-forsaken holes in Polesia that Wanda Wasilewska had written about. And so I don't know whether, despite the information Soviet intelligence supplied him, Stalin issued that order under the influence of her book, which he might have been reading at the time.

In any case, they were looking for her everywhere. Where is Wanda Wasilewska? That's all you heard. Another possibility is that she might have been connected with some Soviet institutions before the war. She was not actually in the Communist party—she was in the PPS—but, as I told you, she had written a communist work as early as 1936; *The Face of Day* was a thoroughly communist book. And so perhaps she was connected in some way.

She turned up in Lwów and was given all the honors; she was also co-opted onto the board of the Writers' Union, where she behaved very decently. In general, in personal matters and in her dealings with her colleagues she had firm moral principles and *Kinderstube*. She was the daughter of a government minister, a socialist, and she had carried on the family's good traditions.

She even put me to shame once. Quite painful to recall. I was busy handling organizational matters, housing, food—so I would not have to write or deal with anything ideological. I had nothing to do with ideological matters. My duties included registering people for the Writers' Union. One day old Purman, an economist I knew quite well, paid a call on me. We'd been at the university together; he was my age though he had been ahead of me. He was called "Wig" because he was bald and wore a wig—once one of the threads had come out of the wig, and that was how he got his nickname. A very nice man, a philosopher. His brother had been a prominent communist, one of the leading communists; he was killed in Russia. Purman had been present at the birth of *The Literary Monthly* and then later disappeared from sight. I was not even aware that he had gone on to become a Trotskyite and had joined the PPS along with Deutscher and the other Trotskyites. (A whole group of Trotskyites had joined the PPS in 1934.) I registered him, of course, not knowing that he had something on his conscience. Had I known, I would have warned him against registering, as I had a couple of other people—not always successfully, though, because they had absolutely wanted to be in the union. And so I registered Purman. Had I known, I would have advised him against it. Then there was a great scandal because he was one of the most important Trotskyites. And they complained about me; they went for my throat because I had been the one to approve his membership in the union. He was discussed at a union meeting, and Panch asked me what the real story with Purman was. I said that I knew he was an old communist and that a short while ago I had learned that he had joined the PPS, but I hadn't known that at the time. I didn't condemn him; I only said that he had joined the PPS. At that Wanda Wasilewska turned red and went after me in a fury: "So what if he had joined the PPS; I was in the PPS, too." And so I explained that I wasn't saying that that was bad; I was just repeating what I'd been told. This is one of my more unpleasant memories, because Purman was arrested the same night I was. But he never came out; he died in a camp—from typhus, I think. And so Wanda Wasilewska behaved decently on that occasion.

She was an impassioned woman. Around that time she published an article, a sort of absolutely fantastic hymn to the Red Army. The mysticism of the Red Army, the exaltation of a Saint Teresa.

MILOSZ: Explain that to me. It was extremely difficult for anyone who had been raised in Poland and who saw the Red Army to be in ecstasies over it.

WAT: Yes, all that rabble, Asia, ragged, illiterate Asia. It turns out that the elimination of illiteracy was hogwash, as I saw for myself in Russia. It had been eliminated in the statistics, but there had been a marked lapse into illiteracy, especially among those who had been through the seven-year schools. I myself knew a great many young people in Russia who had graduated from the seven-year schools and weren't able to write a few years later.

No one has made a study of the women fanatics, the Saint Teresas of communism, La Pasionaria [Dolores Ibarruri] especially. As for me, I saw Wasilewska; I spoke with her. The air was full of lies; many of the old communists were lying, but I am absolutely certain that she was sincere. Those are mystical women who don't see reality—or rather they see another reality, one we don't see.

She went to Kiev soon after this, where she was given a triumphal welcome. She went with her husband, Bogatko, a former bricklayer, a fantastic athlete, a truly handsome young man, always game for anything. He was intelligent, quick, with a sense of humor, strong, cheerful. She was popular with those strong guys. Apparently she loved Bogatko very much.

After they came back from Kiev, one afternoon there was a mass rally out on some square; Wanda was going to give a report on Kiev. I went with Broniewski and Bogatko. It was the usual bombast—a happy life, everything is rosy, all the clichés that were ever used in the press. But she spoke with real passion, fire. A tough, dry, big-boned woman, with a broad, flat face, large powerful eyes; her gestures were passionate.

Afterwards, Bogatko said to Broniewski and me, "Let's go to a bar." And so he dragged us to a bar; he drank like mad. And just imagine, in a bar full of Soviet officers, Bogatko started telling us all sorts of other things right after that meeting, his voice booming, "Remember when you go to Kiev, as soon as you get to Kiev, when you take your first step off the train, grab onto your bags with one hand and your cap with the other, or they'll snatch it right off your head." I'm only telling you of one incident, but there were many such incidents with Bogatko.

Later on, when I was already in prison, they put a Ukrainian in our cell who told me about Bogatko's death, a story that would later be confirmed by Broniewski. Two NKVD men went to Bogatko's place and shot him dead. The culprits were never found, which must be unprecedented in the annals of Soviet crime. It was always the crimes that were not discovered, though the culprits were always known—but in this case the culprits were not found, a first. The newspapers said that Ukrainian nationalists had killed him. But there's no doubt that it was the NKVD. Broniewski, who always maintained good close relations with Wanda, right to the end, confirmed that to me.

This is an interesting story because Bogatko's death was real first-rate Stalinist training—so that she would have no illusions. *Point de rêveries.* Immediately. A one-time shock. Zen. A whack on the head and your entire consciousness is restructured. Then comes the reforging of the soul.

But I'll say it once again: after we were arrested, Wanda made great efforts and ran risks to get us out. Apparently Khrushchev warned her not to interfere. There was a sort of subliminal antipathy between Wasilewska and me; we were never close. But she had drunk a sea of vodka with Broniewski.

I had many conversations with Soviet writers in Lwów. Shklovsky, who knew about me from Mayakovsky, was very warm to me, but he was the most careful of them all; he hated like hell to get onto political subjects. He was enchanted with Lwów, however; one time he asked me to show him Lwów's historical sights. He had tremendous admiration for the Armenian chapel and in general he admired Poland for its authentic baroque architecture and for preserving it. I was even a little surprised, because both Moscow and Novgorod have their own antiquities. For all I know, it might have been the monuments of Western culture that sparked his passion.

And now to skip ahead a little for a moment to Izak Feffer, who was liquidated later on with all the other Jewish writers. I knew him from before the war; he had passed through Warsaw. In Lwów Izak Feffer threw himself on me and asked if he could come see me at home. And so Ola had to make a dinner, and we invited Górska too. Feffer never showed up. The next day I was walking down the street, and I saw Feffer coming toward me about a hundred feet ahead. He was a Jew; he had a nice face. You know Orthodox Jews wear *shtreimlech*, fox-fur caps. He was wearing a fox-fur cap but a luxurious one, a sign of the "new man." He was not in uniform, just dressed like an important person. A wonderful fur coat, a fox-fur cap; he was a tiny man, and he was swimming in that cap. As soon as he spotted me from a distance, he immediately stopped and turned around. And then and there I said to myself, the axe is falling. And that was true; I was arrested about three days later.

All those writers were of course buying up everything in Lwów. They liked antiques best. This was after my time but they say that Alexei Tolstoy had two or three freight carfuls sent back from Lwów, and apparently Stalin tongue-lashed him for that. That was going too far.

Broniewski was already having problems. He was walking around Lwów in a daze, seething, gritting his teeth, reciting his poetry wherever he could. They arranged a New Year's ball for the children, and he was to be one of the performers. Panch forbade Broniewski to read any patriotic poems. All the same he read "Goes the Soldier out of Bondage." Finally, Panch got up and made a point of leaving the auditorium. That was right before Broniewski's arrest. But still Broniewski was raving on about a Soviet Poland and singing songs like "Moskva moya, Moskva moya" (Moscow, my Moscow"). He had all that inside him at the same time, meaning that his emotional experiences were in a frenzy before he intellectualized them: a patriot, Poland, Poland's defeat, the Soviets, their friendship with the Germans, not being allowed to read anti-German patriotic poems. But it was a long way from his guts to his head. When it finally got there, he could think quite logically. He had horse sense, common sense. But it took a very long time for it to get there.

There was terrible hunger and poverty in Lwów at the time I was arrested; everything had been shipped out to Russia. The terror had been greatly stepped up and was still going on in April 1940 when Ola and Andrzej were deported. But it must be admitted that after that the material situation became perfectly fine; they started supplying the city as part of a general policy of winning the people over. I guess the change took place in the middle of 1940. The mass deportations began a few months after the Soviets arrived.

OLA WAT: There was a very bad deportation in February, mostly peasants.

WAT: Yes, Ola was in the first transport of wives of men who had been arrested. It took place on the night of April 13, 1940, and there were a few more deportations after that.

MILOSZ: They didn't start deporting large numbers of people from Wilno right away. There was an initial wave of deportations, but then there was a long interval while the lists were being drawn up. The great deportations only occurred shortly before the German-Russian war broke out.

OLA WAT: The first deportation from Lwów came in February. You were arrested on January 23. The February deportation was terrible: people froze to death in the train cars; women were giving birth; dead children were thrown off the train. Then there was the April deportation, the one Andrzej and I were in.

WAT: Now we're getting near the satanic tale of provocation and arrest. The hard-nosed communists in the editorial office were afraid to talk to me. I even remember that Stryjkowski was afraid to talk to me; he kept giving me the slip. I was no longer a secretary at the union, and Panch would barely see me. There were many signs that I would be arrested. I was certain that Broniewski would be picked up too. In the Soviet Union you can tell about these things because a void forms around a person.

I remember the day I was arrested, as clear as can be. In the morning I went to the union; I still had various functions that I hadn't handed over to anyone yet, like dealing with fuel. I had an appointment that I didn't keep. I knew that I was being followed. I'd been paranoid for quite a long time, and, I'll tell you, if it weren't for that paranoia I would have fled from Lwów with my sister and brother-in-law and probably would have been killed during the German occupation. I would certainly have been killed because we would all have stayed together, and it was hard for an entire family to escape destruction. I remember that Ola tried to persuade me to flee from Lwów, but I was sure that I was being followed—they'd catch me along the way and then there'd be no question about finishing me off. But people were fleeing, even communists. Polewka fled. Right before my arrest he said, "You know, Aleksander, there are only two choices. Either you join the NKVD, or you run away." He ran.

17 LWÓW. ARTICLES FOR *THE RED BANNER*. DIGRESSION ON MONGOLIA AS A PEOPLE'S REPUBLIC. MY JEWISHNESS. PROVOCATION AND ARREST.

WAT: I don't remember the last time I had to regurgitate what I consider the greatest sin I committed in Lwów. One sin was that self-criticism, and now I'll tell you about the other one. Well, you see, one day the editor of *Literaturnaya Gazeta* showed up in Lwów. Obviously after talking with some of the local Soviets, he approached me and Borejsza as two people with a good command of Russian to write about Lwów for his paper. I didn't want to at all, but again Dan and others advised me not to refuse, saying something could be written somehow or other. And so I wrote feuilletons in Russian. I found a good dodge—to write, so to speak, with dignity, a bit the way Ehrenburg did in his reportage. A certain distance, a bird's-eye view. Some yarns about that city itself on the Peltev River, a city at the watershed of rivers, a bit of topography, people immersed in the topography, or as a part of it.

They printed it, but they did fiddle with it a little. I have to say that it was done delicately, but the changes were crucial. After the war I somehow managed to get hold of that issue, and so my memory's been refreshed on the subject. They threw out a couple of sentences, added a few words here and there, and made some of the adjectives stronger. Though the truth is that even in that form, it's not a scandalous article. What's in it? I describe on the one hand the old bourgeois society (which I don't call bourgeois), that mourns Poland's tragedy, and on the other the workers and so on who are building a new life. As I say, I tried to do this with a certain dignity, but it was those changes and cosmetic touch-ups that made the article very unpleasant. There's no abuse in it, no elegiac, mournful tone, though there is some estrangement, an a priori attitude. You know what I mean. Meanwhile, they added some very strong adjectives where I described the people building a new life. And that caused an absolute shift in emphasis. It made me very ashamed. Poland was undergoing a tragedy, and there I was taking the grand tone. I had written from a bird's-eye view, all a literary trick, but they had stepped up the grand tone. The new adjectives, a few sentences thrown out, and a couple of words changed nearly made this sound like contempt. A very sorry state of affairs. I would have protested in People's Poland—I did protest in other cases—but I didn't even think of protesting or sending in a correction in Lwów.

And so those are my sins. I speak of those sins, those shameful acts, those wrongs I committed, for two reasons. I want to stress this point. In prison, until a certain moment—in any case in Lwów though not in Moscow—I kept to a certain line. I was interrogated nonstop; it was incredibly wearing, all-night interrogations, very long. No brutality; they yelled at me, but they never struck me. Once they came flying at me and I thought they were going to beat me, but they never struck me or used those lights on me. But the interrogations were mentally oppressive, unrelenting; they dragged on and on. Time seemed endless. I used awful tactics at those interrogations, which is why they tormented me so much. One of my tactics was to say that I was a leftist. I didn't say I was a communist, but a leftist, and that I had regained my faith. Sincerity was another one of my tactics. I openly admitted everything I had said against the Soviets.

Not everything, because I denied comparing Stalin to Hitler on the day the pact was signed. (That had to be Daszewski's testimony; they didn't say that, but I had spoken to him about it.) In fact I admitted 90 percent of everything about myself; I beat my breast because basically I thought those things didn't matter much in interrogations. Because in the end those were things that I had said and done before Lwów when I was a Polish citizen, though they didn't care about that. Still, it did carry some weight, and so I made a tragedy out of my transgressions in Poland. I went on and on. But the range of accusations in the interrogations ran from being an agent of the Vatican through Zionism, Trotskyism, and Polish chauvinism. Quite a range. And that wasn't too good. In fact it was so bad that I tried to keep to certain limits so as not to harm anyone, which meant saying only the negative things about people that were already known to absolutely everyone, things that were black and white.

So, in a word, I tried to work it so no one got hurt. Of course that got me all tangled up and laid me open to their screaming and yelling. For example, when I said that Herminia Nagler was a progressive writer. At that, the interrogator pulled out a brochure—they'd been very well supplied by our people. You see, Gebethner had published a scholastic series of little books, *Poland and Today's World,* one of which was by Nagler. And the interrogator said, "But you published this!" Nagler had written about two members of the POW who were tortured during the Russian Revolution.* The interrogator said, "And you call her a progressive writer, the way she describes the Soviet Union and the Revolution!" So, you see, terribly difficult situations.

Later on, I not only learned my lesson, but I became a fanatic. Specifically that started in Saratov, where I had religious experiences, mystical ones; everything within me was turned upside down, and I began to sense the diabolical nature of communism. As a result, but also quite spontaneously, I began to renounce all leftism (which also proved to be a perfect tactic).

When I was released, I wrote an uncensored obituary that was published in *Poland* (an embassy publication), in which I admitted my Catholicism. I said that we were eyewitnesses to the confusion of tongues, an apocalyptic shattering of cultures and civilizations that wanted to be

* POW. A Polish military organization created by Piłsudski.

ruled exclusively by the laws of human reason. In that article I used the expression "Mongol faces." They brought that up when I was arrested the second time. "You don't like Mongol faces?" asked Omarkhadzhev, a handsome Mongol. And he also said, "Wat, after all, you were a communist." And I said, "Yes, something like that, but it was so long ago I can't remember now." I stuck to that line and felt wonderfully at peace. And they respected me. That approach proved my salvation.

When I returned to Poland in 1946, after six and a half years in Russia, Poland seemed an island of freedom to me, absolute, unlimited freedom. Besides, I had not succumbed to the same illusion that the magazine *The Forge* had. I had no doubt that Stalin planned to make Poland a puppet. And I remembered conversations I had had with some wise communists, including a shoemaker, a Jew from Odessa, the director of a shoemakers' workshop in Ili, in the desert, who foresaw everything that would happen in Poland. Everything. So I knew that Poland would be a puppet, but I succumbed to the illusion that it would be a puppet on display for the West—for the French, the Italians, and so on. A show window with some freedom left. Besides, I was well aware what a people's democracy was.

I see that I'm talking *à bâtons rompus* today, but perhaps that's better—straight lines are boring.

So, in Moscow, in 1942, I was in prison with a commissioner from the Ministry of Health in Mongolia. He described Mongolia to me. Today *Le Monde* or even the American papers still express surprise and joy that Mongolia is on Russia's side, that it hasn't let itself be talked around by the Chinese, that it was admitted to the UN in return for Mauritania. That was some deal. Independent Mongolia and independent Mauritania. The next day Mauritania voted against the West and America, and Mongolia became a go-between for the Afro-Asian camp. What kind of a place is Mongolia? (I'll make it fast because we might not come back to this later, and it's interesting.)

He was a commissioner in the Ministry of Health. What does that mean? It turns out that collective farms were not introduced in Mongolia, and they didn't touch the majority of the monasteries, and they left the old Mongolian customs alone, they were so old. There were ministries, and the ministers were Mongolians. And in every ministry there was a security commissioner with his own secret office. The Mongolian minister had a limousine, a villa, servants, and girls, and, besides that, as a doctor, my friend the commissioner would supply him with hashish or opium—I don't remember which. He could do anything if it was connected with health. He'd been in power, my cell mate, but there was also the NKVD where all the strings came together, in a little building, not interfering, the NKVD outpost for Russians sent from Moscow. They had orgies there every night in the NKVD building, he and those NKVD people. Well, but then he tripped himself up. At that time no one was permitted to travel to Mongolia, but a group of French communists or progressives arrived there. They took a picture of a cemetery where dogs were ripping apart the corpses that hadn't been buried deeply enough out of sheer slovenliness. The ground was stony. The delegation of progressives returned to Moscow with that photograph, and there was a scandal. He probably had other things on his conscience as well. For example, he was also accused of stealing a beautiful and very ancient ivory sculpture from a monastery. He described that sculpture to me: it was of a monastery with a great many monks. He said, "All right, but we all did that, all of us; I went to that monastery with my friends from the NKVD." Of course he said that he had sent the sculpture to his wife in Moscow, and his wife was supposed to donate it to a museum but hadn't gotten around to it yet. They all stole. And that was a People's Democracy. Without collective farms, where the customs and the religion had been preserved.

And so I thought Poland would be a sort of Western European Mongolia. I deluded myself. Besides, after six years on my back, six years of lying on the floor, I needed activity, and I was very active during those two years in Poland. I was on the editorial staff of *Rebirth*, in the Writers' Union, in cultural associations and on commissions, the PEN Club, the State Publishing Institute, God knows what else. I was active. But even in that period I protested when I was called "comrade" in the newspapers. I constantly stressed that not only wasn't I a communist, I wasn't even a Marxist; I wasn't a materialist. I was very glad when they called me religious or a Catholic. Right after I returned from Russia, a delegation of French progressive Catholics arrived in Poland, including Marek Schwarc, Fumet, and that priest like the one in my story, "The Wandering Jew," who was a priest, a Jew, and a communist. Borejsza introduced me to that priest very cleverly: "This is one of our Catholic writers!" Naturally, I protested at once. They were ready to use me like that, but I wouldn't go along with it. Of course I deliberately encouraged my reputation as a religious person, a Catholic, but I avoided Catholic circles so as not to be made their tool. That proved to be an ideal move, very shrewd.

Why do I emphasize my sins, my guilt? I've mentioned that I had too many scruples. I suppose that's my Jewishness coming out. I don't know—it's part of my psychology. As I told you, I had total freedom at home. I was already a Darwinist by the time I was a six- or seven-year-old brat. I'd tease our nursemaid Anusia and say there was no God and man was descended from the apes. To which she would very wisely and calmly reply, "So go climb a tree!" A very good argument, a philosophical argument. My father's philosophy was not to interfere with our lives, and all my six older brothers and sisters were atheists.

But I also had another legacy, because some of my ancestors had been great rabbis. I'm related to Solomon ben Isaac Rashi of Troyes, who was educated in Mainz in the eleventh century. His commentaries are still authoritative after almost a thousand years and are found in every Hebrew Bible. Then, in the beginning of the nineteenth century there was Izrael—I don't remember "ben" what—a wonder-worker from Kozienice. Prince Czartoryski used to go to him for advice because he was a clairvoyant. Kozienice is in Radom province. (My grandfather had property there, meaning some land and a smithy. My grandfather was very rich; my father wasn't.) My mother's great grandfather was a very great rabbi from Kutno. I once visited his grave. He had a splendid tomb covered with many little slips of paper. Not ex-votos, just supplications for him to intercede in an illness. When my mother was sick, my two aunts from Kutno also put little slips of paper on his tomb so that our ancestor would save her. So that's my Jewish legacy.

Generally speaking, I perceive the world, life, and myself through categories of guilt and punishment. And that isn't good. Always, in the last analysis, as Engels used to say, I'm always coming up against those two terrible extremes: guilt and punishment. That's why I'm inclined to stress these things so strongly, not because I'm a repentant intellectual—this has nothing to do with repentant intellectuals. I'm neither a repentant intellectual nor a masochist—this is simply my burden as a Jew. And I think that a great many Jews, even the Jewish philosophers, scholars, and writers, bear that burden, too, without realizing that it's an inborn conception of the world. Does that ring true to you? The last analysis. Not the Last Judgment, which is Christian. This has to do with the past, the past tense, fate.

MILOSZ: A dialogue.

WAT: Yes, a dialogue with God. A menacing dialogue. That menacing Jewish God. What does the Bible say? "Vengeance is mine." Do you remember that from the Bible? Guilt and vengeance. And sin. That's why I keep stressing the point.

But all this is getting a little too general, so let's go back to Lwów. I was acting like a coward, frightened, foreseeing the loss of Ola and Andrzej. Ola was very pretty then, and Andrzej too had a subtle, delicate beauty. Someone once called him a little Proust. Besides, I really didn't know Ola yet; I mean, I was used to thinking of her as orchidlike, a delicate sensibility, neurotic. Before the war she had been going through great metaphysical anxieties—what is the purpose of life and so on. She agonized a lot before the war. Kazakhstan cured her of all that. Her home life had been wonderful, her parents were wealthy, she was the favorite, the prettiest of all the daughters—and all the daughters were pretty. I was good to her then . . . Now I'm an old dog and a pest . . .

OLA WAT: That isn't so. It isn't!

WAT: I was good to her then. I took care of her; I thought she needed to be taken care of. I was terribly afraid that she would die. And she was alone in a foreign city without any money. I had nothing then; I had fled Warsaw with very little money, and I lived on what I made at *The Red Banner,* that rag. Besides, I knew what they did to the wives and families of condemned men. That ate at me. In prison that ate away at my health, because I was always picturing horrible scenes: her in the hospital, Andrzej in a children's home, an orphanage—I knew that the children's homes were schools for bandits and thieves. Or that they both had been killed, that sort of thing. Constantly, constantly, that gnawed away at me in prison right to the very end. Meanwhile, Ola turned out to be incredibly strong and brave in Kazakhstan. In the worst possible conditions, with people dying around her, she was able to take care of Andrzej and herself. That's her nature: a head cold does her in, but she bears disaster much better than I do. Women are often like that, you know.

Was I petrified when they finally arrested me? I had quite a banal dream in the cell after I'd been arrested. I dreamed I was surrounded by guards on all sides. I woke up with an enormous sense of relief, drenched in sweat—Ah! I'm in prison. I've spoken about Ola's beauty and Andrzej's delicate beauty contrasted with the increasing ugliness of Lwów. Lwów was growing uglier by the day. Then came my arrest, the epitome of ugliness, hideous. And when I was arrested, I really did think, tough, but it's all over; I don't have to worry about that any more. But it wasn't being arrested that had me by the throat, not the threat of arrest, because that didn't matter to me anymore, I was only afraid for them. And there was the ugliness of the arrest that affected my attitude toward communism. The first level on which communism repelled me was that of ugliness. Not the esthetic level but the moral-esthetic level. Its ugliness—people, cities, things—everything became shabbier. Perhaps that's the Asiatic element, that inferior Asia of the steppes, which is always shabby.

And now I'll tell you the demonic story of how I was arrested.

117

Czeslaw, I didn't go to bars, not even in Warsaw. I can't stand the smoke and I can't stand vodka, and besides, I had stopped drinking a long time ago. But I did go a couple of times in Lwów. Daszewski and I didn't see each other much in Lwów, but once in a while we did. One time I went to see him in the belief that we thought alike and I spoke very openly with him. He had immediately become a director in the Polish Theater. His boss was a Soviet—from the Ukraine, I think—but Daszewski was the Polish director, his assistant. And I even asked Daszewski to slip me into some job at the theater because I wanted to get away from *The Red Banner* under any pretext. As I told you, I met Daszewski in Warsaw on the day the Molotov-Ribbentrop Pact was signed, and I had grumbled about the Soviets. During the years of *The Literary Monthly* our friendship couldn't have been closer. Later on we saw each other less often but we stayed in touch right to the end. And Daszewski and Broniewski had been inseparable for a long time. They drank a sea of vodka together.

And then all of a sudden one day in Lwów, Daszewski comes to see us and says, "I'm having a party, can you come? I'm inviting a few people."

"What is it, your birthday?" I asked.

"Doesn't matter. I'm not saying."

And I said, "We don't go out, especially at night."

"You absolutely must come." He made us promise to come.

A couple of days later I was in the union where I still had some unfinished business. Later that evening, around five or six, there was to be a poetry reading—Leon Pasternak, Stanisław Lec, a few others—but it was Lec and especially Leon Pasternak who urged me to go to the party.

And so we went. Daszewski arrived. Ola wasn't sitting with me, and Daszewski took Ola—he knew that if she was there, then I'd be there, too—he took her, Peiper, and Broniewski's wife, Marysia Zarembińska, out to the theater's black limousine and brought them to the club. The reading was over. I looked around for Ola; she wasn't there. They told me that she had gone on ahead with Daszewski and had left word for me to follow. And so of course I followed. That was a foregone conclusion since Ola was already there. Then Dan grabbed me. He was very pale, and he said several times, with great emphasis, "Aleksander, I beg you, don't go to that bar!" I had suspected I would be arrested; I imagined that they would come at night, drag me from the house, search the apartment. It never entered my mind that it would happen in a bar. And so I glanced over at Dan in surprise. Why was he insisting so vehemently, I wondered. Was he concerned about my reputation with the authorities; was he watching out for me, trying to keep me out of trouble? And so, because he made such a point of it, I am absolutely convinced, beyond any shadow of a doubt, that Dan knew about it, meaning that Dan had been assigned to me. But still he was favorably inclined toward me.

And so I went to the restaurant. There was a private room for the party. Who was there? The Broniewskis; Leon Pasternak (his wife was an actress who used to play theater); the Szemplińskis (Szemplińska and her husband, an athlete who, by the way, conducted himself splendidly); Peiper; Balicki, the actor, and his brother, who worked in publishing; Siemaszkowa, a graphic artist who became known after the war—she illustrated children's books; and Wojciech Skuza. The Sterns had not been invited, but they were there in the restaurant. We were all at a very large table in that private room. There was another smallish table in one corner of the room. After a while a tall bald man came in and sat down at that table with an actress from the Polish Theater who was known for whoring with the Soviets and everybody else, a good-looking blonde.

Daszewski was distracted, nervous, in a state of excitement. He was constantly moving, making the rounds, asking if people had enough or wanted anything, saying he'd order this or that. A sumptuous feast. "A feast in time of plague." Two or three times I asked Daszewski, "Come on, tell me, what's the occasion?" And he would rub his hands and say, "You'll see! You'll see!"

At one point he was talking with that actress and the Soviet. Then he turned to us and said, "With your permission, a well-known art historian would like to join us." A tall, thin Leningrader, one of those thin Russians, wearing a shapeless suit. A dry face, a bit consumptive-looking, a very caustic expression. With your permission, an art historian very interested in literature who would very much like to meet you and so on. And so everyone said, Of course! He sat at one end of the table, with a door covered by a curtain behind him, the actress on one side of him, Skuza on the other, the Broniewskis a few places from him, and me at the opposite end of the table facing him.

There was so much talk I couldn't hear a thing. At one point there was an unpleasant exchange of words between the Soviet and Władek Broniewski. I could see Broniewski clenching his teeth, talking through his teeth. Now their conversation had started to turn nasty, really nasty. I could see Skuza lean in front of the Soviet and say something to the actress. And the Soviet slapped Skuza's face and yanked the tablecloth—everything went flying, bottles, glasses, plates. (My memory is eidetic in this case. I'm not telling you anything but what struck my retina.)

That was probably a signal, because just then two short, athletic, square-headed types wearing dark blue suits came rushing out from behind the curtain. There was something dancelike, almost slow-motion about the way they burst in, and then they began throwing punches left and right. I saw one of them struggling with Szemplińska's husband, who was giving him a good drubbing—her husband was an athlete, a boxer, I think. Just then I was struck in the teeth and fell to the floor. Such a strong blow that even though I had fantastic teeth, hard as oak, I had a loose tooth for eight years after that. It came loose right away, but it didn't fall out. My nose and teeth were covered in blood. Then I blacked out. In despair, Ola poured water on me. I didn't know what was going on. She wanted to drag me out of there. A total panic—people were shouting in the other rooms, but no one was being let into our room. The door was locked, and it was only then that I saw that those two boxers were on the floor dead drunk, pretending to be drunk. They were lying on the floor pretending to snore, their eyes closed.

Ola saw Władek Daszewski slipping away and grabbed him near the cloakroom, saying, "Władek, what's going on here?" But he—all he could think of was getting away. He didn't answer. He grabbed his coat, which the attendant had ready for him, and flew out the door. But then Ola saw police on the stairs, the entire staircase lined with police, and they had let Daszewski pass. A moment later the police came into the restaurant and allowed no one to leave. That's important. Because later on, Słonimski, Broniewski, and Schiller conducted an investigation of their own.

MILOSZ: I don't understand. Schiller was in Poland and Słonimski was in England.

WAT: My dear Czeslaw, Schiller, who was Daszewski's closest friend, looked into the whole matter during the Nazi occupation, since Daszewski had stayed in Lwów under the Germans. Almost immediately the story of our arrest turned up in some underground song, in Warsaw. Not entirely accurate, but with Daszewski playing the role of provocateur. The Germans took Lwów; Daszewski didn't leave with the Soviets, or he couldn't, or he chose not to. I don't know. He hid out somewhere in the countryside. After I returned to Poland, Schiller assured me that he had investigated the matter, and it turned out that Daszewski hadn't known what was going to happen. Schiller came to the conclusion that Daszewski had been told, "There's an art historian here; he wants to meet some writers." They told him to arrange a meeting and said that if he did, they'd get his wife out of Warsaw. Not aware of what was happening, not suspecting that the NKVD was behind it and supplying the money, he had invited us in all innocence, believing that the man really was an art historian. That was Schiller's version and people accepted it. After the war Słonimski and Broniewski said that Daszewski wasn't to blame. But they're his friends.

I would believe all of that, except that I was already in the corridor myself when he was running from the restaurant. You see what I mean: they let no one out, but he flew out the door. And then there had been that "You'll see!" of his. The odiousness of it! An old, close friend took on that odious role. It simply made me gag. I couldn't rid myself of that feeling the entire time I was in Zamarstynów prison. I mentioned that before the war in Warsaw, Mietek Kwiatkowski had told me that Moscow had sent a list of provocateurs and counterintelligence agents. And Daszewski's name was on it. A few days later Daszewski's name was taken off the list; it had been a mistake; Daszewski wasn't involved. I also recalled Daszewski's telling me in confidence that when visiting Moscow in the thirties, he had put the Polish poet Wandurski in touch with the Polish embassy. And so when I was in prison, I told myself that he had simply been playing both sides of the street.

I must stress that during the period of socialist realism Władek Daszewski behaved with extraordinary decency. He had a lot of power then; he was a real mover, stood high with the party, an important figure, but he never harmed any of the painters. I have a feeling that what had happened in Lwów—by nature he was amoral; I knew him very well—must have been a moral shock to him. Because after the war in Poland he acted very discreetly, very decently. Except I have proof against him: his running away.

That was rough, don't you think? The first thing they do is knock you off your feet. And that's exactly how you turn people into rags. In Moscow, in Lubyanka, I saw old heroes of the Revolution who served as informers in their cells. For example, there was a former vice-minister of electricity, an old Bolshevik, one of the ones who had been active during the Revolution. Everyone in the cell knew he was an informer, that for a glass of tea or a smile from his investigator he would report what his cell mates were saying. Maybe that wasn't true, but that was the cell's opinion of him, and some of them were old communists who were expert in such things; otherwise they wouldn't have cast aspersions on him. The terrible degradation of those idealistic heroes. That process of swift degradation began when the ideal had been realized, when those idealists had dirt and blood on their hands.

Daszewski introduced me to all that, and the way I was arrested always left me with a bad taste. What was the point of it? They could have arrested me that night at home; they arrested thirteen or fifteen other writers, most of them at home. Peiper, me, Skuza, who died later in a camp, Broniewski, and Stern, who was in the main room, were all taken in right from the restaurant. Stern was in for a few months, but he was the only one who was released. Leon Pasternak wasn't arrested, and apparently he was very indignant the next day at the *Red Banner* office. Szemplińska wasn't arrested either; her husband spent one night in jail for striking an NKVD man.

I was stunned by the unusualness of the arrest. As soon as I was thrown into the cell, a prison nurse, a Jew from Lwów, came to see me. She knew my name. She shook her head and told me to exhale so she could list me as a drunk on the record. I'd been drinking like everyone else, not too much though. For a few hours that night I kept thinking it was some sort of misunderstanding, a drunken brawl. But a drunken brawl was just what they'd needed: a couple of days later *The Red Banner* published an article saying that we were all low-lifes, womanizers, that we caused the waiters trouble every night and roughed them up, that we were Trotskyites, counterintelligence agents, drunks, the lowest of the low. They needed all that for the article.

Now the first of my prisons. I really don't know whether I should start in on that. There have already been many descriptions of prison, and they can be interesting only if they've been interiorized, seen through the particular prism of my own experience. First, this is difficult to describe, and, second, it's here that you really need details. Leaves—leaves, not branches.

All told, I spent time in eleven prisons. Ola argues that I can't say it was eleven because I spent only twenty-four hours in two of them. And she's right. But for the sake of statistics, the beauty of statistics, say eleven. And if I add the two Polish prisons I was in, that makes thirteen. A nice number. As a matter of fact, two of my most important prison experiences were in Lwów—mainly Zamarstynów, of course, because I wasn't in Brygidki very long. That's two. The third one was in Kiev. Not long—ten days—but extremely interesting, very instructive because that was a transfer prison. That makes three. Lubyanka was the fourth, Saratov was the fifth, and Ili the sixth. The Third Section was the seventh. And so on. Each different, a variation on a theme, a world of its own. A wealth of material. (My illness and the Percodan, especially this past year on Percodan, makes me have to struggle to remember, but what I'm saying is accurate.)

Zamarstynów. I'd like to start fresh on that because once I start, I won't stop. So, before I start on Zamarstynów, ask me some questions about Lwów.

MILOSZ: In the first months after September, which I also know from my own experience, the state of shock, really of rage, fury at the Polish government, was a strong factor that undoubtedly disposed many people to submit to the new world that had come from the East. No question about it, that was a strong factor, that absolute sense of having been made fools of. We had been utterly defeated. The old illusions that Poland was a normal country. It was a different story when France fell; people gained a certain distance. Great France had fallen so quickly. Like Poland. But the rage, the fury, was very strong during the initial period. That was a period of the wildest intellectual and political speculation, café strategy. What was going to happen, what form would it all take? I'd like you to say a few words about that.

WAT: What . . . about those speculations? It's true, people sat in cafés and constantly talked about the future. People kept pouring in from Warsaw; then they started going back, even Jews. My own brother, the younger one, came to Lwów with his father-in-law, but after a while he saw that things were better in Warsaw and so he went back, and later on he was killed. You're right, people felt that they had been made fools of. Some people were furious and some were elegiac. Most of the intelligentsia felt that they had been made complete fools of. For me those years between the wars had been a stage set, with dummies made of plywood and cardboard. It was all so theatrical and fake, those twenty years of Piłsudski-ism. Independent Poland was so unprofessional, especially with its demented fantasies of a Poland from the Baltic to the Black Sea, that slogan—"doomed to greatness."

MILOSZ: Was the idea that war between Germany and Russia was inevitable in circulation early on?

WAT: In Zamarstynów there were people who considered it absolutely certain. At night we listened for the tanks—which direction were they taking? If it was west, that meant war!

MILOSZ: But the official Soviet opinion was that Poland wouldn't rise again.

WAT: Poland will never rise again. And they were saying that openly!

18 COUNT BIELSKI. MY CELL IN ZAMARSTYNÓW PRISON.

WAT: This morning I remembered certain things about Lwów on which I might put a finer point. First, the Writers' Union was in the writers' club and then in Count Bielski's palace. The count and countess lived upstairs, on the second floor, and the union took over the ground floor. At first the stairs to the second floor were open and there was an occasional flow up to the count's for a half hour or an hour of conversation. Polewka was one of the ones who went to see the count. Later on, because there was too much of this back and forth, the stairs to the count's were blocked off. He was a splendid count, one of the leading hunters in Poland. The walls in his palace were covered with trophies. By the way, a couple of times the count came down with his wife, and—I heard this with my own ears—Polewka called her "comrade countess." The countess was still a very beautiful woman even though she was no longer young. She'd been a famous beauty at one time, and her lovers apparently died in duels over her.

The count and the countess were deported later on, on the same night as Ola, April 13, 1940, and they were together later in the settlement. He was allowed to take a lot of his possessions, crateful. Count Bielski died before the end of the war; the countess took up lodgings in Ushtob, a few hundred kilometers from Ili, where we were. We would hear news about her. Her sons were high Polish officials in London, and they had obtained permission for her to leave Russia, but she had vowed to return to Poland by the same route she took when she left. And she stayed there until the very end, the repatriation.

Bielski was splendid, tall; he looked like a count. How you look has enormous importance in Russia. No European could ever comprehend the magic a good appearance has there. At one time the way I looked saved my life. It's the look that matters, good or bad. At that time I was terribly thin; I was like a skeleton; you could see my entire skull, which made my eyes seem huge. My eyes blazed; I was burning with moral indignation. I have a photograph of me at that time, my eyes ablaze. My head had been shaved in prison, and, especially in Kazakhstan, people thought I was a sorcerer; they were afraid of me. One time I made some gesture with my hand that frightened a policeman, and he asked if I were casting spells. The way a person looks is of enormous importance in Soviet prisons.

But I want to go back to being arrested. Before they arrested me, I was brought into the restaurant owner's office. There was a police captain there who, I suppose, was an NKVD man in a police uniform. All in all, appearances were preserved that these were policemen. A large squad but all police. First, he ordered me to empty out my pockets. He didn't frisk me. He was interested in my wallet. He placed the money in a separate pile and tied it up with a piece of string and then tied up my papers and documents with another piece. Not a new wallet or an elegant one but still a good one—it was made of goat hide—from a store in Warsaw. Calm as can be, he pulled out his own shabby cloth wallet, emptied it out, and very coolly, without even a glance at me, placed his things in my wallet and then stuck it in his pocket. Then he gave me a statement to sign that said that I had taken part in a drunken brawl during which windows had been broken and so on. I refused to sign. Even though I'd been stunned by the blow and dulled a little by the vodka, I still could see that his approach was an excellent sign. I refused, saying that I hadn't taken part in a drunken brawl; I'd been the victim of one. He spent some time trying to persuade me to sign, but without putting any special energy into it, not insisting. Finally, he said, "All right, if you won't sign, you won't."

Then they took us out. I could see, or rather I could hear, Broniewski. The stairs were full of policemen. I was brought outside. Ola, Broniewski's wife, Peiper's girlfriend, and a couple of other women were waiting on the sidewalk by the police limousines. Ola claims that I bowed and tipped my hat. But in prison I was tortured by regret: we'd never see each other again and I hadn't said good-bye to Ola, even with my eyes.

Well, then we came to the gate to Zamarstynów Prison, a second gate with a prison guard armed to the teeth. It was already late at night, one or two o'clock, when we pulled up to the prison. Then a quad, very tall iron stairs, and cell number forty-eight or fifty-eight, on the first floor. The key grinding in the lock has been described a hundred times, and besides I already knew that sound from Polish prisons. But it's still a shock. Your soul turns around with the lock. But that time it left me with a different feeling because, despite my doubts and my belief that it might have been a chance event, that it might in fact have been a drunken brawl, I still had the leaden feeling that there'd be no getting out of there.

And then I was in a cell that I later found out was eleven and a half square meters; it was rectangular, the window barred of course, a rather long cell—it would have been twelve square meters, but more or less a half square meter was taken up by the potbellied tin stove, just part of the stove. The rest of it, including the door, was out in the corridor.

And that sometimes had unpleasant consequences for us. At night when one of the guards, a young Komsomol member (he was called Josek by the people in the cell—which was anti-Semitic; apparently he was a Jew, or at least they thought he was), was very bored, he would amuse himself by burning straw in the stove. Naturally that made us choke and gag. The smoke was terrible; the window was locked. He'd watch us through the peephole until we were reeling from nausea. He'd make no secret of watching and he laughed wildly. Then he'd open the door wide and the smoke would go out the window, which looked out onto the courtyard. But it happened again and again. Sometimes there'd be a woman in the corridor, a Russian woman from a camp who worked as a cleaning woman there; he'd screw her at night.

And so the cell was eleven and a half square meters. Quite a lot of room at first. When I arrived, there couldn't have been more than a dozen other prisoners. But soon it filled up to twenty-eight. Twenty-eight people in eleven and a half square meters.

At one point after the war Mrs. Morris, you know her, sent me documentation on the terrible fate of Greek prisoners on those island prisons and asked me to start a campaign on that issue in Poland. One of the things that had shocked her was that there were eight people in twelve square meters in those prisons. So I wrote back saying that was truly horrible and a protest was necessary, but that I had spent nine or ten months with twenty-eight people in a cell that was eleven and a half square meters. All in all, Zamarstynów was the worst of my prisons.

I make two assumptions here. One—and this was quite common in Russia during a campaign—was that overcrowding was used as a form of severe torture. In Russia that was mitigated because the regulations were honored there; in all the prisons I was in there, the prisoners enjoyed the right to a twenty-minute walk during the day. But in Zamarstynów we were allowed two or three walks over a period of nine or ten months, and very short ones too. Another thing was the prison guards, the warders. It was clear that they had picked out the sadists and sent them to Zamarstynów, whereas in Soviet prisons the guards are mostly either indifferent or even have pity for the prisoners. That pity for prisoners that Dostoevsky described is not uncommon among prison guards in the Soviet Union.

There were still two plank beds in the cell when I arrived, but later they were taken away. We had straw mats, but there was practically no straw in them. The prisoners slept on their own things, piles of dirty rags.

I was afraid. My eyes were gaping and my instinctive reflex fear in those first few moments was very bad. I was frightened by the prisoners' faces, by the way they looked. My first instinct was that they were bandits, convicts who'd already been in prison for years. But everyone in that cell had been arrested during the first and second wave of arrests in October, and some even in September. Right at the very beginning. That terrible grayness of Russian convicts had come out in them in such a short time, in the space of three months. Those gray faces. And that criminal look. I don't know what made that happen. Their heads had obviously been shaved with clippers but stubble had grown back on some. Dead eyes. The Russian painters of the Peredvizhniki school did paintings of convicts being marched off over great distances to hard labor and exile. And their faces were like those in my cell.*

Who was in the cell? The oldest might have been seventy. During the first few days it's difficult to tell a man of forty from one near seventy. It takes some time for the eye to acquire that skill. But still a man around thirty could look as old as someone sixty. So there was Colonel Słonecki, who was around sixty-five and the oldest man in the cell, followed by Róg, a lawyer from Lwów. The youngest person in the cell was fifteen. His name was Piątek, a school janitor's son. There were some four or five young people, all from underground organizations. And there was an assistant prosecutor from the Military Tribunal, the director of Internal Revenue in East Galicia or Lwów, a lawyer, a railroad worker, a railroad official, some high school students and teachers from Lwów—that's more or less the basic group.

They were all sleeping when I came in. Some of them didn't even open an eye or make any movement; others opened their eyes but closed them right away; and a few seemed interested in me. Colonel Słonecki, the senior man in the cell, was on his plank bed too. In a very kindly voice he told me to go to sleep and pointed to a place where I'd be more comfortable, near the door and away from the slop bucket. I told him my name and my profession, which certainly was the wrong thing to do, since someone in the cell might know who Aleksander Wat was: a "commie Jew."

Charisma comes out in prison, especially in Soviet prisons. There

* Peredvizhniki (Wanderers). A school of Russian realistic painters focusing on social ills. Group founded in 1870.

are people who are liked immediately and have great authority in a cell. I was in many cells, but it's hard to say exactly what causes it; it's really some kind of personal magnetism. And facial expression plays an important role, too. There are people who are simply liked, and there are those who have authority and are obeyed. And there's one other category, more or less what Hempel was for us in Central Prison: the father figure. Good people, older people. Someone is usually found to play the role of the father. It's not so much wisdom that counts here—Colonel Słonecki wasn't especially distinguished by intelligence—but goodness. Character has enormous significance. Others, like that lawyer Róg, had great intellectual authority but were disliked intensely. On the other end, there are people who immediately evoke terrible antipathy. These are simplifications and require closer analysis, but, as a role, egotists are disliked intensely. There are other reasons as well. Needless to say, in every cell there are quarrelsome people who are always at odds with everyone else.

In general, I should say that I had good standing in prison. Perhaps because I have an expressive face. I wasn't liked, but I had a certain authority. These things happen right off the bat or not at all. My situation in Zamarstynów Prison took a turn for the worse later on when a young ONR-ite came to the cell. That was a bad stretch, but it didn't last very long. My position in the cell was such that I had a certain intellectual authority right from the start. It wasn't that they got to know me or that I made any efforts to display my intelligence—those things are established immediately, instinctively. There might also have been a bit of fear in that. They were probably afraid of me because someone must have known that I was a Jew and a communist and so forth. I simply infer this from certain faint hints, things that I didn't even really feel at the time but that I suspected. Maybe it was all in my head, but there was undoubtedly a certain element of fear in any case. I think it was rather weak, though, because fear did not play an important role in that cell.

The former director of Internal Revenue was thought to be an informer. No one could stand him, and the young people had a special hatred for him. He was treated with contempt even though they feared him as an informer. He was summoned very often and was, in any case, an unsavory person. But still they made a point of treating him with aversion; he was practically boycotted. And so I could see that that cell would not let itself be terrorized easily.

That first night Słonecki asked me why I had been arrested. A few people were listening to us. I said I'd been in a restaurant, a drunken brawl had broken out, and people had been arrested, including me.

And then I committed the same sin that I had in Mokotów Prison: I said that I'd be released soon, that it was all a misunderstanding. And that caused an outburst of genuine laughter. I'll never forget that laughter. And it was only with that outburst of laughter that my stupor—the effects of the vodka and having been knocked down—suddenly wore off, and I came to my senses.

But I was in no mood for laughing; I didn't even begin to laugh. Daszewski's odious role and all the rest of it were still too much with me. By then the fear was gone—I was less afraid for Ola and Andrzej—but the ugliness, the odiousness of it all . . . When I heard the key grind in the lock, I knew that was the last grind of the lock, Judgment Day. That certainty was at the base of my consciousness, not in my unconscious. But uppermost in my mind was the desire to believe—they had told me to sign the statement; the nurse had wanted to check my breath. The delusion had been on the surface, but it had been dispelled by that laughter. And then I no longer had the slightest doubt that it had been a provocation. My memory re-created the scenes as they had been played out in the club. I was no longer dazed. The whole thing had taken a couple of hours.

Colonel Słonecki shouted at the ones who laughed. He said, "Who knows, it might well be true; we don't know anything in here." And he told me that I should go to sleep, sleep was best. I fell asleep and, as I told you, had that dream—no story to it, but a realistic dream—that I was surrounded on all sides and about to be arrested. Then I woke up in a sweat, already in prison. The two-month nightmare of waiting for prison was now a thing of the past.

The routine, which has been described in all sorts of memoirs, began the next morning. Reveille was very early—I don't remember what time. Then a guard came in—actually, one of the head guards; there were often two or three on a shift.

One of them, the head man, was like a light from a better world. But he showed us no compassion or kindness. On the contrary, he was dry and formal, very clean and well dressed, smelling of eau de cologne like all of them did but less than the others, rather handsome. We called him the Englishman. He was the only one who always said hello. He never raised his voice at anyone, never cursed. He was fair if there was some problem. He would ask if we had any complaints, if we wanted anything, and he'd make a note of it. Of course, our complaints never reached anyone's ear, but he wrote them all down quite seriously and then would walk out, salute, and say good-bye to each of us. We loved him.

And then there were head counts. He was efficient, but some of the others made a lot of mistakes; they had trouble counting; two of the day men were good, but the rest were really sadists.

Then came breakfast, meaning they'd give us something like coffee, chicory—but they'd bring the boiling water for it only later on—and those four hundred grams of black bread, baked Soviet style—by that time, the bread was like wet clay. It was so wet because they used a lot of water in baking, a very high percentage, to cover their own theft. I know because I worked for a while in a bakery. That was Soviet bread, not Lwów bread.

We had to pile up those miserable straw mats by the wall for the day, and people mostly lay on the floor or leaned against the walls. Aha, and then you went to the latrine. Those are some of my fondest memories—walking back from the latrine and waiting for lunch. They invariably gave us a big lunch in that prison, food that later on would have had me licking my chops, but at that time I had reserves; I was still quite strong, and so I couldn't eat that food, that hulled barley. A spoon would actually stand up straight in it—no butter in it, nothing, just a dash of salt. You divided your bread into little pieces so that it would last you the day. There was another trip to the latrine in the late afternoon, then dinner, but not at any regular time, because it depended at which end of the prison they started. Sometimes dinner was before the trip to the latrine, sometimes after. You got hulled barley again for dinner. Later on the guard would come to count us.

And then it was night. The bulb, of course, was always on, very glaring. Someone always went to be interrogated during the night, and so the key would turn in the lock, the door would open, they'd call you by your letter—not your last name, only the first letter of it—and you had to answer to that. It turned out that an amazingly high percentage of the guards were illiterate; they couldn't read well at all.

Another part of the routine was the occasional search. We'd be herded out into the corridor, which was very wide. They'd order us to strip naked and bend over; then they'd look up our asses to see if anything was hidden there. Going back to the cell was awful. The guards were sadists; there was never anything like that in Russia. All our things would be tossed in a mess on the floor. All our treasures—everyone had some sort of treasure. Everything crumpled and stepped on, boot marks on our things. And then the whole rest of the day would be spent collecting our things and sorting them back out. But there were a few smart ones who knew how to hide things so they wouldn't be found—pieces of iron, homemade knives, chess men made of bread, pencil leads.

There were also people who had never been in prison before but who had certain fantastic talents: they could split a match into a few pieces, make needles out of just about anything. For example, sometimes there'd be some fish in with the hulled barley and they'd make needles from the fish bones or from matchsticks! Masterpieces of every conceivable sort.

The nurse would come to the cell, but she wouldn't enter it; she'd pass the medicine on through the guard. It was usually aspirin or something of that sort. It was very rare for anyone to be taken to the doctor, who was local, a Jew from Lwów, a communist.

Before April, before the deportation, we received packages every two weeks, but that wasn't regular either. A couple of times there were none. Packages meant that you could be sent underwear and tobacco. Families could send you cigarettes, but you had to send them back your dirty underwear. I had been taken right from the club and had none of my things, and so I was able to get some warm socks from home and to exchange my suit. I had been wearing a new suit that night, and I thought that Ola could sell it if she needed to. Besides, I had another suit that was like iron, excellent material, really. Ola sent me that suit, and I changed into it, got clean underwear, and so forth.

You could also have money sent. There was a canteen for a while, though it wasn't open regularly. With the money in your account you could buy salt, onions once in a while, and tobacco, but you couldn't always get matches. In any case, the matches went to the guard, and a couple of times a day you could ask him for a light. They had candy a few times. I wasn't a smoker, but cigarettes were the most valuable item.

Of course, in the Polish prisons run by the Polish "fascists," the principle of the prison commune went right into effect without a word on the subject. All the prisoners had families, and they all had money to buy things, and so everything was pooled. That wasn't allowed in Russian prisons; there was no such principle there. It wasn't allowed, and no one was so inclined.

And so what else was part of the routine? Sometimes a barber came, and there was a trip to the bathhouse every once in a while. Trips to the bathhouse are quite regular in Soviet prisons; in Moscow, in Lubyanka, only once in nine or ten months were we not taken to the baths at the designated time, while in the nine months I was at Zamarstynów we went six, maybe seven times, but no more than that and maybe not even that many times. The baths were something you longed for and were afraid of at the same time.

So what were the baths like? The main thing was the water. We were horribly dirty, of course, covered with a layer of dirt and sweat. But the water there was always dirty. The showers worked badly, probably on purpose. Sometimes the guard in charge would set the shower too hot, almost boiling, or suddenly turn it ice cold. He was probably amusing himself, or else the machinery was no good. You really had to be on your toes.

The worst part about the baths was the delousing. The guards, and not only the guards but Soviet people, the prison help, and the NKVD men thought that Poland's low level of culture and backwardness was demonstrated by its lack of delousing stations. They had to be brought in from Russia. The delousing station was a sad affair; they took your clothes, which took a beating from the heat and came out wet. Then everything—all the underwear, clothing, coats—was thrown out, everything jumbled together. You had to be quick; you had to grab your own drawers, shirts, clothes on the run and dress with incredible speed. Everything had a weird smell; everything was hot and wet. Then you had to go out into the freezing cold in those wet things. But for some reason people didn't get sick from that.

The worst thing about the bathhouse wasn't those jets of dirty water or those wet, smelly clothes thrown on the floor but that the process infuriated the lice, a rage that would last at least two days. They never bit you as they did for those couple of days after the baths and the delousing. Not only was the delousing absolutely useless, but the baths seemed to increase the lice's sexual vigor. I assume that with lice the two things—sexual vigor and anger, aggressiveness—go together. Before the baths everyone had his own lice, though of course there were lice that liked to roam and change hosts. But for the most part each person had his own lice and their descendants. They multiply very quickly so that there'd be great-grandparents and grandparents, a few generations on you all at the same time. Meanwhile, the baths and the delousing threw all that into utter confusion. The worst species of lice we had were marked by a special vitality. We counted what must have been four different types, but the most dreaded were the ones we called the "blondes." The blondes were very puffy, light-colored, fat, bloated, and it was their vigor that increased the most.

There were a lot of lice. Our day was taken up with killing them. At first with disgust and then later out of habit and with pleasure, great pleasure. It almost became a delight, like vodka, alcohol. Very accurate counts were kept; the number of lice killed during the course of the day was written on the wall along with the date. Sometimes the number was very high; other times it would fall. Occasionally the number would exceed four hundred, but I don't remember it ever reaching five hundred. But it did pass four hundred, especially when new prisoners were carriers.

The cell started filling up quickly, awfully quickly, and in a very short time, in just a couple of weeks, it reached the limit: twenty-eight. From time to time, sporadically, they'd add a twenty-ninth or thirtieth, but that wouldn't be for long, just a few days or so. There was a brilliant mathematician in the cell, Kmiciński, a seventeen-year-old high school student. He had a wonderful sense of geometry and somehow he was able to arrange us so that there was room for everyone on those eleven and a half square meters. He fitted us together by height so that none of the space went unused. A terrific jigsaw puzzle. Twenty-eight men to eleven and a half square meters—that's a form of torture.

The winter of 1939–1940 was terribly severe as you know. The nights were hell in winter, and especially when the weather turned suddenly hot in the spring of 1940. As a matter of fact, the most abominable physical memories that Soviet prisons left me with are those nights in Zamarstynów. Sweat streamed down both sides of you, your own mixed with other people's. That's terrible. You have to experience it to know what misery that is—somebody else's sweat mingling with your own. We really were packed in like sardines. You can imagine what the air was like, especially since the kasha had a certain effect and especially on that lawyer, Róg. By day he spoke wonderfully, raising our spirits, but at night he was a "ventriloquist," meaning that he suffered from flatulence. Horrible. One time a commission arrived from Moscow, probably prosecutors, but, judging from the behavior of the wardens who escorted them about and from the guards, they were big shots. A few of them wore workers' caps, drab coats. They opened the cell door, but none of them dared to enter. I suppose that was also the reason our jailers splashed on so much eau de cologne. (That was in style in the Soviet army, but that's another story. It wasn't the soldiers who smelled like barbershops; it was the noncoms. Cheap eau de cologne.)

Well, so you can imagine what leaving that air for the latrine meant to us. You know, in everyone's life there are moments he's nostalgic for, that he yearns for . . . first kisses—it's different for everyone. Most nostalgia doesn't last. But one moment has kept coming back to me for many years, even when I was abroad, even fairly recently. To be there once again, to experience it one more time! I'm referring to coming back from the latrine in the summertime, down that long corridor. The cell was quite a ways from the latrine. I don't know how many meters it was. Maybe fifty or sixty steps, but we walked them at an extremely slow pace, to the annoyance of our guards, who would shout and even hit us. They'd beat us, but still we'd walk at a snail's pace.

The latrine itself was horrible. They gave you very little time. The floor was covered with tiles, but everyone sat down wherever he happened to be standing. It was supposed to be the obligation of each cell to clean up after itself, but that was impossible. And so if they brought you to the latrine late, there wouldn't be even a clean place left to stand. There was also a water faucet in the latrine, but there was no time to wash either. But you could put your hands under the cold water and then bring your hands to your face.

The windows looked out onto Zamarstynów Street. The latrine had barred windows, quite high up. We would grab onto the bars, and of course the guards would start yelling at us because they watched us through the peep holes, but anyone who could would grab onto those bars for a glimpse of free people walking down the street. With mixed feelings, for all I know. Sometimes when you've been in the hospital for a long time and you look down from a balcony or out the window and see healthy people, you think, You fools, you don't even know you're sick. Sometimes there were feelings like that about the people walking down Zamarstynów Street. It didn't matter that Lwów was becoming shabbier and shabbier, especially on that street. People were ragged, gray, gloomy. But all the same, that was the world of freedom. That was one way of looking at it.

And then, you know, especially in the evenings, summer evenings, when it was still light, with those windows looking onto the long, clean paved courtyard . . . There were three mulberry trees in that courtyard. Then those Soviet barbarians cut down one of them, a perfectly healthy tree. No one knew why. There were some hills close to Zamarstynów Prison and in the summer you could smell the meadows, especially the hay. Imagine those trips between the stinking latrine and the stinking cell, walking as slowly as possible with the windows opened wide to that courtyard and the hot smell of summer. That was happiness. Not only was that happiness, but it was a *katharsis* as well, an inner cleansing of the mind and spirit. Those moments weren't very long, but they lasted long in psychological time. Those are dear memories for me and I truly have been caught up in them. Oh, to experience it one more time!

But let's go back to the people. I'll give you profiles of them. Let's begin with the negative ones. Why was the director of the Internal Revenue office hated? He had been a great dignitary in Lwów; everyone knew of him. A son of a bitch, a supreme bureaucrat. Out of the bureaucrat's blindness and deafness, he told us the most revolting things, to wit, that he had made sure that his department wasn't a single penny short so that everything could be turned over to the Soviets. For, you see, Lwów had surrendered; General Langner had officially surrendered. And that bureaucrat had seen to it that all monies belonging to Internal Revenue in Lwów were turned over. He told us himself that the employees in his office had asked him, since bad times were coming, to advance them three months' salary, or at least a month's. A legalist, he wanted to keep the accounts straight; the books had to balance. He might have been boasting in the belief that there was an informer in the cell—that might have been his line of defense—but that probably wasn't the case. He had great self-assurance; he was a real dignitary. He had the impersonal sadism of the ideal bureaucrat. Psychologically, he was a sadist, but the bureaucracy demands a certain sort of sadism, a certain sort of ruthlessness. Later on I came to know Soviet bureaucrats, but he was the first pure bureaucrat I had encountered in Poland.

It turns out that bureaucrats are identical in various social systems. Except that there are systems that favor the bureaucracy, where the life of the state and the society is bureaucratic, and there are systems where the bureaucrats are only a small part of life. But the bureaucratic type, the bureaucratic ideal, is the same everywhere, which is what emerged from Eichmann's trial in Jerusalem. I have the impression that there are not many types, that there is one Platonic type of bureaucrat, identical in all societies, a single prototype.

That bureaucrat also repulsed people with his selfishness; he was very concerned with what was and wasn't his. Colonel Słonecki was at the opposite extreme. An old cavalryman, crazy about horses, he could talk about horses for hours on end. Colonel Słonecki loved to tell about his days in the cavalry. He was a great expert on horses. It turns out that horses are an enormous field of knowledge, not just of knowledge, but one bordering on art, literature, almost poetry. Actually, he couldn't have been further from poetry, but what he said was intensely poetic in essence. He had been in the cavalry in the part of Poland ruled by Austria, and he had been one of the archduke's aides-de-camp. One of that archduke's traits that has stuck in my memory was that he was an obvious festering syphilitic, and quite often he would give drinking parties for his officers and force them to drink champagne from his glass.

Colonel Słonecki was the father, the father figure; he was enormously fatherly to us all. Terrible hatreds develop in a cell, the result of strangers having to live together in such close quarters. He was able to defuse all those hatreds with just a kind word or a gesture.

Colonel Słonecki soon found an ideal partner for conversation. A young Ukrainian peasant was put in our cell, one of the ugliest people I have ever seen in my life. A gnome, an earth spirit. He was small, with a nose that was long and lumpish at the same time. One eye was higher than the other; one looked to the right, one to the left; one was large and the other small. His mouth was distinctly crooked, but only one half of it. An extremely pointed jaw, which looked like a beard. He might have been in his twenties, or thirty. His voice was a beautiful, almost feminine, contralto. Who was this little peasant, this gnome? He was a very poor poacher from a farm family with no land of its own who hired himself out as a farmhand. In addition, he'd go around the villages in the summertime with two or three friends and paint huts. That was how they made a living in the summer. But above all, by temperament, passion, and, who knows, even by calling, he was a poacher. He had an uncanny love for animals. Naturally, he'd been in jail a hundred times for poaching, but that hadn't broken him of the habit.

How did he end up in the Soviets' hands? He had set out with his friends to paint huts on the other side of the Bug River or in some other area that was cut off later. He was cut off from his home and he tried to go back. They grabbed him at the border and put him in jail as a Nazi spy, which was common.

He loved animals so much that he begged us to give him our clothes and underwear to delouse (by then we were competing for fun to see who killed the most lice). You see, his love of animals did not preclude killing them. On the contrary. As you know, poachers kill animals. And so he killed those lice; he could never get enough of them. He had his own lice, but that wasn't enough for him. He made up a game for himself that he played often during the day, but it was at night especially that I heard him playing it. Frequently I had trouble falling asleep. Colonel Słonecki and the poacher suffered from insomnia, too. So, the game was that when he caught one of the larger "blondes," a pregnant one, for instance, he'd start playing the part of an investigator with it: "Confess! What assignment did the Gestapo give you?" He retraced the entire course of his own interrogation with the lice. He was in no hurry to kill them.

But the conversations he had at night with Colonel Słonecki were really lovely. Słonecki would tell him about horses, and he would tell Słonecki about various forest animals. There was a certain natural connection between them, an attraction, a *Wahlverwandtschaft* of souls. Słonecki, who had been the archduke's aide-de-camp, a colonel in the Polish army, and that genuine illiterate, a peasant, a poacher, immediately became the closest of brothers out of their love for animals. Very beautiful!

I still didn't know how to deal with prison. I learned that very late, and I let things eat at me. I was eating my heart out and trying somehow to live my own inner life, to separate myself from everything. The cell was a madhouse. The mornings were relatively quiet; everyone seemed to be hung over; everyone was melancholy in the morning. But a person remains human despite that terrible degradation, really the bottom, despite being treated like dirt. The guards and the jailers walked all over us, walked all over our things, spoke to us in the most horrible language, terrible curses. Like a neurasthenic, a person would be dull, deaf to the world, demented during the day, but toward evening some sort of divine spark would flare up in him; he'd become incredibly extroverted, laugh, tell jokes, stories. The cell really buzzed like a hive; sometimes the guards would yell and pound on the door to quiet us down.

Prayer and the singing of morning and evening songs became quite quickly a custom in our cell, especially songs connected with the Virgin Mary. Yes, prayers because there were religious people—Catholics and Uniates—in the cell. But their religion was beautiful, pure, without any obscurantism. Those were Ukrainians, Uniates. The Ukrainians came over a period of time, until, toward the end, there were five or six of them. In comparison with Poles and Jews—later on in Russia I was in prison with Jews—their group made for a beautiful little community, one with excellent traits of loyalty and solidarity, with a natural sense of human hierarchy, not one that had been imposed on them.

I think I've already told you about that young, skinny, average-looking Ukrainian who was put in with us one day. Despite the significance that faces have there, all those Ukrainians knew—God only knows how—that he was somebody, a leader, and that he would take charge of them. Natural obedience.

I spoke of the songs about Mary, the devotions. Naturally, they sang "When the light of a new day comes." They also sang folk songs, not so much folk songs as popular songs. You have to know the degradation of prison to appreciate what songs are and what they can become, songs like "Time to go home now; they're calling us home. Mother's in the doorway; it's dinner time now." Or the old song "Though the storm roars around us, we lift up our faces." You know that refrain—the bells are ringing—it's a whole world, a cosmogony, a cosmos. The bells call us to prayer, mother calls us to dinner—you see, that's the natural way of life. Even in the degradation and misery of prison, you knew that was the way of life to which people are destined by nature. To prayer, to mother, and the evening meal. Time to go home now.

19 RELIGION IN PRISON. *ÊTRE* AND *PARAÎTRE*. LITERATURE IN PRISON. SOCIAL BONDS. POLES AND UKRAINIANS.

WAT: I have spoken about my cell mates. I have spoken about the religious and patriotic songs. And about myself . . . It's really too soon to start talking about myself. I would rather tell you what the others were like. So, to make a long story short, in that terrible abject misery, the prisoners sang songs to the Virgin every day. They were all religious, while I just lay in my corner, excluded from that community. I was the only Jew in the cell at that time; another one came later on. But that's not the point. I was excluded from the believers. They prayed, they sang hymns to Mary.

One Ukrainian sang particularly beautifully. He was probably a deacon. He was a minor official, a very modest man, very religious. The type of person who is always singing hymns—at work, out walking, on the way home—that type probably doesn't exist any more. He was a Uniate. His religiosity was different from that of the Poles; his was more inward, more mystical. That's probably something the Uniates got from the Eastern church, some mystical sense, while the Polish Church is more social, ceremonial.

Excluded from that community, I felt enormous envy for them. I sat in my corner and wept, though I shed no tears. I've cried very little in my life. But, to be rational about it, this was all really a paradox. I found within me no belief in the existence of God. But I had a vivid, strong sense that I had been rejected by God because I did not believe in His existence. That is, I believed but had no faith; my only faith was in that sense of rejection. I'd like to return to this, because later on I was to undergo a conversion in Saratov that was probably already in the ripening when I experienced that sense of rejection, and especially that feeling of exclusion from that human community. I must also say that Zamarstynów was neither a Soviet nor a Polish prison; it was a special sort of prison. There was community in Zamarstynów, but there was none in Soviet prisons.

I'll return to the other people in the cell, a rather interesting assortment, and to the relations that formed among them. But, my God, it's

138

not so much the people that concern me here—there are novels and so forth for that—but the specific character of experience in Zamarstynów, which, as I say, was unlike that of any other prison.

And so, the lawyer Róg of whom I've spoken, an old lawyer from Lwów, was greatly disliked, especially by the young people. I've said that charisma plays a very important role; it's a mystery why some people are liked in prison while others are not. It has to do with the aura around a person. But certain traits can be acquired, though they don't explain everything either. Prisoners always love gentleness in a person. If there was a good aura around me, that might have been because of my gentleness. It was not even a question of my basic character. I told you about the walk I took right after my mother's death. The two rabbits that ran right by my feet, the birds that weren't afraid of me. That was a state of grace, independent of my character, a state that could descend on anyone. A state of grace, as when I cried. Only when I cried did I understand why people speak of the gift of tears. That was the gift of tears.

One other thing about prison: the way one looks and the way one really is. That is, *être* and *paraître*. It's not that a person ceases to *paraître* in prison. On the contrary, in prison what is sham about a person, the roles one plays and imposes on oneself, stands out all the more clearly. But there's something pathetic about *paraître* in prison. Like a provincial theater company's cheap costumes, medieval armor made of cardboard. *Paraître* comes unglued; it can't adhere to *être*. People present themselves in certain ways, play their roles, but you immediately see that their roles are not important. You don't give them any weight. You see their *être*, which is obvious; either you become naked, or you can be seen through your costume's holes and patches.

How did Róg turn people against him? I mentioned that he had a tendency to flatulence, but that wasn't the reason. He was an old bachelor. Individual features are magnified in a cell like that one in Zamarstynów, where space was short and where there was no escaping all those strangers. A prison cell multiplies an old bachelor times two. Besides, it was clear from his stories that he was miserly. Or maybe not so much miserly as thrifty; he knew the price of everything. Obviously, he earned a lot of money, which he saved up to treat himself to some extravagance once a year. He traveled abroad as a tourist once a year. To a different country every year. And though his stories were interesting, the young people were particularly put off by Róg's buying his postcards for his colleagues, acquaintances, and relatives in Lwów before he left so as not to waste any foreign currency when he was abroad.

Besides, those trips were now costing him dearly. He was treated

139

well during his interrogations; the Ukrainians spoke very well of him and apparently stood up for him. He had even been a very unselfish lawyer, a good lawyer, and had a good reputation. But the Soviets were unwilling to believe that he could go abroad every year and not be connected to counterintelligence. And to Róg's misfortune there was a certain Mr. Bartou of France in his address book. That caught the eye of some high-ranking Soviet investigator who took it into his head that this was Premier Barthou who had written up a project for an Eastern pact in the mid-thirties. The Eastern pact was to have been concluded with Russia, but Poland prevented it. And so Róg was questioned by some Soviet NKVD general, for they suspected that he had been the emissary who had torpedoed Barthou's pact. The follies of the NKVD, that brilliant institution.

Each of us had something he could talk about. In Zamarstynów I talked about a variety of literatures: Polish, French, German, Russian. Róg was very well versed in history. He knew the history of the borderlands and Lwów down to the finest details. And he spoke wonderfully about that history, beautifully. How can I put it to you—those weren't the usual platitudes: those lands had always been bloody, battles and wars had always been fought there, the generations pass but Poland remains. It wasn't that; he wasn't a nationalist. And, besides, there were Ukrainians in the cell. When he spoke of the clashes between the Ukrainians and the Poles, it was from an objective standpoint, not taking either side. It was as if he were speaking on behalf of the land itself. That had enormous value for all of us. I could see that everyone learned an essential lesson and derived great consolation from it. Your own fate, your own misfortune, when seen against that immense historical panorama that was bound to that soil, that land, seemed less crucial when thought of in terms of generations and centuries. That was very valuable for us.

The lawyer Róg gave us one other thing, something perhaps even more important: the consolation of the philosophy of history. His presentation revealed the underpinnings of communism. We philosophized: what is communism? and so on. But he demonstrated the basis of communism as fact, the communists as invaders from the land of the barbarians—Genghis Khan. Genghis Khan was not a savage. He was a barbarian, but he had his own culture, his own civilization, an excellent organization, as you know. But that was an aspect of the East, Tartaria, that had attacked Christian Western civilization. And in Róg's view the Red Army was nothing else but that—all Marxism, Leninism, nothing else but that. Of course, there was more to it, but that was the basis. First you have to see what the basis is: invaders from the land of the barbarians.

MILOSZ: But that's not what communism is for Latin America!

WAT: Or maybe it is for all I know. All communism, Chinese or Latin American, is against our civilization. But that would lead us off into politics, polemics. Communism's anti-Christian aspect was fundamental, and that was brought home to all of us, from the most overly intellectual to the simplest. Róg did not say this in so many words; he did not speak so explicitly. It just emerged from his way of looking at things.

Another thing that stood out in his little talks was the retrograde, archaic side of communism. When he went into detail about the Cossack wars, for example, there were some striking analogies with the Soviets. And that accorded with my own intuition, my vision.

Well, since we're on the subject, I'd like to say a few words about the little talks I gave. I spoke about what I remembered—certain clichés that I had fashioned for myself about Polish literature, for example. This and that, Mickiewicz, romanticism, Young Poland, and so forth. And then I hit on a certain trick. Tell me what you think of it. It seemed right to me—I mean, fruitful in some way—as an attempt at reassessment. I was supposed to give a history of Polish literature, and I began at the end and went backwards. I began with Skamander, then Young Poland, then positivism, then romanticism, then pseudoclassicism, the baroque, the Renaissance. I had the impression that if this approach were worked out more, done in a more documented way, with supporting materials, it wouldn't be a bad way to attempt an exposition of literature, because you'd be segregating things according to whether or not they had a future. You'd separate what had a future from what didn't at various stages. And there'd be a sort of treelike structure; you'd see the branches, the boughs. And what is it that you'd see? The lack of ethics in literature, Tolstoy's literature versus life, literature as something immoral, literature as lying. An empty shell! That means that literature does not measure up to certain existential situations. Literature is for women and children, but for grown men it's an evasion, a way of forgetting, a diversion.

MILOSZ: History is for grown-ups. History and theology.

WAT: History and theology, you're right. But literature is for women and children.

When you're bored, you can fill the empty hours by retelling plots.

My memory was still good then and I could remember a great many novels. That helped me achieve a stunning success in a unique situation in Alma-Ata, in the Third Section, with some bandits. They pleaded with me to tell them the story from some novel every day. *The Red and the Black*, for example, delighted them. They were intelligent bandits. But I had already begun telling the plots of novels at Zamarstynów. That was entertaining, whereas my philosophizing on the baroque or Skamander was dry, no juice. Here I should like to mention that of the Polish novels I retold (not many Polish novels bear retelling—the *Trilogy* was not for them and, besides, I never read the whole *Trilogy* anyway; it always bored me), they liked *The Pharaoh* very much.*
O. Henry also had special success with them. At one time I had translated it must have been fifty of O. Henry's stories, and I remembered them well. Those bandits in Russia were especially fond of them, but even the Poles liked them. O. Henry's stories are perfect for prison. And in fact he started writing them in prison. Conclusion: what is begun in prison goes over well in prison.

I remember another aspect of my talks on literature. I told them the story of *The Robbers*. Most of them knew it, but they wanted to be reminded of Schiller's version; they wanted to be reminded of certain plays. And so I began telling them *The Robbers*. I remembered the play well. And suddenly I was struck by its absurdity—a play that had influenced humanity, the French Revolution. After *The Robbers* came out the government of revolutionary France awarded Schiller honorary French citizenship, which he rejected. A play that had been thrilling young people for generations. Because his scheming brother had turned their father against him and because he is outraged that normal people—workers and townsmen—are unhappy about their family rows and arguments at night, a young dolt joins a gang of bandits. They kill and rob. And not only do they have the right to do that, but they're heroes as well. It's their sacred right. The absurdity of literature. Seen in prison, it's absurd. Well, naturally, I don't want to generalize from that.

Milosz: But it's held by form that lends it a certain nobility.

Wat: Yes, form, language. Language, structure, certain elusive things, imponderabilia.

Now I'd like to tell you about the assistant prosecutor from the military court. A very beautiful person, even physically beautiful. The sort

---

* *Trilogy.* Three historical novels set in the seventeenth century, by Henryk Sienkiewicz (1846–1916), who was awarded the Nobel prize for literature in 1905; *The Pharaoh*, by Bolesław Prus (1847–1912).

of Polish handsomeness you see in Wyspiański's drawings. A great finesse in the profile of the nose, the nostrils and lips finely finished. Polish handsomeness. He also had the handsomeness of those times. Probably nothing could have seemed a less likely career for him than that of prosecutor. A greater contrast would be difficult to imagine. A person of great goodness, delicacy. An amateur astronomer. He knew everything. He was more than an amateur; he was practically a professional. He was able to speak about astronomy in a way that was accessible.

I was very partial to him. We had certain affinities. Astronomy, for example. When I was young, I had been very taken with astronomy, and as a boy I would sit over a Flammarion, a map of the heavens. I learned all the constellations very quickly and in an odd way. It was all connected with Greek mythology, with names like Cassiopeia. So much so that it gave my thoughts a certain astrological coloration. That prosecutor worked at the outer limit of astronomy where there was no technology yet and there were still some underground ties with astrology. That brought us together.

And something else that connected me to him, another affinity, was that we both had had a happy family life. Once again, in prison everything becomes more condensed, fuller. On the street, in the café, in life, everything is mixed together, happy lives with unhappy, unsuccessful lives. In prison, people who have happy family lives stand out. Why is that? How can it be defined?

Something very important was operating and revealed in Zamarstynów: the essence of socialization. One has a vivid sense, actually a fundamental intuition, *intuitus originalis*, that individuals cannot be sufficient unto themselves. To put it simply, people are social creatures. There was a tremendously condensed sense of social existence at Zamarstynów. If you're going to study sociology, there's no better place to do it than in prison, one just like Zamarstynów. All social differences, the various social circles and levels—their essence is bared.

Socialization at Zamarstynów: it was those who had had a happy family life, like that prosecutor, who were full, rounded, complete people. And no doubt it had been a happy family life that had provided that completion. I don't know what his wife and son were like; he spoke of them at times but said very little. But there's no need to talk about that; a very few words are enough, the tone used, what's said. Prison is a catastrophe for a single man or a man whose family life isn't close, but there is also a certain sacral tragedy, the destruction of a world.

MILOSZ: When the man has had a happy family life?

WAT: Yes. Prison was a catastrophe for most of the people there. But there was something else here; this really was a tragedy, a sacral tragedy. Something truly sacred had been destroyed here, certain taboos had been broken. It was a kind of crime. That doesn't mean that the prosecutor displayed any greater despair than the others. No. But it was the depth of his experience. His experience of the tragedy went incredibly deep. And besides, he had good reason. His only son, a sixteen-year-old boy with tuberculosis, was there in that same prison.

MILOSZ: In the same cell?

WAT: No. One time the prosecutor came back from an interrogation and a confrontation with his son. For a day or two he didn't utter a single word. He was a changed man after that. His interrogations were very rough. It's an odd thing, you know. Ukrainians, for example, were beaten, and some were tortured. But Poles weren't beaten. At least not in my cell. I don't want to generalize, but no one in my cell was beaten, except for the kids who were smacked in the face. They'd use the conveyor belt system though: you stood on your feet for long hours during the interrogations by a very hot stove with your back to the fire all the time, and with a light shining in your eyes. But basically there were no beatings. Since he was an ex-prosecutor, his interrogations were rough, and he had to deal with that stove. It wore him out. He came back gray as the ground, his eyes sunken after the confrontation with his son. He told me about it later. His son had not only "sung" but had signed everything he was told to, even the pure fabrications. All those boys "sang" right away. And I remember perfectly well the prosecutor said to me at the time, "When I'm back out free, I'm going to track down General Januszajtis and shoot him."

He told me that General Januszajtis had created an organization of high school students. There were four of them in my cell. One was a fifteen-year-old named Piątek. The guards were fond of him; he was the only one they treated well. A great kid. That fifteen-year-old boy melted their hearts. Russians are like that—Ukrainians too, for that matter. I'll give you an example of what had happened with those kids.

Piątek had been in a high school. He was reading something in front of his teacher during a class, and a piece of paper fell out of his book. The teacher, a Soviet, picked up the paper, and there was a beautifully drawn map, boy-scout style. The forest, little marks. Of course he was brought at once to the NKVD and then taken for a ride in a limousine. First, he betrayed his colleagues, then he brought the NKVD to the forest and showed them where the weapons were buried. Those bandits, those dolts. Unfortunately, that's the Polish psyche. "The children of Lwów." Disgustingly bankrupt themselves, the adults in Lwów didn't know how to deal with an army, defense, anything, and so the obvious thing was to sacrifice the children. That's the Polish magical mentality. Sacrifice the children—an old story, pre-Homeric—so that the nation will endure, to create a legend.

MILOSZ: I saw plenty of that during the occupation.

WAT: The entire Warsaw Uprising! But here that was idiotically criminal. The mighty Russian army was there, and those high school students from Lwów were supposed to overthrow the Soviets.

I'll return to the question of socialization now. And here I would like to make a few small distinctions about the various forms of prison society. The world of social relations in Polish prisons was different from that in Zamarstynów. The Polish prisons corresponded to Gorky's formula in *My Universities*. They were educational institutions for revolutionaries and for those who would rule later on. That's what Gorky meant by "universities." What was that? Tremendous solidarity. I've already told you about the first of May in that Warsaw prison: we were marching, and the policemen seemed ready to open fire on us, to provoke us. And we kept singing in Russian "Higher and higher!" and walking like soldiers. So, you see. But there were also those majorityites in the cell who weren't even allowed to take part in the hunger strike. And so that society had immediately formed into an in-group and an out-group, a primitive form of socialization, friends and enemies in one cell. Not only the enemy above you, your oppressor, but your enemy right there in the cell—the dialectic, thesis and antithesis, on the same level.

For the revolutionaries in that Polish prison, the police were not the antithesis, but the majorityites. The police were the synthesis, but not the Polish police; that synthesis remained only a dream for the time being. That would be something else, another level—a society of people marching, walking in step, a society of cadres. A society—*mutatis mutandis*—like the one the Nazis had created.

Now another type of community: community in Lubyanka and the Soviet prisons. It's my little theory of communism that Stalinism is actually Marxism-Leninism in its most developed phase. Communism is too broad a word. Not to be paradoxical, but this is socialization through desocialization. The principle here is the introduction of a third party, meaning where two of you gather, I shall be there with you. That comes out in prison, that Soviet upbringing. That means that my friend and fellow prisoner is my friend through the NKVD, and my brother is my brother through the NKVD, that is, through the police, the party,

Stalin. It's evangelic: where two of you gather, I shall be there with you. A husband is a husband through the party, through Stalin.

In the Soviet prisons—in distinction to both of the previous types I had been in, meaning the Polish ones and Zamarstynów—there is no question of any community. There the greatest crime is a joint petition, even one from two people. Of course, you could do everything; you could file complaints. If you wanted to write a statement, they would bring you to a cubicle, give you paper and ink, and you could write to Stalin himself. I must have written about a dozen petitions to Stalin when I was in Lubyanka. I asked Stalin what was happening to my wife. Where are my wife and son? That you could do, but only alone. Two people, that was already dangerous.

Besides, those are old Russian stories. Do you know Shchedrin? In one of his novels or sketches some progressive members of the provincial gentry attend a fair, and when they meet in a Moscow hotel, they naturally begin talking about reform. All of a sudden they realize that this is a very dangerous subject, and so they all stop talking. Finally, after a couple of minutes of silence, one of them says, "For the love of God, let's not all be silent at the same time!" An old story. It's not just Shchedrin; it's a pattern.

In Zamarstynów, in contrast, a very deep and natural community was formed, with all the usual subconscious currents. The full range of human social relations came into play, and there was nothing forced about it. Even there, there were two groups, of course: the Ukrainians and the Poles. That was the only place in recent memory that a natural harmony existed between the two nations, the harmony of which Giedroyc dreams. Not without certain "buts," however. I'm speaking about solidarity and socialization, along with their negative aspects. The Poles are a quarrelsome nation. Quarrels would erupt from time to time, but not very often. There were some intrigues, but not that many. Antipathies, sympathies. But it was all within peaceful limits. The dominant motif was solidarity, even among the Poles.

Of course, I saw other types of Poles and Ukrainians in Kiev, in a transfer prison, a real inferno. Have you ever been to the zoo in Vincennes? They have some mandrills there, a colony of mandrills living on rocks, which, by the way, aren't even real but cement, I think. Have you ever seen those mandrills? They lead a terrible life. Incredible hatreds erupt, then die down, then erupt again. Back and forth. In the morning you're friends, and by evening deadly enemies. At each other's throats. Those people [in Kiev] were the elite, mostly members of parliament, lawyers, but they had been tormented, reduced to an absolutely biological level of existence. Such things happen in certain tribes—Ruth Benedict writes about them—those Dionysian tribes in Melanesia where everything is based on hatred, where the social bond is hatred, envy. It was absolutely terrible in Kiev, but those were special conditions.

But in Zamarstynów there was total solidarity, though not everything was so simple there—it was rather complicated, in fact. There was discord among the Poles, and subterranean conflicts were constantly breaking out and being smoothed over by a few people like Colonel Słonecki, the assistant prosecutor, and Drobut, of whom I'll speak later.

But the Ukrainians created an excellent community. In addition to their solidarity, there was also a sort of profound respect among them. You see, I'm not nostalgic for the medieval world, and I don't have a high opinion of Ukrainians. After all, its no secret what the Ukrainians did in Poland, how cruel they can be, and so on. For example, in Paris Paustovsky said that he dreaded to think what would happen in the Ukraine when Bolshevism came to an end and the hour of great retribution came—the Ukrainians would slaughter all the Jews and Russians. And I don't have any nostalgia for the Middle Ages. But there was a certain analogy to the medieval world there, in the sense that among the Ukrainians (in their hierarchy) the lower respected the higher, but with a respect that had nothing servile or obsequious about it. Let's say that this was a respect for the order created by God, respect for the higher person's place. But the higher had enormous respect for the lower. And there was a certain emotional tone to it all, a tenderness. People who didn't know each other at all, militant intellectuals and peasants.

How were relations between the Ukrainians and the Poles? The Ukrainians related to the Poles with reserve but with incredible loyalty. We are enemies, but not here. Here we are persecuted in common. Relations were cold but very polite. In general there was no closeness between the Ukrainians and the Poles. The Ukrainians were anti-Semitic, but since I was the only Jew and so also a member of a national minority, a couple of them were somewhat close with me. And now: the Poles' attitude toward the Ukrainians. Again, unfortunately, another ugly trait emerged: the ingratiation with which the Poles relate to minorities.

MILOSZ: A patronizing attitude?

WAT: No, on the contrary. Things had been turned upside down, after all. They were afraid of the Ukrainians. Here's a little of what Dostoevsky said about Poles: ingratiation but with hidden contempt, one kept well under control, however; it only came out among themselves; and so, that sweetness of Poles to minorities. Quite often they're that way to Jews. You know: a Jew but a decent person, a Ukrainian but a decent person. That went on. I'd like to generalize here, philosophize a bit, the way I like to, some pure reasoning. That society existing through a third party—that atomization of society, as the Sovietologists call it—that triangular social structure has yet another side to it. This is connected with their methods of questioning. I want to tell you that everyone underwent the most absurd questioning. I was interrogated simultaneously as a Trotskyite, a Zionist, a Catholic, a nationalist, a Polish chauvinist and so forth, all at once. Utterly absurd.

When they write about being questioned, the majority of memoirists ridicule the illiteracy and stupidity of the investigators, which always makes me furious. There's one thing those people fail to understand. The person questioning you, that rank-and-file investigator, is a guy who may even have attended a university, but he is a lout. A primitive. And that primitive took a course, and he questions you according to certain forms. I never saw this myself, but some people swear to have seen an investigator forget something and look into a list of sample questions. Of course, they learned them by heart. But the people who composed those forms were people of the highest intelligence, disciples of Pavlov, experts on reflexology. I don't have the slightest doubt about that. There was incredible intelligence behind it.

Not to go into too much detail, I would say it was like Zen, acting through the absurd, the remaking of souls—the reforging of souls, as the Russians say. But where does that reforging of souls begin? What specifically is the nature of Bolshevik socialization? It has to begin by killing the inner man. What Lubyanka is all about is breaking down the mind, to cause death within. The killing of the inner person, very intelligently done, thought through.

And to philosophize a little about communism again: in distinction to what we call Western civilization—the name doesn't matter—our civilization (maybe it's not Christian, maybe it's not Western, but it is our civilization), communism is space, spatialization. For example, in my book *My Pug Iron Stove*, there's a passage that says, "I proclaim myself the tsar of space, the enemy of inwardness and time. I burn with a single passion—to be manifest." And that's why numbers matter so much, mathematics, numbers. Spatial relations, not temporal relations. Lubyanka is a factory that destroys your sense of time. But I will speak of that later when I tell you about Lubyanka.

I'd like to say a little more about the young people. I mentioned little Piątek, the one the guards liked. Sometimes they gave him candy, the only one they ever treated like that. But they were not shocked in the least that he was in prison. They did it out of affection, not pity. That's the Russian (not Bolshevik) acceptance of prison.

One time we had to choose a cell leader. I was nominated because I spoke Russian well. Nobody else spoke good Russian. Hardly any of the investigators spoke Ukrainian. They were "Ukrainians" who had been assigned to the Ukraine, like Nikita Khrushchev. Anyway, they chose a railroad worker to be head of the cell but quickly removed him because as soon as the guard would walk into the cell and our leader had something to say to him, he would tremble and always address the guard as comrade, even though he had been yelled at a hundred times for that. They always answered him, "Your dick's your comrade" or "A Siberian wolf's your comrade." Prisoners did not have the right to address people as comrade.

The younger people stood up to prison much worse than the older ones, much worse. It turns out that a grown man is like a camel, with enormous reserves in him. But, just imagine, after the war I was in Wrocław for a writers' conference. I went to a restaurant and a young good-looking waiter said to me, "You don't remember me, but I'm so and so. We were in Zamarstynów Prison together. I'm a student now and supporting myself by waiting on table." And he told me his story. It turned out that he was the only one not deported from Lwów. He was in Zamarstynów the whole time, right to the very end. And then he was taken to a hospital and brought back to life; he spent a very long time in the hospital. Perhaps that's why he was still there when the Germans arrived. He described the departure of the Soviets, their flight. They took people out of their cells, a whole crowd of prisoners. There was a machine gun in one corner of the courtyard (the courtyard was long, just as in an army barracks), and they opened fire. And so some of them went back to their cells and slammed the doors shut behind them. The Soviets tossed hand grenades in through the cell windows. He was one of those who had gone out to the courtyard, but fortunately he ended up with other people on top of him. He fell to the ground immediately, and that saved his life. He was the only person from prison I ever ran into.

20 A NEW SPIRITUAL LEADER IN THE CELL.
CHARISMA AND HIERARCHY. INNER LIFE IN
PRISON. AN INFORMER. THE PUNISHMENT CELL.
BRONIEWSKI AS HERO.

WAT: I realized that I've skipped one of my more important cell mates.
He came two months after me. A power-plant worker, a little over fifty,
his last name was Drobut. A member of the PPS, a union activist. And
in a group that included colonels who certainly must have thought
themselves something special before the war, Drobut immediately became our mentor, our leader, the first among us. How should I put it?
Our spiritual leader. He had not been especially involved politically
and hadn't done anything against the Soviets. But he was arrested for
being an old PPS member; I guess he was known as an activist. He
came from that fine tradition of the politically conscious Polish proletarians, even-tempered, thoughtful people with no taste for the extremes of communism. Not utopian, very realistic. It was he who told
me that a Soviet officer had shot and killed the director of the power
plant, thinking that he was reaching for a gun. And it was from him too
that I learned about Soviet economic operations in Lwów. All new machines were shipped out to Russia and replaced by ancient junk from
the sticks of Russia. It's hard to picture all the riches the Soviets acquired in that part of Poland, which had a reputation of being poor. In
Ili we lived near the railroad tracks, and probably half of all the freight
cars we saw in Kazakhstan in 1944 and 1945 were marked Polish State
Railways.

How did Drobut win our esteem? Not through any charisma or a
striking appearance or an unusual personality. It was simply a matter
of his human qualities: he was wise, very kind, even-tempered, and
brave. By that time, a classless society had formed in our cell, perhaps
the only instance of it in Polish history. (Well, not the only one, because the same thing happened during all the uprisings and in times of
disaster.) Family, wealth, and education had no significance for the
people in our cell at Zamarstynów. The human hierarchy was formed of
the old virtues: goodness (especially goodness), wisdom, a sense of
measure. And it is only when I think of that classless society in our cell

at Zamarstynów that I realize how much Poland is a class society and what a role all those distinctions, gradations, and privileges play in normal Polish life. A cell like that one provides a standard of measure.

To digress for a moment and narrow the focus, the Russian stereotype of the Pole is the "haughty Pole." Not so much haughtiness as something between haughtiness and putting yourself above others, more the latter. When life is normal, Poles have a need to feel above somebody else. The same can probably be said of any country, but it's very strong with the Poles—at least that's how I see it. Here quantity turns into quality, to the degree that the Poles have earned the epithet "conceited" even from those Russians who were favorably inclined to Poland.

So, you see, it's pressure and crises that create these miracles. All barriers, everything that a man was before, turned to dust at once in that cell. There, you had to be. Être! Et ne pas paraître! And I was staggered by all that because I had seen nothing of the kind when I was in prison in Warsaw. Russian prisons are class-ridden, of course, with various degrees and blends of contempt: everyone has contempt for those beneath. In fact, for all the terror it brought, the Soviet invasion also brought out the best in Poland. You have to remember that I'm speaking of the special conditions in a prison cell where there were twenty-eight people in eleven and a half square meters. An extreme situation.

But Ola is right, too, when she says that all the worst Polish features—highhandedness, status consciousness, anti-Semitism—came into play in those steppe settlements where people were doomed to starvation (which was why they'd been deported there), where Ola never saw bread all the time she was there. And there was Kiev prison where I saw Poles, and Ukrainians, reduced to animals.

The situation there was even worse than in Zamarstynów. But something made our cell noble, some existential depth. But as we know, every depth assumes the existence of another one beneath it. But there is also a sort of ultimate limit. And beneath that limit men become animals.

Now I'd like to go back in some detail to those hours of reverie in the cell that I've spoken of already, though rather sketchily. Our private life, our inner life. I assume that certain general features were common to us all. Memories were the main thing. Memories were a part of our conversations, but of course not everything was spoken of. Your most intimate memories were kept for those hours of reverie. A great many memories would come to you then. Your memory would become incredibly precise, microscopic. Things that you had remembered only in rough outline now seemed under a magnifying glass—scenes, experiences, feelings.

For a very long time I was captive to a single idea: I could think only about my family, who seemed not only doomed to extinction but to all the ugliness of life outside prison. And there was something else that tormented me: I could recall all the faces of the people I knew, but for as long as I was in prison I could not fully summon Ola's and Andrzej's faces to mind. That was exceedingly painful. I made bizarre efforts to overcome this; I went as far as using certain yogalike techniques. But nothing worked. I could remember only Ola's eyes when she was standing at the edge of the sidewalk as they put me in the black limousine. But those weren't Ola's eyes; they were just eyes. Two eyes full of compassion and a certain consolation—that everything will pass, and these too were things that would pass. That's what I read in those eyes. And, as I've already told you, I couldn't stop thinking that my own eyes had somehow not been in focus at that moment; I had been in a stupor.

Memories. What they say about the dying seeing their whole lives pass before their eyes like a movie in their last few minutes of life isn't true. But in prison it is. Not in a few minutes, but over the course of time—time that grows incredibly distended and loses its substance. Time has to be endowed with substance; in prison, time is empty and has to be filled. And you fill it with the movie of your life, which is sometimes vivid, sometimes not so vivid.

Here we must distinguish between memories and soul-searching, pangs of conscience. Right now it's pure memories that I'm speaking of, memories unaccompanied by pangs and that make no distinction between good and evil. Visual, or rather artistic, memories, free of morality. Another and more vulgar form of inner life is "if-onlying": if only I hadn't done this or that. You can fill many hours by dwelling on that sort of thing. You know it's stupid, that you shouldn't be doing it, that those are useless thoughts, but they intrude themselves. And, lastly, there's soul-searching, and, in prison, that's rough. There are two separate film strips: memories without any moral evaluation and those same memories accompanied by a moral judgment. And you don't know whether you're doing the judging or if it's that *judex ergo cum sedebit* in you that's speaking. In a grim, stinking, humiliating cell you start thinking it might be *judex ergo cum sedebit*. The highest judge, the omnipresent. Moral evaluation, moral judgment, is only partly obscured by what we refer to as our normal judgment.

I've done some nasty things in my life. But it was one trivial incident that caused me the most anguish. I was fourteen years old and coming back from a friend's house on Ceglana Street. You couldn't call me an anti-Semite, but at that time I wanted no part of Jewish customs and culture. I was not an assimilationist and had considered myself a cosmopolitan since I was a child. And so this didn't come from any desire to be sophisticated; it wasn't snobbery. I grew up right at the boundary of two worlds where each was very distinct, condensed, developed; and the point where they met was on a high level. I wanted to leave one part entirely behind. And so I moved very far away from Judaism.

Ours was not a Jewish home even though my father was very religious. Our home had been transformed by literature, Polish literature in particular, but other literatures as well. The horror of my childhood was that my sisters were always reciting poetry. And we had picture postcards of sunsets with [Słowacki's] line, "Sad am I, O God." I hated all that, and it still upsets me to talk about it. Our home was somewhat literary and very imbued with the theater (which was why my sister became an actress).

But I loved the High Holidays. I remember my mother blessing the candles on Friday when I was little, though she stopped later on (by the time I was seven, our home was not religious any more despite my father's piety). The High Holidays—Passover, the Jewish Easter, the Day of Atonement, an ominous day! You see, the Holidays are very sacral for the Jews. The Jews' sense of the sacral is incomparably higher than the Christians'. When you go to church, you see religious people who've taken communion, and their faces, especially the older people's, are radiant. And you can also see them straining to take that purity back outside with them, to walk from the altar through the church and take that state of innocence at least as far as the doorway. On the Holidays, and on Saturdays too, every Jew, and especially the pious ones, casts off his dirty garbardine and all the dirt of business, the pursuit of money, *parnose*.

I don't know whether you were familiar with the Jewish ghettos. The young Hasids had beautiful angelic faces, pale, utterly bloodless faces with those *peyes*. They'd spend something like a dozen hours a day studying the Talmud, and they'd be in that state of incredible purity until they entered the world of business. But even a businessman, if he was a religious Jew, has those two days, or that day and a half, or a week during the Holidays, when he casts off the old Adam and is purified. There is enormous value placed on purification in Jewish life.

Certain Jewish customs were still observed in my house when I was very young. For example, I was very fond of Purim. We had a little wooden house with a roof that we put up every year, and inside were fragrant mats that smelled of camomile and open fields. In the middle of that little room, which was out in the courtyard, there were primitive paintings of fruit, flowers, and symbolic biblical animals, a *bestiaire*. Lions, of course, and deer. For some reason I became very attached to deer when I was a child and identified with them.

And so I was on my way home on a bright summer evening and I felt like a young deer. I was even making my legs move like a deer's. Passing a ground floor window, I saw the beautiful angelic face and *peyes* of a Talmud student, a white, transparent face. He wasn't wearing one of those flat skull caps but a bulbous one, like the ones little children wear. He was bent over a book on the window sill, the Talmud, or maybe something else. I was in excellent spirits, without a care in the world, and feeling like a deer. But by then I had begun to reject Judaism, no matter what the cost to me, and so I stopped and began mocking that student, the way you mock Talmudists. And then I saw into the room where an older woman, looking utterly waxen, was lying out flat on a bed. She couldn't have been dead, because her face hadn't been covered, but the end was definitely near. There were bottles of medicine beside the bed. No question, she was dying. His mother. And suddenly in Zamarstynów I saw all that as a verdict, a condemnation, unforgivable.

Not all the soul-searching was so extreme. No doubt I had done Ola a great many wrongs, but for some reason I never reproached myself for any of them there. It was strange, but my conscience was clear when it came to her. There was one little incident with Andrzej, however, that gave me a lot of pain. We were fleeing Warsaw, near some lake, outside of Brześć. Andrzej was very ill-behaved, capricious, especially to his mother. Conditions were bad. And for the first time I grabbed him by the shirtfront and shoved him so hard he fell over. The poor thing ran off toward the water. He ran away. And in prison I worried that he might hold that against me. So there was that sort of thing, normal self-reproach. But in regard to my mother my self-reproach was deep and acute because I had not been a good son. And that weighed on me all the time in Zamarstynów. Not only that, but I kept dreaming about my mother. My initial severe pangs of conscience had to do with being a communist before the war and with *The Literary Monthly*. But, paradoxically enough, I did not reproach myself in the least on that account in Zamarstynów. I don't understand that myself, for I had greater and more immediate cause to do so in Zamarstynów. As if I had drawn the Red Army in by magic and therefore should have been reproaching myself. It was only later on that I drove myself crazy over the sins, crimes, and transgressions I had committed as a communist.

I had other inner experiences too; there were certain practices. I'll tell you one: we had worked out an ingenious system for arranging ourselves to sleep in that cell. There was a terrific racket in the evening; the cell would become as lively as a café. Almost cheerful. That curtain of mingled sweat would come over our bodies only as we were trying to fall asleep. But this was the time before going to sleep when I would close myself off from everything. After two or three tries the racket in the cell stopped bothering me. Mentally, I would walk out of the cell and down the corridor to the courtyard. I would retrace the steps that had brought me there except that I wouldn't go back to the club. I would pass through every street at lightning speed but not miss a single inch, a single street, or any part of the way. I knew Lwów well. I would go to 9 Nabielak Street. The doorkeeper would open the gate for me, and I'd exchange a few words with her. I'd go up the dark stairs; the door to their room would already be open. Ola and Andrzej would be waiting for me. There was a great sense of calm about it all, a calm joy, a feeling of concentration, a nearly carefree joy, with no regret that I would have to go back. I would make full use of that joy. I would sit at the table, a round table, with Ola on one knee and Andrzej on the other. But first Ola would have given me a glass of tea, very hot, very good bitter tea.

I fantasized about tea. At that point, before I had really known hunger, my food fantasies were about tea. But tea meant more than something to drink; its meaning was magical—purification. I thought that when a stream of hot bitter tea went through me, all the filth of the cell that had gotten into me and permeated me to the core would be washed away. Tea was a symbol of purification for me. I felt horribly grimy. And that grime was so great that it became moral and mental grime.

OLA WAT: It's interesting that in his dying moments Stawar begged for a glass of tea he wasn't able to finish.

WAT: So there's something to that then. I fantasized about tea. I also fantasized, but much less, about sitting with Ola and friends in some outdoor café on a summer afternoon or evening and drinking iced coffee. That was rather a secondary fantasy, a luxury. But tea I needed body and soul.

We would talk calmly, and then soon it would be time for me to leave. I had to be back in the cell when they came in in the morning. That was the "agreement." I'd take the same route back, straining not to miss or skip anything, return to my place in the cell, and fall asleep immediately. Rather soon—I don't know just when this started to occur, because these practices were successful from the start—but rather soon I had the sense that I had a double. That was a substantial physical feeling, tangible. A sense of really being present there with them. This went on night after night. I started in the beginning of February and it lasted for quite some time.

On April 9—I made a point of remembering the date—I performed the exercise: I entered the building, but the apartment was locked. The doorkeeper opened it for me and then she disappeared. I went in and had an absolutely physical sense of a void, the presence of a void. But how can that be? Absence is an emotion, not a physical sensation. But at that moment I had a palpable sensation of absence. Emptiness. Absolute absence. I kept at it desperately for the next few nights, with great despair, a twofold despair. Part of that despair was that this was something I needed, and the second and greater part came from the belief that some terrible disaster had happened to them. I made three or four more attempts; it couldn't have been more than that. But when I encountered that void again each time, I lost my desire to continue. I didn't want to be a shaman any more. For that was shamanism. And it turned out that Ola and Andrzej were deported on the night of April 13. A difference of four days. There is some sort of link between those two events, though the exact explanation would be difficult to find. Maybe the decision to deport them was made on the ninth. Or maybe that's when the order was signed by the chief, the NKVD.

Those spiritual practices, those spiritual experiences, increased in intensity, though now they took a new form. I knew I had to stop. For example, seeing yourself from the outside, well, that's easy. The ego sees. You see your own ego being seen. That's nothing special, simple stuff; you can do that any time. But after getting deeper into those practices, I reached a state where I could simultaneously see the ego seeing and the ego being seen. There was no fusion of the two—that sounds laughable when you say it out loud, even pretentious, and maybe even illogical but that's the way it was. I can't put it into words. But not because that was a higher level of visual perception. No, that would be a bad way of putting it. And that's why I can't express this idea in words. I can't even reconstruct that state exactly from memory. But it was all very clear.

MILOSZ: Do you mean visually? To what extent was all that visual?

WAT: That's just the point; it wasn't a visual experience. Visualizing is easy. You close your eyes, or you don't even have to, and you can see yourself talking or walking or doing something or lying with a woman. You can do anything, you know. But this wasn't visual, this was a non-visual experience. It's a state that probably can't be remembered. And then at one point I quit those experiments because I knew they were leading me either to schizophrenia or to some yogic state. It's a very fine line there.

I'll say a little more about those hours of self-immersion, inner life. I think it was the same for everyone. That feeling of metamorphosis, like a butterfly . . . the feeling that you've become a different person, different from the inside out, not the same person who walked into that cell. The feeling that you'll really leave there a different man. It's just what I said before about the guillotine blade. It's already at the back of your neck. But you're certain that the guillotine blade will cut off him, Aleksander Wat, with his irony toward the world, his manic-depressive personality, what have you. This transformation does not depend on a change in your psychology—maybe you'll still be a manic-depressive and still be ironic—but something more important than that changes. The foundations of your psychology change. Am I making myself at all clear?

MILOSZ: You are, but be a little more exact about the guillotine. Just what do you mean by that?

WAT: That was a bad choice of words, the guillotine at the back of your neck. Once again, it's not visual. It would be nonsensical if it were visual. What can I say here—it's like you're a snake. That may be more like it. You're chopped in two and each part is still alive. But one part of you is far away.

Aha, I've forgotten to say anything about dreams. You dream a lot. People remember their dreams and tell them the next day. At Lubyanka we even came to the conclusion that there are certain prophetic signs in dreams. I dreamed of my mother very often. But those were banal dreams in the sense that they came from my uneasy conscience, and so I dreamed of her as a menacing, implacable figure even though she was a very kind woman. I don't remember my dreams now. I do know that I dreamed every night and that I would remember them the next day. And that I had nightmares all the time.

I've spoken of certain states of mind, certain experiences, but a little more about the cell. All sorts of people kept coming, including one named Majteles. He made for one of the few events that happened; nothing much happens in a cell, you know. Majteles was perfectly typical of the Muranow district of Warsaw: working-class, a perfectly deplorable communist fanatic. He was very lean, gaunt, dark, quite small. His eyes burned with hatred. He was a breeding ground for enormous colonies of lice, a new type of lice, tiny as poppy seeds. He was completely covered with them; they were moving all over on him. Where did he get all those lice? He had fled from Warsaw without a cent; he had no money, no friends, and so he spent the nights in shelters. And the lice were terrible there. But even that doesn't explain their numbers. Lice just loved him, that's all there is to it. That's very important. I had relatively few lice; they didn't like me. The bedbugs, however, loved me. They can smell your blood; they know what kind of blood you have.

Majteles viewed us as enemies from the start. He was there by mistake! He had signed up for labor in the Donbas. On the day before he was supposed to leave, the NKVD came and took him. And they accused poor Majteles of being in contact with the head of the Gestapo. What assignments has the head of the Gestapo given you? He was utterly deranged by those interrogations. He had no idea what was going on. He was one of those who thought that it was right to put the Trotskyites on trial—traitors, they sold out to Japan. But then all of a sudden it's he who sold out the fatherland of the proletariat to Hitler! And so he had no idea what was happening any more. But he saw no connection between those trials and his own case. His was an absolutely isolated instance, one big misunderstanding. The world is logical, rational. In the entire world there was only one exception to that rationalism—him, Majteles. Something had gone wrong. And us? We were the enemy. His hatred for us was implacable.

MILOSZ: You said that at first your own attitude was that you were in there because of some mistake.

WAT: Not at all! Not because of a mistake, but just that perhaps they hadn't meant to put me in prison. I didn't think I was any sort of exception, and, as you know, I was waiting to be arrested at any moment. But because of the scene, the bar, Daszewski being my friend, I wanted to believe (but I didn't) at the beginning that it might not be what it seemed, that it might all be absurd, that I might be released. Why not? Maybe through my connections, maybe Wanda Wasilewska—I knew she felt responsible for her colleagues. I wanted to believe that that wasn't the end of it. But it didn't take long for that to pass. But it did last for a few days, because when they wanted to give me a prison haircut, I somehow managed to postpone it for three or four days. I was still figuring they might let me out. I lost all illusions when they shaved my head. I thought to myself, They're not going to let out a writer, a former board member of the Writers' Union, with his head shaved clean. And so since they had decided to shave my head, that meant that they had no intention of releasing me. And it was when I was out in the corridor with the barber, who had put a dirty sheet around me, that I suddenly saw all the gray hair I had after three or four days in prison (my hair was dark brown when I went in).

MILOSZ: How old were you then?

WAT: Thirty-nine. All that gray hair. I haven't actually grayed much since then, though perhaps recently I have a bit. I never thought that everything was rational—on the contrary. It's just that I deluded myself that I had a chance of getting out of that madhouse.

But back to Majteles. He was such a picture of poverty and despair that I suppose even the anti-Semites felt sorry for him despite their hostile looks. I felt a special obligation to take care of him if only because we were both Jews. But for some reason he was given a warm welcome in the cell.

Majteles took offense at me because when he sat down on my blanket (Ola had gotten a blanket to me), I asked as delicately and courteously as possible if he would move away just a little because he had a lot of lice and I didn't have many at all. But that's how you acted with people who had lots of lice.

Then one day—it must have still been in January, it wasn't long after I'd been arrested—I heard the people from the next cell walking down the corridor to the latrine. And then I heard Władzio Broniewski's voice. When they were coming back, I stood by the door and said in a loud whisper, "Władek, have you heard anything about my family?" And he said, "We'll talk tomorrow." I was tense the whole time. The next day they went to the latrine in the evening, right before us. I was by the door and heard them leaving. On the way back, Władzio said, "There's a note for you by the handle of the third (or the fifth—I don't remember) toilet from the door." The whole cell knew. They had heard us talking; everyone was curious. A little life. So I looked around in the latrine, and there it was pasted to the toilet with a daub of bread. The note was just the prison alphabet. I went back to the cell and Broniewski started tapping. It takes time to learn the code and I was no expert. But young Kmiciński, who was a scout, a mathematician, and an electrician, had it down pat. I gave him the note just in case and sat beside him while he told me what Władek was saying. Then I'd tell him what to say back. Naturally, Władek hadn't heard anything about my family. But he did tell me what he was thinking about our case. We tapped, we talked.

Later that evening, all of a sudden the cell door opened with a grind of the lock. We all jumped to our feet. The guard was coming in for a head count. Majteles began yelling hysterically, "He's tapping messages, he's got a paper!" The guard was probably an anti-Semite and began shouting at him. Majtełes kept pointing at me: "He's got a paper!" In the meantime I'd managed to swallow that piece of paper. The guard was a decent guy, but Majtełes wouldn't leave him alone and kept saying the same thing over and over, absolutely frantic, deranged with hatred. The guard took Majtełes out.

Fifteen minutes later Majtełes was brought back accompanied by two men. Majtełes pointed at Kmiciński and told the whole story. Poor Kmiciński was trembling; he'd probably already gotten it in the face a lot during the interrogations. While Majtełes was making his accusations, I kept saying, "There's nothing to it. You can see that he's crazy. He's deranged. Nothing happened; there was no paper. You can search me." But Majtełes pointed at Kmiciński again. Kmiciński quaked and then he said, "It wasn't me, it was him!" Poor Kmiciński, he felt like a terrible fool afterwards; he kept trying to justify himself.

My cowardice in Lwów had a disastrous effect on the course my investigation took because I kept pretending to be a leftist. I didn't pretend to be a communist, but I did pretend I was a progressive. And so of course now, once Kmiciński had said that, I did not contradict him. I told them what had happened, that I had heard Broniewski's voice and so forth. That I didn't know what was happening with my family and wanted news of them. I said that Broniewski and I had talked about our families but that Broniewski hadn't heard anything either. I was told to put it all in writing, which I did.

I went back to the cell and thought that was the end of it. A couple of days passed and then they came for me and brought me to the punishment cell. It was in the basement, a very small cubicle with a window at sidewalk level. The glass was out in the window. And that was a horrible winter. There was a wooden plank bed, a slopbucket, and a pail. Each morning the guard filled the pail with water and poured it out on the concrete floor.

MILOSZ: Did you have any covers?

WAT: No, there weren't any. Fortunately, they hadn't stripped me; otherwise I would have certainly died. I had fled Warsaw in my summer jacket, but in Lwów, a Jewish writer, Debora Vogel, a very intelligent woman, a subtle critic (I don't know what happened to her) had given me her husband's fur coat. The coat was getting old, but it was lined. I wore it all through Russia, and it saved my life. I had to have been as strong as a horse to survive that punishment cell. It was terribly cold. I was only able to lie on that plank bed for a few minutes at a time at the most. Sleeping was out of the question because I had to keep jumping up and walking around. I plucked out a little padding from my coat and stuffed it in my boots. It was toughest on the feet. My nose was freezing. But that was it. Doctors still admire my *carcasse*.

I kept walking for five days and nights, lying down for a few minutes at a time. And of course I had been put on half bread rations. Broniewski was in the next cell. He didn't want to talk to me. He said through the wall that he had nothing but contempt for me for confessing (of course, he had no idea of the circumstances or about Majtełes and Kmiciński). Broniewski had not confessed to anything.

I used that method afterwards. I'd deny even the most obvious things. They could show it to me in black and white and I'd still deny it. That's the only way to act with the Soviet authorities, the communist police. You say "No!" brazenly, right to their face. Then they leave you alone, unless you've been selected for torture. At Lubyanka I saw what torture could bring a man to, the bravest man I ever met, a Soviet citizen. But I was not in the category of those to be tortured.

Władzio was incredibly brave, enormously strong, a young eagle. But that wasn't the only reason I admired him. I walked around my cell in circles, intellectual style. But Broniewski—and I envied him for this—marched like a soldier, beating time, and singing all those Legion songs. He sang the whole time; he sang for five days and nights.

MILOSZ: Fantastic.

WAT: And so I felt like a miserable weakling. Broniewski had shown me how to retain human dignity, strength, and fighting spirit. But I wasn't a weakling all my life. By the time I was imprisoned for the second time, I had learned my lesson from all this. But back then, compared to Władzio Broniewski, a full person, I felt like a worm. I never saw anyone bear himself better, with more dignity, than Broniewski did then. Communism is all the more horrible because it was able to turn that splendid man into a rag during the last years of his life.

MILOSZ: It turns out that official privileges are more dangerous than prison.

WAT: A hundred times more dangerous. And so he had contempt for me and wouldn't talk to me. He brought it up again later once when we ran into each other in Lubyanka, when they were deporting us. Actually, it wasn't at Lubyanka but at the deportation point. We were in a very small cubicle, pressed up against each other during the entire night. The next day we were taken to Saratov. Our meeting was friendly even though he did bring up the subject . . . I guess I explained Majtełes and everything to him. But there are no excuses! He gnashed his teeth. No! You can never admit anything!

Anyway, I survived the punishment cell. I was barely alive on the morning of the sixth day. The janitor came—we knew him from before—a Ukrainian, a country boy with a face like Simple Simon, a very kind person. He brought me a pail of water and a rag to clean that cement floor. I took the rag and wet it but I couldn't wring it out. He was standing in the doorway and could see that I had no strength left. He took the rag and did the job for me and then brought me back to the cell.

It was daytime; the cell was very lively. It must have been around eleven o'clock. They made a place for me right away. I was very weak, more dead than alive. I felt miserable, half alive, in a daze. I fell onto a mat and went right to sleep. But not entirely. I was asleep, but I could hear what was going on in the cell. It must have been only for a minute or two, but it seemed quite long to me. I heard Lenc-Lenczowski, another young man with aristocratic airs, say, "So they threw that Jew back in with us again." Then I fell asleep and I don't know how the others reacted to what he said. I noted that remark, but I didn't react to it, and I had no attitude toward it either. It neither disturbed nor interested me.

MILOSZ: How did the others react to Majtełes?

WAT: Majtełes wasn't there when I came back. The cell had divided. The positive types, the people with dignity, hadn't talked to Majtełes. They didn't insult him or boycott him, but they did treat him coldly. There were, however, a few people, probably two or three, who sucked up to him, smiled at him, ready to be of service. The rest were polite to him. They were all afraid of him, but they still behaved with dignity. No one reproached him; that would have been absurd; he really had been deranged by hatred.

That's not the end of the story. In 1943 I was working in the Polish delegation in Alma-Ata. There were tremendous warehouses there with aid packages from all over the world. I was a school inspector, setting up little schools. That day I was sitting at my desk. Poverty-stricken people were constantly coming in from the kolkhozes, swollen with hunger, covered with sores, wearing rags. The delegation gave them a lot of help. And in comes Majtełes; he sees me, recognizes me. He was terribly frightened. He walked over to me and began jibbering. As I remember, he was working on a kolkhoz not far from Alma-Ata. He had come to get what he could from us. And so I told him that he had nothing to fear, but that he should clear out; I didn't want to know him.

The other incident I was involved in was very distasteful. There was a new prisoner named Fischer or Schultz, some German name. I would have even liked the man on the outside. He was from a little town near Lwów. An active member of The Rifleman [a provincial government organization]—almost illiterate but incredibly shrewd. A Gypsy type, the soul of a Gypsy. Without any embarrassment, he talked about the dirty tricks he had done for The Rifleman. He was a common thief, but a jolly one, a joker. Witty, cynical. He talked about women; he was the first one in the cell to bring up the subject.

He was married to a Ukrainian, a gigantic woman, a wealthy peasant; she owned a little house and a farm in some small town. He told how he had tricked her out of money to spend on girls. He talked a Gypsy woman into going to see his wife to tell her fortune with cards. His wife was very superstitious and loved to have her fortune told. He told the Gypsy woman what to say: that she had a husband who was jolly and seemed like the type who chased women, but you couldn't find a more faithful husband if you tried. He might look like a womanizer, but when it came right down to it there was always something that stopped him. That sort of thing. A joker, a swindler, a crook.

He told disgusting stories. If what he said was true, those organizations in the small towns were unbelievably corrupt. Of course, you had to discount a good portion of what he said. He was a pleasant guy, but the moral atmosphere in the cell had started to go bad. You shouldn't think we were puritans in there, but now some corruption had crept in.

I was on good terms with him, though there was something between us, some snag. There had been something I hadn't liked and I'd said something about it. Right after that a new man was put in our cell, a little runt, though he was clearly strong. He had only one arm; he was the son of an ND member of parliament and had himself been one of those student rightist thugs. And so he and that Fischer, or whatever his name was, started getting their heads together right away. They'd sit side by side and had a lot to say to each other. Naturally, the runt kept scowling at me. Some of the others may even have been ONR sympathizers or members, but in prison the prevailing tone was that all that had been left on the outside. But he didn't see it like that.

I was to give one of my little talks soon after he came to the cell (these are trivial incidents, but that's really the only sort there is in a Soviet prison), and it so happened that I spoke about Russian literature and Russian, Soviet, poetry. I spoke about the great poet Mayakovsky. At one point he interrupted me and said that this was a provocation and that I was a provocateur. That infuriated me. I ran over to punch him in the face. I took a swing at him, but he pushed me away with that one arm of his; he was terribly strong. He got in a punch to my side and I had pain there for as long as I was in Zamarstynów. That was the only fight in our cell. I felt very isolated. I was angry at the people in the cell and started associating with the Ukrainians.

But it all passed quite quickly because Drobut stepped in. He gave a very calm little talk about the ONR, the fascists. He demolished that one-armed man with that talk and demonstrated that he had no right to complain about communism and Soviet power. Drobut, that simple, wise, intelligent worker. He spoke astutely about the ONR's influence on the people and about the proletarian ONR members, those bandits. The one-armed man didn't dare to respond. I was in the good graces of people like Słonecki; they expressed a certain solidarity with me. And so the incident passed fairly smoothly.

MILOSZ: Did Drobut have a higher standing in the cell than Słonecki?

WAT: No question about it. Drobut became the supreme moral authority in the cell a few days after he arrived.

MILOSZ: For the Ukrainians too?

WAT: Yes. He was kind, wise, calm. And it was clear that he had dignity and courage. One man. He didn't have to do anything special. Through the very fact of his existence, the old values—goodness, wisdom, courage—crystallized around him. What he radiated was enough for a magnetic field to form. I have mentioned that Colonel Słonecki did not have an outstanding mind, but he was very kind, very pleasant, tactful, democratic. He put on no airs at all even though he had been the grand duke's adjutant and had good reason to. And that assistant prosecutor was also wise and very noble. But Drobut had something else. He was more powerful than they. The assistant prosecutor had a certain finesse, the finesse that comes of weakness; he was handsome in a way that was more refined than decadent. But Drobut had both the strength and the earthiness of a proletarian. He was a beautiful specimen of the Polish workingman.

MILOSZ: Tradition.

WAT: Yes, tradition.

Aleksander Wat as a philosophy
student at the University of
Warsaw, 1918.

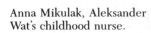

Anna Mikulak, Aleksander
Wat's childhood nurse.

Ola Wat in 1928 or 1929.

Wat (on sofa, second from left) and Ola (third from left), before their marriage: Wat's sister Joanna, fourth from left; Władysław Broniewski, far right.

Władysław Broniewski, 1919.

Stanisław Witkiewicz (Witkacy).

Futurist portrait of Aleksander Wat, by Tytus Czyżewski (date unknown).

Wat, Ola, and Andrzej in 1931.

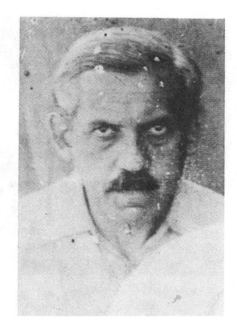

NKVD photograph of
Aleksander Wat, taken during
the period of passportization.

Ola Wat in 1948 or 1949.

Aleksander and Ola in 1956.

Aleksander Wat and Antoni Słonimski at a Polish Literary Congress ca. 1948.

Czeslaw Milosz, Aleksander Wat, and Gustaw Herling-Grudziński, Portofino, 1959.

Aleksander Wat and Czeslaw Milosz in Berkeley, 1964. Wat the teetotaler is toasting with a small flowerpot.

Aleksander Wat in Berkeley at the time of the taping, 1964.

Wat playing with his grandson François, 1967.

21 KIEV IN AUTUMN. TRANSIT PRISON IN KIEV. CHILDREN IN PRISON. GRAFFITI. TO MOSCOW BY TRAIN.

WAT: And so then I was in Kiev.* I was loaded onto a Black Maria at a side track. A tin box, a few little cells hermetically sealed off from each other. Mine adjoined the cab. So cramped and low that I was bent over double, my head pressed against the partition. At face level the sheet metal was perforated with little holes arranged in a concentric circle a few centimeters wide. Later on in my travels I would press my mouth to those little holes. But this time there was no need to: the door to the cab was open a little. I was grateful to my escort for his mercy. He was sitting beside the driver, excited to have company, talkative. A real chatterbox, he talked about people, using their names: Vasya, Natasha, Fedya, Tanya. Andrusha did this, Fedya said that. They were laughing. And that was good. After cruel Zamarstynów, there I was crouched over in a little tin coffin, and all it would take to suffocate me would be to slam the door shut. And what torture chamber were they taking me to now? And "Vasya said to Tanya: Kiss my . . ." The world was going its own way, and that was good.

Kiev itself was bucolic. I could see out through a crack in the Black Maria. We kept driving and driving and stopping at various prisons, one, two, three, five of them. The escort would get out and be gone quite a while. The driver would light up a cigarette—the strong smell of cheap rolling tobacco—and open the door a little wider; he was doing that for me. The escort would come back, throw up his hands, in the mood for a laugh: "You see that, no prison wants to take you. What

---

* The chapter preceding this one, concerned almost entirely with the grueling investigation Wat endured in Lwów, has been left out because of technical problems with the taping. After the conditions in his cell at Lwów, the journey through a sunny fall landscape he recounts here seemed entrancing to him. This chapter and the two that follow were revised by Wat during the last months of his life. These sections differ in tone from the book as a whole, being more "written" than "spoken." I hesitated, wondering whether to keep to the taped version for unity of style. Respect for the author's will prevailed. Besides, this more literary expression of the material provides some idea of what the whole book would have been like had Wat revised it as he had intended—Czeslaw Milosz.

am I going to do with you? Drown you in the Dnieper?" I assumed that my papers hadn't been drawn up properly—oh, those prisons there follow the letter of the law.

We were driving around on the outskirts of the city. The roads were packed dirt, mud; sometimes there'd be a few kilometers of cobblestones. Crooked log cabins with misshapen thatched roofs, a barracklike brick building every once in a while. I would have thought I'd been transported back a hundred years to some godforsaken province straight from *Dead Souls* if the area hadn't been so depopulated. Early afternoon. Golden autumn. Everything quiet and deserted. When a human form flitted past, it would be dark, indeterminate. The hands on the clock had stopped for good or had been broken off. The clatter and rumble of our vehicle was accompanied by dead silence. We must have passed some trees, but I didn't notice them; birds must have been chirping, but I didn't hear them.

A broad street, not entirely devoid of life. Whitewashed huts, two-story brick buildings, a line in front of one of them—it must have been a food store. Old women, old men, a strikingly thin teenager—all of them looking as worn-out as their clothes. Two old women in the doorways of their huts, both of them bony, tall, stooped. They seemed to be standing and waiting for the hearse to take them away to the cemetery. Four children playing in the gutter; they might have been floating a rat down the stream of water. What was there for children to do in a landscape like that? No doubt I had seen similar sights on the outskirts of other cities in the regular world, but we kept covering kilometer after kilometer, moving toward the center of the city, and that was all I was seeing.

At the third prison we had picked up two Soviets, obviously man and wife. They were both tearful. Jews, middle-aged. He was wearing a stiff Soviet cap with a visor and a black overcoat that reached his ankles. Her eyes were very dark and may have been beautiful once, but they were red from crying now. I had seen that sort of clothing, those "trusted-employee" faces in Lwów: faces that were always perplexed, sober, and simple as multiplication tables. And there was always a certain watchful gleam in their eyes, eyes that were melancholy by nature, watchful, always on guard.

We kept going, not a murmur, not a sigh from their little cell; the driver and the escort were quiet now too. We drove another fifteen minutes or so. The couple were taken out at the next prison, the escort hurrying them along: "Quick, move it"—but he said it lazily, without much conviction. They both lowered their heads; it was so hard for them to keep on. Two Everymen, deported and dragging themselves to the grave. My eyes were rapacious: there was something terrible and comic about their Soviet clothes—black, square, and "with room left to grow"—about the way they dragged themselves along, their reluctance to go, their obvious desire to take refuge in the Black Maria, and even about the way the guard said, "Move it." Was the man a dignitary? A poet? A Soviet Orpheus and his Eurydice? Adam and Eve exiled from the Black Maria? I mocked them while my heart bled for them and for my own unhappiness, our unhappiness.

The fifth, or maybe it was the sixth prison, agreed to take me. The escort was pleased and laughed to me. And even though my malevolent eyes still had not seen enough of that new world, I was dead tired and could barely stand on my feet.

We drove into something almost like a town, quite extensive. The buildings were solid, heavy, well proportioned, decently kept up. What had this place been under the tsars? Certainly not a prison or a barracks, perhaps a scientific institute. A broad lawn, in the center of which was an enormous, branching, bird-filled tree. "Tree, tree, tree," I repeated aloud as if I had just learned the word until finally my escort, who was used to my being silent, as required by regulations, began looking at my lips in amazement. The leaves had curled into golden scrolls under and around the tree. Had I been able to stop and lie down under that maple tree, to listen to its million leaves rustling and the birds singing in that beautiful October twilight, then all my exhaustion, all the sweat and nightmares of Zamarstynów would have fallen away from me. But I had to keep going.

After the formalities, brief this time, I was taken to a cell. And what a spacious cell. Naturally, it was packed, but it seemed roomy to me after nine months with twenty-eight people on a floor eleven and a half square meters. I was glad of the space and the air, which didn't seem to reek too badly. I was glad to have a wooden plank bed and to be with fellow Poles. There were Poles and Polish-Ukrainians in that cell—prosecutors, lawyers, judges, policemen, a Ukrainian member of parliament.

I was met by cold, piercing eyes. I was taken aback as I read defiant hatred and mistrust in those eyes. Was that hatred for the intruder, someone not of their world? I lay down on a plank bed and closed my eyes so as not to lose the harmony I had just miraculously attained, to hold the rich harmony of the tree and the chirping birds in my mind. To no avail. Arguments kept erupting; my cell mates were always at one another's throats, fury, nothing but fury in their eyes.

167

The man beside me whispered in my ear, "The one across from you is a rich man, a lawyer from Sambor. But I'll tell you, sir, he's no good; he'll steal anything he can get his hands on. A real snake; he even steals bread; he stole seventeen lumps of sugar from me. The one by the window was the chief of police, and the one he's always whispering with was a judge. They're the informers here, *stukach*, as the Russians say. Watch out for them, sir."

I heard the same thing said of him by the lawyer, the police chief, and the judge. I have no doubt that I too had been immediately classified as an informer. They regarded me with a double hostility: I was a newcomer, I was not of their world, I'd already been sentenced, I'd be relocated, and, besides that, someone there may well have known my old reputation as a "commie Jew." How to reconcile that cell with the brotherhood we had in Zamarstynów? The spreading maple tree that had so delighted and purified me, the spaciousness of the cell, the daily walks, the hopes, the new hopes—all those things lost their charm, and I longed for the piercing stench and the packed, lice-ridden cell at Zamarstynów.

Their story was simple. They'd been picked up right after the Red Army had arrived and then had been subjected to a unique form of torture: for a year they'd been shifted from one prison to another. They'd already been in Arkhangelsk on the White Sea and in Astrakhan on the Black Sea, in Krasnoyarsk and Krasnodar, Omsk and back to Kiev. They never had time to warm up to a place: short spells in prisons crawling with bedbugs, each one worse than the other; thousands and thousands of kilometers, weeks and weeks locked up in cattle cars, plagued by *urks*, even more thirsty than hungry, and then back to bug-ridden transit prisons. Never knowing why, where, for how long or what reason. Their only dream now was to be in a camp. They had become like *urks* themselves, worse, because the *urks* are bound by an implacable decalogue of solidarity while they, always "traveling" together in the same group, hated each other, virulently, murderously. Civilization was crumbling away in them, layer by layer. The most monstrous thing I witnessed were the vestiges and remnants of their former decorum, like the still-chic cut of their clothes that now were rags, all that "please, my good man," "permit me to introduce myself," "would you be so kind"—that sickening courtesy that would suddenly turn into fights, insults, yelling, hysteria.

Was all this the bright idea of some jolly Soviet sadist? Or perhaps the idea of Khrushchev, then the governor? Or was it perhaps an experiment in reforging souls under laboratory conditions, an attempt to utterly destroy social, family, professional, and national bonds in record time? To see how normal, honest, civilized people can be reduced to complete moral savagery?

Attempts of that sort had failed in the prisons of Lwów. The converse held there: over time in that cell in Zamarstynów we began to feel like Christians in the catacombs. There was a certain solidarity in the other Soviet prisons I was in later on, and when it came under threat, it was protected like a candle flame. But in Kiev it had been entirely extinguished.

It was the only cell I was ever in from which I cannot recall a single face or name. Would I have been any different if I had been through what they had?

Bedbugs were another plague there, bedbugs about to burst with the blood they'd drunk. Not the least like the bedbugs I was to know later on in Saratov, which were apathetic, philosophical, pensive. Their stinging bites were more irritating than those of the lice in Zamarstynów. I remembered the old Russian saying: the best remedy for bedbugs is to get to like them. You could get used to your lice, but bedbugs? Their stink in my mouth kept waking me up at night—they were practiced in falling from the ceiling into the mouths of sleeping people.

They walked along the walls in ranks, row upon row of them. In 1929, in starving Berlin, in broad daylight, tall, busty prostitutes had walked down Leipzigerstrasse in a similar formation. That association disturbed me; succumbing to the zoological atmosphere in the cell, I was comparing human beings to insects. But there was something human and dignified about their silent maneuverings in comparison to those constant quarrels in the cell.

The children were my consolation in Kiev Prison. There were whole swarms of children there. A bunch of them went past us on the morning of the second day when we were being taken out for our walk. They were uninhibited, noisy as kids at recess, raggedy, though somehow I wasn't struck by their rags. They didn't look undernourished and did not match my picture of homeless waifs. A lot of nice, bright, likable faces, probably more than in the average school. Four or five looked degenerate, syphilitic, but a good many had lively, attractive, warm faces. One had curly hair and brown eyes and bore a striking resemblance to my own son, Andrzej, and it was that one who ran over to us and said, "Hey, pop, give us a smoke." Winking at his cohorts, he said something about us, some crude remark about Poles, but in a friendly tone of voice. They chuckled and cursed in response; they were merry and abusive, too, but not unfriendly. The sight of them lit up the world for me. But then a second later I thought, Could Andrzej already be in with a gang like that? I knew that wasn't possible now, but in a year or two? So many months had gone by; so many bad things could have happened. So many bad things were happening, inevitably.

These juvenile criminals received special treatment. They had a sports field and rights that had either been granted them or that they had fought for and won. They spent many hours in the open air. We were taken for our walks to a special area enclosed by high palisades with turrets at the corners. It was quiet, dead silent, in our area, whereas shouts, laughter, an incessant hubbub reached us from theirs. How many juvenile convicts were there in that transit prison? Tens of thousands? A few days later, on the way to the latrine we passed their open cell—swarms of them on the three-tiered plank beds, smoke, darkness. They had just been kicking up a row, storming the door with tables, chairs, what have you, protesting against something—protesting in a Soviet prison! The guards seemed helpless; they stood in the doorway using patient persuasion, ignoring the curses. I had already observed the special warmth the NKVD men had shown the kids in Zamarstynów prison. Was it because so many of the NKVD men were former waifs themselves? I had been so taken in by Makarenko's *Pedagogical Poem*, *The Republic of Shkid*, *A Start in Life*, all those teachers in leather jackets who wisely and humanely eliminated Russia's plague of homeless waifs. When was that? Right after the civil war, I think. Now, twenty years later, there were thousands, tens of thousands of children in just that one transit prison alone.

The uproar in their cells quieted down late that night and started up again long before dawn. They called to each other from cell to cell, from floor to floor, from block to block. They had been herded there from all the ends of Russia; some of them knew one another or came to know one another by their long vagabond nicknames. I didn't understand much of their lingo—all I caught was scraps of their stories. An immense pararepublic of criminals (*urks*) was revealed to me, a dense network covering Stalin's tsardom. Was this the ferment of life, irrepressible, forever alive? I had no inkling then that three years later a friendship would spring up between *urks* and myself. The contrast between their pleasant chirping youthful voices and their foul language did not grate on me then, but I was struck by the clash between their "gay knowledge" of life and my hellish cell—ex-prosecutors and lawyers snarling at each other.

Voice was not the only means of communication. Our entire cell block and the one facing it were strung with threads from top to bottom. A year later I was in Saratov Prison with a young thief who would throw matchboxes containing my notes—"Is there a Polish citizen, Ola Wat, in your cell?"—through the high barred windows to the other cells, even to the floors above. I constantly had the feeling that Ola was in there someplace. But the prison in Saratov was for politicals, and the prison guards were always cutting our lines of communication. In transit prisons, however, this practice was tolerated; in fact, quite a lot was tolerated in them.

I had no dealings with investigators in Kiev. When I compared the prison staff there with that in Zamarstynów, I came to the conclusion that the elite of the sadists had been sent to the annexed territories; in Lwów they felt like soldiers in a captured town—there was plenty of booty but ambushes were frequent. Perhaps the jailers in Kiev were lazier, simply sluggish from undernourishment. Or could they have been softened by their contact with children? And with the "regulars" who had been sentenced under privileged statutes since they weren't politicals? Everything probably played its part. There were exceptions, however, even in Lwów. Like the Ukrainian who, after I had spent five full days in solitary during the severe February of 1940, washed the cement floor for me. I was too weak to do it, and I was very moved by the goodness of that gesture, so unexpected, so exceptional there.

My subsequent mentor in Lubyanka, the writer Dunayevsky, explained to me the reasons behind these new generations of waifs and *urks*, whose numbers kept increasing. There were several reasons, but they all arose from the nature of the system and the way it operated.

The psychological reason. With the breakdown of family life and the obligatory cult of Pavlik Morozov (who informed on his parents), any young person in Russia with a wild streak in him who wanted a life of action had only two paths open to him: either make a fast career in the Komsomol by climbing over the backs of his peers or run away and join the *urks*, the free life. Those who in a normal society would have been led by their temperament to become artists or revolutionaries, especially communist revolutionaries, were in the USSR forced into crime.

A second reason. Every "campaign" and purge increased the population of the children's homes, the orphanages, which were, as a rule, hotbeds for *urks*. There were a dozen or so, maybe a few dozen, maybe even a hundred model children's homes that were shown to visitors from abroad, but there were tens of thousands of others, the regular sort. In many respects the children's homes were worse than prisons because even though there was no more to eat in prison, at least there was no military discipline, no forced political or moral make-believe, and the guards, on the whole, were more compassionate toward young people than their hungry, ill-tempered teachers.

A third reason. Government or factory functionaries would travel on assignments that took them hundreds or thousands of kilometers from home; they would go for a couple of weeks and stay for months, years.

The further they were from the local police files, the safer they were. It was also a chance to escape the daily grind, to earn more money. They'd start new families, the only way to deal with daily life. There was a surplus of women everywhere. As a rule, children abandoned by their fathers went to the children's homes.

In 1944 in Ili when people were being rounded up to be sent to the mines in distant Karaganda, our neighbor, a soldier's wife whose pregnancy was close to term, was picked out of the crowd. "My husband's at the front!"

"So what," said the civilian in charge of the roundup to console her. "You'll find a new one there, one just as good . . ."

"I'm pregnant."

"The hospitals are better there."

"What will happen to my children?"

"They'll get along. Did you ever see anyone who didn't get along in our country?" he added with pride.

I still had so many illusions to rid myself of in the fall of 1940.

There was one other means of communication. Writing on the latrine walls. Quite a lot of pornography, but it didn't predominate. A lot of messages in Polish: names, ages, dates, place and length of sentence. There were dozens of young people among them, fifteen-, sixteen-, seventeen-, nineteen-year-olds with sentences from eight to ten years, mostly in Kolyma and Kotlas. The Polish messages were practical and to the point: "If any Pole reads this, please pass on word of me until it reaches my family." The exact address was often provided. Another read, "My parents were deported to Kazakhstan in April 1940." And that is how I learned beyond any doubt that the families of prisoners had been deported in April 1940. And so my intuitions, my nightly telepathic trips to Nabielak Street, and my sense of a sudden terrible emptiness in our apartment on the night of April 9 had proved true. I was constantly worried about Ola and Andrzej, but there in that latrine, those messages stabbed me in the heart twice a day.

As for what the Russians wrote on the walls, it was either in underworld slang and indecipherable, or philosophical. A lot of poems, *chastushki*. Mostly obscene but with a certain wild energy, real *urk* poetry, and some imitations too, written by intellectuals. I can still remember some of the words:

> Ot Vorkuty idut katorzhane,
> Vory, blyadi, millionaya rat'.

> Prisoners are coming from Vorkuta,
> Thieves, whores, an army a million strong.

A lyrical poem, the work of a true poet, poignant.

I was most impressed by philosophical maxims, which I was also to find later on in every provincial prison.

> Bud' proklat kto vydumal nazvanie
> Ispravitel'no-trudovye lagerya.

> A curse on whoever invented the name
> Corrective Labor Camps.

That's how the poem begins.

The most beautiful was an age-old maxim:

> Ot sumy i tyur'my ne otkazyvaysya.
> Vkhodyašciy ne sumis',
> Vykhodyašciy ne raduysya.

> Do not reject the beggar's bag and prison.
> Entering, do not lose heart.
> Leaving, do not rejoice.

This is like the antiphon of the chorus in the ancient tragedy of the Russian people. Now this old maxim once used by runaway serfs and pilgrims expressed the fate of the entire nation, fully, truthfully, and with great dignity. I was fascinated by the dignity in the maxim, its severe truth. But I had come there from another world, and I fought against that fascination. Bolshevik terror could not be sustained without that national acquiescence to the beggar's bag and prison: *les idées forces*—formed in the West under the monstrous pressure of injustice and vengeance—found their promised land in Russia, I thought scornfully. But, returning to my plank bed and the quarrels of my miserable cell mates, so Western until recently, I repeated the maxim with its solemn anapestic cadence and knew that this was a holy thing. I closed my eyes and tried to visualize the face of that prisoner who on the filthy wall of the prison latrine had written not "Every man for himself" but those solemn, humble words. A man of the people, condemned to death? One of millions? He had found the meaning of his nation's fate in the midst of meaningless chaos and in the random calamity of his own suffering. Twenty-five years later, when I read *One Day in the Life of Ivan Denisovich* and *Matryona's House*, those words came back to me and with them the face that I had imagined then, the face of a Christian, a stoic sage of Gulag Russia.

"A curse on whoever invented the name. . ."—anger about a name, the meaning of words, semantics. The loss of freedom, tyranny, abuse, hunger would all have been easier to bear if not for the compulsion to call them freedom, justice, the good of the people. Mass exterminations are not an exception in history; cruelty is part of human nature, part of society. But a new, third, dimension had been added that was more deeply and subtly oppressive: a vast enterprise to deform language. Had it been only lies and hypocrisy—lying is part of human nature and all governments are hypocritical. The rulers' hypocrisy can cause rebellion, but here any possible rebellion had been nipped in the bud once and for all. A lie is an infirmity, a disease of language. The natural function of language is to ascertain the truth, or truths. Lies, by their very nature partial and ephemeral, are revealed as lies when confronted with language's striving for truth. But here all the means of disclosure had been permanently confiscated by the police. The customary or even just the logical, natural connections between words and things, facts, had been taken from the individual, expropriated everywhere, and nationalized for good, so that now any word could mean whatever suited the whims of the usurper of all words, meanings, things, and souls. The viler the deed, the more grandiloquent the name. But if only this procedure were used just to mask criminal means and ignoble ends—that too had happened often enough in history, the history of wars, tyrannies, and annexations; Tacitus knew about all that. But in this case a coherent set of grandiloquent terms and the opposing monstrous reality were kept side by side, ostentatiously and with diabolical thoroughness and perseverance, and under threat of extermination a person was coerced into fully believing that the terms and the facts were identical. Such things had been anticipated and attempted in history's darker hours, but this was the first time that the "reforging of souls" was carried out by the police on such a colossal scale, with such speed and such logic. Collective farmers dying of starvation were herded to films in which the tables buckled under the weight of food; under threat of death they *had* to believe that these banquets, and not their wretched poverty, their collective farms, were true and typical. Young enthusiasts sang rapturously: "I know no other land / where a man can breathe so free" while their fathers perished in the camps. But for souls that had not been reforged yet, nothing was as hateful as that total corruption of language. It drove them to their wits' end. It suffocated them like a nightmare, like a noose around their necks.

When I was at liberty in Russia, which by then had been pacified until it was like a cemetery, I saw some old people who risked their lives to shout out, if only once, that slavery is slavery and not freedom. That was to be a common thing later on in postwar Poland, even during the blackest years. I was one of that large number, and I paid dearly for it.

So in the prison latrines you could read the plain human truth about Stalin's Russia—there, and only there.

When leaving me at the prison, my escort had said, and not without a certain protective warmth, that he'd be coming for me in two days to take me elsewhere. But where? To Moscow? Was my case going to be reopened? Seriously this time, not on any trivial Paragraph 58.10! Would there be a confrontation with the ghosts of people like Hempel, Warski, Stande, who'd been liquidated a long time before? And with all that throng of other ghosts who are constantly there in the investigators' offices, in that nocturnal zone of the living and the dead, that *città dolente*. Had Zamarstynów been only a prologue, a game of cat and mouse? "I didn't know you were such a big fish." That's what my last investigator, attached to our case from Kiev, had said, and not without a certain dry esteem. He had made a show of closing the file that contained mean, shabby documents on me, the abject testimony my friends had given, depositions that had already caused so much trouble and pain. The USSR has other places for a "big fish" than a tank in some godawful province.

Two days, three days, five days passed, and no one came for me. Perhaps it would be just the opposite, and my wanderings had come to an end. Would they strike down the charges and say, You can live here in Kiev or somewhere else in the area. In Lwów you were in our way, but you're an honest person—though, as my first investigator, a philosopher, said with a sigh, you lead "a socially dishonest life."

Finally, the escort came for me late in the afternoon of the seventh day. And just in time too! My situation in the cell had become unbearable. Everyone hated me, and they were showing it in ways that were increasingly brutal. They were treating me with contempt. The most ominous arguments were erupting over the soup pot. When portions were doled out, intricate but rigorous rules were observed, supervised by twenty pairs of watchful eyes. I always got the dregs, without even one glob of fat; my chunk of bread was always in pieces. Where did that hatred come from? I've trained myself to observe myself with a "third eye." This I do as a matter of principle and with a passion to detect everything negative about myself, but in that case I found nothing to reproach myself for! I had acted with simple discretion and natural tact, not an iota too much or too little. I didn't accost them with talk; my answers to questions couldn't have been more ordinary: complete, neither aloof nor overly familiar, like a timid student but one who knows the lesson. I didn't once snap at anyone picking quarrels.

It had been just the other way around in my cell at Zamarstynów—I had been irritated and irritating, hysterical at times. Over a long period, inch by inch, with great difficulty, I learned the art of coexisting in prison. To a select few, that art was second nature. Each step forward cost me great effort and sometimes came with a lashing of painful lessons. I was egocentric, consumed by myself, by my own afflictions and constant recollections—an unforgivable sin in prison. I did not see my own suffering as part of the nation's total suffering. And worse, I saw my own suffering as incomparably greater than that of my cell mates. I was even like that when the major, the military prosecutor—I've told you about him, a brave and beautiful person—came back to the cell after being interrogated; the investigator had kept him sitting by a red-hot stove all night, under blinding lights, on a chair with one leg broken off. Regularly, every fifteen minutes, the investigator struck him in the face, not even interrupting that automatic act when the major was confronted with his tubercular sixteen-year-old son, who was a prisoner too and who, when beaten, had spilled everything. This moved me to my depths. I admired the major, and I truly loved the man and that day, of course, I didn't think once about myself. But I can't deny that I still didn't know how to act in prison, and I had not deserved the warmth that was shown me at Zamarstynów.

But there was something else entirely going on in the Kiev cell. When I walked in, I was immediately shocked and depressed by how severe their animosity was, and that depression always colored my relationship to that cell. The next day when I found out what they'd been through, I was filled with a sense of how utterly helpless they were against fate and how utterly helpless I was toward them. My sympathy could not wound them; it was beyond pity and contained more dread than compassion. Anyway, I never expressed that sympathy in words or with my eyes. I made no effort to conceal my difference, my superiority, precisely because I didn't feel the least bit different or superior. My clothes were as ragged and foul-smelling as theirs; my face was as ravaged as theirs. I hadn't seen a mirror for almost a year, but I had seen my own face reflected in the faces of the Lwów intellectuals, a group of old convicts, something out of a Peredvizhniki painting. There was nothing to envy about the way I looked. To me, they were all still lawyers, prosecutors, members of parliament, and what had made them what they were there in that cell was beyond the human order. They had been subjected to forces that were beyond the human order.

I made no attempt to bend to them, to adapt to them, which might have offended them. I didn't do that out of humility or from a sense of guilt toward those who had been wronged more than I had. It happened by itself, without my intending it—I felt that I was truly a nothing there, without virtues, faults, or backbone. They must have thought me a weakling, a dolt, a nothing. As a matter of fact, any one of them should have felt superior to me, more human. They were men to their bones; they had mettle, passion, intelligence, sensitivity.

Why did they hate me so? Not because I was a Jew, not even because of my reputation as a communist, and they were not afraid of me. I'm not even certain that they still hated the people who were torturing them—the torturers were from the world of the gods, barbaric, monstrous, but still gods.

I didn't play the observer either, didn't steal any glances at their suffering. I did take one look at them, just for a moment, but I stopped there; that was no place to indulge literary habits. But they knew about that one glance, not because they observed it or felt it on their skin, but they were always mindful of it. They were fatally at odds with each other, but in relation to me, a witness by chance and necessity, they felt like a community. And it was their own community they hated in me. They didn't want any witnesses. Had they been *urks*, they would have strangled me in my bed.

I was glad to see my escort's coarse Russian peasant's face, grateful to be out of there. It didn't matter where I was going, anyplace but there. I made a promise to myself, and to them, to forget them forever.

Then by Black Maria again to a side track, a few kilometers from the station. A Stolypin car on the tracks by a building guarded by soldiers. I boarded the train, glad to see I was alone. A clean car, wooden compartments, wooden bunks, iron bars. No lice, no bedbugs. It was a cold night; I didn't sleep. But then there was the morning and the world outside the window: fields, stubble, groves, woods, now and again some hills. It was still warm, still sunny; it might already have been October. Because of the trees I seemed to be traveling through Poland: pines, birch, willows, linden, oak, poplars. I repeated their names in various sets like incantations: elm-larch-alder, birch-linden-maple. I once saw a poem by a young mental patient, a whole page in a notebook covered with nothing but "The sadness of trees." But I didn't feel any sadness. On the contrary, their serene dignity, their radiance triumphed over the antiworld of prison into which I, who belonged to the world of the trees, had been hurled.

A river, ponds, brooks. I longed to throw off my sweat-soaked clothes and dive into that smooth, pure, living water. I was tormented by that desire, obsessive as the vision of a glass of hot tea had been at Zamarstynów. A need for religious purification.

In Greece I would have been a tree worshipper. I would have made pilgrimages to the sacred oaks and used the rustling of their leaves to

177

divine my future and what to do, even though I would get the future I deserved. Twenty years before, as a dadaist, how I would have laughed and jeered at such platitudes.

What had happened to the young who had set out early, too early, on an adventure, the adventure of overstepping all bounds. I called him back to me; he wasn't alien to me now. On the contrary, he was closer to me now than ever. I was finally reconciling myself to him, as if he were a reckless son. But if he could have seen me then and heard my thoughts, he would have disowned me out of despair and shame. The way a son is ashamed of a father who's gone bankrupt. Now I can see myself during those feverish nights in Niecala Street, sitting by my pug iron stove, in a trance of *écriture automatique*, getting my "voices" down on paper. All the mirrors were broken, the values splintered, the world shattered, and I saved myself with mockery and despair. What a long way I had traveled since then! It was as if that young man had not stayed still but had gone off in the opposite direction. But fortunately the world is round and we met again twenty years later in that prison train. I recognized him in me as I never had before, and he disowned me. I had traveled a long way with scoundrels. I had feasted with them, and I was, or rather we were, now wandering the penitent's road. And if that nineteen-year-old had recognized himself in me, in that old convict, he would have hated me just as my cell mates in Kiev had.

My escort, Vanya, was clearly pleased with me, a peaceful prisoner, no trouble. Vanya had a good appetite; he was always eating. By then I could no longer stand to watch people eating, even if they were just chewing a piece of fresh bread; the sight made my stomach turn.

We weren't in steppe country yet; the flora had a certain modest beauty. No people or animals anywhere. Of course there were people at the stations we sped past: railroad workers, a few bearded men, peasant women of indeterminate age. Did Plyushkin's serfs in *Dead Souls* look that wretched? How swiftly Russia flies, forward through space, backward in time.

We sped past a station, the outlines of a town, cupolas. A short while later the train stopped in a field, and two prisoners were brought into my compartment. The other compartments were already packed, nothing special about the people in them. I'd get glimpses of them on their way to the lavatory—expressionless faces, grimy clothes, one or two politicals. My new traveling companions: one short, stout, and blonde, the other tall and thin, with brown hair. The blonde one was fat, firm, a crudely carved hunk of lard; in his early youth he might have been good-looking in a Komsomol poster sort of way. Both well dressed, Soviet style. Higher-ups, no doubt about it. The blonde one's bulging eyes still glowed with the pride of a man who'd worked his way up from the bottom. "Just look how high I've risen, me the son of a sewer worker!" He was on the way down now; he would come alive at times, become brighter, then fade out. They introduced themselves quite formally, with a touch of servility.

I found out the fat one's story. The son of a sewer worker, he had been an engineer who'd risen quickly to become the director of an arms factory in Tula. And he'd also been a deputy to the Supreme Soviet for the last few years and had been decorated. He sat beside me, his mouth hanging open. His thick lips were parted; his shrewd eyes expressed endless puzzlement: "The Order of Lenin, which I earned by hard work . . . Deputy to the Supreme Soviet of the USSR . . ." he repeated again and again. "And that kid, twenty-six, twenty-eight years old, that lieutenant dared to rip the Order from my chest, to throw the Order of Lenin on the floor." An incantation without feeling, he spoke in an even, dull voice.

The brown-haired one backed him up: "That's exactly right, Platon Sergeevich." He'd been the blonde one's subordinate, his right-hand man; you could see that. Since they'd been arrested together on the same charge and hadn't been separated, the subordinate was undoubtedly informing on his former boss, who was aware of it but still had to speak his mind.

Gradually I found out the details. The explosion of an expensive boiler had caused the destruction of the machine room, the deaths of a few workers, and a long standstill. Commissions, examiners came in from Moscow. A simple affair, it was cleared up quite quickly. The accident was caused by the carelessness of a mechanic who hadn't been sober and who had, in any case, been killed in the explosion. At the time, the director had been at the Supreme Soviet in Moscow. All the evidence was gathered, written down, sealed, and filed. Then he was called in to the NKVD—not to the chief, who was his buddy, but to an ordinary lieutenant, "a kid." The lieutenant immediately accused him of sabotage. The deputy grew indignant and pointed to the order on his chest. The "brat" ran out from behind his desk, ripped the Order of Lenin off his chest, and threw it angrily to the floor, cursing him up and down.

He still couldn't make any sense of it all and mumbled, "That snotty lieutenant, fresh from the Komsomol, that kid—and me, a deputy to the Supreme Soviet of the USSR, the Order of Lenin on his dirty floor."

I couldn't share his amazement, and I almost broke out laughing once, but I stifled it in time. There had been a certain ritual in Zamarstynów Prison: whenever a naïve prisoner would appeal to Stalin's constitution, the interrogator would pull a rubber truncheon from his desk drawer: "Here's Stalin's constitution for you." And sometimes he'd use it before he put it back. I once quoted the constitution myself, but only in regard to the elementary rights of prisoners; from the conceit of my investigator I concluded that this attitude toward the constitution on the part of the NKVD was not a sign of cynicism, as we in the cells supposed, but the necessary result of their deep conviction that both the constitution and the Order of Lenin (in this case) were only concessions to the weakness of human nature. That unconsciously rooted conviction allowed my interrogator to employ the most perfidious lies with a clear conscience.

After the evening meal the thin one started to gab. Incidentally, I was struck by how uneconomically they ate; they clearly hadn't done their apprenticeship in prison yet. I had already forgotten that a person could eat so unintelligently. They had their own food with them in a large canvas bag that must have belonged to the director, as did the food: slices of lard, an onion, bread—not our claylike prison bread; the way his had been baked and its smell reminded me of prerevolutionary soldier's brown bread. They shared the food like friends but didn't offer me any.

To my surprise the one with the brown hair turned out to be an intelligent person; when he spoke, he was concise and to the point. Since for the first few hours he hadn't said much more than his usual "That's exactly right, Platon Sergeevich," I had taken him for a humble official right out of Chekhov, but we often find that when relating to foreigners we superimpose characters from literature on them, which distorts our perception of them as real people.

With great clarity he explained to us (speaking to both of us and as if to neither of us) the organizational differences among all the different categories of penal colonies and also among the different types of camps. It was obvious he knew what he was talking about. From what he said it was apparent that their arms factory employed convicts from the numerous colonies around Tula; one department was even staffed entirely by prisoners under guard. Moreover, the factory had connections with some of the more distant camps. He (also an engineer) had been responsible for this department, and his duties had often taken him to Moscow and Siberia. He spoke only about the organization and his work, saying nothing about the living conditions in the camps. With one exception.

I observed the director curiously as he listened avidly, sometimes flushed, sometimes pale, but always with close attention, though it couldn't have been the first time he'd heard it all; it was as if he were constantly trying to find what would be the best place for himself in that network. He was particularly disturbed when his subordinate dryly and matter-of-factly—and in my opinion with some sadistic intent—praised the recent repeal of the policy of releasing prisoners before their terms were up for working well. A blessing that had been permanently repealed. He mentioned that political sentences had recently been increased from ten to twenty-five years. I interrupted: "But I was sentenced under Paragraph 58:10."

"Doesn't matter," he answered. "In Moscow they'll tack on the rest!"

Naturally, I'd known about the camps and how widespread they were for a very long time; only my way of viewing them had changed. There was a time, a rather short one, when I had soothed my engagé conscience with the "epic poetry" of the Belomor Canal and Maxim Gorky's idyllic descriptions of depraved people becoming moral and "growing" in the educational camps in Bolshevo, which had been toured by foreign delegations. Even back then, however, I was disturbed by the enigmatic stance of my communist friends: they simultaneously denied the existence of the camps and sporadically accepted their severity with a certain dull-witted approval. "They don't fool around over there. Over there, they don't pat you on the head," Stanisław Ryszard Stande, the poet, used to say with delight, in his fine diction (he perished "over there" a few years later). To have pressed them on that essential point would have been tactless. They would have wriggled out of it anyway, saying, "Reactionary slander." They invested their hints and their silence with a deep sacral mystery, to which I, only a sympathizer, had no right of access. They didn't want to deceive me. The attitude of the communist intellectuals was irrational—in its very assumption, its very origin. Their assumption was that the slogan of the party simpletons—"They're in a better position to judge"—was sensible, if obtuse. It's a waste of time for us to philosophize; the Kremlin was in a better position to judge. "They see things better"—that's how they put an end to discussions, to other people's doubts, and to their own scruples during the time of the great trials. Although that formula disgusted me (I was a renegade by then), it was more straightforward, a simple article of faith, than the sophistries of the communist rationalists, Stalinists, and Trotskyites alike.

In Lwów, during the short time I was free, I attempted to allude to all this in conversation with an eminent Soviet writer. From several of his veiled hints I took it that, without exception, everyone in Russia knew about the horrors of the camps, had to know and had not to know about them; the camps were horrible chiefly so that everyone would know about them and never forget them for an instant. (And so the name "corrective labor camps" was not a complete misnomer: they really were educational—not for those already in the camps, but for those who hadn't been in yet, for the country as a whole.) It was most essential that the subject of the camps be constantly present in people's minds, while even the very word *camp* was under the strictest taboo; it was precisely this duality that, by causing religious dread, accelerated the "reforging of souls" to maximum speed.

In our cell at Zamarstynów the camps were naturally discussed a good deal, and it turned out that the "reactionaries" knew incomparably more about them than I, the "progressive," did. But at the time there was no way to distinguish between what was true and what was just talk. Strange as this may sound, as soon as I saw the first Soviet airplanes on September 17, 1939, I had no doubt at all that I'd end up in a camp, and yet I wasn't much interested in them. Could I have been wearied in advance by the monotony and dullness of mass atrocities?

Nevertheless, with my fondness for hyperbole, I listened to the engineer's matter-of-fact account about the camps' organization, and I envisioned a huge map of Russia dotted with islands of repression, just as in my cell in Kiev I had pictured it covered with a network of thieves' dens. Autonomous structures, super- and substructures, how many of them were there? And what were the connections, fine as a hair and strong as steel, that bound them together into a single world? In my early youth there was a long period when I delighted in reading the literature of cruelty from Lewis's *The Monk* to O. Mirbeau's *The Torture Garden*; evidently, in my readings I'd consumed my portion of sadism, and the world of Soviet tortures bored me like a hackneyed novel. As for my own fate, I had no doubt that I was one of those who would die like flies in the camps, or while being transported there, or in the first stages of adaptation. Three years later I was assured of the same thing by Colonel Omarkhadzhev, the chief of the NKVD, and by the bandits who were my fellow prisoners in Alma-Ata. Suffering, which had an end to it, seemed bearable to me.

I was sure by then that we were headed for Moscow. We were put off the train on a side track again. Behind a cordon of soldiers, peasant women were carrying railroad ties. The two men who'd been in my compartment were taken away at once; I waited with my guard, who was feeling dejected now. I could see a suburb a half a kilometer away—a tall yellow apartment building, some wooden huts beside it, and a lot of people—the first crowd of free people I'd seen. On the corner closest to me there was a stand; I wondered if they were selling ice cream there. These signs of life's beauty consoled me.

Back to another Black Maria. This one was much larger and my compartment higher than in Kiev; the door, however, was shut. But the little holes in the door were considerably larger. Even though I could stand up straight in there, I bent myself into the shape of an "S" and took turns putting my eyes and mouth to the perforations. My box was pitch black, but the one next to it was large and had a light on. Three women: one old, two young. I could see one of the faces clearly; the light from the bulb fell right on it. A young face, boyish-looking, probably because her head had been shaved, though that didn't spoil her looks—delicate, regular features, sweet, round eyes, very Slavic beauty. We started moving; it was night in the city though I couldn't see it, separated from the cab by the women's cubicle. The Black Maria kept stopping in front of one prison after another. The beauty was taken out first. The other two women began whispering with feverish haste: so young, so nice, but a gang leader; they slaughtered an important official's family. Then, their voices louder, they began to confide their troubles to each other. They were both on the way from court and they'd both been sentenced for "malingering." A new ukase. At the beginning, as a rule, the judges hand out the stiffest possible sentences.

The young one lamented, "I'll never get married again! My boyfriend was on leave, and so we went to Zags and got married. In the morning he keeps telling me, 'Don't go to work. We'll have some more fun; don't worry about being caught for malingering.' The next day, the same thing, and the third day they came and took me right out of my bed. I went to court and got six months. I'll never get married again!" She was sobbing softly even as she told her story. The old one, wearing a kerchief, which kept me from seeing her face, had been taking care of her four grandchildren—their father had disappeared; their mother had died. She was a lavatory attendant. One morning, two of the children were running a high fever; she didn't go to work; the doctor didn't come. Two days later a delegate from the factory crew arrived with a policeman. Six months. What would they do with the children?

Bent double, my legs in pain, my ears ringing, sweating, with my eyes glued to the specters chatting on the other side of the tin partition, I listened closely to that woman, and what she said was a revelation for me. All that I had seen so far were prison phantoms, hallucinations seen through eyes half closed like the door in that Black Maria in Kiev. This was the Land of the Soviets, the homeland of the worker and the underdog. Once and for all . . . once and for all? . . . the dregs of my doubts, my qualms of uncertainty, my addiction to the dialectics of justification—war, historical necessity, "you can't make omelettes without breaking eggs," encirclement by the enemy, the country is backward, the dark legacy of the past—all that fell from me like dry scabs. Those backward, ignorant women were the only light in the darkness.

Even during my first ride in a Black Maria, on the way out of Kiev, listening intently to my inner voice, I repeated with that voice the seed of a future poem: "A base city," "A city of the base"—base because debased, because they let themselves be debased. In Zamarstynów we summoned up a vision of Poland—and that saved us from despair! Poland for centuries the "rampart of civilization." And Iranian, steppe Russia in convulsions, continually stirring up new hordes of invaders. It delighted us to recall the Soviet soldiers in their pointed Mongolian caps, reeking of birch tar and cheap rolling tobacco. We recited Mickiewicz's poems, his vision of a faceless Russia, a Russia without culture. At one time I had been repelled by the arrogance and false rhetoric of that patriotic *imagerie*, but in my cell in Zamarstynów, I touched the living, bleeding heart of it.

We were so vindictive, so small-minded! One of us would quote a striking analogy from Zatorski's book about Genghis Khan; someone else had read somewhere that Russians are a mixture of Mordvinians, Chuvash, Pechenegs, Khazars, Mongols, and Tartars. The filthy square of our cell floor became the battlefield for the enormous thousand-year war between the barbarians and civilization, between nomads and settlers. And bolstered by that far-ranging vision, we were ready to enter our Tartar captivity.

Even in that Black Maria in Kiev, observing those anguished Soviet citizens, I perceived, and not without a certain secret satisfaction, the comic contrast between their despairing faces and their overcoats that reached their feet and were made of stiff Soviet cloth, their angular visored caps. Now the laments of those women seemed to illuminate those other despairing faces as if with a painful inner light. Did I leave that Black Maria cured of my vengefulness?

How many prisons are there in Moscow? "Taganka," said the older of the two women when she got out at the third or fourth prison. Wet, shivering, my lungs barely working, my heart in my throat, I beat my fists in despair on the cold partition. The driver came around back, opened the rear door halfway, and shouted to me to stand by the door for a minute and get a breath of fresh air. I saw two small streets forming something like a square: high walls, a small, brightly lit gate at the corner—it too was a prison. The last woman got out there, still weeping. I was left alone. Why was I always the last to be taken? "Not far now," the driver called out to me, sounding encouraged himself.

22 IN LUBYANKA. DUNAYEVSKY AND OTHER CELL MATES. THE "IRON BARRIER." POLISH CATHOLICISM. SOVIET LAW. JEWS.

WAT: Then I was in the center of the city, but it was silent, empty; dark silhouettes moved along the walls. The gate opened, a heavy gate, its lock and metal squeaking. We passed through a second gate, and a third. A small dimly lit courtyard. I was taken through a larger court-yard to a large room on the ground floor. An officer in uniform, a middle-aged Jew wearing glasses, an intelligent face—the photogra-pher. He was polite, even friendly. He took the photographs and the fingerprints without saying a word. My escort had disappeared back at the station. Now I had a new guard, two of them. After taking the pic-tures, the photographer asked me a few friendly questions—where I was from, what I did. He nodded his head when I said I was a writer. "No need to worry then; they'll clear things up and let you out." Such sincere, human eyes, so friendly; then why did he lie?

I was searched closely but with no effort to humiliate me. There was no shouting, as at Zamarstynów. I was taken to the shower room. Blue green tiles! There were showers, the place was perfectly clean, hot and cold water. I could regulate the temperature myself; I wasn't scalded or doused with ice-cold water. No one hurried me; the guards waited pa-tiently, silently. Then I was searched again in complete silence, deli-cate fingers. Then forms, signatures—everything efficient, no wasted words, quick but not rushed, as in a movie.

And then finally the cell door opened in front of me, no grinding lock. And what luck—solitary! I didn't notice how small the cell was at first or that there were no windows. It was three paces long. A plank bed, clean bedding, a fresh sackcloth mattress, even a little pillow. A small window in the door. Above the door a powerful bulb protected by a grille. Too good to be true. I began to grow suspicious.

I remembered what a Georgian, who knew the GPU prisons of 1925, had told me in Brygidki to frighten me: "They'll send you to Moscow for sure. If you're lucky, you'll end up at Lubyanka. Lefortovo is the worst. And Sukhanovka is even worse. It's in the forest. No one comes out of there. But why should they torture you? You'll go in your cell, everything'll be neat and clean and beautiful, and then suddenly you'll start feeling hot—sweat will start pouring off you; you'll rip off your jacket, everything down to your underpants. Then a second or a quarter of a second later it's cold as Siberia—your teeth will start chattering, your hands will shake so badly you'll barely be able to get your clothes back on. You'll start running around the cell to warm up, and then it'll turn unbearably hot again."

I considered that a joke, but now I readied myself for it just to be on the safe side. I waited. It didn't become either hot or cold. The little window in the door went up, and someone in a white uniform on the other side handed me in my dinner on a tin tray. Thick pea soup, my favorite. Unbelievable. No more than three or four spoonfuls. The second course was a Russian mixed salad of finely chopped potatoes and vegetables, a vinegar and oil dressing, a few shreds of herring and two grapes. Not a large portion, but a human meal. The world of taste came back to life in me; I didn't have to suck imaginary flavor through a hunk of black bread. The waiter in the white uniform collected the tin tray and the spoon, both licked clean, and then he placed four or five cigarettes on the tray and, idiot that I was, I refused, saying I didn't smoke.

I hadn't slept so soundly, so grateful to creation, for a year, since that ill-fated September. I had a last facetious thought before falling asleep: wisdom ended with Leibniz. Not only wisdom, decency—we should be grateful to the Creator, and evil exists so that the good can be appreciated. But then I woke suddenly, as from a nightmare, ashamed of how content I had felt before falling asleep because of the pea soup, the shower, a kind word. The light from the bulb, though encased in iron grillwork, was exceedingly bright and somehow different from the bulbs in the other cells I'd been in. I had the impression it must have been an especially dark night outside for it to have been so bright in there. I told myself that this was just a case of nerves. There was a racket going on in my mind—voices arguing, fears, memories, regrets, contrition: there I was praising creation, and what could I see of it? And how about Ola and Andrzej? The darkness outside was as impenetrable as the light in my cell. The impenetrable stillness of my cell at the very heart of the night.

A day passed, then another. I would walk the three paces of the cell ten or twenty times, sit down on the plank bed, and try to think about my situation, to prepare myself for what might await me in Lubyanka. It was pointless. I didn't know anything. I couldn't assume anything; the reality would be different from anything I could imagine. There was no defense against anything there, but I could—and I should— prepare myself to defend my inner life. In point of fact, the aim of the entire procedure there was to degrade the inner life and make it empty—to muddle the mind with trivial nonsense, to debase your memory of your own past. You had to be vigilant in defending your inner life in that place where everything was tidy, discreet, quiet. But was I up to the task?

The air felt increasingly stifling to me when I went out to the latrine, even though there was ventilation there. If there had been a window in that solitary cell, I would certainly have had everything I needed. The third day passed, the same ritual, except that now they no longer offered me cigarettes. On the fourth day that provisional state of mine started becoming unbearable. The guards didn't respond to any question, any complaint. They were all like deaf-mutes.

They came and took me when I least expected it—in the early afternoon. A corridor, an elevator; long tidy corridors with woodwork along the bottom painted a poison green; the walls were a light color. When footsteps could be heard from a distance, my escorts would strike a key on their belt buckle; a human sound, it would break the spell. Twice they put my face to the wall. That meant another prisoner was being brought past. I knew that I wasn't allowed to see the faces of other prisoners, nor were they allowed to see mine. A well-ordered world. But where were they bringing me? A sinister stillness in the house of the dead. Full of grim premonitions, I might even have consented to walk forever through the labyrinth of Lubyanka with those two silent guards clanging their keys. Sometimes they would click their tongues. The guards' hands were warm, human hands radiating security. But the stillness was dead, and, instead of putting me at ease, it alarmed me. We stopped in front of cell number thirty-four.

A rather large cell, on the long side. Maybe twelve square meters, maybe thirteen. By the wall four iron beds with blankets, a night table by each one, an oak parquet floor waxed to a gleam, and a table with a large teapot on it by the window. And books! I counted them immediately—five thick volumes. Two men were playing chess. The third one was lying on his bed. A tiny Korean, he sat up and stared at me. An impression of harmony, human geometry. It looked like twelve square meters and only three prisoners; I would be the fourth. And clearly the cell had everything a person could need. They introduced themselves. The Korean made a low bow and then lay back on his bed, closing his eyes. The other two stopped playing chess and struck up a conversation. One was tall, stooped, with a refined look to his long, somewhat horsey face, the lips its only flaw, too soft, the lips of a gossipmonger, a gourmand. His movements were elegant but oddly jerky, like those of someone trying to remove his shirt with his jacket still on. This was

Evgeny Yakovlevich Dunayevsky, a writer and a translator of Persian poetry. The other man, a Pole, had been the chauffeur at the consulate in Kiev (or was it Kharkov?). He had a hounded look in his eyes, a network of deep creases on his face. The guard stood in the door, a middle-aged man, on the stout side, with a face like a large bun, bulging, kindly eyes, his uniform made of decent material. He pointed to the list of regulations on the door—my rights and my duties. He asked if I had any special wishes. I spread my hands.

I inherited my bed from General Anders [Polish general Władysław Anders], who had been taken from that cell not long before. Dunayevsky began by telling me about the general, speaking with enthusiasm of him; courageous, gallant, he was impeccable about treating his cell mates as equals and he bore the severe pain from his untreated wounds with dignity. The general was respected not only because of his reputation but because of his rank as well. "A general is a general," said Dunayevsky. And so he was given special rations. Milk every day, a meat dish for lunch, usually chopped meat. He was also taken to a cubicle where he was supposed to write a professional account of the September campaign. I found myself in one of those cubicles a couple of weeks later: you could write requests there, you were allowed to write to your investigator, the warden of the prison, the procurator, the presidum of the Supreme Soviet, and to Stalin himself. There was a table there, an inkwell, and a chair. An old jailer would hand you a sheet of paper, always with a sense of ceremony.

The white roll on the night table was Dunayevsky's. Like every prisoner in Lubyanka who had money on deposit or received money from home, Dunayevsky could buy things in the prison canteen. For seventy rubles—I think it was—he got two loaves of French bread, one hundred grams of butter, one hundred grams of sausage, cheese, onion, garlic, and, every once in a while, herring of a kind seldom available to Moscow's civilian population. Our canteen was somehow connected to the NKVD distribution network.

Dunayevsky initiated me into the routine: every ten days the librarian would come with a stack of books. The cell could have the same number of books as it had prisoners, though often the librarian would throw in an extra book. Every ten days they were taken to the showers and given a change of underwear and sheets. The prisoners had to keep the cell clean, wash the painted part of the walls, and every day they were given a chunk of wax and a cloth to polish the floor. The prison guards were polite, beyond reproach. A doctor could be seen every few days. There was a twenty-minute walk every day.

New books came that day. The librarian, who wore a light blue smock, was an old man, with the look of an anxious librarian on his face. He stood in the half-open door holding a stack of books with a guard beside him. Clearly a trustee, the librarian waited patiently until we had made our selection. Not an easy decision either; they were all excellent books, but Dunayevsky had instructed me to be careful to choose the thickest volumes so they'd last the whole ten days. A conflict between quality and quantity. But why do they give prisoners books in Lubyanka? For me that's an enigma, a *mysterium tremendum*. I had a constant inkling of some menace lurking behind all those amenities, those humane conditions. What was in those books that they gave them to the damned?

I awoke the next morning full of life, refreshed. I literally felt at home. Breakfast: black coffee, the daily portion of bread, and two lumps of sugar! Dunayevsky borrowed the obliging guard's pocketknife to cut his bread into pedantically even slices, then buttered them, laying a slice of sausage on one, cheese on another, his gestures pontifical—you could tell they never varied. With the same sort of gesture he broke off a good-sized piece of his prison bread and, along with two chunks of garlic, handed them very ceremoniously to Stanisław, the chauffeur, who didn't understand the game and snatched them greedily. Prospero and Caliban, the full and the hungry, in one cell at Lubyanka.

Dunayevsky persuaded me to take fifteen-minute walks around the cell, not only for exercise but for morale. I had grown slothful from idleness at Zamarstynów. I flipped feverishly through the books. I remember the first batch quite clearly: a volume of Tolstoy's moral and religious letters; the first volume of Proust's *Remembrance of Things Past*, the Academy edition, with a foreword by Lunacharsky; Selma Lagerlöff's Neapolitan novel; a thick volume of Nekrasov's prose; a selection of Machiavelli's letters, another excellent Academy publication. I was beside myself with joy. Dunayevsky and I were the only ones in the cell who read. The Korean didn't know Russian, and Stanisław, the chauffeur, had no desire to read, or maybe he was boycotting Russian books. He did speak Russian smoothly, sometimes even with me. He probably couldn't tear himself away from his own thoughts and worries even for a second. At that time my own thoughts were in such disarray that for a while it was enough just to stroke the pages, some smooth, some ragged, to gaze at rows of black letters on white paper, and to breathe in that library smell.

We were given a chunk of wax and a cloth, and we each took a turn polishing the floor, which was more than it needed. Dunayevsky closed his eyes halfway in delight; his movements lost their angularity, becoming fluid, dancelike. My legs were rubbery at first and I was sluggish, but later on I acquired a taste for polishing the floor, a pleasure to the legs, like a skating rink.

I admired Dunayevsky. He bore himself handsomely, with dignity. I identified what seemed to me typical about him: he was surely the only child of cultured and well-to-do Moscow Jews—patriarchal kindness, cultivated artistic tastes—and he was maintaining his individuality in Soviet prisons. The Korean was built like a sculpture from the period of Indian Hellenism. Subtle physical articulation—the hands, feet, and fingers looked sculpted—his complexion the color of ivory. A youthful body. How old was he? Thirty, fifty? One side of Dunayevsky's body was crooked. He was good-looking, but he was disfigured by that one side that was lower and more protruding than the other. A flaw like that in an esthete disturbed me—it had to be compensated for by some resentment.

The afternoon meal was consommé—there wasn't much, but it was tasty—and, for the main course, dark buckwheat kasha! Just four spoonfuls, it left you wanting more; it left you with regret and a whetted appetite. If only there'd been five spoonfuls! One spoonful of buckwheat kasha could change your *Weltempfindung*—"existence determines consciousness"; how easy it is to rule a nation when there are shortages of everything. That meal only left me hungry, but, at the same time, I savored the taste of it, and somehow, in a peculiar way, the memory of what I'd tasted made me full. Stanisław, however, kept saying, "I'm hungry, I'm hungry." A wolfish gleam flared in his burned-out eyes. I had seen him in the showers, and he really was nothing but skin and bones. But he was small and slender in build and he'd been in prison only a year, not much longer than I had. He was one of those skinny people with appetites like wolves.

I was suffering from hunger, too. I looked greedily at Dunayevsky's shelf and averted my eyes when he was eating. He had a nasty way of eating, the only ugly thing about him (apart from his crooked side). He would methodically chew and rechew his food, his soft lips looking even softer. Clearly, my body still had some reserves from before the war; people are amazingly camel-like by nature. Much later, in Saratov prison, and to a greater degree in Ili, in Kazakhstan, I experienced what chronic hunger means, when it's taken permanent hold on your brain, constantly sucking at you like a suckling. Stanisław's flagrant hunger irritated me; it seemed indecent there.

The relationship between Dunayevsky and Stanisław struck me as strange as far as food went. I knew that in communist prisons sharing was a punishable offense, but Dunayevsky was a kindhearted person and he had deep compassion for Stanisław's suffering and, besides, he liked him. Still, Dunayevsky would dole Stanisław the skimpiest portion—a quarter of his prison bread ration, a clove of garlic, a thin slice of onion, and sometimes a sliver of herring. Dunayevsky always made too much of it, as if he were holding the food on high. But the chauffeur did not repay him with hatred; on the contrary, he treated Dunayevsky with respect and esteem.

Another mystery: the three of us were hungry, and, as I was to learn, not even the friendliest investigator could be of any help with that. But Dunayevsky had first-rate food because he had money, and General Anders had been fed like a human being because he was a general. And so it would appear that hunger is not specifically used at Lubyanka as a means of terror but was part of the general routine of the system whose secret I may never fathom.

The guard came to the cell after the afternoon meal. I studied him from close up: stout, over fifty, a paterfamilias, the broad face of a down-to-earth Russian merchant. In a pleasant tenor voice, he said, "You've eaten; now get some rest." We lay down on our beds, one person reading, another meditating, staring glassy-eyed into space or dozing off. Unable to read that day, I lay on my bed staring senselessly up at the ceiling. My excitement had died down; I was depressed again, even more than usual—there were too many mysteries. I could literally feel my weary cortex. I didn't think about anything, I didn't care about anything, I wasn't trying to detect torture lurking behind everything; I was just weary. I must have looked like a broken man because before I was even aware of it, Kim, the Korean, was standing beside me, lightly stroking my brow, and with one finger of his other hand, touching his own chest then mine while repeating, "*Chryuki akani kari.*" Dunayevsky, a linguist, the only one in the cell able to talk with Kim, translated for me, "There's a flame that burns inside the chest."

Chryuki akani kari—he said that to each of us often, but, apart from this one time, he was always referring to himself. I learned Kim's story from Dunayevsky. Fifteen years before, he had been a peddler and had lived in Manchuria near the Soviet border, which he crossed often carrying his goods; he had a permanent pass. In the end he was arrested as a Japanese spy. He had a wife and four or five children at home. After a couple of years in a camp he had escaped. They caught him at the same border point. He escaped again and headed in the same direction. Another camp, a more severe one. After a few years, he was transferred because of his model behavior and Stakhanovite labor to a penal colony in the far north. He escaped, but that time he headed west. He covered thousands of kilometers without knowing the language, in his quilted camp jacket, with no money. By a miracle he reached Moscow, where he went to the Japanese embassy. He barely had one foot out the door when they grabbed him and brought him to that cell in Lubyanka.

He still looked young; all the escapes hadn't left any trace on him. He spoke of his family as if time had stood still, as if his children were still little and were waiting for his return to grow up. He had left his house in 1925 loaded down, as usual, with his wares. He'd said to his wife and children, "See you tomorrow or in three days, a week."

Dunayevsky did not know Korean, but he was a linguist by calling and was the only one who could understand the way Kim spoke Russian. And, besides, Kim's fifteen-year odyssey could be summed up in just a few words: camp, escape. family. And *chryuki akani kari!*

Kim was taken away a couple of weeks later, this time, I assumed, to a camp from which even he could not escape.

After we rested, Dunayevsky would play chess with Stanisław. They played halfheartedly, for something to do. The game bored me.

Later on we'd be taken out for our walk. Only then did I get a good sense of the staircase: a wide staircase surrounded by a thick steel net from top to bottom. According to Dunayevsky, it had been installed after Savinkov's suicide jump. While he is under investigation, a prisoner's life is priceless goods; the warden is held responsible for every head. After sentencing, that same prisoner becomes one figure in a calculus of many millions and sometimes does not even reach his destination—people who died of starvation were simply tossed off the trains.

A few months later, when the cold, rainy days of early fall began, we took our walks on the roof of Lubyanka for a week. When we returned to the courtyard from our walks, we noticed that the drain pipes had been raised level with the third floor. The rain lashed the walls; chunks of plaster would fall off in the course of the day. Later on I learned the purpose behind that: during his walk time, one acrobatic prisoner had shinned up the drain pipe and leaped from the highest point to the ground.

The evening meal was the same tasty food, in somewhat skimpier portions. I had eaten my bread ration, and this time I kept each morsel in my mouth as long as possible so that its taste and substance dissolved even before I swallowed it. Islands and continents in my buccal cavity, a wealth of sensations in each square micron of my mucous membranes. There was an additional element to the evening meal—the despairing awareness that there would be no more food that day. Tomorrow there would, but you died there each night.

The morning trip to the latrine left no impression on me. The chief thing we thought about in the morning was washing up. And we were still full of voices and ghosts from our dreams. In the evening, on the

192

other hand, one's powers of observation grew keener. The lower half of the walls was painted black in the vast shower rooms; toward the rear were three very steep black cement stairs that extended the entire width of the room. There were five round holes on the top level. While the three of us washed our hands with tap water, Dunayevsky was still squatting over the center hole. He rose up like a dervish and came back down on his heels, massaging his stomach methodically from bottom to top. Those high black stairs, the solitary figure of Dunayevsky, his solemn gestures—a hero on stage, a modern production of a classic. At one moment he propped his head on his hand, and I realized that he looked like Rembrandt's *King Saul* in the Rotterdam museum; all he needed was a beard, a crown, and a spear. The throne he had.

It was only then, after coming back from the latrine, that I immersed myself in reading Proust. The translation was so-so, but I knew the first page by heart and could almost see that early, nearly marginless edition before my eyes: "Longtemps je me suis couché de bonne heure. Parfois, à peine ma bougie éteinte, mes yeux se fermaient si vite que je n'avais pas le temps de me dire je m'endors"—followed at once by a cascade of Proustian sentences with their semicolons and colons. The cadence of the French replaced the Russian and was with me through the last word in the volume. It calmed me; its undulations made me ready to sleep. Que je n'aurais pas le temps de me dire je m'endors. After I'd read the first three pages, we were told to go to sleep, but the light couldn't be turned off. We had to lie on our backs like naughty children, with our hands outside the blanket, eyes closed. In spite of that, I fell fast asleep quickly, a healthy sleep. Before falling asleep, I listened with pleasure to my cell mates snoring—as opposed to Zamarstynów, where all human sounds—snoring, farting, whispers—had irritated me. Things can't be so bad if people are snoring, praise God.

A final incident from that day rich in impressions. During the night the guard woke me up with a light touch, gestured for me to keep my hands outside the blanket, then left silently without waking anyone. Even though I'd been searched so many times already, could I have smuggled in some implement for taking my own life?

The next day the same routine. I decided to treat the books like bread—with studied economy. I counted the number of pages in all the volumes; they had to last for ten days, and so no more than such and such number of pages per day. Zamarstynów had trained me in will power. Stanisław lacked practice; he had gone right from freedom to the palatial conditions of Lubyanka. He hadn't learned how to eat and he didn't know how to read.

On the third day my own memories came back to me in waves, for the first time. They really were waves; no sooner had one reached the shore of consciousness than the next one would break over it. Memories of lost happiness—the happier the time I remembered, the more painful it was. But the pain was really the pain of the present brought out of the mists and clouds by the brilliant light of lost happiness. And so when I would pick up my reading of Proust in the afternoon, my own memories and Proust's would match like the halves of a banknote torn in two. And in the narrator's tears as a child each night when parting with his mother, tears that he realized when writing would be somewhere deep in him for the rest of his life, I recognized my own tears that I had concealed from myself.

So, apart from reading, polishing the floor, the walks, dealing with the routine, ruminating on memories, or thinking, I'd spent the whole day talking in a whisper with Dunayevsky. I said that Dunayevsky was quiet, but in fact from time to time he would interject a question when he didn't understand something. In the evening I would feel Stanisław's hostile gaze on me. I thought I knew what it meant: of course, two Jews getting their heads together. But I don't think Stanisław was an anti-Semite, and I was very sensitive to that after Zamarstynów, much earlier than that. This was something else: intellectuals!

The Polish proletarians' typical hatred of the intellectual seems to me deeper than their hatred for the middle class and the gentry. It may not be chance that it was a Pole, Machajski, a revolutionary intellectual, who preached the extermination of the intelligentsia to the point where Lenin had to condemn his excesses. Many years later in People's Poland, I observed that the workers hated the party not only because of its alienness, its betrayal of the nation, but also because they considered communism a movement of intellectuals, the party cloaking itself in the name of the workers—all those stylized images of the worker and the presence of former workers at the top only fueled that hatred.

That's nothing new. In 1932, of the twenty prisoners in our cell in Warsaw Central, the only Polish proletarian was a sandhog. The boys from Murdziel imitated his accent, his gestures, even his voice—they made a fetish of him; after all, they were in prison for his sake. The sand dredger himself stumbled diligently through brochures and books and listened closely to our lectures, but you had to see his contempt, even disgust, when he looked at his mentors. That's probably a typically Polish phenomenon. There's no analogy to it in Russia; there the party hates the intellectuals and the *urks* hate them, considering intellectuals part of the ruling class.

Stanisław's hostility toward me increased every day, and some of it was my fault. I had all the failings of the intellectual, one of which was particularly galling: I couldn't talk with people who didn't interest me.

And Stanisław's fixations also irritated me. Oh, I still didn't know how to act in prison.

Stanisław was very typical of the Polish peasant, the worker of peasant origin. He was too hard a nut for the NKVD to crack. (And here you can see how much Broniewski was of the people. A Pole of the people, though he was of gentry origin.) Stanisław could not be cracked because he had only one idea. Or rather two. Ideas that were very limited and very just. They were all that mattered to him; he didn't want any part of anything else. One idea was that he wanted them to let him go back to Poland. And so they told him that the Germans were in Poland, that they were murdering Poles, and so on. They were very gentle with him.

At certain stages, if a case isn't serious and there are no political needs involved, honorable people were well treated by the NKVD, respectfully. I have the impression that this was also characteristic of Stalin's style. And that's why he spared Pasternak. Stalin tried to throw people like that into the mud, but if the mud didn't stick to them, Stalin would be inclined to spare them. That happened during the purges too. He destroyed only the people who had let themselves be dragged into the mud in their former lives, before their arrest, or when they were in prison, like all those leaders, those old Bolsheviks, who were up to their elbows in blood, mud. That's my view of Stalin, a very risky view. I don't insist on it, but I deeply believe it to be true.

And so that was one of Stanisław's ideas: let me go home. The other idea was like something out of Kleist, a rather German idea actually: the sense of law and order. You had no right to arrest me because I worked in the consulate. Of course, you declared war on Poland, but members of the diplomatic corps and the diplomatic service are sent back to their country or allowed to go to neutral countries. Other than that, all his days and talk were full of his wolfish hunger. A hunger that sucked away at you, which I hadn't known yet but would know later on in Kazakhstan.

I still wasn't being called in for interrogation. For the time being I was glad of that—I could rest. But day after day passed. There was a rankling anxiety at the back of my mind—why had I been brought there when the investigation of my case had been completed, the charges formulated, the sentence ten years, five years, whatever. And there I was in that elite Lubyanka, with all that *moderne* comfort. Was my case being reviewed? Or, on the contrary, would there be a new investigation, this time one much more severe and wearing?

In Lwów I had been constantly surprised that the investigators made no mention of the most sinister thing: *The Literary Monthly*, my connections, my collaboration with so many people who had rotted in jail a long time ago—Jasieński, Hempel, Stande, Wandurski, Warski, Żarski, Fenigstein-Dolecki, and so many other leaders and ideologues. There seemed to be a taboo on the subject. Only once, at the end of my investigation, did they read me Jerzy Borejsza's deposition that stated that in Lwów I had "forbidden" him to speak badly of our Polish colleagues in front of the Soviets. To which Borejsza had modestly added, "Wat was the founder and editor of the magazine *The Literary Monthly*, whose contributors included (the names I just mentioned) . . . who were exposed in the USSR as Polish counterintelligence agents." That sentence alone could earn you the death penalty, but my investigators did not pick up on it. Evidently it was too grave a matter for a first lieutenant. It was only in Lubyanka that the dance started.

Meanwhile, Kim's place had been taken by a new prisoner, a Pole. Now that there were three Poles, would Stanisław let down his guard? I was repelled by my first impression of the new man. He looked perfect for the role of Tartuffe—even his coat, long as a cassock. All his clothes were covered with dust, threadbare; he smelled of church. A very pale face. His eyes were usually lowered and they had no light at all in them, eyes that seemed to see everything, then nothing. As soon as Kim's bed was pointed out to him, he sat down on the edge of it as if fingering an invisible rosary, his lips moving: he was singing hymns or reciting texts from the missal. His piety was overdone. My negative impression of him increased when he told me his last name was Januszajtis. He was the general's brother. General Januszajtis had been hated in my cell at Zamarstynów, blamed for founding an organization of high school students to fight the Red Army.

How mistaken our first impressions can be! This Januszajtis was a gentle, modest, serene person. From his infrequent confidences, I gathered that he had been through an exceptionally long and severe interrogation in connection with his brother, the general. I had no doubt that he had shown steadfast resistance even though he was clearly cowardly at heart and stuttered when he spoke. In spite of his dire experience, he did not flaunt his "forgiveness" of his interrogators' sins; vengeance and hatred simply did not breed in his pure soul. He was respectful and carefully deferential to each of us; he had compassion for others and their problems even though he had strayed in from another world, a world where he thought only of God. He was a religious zealot, no question of that.

Mistrustful, I was critical of him for a long time. Moreover, that was a period when the charms of religion had absolutely no effect on me. Just the opposite. Still, from one day to the next I grew increasingly convinced that Januszajtis was pure and simple, that he had no religious exaltation about him, that affectation that repelled me in people otherwise saintly.

I couldn't explain my own state. In Zamarstynów, I had been caught up by the religious atmosphere in the cell—me, an unbeliever—and so irresistibly that when hearing them sing the songs devoted to Mary, I would cry in my little corner, all the unhappier because I wanted to believe and could not. In Lubyanka there was nothing left of the religious feelings I'd had in Zamarstynów, and I was moved only esthetically by Januszajtis's piety—meaning from outside, from the standpoint of an observer—but my heart was not moved. So then, had my religious experiences in Zamarstynów been essentially superficial, a literary impressionistic mood? I couldn't accept that. Had that been the dry time, the dark night of the soul known to the mystics? No, it wasn't that either.

At that time I was suffering from terrible migraines. The pain was battering at my temples; I had to put my reading aside. Januszajtis, who didn't seem to know Russian well, offered to read aloud to me. I don't know why, but that sent me into a blind rage, and I asked him straight out if he was a priest.

By then I had great respect for him in general, but I was constantly rough on him; I couldn't help it. His sheeplike serenity irritated me often, and I mocked him to myself: "A Polish Catholic version of Prince Myshkin!" But the contrast between Januszajtis's blandness and the beauty and fantasy in the Russian *innocent* Myshkin activated my inferiority complex toward Russians, which, after all, is the deeply concealed impulse behind Poland's ostentatious contempt for Muscovites. Angry at how I was acting, I became twice as rough on Januszajtis, all the more irksome because he chose not to notice.

So I asked him point blank in a moment of particular malice if he was a priest. No, he said, he wasn't; he had graduated from a seminary but he couldn't take holy orders because he was an epileptic. From then on, I avoided talking with him, afraid to bring on an attack by saying the wrong things.

The epileptic attack Januszajtis had was a mild one, with nearly no convulsions, scarcely any froth. He simply fell without a moment's notice. There was no external cause; the cell was peacefully quiet. A short while before our guard had spoken his sacramental words, "you've eaten, now rest." Dunayevsky and I were both reading; Stanisław's thoughts were far away, fixed on his two obsessive ideas. By the way, he didn't engage in any long conversations, even with Januszajtis; he was just a loner. Nothing had been happening for quite some time; no one was being summoned for interrogation. But like a scene from childhood, white flakes of snow were falling outside the window that was screened by a slanting shield. It must have been a big storm and there we were, well provided for in the very heart of the terror.

If epilepsy is diabolic, then Januszajtis's demon was as bland and inconspicuous as its victim. He was taken away maybe an hour after his attack and never returned to our cell.

He was replaced by a young pimply faced Soviet sailor. How could that be, a semiliterate common deckhand in our elite club? Even the all-knowing Dunayevsky couldn't fathom it.

The sailor hummed incessantly, for days on end, even though the guard had admonished him on his first day, good-naturedly but severely: "No singing here!" He took turns humming vulgar little ditties, *chastushkis,* and solemn Soviet marches. His humming was obsessive to the point of being pathological. He would start as soon as he woke up, and he would fall asleep humming. On the whole, during my six and a half years in Russia, I was struck by the importance singing had in the life of the Russian people. Of course, the Russians, like the Neapolitans, are a singing people. It wasn't only that people sought some relief, some escape from their cares in singing, but it worked the other way too; they sang to accommodate themselves to the system because "a person can live anywhere," and by singing a person could merge with the system in "mystical participation." Perhaps there was something analogous here to the black slaves in America, and so those obscene *chastushkis* and grand military marches may have been the Soviet equivalent of Negro spirituals.

The sailor's story was quite banal. He had gotten lost in the taverns along a canal in Copenhagen. He liked everything there and was most enchanted by the shapely girls—"We don't have them like that in Russia"—girls who, moreover, drove to those taverns on bicycles, the height of culture. On the fourth day he'd had enough of foreign *urks* and foreign culture; it had never crossed his mind to forsake his country, but meanwhile his ship had left without him. He made his way to the Soviet consulate, no easy task. They understood. They laughed paternally at his adventures and sent him back home on the first fishing boat out. The boat had scarcely set to sea when they put him in chains and shoved him into the hold where he was fed on bread and water. He had already been through the first few interrogations, accused of having been recruited by British intelligence. "You're a big fish," they shouted at him. I took comfort in that because that was precisely how my second investigator had classified me, and so that was clearly part of police routine.

The sailor thought that everything that had happened to him was not only natural but even fair, for he had done the forbidden. Later on, when I was out of prison, I observed innumerable times that in the young Russians' minds there was an iron barrier between the large and the small prohibitions. The large prohibitions were taboo and were surrounded by appropriate numinosity, as in primeval times. But by breaking the small prohibitions a person proved his toughness and defied the good manners that he thought had been condemned by history; this was the compensation for obeying the taboos.

In 1944, in Ili, in Kazakhstan, a disabled veteran I knew raved about the riches and pleasures to be had in the small Bulgarian towns in which he had been during one campaign. "Would you like to live there?" I asked. "Not for anything in the world. There's no freedom there." It cost me little effort to determine that what he had in mind was the freedom to get blind drunk in a public place, to spit and blow his nose on the floor, to shove old men and women aside in a streetcar, to curse without restraint and so forth. Other freedoms were not only of no use to him but would encumber him and, worse, would force him to make his own free decisions about his life, which he had been taught to relinquish forever. In that way, Stalin's paternalistic terror reduced a few Soviet generations to the level of the Guarani Indians in the eighteenth-century Jesuit communistic republic.

The mental barrier I am speaking of here could, however, be shifted. For example, in 1942 the word *zhid* [Russian for "kike"] was under a rigorous taboo, but two years later, the Polish Jews deported to Ili were showered with that insult—and from time to time with stones as well—by children and the teenagers from the local high school. Today, in 1965, those Young Pioneers from Ili are young engineers, literary critics, apparatchiks. People in the West who are not aware of that mental "iron barrier" will fail to understand much of the relationship between mentality and ideology, or much of the young people's rebellion in the USSR.

In order to liberate themselves from Stalin's heritage in their souls, they must first "detach themselves from the enemy." Like a snake shedding its skin in the springtime, they must throw off not only any concern with Stalinism, communism, revisionism, but those ugly words themselves. In that sense, the free people are not Andrei Voznesensky, Yevtushenko, or Tarsis but people like Joseph Brodsky, the Solzhenitsyn of *Matryona's House*, the Tertz-Sinyavsky of his last (apolitical!) works. Political thinking has become so distorted and corrupted during this long, long half century that one has to begin by tearing it out, roots and all, from one's soul to prepare the ground for a healthy and humane politics that fosters the *virtu* of the free citizen. Anticommunists in the West do not understand this. Of course, acts of political rebellion, and, even more so, a political rebellion in the mind, are useful things because they can squeeze concessions from the rulers, but, nevertheless, in the Russian Empire those rebellions will remain abortive, powerless to touch off a movement of the masses for many years to come. Personally, I see the hope of Russia not in them but in life itself, existence *(Sein)* in an utterly different spiritual space.

How delighted Joseph Brodsky was as an adolescent to discover John Donne, and what beautiful fruit that discovery bore! And how effective Sinyavsky was (in his aphorisms) in liberating himself from the nightmare of anti-Stalinist neuroses, renewing himself at the sources of ancient Russian folk religiosity! What great inner beauty emanates from Solzhenitsyn's folk-Christian *caritas!* How moving was Pasternak's identification with the suffering of the whole, vast, long-suffering Russian people! And Akhmatova setting herself and the world aflame with the depths of suffering while waiting outside her son's prison! Russian literature had not created any values like those since Blok's "The Twelve," a period of nearly fifty years. Enlightened young people in the Soviet Union know the miseries and monstrosities of communism incomparably better than Western Sovietologists do, but every word of authentic religion, idealistic thought, disinterested beauty in poetry or ethics falls on fertile ground there. And though I personally esteem Beckett, Gombrowicz, Genet, Sartre, all that literary strip-tease can only blight the young shoots sprouting there.

Communist Poland cannot be compared to Russia, since it never actually went through Stalinism. The process of Stalinization, though accelerated, lasted barely four years (1949–1953) as opposed to thirty years in Russia; similarly, Poland's mainstay was not in revolts but in "disengaging from the enemy," specifically, the country's overwhelming Catholicism, precisely that parochial, obscurantist, and often vulgar Polish Catholicism, which, however, purified itself and grew deeper "in the catacombs" and truly found its shepherd in the person of the Primate, Cardinal Wyszyński. That Catholicism made the Polish soul impervious to the magic of "ideology" and the knout of praxis, and it was not the rebellious writers and revisionists who caused the Polish October but—apart from Stalinism's crumbling power and cohesiveness—the steadfast, constant, unyielding mental resistance of that Catholic nation, its "dwelling" in transcendence.

Let's go back to the cell. If I keep launching into digressions and often needless rationalizations, it's not only the result of my bad habits or my literary failings, but also because it's not easy in the least to return to prison voluntarily. To return to prison after twenty-five years by

200

the faithful exercise of memory involves my entire being and is almost a physical act; it requires the greatest concentration I'm capable of, and I'm already so much older now, so much more devastated . . .

Back at Zamarstynów, I had already begun to theorize that the fundamental but unwritten assumption of Soviet law is that everything that can be conceived is possible and everything that is possible is real! To that knotty principle a simple working principle can be added: "Give us a man and we'll find a case." There you have the pattern of Soviet legal behavior, in its entirety, from A to Z. Two things interest me most here: one, rather trivial, concerns the dislocation of concepts that is typical of communism: for example, winged lions had populated poetry from time immemorial whereas they were barred from science and practical knowledge, at least after the end of the Middle Ages. It's the other way around under communism: driven out of poetry under the lash, the chimeras set up housekeeping in the criminal code. Similarly, all myths and ordinary lies had to be given an appearance of verisimilitude in the Soviet novel—that's what's meant by realism; the most adroit socialist realists were paid well indeed for that. On the other hand, in the judiciary, verisimilitude was branded malicious counterrevolutionary hypocrisy, and the judges (as opposed to writers and Chekists) were paid poorly.

Another thing that was of particular interest to me, a meatier issue, was the peculiar crossbreeding of post-Hegelianism and the "primitive mentality"—it would be monstrous if it weren't so comical! By means of a few mental operations, the Soviet dialecticians descended from that confounded Hegel's "Everything rational is real" into the very depths of paralogical folk thinking. Long ago, and reasoning in the same manner, people lynched the village witches in Penza and Salem. All the diabolical qualities that the popular imagination ascribed to the Jews, for example, were now ascribed to the "enemies of the people" by Soviet judges and members of the Komsomol. It's possible to conceive of a folkloric sabbath in which the Jew is the "enemy of the people." And indeed a Jewish "enemy of the people" was treated worse under investigation than a non-Jewish one, even though there was no shortage of Jews among the Chekists. And that fact carried an additional burden, for since some Jews had attained the honor of being among the "best sons of the people," every Jew who was an "enemy of the people" was doubly cursed, for he was also an ingrate and an apostate. A Jewish NKVD man would vent particular rancor on Judas-Jews, the disgrace of Holy Russia, and he would be more ferocious the more that he felt he was himself a Judas and a disgrace to Judaism, the more that he felt that way at night, in the depths of his conscience. I committed an error in saying "at night" because the Chekists worked at night, perhaps not only to disorient and harass their victims but also to protect the torturer himself from night's spectral companion—conscience.

There were exceptions, of course, and often a Jewish investigator would, if he couldn't save a fellow Jew, at least try to ease his misery. In communist Poland especially, there were many such Maranos, as I called them, at the top of the party and it's probably due to them that I was not ground totally under.

In Zamarstynów when my first investigator made an insulting remark about me as a Jew, I reminded him of Stalin's telegram—in 1931 I think it was—to the American Jews, which was published in *Pravda:* "Anti-Semitism is a vestige of cannibalism and punished in the USSR by death!" Raising his fist, the investigator answered spontaneously: "Then why don't you respect Stalin!" Khrushchev's splendid explanation for the slaughter he wreaked in Budapest (he said this in 1963, I think) is worth bringing in here: Under Nicholas I, Russian troops suppressed a revolution in Budapest in 1848, and we had to wipe that stain from our honor and suppress counterrevolution in Budapest! I don't see any of Lenin's sophistry here; this was not a statement made in bad faith. It had a sincere ring to it (and was all the worse for that!): when reaching for the higher spheres of history, Khrushchev's peasant common sense fell at once under the spell of primitive paralogic. In his Paris lectures, Mickiewicz told the story about Genghis Khan ordering the massacre of a hundred thousand citizens of Bukhara, which had voluntarily surrendered to him. Genghis Khan said to the elders of the city: "You must have sinned greatly against God if he sent Genghis Khan down on you." You Russians must have sinned greatly against God if he sent Stalin down on you. Stalin could have said that himself, in a quiet moment of conscience—insofar as he had one.

To end this ugly inventory with a non-ugly example: in my cell in Alma-Ata, my bandit friends told me about a kulak who was felled by a stroke that hit him like a bolt of lightning while he was out working the fields. When he was cured of his paralysis and had regained his speech, the kulak explained that God the Father had appeared at that moment and said, "There is no God. Go and preach that to the ends of the earth." That happened in the late twenties. He abandoned his farm and his family and set off into the Russian heartland, going from village to village preaching. Always in danger of being lynched by peasants, he was cruelly beaten by religious people and betrayed to the authorities by the unbelievers. For a long time the authorities tolerated his peculiar brand of atheism but finally exiled him to a copper mine in Siberia, where he was murdered by *urks*. A defender of the faith and the Living God.

*This chapter is made up of taped sections, a separate sketch found in
Wat's papers, and a part of the taped text that he reworked.*

WAT: We had no communist literature the entire time, no Marxist
literature at all. I was in many cells where prisoners were given books,
at least a few, and everyone confirmed that they were never given that
sort of book. My fellow prisoners had a very intelligent explanation for
that: it was simply to keep the investigators, who were not terribly intelligent, from being nailed to the wall by Marxist arguments. There
was no shortage, however, of religious literature. I read Solovyov there
and a great many others. I read the church fathers, St. Augustine on
the Kingdom of God.

As I'll explain later, the books I read in Lubyanka made for one of
the greatest experiences of my life. Not because they allowed me an
escape but because, to a certain extent, they transformed me, influenced and shaped me greatly. It was the way I read those books; I came
at them from a completely new angle. And from then on I had a completely new understanding, not only of literature, but of everything.

Literature is insight and synthesis, which means that poetry, ultimately, is heroic. Naked, weak, hungry, trembling, endangered by all
the elements, all the beasts and demons, the cave men performed that
act of heroism for consolation, in the deepest sense of the word. And at
that time there in Lubyanka this seemed to me the essence of literature
and the source of its legitimacy in the world. Consolation for a weak,
naked cave man.

A Sketch Found in Wat's Papers

As I've already mentioned, *Swann's Way* was in that first batch of
books. My first book in a year. To my surprise and, later, almost to my
horror, I realized that my entire value system had not been destroyed
but had simply been left outside the prison walls. All my knowledge of
people and society, all the circuitous paths of psychological inquiry, my
industrious study of the passions, my oversophistication—everything
in which I had taken so much delight—in Lubyanka seemed atro-
phied, pretentious, and irritating at times. After the misery of Zamar-

stynów what did I care about a satire on the Vedurins' salon? What did I care about a world enclosed in a salon like a ship in a bottle; what did I care about lifeless thoughts turned into elegant conversation? It was absorbing, of course, and helped to kill time. But everything in that book that was not poetry, that did not have poetry's energy and movement, was just costume drama.

Swann's Way did not emerge diminished from that reading. Quite the contrary, I was more charmed than ever by the power of its energy, its beauty of movement. The poetry in Swann's Way made everything intimate, an "inward vibration," and was all the more unusual in that it played off the outermost layers, the epidermis of the sensibility. And what was of more importance to me was that in its experience of time past, the book was, first and foremost, a state of constant agony in which nothing had yet died but everything was dying. An unbroken moment suspended between life and death, a final breath hellishly protracted beyond all measure—it is that alone that gives the book its depth and stirs the reader to his depths; without this, Proust's entire work would be no more than an enormous fresco of vanity, in both senses of the word. While reading Swann's Way, I began to discover a model for the agony I was suffering in prison, and Proust's long sentences and time periods recaptured their original power for me. An exchange of form and power—the archetypal relationship between author and reader. As if in mockery, it was everything flimsy about Proust—his quasi-Balzacian side, his descriptions of human life in "decadent capitalism"—that Anatoly Lunacharsky praised in his introduction and that was seen as the sole justification for publishing the book. Like all Marxist critics, Lunacharsky, the last of the Bolshevik esthetes, did not write about the work itself but treated it as a sociological "trot." When reading his introduction, I realized that I was repelled as much by communism's reduction of everything to the flat and the linear as by its atrocities.

By the way, the clichés used in introductions by Marxists—"subjectively reactionary but objectively progressive"; "a genius conditioned by the limitations of his time" or "his class," and so on—are sordid and arrogant, but, after all, they have saved and continue to save literature in those countries where, as Gobineau put it, "the inquisitor functions as a critic."

Machiavelli, in the Academy edition, was also in that first batch of books. Not long after that I happened on a large selection of his letters, a prerevolutionary edition containing his correspondence and a detailed biography. At one point I had read Machiavelli like tout le monde, through the prism of the epithet "Machiavellian"—"the genius of political corruption," "the severe masculine world of the condottierri . . .

204

virtu . . ." Machiavelli the poet came as a real revelation to me in Lubyanka. Not because of his verse itself, which was rather weak, but because he was a poet. "Dichterisch wohnt der Mensch auf dieser Erde" (Hölderlin). A poet of action, Machiavelli tried to make his earth *dichterisch.*

That book came to me at just the right moment. On the dunghill of Zamarstynów I had trained myself in hatred and disgust for politics, all and any. We had seen its ugly pockmarked face; it had come to the old refined city of Lwów from the Bolshevik steppes, the plains of Muscovy, and that was the source of our suffering. We heaped abuse on the politics of Poland, on the politics of the West, embroiled in a thousand petty intrigues like those that tore Machiavelli's Italy apart, that weakness that had helped give rise to two monstrous waves of barbarism.

It would be an exaggeration to say that reading Machiavelli in Lubyanka cured me of the hatred and disgust for politics I had acquired in Zamarstynów. That still comes back in me to this day and sometimes literally chokes me and makes me stammer; to write on political subjects is torture for me, but I was always doomed to have to speak my piece. The power and glory of reading come from those moments of illumination, when it clarifies the obscure, when it breaks things into their parts, but it is powerless against strong feelings. Once strong feelings have taken root in us, reading can only influence the direction they grow in, inhibiting or enhancing them, raising them to a higher level. Reading Machiavelli restored my equilibrium; I regained my sense of proportion and distinction, albeit sporadically—and what more could I have asked for? I learned to distinguish between politics as collective fate and as political instrument. Machiavelli showed me politics against a different sky, against stars that could not be seen from prison.

"Politics is fate." When, in 1808, at a gathering of kings in Erfurt, Goethe praised Voltaire's *Mahomet* as a *Schicksalstragödie,* the emperor Napoleon interrupted him to say, "A tragedy of fate? That's part of the past now. Politik ist das Schicksal."

Machiavelli and his city-state were faced with the same hopeless task as the Athenians of the fifth century: how to safeguard the polis, the beauty and harmony of its logic when, by the nature of things, large groups, large numbers, were fated to enter history, and vast dark forces came into play threatening the polis with subjugation and degradation to the conquerors' own low level. Machiavelli then became the poet of politics as Plato had once been its teacher. But, as opposed to Plato, Machiavelli was no longer able to believe in educating the rabble: "A corrupt people is unable to maintain the freedom it had once secured for itself." He no longer believed that the Ideal could be realized, and he believed neither in the wisdom of the philosophers nor in the virtue of the knights. The prince had to be educated.

Dramatic circumstances attended the writing of *The Prince:* [Machiavelli was] thrown into a dungeon, subject to torture that he bore with courage and with such sarcasm at his own expense that he could say when writing from prison in supplication to powerful people, "I acted so well that I felt a certain tenderness toward myself."

Released, finally released to a miserable little village, he described his life in a letter to Francesco Vettori: "In the afternoon I go to the inn, play dice and backgammon with the innkeeper, the miller, the butcher; we argue over pennies, exchange the most obscene of insults, and cheat each other. And thus do I defend myself against Fortune's spite . . . content that it has cast me low, as it peers at me to see if I blush with shame."

He would return home in the late afternoon, cast off his stinking clothes, don courtly attire, and then settle his accounts with Livy and Seneca, whom he treated as equals. In those evening disquisitions after his days at the inn, he wrote *The Prince,* a crystal of poetry and logic, in one burst of genius.

Machiavelli, our contemporary, with our passion for self-degradation—"Content that Fortune has cast me so low . . ." He put the entire *esperienze delle cose moderne* to the test and in that he resembles the people of today. When in one letter he describes with scrupulous naturalism an adventure in the dark with a lame, festering old prostitute, one suspects that this could have been Baudelaire's model for *The Jewess.* "For a long time now I have not been saying what I think and not thinking what I say, and, if a true word escapes me, I wrap it in so many lies that it cannot be found," writes Machiavelli to Francesco Guicciardini, a ready-made epigraph—and perhaps an epitaph as well, for Russian or Polish writers under communism.

Nowadays one speaks of "Stalin's Machiavellianism," a single phrase that joins the height of Renaissance thought and virtue (*virtu*) with Tartar customs. Although at that time I was still avoiding making any allusion to Stalin, since the principal accusation and perhaps even the cause of my arrest was my prewar statements about him (as numerous witnesses, my colleagues, had testified), in the cell I did read aloud the passage in which Machiavelli advises the Prince to commit all the atrocities he will have to commit right at the beginning, in one fell swoop, or else end up in a vicious circle of constantly renewed atrocities.

A Section of Wat's Memoirs

The pendulum of prison time swings between agony and nothingness, but in Lubyanka time has other laws and moves in a different way. But books brought us back to life, immersed us in the life of free people in the great and free world. We took fictional reality naïvely, like children listening to fairy tales. Could that have been the reason they gave us books in that laboratory of prison existence, where every detail had been thought out, quite possibly even by Stalin himself? Perhaps the experience of two such antithetical realities is supposed to induce a schizophrenic dissociation in a prisoner, rendering him defenseless against the investigation.

Could this be one means by which the investigator fires the desire to live, which is otherwise extinguished in a prisoner? I had a great desire to live because I found Nietzsche's *amor fati* in every trifle in every book, even the pessimistic ones. The more pessimistic the book, the more pulsating energy, life energy, I felt beneath its surface—as if all of literature were only the praise of life's beauty, of all of life, as if nature's many charms were insufficient to dissuade us from suicide, from Ecclesiastes, and from Seneca's "better not to have been born at all but, if born, better to die at once." I came across books that I had read before prison and that had sapped me of my will. For example, *Notes from the Underground.* But there in my cell even those books sang hosannas. In Lubyanka freedom seemed a hundred times more alluring and a hundred times more desirable than in Zamarstynów, where I had hit bottom. Could that have been the influence of the books I read? And wasn't that the investigator's intention: to fire the prisoner's desire for freedom so that he would be ready to do anything that was required of him?

But no doubt the secret behind our being given books was less complicated than that. Perhaps in Stalin's ark, which contained the prototypes for everything—wealthy collective farms, model cattle feeders, the most modern factories—there was also a place for a model prison in which the prisoners had a right to culture. Perhaps Stalin's personal fondness for reading as well as his Byzantine sense of decorum were significant here. Or perhaps this was an instance of chance and disorder in his global strategy. Or perhaps all the above operating together.

And so I think that reading had a twofold effect in Lubyanka, whether that was the investigator's intent or not. This isn't just speculation on my part; I observed its effect on my cell mates. Primarily, books stimulated a keen desire for life, life of any sort, at any cost, to live and move with the Rastignacs, Rostovs, and even the heroes of *Notes from the Underground,* an insatiable desire to live in freedom, even if that were the miserable freedom of the camps. I encountered many prisoners who had been pulled out of the camps for a review of their trials; despite their having no faith in being released and despite the great wretchedness of camp life, they would still grow nostalgic about being able to move freely about the camp, about the chance to work and be in contact with large numbers of people. A second and opposite effect of reading was that it disordered a prisoner's mental structure by causing him to experience two entirely different realities simultaneously: the world of books—free, full of movement, light, change, colorful, Heraclitean—and the world where time stood still, lost all sensation in captivity, and faded into a dirty gray. The sum total of both opposed effects worked to the investigator's advantage because it disturbed the victim's entire soul.

But reading had the opposite effect on me. It marshaled my intellectual and spiritual resources and made me stronger. It truly was like touching the earth for Antaeus. No doubt that was because what I primarily filtered out from books, any sort of book, was the poetry they contained, and it was only in prison that I became aware of a certain banal truth, one that I had often doubted, namely, that I am a poet.

I am not a poet because I write poems (besides, I only did so in periods that were few and far between) or because I composed poems in prisons to condense my spiritual states. And not because I had loved poetry since I was a child and had a high respect for excellent verse. Both of those factors, though important, were secondary, incidental, here.

And not because I had wanted to make my life into a work of art, a poem. On the contrary. I never could bear the Oscar Wilde brand of dandyism, and there were times when I had felt a need for the ugly, the low, a need to go slumming. And my early reading of *A Seducer's Diary* and Kierkegaard's *Either/Or* had made me aware of my natural aversion to "esthetes." In my early youth, I wanted to end up as a drunk in the gutter, a *clochard* (and I came close to it in my dadaist phase) or, alternatively, as a hermit philosopher living in the extreme poverty that I thought probably lay in store for me anyway. I also had long phases in which I needed to take refuge in mediocrity, and that was bad, very bad. On the whole, my life was a patchwork affair, and there was no question of its being a work of art.

In Zamarstynów I not only examined my past in the light of conscience, an old habit of mine, but I undertook a spectrum analysis of all my failures, sins, disgraces—both those I could remember and those that I had to wrest from oblivion because that truly was a *dies irae, dies illa* . . . And everything that had been hidden away came up to the surface. It was then that I became fully aware that I had always experienced things as a poet. Mine had not been the philosopher's life: at the university I had concluded once and for all that it was pointless to dream of universal knowledge, *mathesis universalis;* I had lost faith in that, and partial, relative truths held no attraction for me. Mine was not a religious life either, a search for God, as one critic has imputed: heaven is either taken by storm or step by step and even in my religious ecstasies in Soviet prisons and sporadically later on in communist Poland, I was passive toward religion.

But my life, oh, my life, had been a constant search for an enormous dream in which my fellow creatures and animals, plants, chimeras, stars, and minerals were in a pre-established harmony, a dream that is forgotten because it must be forgotten, and is sought desperately, and only sporadically does one find its tragic fragments in the warmth of a person, in some specific situation, a glance—in memory too, of course, in some specific pain, some moment. I loved that harmony with a passion; I loved it in voices, voices. And then, instead of harmony, there was nothing but scraps and tatters. And perhaps that alone is what it means to be a poet.

And so Lubyanka made me sensitive to everything; in poetry, novels, works of philosophy (we had books by Solovyov and Losky there), and in the handbook on minerology I read, I read both the poetry and the reflections they contained. As two sides of the same thing, since poetry without reflection is empty, just word games, and reflection without poetry is blind, its bearings lost. I said "reflection" but it would have been more accurate to say "philosophy," as a consolation for life's misery, as it appeared to Boethius in prison—in a robe with the letters T (*Theoria*) and P (*Praxis*) embroidered at the bottom. "Two sides" of what? Human fulfillment? Spiritual life in the state of becoming? The modus of existence? Consolation? In the end when asking myself those questions I applied to poetry what St. Augustine had said about time: "When no one asks what it is, I know what it is; if someone asks me, I don't know." *Nescio:* and if asked what poetry is, I wouldn't know either, even though its substance was so self-evident as to be almost palpable in Lubyanka. I could detect its presence with my fingertips, even though poetry's spiritual content is perhaps even purer than that of religious experience since the latter contains psychological elements—a person's feelings toward his father, his relationship to nature, and so forth. Poetry, however, can feed on those elements too, but it can also do without them. Perhaps poetry can do without everything and is a state of nirvana, not meaning nothingness but, on the contrary, the highest fullness. "*Gesang und Dasein*," I repeated after Rilke, and that was enough for me.

That was what I thought and felt about poetry in Lubyanka. Clearly my views have changed a great deal since that time, but still now, if asked to, I can't define what poetry is. For me it is still a state and not a fact, the highest value in literature and language. I would replace the poet's fashionable clamor to *réinventer la poésie* with the simpler but more difficult *réinventer le poète*.

Even when reciting poems to myself in Zamarstynów, where it was a crime to possess a scrap of paper, I knew poetry was a consolation, and something more than that as well: a wretched creature, subjected to misery of every sort, struggles toward beauty from the abominable depths of his misery . . . Let the critics discourse on the structure of poetry, linguistic entropy, metonymy—poetry fulfills itself when it is an act of heroism. That lesson on the ontological meaning of poetry was not lost on me. When we go back to the twenty, fifty, or hundred greatest works of world literature that we read as young people, we cannot, nor do we wish to, be freed from the charms of that initial reading. Still, we were prematurely exposed. What could we have known of their roots in human life? Under conditions like those in Lubyanka—cut off from the world, aware of the vast roaring world outside, the deathly hush inside, where time slows terribly while we continue to grow terribly old biologically—under those conditions we sought to recover our initial freshness of perception, the way Adam saw when he saw that "it was good."

Here I should interject that my experience was very much my own, and not typical. Not because I had been devouring books all my life or that the history of my childhood and youth could be told by the books I read, or that for my last seven years as a free man I had been the literary director of Gebethner and Wolff. I had acquired such a taste for analyzing and restructuring other people's work that I had stopped writing myself (or perhaps it was the other way around, and I had become an editor in order to stop writing). I felt in charge only when I had taken hold of the actual end of the thread and could see an entire work unravel into its components. And I gradually became cynical about what I considered the spurious integrity and unity of a given work; it was nothing but a skillful montage of various elements and tricks. In Lubyanka, to my joy, I rediscovered the sense of integrity—the whole that "precedes" the parts and is their soul. I had fully recovered my ability to see things synthetically.

24 DUNAYEVSKY'S THOUGHTS ABOUT RUSSIA. A HIGH NKVD OFFICIAL. DUNAYEVSKY'S STORY; OR, THE ABYSS. THE FLOW OF TIME IN PRISON.

WAT: I've spoken of Dunayevsky and his hobby, linguistics, and I've spoken in general of the Russian intellectuals I met in prison who had a second area of expertise that they kept concealed. I spoke of Dunayevsky's interest in linguistics, which was more an official field for him, but his knowledge of Russian history, Oriental history, including China, was fantastic. At the same time, his erudition and memory were directed primarily by his effort to understand communism (that's my conclusion) and, secondarily, its demonic aspects. He considered himself a disciple of Leontyev and Solovyov. He also had considerable knowledge of Russian Orthodox theology even though he was a Jew, 100 percent a Jew, with no inclination to convert, but he was also able to reconcile this with a certain admiration for Russian Orthodox mystical theology. I learned a great deal from him as far as historical connections are concerned. It's not what I learned that matters, but his helping to launch my imperative, my conviction, that absolutely none of the phenomena in our history, meaning the history of communism, can be understood if one does not accept the premise that communism has a hundred, or a thousand and one, roots in history. I owe him my inclination to examine every banal symptom, not for analogies and influences, of course, but for echoes, resonances, things that reach far back into history, even into the archaic.

He had not read Berdyaev and his view of communism was not Berdyaevan. According to Berdyaev, communism is a typically Russian phenomenon. In my opinion, Dunayevsky took a wiser view, namely, that Russia is not a communist phenomenon. Quite the contrary. He did not show all his cards at first; he was very cautious, very suspicious. I was something new for him. He was firmly convinced that none of the others in the cell were informing, not even the counterintelligence officer. But I was new and he was not sure of me. He spent quite a lot of time feeling me out but later on was very open with me and even admitted certain things that went rather far. And therein lies the whole drama of it all—later on, much later on, from certain nearly unmistakable signs, I came to the conclusion that Dunayevsky himself was telling his investigator what went on in the cell. That was many months later. I was absolutely certain that Dunayevsky deceived him and spoke well of us. But he was telling him things.

Well, a day passed, a week, two weeks, three, and for the time being I was happy just to vegetate after all those other terrible prisons. But anxiety and memory kept trickling in; my family, Ola, Andrzej. And of course all the obsessions kept coming back to me, all the combinations of disaster that could have befallen them. And if I wasn't imagining that, I was picturing Ola's grief.

At that time I was very important to her; later on she became my support. But at that time she had a great need of my support. Her childhood had been very comfortable from the material point of view but terribly difficult psychologically. Her painful childhood experiences, which had even become something of a neurosis, were only finally cured in Kazakhstan. She had a great need of me, and I could imagine her despair. I was already living in a world not so much of symbols as of religious presence, and so *Stabat Mater*, of course, those identifications that in any case you have to be wary of, very cautious about—they can be very dangerous—but still, at that time, they were very much at work in me. I saw Ola beneath what she might have thought of as my cross, even though things weren't so bad for me at the time.

But she knew that I had a talent and a passion for suffering. And so I could imagine her despair. That began to fill my time, my thoughts. I still couldn't remember her face. I could remember all the faces of casual acquaintances, but I was absolutely unable to recall hers. Absolutely unable. I couldn't even say what color her eyes were. Nothing. Maybe her smile, but that was like the smile in *Alice in Wonderland*, the smile of a cat that has vanished. And so the monotony began, days filled with painful worry.

The monotony of the days—slowly I began to feel the grim reality of existence in Lubyanka, even though only two or three weeks had passed. I already knew that this was the modus operandi in Lubyanka. Absolute monotony. I talked about that and other things with Dunayevsky, with whom I was quite close after a few weeks. When I spoke about the monotony, his reply was, "I'm coming to the end of my third year here, and I know what it is. You can't know yet. A person can go mad here." Dunayevsky foresaw his own fate. I asked him other questions, practical ones: why am I in Lubyanka if my case was closed?

MILOSZ: How did you know it was closed?

WAT: Because they had read me all the testimony. No sentence had been passed, but they had read me the testimony. In fact, the whole procedure was such that they should have sentenced me right away and sent me to a camp. So why did they bring me to Lubyanka? Dunayevsky had tremendous experience of the NKVD and said that certain things were out of the question. Two alternatives remained. They might be implicating me in some larger, more important, case in which I would be a witness or a codefendant. That, obviously, was a terribly ominous hypothesis, for, as I've said, I lived in constant fear because of the period when I had been close to communism, because of my relations with the embassy, the people who had been executed, *The Literary Monthly*. There was one other possibility, he said: they wanted to study me closely, to prepare me for some future role. Another ominous prospect. And so I was expecting either a bolt of lightning or a long painful haul in which I would resist being used. But time kept passing; no one summoned me—it must have been the off-season.

Dunayevsky and I told each other our dreams, some of which proved prophetic as a matter of course. So, for example, if someone heard a shot or an explosion in a dream, then something was bound to happen the next day. Dreams proved to be prophetic during my entire time at Lubyanka. It was rare for anything to happen there, and so that provided a standard. For example, one morning the chauffeur said that he had dreamed of cannon fire, and that day he was summoned for interrogation.

People had the right to write requests every two weeks, or once a month. To anybody. To the national Soviets, the presidium, Stalin, the warden, the prosecutor, the investigator, and so on. Dunayevsky exercised that right often. You were taken to a windowless cubicle. You reported to the guard in the morning and were given paper and pen. And so Dunayevsky said, "You should write and ask to be summoned." I wrote that I had been there more than a month. (I had no idea that a woman by the name of Lipper had spent eleven years in prisons and camps and never been summoned once. Not once!) But I had grown used to being interrogated and found this surprising. What had they brought me there for?

And in fact I was summoned rather soon, a few days later, at night, but at the beginning of night, somewhere around eleven o'clock. That was my first time in Lubyanka's Kafkaesque corridors. The guards who were escorting me clicked their tongues before turning a corner, to alert other guards escorting other prisoners. Sometimes they used their metal buckles to make a sound. Everything was quiet at Lubyanka, perfectly quiet, and it was only in that corridor (it was around eleven o'clock) when passing an office door that I heard a woman scream, a woman being tortured. She had a beautiful contralto voice; I wrote a poem about it. A terrible scream, just one. Later on I learned that, supposedly, screams like that were stage-managed. They weren't always authentic; they were done to induce the proper mood in the prisoners in the neighboring cells. Anyway, that was the first scream in the night that I heard at Lubyanka.

I was brought into a very large, almost luxurious office. I had been in offices like that only twice before. Persian rugs. A very important dignitary. A good-natured fifty-year-old man with a nice broad Russian face. A family man. He was in uniform, the collar unbuttoned a little. A fleshy neck, an apoplectic build. He received me with a jolly smile as if the whole thing were a big joke. I wasn't there long—twenty, thirty minutes, even less—but that farce went on the whole time, that farcical tone. He looked at me and laughed. The sight of me, my person, my being there, all put him in good humor. At first that lifted my spirits; I thought, So there's no danger. No danger of being implicated with those who had been executed. But I had the impression that he knew nothing about my case. He knew nothing about me. And he asked, "Well, what about it? Were you spying for Hitler?" But with a laugh.

I spread my hands and said, "What, what do you mean?" No one had accused me of that; it would have been absurd. I told him more or less what I had to say: I was a writer, I'd been arrested in Lwów. Yes, I had engaged in anti-Soviet conversations, but that was when I had been a Polish citizen. Yes, I admit it. But in Lwów I engaged in no anti-Soviet conversations. And the testimony? Some of the testimony was false.

He was laughing constantly. He made a little joke, then said, "Yes, but you Poles are terribly corrupt morally. You should all be isolated." And he laughed. He wrote down my name, a little personal data, when I was arrested. "We'll look into it; we'll look into it while you're here. Are things all right here?"

I answered, "The cell is all right."

He said, "So stay awhile, why not. Things are all right, aren't they? Are you getting what you need?"

I said, "Yes, but I have a family."

He said, "A family! You'll start a new one. Anyway, you'll be reunited with them. You're still young; you've got plenty of time."

I remember that perfectly. His was a completely different sort of face. My other investigators had been more on the Asiatic, brutal side. And here was that Russian good nature, that great patience—all that time we have ahead of us. An enormous amount of time. Why hurry things that will happen of themselves? That philosophy, right from the start. Besides, I was prepared for that because my only link with the NKVD, the world of communism, before this had been our warden. He was a paterfamilias too. Only a little older than I was, the one who'd say

214

after we'd eaten, "You've eaten; now take a rest!" The one who came into the cell one night like a cat and, so as not to disturb anyone, whispered in my ear that my hands had to be outside the blanket. That same good nature, that fatherly quality. More like an uncle. Only Stalin could be the father. In that configuration Stalin, with his fatherly smile, was the only father. The others were like uncles. Big uncles and little uncles. The warden was a little uncle. Of course, it's my fault, my Polish moral corruption, that I could not in the least separate that world of the father and the uncles from the lice, the filth, the misery, and the way we were trampled on in Zamarstynów. A hierarchy of emanations, in fact like the gnostics' system. High emanations that diminish and descend as they reach into hell.

I suspected there was a system to it, but I couldn't discover how it worked. I told Dunayevsky about it. He said that no conclusions should be drawn; it proved nothing. It meant that I had not yet been assigned to anyone. It was just that some dignitary saw my request and wanted a look at me, to see a writer. But if he was well disposed toward me—and he clearly was, his good-bye had been almost tender—that would in fact speed things up. Dunayevsky added, "You should remember one thing: admit everything they demand you to."

I knew that Russians gave advice like that, but Dunayevsky was a very upright man, even pedantic about it, and coming from him that advice made me indignant. And I replied very sharply to him, with a sort of Polish conceit. Very stupidly, arrogantly—that you Russians admit to everything, but Poles don't. Poles don't admit to crimes they didn't commit. I could see that this hurt him very badly. I thought it was due to some Russian patriotism on his part.

But not long after that—in fact, after that he spoke very little with me; he had been hurt—he told me in a near whisper (the others were sleeping) about his case in very general terms. What the grounds were, what the charges were, I don't know. They stemmed from his past, from 1915 when he had been in Iran with the Red Cross, with Princess Radziwiłł, of whom he spoke with great affection. He said that Radziwiłł was an extraordinary person. She was the head of the Russian Red Cross in Iran. He was very indebted to her morally. Everyone has some person who is a moral influence, serves as a moral example. Dunayevsky was a secretary there for a year or two. And so that was old business.

And so what had happened? Of course, I don't remember his exact words, but I remember the drift well enough. It was really quite simple. He had a wife and they loved each other very much. And he had a friend whom he and his wife both adored. In the end, the wife left him for the friend. All three of them loved each other very much. Those were very morally pure people and so that wasn't a sexual triangle, but genuine mutual adoration. They had tremendous respect for each other.

I don't remember which of them was the first to be arrested in an important case—he didn't say what the case was, but it was one of the major ones in 1937. It might have been his friend or him. And then his hard times with the NKVD at Lubyanka began. Now I remember—his friend was arrested, then his wife, his former wife; she was his friend's wife by then. He was still a free man, working in some ministry and also doing translations from the Persian. He was still at liberty when they first summoned him. Because he was stubborn about giving testimony, he was threatened and finally put in prison, but not for quite some time. After numerous interrogations, they put him in prison, and what they principally demanded was that he turn on his friend. He refused. And he was tortured. Possibly first on the "conveyor" but then tortured in the literal sense. He gave evidence. Then he recanted. They tortured him again. He didn't go into details about the torture or how long it lasted.

He said, "Morality has its own arithmetic too; it's easy to figure. There are situations where the morality had to be figured in. I took a stand on not dooming one individual. Had I given testimony then and helped doom that person, I probably would have been arrested too and sent to a camp, but since the major case we were linked to was already a thing of the past, probably I, my friend, and my ex-wife, too, would have been able to live peacefully in a camp. Either we would have survived or we wouldn't. Now I'm coming to the end of my third year here. I did not wish to betray one individual and I betrayed eleven. Eleven versus one!"

I assumed that the point here was to explain why he had advised me to admit to everything right away, immediately. All the horrors of Lubyanka and the NKVD that I had read about before the war and what I had been told in Lwów and Zamarstynów about torture—all that did not so much pale as somehow lose its importance in the face of what Dunayevsky had been through. But this was of another order entirely. The other was a Grand Guignol, a menacing Grand Guignol but still Grand Guignol. But this was the abyss.

And so day after day passed. Literature. Of course, it's an escape; the brain functions. In prison the aesthetic sensibility is purged of various fashions, all that experimental volatility. Everything volatile seems somehow illusory, almost nonexistent. And what's left are things that exist in themselves and derive from what is stable. You have to find a stable point; otherwise it means death and terrible suffering. Emp-

216

tiness. A deserted world. You have to find some stability as quickly as you can. It's a long, hard process. But the thing is to start in on it. Search yourself, your memories: one thing, two, three.

Besides literature, there's that review, that military review, your life almost on parade. Or like a film—you sit on your chair, not on a chair, on your bed or a stool, and the film of your own life flashes before you with different meanings, different subtexts, a different basis. And you sort through that life for those places that can provide some way out, some salvation. It isn't easy. A person is so lost in his own life. You've probably read Exupéry when he tells about being lost over the sea at night. There are no signals; he doesn't know where land is—nothing but water and more water; he keeps circling, and suddenly he sees lights, a great many lights. It turns out to be a fata morgana; the Sahara is nearby . . . I don't remember if he was over the Sahara or the sea— it's been so many years! But in any case it was a fata morgana, boundless space, and he doesn't know where to land. But he does know that some of those many points of light belong to the airfield. But which ones? And that's how it is with your own life in Lubyanka, reviewing your own life. You know there's a single point somewhere, but which one is it?

And so I began to experience monotony as a confusion of time. The experience of the present, the present moment, extends almost infinitely. A terrible, monstrous expansion of every minute. You think you won't make it, if not to the next minute, then to the next hour. How can you live through an entire hour that grows longer with the passage of time? What I mean by that is if it's five after ten now, it will be six after ten next, and a tremendous amount of time has to pass for that to happen. But eight after ten, the minute ahead of you, is even longer because of that. And of course there are various combinations; you think what it will be like in a month or a year. But when you reject all those combinations, that conniving mechanism that is always at work in you, the future becomes limited to a small stretch. The farther away a point is on that stretch, the longer that stretch of time becomes. Each successive minute you have to live through becomes longer every few moments. Am I being clear about this?

MILOSZ: I understand perfectly. I know about that more or less from experience, but if you read and lose yourself in reading, in another world, then all that stops.

WAT: Naturally. But you can't read all the time, not because you're not allowed to. You're allowed to. But you mustn't. Just as you have to know how to die on your feet, you also have to go on living. Reading was paradise, a delicacy, but it was an attempt to trick fate. A narcotic.

217

An escape into anesthesia, despite everything. Though it was more than that too. Obviously, for me in that cell it was an anesthetic. And also like a gift from heaven and something else, too—I was an isolated monad in that cell, and through reading I established contact with history, the works of humanity, the human race. And so reading was not only an anesthetic; it also provided considerably more than that—but my first obligation was to go on living. Not just an obligation, but a necessity, a need. I overstate the case by calling it an obligation. Because it's not necessarily even conscious, but it truly was a need, an absolute need. And so the books would be put aside.

And the past contracted. All those months, a month, two, three at Lubyanka, four, five—all that had for the most part contracted. Not that it happened all at once—it was a process in which the past contracted and the future grew incredibly protracted, the immediate future, the future of minutes, hours, days. Obviously that can't occur without damaging the brain; you pay for this with certain mental deviations. A certain mental restructuring takes place. Everything takes a different mental form. And that takes its toll. Every bad thing can at the same time be good, as you know. Absolutely everything. What causes the modulation from bad to good is of course imperceptible. But in Lubyanka it was a case of something very bad. And that leads to a certain insanity, at least to moral insanity. In Dunayevsky's case it led literally to insanity, clinical insanity. I assume that it was not so much, or not only, his moral scruples that undid him, not only that moral torture he suffered when he found that he no longer had the strength to stand still on an inclined plane, that he had started moving down that inclined plane, had crossed a certain boundary, and where he stopped depended solely on his torturers. No further resistance was possible. He had crossed a certain line. He saw no possibility of resisting any longer. Probably that was what caused him to go mad after three years in Lubyanka, but from what I observed, I assume that those strange changes of structure (not the right word here, "structure"), those paradoxes of time, also had their effect.

25 THE WEIGHT OF WORDS. THE RESEARCH OFFICE AT LUBYANKA. INTELLECTUAL SNOBBERY AND FAMILY EGOISM. EINSTEIN'S THEORY AND PRAYER.

WAT: Let's go back to Dunayevsky. I wanted to bring a few features of his out a bit more: his relation to the authorities and the Soviet system. Anders wrote that Dunayevsky had been a vice-minister in light industry, but I rather doubt that. He didn't give the impression of being a high official; on the contrary, he seemed like the quiet former intellectual who is tolerated in a ministry as an expert, a specialist. But that's not even the point. At bottom, his attitude toward the system was, I wouldn't say positive, but accepting. He accepted it. And he, a follower of Leontyev, prophesied that a new slavery, more terrible than anything humanity had experienced so far, was awaiting Russia and the world. A cruel one because created by the collective. That was Dunayevsky to a tee. Probably that was also the influence of Marxism, the basic Marxist ideology of historical necessity. History as a necessity against which nothing can be done. You cannot fight history. Deep down, that's the basic Marxist sense of the world. And Dunayevsky acceped that. Of course, in a certain way this is connected with Russian, Eastern fatalism. But it's not the same thing. Both are there in Leontyev. And I suppose the same was true of Dunayevsky.

Another feature of his, a very strong aspect of his character, was his pedantry—almost like Molière's—which showed even in the way he moved. I don't know why I associate that pedantry with his crooked side, with his physical shame, which probably had a great influence on his life. I mentioned his main hobby, philology. He was mad about etymology; it's what he lived for.

Being completely closed in a cell in Lubyanka with a man mad about etymology had an enormous indirect effect on me as a writer. That well may have been the end of my avant-gardism. The result of spending many months with a man who tracks down the roots and history of each word, who re-creates a certain historical and anthropological reality in the roots and history of each word, was, at least for me, the sudden falling away of the essence of avant-gardism—it began to fall away from me once and for all—all of what Marinetti had unleashed with his slogan "The liberated word": nihilism, linguistic materialism, the word as an object with which you can do as you please. For me that's a basic distinction in poetics—in even more than poetics, for what distinguishes the worldview of the avant-garde writer and poet from the traditional or classical view is precisely the concept of the word as a material thing. Living close by Dunayevsky, I was pulled into his game, a wonderful game for killing time. But that game also caused a regression into feeling the biological connections of words on a higher level, not a mineral, biological, or even archetypal level but in connection to history, to the incredibly alive tissues of human destiny, the destinies of generations, the destinies of nations. And the responsibility for every word, to use every word properly. And then, intuitively—for I realized all this only later on—I had an intuitive sense both of the responsibility and of that which is perhaps the only thing that distinguishes a poet from the others who speak the language: the poet's task, or mission, or instinct to rediscover not the meaning of each word but only the weight of each word.

I learned a great deal from Dunayevsky about Russian sectarianism. Primarily what I learned was that before the Revolution there had been thirty million sectarians in Russia; that was the figure he used. He also told me about a fellow prisoner, an ex-monk, expelled from his order, who had a theory about the Jews. And it so happened that after the evacuation of Lubyanka I ran into that monk. He was very interesting—I'll return to this later on.

But let's go back to the cell now. Day after day passed and I was already starting to feel that something was happening to time, that confusion of time and its incredible importance for all human consciousness. Lubyanka as a laboratory for a total change in the way time is experienced. And my camel period was over too; I'd used up my own reserves and had started to feel undernourished.

It wasn't long before I was summoned in again by a general or a colonel—I don't remember which, but he was in uniform. I entered a relatively large office, furnished like an official's office, but quite bright. Two NKVD men sat at desks at quite some distance from each other. One had a very Oriental face, the other a very Russian face. The one with the Oriental, Georgian face—a good-looking face but one without character, a rather superficial face—was relatively young, somewhere around thirty or maybe more; it's hard to tell. A face so without personality that today I would know immediately that it was Georgian, but I certainly wouldn't recognize him even though we were together so many times. I would definitely recognize the other one, however. A Russian intellectual, the face of an eternal student, a revolutionary from the old days, a perfect consumptive face, sunken cheeks, a sunken chest, large, feverish eyes full of *nieutolimaya toska,* unappeasable yearning, a hectic complexion. Definitely a consumptive. You could imagine Raskolnikov looking like that.

And here we might ask ourselves whether a Raskolnikov living in Soviet times would, after committing his crime and being tried for it, go out onto a public square to do penance or enlist in the Cheka? Maybe the latter. I can give you a little story as a footnote. Andrzej was in Moscow talking with some young writers and painters. And he met the head of a band of painters who was also a painter. That was a special sort of gang, based on not having any residence. So they wandered all over Russia, staying with friends and hanging their shows there—their paintings were abstract of course. The leader was a bearded man; he was the oldest, past forty, a former NKVD and KGB officer. He had been put in a camp for five years for shooting a prisoner in a camp for no reason—that was still in Stalin's time, before Stalin's death. He was released in an early amnesty; he went to a public square and began to repent. He began speaking of the terrible crimes of the NKVD, the KGB, the Cheka, and so on, and about the crimes he had committed when in the NKVD. Naturally, he was arrested again, but he was released soon after for being insane. They left him alone. So there you have it: Raskolnikov in Soviet times.

The Georgian, Lalashvili, introduced himself to me first because, in fact, I belonged to him; the other one was there more for show. I don't know if his rank was lower or whether I just hadn't been assigned to him. So Lalashvili introduced himself first and in a very elegant, almost salonlike, manner. I was expecting one of the two alternatives Dunayevsky had presented to me, meaning either a bolt from the blue, some threat to implicate me in the case of Jasieński, Hempel, and the others, who were dead by then, or a reprocessing of my case. I was suspicious, wary as a hedgehog, closed, stiff, and besides I was used to sitting before the investigator in the proper manner, hands folded properly. Lalashvili kept telling me to relax. He had the face and the manner of some friendly person in a salon or café. He also introduced me to the other one, Nikolaev—I don't remember his name exactly, something like that.

And so a conversation started. It started with how am I, am I all right. As all right as you can be in prison—I said that I was all right, the cell was clean, and my cell mates were, of course, very decent people. But I had some very painful problems. My family! What was happening to my family? I said that was eating me up. And then right away I bit my tongue, for I thought I was showing them my weak side, which they could exploit cruelly. But what was done was done, and besides, I had to ask that question. He said, "I don't have any precise information, but I do know they're alive and well!" And then just as automatically I asked, "Both of them?" Then he hesitated for a second before answering, "Both of them."

But that hesitation was enough for me to see an abyss open up before me. Especially after I was back in the cell, I began ruminating about which one of them would be worse to lose. I kept repeating, Both, are you sure? Yes, both, he just didn't have exact information. At Zamarstynów I knew that the families of prisoners had been deported, and, besides, my parapsychological experiences had told me that.

I asked where they were, what they were doing. He said they weren't in Lwów, they were in Asia, he didn't know where, but he would try to find out and then said sincerely, "I won't hide anything from you. I have no intention of hiding anything from you" and so on. In general, he tried to show me that I ought to drop my distrust of him, on that point especially.

The second point I spoke about was undernourishment, which had become very painful. He said, "Yes, it really is hard. Most of the people in Lubyanka are Russians who are sent money and, as you know, the canteen is well supplied. I will try to have your money from Lwów transferred here as quickly as possible. It will take some time, but as soon as the money arrives you can start using the canteen." That melted me.

I could see a lot of books on his desk. Naturally, Czachowski's *History of Contemporary Literature*, which I'd published at Gebethner's. But I had already seen Czachowski's book in an investigator's office in Lwów. I saw other books there, including, I think, Bobrzyński's *History of Poland*, mostly works on things Polish.

Questions about literature, writers. Nothing about my case. What did he ask about? Everything. And, apparently to disarm me, he began with writers who were dead. It was only later, in the following sessions, that he switched to living writers. And somehow right from the start he connected things to international events, right away to Paris—the food situation isn't good here but what about France. He spoke with enormous compassion about the misery of Paris, the misery of France; he said they were eating rats there. He made references to 1870, and, maybe this is my own addition, but it's not out of the question that he mentioned the Goncourts' memoirs, which described the misery of that time. In any case, after that session about the rats, I was left persuaded that he was flaunting his erudition. In their conversations with each other—and I assume with any writer or intellectual—NKVD people like very much to display immediately how well read they are.

He had genuine compassion for Paris, and what struck him most was that Parisian women were wearing wooden shoes, sabots. That was because he imagined Parisian women and Paris from Balzac's novels. And now suddenly those princesses, those great coquettes were wearing wooden shoes, peasant sabots as he imagined them. Clearly, that was his image of Paris. Sincere sympathy for France. And so this was something that seemed to go against official policy. At that time the official policy toward France was very harsh. And so that was a point that caught me by surprise and that he pushed a great deal, probably to loosen me up and disarm my suspicions. But I was suspicious again, thinking, He's cunning. But that wasn't true; he really wanted to talk with me like one human being to another. Nikolaev cut in on the conversation; his way of speaking about people and things was warmer, very Russian.

And so there were questions about Polish literature and writers—but not only writers, the problems of literature as well. They were very interested in Żeromski, which I liked, and I gave them my analysis of *Early Spring*, which I could see was very much to their taste. I didn't speak as a Marxist. Lalashvili had been through my records very closely and knew my whole biography quite well; he knew that I had strained to be Marxist in the testimony I gave in Lwów, and he made great, almost intrusive, efforts to keep me away from Marxism. He couldn't say, The hell with the Marxism—but that's what it came down to. What he wanted from me was a real image of the real reality.

Here I should correct the generally accepted opinion about dogmatists among top Bolshevik figures. On the lower levels, dogmatism was obligatory, of course. Those were narrow minds, dogmatic minds formed on the ABCs of Marxism. But on the upper levels . . . Even though Lalashvili was an ordinary captain, he was part of a very high-level institution, the highest level, meaning intelligence or NKVD.

In any case that was a research section, not a detective bureau. I served as an assistant teacher. The office was called either the First Section of the Third Department or the Third Section of the First Department, and that definitely was the Polish Problems Research Office. And they had probably brought me there for their own purposes. That was why I had reached the heights of Lubyanka, as I realized later—simply because I was a specialist in literature who could refute everything they had heard from the Polish Marxists. They disregarded those Marxist approaches. On those levels, at that time, they were all certainly Marxists, with very deep Marxist beliefs and convictions. But that was Marxism along with some skepticism; that was the Marxism of Engels's expression "in the last analysis." Of course economic forces, of course social relations, of course class struggle—but later on, in the last analysis. But here and now there's a terribly complicated reality. And so Marxism was left somewhere in that last analysis. What actually concerned them more was the real world. That first interrogation where I took no Marxist approach whatsoever was proof that I could be of valuable assistance to them. I didn't realize it at the time.

And so that was the sort of conversations we had, just like in a literary café. You know, I love to chat about literature; I grew up in the cafés—that's my weakness. And so when I'm in that atmosphere, I'm capable of kibitzing with my worst enemies, people who have done me the greatest harm, even Putrament, not to mention Borejsza. Sitting in that imaginary or real literary café, I was so disarmed that I immediately felt friendly toward them, a great rush of genuine affection. All the grievances and injuries just disappeared. And so he really did melt me. I left him in a sort of blissful mood; I wasn't even thinking about my family as I left. Because that's something you think of, then forget. You remember again, then you forget. But I went back to the cell feeling on top of the world. I suppose that's how a river feels after the winter when the ice starts breaking up, cracking and flowing. A state of delight, melting, I enjoyed it very much.

Naturally, I repeated the conversation to Dunayevsky, and then, as if he were a rabbi, I asked, "So what does it all mean?" And then, rabbinically, for there was a little something rabbinical about his mind, he said it's either one of two things. Either very bad or very good. Those same alternatives again. By Zamarstynów, I had already stopped pretending to be a Marxist in the hope of convincing them that I was, after all, one of them. I no longer had any resistance at all; I still wanted to be released; I wanted to live, even in the Soviet Union, and save Ola and Andrzej.

But Dunayevsky, on the contrary, thought that if they wanted to prepare me to be a good Soviet citizen, I should aim for that; I'd be crazy not to. I had a different but equal fear of that as an alternative to being implicated in old cases. Of course, I was smart enough that when Lalashvili asked me to compile a bibliography of the books he should read for an overview of Poland, I did so willingly, and I had no misgivings about helping him with that. Especially because in a twinkling of an eye I somehow felt, maybe intuitively, maybe even unconsciously, that by doing that I would be counteracting the falsehoods, the dangerous deformations that the communists in Poland make in Polish history, society, in the presentation of the image of Polish society. I didn't have the slightest misgivings about helping him then, telling him things, initiating him, and so on. Instructing him.

Aha. Tea. Russian tea drinking. Nikolaev was brought tea and sandwiches. He had ordered that sandwiches, and plenty of them, be brought right away, and three glasses of tea. The ideal tea I had dreamed so much about at Zamarstynów, the tea that was to cleanse me, body and soul. Hot, strong, freshly brewed tea, real tea. And so of course I drank it without the slightest misgiving, but I didn't take any sandwiches the first time. I don't know why, but I said, No thank you. He didn't insist, very tactful. But later I did eat the sandwiches.

He had me brought there quite often—well, not often; it would be hard to say often, but every once in a while—for conversations. One time I wrote a request to be summoned. He summoned me at once, the same night or the next day—in any case very quickly. That was the third or fourth conversation, and I had called for it. He was very busy and so was Nikolaev—they were both up to their ears in paper work—and, imagine this, he sat me at a table and gave me a copy of *Nowe Widnokręgi* (*New Horizons*), which I didn't even know existed. And he had asked me to read it carefully. That's all I needed to hear; I devoured the journal.

I had extremely mixed feelings, because there were the names of all my friends, all my ex-friends, alive, doing wonderfully well, all of them writing—Ważyk, Rudnicki, Boy (I think he was in it)—and not necessarily communists. My friends. Suddenly, I had an image of their life, living in freedom with their families, getting together, arguing, writing, not only writing but writing with great freedom, some of them making no special attempt at all to be Marxist, some of the pieces almost nonconformist or in any case not dealing with Marxist problems. On the contrary, some very good pieces. Somehow, they were still developing—even somehow making progress. And I was disconnected. They were all out in the world of life and I wasn't. That struck a very deep emotional chord, probably connected with childhood memories. Everyone's been in that situation, excluded from the fun, heartbroken. They're having a good time and I'm not part of it. That was exactly the childish sensation I had. And despair that prison would probably never end; prison was where I would die. It was winter then, and they took us for walks on the roof of Lubyanka, where there were horrible Moscow winds. But when reading *New Horizons*, I could see them all in summer cafés, gardens, in summer twilight. And I wasn't there. Everyone's there, absolutely everyone. I'm the only one who isn't there. I'm the only person in the whole world who isn't there.

But at the same time there was another feeling. Because by then I knew something about how diabolical all that was as a historical phenomenon. In the end I had read a bit of history, and I knew that evil takes one incarnation or another in every epoch. And I thought that in the twentieth century evil had incarnated itself in history and that Bolshevism was the devil in history.

Yesterday you asked me about Nazism. I didn't know about Nazism, what it was. I tended to minimalize Nazism all the time I was in Russia. I knew it from before the war. I was very interested in it. If I took any social action in those years before the war, it was anti-Nazi action because I thought that no harm should come to Russia—my work in the Human Rights League for example—to such an extent that as soon as the Germans arrived, they came right for me. I think it was during the first week, they came looking for me at Gebethner's (I even have a letter from him about it). And so I was on one of the first lists; I don't know why, for I really had been very passive at that time. Though I did take part in some mass meetings and so forth. But, you see, I considered Nazism a provincial phenomenon. I hadn't imagined its dimensions. But the phenomenon itself, its nature, was not the essence and the danger of Nazism; in fact it represented a certain regression, one well known in Germany. And not only in Germany. A repetition of something; only its colossal dimensions made it new. And I hadn't known about those colossal dimensions; I thought what I read in the Soviet press was bunk. All Poles proceeded from the assumption that you had to read everything that was printed in the Soviet press in reverse. It was only when I returned to Warsaw that it hit me like a bolt from the blue. It was only then that my mind was rent by the revelation of what Nazism had been.

MILOSZ: But as far as Russia goes, you probably saw it as the incarnation of absolute evil because communism was future oriented.

WAT: No, no. I knew that it was a terrible calamity, a monstrous calamity, a monstrous regression reaching far back. In the beginning at Lubyanka, even back at Zamarstynów, I thought—and everyone at Zamarstynów shared that opinion—that war with the Nazis was inevitable, and even at night when we heard the tanks going by, we'd think, So, it's war. And I thought that Gog and Magog would devour each other. I don't believe in permanence, but I knew that communism was a phenomenon that had come out of history, that it was a disease that was surfacing—but a disease of European, Christian, Western civilization, whatever you want to call it. That a deeply rooted disease was coming to the surface. And that means the presence of the devil, the constant presence of the devil in history, to put it mythologically. And so of course I considered them servants of Satan, the whole lot of them, all of them who worked together. By then, I thought that literary cooperation—writing, feeling at home with it, settling down with it, for Polish writers to further their careers in the Soviet system—was treason. And not in the easy Polish sense of the word, but a fundamental treason, not against Poland, but treason against some principle of the good. The most elementary, simplest, bare-minimum good. And so in that way I didn't envy them; on the contrary, I was happy to have been left out. Those were very contradictory feelings, very contradictory.

Then Lalashvili asked questions. He had torn himself away from work with incredible interest, greedily, looking me right in the eyes—I remember that well—to see if I were speaking frankly; he would ask me for a frank, sincere opinion: what did I think of this or that. I don't recall the details any longer. Also questions, I don't remember the wording, about how I viewed one periodical or another, its strengths, its shortcomings.

And from what he said I inferred that he wasn't so much concerned about the literary level, even though there were people intelligent and wise enough in that office to know that a good literary level is a minimum requirement for political usefulness and that a low literary level destroys political usefulness, becomes counterproductive. But that didn't matter to him. He was concerned with literature's effect on society. And it was clear from what he once said that he was not concerned in the least with Polish society in Lwów—that was of little interest to him—but about society in Poland.

And so there were two striking things about that research office in the heart of Lubyanka. One, that in the heart of Lubyanka there were typical old prewar intellectuals like Nikolaev, and even that Georgian, with the entire psychology, mentality, and sensitivity, and even the fine humanism of old Russia. And second, these intellectuals, at the beginning of 1941, were taking an interest in the effect of literature on society in Poland itself. That is, they had plans for Poland.

I returned to the cell and conferred with Dunayevsky again. I was back on good terms with Dunayevsky; relations were very warm, truly warm, nearly brotherly. We talked a great deal, with him maintaining his discretion about his own life, of course; on the whole he was very discreet when it came to his own life. I apologized for my Polish haughtiness. I admitted that it was an ugly character trait and, moreover, one that in an ugly way covers something beautiful in Polish people—perhaps the most beautiful thing about them: their resistance. Resistance, the spirit of resistance. That Polish toughness in prison, during the occupation, and so forth. That's what I consider the most beautiful, purest thing about Poles, Poland. But it's overlapped by the ugly trait of conceit—"We Poles don't confess!" We had a general conversation about Polish conceit.

And so relations with Dunayevsky were warm, but the chauffeur couldn't bear the sight of me. He had a hundred reasons for it. Basically, I was unbearable. Even then, despite the good, hard lessons of

Zamarstynów, I still hadn't learned how to live in a group. And why was that? Irritability? No, not that. Impatience? That's worth some thought, because again that's not only a Polish trait but one common to all intelligentsia, intellectuals and so on. The chauffeur kept repeating one thing: "I'm an employee of the consulate; they shouldn't have arrested me; I want to go back to Poland." I explained to him that he was making a fatal error, that he'd never be released that way. First, I asked him if they'd accused him of spying, espionage activities.

"No! At first they did but not afterwards!"

"So what do they say?"

"They say that it's wartime and they can't let me out."

And so I said, "Well, of course, they can't let you out to go back to Poland. Don't start by demanding to return to Poland. Tell them to let you out so you can work as a chauffeur in Lwów."

They had convinced themselves that he was loyal; he never said a bad word about the Soviets. Of course he hated them, but clearly he had been trained in the consulate never to say a word, to have no dealings with a foreign power. He's a Pole; he wants to go back to Poland. That would seem very straightforward, very logical, but for his own good I, as an intellectual, found a deeper meaning. His obtuseness irritated me.

When dealing with simple people, intellectuals have a certain air of superiority that infuriates some of those simple people, and rightly so. Nobody likes a turned-up nose, a nose up in the air. That sort of thing is found everywhere but especially among Poles, because Poles are incredibly sensitive to their social career. Polish writers advance by entering a salon. And that's what ruined Skamander, in my opinion. It didn't ruin it, but it curbed all its poetic and literary ambition. To break into the salon. They broke in too early and that was all it took.

I was a typical intellectual in relation to the chauffeur; he hated me and rightly so. But I had a worse trait: I was immersed in myself, which is not allowed in a prison cell; it goes against the grain of every social being. People are social. Of course, I put myself in other people's positions, I gave advice to this one and that one, but that was only half the battle. I did their thinking for them—yes, often I did. But I didn't think about them. Maybe I'm not finding the right words here. There was no closeness, equality, communion. I was absolutely incapable of that then; I learned that only later on, in that cell full of bandits. That's where I actually passed the test. But only there. Besides which, it saved my life.

But not in Lubyanka; there I was immersed in myself. An egotist or an egoist. I rarely felt any love for myself. Somehow or other, that's how I'd been raised; for me, *le moi* was always Pascal's *le moi haïssable*.

228

I easily overcame my egoism as an individual, but I had a worse form of it, the most powerful, animalistic form: family egoism. I must tell you that I was cured of that too, because in Ili, during the passport process, I had reconciled myself to the fact that both Ola and Andrzej would lose their lives. And besides, Ola had agreed to it. And so in the end, in that Russia that was such a great and excellent school for me, that changed me from a fainthearted intellectual into some sort of human being, I managed to overcome that. But in Lubyanka I was filled with family egoism. It's terribly powerful, biological and instinctive, and very bad. It sows a terrific amount of evil because it leads to animal egoism. Even if that's noble in an animal, even if there can be something noble and sublime about it in a human being, in a powerful person, a bad person, still, it leads to territoriality. Any other animal that approaches must be destroyed.

Dunayevsky was in the cell the entire time. The chauffeur was there a very long time, but in the end he too disappeared. They took the Korean away, they took the Lithuanian away, others came, and so there was a certain change. A major change, but one spread out over months.

One day a young man arrived, terribly likable—he didn't look like a Jew but he was. An open, very sincere, even Russian, good-looking face. (You know, sometimes young people in Russia are very good-looking; they have broad, open, sincere faces, straight from the steppes.) They lose their looks later. He was a student. An extraordinary mathematician, a physicist, with enormous knowledge. And do you know that he had never been either in the Komsomol or the Pioneers. All the same, he had graduated from the university and had a splendid career ahead of him. In fact, in the cell he showed his mathematical abilities, even his ability to make calculations. There are people who are able to do complex multiplication problems mentally with lightning speed, and he was one of them. Besides that, he also gave us an excellent lecture on the theory of relativity, in quite popularized form but, at the same time, with great subtlety. Einstein's theory. I learned from him that he knew the theory of relativity well and that he knew Dirac, de Broglie and so on, even though he had no right to. They have excellent knowledge of those things, but it was only for trusted students, meaning those who come up through the Komsomol and so on.

And a very strange thing. He lived in Malakhovka. From what he told me of the place, I visualized a Chagallesque Jewish community, a Chagallesque world. Old Jewish men and women praying in a temple that would be destroyed during the anti-religion campaign under Khrushchev. I was in Malakhovka on my way back to Poland. A pine forest, rather sparse (bare, actually), sandy ground. Most of the young people did not keep to the traditions, but there were a great many homes where even the young people kept to the traditions of the pious Jews.

In fact, in Russia it's not so much Hasidism you find as orthodox, rabbinical Judaism. His family had probably not been Hasidic either, but very pious, very orthodox, very observant. And from what he told me, nothing had affected them. It had all just rolled off them. It dawned on me that in Russia, in those most dangerous Stalinist times, there were islands, and not only islands, rocks against which all that reforging of souls was smashed to pieces. Nothing had any power there. And those weren't old people.

It was clear that this young man was rooted in the good Jewish tradition. You know, people are very well brought up in that patriarchal-patrician tradition. As I already told you, Jews with chutzpah, those are Jews on the road to assimilation. Good Jewish orthodox families, however, bring up their children wonderfully; those are the traditions of generations that produce sui generis gentlemen, and he was proof of that. Another thing: I could see from his face, his expression, that he prayed—at sundown, for example. Of course, he had already been through a Soviet university, he was extremely careful, and he also accepted Soviet power completely, sincerely, in his heart. He was absolutely loyal. A Jewish loyalty, meaning God gave us this, perhaps God will take it away, people have to live, people do live, you must be a decent person and do your duty, and so on. A good tradition. And he prayed to himself not even moving his lips, but I could tell; it's easy to spot, especially since I was doing it myself.

At Zamarstynów—even though I didn't pretend to be Christian, I did envy them—I got used to saying a prayer before going to sleep, a habit that's still with me today and probably always will be. So many years! And I didn't miss saying my prayer on a single night. Most often in a distracted state, but not always. I said my prayer even at moments of total disbelief, complete atheism, even at the times when I felt a very strong need to return to Judaism. But I didn't stop. You might think this was a magic incantation, magic. But it probably wasn't.

MILOSZ: You learned it from the Ukrainians?

WAT: That's right. That came out yesterday without my meaning it to. I told you that I said "Our Father," "Hail Mary," and another one I can't remember even though I recited it for so many years. Yes, in that cell at Zamarstynów I was fascinated and shaped by the devotion of the Ukrainians, even though there were also some very devout Poles there, like that assistant prosecutor. But the Ukrainians were more devout—perhaps because they were country people; there was something crystalline about their devotion, and their devotion influenced me much more strongly than the Poles'. You said this was probably because, fortunately, they were unaware of Thomism, as you put it—and as I would too. But I rather suppose that it was also a closeness to the earth and the peasantry, the good peasantry—what is very good about the peasantry.

Why was the student arrested? What happened? The family was living in a single room, in some dacha hut, and they had the misfortune to quarrel with the woman who owned the house, after knowing her for years. And she wrote a denunciation—the student had said that General Golikov was a total drunk. The general was always drinking until he passed out. And so they put the student in prison. His political situation was probably shaky anyway; he'd never been a Pioneer. That was enough.

26 PLATO'S REPUBLIC. TIME AND ST. AUGUSTINE. EARLY SPRING IN MOSCOW AND MUSIC.

WAT: As a country with enormous distances and with an enormous number of people, Russia can't be ruled without the making of large numerical calculations. And large numerical calculations require allowances for figures that are unnecessary or imaginary, for excesses, eccentricities, and chance events. Stalinist planning, the so-called planning on a higher level, required the making of an antiplan—in the same sense as one says antiword, antimatter. The arrest of a young man who had the makings of an excellent specialist only because he said that General Golikov was an alcoholic belongs to the sphere of accepted illogicality, antilogic. Why were a student, a sailor, and a consulate chauffeur in Lubyanka? I wondered about that and may have been a bit irritated by it. How could it be: I had achieved an honor, Lubyanka, for the elite, the greatest transgressors against the Soviet state, and there I was with a sailor who by chance had become a deserter for a few days? That pricked my vanity a bit. What was this? Well, we know that Stalinist logic is not Aristotelian logic, and that it operates on the basis of contrasts, planned contrasts. No doubt this too had been planned by specialists, disciples of Pavlov, perhaps even experts on Zen, because Russia has a great many first-rate experts on the Orient, and not just on economics but on Oriental philosophy and religion. They probably all worked somewhere there, in the top section where the models for terror were worked out. They operate on a basis of Zen and Pavlov. They operate by employing shocks and contrasts to confuse the mind about everything.

What is the basis of a revolutionary's faith? To build the new, the old must be destroyed to its foundations, its very foundations. To uproot the roots. That's easy in the material world, economics. In the world of the mind, the soul, you can't destroy things like that. You can't begin from *nihil;* that isn't doable. The soul truly cannot abide a vacuum even for a single second. The remaking of humanity can only begin with confusion. The rebuilding of the entire old mentality, the entire old soul, I repeat, soul, because, despite accepted opinion, the Bolsheviks never denied the existence of the soul. There was argument on the point. I remember reading articles when I was young in *Under the Banner of Marxism,* long articles by the Pavlovians, the reflexologists, against the American behaviorists; they said the Americans denied the existence of the soul, but the soul exists. What prospects would Bolshevism have had if there were no soul? Bolshevism is the reshaping of souls. And if souls don't exist, what's there to reshape?

MILOSZ: In cases like that of the sailor being held at Lubyanka, or even the student, I would allow for a certain margin of foul-up and accident.

WAT: You're absolutely right. But I still wished to speak about the reshaping of souls because it was a chance to seize on something I had suspected while in prison. I want to stress this point: the essence of Stalinism is the reforging of souls. Meaning the educational aim on which Rousseau reflected in the *Contrat social.* And Marx even quotes Rousseau in that regard: everyone who has the courage to rebuild society and the state should have the courage to rebuild humanity. And that's what Plato's *Republic* is all about. And the term "corrective labor camp" was absolutely on the mark. Those are corrective camps, but with one proviso. The point was not to correct the five or fifteen million prisoners in them because they were a minority and Stalin was concerned with large numbers, large percentages; the only point was the population as a whole. Someone from every family was in a camp, and everyone could expect that. The point was for everyone to feel that threat at every moment, to know that the camps were terrible and that this could not be spoken of because this was something holy, sacral. To use the prisoners to educate the rest of the population who had not yet been put into camps.

Of course, you were right about foul-ups. There were terrible foul-ups in Russia—and those foul-ups had probably even been planned for, accounted for. That was obvious to me later on in civilian life. All that theft was tolerated to a certain degree; it was under control—that

232

entire paraeconomy in the Soviet Union. Stalinism had cast an iron net over Russia, but there were large gaps in the net that wouldn't have existed under German communism. People wouldn't have been able to live under German communism; everything would have come to a stop and died. But in Russia the gaps were large and you could wriggle through them. And people wriggled through. It's wrong to think this was at the price of depravity, crime, betrayal. Nothing of the sort. I met people in Russia who had never made any compromises, people who were pure. And somehow they had wriggled through. Chance, the grace of Providence. A cunning in their honesty, a certain flair all their own for making that sort of life.

A new change in the cell. A very interesting person arrived, a doctor with a Kalmuck face, a Russian-Mongolian cunning about his slightly slanted eyes. He was around fifty. Not tall, but strongly built, a bit like the iron build you see on NKVD men. I remember that nearly the first thing he said was, "Life, life! Under any conditions. In Lubyanka, in a camp, as long as it's life." That's the Russian nature. Life at any price! Imagine, many years later I translated *Vasya Zheleznov* and old Zheleznov says the exact same thing there. He's an old drunkard who's destroyed by his wife; he's afraid that she's poisoning him, which she is. She poisons him because he is facing trial for raping a minor; to avoid that compromising situation she poisons him. He's afraid of that, but he's not afraid of the trial and he's not afraid of prison. He even says, "Life at any price. Siberia, as long as I'm alive!" And so this was plagiary though I wasn't aware of it at the time. That's very widespread among the Russian intelligentsia—plagiarizing their own literature. They don't even know they're doing it. Literature has an enormous influence on them.

Days passed, weeks, the time-torture became more and more terrible. It was a gift from God that every once in a while I went to see my dear friend Lalashvili in whom I was now slowly losing confidence. My persecution mania came back to me at various times. I recall that someone told me—it might even have been Dunayevsky—about a great Chekist who introduced a new method. The Chekist was a very elegant gentleman, with a very handsome face, and he spoke refined French— and then suddenly, like lightning, his face would change and he'd either grab you by the hair or smash you in the teeth, his face wild as a Mongol's. An elegant conversation in French; then he'd grab a woman by the hair and rip out tufts of it. His face transformed. Clearly they'd been taught that. And so sometimes I didn't trust Lalashvili—maybe something like that would happen with him. Or with Nikolaev? Would I suddenly see the faces of beasts instead of those nice, intelligent, gentle Russians? I would give a lot to know what happened to all those people I met in Russia. Nikolaev must be dead, but Lalashvili might still be alive. Maybe he's some high official now. I'd be glad to see him; I'd shake his hand. He really was exceptionally kind to me all the way through.

And so, time-torture! Actually that's hard to talk about. I can't see it discursively. Time is an abstraction of God, duration. Can you imagine, I read St. Augustine's letters in Lubyanka. I was constantly reading. I had that thick volume of St. Augustine that contains his discourses on time. Have you read them? Very wise. On the whole, St. Augustine was a wise man. He perceives three present times. The present in the past, the current present, and the present in the future, which was very much in line with my own experience. Because I lived in the present—but in those three presents. My eyes had been opened, and I saw that I was basically living solely in the present, but in those three presents. Pure past and pure future do not exist in Lubyanka! That's one thing. But a second and perhaps even more essential thing was the tremendous blow he inflicted on Socratism. St. Augustine had come out of Greek philosophy, but it was he who negated it most radically (that's my opinion, despite the popular view). He used the terminology of Greek thought to destroy it; he undermined it, destroyed its very foundation. He makes this definition: what is time? As long as no one asks, I know what it is, but as soon as the question is put, I don't know a thing! Ultimately, this applies not only to time but to love or to God or to poetry. It's very important. It totally changes the mind's orientation.

Lalashvili's promise was kept; some money arrived. It wasn't an especially large sum, a few hundred rubles. Prisoners had the right to spend fifty or seventy-five rubles per ten-day period. Since I didn't have a lot, I of course tried to spend as little as possible each time we had canteen privileges. I limited myself to onions, garlic, bread, and especially lump sugar. It's a wonderful thing, lump sugar. I still have a weakness for it. Even in cafés I'll catch myself, completely unconsciously, slipping some lump sugar into my pocket. I'm not a cheap person; it's just that since Lubyanka I've loved lump sugar. Those lumps of sugar are beautiful. You have to admit they have a certain beauty. And you can see by their very form that they contain sweetness. They're well constructed; there's nothing superfluous about them. Those lumps of sugar were a delicacy for me, and here of course the beautiful and the useful were united—not as they are in constructivism, which I detest, but as they are in human life. A primeval unity. The naïve unity of the beautiful and the useful, the enormously useful. I was sparing with those lumps of sugar; I built up a reserve in case things became worse. I allowed myself delicacies a few times—those herrings that Dunayevsky contended the average Muscovite couldn't get. A few times. The time I had spent in prison in Warsaw and then later in Zamarstynów had accustomed me to being communal, to sharing with my cell mates.

I'd lost that habit and of course I did not share with the chauffeur, though I did give him something. He accepted food from Dunayevsky with gratitude and great dignity and did not feel in the least offended. But when he took food from me, even though I was more generous than Dunayevsky, it was clear that he felt offended. He accepted it, but with hatred, because for the most part he hated me. More and more all the time. I've mentioned the reason: my intellectual ways. And besides, he saw that I was always buzzing with Dunayevsky and talked to him very little even though we were both Poles. He wanted contact with his own people. For him Russia was hostile and alien—primarily that, alien. He didn't want to know anything about it. And so naturally he thought, two Jews, naturally the Jew is a traitor, and so on—because every Pole is *naturaliter* an anti-Semite; there are a great many Polish philo-Semites but, *naturaliter*, every Pole is an anti-Semite. That was the background that fed his hatred for me. That was terrible for me, for I could see that he felt offended when he took food from me and repaid me with an entirely natural hatred. I realized that he hated me for giving him that piece of bread. But what could I do? I kept on giving him food. And besides, he was very closemouthed; I didn't know how to get him to open up. Later on I was in all sorts of hospitals in Poland. I was often in the Ministry of Health's clinics for the elite. I was also in ordinary hospitals, and I know how easy it is to prompt a common man who's taciturn into talking, into opening up. It's easy. It's mostly a matter of ridding yourself of a certain arrogance. You must be sincere and authentic, for they feel it immediately if you're doing it to be democratic. You can't think of yourself as superior; you simply have to feel that if I occupy a higher position, that's because of the vagaries of fate, and I offset that with faults that my colleague from the people does not have, and he is thus superior to me in that respect.

Dunayevsky was in a melancholy turn of mind. Now he spent most of his time lying down and had to drag himself out for our walks. He would be mumbling as he woke up. What was he mumbling? Sometimes I heard him saying the four famous sounds that Marr thought were the source of all human speech, then words in various languages—Lithuanian, Greek, Persian, Polish, Russian. Always doing his etymology. There was something of a vacant look in his eyes now; he was demanding to be called in for an interrogation. He would come back very serene and peaceful from those interrogations, and so that probably meant that he now had a Lalashvili of his own.

One time he came back from interrogation exhilarated and said that he had finally been given something he'd been demanding for a long time. Specifically, he had been trying to convince them that he had a very materialistic theory of prehistoric times. He wanted to write, to be given permission to write. He could even get along without books, if only they would allow him to write. And now his investigator had told him that he had permission, that he could work in the cubicle every day for a couple of hours, as long as he liked, three hours, four. And that promise was kept; a few days later he went to the cubicle and started going every day. I think I've mentioned this already, but it was then that Dunayevsky told me that General Anders wrote his observations, his concept of the September campaign in the Polish-German war, in a cubicle of that sort; Anders makes no mention of this in his memoirs, which means either it's not correct or Anders was ashamed of it.

Dunayevsky became markedly calmer when he began writing in the cubicle. He'd been disturbing until then. The harmony between us had started to sour simply because I was afraid of his hysteria. I'm a hysteric by nature, and I was afraid that his hysteria would unleash mine. My hysteria was locked up tight.

No one would have said that I was experiencing states of hysteria because I knew how to keep them from showing, but it was genuine hysteria, connected to the fate of my family. My imagination ran wild. I knew that Ola had enormous strength—morally she was much stronger than I—but I was worried about her nerves, which were weak. I underestimated her physical strength and her nerves. I underestimated the degree to which moral strength can form, dominate, control, and rouse both the nervous system and the body itself. Ola performed labor that would have been difficult even for the peasant women in Kazakhstan. I tried to establish parapsychological contact with her but that didn't work, and so all I could do was use my imagination. Nothing worked; I couldn't locate them.

And so I was terribly despondent; I saw no end to any of it. There was Lalashvili, of course—our talks. I had already been to him four or five times. When I regained my trust in him, I asked him what was really going on with me; what was the point of all this? I don't remember his answers exactly, but in essence he said that my arrest had actually been rather a matter of chance. From that I concluded something I already suspected—that there had probably been orders to arrest a certain number of Polish writers, mostly people on the left, and the local people had made the selection. Rather a matter of chance. I never mentioned that I had been a communist at one time. That was an odd thing: all the time I was in Russia I never made a peep about having been a communist or about *The Literary Monthly*, Jasieński, Stande,

236

nothing, and no one brought it up—a sort of absolute taboo. I was very glad of that; I was intelligent enough to know that this was all to the good.

That I could ask Lalashvili about my case clearly meant that it had been a matter of chance, not only an accident but a stupid one as well. And so they had no special accusation against me. He said, "You'll get out; I can't tell you when, but it shouldn't be long now." It was March then, the beginning of April.

I asked, "What does that mean—not long? I keep hearing people say soon, soon, here, but soon can mean a day or an hour or a year or two years or five years." I was already a little angry. We were talking like human beings, and that meant I could get angry once in a while, truly show anger.

He said, "No, it might be a matter of weeks, it could be very soon." What did that mean? The end of April? Lalashvili said, "It's not out of the question, highly possible." I believed him and returned to the cells with spirits raised. I was constantly torn because inwardly I also knew that in principle people didn't get out of Soviet prisons. For that you needed a fundamental stroke of good luck. I knew I had little chance of winning that lottery; I wasn't lucky. But of course I went back to the cell with spirits raised.

Meanwhile, it was early spring. My only experience of early spring in Moscow was in Lubyanka, in a stifling cell. In that stifling, choking building. With very sporadic exceptions, our walks always took place down below, in a small, narrow courtyard, surrounded by large, tall buildings. But still the early spring penetrated the walls. I don't know if any other place has an early spring like Moscow. The winter is severe there. Some very odd things occurred—phantoms of the brain, the cerebral cortex. A falsification of organic, natural processes by the cerebral cortex. Illusory experiences. You know, after your arm is cut off, you feel what they call phantom pains in that part of your arm which isn't there any more. The cerebral cortex hasn't realized that the arm is gone, that cutting it off put an end to the pain, and so it stays on the most recent level of pain. It's the same with early spring. Early spring in Moscow really does melt and burst out with tremendous force. On the whole, those people in Russia who ascribe a great role to the climate in the formation of the national character may be right, because those severe winters followed by that sudden break-up of the ice, those early springs, elicit an incredible outburst of vital, organic forces. Libido, but not only libido in the sexual sense, a mighty libido—to live, to live at any cost, as the official from Mongolia had put it.

Sometime before Easter we were taken up to the roof—I don't know why—it was the first time in daylight as well. Darkness was falling, dusk. But the sky and the air—the early spring easily overtook its victims there, for we were its victims. My feelings grew keener. I felt the early spring around me, and I could also hear music. They were playing Bach's *St. Matthew Passion* on the radio for Easter—can you imagine? It was just coming to an end, but it reached my section of the roof. It was the second time I had heard music since being imprisoned. Unfortunately, it was the finale and then came some Russian music— maybe Shostakovich; I don't know. But something very beautiful, very solemn, in keeping with Easter. I spoke of illusory experiences because the prison regimen caused your biological juices to dry up. There were no juices in me, and so that was an unreal experience. It was the brain, the brain that had given me that sense of effervescence, the feeling that my juices were flowing even though there were none to flow. I had a twofold feeling. On the one hand I could feel my juices, the juices of life, of real life, and on the other hand I had a physical sensation like the one that everyone has in winter, the feeling that the inner vital forces have been completely dried up for a good long time. I had a body but a dried-up body that craved real food, a vexatious burden of a body. The soul, the spirit, was completely separate from the body; there were no juices in me, no archer in me, no biological vitality, nothing that makes for real life in a person. And so, experiencing those two aspects, one dried-up, the other juicy, I realized that the juices were fictitious. It's a question of sex, of course. And clearly this was the effect of the prison regimen, especially a Soviet one—there was no sexual libido.

Later on I learned that this causes color to disappear. You don't see the colors. The world is only gray or black and white; you don't see color. The first color I saw as a free man was in Alma-Ata. It was then that I realized I was seeing colors for the first time, that I hadn't been seeing them before. A world without sex is a world without color. That was my experience. I don't want to talk about this, because it's part of my autobiography in the strict sense, but I was tormented by sex, meaning that I was terribly excitable sexually. I had been highly excitable all through my youth, especially since I did not come from a puritanical home. For quite a long time, in any case for a few years, I imposed certain ideals of castration on myself. I thought that Origen had done exactly the right thing. You know what I mean. Then came the fall, what I thought was a fall. I told you that I used to dream, very often if not always, that I was flying along, an inch above the ground. You said you still had those dreams but after my first "fall," as I called it, I stopped having those dreams, and I never soared above the earth again. But in Lubyanka peace had finally returned to me; I was like a eunuch there. Then, suddenly, it was early spring. That false intoxication or, actually, that purely cerebral intoxication, again as if by magic—not like the paintings of St. Anthony; this wasn't bad, it was lovely, the world of sexual beauty. And that was connected to the music I heard. The first music I had heard had been in Zamarstynów, and it had made a powerful impression on me. One of the NKVD men had a phonograph and one record. Some hit song of the time, the counterpart of the songs of those American women singers who sing from the uterus, the womb. A womb, a hungry, starving womb. A womb that desires a spasm, that's waiting for a spasm. In reality, that's what life is—a spasm.

27 BACH AND NATURE. A VISIT TO ERFURT. DUNAYEVSKY'S MANIA. THE MONGOLIAN DOCTOR. QUESTIONED BY A HIGH PARTY OFFICIAL. THE WRITING CUBICLE. THE GERMANS INVADE YUGOSLAVIA.

WAT: So there we were on the roof, our twenty-minute walk. We were talking about early spring and that rush of life's juices in nature, in the air, all around me. My God! I was only forty-one at the time; physically, I didn't feel old, but aged past my years. And so those juices were false, fictitious, but they gave me an incredibly strong rush. And during that walk, on that narrow space, at twilight, on the roof of Lubyanka, the Kremlin's towers visible, I could hear Bach, the finale of *St. Matthew Passion*. At a point where the Passion was still occurring but already at the beginning, the promise of the Resurrection. In my relationship to Christianity the Resurrection had always been the greatest sticking point, the resurrection of the body and the Resurrection of Christ. To tell the truth, for me, Christianity always basically ended on the cross. And here was the promise of resurrection. The Passion is one thing but, as in Bach, there is also exaltation, *exultavit*, and what would seem to be a harmony with the juices of reawakening life. To all appearances this is the archer, that is, an Egyptian or Attis-like sun god, who dies in the winter and who is resurrected (rises) from his separate parts again in the spring. Scholars of religion and anthropologists relate Christ's death and resurrection to those archetypes of the god who dies and is resurrected, the sun god. But it's nothing of the sort.

It was at Lubyanka, there on that roof, and precisely because I had such an incredibly keen sense of how juiceless and cut off from nature my body was, that I saw in Bach's *Passion* the essential and immense difference between Christ and Attis. Because something else comes into play; whether it's dialectical or not, I don't know. All right, there's nature. I am a *Naturmensch*. Nature rises from the dead. In the music I heard, God was rising from the dead in some higher superstructure. There is a harmony between me—nature that rises from the dead— and God, who also rises from the dead. But because I also had a terrifically strong feeling that this was a temptation by the devil, I also felt that nature did not exist; it was an illusion. The body had no juices— the body, not the soul; that meant that Bach's God is not the God of Nature. He is anti-Nature. That wasn't well put. Now you would use expressions like antimatter, antipoetry. So, let's say, transnature, the transubstantiation of nature. The pagan cults of the God who dies and comes back to life are cults of nature. Of *Naturmenschen*. But Bach is something else.

And this is another case of something that occurs frequently—things are identical on the surface but in reality belong to two entirely different worlds. In Bach's music I also heard an earthly joy, dignified, like Bach's family life, where people eat and drink—and like to eat and drink—a sense of life, life lived with decorum. Bach is religious music, but in Bach's work, even in the *Passion*, religion and faith are hemmed in by all sorts of doubts. Anyway, all our problems and troubles certainly are better expressed in music than in words.

It seems to me that music, generally speaking, is the proper language for philosophy. I'm not talking about today's scientific philosophy, logic, but what lies beyond logic, metaphysical philosophy. Maybe I'm launching into too much commentary here—there are times when I can't stand it either, but somehow I have a weakness for digression. Schopenhauer's definition of music as architecture in time. Metaphysical philosophical thought is speculation in the good sense of the word, not speculation occurring in space but in time. Logic is rather spatial, but traditional philosophy is temporal; music is a better language for human thought; it expresses what words cannot.

I was convinced then that for the first and last time I knew what infinity was; to be more precise, I knew infinity. For a long time I thought I had heard a piece of the finale of the *St. Matthew Passion*. I was mistaken. In spite of, or perhaps precisely because of, my experience of it coming as such a shock, I couldn't remember anything of the music itself. Now I think it might have been the fifth, or the fourth cantata of the *Christmas Oratorio*. I seem to remember that the singing broke off at the words *im jüdischen Lande*. One way or the other, it was Bach. If Dunayevsky hadn't confirmed it, I'd have thought I'd been hallucinating.

If the human voice, manmade instruments, and the human soul can create, even once in all of history, such harmony, beauty, truth, and power in such unity of inspiration—if this exists, then how ephemeral, what a nonentity, all the might of the empire must be, that might that a beautiful Polish carol says "quakes in fear." It's a commonplace line, but I'm an old man and I stopped being afraid of the commonplace a long time ago—what the critics call a commonplace. That wasn't a thought I had while listening to Bach because I simply wasn't a "thinking being" at that moment. I was listening. But that thought did come to me as the last chords were fading. With desperate nostalgia I tried to summon them back from memory, but to no avail. The only sound was the wind howling over the roof of Lubyanka.

Since that time I have heard a great many of Bach's cantatas and I can't say with inner certainty of any one of them, That's it! I did not conceptualize my experience of the music at the time, and a memory untrained in music is not dependable. When I listen to the cantata from the *Christmas Oratorio* and I bring myself to a state of receptive spiritual emptiness, I am of course penetrated by its beauty and its power, but the structure of the original experience has been lost, and I can't find any way to even begin getting back to it.

But the shadow of memory's wing did pass over me once. It was in 1949. I had wangled my way into a delegation invited to Weimar for a Goethe festival. At the time I was writing a novel about German society under Nazism, intending to analyze Soviet society by analogy, a futile plan because it would be too transparent not only to the censors but to everyone else as well. After two years of work and after publishing two or three chapters in *Twórczość* [*Creative Work*], I had given up on the idea. The book's point of departure had been a bronze plate I had seen on a crematory oven at Auschwitz. It read, "Topf und Söhne, gegründet in 1886, Erfurt." I imagined the two junior Topfs, one of whom I saw as a classical philologist by education and calling who had ordered reliefs of the Grecian image of the spirit of death to be put on the doors of the luxurious ovens and who would have used quotations from the *Iliad* on his brochures, in particular the passage in which Hector's spirit implores Achilles that his remains be burned. [While in Weimar, I went to] Erfurt and was in the office of Mr. Topf, who had taken refuge in West Germany, and on his book shelf I saw Sophocles, Epictetus, Seneca, and so forth in German and also Kiesewatter's books on Homer. His younger brother had committed suicide as I had planned for him to do in my novel. I knew that this would be my last trip to the

West, the Sovietization of Poland having been accelerated that year. I was preparing myself to take the life test I had failed in Lwów and pass it this time, at any cost. So, I traveled from Weimar to Erfurt; I had only four free hours. I was to make the concluding speech at the [Goethe festival] banquet, but I didn't know what I was going to say. That was the fastest speech I ever wrote, and the most ambiguous one as well.

I visited the [Topf] factory, but even though that was the reason I had undertaken the journey, I gagged with disgust and renewed hatred for the Germans. The chief engineer said to me, "There's nothing to see here. Yes, we exported crematoria during the war, and they were used in Buchenwald too. Buchenwald is a small German town; people die there like they do everywhere else. They used to bring the bodies to the cemetery in Weimar, but transportation is expensive in wartime and so we installed crematoria there." I rebuked the engineer, who was pasty from his fear of me. Then I ran out with a welter of emotions and wandered around the old city.

At one moment I was paralyzed with fear: I found myself on an enormous square of medieval cobblestones, facing the huge soaring stone mass of a cathedral and the Severinkirche adjoining it; the low, even line made by the fronts of the patricians' houses was miniaturized by the distance between them and the cathedral. This is the real Gothic, I thought at first, the might and mass of a sacred thing, faced at a humble distance by secular things. ("Secular" cannot convey the essential connotations of the Latin *profanus*, the first and basic wording of the mysteries: *Procul este profani*.) A moment later, the memory of my experience of Bach seemed to stir in the dark depths of memory. Of course, there is no sensible analogy here: the severe mass of the cathedral, no doubt purposely left unadorned by the architect, and Bach's refined Baroque; moreover, what could there be in common between a medieval patriciate and the rabble of bolshevism. Above all, I think that the tension between the sacred and the secular was revealed to me for a moment on the roof of Lubyanka.

Despite all the terrible obsessive monotony of the days and weeks in Lubyanka, those twenty minutes on the roof were a very rich experience, incredibly rich. Twenty minutes can hold so much! Twenty minutes is enough for the most important thing in your life to happen. Isn't that so? That does happen. I had been emotionally stirred, but that was a very hard period in my life. I probably had never suffered like that before, not even in Zamarstynów when I felt people's sweat on me, men's sweat—another man's sweat is a terrible thing for a man to feel. I had not suffered in that commune of male sweat, lice, and anxiety as I did in Lubyanka. I suffered terribly. Before that, I would never have believed that you could suffer to that degree, that acutely, and not die, that you could bear it. I had never been through a time that painful before. (It was to happen once again, in perhaps an even worse form, many years later, in your Arcadian Berkeley, where I was given ideal living conditions. Very strange, it's a mystery to me. Yes, in Berkeley it was probably even worse. But it was terrible back then, terrible.)

Why had it been much better in Zamarstynów, and then infinitely better later on when I was in jail with those bandits? It was probably better in Zamarstynów because I was living a social existence there. I was forced to be social. Not in the socialist sense of the word, but really in the Christian sense. Lice, hunger, malnutrition, and yet that was agape. The agape of people who aren't of the proper religion and who are thrown *ad leones*. And so there was real community. By the time I was in Lubyanka I had a keener sense of the main law of social relations under Stalin. I called it the law of third. Wherever two of you gather, I shall be there with you, "I" meaning the party, Stalin, an agent. It is through the police that a brother is a brother to his brother, and a friend a friend to his friend. The law of the greatest possible disjunction of the social bonds between people.

There had been some social relations there at the beginning, thanks to Dunayevsky and that Pole, but they deteriorated from one day to the next. The main reason was that Dunayevsky was acting odd. He'd stopped talking; he spoke out loud to himself—actually, he mumbled. Sometimes there was hatred in his eyes when he looked at any of us. Sometimes, especially when he'd begun writing, his linguistic obsessions would get on my nerves. Writing gradually brought him to a state of complete hysteria. He'd come back excited every time he would discover something new about prehistoric man and the history of language. One time he came back after making a great discovery, and he told me about it. I said, "Méfiez vous de cette facilité."

I forgot to mention that we often spoke French and even more often German, of which he had a very good command. It's like that sometimes in Jewish families where German is basically the lingua franca—maybe because Yiddish is actually a distortion of Old German. And so when we were talking about political beliefs or, for example, his view of the arithmetic of morality, Dunayevsky would speak German. And sometimes, when the issues were just too delicate, to spare each other's feelings we'd speak a foreign language. What I had said, *méfiez vous*, infuriated him, and he nearly lost control of himself. He was also surly and rude to the chauffeur, to whom he had always shown great tolerance and human sympathy. There was an irritable, argumentative air about him, and we all had it too. We radiated mutual vexation: people who are closed up together for a long time begin to hate each other.

243

At that time my most enjoyable companion was that doctor from Mongolia, a jovial man with an enormous sense of humor. When I'd come back from Lalashvili cheered by the prospect of my release, the Mongolian would not want to dampen my spirits, but he was skeptical. A jovial skeptic, unlike Dunayevsky, who took everything seriously. I don't remember exactly but the Mongolian said something like, "They'll squeeze the various things they need out of you, information, technical questions, and then you'll be put in a camp, of course."

I'd say, "All right, but Lalashvili is a wonderful person. You don't believe that. Do you think that Lalashvili is like all the rest of them?"

He'd say, "How should I know? I've never seen the man. I have complete confidence in you when you say he's different, that he's not a bastard and a liar. But one day when he's found out everything he wanted to know, he'll pass your file on to someone else. That's all. He won't even pass it on himself; it'll just go from him to someone else. Or maybe it won't; most likely your sentence is already in your file; it's just been postponed. But people live in the camps, people can live anywhere."

He was very intelligent and witty; he had a sense of humor, very jovial. He didn't take anything tragically, even his own fate. Sometimes he'd be terribly upset, seething; he'd say, "I drank with them all the time, every night, and now they punch me in the face and fire their pistols at me." He'd be furious and then immediately he'd burst into laughter. After the indignation, a good joke, a farce! I was very fond of him—an enjoyable companion; they're the best sort in prison.

Meanwhile, Lalashvili called me in to see him with surprising news. He said, "I have information from Warsaw now. It's very, very positive." Information from Warsaw at the beginning of 1941, and about a pawn like me! What an efficient network they had in Warsaw. "All the information indicates that you're a reliable person." He didn't just have one source, but a few sources, a few people. "That moves your case along quite a way."

And so I said to him, "Have you been able to find any information about my family?"

"I have certain information. They're both healthy; I can assure you of that, both of them. Their life isn't easy; they're living in very difficult conditions."

And I said, "So, do something to get them out of there; let them go somewhere else where conditions are better."

And he replied, "You see, it wouldn't really be worth it because you'll definitely be released, and if your family were released beforehand, that would cast a certain shadow on you; people are suspicious," and so on.

Then my fear came back to me: they're preparing me for something;

they don't want me to appear compromised later on. Although relations with Dunayevsky had soured, I sought his advice again and told him my fears. He reassured me, said I was exaggerating and that there were all sorts of ways of exploiting people. He had suddenly taken it into his head that I was someone of great distinction and he said, "They don't force people who are on a certain level to collaborate in anything. They can be handy to the Soviet Union just by doing what they do."

Aha, another thing! All the time I was in Lubyanka I let it be known, discreetly, not flagrantly, that I was no longer a writer, that I had stopped writing a long time ago, that I had lost it and was finished with it. I was an editor now. Because I had an idea of what to do in case I was released. Dunayevsky asked me, "What do you actually want to do when they release you? What are you going to do? How do you picture it?" A direct, realistic question. I had an idea; namely, I very much wanted to work as a specialist in a publishing house, not in Moscow but in Novosibirsk or someplace where there are quite serious publishers. And so when giving my opinions and analyzing literature for Lalashvili, I would manipulate the conversation to make him think, let him know, that I was a good editor, that I knew how to analyze a work. Of course I made my usual blunder. I'm a blunderer. I bragged that at Gebethner's I had published at least twenty titles a year with only six co-workers, none of whom was an editor. I was the editor. I never gave anyone anything to read; I had no confidence in them. Of course, this was a blunder here, because a Soviet publishing house that puts out twenty books a year has to have two hundred workers; that's the basis of the Soviet economy. Otherwise, there'd be unemployment. That's the basis of the entire economy. A person who replaces two hundred people with six is death to the Soviet economy and isn't smiled on. On the contrary.

Lalashvili summoned me again and said very ceremoniously that someone wished to see me. He took me by elevator to a floor above or below. He knocked at the door with a sort of official respect. Another office with rugs, clean and tidy, nice smelling; a man in civilian clothes at a desk. Lalashvili held himself straight as a ramrod; then he left the two of us alone. A very important person, I thought, for Lalashvili to treat him with so much respect. Meanwhile, the impression the man made on me was that of a leftist shoemaker, a Warsaw Jew, wearing his good Saturday suit. A self-educated man, intelligent, but a tailor or a shoemaker. The face of an honest Warsaw Jewish tailor, not the owner of a tailor shop but a master tailor, a union activist.

Speaking Polish with a Yiddish accent, making grammatical errors, he said, "Tell me, has Warsaw changed a lot in recent years?" Another surprise. He had the face of a respectable man, a father, a paterfamilias. The face of a traditional Jew, but of a communist too.

We talked. I told him about Warsaw, almost tenderly, without hiding it. I asked him, "When did you leave Warsaw?"

"Oh," he said, "years back!" It sounded as if it was sometime during the First World War. He spoke Polish very badly. But he spoke Polish and he wanted to speak it. He would switch to Russian when he had to be exact. He said, "Your case isn't so bad, of course, but we still haven't come to an exact judgment on you." But he said that I could improve my lot. He said, "I'd like to propose something to you. Agree if you want to and don't if you don't. You've spoken with your investigator a lot about literature; he's told me a little about it." I had the impression that he wasn't NKVD, but from the party. But the respect Lalashvili showed him meant that this was someone highly esteemed in the Kremlin. He clearly wasn't part of Lubyanka; the office wasn't his. That was completely obvious; it was not his office. And so I thought he was someone from the top of the Polish or Russian party who worked on Polish affairs. "I want to propose—and this can change things a great deal, speed things up a lot—that you put what you tell the investigator in writing."

I didn't know how to respond to that proposition. Evidently Lalashvili had told him that I was still mistrustful and stubborn, because he said immediately, "Please understand that this isn't a matter of denouncing anyone. The point here is to give us some idea of what you're about and how you view these things." That came out of a slightly different barrel than Lalashvili's approach. Lalashvili was clearly interested in learning, but this was something else again; this one, as he himself said, wanted to see who I was. As a mind, a *capacité*. Of course, I replied that basically yes, I could do it.

But then I went back to the cell and began playing Hamlet something terrible again. What to write? Dunayevsky gave me his typical advice, "Make it as interesting and true as you can. Say what you think. Don't paint things too black, and don't make them too pretty either. Tell it the way you see it. Be sincere and honest." Yes, but to speak honestly, doesn't that mean to tell the positive and the negative? And in that echo chamber the negative could have terrible consequences for people. The positive would fade away in time but the negative would emerge in all its virulence. If the man, the pseudo-tailor, who had talked with me, was broad-minded, then perhaps he could be told the negative, though that was doubtful. But a piece of paper remains a piece of paper, and it would go to other departments that would be looking for something else. I was very much aware of that. It was a dangerous game, and there was no possibility of being honest there. What was needed was tactics.

And so I was brought to the cubicle. I don't remember how many times—three, or four? Then I stopped. It had been an error of cowardice—to maneuver and use tactics. Completely off target. I don't remember what I wrote, but I do know those were tactical maneuvers, a covert apologia for the people about whom I was writing. Afterward, Lalashvili would talk with me and tell me what interested them and ask if it interested me. Could I write about such and such. He had an entire list. I'd say, "I know about this, but I know practically nothing about that." And of course I made made my choices accordingly. Since that all happened on the spot, spontaneously, there was also the danger that, influenced by the spontaneity of the situation, I would say, yes, I can write about X, and then on reflection I would see that X was exactly the wrong person to write about.

MILOSZ: Didn't you consider writing something completely abstract, an analysis of some sort, without using any names?

WAT: But it was names that mattered to them. They told me that. And the pseudo-tailor assured me again that there was no question of denunciations here, that God forbid I should cast aspersions or make accusations. I believed him. He may have been right; they weren't policemen. But they didn't trust Poles, were afraid of them, and at the same time they knew that because of the Stalinist system's terrible overestimation of literature and writers, they would have to deal with those writers. They would have to. Because that's incredibly important in education. Literature and writers. But they were very afraid of Polish writers, all of them. Perhaps less of the communist ones, but maybe even more. They were afraid, didn't know them, didn't trust them—you know, the Russian stereotype of the treacherous Pole. Who the hell knows what cunning tricks he's up to! That's the Russians' constant fear with Poles—that something's wrong, something's going on, there has to be some trick.

Since the word on me from Warsaw was that I was a reliable person, Lalashvili and the others stressed that good report, used it to make sentimental appeals to me. Even the pseudo-tailor mentioned that all their references had termed me a reliable person. Obviously, the references had come from communists who were still in Warsaw. In the years after I moved away from the party, I had been semiboycotted, not like Stawar, because I had not been in the party. I had been aware that I was being boycotted by the communist writers, but the old, real communists, even though they did not keep up relations with me, were very warm to me when we met (some even used to come see me). The political people, the union activists—not the writers.

And so it was torture to sit there and wrack my brains over where I should use a little wisdom and where the cunning of the serpent. I didn't succeed. I don't remember what I wrote. As I say, those were inept masked attempts to lead them astray, inept because I was counting on their distrust and tried to put in some of the fine shadings as well.

I remember very clearly what I wrote about Wacław Grubiński; they asked a lot about him. The names that they provided, that interested them the most, were of course the names of people in Lwów, in particular those who had been arrested the same night I had. Both Broniewski and Peiper were in Lubyanka, but I wasn't aware of it, even though I assumed that if I was there, Broniewski would have to be, too. But I never figured that Peiper was in Lubyanka. I was certain the others were gone because at the end of my time in Zamarstynów, and even in the winter of 1941, sentences were coming down and prisoners were being transported to the camps; there were transports every few days. You could hear them in the courtyard. I was sure that my literary colleagues had been in the camps for a long time already. And so the questions about them were probably not part of their investigation; perhaps their trials were under review; maybe they were deciding whether to let them rot in camps or to let them go.

In connection with Wacław Grubiński I wrote about the *Warsaw Courier*, which I analyzed, calling it a bourgeois newspaper, certainly reactionary, but more in the sense of conservative than in the sense of the militant petit-bourgeois fascistic NDs. It was, rather, conservatism, Polish conservatism, peaceful, respectable, middle-class. I wrote that Grubiński had never been an anti-Semite; I was certain of that. Anti-Semites wrote for the *Warsaw Courier*, but not only anti-Semites. Yes, of course, Grubiński had written a lampoon of Lenin, but it was so silly and stupid, so lacking in historical vision—for him history was a Warsaw salon—that it had no significance whatsoever.

And so I used cunning to blend the light and the dark. But that cunning was all too apparent. I know that it didn't work and afterwards it pained me—that I had written anything at all in that cubicle in Lubyanka. That was very bad for me. I don't know how many times I did it, three or four, but in the end I said I wouldn't write any more. I don't remember how many of those profiles I wrote. Maybe five; I'd write one or two at each session. I asked to see Lalashvili again. He made no objections; it was clear he was displeased, but he accepted that it wasn't working, that I could talk but had lost the habit of writing, and there was no point in continuing.

MILOSZ: Did you write in Polish?

WAT: No, in Russian. Naturally, I wrote in Russian.

That was the end of that. Lalashvili accepted it, and it didn't alter his sympathetic attitude toward me, even when I told him I wouldn't be writing any more. But since we had no more to say to each other, I left, without even having any tea that time.

Dunayevsky was getting worse all the time. He was having silent ecstasies, murmuring to himself in silent ecstasy. Followed by rages. You know, sometimes his eyes were red with rage like some kind of mad dog. He practically wasn't talking to anyone. And everyone was a little afraid of him and tried to stay on his good side. His madness was driving me mad.

One morning, after a night full of nightmares, horrible nightmares, like the ones I had at Zamarstynów—my mother with claws of some sort—I got up very upset. I could see signs of madness in me and was convinced that if I stayed in that cell much longer I would go out of my mind. It was early. Dunayevsky was sitting on his bed, saying, "Ish, shaa, shashaai, isha." He kept repeating "shaa, ishaa." He saw that I had wakened, and with a burst of his old good feeling for me, he said, "That's how it started, that was the first word. The males were crouching in the reeds waiting for the females to come by. They could see a female coming along the water. And not to frighten her away, they said 'sha' to each other. Later on *sha* became *isha*. In Hebrew *isha* means woman."

A shudder went through me. I couldn't take it any more. His eyes were wild, on fire. He was in some sort of eureka state. He had discovered the origin of language. I couldn't take it any more. I told him to stop, that this was no discovery; it was madness, a mania. I argued angrily; I was overcome with rage. I was trying to save myself; soon I'd be saying "shsh, sha, sha." I wanted to, I was tempted to repeat after him "sha, sha, isha." Something in me was already starting to. And so I was overcome with fury. It was terrible. Deeply wounded, he just fell back on his bed and closed his eyes, pale as a corpse. He didn't say a word the whole day; he didn't eat. They took him away not long after that.

MILOSZ: For what reason?

WAT: Because of what he'd written. They already knew that he was a madman, but maybe they believed he had something to say. He had studied with Marr.

He told me a great deal about Marr, things I hadn't known. Namely, that Marr was self-taught; he was not a linguist, he was an autodidact of genius. He knew countless dialects and had really made certain discoveries. It was he who discovered the astonishing similarity of the languages and etymologies of the Basques and the Causcasian mountain people. And they certainly shared no ethnic origin. Of course, Marr took a Marxist, socioeconomic approach here, saying that economic conditions were responsible.

249

Actually, Stalin owes his design for a Soviet language, a communist language, to Marr. In something Marr wrote, I read that society and human consciousness could be changed by language, by giving words other meanings. Semantic displacement, he called it—*semantichesky sdvig* in Russian. That was his formulation. And that no doubt gave Stalin occasion to develop his theory of the superstructure further. Another one of Stalin's contributions to demonic derision is that it was Stalin who started the thaw and de-Stalinization with his pamphlet on linguistics in which he attacked Marr's entire theory; Stalin argued in his own fashion that human language belonged neither to the base nor to the superstructure. A revolutionary thing in Marxist philosophy. If language does not belong to the base or the superstructure, then the entire theory of the base and the superstructure is, essentially, destroyed. And the course Stalin's writing and thought took later, his last pamphlet on the Soviet economy, indicates that he was slowly but steadily moving away from all Marxism. That's my guess, but it's a minor point.

Dunayevsky was taken away. The chauffeur was also taken away a bit later. Of the old crew only the doctor from Mongolia was left. He had a very good effect on my nerves. But I was suffering, suffering terribly. For some reason, the dynamo of my problems and religious feelings that had started up in Zamarstynów was now spinning faster.

Enough time had passed for me to be released, according to what Lalashvili had said, and so I wrote another request for him to see me. As always, Lalashvili was quick to call me in. During the day. I think that was the first time for that.

Something very strange happened in those corridors. I had never seen a single investigator in the corridor—they were always walled within their offices—but this time they came running out; their doors were open. They must not question people at this hour, I thought. Open doors and a group of officers in the corridor discussing something with enormous excitement. Something's happened, I thought. I kept walking—and as I've already said, before the war I had become sensitive to animals, to signs that came through animals. The corridor was empty now, and in that very long corridor, in that incredibly tidy building, something too big for a mouse and too small for a rat darted across our path a short distance ahead. It stopped in the middle of the corridor and then immediately ran back. One instant of reflection. The way mice and cockroaches reflect—especially cockroaches when they're in a panic; they stop and fall into philosophic reflection. One second of philosophical reflection and then they immediately run away. And nearly always back to the hole they've just come out of, without looking for any other one. Though sometimes they do look for another one. I thought, Oh, this is something important.

But I didn't see anything different about Lalashvili or about Nikolaev, except that Nikolaev was up to his ears in work again. Lalashvili greeted me with a nice smile as he always did. He clearly liked me, and I liked him; we were simpatico. He asked me what the matter was and I said, "The time limit you promised has passed; you set the deadline, and it's passed."

"But you see, the international situation has changed." What had happened in the international situation that could prevent my release? The Germans had done something very bad in Yugoslavia. They had information on it now. They had expected it, but not to that degree. And so that tells me the date—the taking of Yugoslavia. Evidently there had been a pact like the one Churchill proposed to Stalin later on, a fifty-fifty split on spheres of influence, and the Germans hadn't kept it.

And so I said to him, "What do I have to do with Yugoslavia, and what does Yugoslavia have to do with me? I was never in Yugoslavia, and I don't think I know one Yugoslavian—one Albanian, all right, but he didn't live in Yugoslavia. And that's all."

"But you see, people aren't let out of prison when the international situation takes a bad turn." He said this in such a way that I could see this was a hard-and-fast rule, and that put an end to the discussion.

Because I take the dark view and because everyone was predicting that Soviet-German relations would get worse and worse, I saw no hope of the international situation improving. And so that killed my hopes of release. How was I going to stand the torture of empty time in a cell in Lubyanka? How much time could I stand? I had already realized that I wouldn't be sent to a camp, that I'd be there in that tin can. Dunayevsky had been there more than three years, and I knew of people who had been in Lubyanka for five years. I had already heard about Orlovsky Central and Omsk Central, prisons that were like mausoleums. They tell a guy's family that he's dead, but he lives another twenty years, or ten, or fifteen, and no one knows. An airtight tomb for the living. Lubyanka was very tight too. And so the prospects were not very rosy. After my experience with Dunayevsky, my reaction to him, where would it end? In madness. Once again, I was not feeling very light-hearted. New prisoners came. Our cell had been broken up. Even the Mongolian doctor had vanished.

By then I knew that there were worse prisons than Lubyanka in Moscow. Lefortovo. People are tortured at Lubyanka too, as I learned later on when I was in another prison with people who had been tortured. People were tortured physically, not only morally and mentally. But Lefortovo was designated especially for those who are to be tortured. Lefortovo has luxurious cells, solitary cells; it's actually an old military prison. A toilet in every cell. Luxury. But they torture people there. And there's one prison the Russians fear even more. Sukhanovka, in the woods outside Moscow. It's for those who are to be shot. I assume that none of my cell mates ended up in Lefortovo, or especially in Sukhanovka. They might have been transferred to Butyrki; there are plenty of prisons in Moscow.

28 NEW CELL MATES. THE EZHOV TERROR. A FORMER POLISH INTELLIGENCE AGENT. TAITZ. BERIA. KIRSANOV. GOG AND MAGOG.

WAT: I had new cell mates now. Such indistinct personalities that none of them have remained in my memory, with one exception, who was rather drab himself. He was older than I, or maybe my age. A high-ranking dignitary, a typical apparatchik. A high-ranking apparatchik from Kharkov. From a very important department, a second or third secretary, something of that sort. A bean pole, good-looking in a skinny way. I don't trust people with that bean-pole look. But he was a communist, an old communist, absolutely honest, an idealist, very straightforward. When he came to the cell he looked enormously depressed but, more than that, surprised.

He had just come from a camp, which I found hard to believe, because he looked perfectly fine; he had on good clothes and was in good physical shape. Maybe he had some office job in the camp.

He had been brought to Lubyanka for a review of his trial; he was a victim of the purges in 1937, 1938; he was one of the victims of the Ezhov terror of that time, and though they were a negligible percentage of the prisoners, there were still quite a few of them, of course. The prosecutor, not the investigative authorities, was bringing them in from the camps for a review of their trials. My new cell mate had important evidence to give, and, since he had been brought specially to Lubyanka, he was hoping for a positive outcome because he was not guilty of anything and now finally that would be brought to light.

But he had that look of surprise. Because he was a person who with all his pure heart believed in the justice of the Ezhov terror, and it was only as far as he was concerned—and of course the other honest comrades like him whom he knew—that a terrible, calamitous error had been made. He believed that with all his pure heart, but somehow that didn't fit in with his look of surprise. And so I think that constant look of surprise in his eyes and the way he hesitated occasionally when speaking were the result of doubts that had come upon him in the camp— some things were out of whack with the theory. He really thought that Comrade Stalin didn't know about any of it.

He was not like that old liar Ehrenburg, who lied in the memoirs he wrote in his old age when he said that at that time he had believed that Comrade Stalin didn't know. A good tsar but with no idea of what those scoundrels his ministers are doing. That old peasant legend dates back to Pugachev [leader of peasant uprising, 1773–1775], and that's what the old cynic Ehrenburg, who had wallowed in all the gutters of Paris, was supposed to have believed. In his memoirs, Ehrenburg even says that Pasternak had said the same thing to him. But Pasternak isn't alive to refute that. And that Pasternak was able to believe this—that's something else again. Apart from his immense acuity and the intuition of a born poet, Pasternak had a certain mental ceiling; there was something almost retarded about him. But Ehrenburg? My cell mate, however, absolutely believed it.

By and large the Ezhov terror was discussed in the cells, but the names of its famous victims were not; names like Bukharin, Trotsky, were not mentioned. Moreover, it was rare that we got any books that were current, and the few that weren't Marxist, just some general histories, though the introductions were current. Some of the introductions to the wonderful books published by the Academy had even been written by people who had since become victims of the Ezhov terror. And the names of the damned had been meticulously blacked out with India ink, a sign that very intelligent people were working in the prison library and reading everything. Loyal, obedient, intelligent people, and reading everything.

Word went around Lubyanka that Fanya Kaplan was a librarian in Lubyanka. Fanya Kaplan was the SR [Social Revolutionary] who tried to assassinate Lenin and whom Lenin would not allow to be executed. Stalin respected Lenin's will and did not execute her. She was supposed to be in Lubyanka working as a librarian, and I assume that this was done with an eye to history. The good emperor who had pardoned his would-be assassin. But of course nothing was written about it— what a terrible example that would set for Soviet citizens. [Kaplan was in fact executed in 1918.]

I had my own dream. Since Lalashvili was so good to me, I hinted that I was an expert on librarianship. My dream was that they would take me on as a librarian, because at Lubyanka the librarians were prisoners.

Back in Lwów my second investigator had spoken to me of the Ezhov terror; he either said openly or let it be understood that my first investigator was now himself in prison. In speaking of the Ezhov terror, he said, "We've made mistakes. But we must learn from our mistakes." The "we" in "we made mistakes" even made it appear that the NKVD might be including Stalin in that number. People in the West think that Khrushchev started all that—we made mistakes, the period of mistakes and distortions. No, under Stalin, every so often a purge would be made and then people would say, we made mistakes. It's an old story that keeps coming back around.

It was a very bad time for me. I was completely without hope. An absolute state of lost hope—not even lost hope but a state of pure hopelessness. Apart from the apparatchik, none of the new people have stayed in my memory. I didn't form the slightest relations with them; I did not even observe them. I was in some process of withdrawal from the world, maybe a sort of schizophrenia. Lalashvili wasn't calling me in any more, and I hadn't asked to see him since I had resigned from writing. I don't know what I wrote—I suppose nothing bad since I did not rebuke myself for the content but just for writing for them in that place. But still I was afraid that despite everything, what I'd written would come to matter in some way. Lalashvili would not put it to bad use, but it would go on to other departments and some part, some sentence, would be taken out of context. Later, someone else would come and automatically send me to a camp for an indeterminate number of years, as they did in the NKVD. Without malice. My brain wasn't working; I was in a stupor. Maybe that's why I don't remember anyone, because I was in a complete stupor.

But, once again, God was gracious, and a change occurred. One day I was taken to a new cell. That's incredibly rare at Lubyanka. They want prisoners to have as little contact as possible. And so a change of cell is a great event in Lubyanka. A new world. As I've already told you, every cell has a different social makeup, and in those conditions of isolation and separation from the world, in those ideally monadic conditions, every human social unit is a new world. And that really was a new world. But I wasn't in that cell long; the war caught up with me.

I entered the cell. It was like the other one, three people, and a fourth bed waiting for me, the same furnishings, a perfect twin of the other. And so from the doorway—this is a prison custom—you look for the person senior in age and stature. They're not always the same, but they often are. Stature is more important, a person's standing in the cell. Here the oldest man proved to have the lowest stature in the cell.

He was a tall Leningrader, a consumptive with a sunken chest. Between fifty and sixty—it's hard to tell the difference in Lubyanka. He had the face of someone who had been well raised, from a good family; he was well groomed and had an intelligent, sedate face, a good face, serious. He said that he was an old Bolshevik. He gave me to understand that he had been one of the heroes of the Revolution and that he had been a deputy minister of electrification.

The second man was a Jew, pleasant, his face not especially striking, but he had beautiful, powerful eyes, very intelligent but wide and open, what they call full Jewish eyes, full of energy and awareness. He was of average height but built like an athlete, as you sometimes find with Jews from the countryside or from the lower class, the so-called *amhaaretz,* which means people of the earth. That includes all who work with their hands or in the small trades. That's the lower caste among Jews; no one from the upper caste ever engages in those trades. There are trades like that of watchmaker—it's almost like India except that there are two castes—which are honorable, but to own a grocery store is not. To own a clothing store is not, but to be a wholesaler is. Very strange things; they probably arose during the Middle Ages.

But I've gone off on a tangent. The third man was also a Jew, a Pole. And of course I began my stay with a confidential chat with my fellow Pole. But my fellow Pole was an unpleasant person. He spoke excellent Polish and told me his story at once. He had been in Piłsudski's Legions, then had worked for Polish intelligence. Later on he left Poland; there was something he didn't like about it. He had been in the East, working for Polish intelligence in the Arab countries; he had an excellent knowledge of Arabic. But then he went back to Poland and worked for intelligence in Berlin. His wife's family lived in Lwów. I don't remember now why he was arrested; perhaps he was living in Lwów just before the war. In Lwów he began trying to make a deal—if they'd release him, he'd work for them in Poland. He said he had set stiff conditions. And I believed that because he was tough. And because of how he acted. One time, he was all keyed up and started beating our guard, who was completely helpless because Lubyanka guards did not have the right to respond. He punched the guard in the face, once, twice, three times, in a hysterical rage. Nothing happened to him for that. He was called in and he came back. No punishment, nothing. He had very strong arms. A man ready for anything.

And so he had set conditions. What were his conditions? Not only that they send him to Warsaw but that there be no hostages; his wife and child would go with him. Either they trusted him or they didn't. They agreed to that, but the other two conditions were apparently more of a problem. One was that for half a year he do nothing, absolutely nothing. Six months, maybe even more, he said, then I'll report. Naturally I'll know who to report to, but until then, I don't exist, period. It was standard practice, he said. You have to get the lay of the land; you have to choose your victims, choose people, keep an eye out, go fishing, go hunting for the big game. That's what their work was all about, he said.

MILOSZ: But what about his being a Jew in occupied Warsaw?

WAT: He didn't look at all Jewish. He spoke extremely pure Polish, and it would be a trifle to forge documents for him. And besides, when he was in Zamarstynów, the Jewish situation in Warsaw hadn't become so horrible yet. Anyway, he was a risktaker; nothing mattered to him. I wouldn't have known he was a Jew if he hadn't told me. I might have guessed because Jews can recognize each other quite quickly, especially by the expression in the eyes.

He told many stories. One took place in Berlin in the Ministry of Defense. There was a stenographer, rather pretty, but the kind things never work out for. Timid, always depressed, she loved clothes but couldn't afford them. He had the information he needed on her, and he singled her out. Nothing could have been easier than starting up a love affair with her. He took her to the movies; he was manly, a prominent nose, muscular. On their second date he took her to the movies, then to a nice, cozy restaurant for dinner and drinks. When paying the bill, he let his wallet stuffed with money be seen and gave large tips to everyone who waited on them. Then to the hotel. The next morning he pretended he was sleeping. He had tossed his wallet on a little table by the door. He's sound asleep after a night of drinking, and the poor girl has to rush off to the office. She got dressed quickly, noticed the wallet, and struggled with herself for a moment before taking a hundred-mark bill and slipping out of the room. Meanwhile, he was on the hotel phone ordering that she be detained in the lobby. He had a list of the serial numbers on his money. He threatened her. He wrote up a description of the incident, which she had to sign in front of witnesses. He would inject sentimentality into his stories, saying things like "I felt so bad for her, but business is business!" This was a cruel reminder, one that made me realize that the past in the noncommunist world I had so idealized had its dark side as well and that I thought Lalashvili a much nicer person than my cell mate and fellow Pole. He spoke very sentimentally about that girl—she was pretty and nice and he was very sorry for her because later on he exploited her cruelly. I don't even know if he told us what happened to her in the end. Maybe we didn't even ask because the athletic-looking one, whose name was Taitz, and I were both a bit disgusted by that time.

MILOSZ: What was Taitz in for?

WAT: Taitz played a colossal role in my life. He had been the deputy director of the Marx-Engels Institute; that was his last job. He was a Marxist, the sort of Marxist who worked at The Book. If Berman, or someone else wanted to use a quote but needed to find out what book it was in and what page it was on, they'd phone The Book. There were a couple of Jews there who, without a moment's hesitation, would say, page such and such, edition such and such, Engels from such and such a year. I had dealings with one of them, and I asked him about a certain quotation. Electronic memory machines. Taitz wasn't a machine, but he was fantastically well read in Marxism. Intelligent, knowledgeable about everything.

He had been aware that his appointment to the institute was the step before being arrested. He had been arrested during the Ezhov terror; specifically, he had the misfortune of being in the trade mission in Berlin. He was not the trade representative, but in fact he was the head man there. The mission in Berlin not only dealt with foreign trade but also financed all the secret communist enterprises in Mitteleuropa, meaning Germany, Czechoslovakia, Poland, and so forth. The money flowed from there. Taitz had not actually handled that himself—it was done by someone from counterintelligence—but Taitz was an expert on the subject.

There was also a secretary working there, a good-looking woman who led a terribly debauched life. She preferred to debauch with emissaries from Moscow. Even with couriers, but primarily with high officials who were stopping over there. One of those officials, who was or had been the trade representative in America, married that woman. Taitz was married, loved his wife enormously, was always faithful, and had never slept with that secretary. He might have been the only one on the staff who hadn't, including the messengers and the chauffeurs. But she was a very good-looking Russian woman, a Russian beauty as he described her. Since Taitz was friendly with the man who later married her, he said to him, "Listen, what are you doing? She's a slut." A banal incident but one that had repercussions.

Taitz showed me the marks torture had left on him. He had been through a great variety of torture. He had been arrested (everyone who had been in the West was arrested) in connection with the minister of foreign trade, Rozenholtz. Taitz was Rozenholtz's friend and advisor, the Marxist brain in the ministry. Even though he worked in Berlin, he was summoned often, often ordered to come to Moscow.

Then he was recalled from Berlin. By then he knew about the great wave of arrests and was expecting it. But he was appointed to the Marx-Engels Institute, no small thing. At that time, the institute was headed by a very decent man who had direct access to Stalin, one of Stalin's old friends; he continued to visit him. And sometimes Stalin would summon him. He could go see Stalin at any time of day, one of the very few, but apparently he would tremble like an aspen the entire time. He treated Taitz very well, but he gave him no work to do. That made it entirely clear.

His appointment was the beginning of his arrest. Taitz was an authority, with a reputation as a Marxist; he didn't write himself but he advised the so-called docents. The Russians were respectful to him, warm, as Russians will be. Then a void started forming around him. One day the man who shared Taitz's office didn't arrive at work; an hour, two, still not there; everybody's face was pale. People stopped talking to each other after that, as if the man had died suddenly from cholera and his house was contaminated.

Someone else became infected immediately: Taitz. A void formed around him, not only metaphorically but literally, physically, spatially. People were afraid to come closer than a few steps to him. Daniel Defoe's *Journal of the Plague Year*, that striking picture of plague in seventeenth-century London, reminds one of Russia in the years of the Ezhov terror, in the circles of the Russian intelligentsia. Even the disposal of the corpses, even the atheists in the tavern who blaspheme loudly and laugh at those funerals at night, with usually only the corpse attending. Those funerals, those carts, those Black Marias, just like Soviet Black Marias. People sit in a tavern laughing at God and the dead, and the next day they're gone too, tossed into a mass grave.

So, later Taitz was arrested. And tortured. I saw where they'd made "hamburger" out of him; he showed me the marks, and besides, I'd seen them in the showers. There's a lot to tell about him, but perhaps it can all be illustrated by one thing. At one point under torture he agreed to sign a confession that he had been a Nazi spy, a saboteur, and had conducted anti-Soviet propaganda. Paragraph 58. And that meant his utter ruin, of course. He agreed, he signed, he went back to the cell. At one point I said to him, "But you seem sort of cheerful."

He said, "But you see, for me the cell is a womb, a warm womb. When I'd come back here to the cell after the torture, after signing the deposition, the cell was truly like a warm womb for me. Peace, happiness, warmth."

There's one detail that may not be known and is worth mentioning here. When Taitz was working there, the Marx-Engels Institute was having enormous problems. Specifically, they were publishing Marx but at a terribly slow pace. They had everything, excellent archives. Taitz told me that sometimes Marxist documents were stolen; if they couldn't buy them, they stole them. Stalin was especially bad at quoting Marx; he didn't know German on a subtle enough level. Lenin quoted badly too, stretching things to suit his needs. Now they were publishing a critical, scholarly edition of Marx's texts. If they tried to make an exact translation, someone like the guys who worked in The Book would immediately say that in such and such a work, on such and such a page, Stalin had used that quote but had cited it in an entirely different form. And it had to be used exactly as Stalin had used it, with the same punctuation. Stalin had to be copied—whether it was an original text of his or whether he was quoting—along with Stalin's punctuation. You went to a camp for leaving out one punctuation mark. So what to do. Only Stalin could decide the problem. As I said, the director of the institute had access to Stalin but lived in fear of him. But then Stalin began to demand that one volume or another of Marx appear in print. A terrible problem. He had to go see him. So the director went to see Stalin, but he came back empty-handed because he didn't dare bring up the subject.

So, Taitz was arrested, he confessed, and then he retracted everything. He wrote a statement to the prosecutor saying that under torture he had confessed to things that weren't true; it was all lies. Beria summoned him, Beria himself. There was a confrontation with a woman named Liza and her husband, who were sitting in Beria's office. Liza was wearing perfume; at least she had been brought to Beria's like that, beautifully dressed, made up, coiffed, quite charming. Beria was very dignified; the conversation was also very dignified. Three people from a good set, brought up with good manners. Tea was served, fruit on the table, and so forth. Then they came to the point. (I no longer remember Taitz's first name and patronymic, but let's call him Grigory Davidovich.) Liza said, "Grigory Davidovich, what are you doing? Why are you being so stubborn? Lavrenty Pavlovich [Beria] promised me, swore to me, that as soon as we admitted everything, made a clean breast of it, they'd give us all our freedom. Prison is very hard on me; you know how I am. And my husband is in prison too. I beg you, think it over. You have a wife!"

And Beria said, "Yes, yes, you heard her, she's right. She's young and pretty; she could be living her life. And you're being stubborn. Think of your own wife!" And then to her, he said, "Lizaveta, tell your story again."

Well, naturally, she immediately told her story again, saying that she had been present at a reception given by a deputy to the Reichstag from a communist splinter group after the Reichstag had been burned. There were people from the trade mission and the Soviet embassy there, the communist ambassador in Berlin, and various others, the elite. A lovely reception—she even described what it was like. She had been there too, invited because she was elegant and good-looking. So, she was there. Later on she was taken up to a bedroom. In came Taitz and a Gestapo officer in civilian clothes. It was then and there that she and the officer enlisted Taitz in the service of the Gestapo. She supplied a few details of what Taitz was supposed to have said and done. Another time she had been at Kempinsky's restaurant on Alexanderplatz (not far from the Soviet mission, where, Taitz told me, all the Soviets went for lunch). It was there that she met with Taitz and the same Gestapo officer, in disguise, to whom Taitz gave information and documents.

That was too much for Taitz, who said, "Elizaveta, have you gone out of your mind? What are you talking about, you idiot?" He even reasoned with her. "How could that have happened? After the burning of the Reichstag, the deputies were either in camps or in hiding underground. A communist deputy giving a large reception in Berlin? A meeting at Kempinsky's? When Kempinsky's was full of Soviets? It doesn't hold water. You're talking nonsense! You're out of your mind, you're an idiot!"

She began to cry and said, "And why did you tell my husband I was a slut?" Beria was furious. Someone came in, and Beria said, "Make hamburger out of him!" Taitz was taken out and they made hamburger out of him. And it was the traces of that last torture that I saw there in our cell. (Incidentally, Taitz spoke German when telling me some of the things about Beria. Because it turned out that the dignitary, the former minister of electrification, was informing on the cell. I was surprised that the cell was so open in its contempt for him. An old Bolshevik, a hero of the Revolution—and he did it for a glass of tea, a few cigarettes. And he accepted it; he accepted those invisible slaps in the face he was constantly being given.)

Taitz continued, "I still haven't retracted what I signed the last time I was tortured, but I will. My trial's supposed to be soon, and I'll retract it at the trial. A military council, the highest court. I'll retract it and I'll tell them about being tortured. But I'll have to be tactful and sensible. I'll admit to sabotage, but I'll deny the espionage. I'll fully admit the sabotage. Though that's not so easy either, because what could I sabotage? I was in Germany at the time."

I thought Taitz was right because on some level the story has to hold water. You can tell them the greatest absurdities, but the connecting links have to be very tight, consistent. And so? I'm a writer and we had someone from the Intelligence Service in the cell. Taitz gave us the elements of his story and asked us to help him formulate a good scenario for sabotage. For a few days the three of us thought of nothing else; we peppered him with questions to find out everything we needed to construct an airtight story that would stand up to anything.

I don't know if he ever used it, or with what results. But I could have found out because Taitz had known Kirsanov well; their wives had been very friendly. It was only in 1965 that an opportunity presented itself: a delegation of Soviet poets, including Kirsanov, was invited to Paris. I wangled an invitation to the reception at the home of a French friend of mine. There were four poets. (I won't describe that pitiful scene—I had the constant feeling of being in Tambov in the 1850s, in the salon of some liberal aristocratic lady.) With the exception of one, who behaved normally and thus seemed strikingly mature and dignified, they all made great pretenses of declining before they would recite their poetry: "No, not me; our brilliant colleague should read first." "Not me, the greatest virtuoso of the Russian language should read first." After that, they would recite, using every sort of theatrical gesture for effect. That went on until after five in the afternoon.

At six o'clock I took Kirsanov aside—he remembered me well—sat him beside me on the couch, and began a conversation, which I'll reproduce faithfully here. Very gently, without mentioning the nasty words "Lubyanka" or "prison," I told him that we had a friend in common, one who had had an enormous, beneficial influence on me, a splendid, heroic person. For twenty years I had been wanting to know what happened to him. Was Misha Taitz alive? And what about his wife?

Kirsanov: I don't know, I don't know, I don't know anything. I have nothing to do with these things, I don't want to know, I never wanted to know. Even now I don't read anything on that subject; it's unhealthy to poke around in it. It was everywhere, everywhere. A wave of cruelty swept over the world, everywhere.

I: But I'm simply asking you to tell me what happened to your close friend, Misha Taitz. And to his wife, who was your late wife's closest friend. I must know.

Kirsanov: I don't know, I don't know the MGB's secrets!

I: For God's sake, you don't understand. I'm not asking about the MGB. This is a purely private matter. You're the only person in the world who can tell me if he's alive.

Kirsanov: He's dead. I don't know how he died or when.

I: And his wife?

Kirsanov: I don't know. I don't know. I'm a Russian, you're a Pole . . .

I (with a dismissive wave of the hand at this coward): . . . and we're
   both Jews.
Kirsanov: No, I'm a Russian. I see the world as a Russian and you see it as
   a Pole . . .
I: You're mistaken again: I love Russians, I respect them, I just don't love and
   respect Soviet people. (NB: out of anger, I provoked him into replying
   to that line of thought.)
Kirsanov: I'm a Soviet man and proud of it. I'm a Russian and as a Russian
   it hurts me and deeply offends me that everyone attacks only the
   Russians! They attack only the Russians! I was at Nuremberg; I saw
   Goering face to face as I'm seeing you now. And all everyone does is
   scream about the Russians! A wave of cruelty has swept the entire
   earth, they're using electrodes on people's genitals in Vietnam, and the
   Russians are the only ones attacked! Twenty million Russians were
   killed, including six million Jews. (He was clever, though evidently
   taking me for a Zionist.)
I: Aren't you exaggerating? Even your enemies figure that no more than fifteen million rotted away in the Soviet camps.
Kirsanov: You shouldn't stick your fingers in other people's wounds!
I: They're not other people's wounds, my dear man, they're mine, and have
   been for twenty years.

That was the unfortunate and stupid end of my investigation.

Gleb Struve, not only an excellent scholar but a subtle poet as well,
shamed me with his forbearance after I had described for him that
scene when it was still fresh in memory. Struve said that apparently
Kirsanov was critically ill, very frightened, and, no matter what else,
he had been true to his friendship with Mandelstam. He had been
under fire lately; he was afraid of his own shadow. But, on the whole,
he wasn't the worst of the lot. Undoubtedly true. Even though I'd like
to, I can't forgive Kirsanov, not because he obliterated his old friends
from his memory—gratitude can go awry under communism—but because of the harm he caused Taitz's wife if she's alive. It was so important that I do not hesitate to call it something sacred: for her to
know how her husband had acted before what had to have been his
death. And if I wrote so much about Taitz, it's not only because he
played such a significant role in my life but also in the fervent hope that
by some miracle—and they do happen in this life—these words will
reach her.

I say that he had a colossal influence on my life because he showed
me it was possible to remain human under any conditions, that this is
given to man. Obviously, there are tortures that are beyond endurance, but a person can retract his testimony. Everything is possible.
Taitz—and later another man, Dubin—were two models for me of how

a person can act if he really has a very strong desire to. Yes, the Gestapo proved that by physical and mental torture a person can be turned into a rag, that people might not really have the strength to rise back up. But a person can rise back up. At least, at the far limits, normally unimaginable, a person can still rise back to his feet after he's fallen.

MILOSZ: Did you ever discuss Marxism with Taitz?

WAT: I learned a great deal about Marxism from him, more than from Stawar. We talked a lot. Taitz was a Marxist. As I recall, he spoke about the young Marx, the young Marx's writings. I'm certain of that because when the young Marx's writings came into fashion, I immediately thought of Taitz. I don't remember whether he spoke about alienation, but it seems to me his ideas about Marx were like those that Kołakowski is expanding on now. But Taitz also had a general theory rich in details, which I don't remember though I do recall the basis of it, namely; *Allmacht des Staates,* as he used to say—the omnipotence of the state, the state machine, is inevitable. Marx was not mistaken that this was inevitable, but he was mistaken about what the result would be. Taitz thought it was only the process of concentrating power, one without precedent in history, because this was the concentration of power over everything. Centralism, the pyramid of centralism, power in the hands of ever smaller groups. Taitz had become an anarchist in prison. He was not a pessimist. He thought that at some point it would break, it would all collapse, and then perhaps humanity would become syndicalist. He didn't go in for predictions; he was a wise man. Rather, he believed in certain possibilities. He not only believed but allowed for the possibility of a syndicalist, democratic solution. As opposed to Dunayevsky, he did not insist that communism was Russian by nature. When I say that communism would have been a hundred times worse and crueller in Germany, that's not my idea; that's Taitz's. He knew Germany well and thought that communism in Germany would be even more dangerous, worse for Germany's neighbors than Nazism, which of course he hated.

I wasn't being summoned. By then I was not in bad shape. A *vanka-vstanka.** It was almost like schizophrenia. The world had already fallen away from me; I had no connection with the world. It was hopelessness, not even despair. The despair was gone before I came to that cell; there was only total hopelessness. The heart of Lubyanka. There's no end to it—that's hopelessness—nothing will ever change. First and

---

* A Russian toy, a doll weighted so that when it is knocked over, it rights itself.

foremost, Lubyanka implanted the belief in your soul that nothing would ever change. And so communism is diabolical in two ways. "Everything changes" as the basis of their philosophy, a very strong side, one in which Marx did great service for world thought. But there is a corrective to this in communist practice, meaning just the opposite: nothing changes. This was even expressed in their theory, which said that the law of the dialectic was no longer operative in the Soviet Union; there was no more thesis and antithesis. That's only for societies with conflicts and antagonisms. But in the Soviet Union there was eternal happiness, eternal harmony. That eternity is communism. That eternity was incarnated in Lubyanka, a foretaste of eternity. Dostoevsky has Svidrigailov imagine eternity as a room with a spider web in one corner, but in Lubyanka our room was clean and swept. But one room. Absolutely hygienic. No trace of any spider web. Where could a spider find a place for itself in that room; where could it have lived? But one room. That's Lubyanka.

Time was passing. Taitz wasn't being summoned. Only the minister was being called in, and all the prisoners knew that it was not only for his case but so that he could tell them what was happening in the cell. We were all convinced that he had not actually been promised anything and was informing for a glass of tea, a sandwich, a cigarette. Two products of the communist machine: Taitz and that deputy minister.

One day we were taken from the cell, and when we returned the cell windows had been blacked over. We knew what that meant. Taitz was expecting war too. So it was war. And of course, spring, hope. Not because we loved the Germans. As I told you, my own belief that Gog and Magog would devour each other, bleed each other to death, was widespread. Even Taitz, who was so intelligent, believed that the system had so rotted from within that it would not survive a strong blow. The intelligence agent rubbed his hands in delight. Of course, his deal would be dead now, but his satisfaction was so intense that he no longer cared what happened to him or his family. He had lived to see the day. He hated the Soviets. I too had a sense of satisfaction. Probably Taitz did too, but in a different way. We were more vindictive— God is just, vengeance on the enemy, on evil. For Taitz it was a little different; his was a more intelligent reaction, not a vindictive one but a thinking reaction. Taitz expected the worst for himself. Personally, he pinned no hopes on the war. He expected that he'd be taken to Sukhanovka or maybe even to some cellar in Lubyanka, and he'd get a bullet in the back of his head. The deputy minister was rather expecting that he might be of some use. There was no patriotism in the cell. Those two Russians displayed no patriotism.

Then, one day: "Get your things!"

For years afterwards I thought that Lubyanka had been entirely evacuated—I mean, I knew that it filled up again later, but I had thought at that time, during the week of evacuation, the entire prison had been evacuated. But I've read of someone who had stayed on there. And so everyone wasn't evacuated.

As to the evacuation itself: the elevator wasn't used, only the stairs; all the cell doors were open. People streaming out. And then came those strange chance events for which the critics faulted *Dr. Zhivago* but which are everyday occurrences in enormous Russia. I saw Władzio Broniewski on the stairs. A few minutes later Tadeusz Peiper appeared on the stairs; I had no idea he was in Lubyanka. Thousands of people and our three faces a short distance from one another. Sharing the same emotion. People streaming out but not only prisoners. A little natural corridor had formed among the prisoners through which NKVD officers, even lieutenants and generals, were walking downstairs, all together, with no regard to rank. And at Lubyanka, rank, the whole table of ranks, had been very closely observed.

29 EVACUATION. WITH BRONIEWSKI AGAIN. A FOUR-DAY TRAIN RIDE. THE CAREERS OF UNIVERMAG DIRECTORS. SARATOV. STEKLOV. ERLICH. THE FIRST URKS.

WAT: The evacuation of Lubyanka. The secretaries were walking downstairs between us, beautiful girls, all young, very well dressed. There was no panic on the NKVD people's faces, but each one of them was carrying as many dossiers as he could hold, dossiers whose covers had been marked that they were never to be destroyed. The courtyard was packed with trucks, one beside the other. The dossiers were tossed into the trucks at random, personal data on millions of people, the dossiers that in fact upheld Stalin's state. I don't know about anyone else, but a certain joyful insight ran through me at that moment. It was obvious—they were afraid! They were afraid! The great power was already crumbling.

Prisoners, prisoners everywhere. When a person gets used to his cell mates, he no longer notices any changes in their faces, their clothing, their way of walking. It's only when you come up against a mass of prisoners from other cells that you see what you must look like yourself. Terrible! Terrible! It's all in the face. A certain grayness, a sallowness, the pain on those faces—more than that, the degradation. It's true there were a lot of fresh, ruddy Soviet faces too. But you could tell right away that they were from the most recent roundups, the ones in the week the war broke out. There were a great many of them. Broniewski and I had maneuvered to be as close together as possible on the stairs. And just as I had recognized him and Peiper, the other prisoners were also recognizing people—a brother, a friend, a codefendant. But no one dared say a word; everyone was still fearful; they only winked at each other. A flash of joy at meeting or—something I also saw—a few glances of mutual fear. And so wordless dialogues rose above that crowd descending Jacob's ladder in Lubyanka, a host of dialogues, an entire network of dialogues intersecting in an incredible tangle. It probably wasn't hatred that everyone was feeling but satisfaction that justice had been done, that Stalin's empire lay in ruins.

From the courtyard where the dossiers were being tossed into trucks, we were taken to other courtyards, an enormous number of courtyards, each with its gate, one after the other, like Chinese boxes, and so I don't know how many there were. We were led through those courtyards to where a great variety of vehicles were waiting for us. Clearly there was no plan now; the plan had vanished, been washed away. Simply because I was alongside Broniewski, they packed the two of us into the same vehicle—us, people involved in the same case. But no one took any notice.

They packed us into the same vehicle and drove us to Butyrki Prison. Of course we did not know whether we were being taken to our deaths or to another prison. But we did know that this was an evacuation, and so chances were that we were going to another city, and most likely we were heading for a train station. But we were going to Butyrki.

And again it so happened that Broniewski and I were locked up together in the same cubicle downstairs. There was cubicle next to cubicle on the ground floor. One person could barely stand being in a cubicle like that for more than an hour or two—there was no air—and the two of us had been locked up together in one. I can't say there was no room; there was an arm's length between us. We weren't pressed up against one another, but we spent a dozen hours or so in there together gasping for breath. We were standing, of course; there was nowhere to sit. That wasn't for harassment, just a lack of space.

Two fellow Poles talking in the night—not a good conversation for me because Broniewski was full of rancor toward me. It went back to

266

the time I had admitted tapping messages. I was even about to tell him the whole story of Majteles, and especially Kmiciński, and say that by then it had all been impossible to deny, but I realized that this wouldn't do any good because Broniewski wasn't a person you could reason with. Once he got something into his head, that was the end of that. So I didn't bother. He was very warm; we hugged each other. But then came the grievances: "Why did you say that you had anti-Soviet conversations with me in Warsaw?"

That I had to answer in detail, so I said, "Listen, all our colleagues who were still free had testified to that, and it would have been absurd to deny that I had anti-Soviet conversations in Warsaw."

"You shouldn't have done it; you shouldn't have."

"Maybe you're right that I shouldn't have. Now I can see that. Maybe I really shouldn't have. Maybe I should have denied everything." (You see, in the end I used the principle discovered by a Dominican at the beginning of the seventeenth century in Terni that was also used by the Jesuits: *reservatio mentalis*. It means you tell part of the truth and hide part.)

"But why did you mention me?"

"That was the main thing they were after in Zamarstynów—who with? And so I gave the names of people who were communists, writers, whom they already knew about. They kept asking, 'And who else?'"

In fact that was the point of the interrogation, the subject of the inquisition. You had to name names. Obviously, I was unwise; I should have held fast and stopped at some point. I couldn't skip Broniewski because they knew we were friends, colleagues, and had been in jail together in Warsaw. And so how could I say I hadn't talked with him? We were always palling around. That's why I mentioned him and said that I had talked with him and besides, I assumed that he'd do the same. I didn't know that he was going to deny everything. Certainly, I talked too much, but it looked as if there'd be trouble; the investigator was foaming at the mouth. I really was a flabby intellectual back then, but I was firm on one point; I have to say that. I didn't allow anything that I didn't say to go into the record, no changes in my words. There were very harsh clashes over that, especially with the first investigator, who always wanted to add something to the record, change the wording. Once it even went as far as his pretending he was going to beat me, and he really was furious. I said to him, "All right, beat me." He became angry immediately and said, "We don't beat people here. That says a lot about your attitude toward the Soviet Union. All those slanderous ideas about the Soviet Union." It did not even occur to me to have the nerve to say that there was a Ukrainian in my cell he was torturing day after day. And so, in the end, I signed only records that were accurate. But I did talk too much. As far as Broniewski was concerned, however, I remember very clearly just what I had said. That had been thought through in advance because I expected to be asked about Broniewski and the others arrested with us. I said that I had in fact talked with Broniewski. And what had Broniewski said? Broniewski had taken a view opposite to mine. That was it.

I repeated all that to Broniewski, who said, "There, you see! That wasn't in there. You didn't say that. They read me the deposition and that extra part wasn't in there. It said that you spoke with me and expressed anti-Soviet opinions."

I said, "Well, that's their usual method. They tell you some things and leave some out; there's nothing you can do about that." I was a little angry; I felt denigrated, lowly, contrite in the face of his heroism, his—how to put it—manliness. But all that had started to anger me a bit and so I said, "Of course I didn't mention anything about your coming back from Russia where the author of *Cry China* had said to you that five or six million peasants had been killed off, exterminated, during collectivization. I had to be on guard not to say a single word about your trip there." (At the time I had asked Władek, "And what did you say about those five million people, those five million broken eggs?" And he said, "Well, that's the Russians for you.")

None of us thought that there might be microphones in those cubicles; most likely they didn't have that sort of microphone at that time. And besides, Stalinism could not exist at that level of technology, the technology of microphones. Because the point wasn't only to know what people were saying; the point was also to have a person who had been degraded into the role of informer in every family, in every milieu, all throughout society. And still more important was that everyone knew that informers could be anywhere. That was the most degrading thing; that accelerated people's degradation; it was an inclined plane so that everyone had the feeling that he'd turn informer too if they put the squeeze on him. Bugging devices would not only reduce the number of informers but would also reduce things to a normal police state, something Stalin did not want. He hated the police. He was sincere when he told Ludwig that it was the practice of informing that had alienated him from the seminary and impelled him toward revolution. That was true. I believe it. There was no satanic mockery in that.

But now for the first time Broniewski had begun to irritate me a little, and I had admired him so much in Lwów. When I was on the way to Saratov, a colonel—I forget his name—who had been in a cell with Broniewski told me about Władek. And from what he said Broniewski had not denied everything, had not sealed himself up like a mute, because Broniewski had been summoned for questioning often and he would come back singing, whistling, in good spirits. It was clear that he had been well treated because a person can't change his mood so quickly after seeing his investigator. That mood would stay with you a long time, and if there had been any discord with the investigator, you wouldn't come back whistling and humming. Moreover, Broniewski had been an officer; he had spent seven years at the front and had always been impulsive, wild, uninhibited. But seven years as an officer at the front, that means you also have a sense of military discipline. And there was another thing. I had observed him in Lwów—his dignity was absolutely fantastic; he maintained more of his dignity than all the rest of us did. But I also remember him at a table in the Café Ziemiańska, when he was very much a communist, talking with Wieniawa and being so ingratiating. Broniewski truly was the poet of the revolutionary working class, but he was also 100 percent the petty noble. He fawned on every high official—I saw that. And so I had a few doubts about his saying nothing at all. Even though I still considered myself something of a weakling at that time.

But, on the whole, there was harmony between us, two fellow Poles talking in the night, discussing the future, what Poland would be like. A just society but not a communist or Bolshevik Poland. He was no longer a communist in the least; he didn't know what he was. Of course he'd believed in the working class, social justice for years, and that belief was true, deep, and strong in him, but there was no question of his having any illusions left about communism.

The next day they pulled us out of the cubicle, exhausted. They'd opened the cubicle up for us many times during the night because we were suffocating in there.

The officers, secretaries, and guards at Lubyanka had not been in a panic. But at Butyrki the prison staff was clearly panicky. Butyrki is like a little town. I saw nothing apart from that one building, but later on we were taken out through Butyrki. Lubyanka had no trees, but Butyrki did. A touch of happiness. A tree can give you a touch of happiness when you're in prison; with all those walls, the cement, the stone, it's a tomb. Happiness. For all I know that could be true happiness. The sight of a tree is nearly always a splendid thing.

We were taken to the railroad tracks; there was no station in sight. Truck after truck, Black Maria after Black Maria, they packed us into cattle cars. As soon as the wooden car doors were slid open on their casters, the whole group of us surged forward like wild men to grab the good places. We already knew what those transports were like. The cars have plank beds and of course the most coveted are the ones by the little window. There's one little window high up, just one. Naturally, Broniewski and I kept together. But somehow Peiper vanished in that enormous crowd of people.

The trip to Saratov had begun. It must have taken four days. Again, no way to measure time. Thanks to using our elbows, Broniewski and I had relatively decent places, not right by the window but not far from it either, and on the same side. The daily routine has been described a hundred times—head counts, officers, NKVD. The lavatory was right in the car, a hole in the floor. We were given bread, rather large portions—I think they must have weighed six hundred grams. The world's worst bread; it was like clay. They also gave us herring. And that too was part of their routine. Someone very cruel must have thought that one up because those herring were covered with a thick crust—not a layer, a crust—of salt. And they gave us very little water. Prudent people didn't eat the herring. I didn't eat any; I ate one piece and that was enough.

Gradually, we began looking around, and it turned out that ours was a very interesting group. Quite varied. A great many of them had been arrested in the last wave, during the first week of the war. What kind of people were they? There was an eminent microbiologist. There was Russia's greatest specialist on the avalanches of mud and stone that destroy cities like Alma-Ata from time to time. Heroes of Soviet aviation, aces, generals, two or three. And a very interesting group of Jews, directors of Moscow's big department stores, the Univermags. They were arrested during the first days of the war. All of them. The chief directors, the chief bookkeepers, maybe eight or ten of them.

"Why were you arrested?"

"They needed scapegoats. Our Russian colleagues weren't arrested; they arrested the Jews."

"Did they have any grounds?"

"Well, we couldn't have lasted as directors if we didn't embezzle."

Then one of them said, "Take me, for example. I was an honest merchant. I came from an honest merchant family. I would have been an honest merchant. I know business inside and out. All right, so I became a director. A specialist. I'm in the party. And of course they have confidence in me. Let's say that I don't want to embezzle; I don't want to steal. But it all starts with my having to accept other people's stealing, because if I didn't, everything would have come to a standstill. My supplier, who went around buying merchandise, would bring me all sorts of goods, and he would never have gotten anything from any warehouseman if I hadn't paid him for more than he delivered. Everything would have come to a stop. I would have been tried as a saboteur, and it doesn't get much grimmer than that. Then you're into political crime. And so I had to close my eyes to it, look the other way.

"Let's say that I'm a very honest man and don't want anything for myself—I still have to let others steal. And so after a while I realize that I'll be caught, because everybody gets caught in the end; you can't go on like that for years. They know about the stealing, but then one day there's something they don't like, and bang! If I'm an orthodox Communist party member, dutiful, loyal, active, hardworking, aboveboard with the party, there's a good chance that I'll end up in a criminal brigade. If I end up in a criminal brigade and I have money, I can bribe people. The political NKVD doesn't take bribes. I'd be put in a camp as a nonpolitical. A criminal. But I can survive the camp only on one condition: if I have money and can grease palms in the camp. And then they'd give me some easy job and I'd have food, everything. I'd survive.

"And so I have to have money. I think to myself, I have daughters and I want to marry them off. To make good marriages for them, I have to give my daughters dowries. And then there's the question of how long before I get caught. Impossible to predict. Maybe five years, maybe one year, maybe a month. But in general we figure we can keep going for three years. In those three years I have to set things up, earn enough money in those three years that I can give my daughters dowries and survive the camp living half decently, and, most important, so that when I get out of the camp, I can get a position making somewhere between two hundred and five hundred rubles a month. A little job, one where I won't have to steal or embezzle or sneak around, where I can live respectably for the rest of my days."

"Could you really steal enough in three years to give your daughters dowries, bribe people in the camps, and then have enough to live comfortably for the rest of your life?"

"It can be done. If you have a head on your shoulders, it can be done."

In a word, that was a lecture on the Soviet paraeconomy, but really on the economy itself, since without that type of deal the whole thing would have ground to a halt. It was all so clear, so Aristotelian: nothing could be added, nothing removed.

We pulled into Saratov, on a side track again. There were no trucks waiting to pick us up; a marching column was formed. We spotted Peiper in the column, a ways from us, and we started maneuvering toward him. I was still sticking with Broniewski. Old Henryk Erlich was near us; I knew him from Warsaw, though I had never really talked with him. He knew Broniewski better.

Empty streets of what was actually a village. I don't know how many kilometers they herded us, but it was a good distance. A typical Russian provincial capital where even the main street has a small-town look to it. The whole thing was really a small town, an idyllic small town. Those tumbledown wooden huts, a lot of them between some of the apartment buildings. Half-collapsed, the wood all carved, all those different kinds of pretty lattices, mezzanines, little balconies, stairs on the outside. Some of those buildings were made of yew wood. You saw only old people on the street; somehow I don't remember seeing anyone in the prime of life, let alone any young people. There were children, of course—that I remember—but other than that, only old people. Everyone pretended not to see us. We were herded down the middle of the streets; most of them were cobblestone, but some weren't even paved.

You could tell that these NKVD men usually dealt with *urks*. They were very jumpy and kept threatening that if anyone stuck out his head, they'd put a bullet right through it and so on, though they never did anything like that. They were afraid themselves—that was it, afraid. I also have the impression that they were afraid of us for another reason: they knew we were from Lubyanka. The lower ranks, the guards, the turnkeys, were afraid of prisoners from Lubyanka because they had no right to deal with such prisoners. They felt helpless with that elite— the elite of the damned, but still an elite. They were very jumpy, but they herded us on. "Move it, move it." Erlich couldn't keep up; he had something like a heart attack; he turned pale, began staggering. So Władzio and I each took one side of him, and we held him up by the arms because he couldn't walk. We simply dragged him; we were just about carrying him. It was a very long line, a column, and behind it was a long column of women.

Now picture this: Peiper maneuvered his way over to us, and he said, "Alexander, I have wonderful news for you. I saw Ola with the women!" He was already mad, paranoid, by then, and he was very happy to have such good news for me. It was midday, sunny, summer. A sunny day, an idyllic Russian country town, wooden huts, and then that bolt from the blue. An abyss opened in front of me. Ola arrested . . . then what about Andrzej? Dead or in a children's home. Which was worse?

And so I left the three of them and again began working my way through the crowd. The guards shouted at me, but I didn't let that stop me. I worked my way to the end of the men's line and then whispered to the woman closest to me, without turning my head—that you couldn't do—"Ask if Ola Wat, the Polish poet's wife, is here." And they passed on the message, because I heard the murmur of voices. But no answer came back. My soul and my mind were in hell. I walked along unable to think about anything anymore, unable to observe, unaware of what was happening around me. I came back to my senses only when we entered the large courtyard of the NKVD internal prison in Saratov.

The yard was enormous, and there were a great many guards and barrels of water. After the herring, nearly everyone drank the water, but I didn't. I was thirsty too, because they had given us hardly any water on the way there. Everyone raced for the water. Later on, my bandit friends told me that large numbers of people would die from drinking water in those circumstances. After two, three, four weeks of traveling, and after eating those herrings, people raced for the water and drank nonstop. Their bowels would constrict and they'd die. They allowed the prisoners to throw themselves on those barrels, but then later it was "Stop and squat on the ground." A head count, but this time with lists of names and cell assignments. That lasted a long time because there was such a multitude of prisoners.

I forgot to say that at one point, as I was working my way toward the women, I heard someone cursing Stalin in a loud voice. I took a quick look around, and I managed to see who it was. An old man, so tall he was stooped, very decently dressed, but not one of those just arrested; you could tell he'd been in a long time. A handsome face, shriveled, bony, the face of a Polish nobleman. Long-headed—a Nietzschean type of face. A long narrow face. A handsome Polish nobleman; all he needed was a long drooping moustache. But in fact he looked rather like an old English gentleman, a graduate of Eton and Oxford. Very refined. Long-legged, he moved with ease, quick despite his age and his obvious weariness. His face was weary, very weary. He walked like a young man, his steps cranelike, but for all that refinement, his language was vulgar; he spoke about Stalin like an *urk*. He was close to the far side of his column. A guard and a soldier were nearby. The collar of the soldier's uniform was bothering him; he was jumpy. "That's enough of that," he said to the old man, who kept shouting. Meanwhile, a whisper passed from prisoner to prisoner until it reached me: "That's old Steklov." He had gone suddenly mad. He had started ranting back in the cattle car. Nahamkes Steklov, hero of the Revolution, editor of *Izvestiya*, a friend of Lenin's and of Stalin's right up until he was imprisoned.

We were sorted into groups in the courtyard. They took more personal data from us, and that took a long time too. But you could rest; you could sit down on the cobblestones. Then to the cell. The doors opened on an enormous cell, three *urks* already there. Those three young *urks* had taken four or five or six beds, the best beds by the window. There were other beds, fewer beds than people but a lot of beds. A terrible first encounter with *urks*. Actually, two of them had rather a likable look to them.

One clearly was a peasant, a country boy, Russian, illiterate, ugly, but it was an earthy ugliness. A gnome, small and scrawny, but strong. Cunning little eyes—they seemed to be looking at you through peepholes, eyes like little peepholes. But you could tell by his face that he was illiterate. There are faces like that. You could tell he couldn't read or write. It was etched in his face.

The other was a handsome boy, pretty, swarthy, delicate, cultivated, well groomed, a type you see in the Café Flore all the time. A young, fresh, pretty little queer.

But the third one! I don't know how old he was. He must have been young, but there was no telling. Everything savage in Russia, everything furious in Russia, all the fury of the lower depths, was in that face. All the depravity of which humanity is capable was in that face. Russian barbarity. A holy fool of crime and debauchery. And a syphilitic face too, clearly syphilitic. The terrible voice of a syphilitic—you know that kind of voice. I don't how he moved the way he did, but it was as if he had many pairs of arms and legs, like a Hindu god. A frenetic dance. Words poured out of him in that hoarse syphilitic voice, nothing but curses. Any word was a dirty word in his mouth. He was fantastically inventive with obscenities, the language of the *urks*. Every third or fourth word was "fuck." An irrepressible flood of words, at machine-gun speed.

Now this is like something from a Chinese fairy tale. That *urk* was like a dragon trying to frighten us with those curses and that dance of his so that we wouldn't come any closer. A question of living space. *Chasse gardée*, not only of the three beds for them but so that they'd be separate. That crowd of intellectuals, generals, heroes, air force aces, they all froze. He was a real dragon. People were frozen by the dragon's gaze. No one dared go any closer. He was still foaming at the mouth even though no one came any closer. And it turned out that Poles truly are brave. Two officers and Broniewski, who was a strong man—so, three strong men—began moving threateningly closer and occupying beds. They left the *urks* the best beds, but they took the ones right beside them. The *urk* was still frothing, but then he ran to the door. The young *urks* liked that; it made them happy. They looked at him with love and fascination—not only the young queer but the country boy too.

He was in fact a country boy—I was in a cell with him later on. He liked the *urks*, he liked the way they lived so much that when he was arrested and found himself with *urks*, he couldn't ask for anything better. He wouldn't have wanted to leave. He wanted to live the life of the *urks*. Freedom, no restraints. He'd gotten a taste for it, his eyes had been opened to the great world; he'd seen how charming life could be.

And so the two of them watched, fascinated, love in their eyes, laughing, delighted by it all. The homosexual, that pretty, pleasant homosexual, with whom I shared a cell later on and who proved to be an unusually nice person, above all, a good person, glanced over at us from time to time. It might have seemed like a guilty glance, but that wasn't it. It was a bit of a knowing glance—to say that's life, or, to say that the *urk* was a decent guy, don't be fooled by appearances, don't let it get to you, he's a wonderful guy. And later on, during the few days we were together, I saw that he really was good to those young *urks*, especially to the younger one, who was probably his favorite lover and whom he loved very much. (This is something of a clue to Saint Genet, and his novel. I realized that recently. Genet's novel *Notre-Dame des Fleurs*. The relationships were very similar. Soviet Russia and France, prison and homosexuality, criminals. *Bas fonds*.)

And so the *urk* ran to the cell door and started making a racket. A tremendous racket! The other two didn't join in. He was shouting obscenities at everyone, at the Soviet system, the guards. Finally, the cell door opened. A woman guard had been assigned to our cell. As soon as he saw her, he immediately dropped his pants in one lightning-quick move, and then he took it in his hand and it really was very big, and he said: "Here's a prick for you!" Then another torrent of curses. I don't know what he wanted because I didn't understand their lingo yet; it was too fast, too specialized. But he wanted something. I think he wanted to be moved out because he didn't want to be in with lice carriers. For them, intellectuals were lice carriers.

He wasn't all that wrong either, because in prison cells it turns out that lice like intellectuals' blood better than the common people's. It's different outside of prison, because out there intellectuals would exterminate the lice. But, whenever they can, lice fasten onto intellectuals; maybe their blood is sweeter for all I know. Intellectuals are hated in prison. The criminals consider that justice, divine justice. Those people deserve it. After the occupation certain Poles said that one good thing Hitler did was to rid us of Jews, and in general the *urks* had the same attitude toward Stalin: the one good thing Stalin did was to destroy the intellectuals. And this made it easy for the NKVD to enlist the *urks'* cooperation against the political prisoners.

But the *urks* settled down, especially when they saw those threatening Polish faces. The Russians began moving too, but only after the Poles had started it. They didn't say anything to the *urks*. It turned out that the young *urks* would have been glad to talk, but the other one wouldn't talk with intellectuals; he was withdrawn, in his own world. This was an excellent lesson. The *urk* had raged, but only at the guards; the prisoners he boycotted completely.

How many prisoners were there in the cell? Maybe a hundred. It didn't take long for an intellectual club to form. Erlich was very calm, objective. An excellent person, wise, and very calm. Not the least preoccupied, or maybe he was, but it didn't show. I, however, was constantly preoccupied with thoughts of my family. The Mongolian doctor used to tell me that people like me die like flies in the camps. If I didn't overcome it, if I didn't stop thinking about my family, I wouldn't last long in prison. As a doctor, he gave me a very strong warning. But Erlich wasn't like that; he accepted his fate; he had the wisdom to accept his fate. He was taken away very soon. In our club we had Władzio Broniewski, a Bundist, the microbiologist, Józef, and an officer whose name unfortunately I can't remember no matter how I try. There were a few of the other Russians too. For some reason I was closest with that Russian microbiologist. An upright, decent person. I don't know whether he was in the party or not; he had nothing whatsoever to do with politics—a specialist very involved in his work. You could imagine his apartment full of books. It was clear that he led a cultured life. You can tell the smell of Soviet poverty right away, and you can also tell those who live a cultured European life, not a luxurious life but a cultured one. Maybe one room, maybe two, but clean; decent clothes; lots of books, music, concerts, a few friends who come by for some good Russian apolitical conversation. You could imagine them, those homes that outlast all the Stalinisms. Some are destroyed, but others survive.

So we had a club, a fine club, interesting, pleasant conversation—you know how addicted we are to that sort of talk. The time passed pleasantly. It tore me away a little from my terrible worry that Ola had been arrested. I talked with Peiper, who was in the cell too. Total paranoia—he immediately told me that in Kraków Gestapo agents, disguised as Jagiellonian University students, had rented the apartment opposite his. Day and night someone was at the window following all his movements. So his paranoia dated back to Kraków. Later on, his condition improved a little, but he's in poor shape now—though, who knows, he writes all the time, and he may turn out a masterpiece yet.

By the way, I didn't suffer from paranoia. Early on, at the beginning, when relations with Dunayevsky were at their best, I had a few intuitive flashes of that sort. I would suddenly be struck by some expression or word or question used by my investigator, Lalashvili; a flash of intuition told me that there was some connection here with my whispered conversations with Dunayevsky. I was wary, and I told myself that those flashes couldn't be trusted. One out of ten is true, but nine are false. A few days after that Pole, the high party official, summoned me and convinced me to write, Lalashvili called me in, three or four times. Lalashvili torpedoed all my arguments against writing, but Dunayevsky was the only one I had shown them to. Moreover, Lalashvili was clearly not part of the investigative service; he didn't know investigative techniques, and so he had just repeated Dunayevsky's words. That was so irrefutable, so powerful, that it made me remember other instances, and then I was absolutely certain. One has to allow for the role of chance in history, miraculous chance. Maybe I'm mistaken. But at the time that was irrefutable proof for me.

30 CELL MATES IN SARATOV. THE PROFESSOR. THE GEORGIAN. GERMANS. A DIGRESSION ON BEDBUGS.

A great many clubs formed throughout the cell, where there were at least one hundred prisoners from Moscow. Ours must have been the biggest and the bravest. We talked freely, perhaps because the core of our group was Polish. But there were also clubs of two people constantly whispering to each other. It was immediately apparent who was social and who was asocial. Each asocial person was a club of his own; he didn't stir from his place. Two or three of them would sit beside each other; they usually slept beside each other, and they never walked around. And there were others, of course, who belonged to a club but who also roamed the cell, going from one little group to another. They already had contacts in many of the groups. In a word, a miniature human society. A fantastic return to life.

I've mentioned that there was no patriotic spirit at this time, not even among the generals and fliers. The Poles were, of course, feeling schadenfreude, a terrific joy that Stalin's empire was collapsing. Some of the Russians felt that way too, but not the majority of them. There were those who thought that the empire was collapsing, but quite a large number, probably the majority, didn't believe that. Those Russians—and the English probably felt the same—had an inner, gut, certainty that the war would give the empire another couple of centuries. A lot of people felt that way. Some of them even remained sincere communists in prison; there were a lot of them, especially because most of them had been arrested only recently and had been high officials or at least in the elite, the well-fed. But even they felt that the foundations of everything were changing. They did not believe that Stalinism would prove lasting, and as communists they probably knew what a great evil Stalinism was. Perhaps some of them took a subconscious joy in seeing the evil drain out of Russia, in knowing that some fundamental transformations would take place.

The cell was noisy, pleasantly noisy. People expected that the evil would finally drain away, that the war would return Russia to normal human life. And so there were frank conversations with Russians there. I didn't talk with all hundred of them, but—who knows—maybe twenty-five, thirty. A large cell, a whole world. Interpersonal relations change along with changes in physical dimensions. They're completely different in a cell made up of four or five people and in one with a hundred people.

I wasn't there long before one day they came and shifted me elsewhere. They were breaking up the cell. Now I found myself in a cell with no one I knew except for those two easygoing young *urks*. Not a big cell, more or less the size of the one in Lubyanka, but there were more beds.

And so who was in that one? Again I'll start with the man senior by age and standing. My eye went right to him, and he made a delightful impression. A Russian intellectual, an old professor from Saratov. Stalin murdered them off, but still they're everywhere. And he was all the more pleasant because the young professors I'd seen with a few exceptions—the cryptologist, the microbiologist, and the academician, the expert on avalanches—were all stained by the corruption of the communist, Stalinist elite, stained by the good life under Stalin, the good life over which a sword of Damocles hung constantly.

So, there was that professor, and there was also a very elegant man with elegant manners, even in the lavatory. First, he had the best technique—there were various techniques—for wiping himself. He had a special handkerchief, which he used to wipe himself thoroughly; he was really making ablutions. He also wiped off his genitals with the well-moistened handkerchief and then washed it out under the faucet. Every day. He washed it out systematically so that it was completely clean and had no smell at all. A very elegant man. And an unpleasant one, a very unpleasant one.

There was also a very nice person with whom I became close friends later on. The difference in age was too great with the professor. He was very old, of a different generation. I was forty-one; the professor was over seventy. But I became friends with another professor, a historian, a Georgian. He was still in that cell when I was released; he'd been in for a very long time.

And there was one other prisoner who'd been in a very long time too, a young Jew, around thirty, with darting eyes. A brash sort of Jew. He said that he was the manager of the Red Army theater in Moscow, a well-known theater. Actually, it was the Soldiers' Home Theater. His eyes quivered but were extremely shrewd. A very odd combination. He had an important influence on my fate. And perhaps it was because of his lack of kindness, his wrath, his almost diabolical wrath, that I was saved, that after a three-month delay I was released from prison because of the amnesty. Evil deeds sometimes turn into good offerings—very often, more often than we suppose. In the last analysis, the Marxist last analysis.

He was a very odd type. Self-educated, but in fact a complete ignoramus. For example, for a long time he argued with me that Marx was French. He insisted on that. Naturally, he was a member of the party. He had taken all sorts of courses. A poor Jew by background. Jewish poverty marks a person for life. That poverty—the family wasn't destitute—those centuries of poverty leave their mark.

There were pogroms in Russia, of course, but there is a certain natural attraction between some Russians and Jews, and the Russians have an enormous natural attraction for Jews. And I have the impression that it originates—to take a bit of a Marxist approach—from both Jews' and Russians' having had a very numerous and extensive class of poor people who lived on the outskirts of cities, a class probably larger there than anywhere else. That theater manager had something of that in him. (I'll call him Josek because he was a typical Josek. It wouldn't ring true to refer to him as the theater manager.) Josek was from the poor class that lived on the outskirts of the city. Not only he, but his grandfather and his great-grandfather. Babel, who was an excellent writer, failed to capture that class and that world. He was more interested in the underworld, but the underworld was just the opposite of that class; those Jewish criminals were the antithesis of that Jewish world. Those criminals were revolutionaries in the sense Pugachev was, not in the sense of the age-old patient poor who rose up in revolt only once. They couldn't stand it any more. And they got a chance. But in general they do not revolt. Those poor Jews went to the ovens with the greatest humility—because of those centuries of patience and poverty.

But as in all classes, there were good people and bad people among the Jewish poor. When they were good, they were saints, true saints. And when they were bad, they were satanic, devils. Josek was one of the bad ones, the fundamentally depraved. His best language was Yiddish; he made mistakes when he spoke Russian. But he knew all of Moscow. He knew everything that went on in the elite, among the Soviet elite, especially the crème de la crème. He was obviously boasting. He liked saying, "Any Russian woman will go to bed with you for a liter of vodka." I immediately distrusted and disliked him, and so I tried to keep him at a distance. But then there was Jewish solidarity. Anti-Semites exaggerate Jewish solidarity, of course. But when two Jews find themselves in a closed situation, they really do rush to each other immediately. But I kept him at a distance. I disliked him very much.

The professor from Saratov was gentleness itself. This was his great misfortune: he had a beautiful daughter, which wouldn't have been a misfortune if he hadn't also had a piano in his apartment. The piano was his undoing, because all the best young people from the university used to meet at his daughter's. Well, one day one of those young people, who had either been sent there or was there by chance, informed on them, saying that they had been discussing the need for a second revolution. That was before the war. They were all brought in, and not only the children. Because that had taken place in his home, the professor and his whole family were brought in, even the wife (later he learned that she had been released). The daughter was in prison; he was in prison. Those young Russians worshipped Mayakovsky and, from what the professor told me, their discussions about the need for a new revolution, a second revolution, were connected with their cult of Mayakovsky, the influence of Mayakovsky. And those are all myths, you know, because in the end Mayakovsky debased himself, and very much so, right before his death.

The Georgian. The Georgian did not tell me why he was in prison. But he and I were very close. He told me about Georgia, and even once confided in me about Stalin. How Stalin had murdered off the Georgian intelligentsia. (After Stalin's death, however—as Paustovsky told me in Paris—this did not prevent a mob of Georgians from booking an entire train to pay their respects to Stalin's mausoleum. They hung up a banner telling where they were from and where they were going: Georgia–USSR. It's very strange, but after Stalin's death the cult of Stalin in Georgia was an authentic one.) The Georgian told me that Stalin had slaughtered the intelligentsia twice. There were only a few survivors, including himself and his family. His sister was a doctor in Alma-Ata. Later, I went to see her to inform her that her brother was dying of hunger. She hadn't known where he was and so had not been sending him any food packages. Then she started sending him food packages. He was released later on, during the war when I was in Alma-Ata. I was greatly tempted to go see him, but I was working in the Polish delegation at the time, and I was being followed and was very afraid. Anyway, that Georgian was a wonderful person. A European. He would have shone in any circle. Refined, with lovely manners, and a certain lovely, typically Georgian lyricism.

As you can see, I'm a bit scattered today. Who else was in the cell? No one was being summoned for interrogation any more. No one. But the theater manager, Josek, was called in very often; no one had any illusions about him. An informer. At some point in October he was taken from our cell and replaced by an ethnic German from Saratov. A party member, an apparatchik from the autonomous German republic, the German area in Saratov. I spoke with him in German. He wasn't very easy to understand because those Germans had been there since the time of Catherine the Great. And for them German literature meant Luther's Bible. They all spoke the German of Luther. Though I did know a little Old German, there were still certain problems in understanding him. A beautiful language. They had not lost contact with their fatherland. But they maintained a very strange sort of contact. They would send emissaries who would then return. Contact with the fatherland through emissaries. That German told me about their terrible hatred for the Soviets. He was a high official, an apparatchik, and very intelligent. He had a Marxist education, but that Marxism was just a removable shell. Not as it was with the Russians. The Russians' indoctrination had grown into their flesh, and that was a terrible thing. But for those Germans it was a diving suit in which they could safely immerse themselves in the black waters, the murky depths of Stalinism. So none of it had stuck to him, even though he had been a high apparatchik.

While I'm on the subject of Germans, there were two others I got to know. That was back in Lwów, not in Zamarstynów, but in the large cell at Brygidki. There were two Germans there, German soldiers. They professed to be Communist party members. One of them never said a word the entire time. But the other one was a raging German, and he spoke a great deal. A terrible anti-Semite. From him you could guess what lengths anti-Semitism could go to in Germany. He wasn't the Polish "kike-baiting" type; he was the "slaughter-them" type. Not slaughter, exterminate. If they burned Jews, it was because they didn't want to waste their knives on them, not to mention bullets. German anti-Semitism. Exterminate them with fire; burn them up. He was that sort of anti-Semite. But he spoke with me even though he knew I was a

Jew. I even told him. He had deserted; he had been at the border. As an old communist he had crossed over to the Soviet side along with his friend and their weapons. Naturally, they threw him in prison as a spy. He was a Nazi by the time I met him in the cell in Brygidki, but I'm not sure he was a spy. I'm inclined to think that he really was a communist and, as such, had deserted to the Soviets, another proof of how thin the line between Nazism and Stalinism was.

The prison cell in Saratov had other occupants as well. I can't call them by any other name because of their great and obvious sense of their own dignity. Those were the bedbugs. Sublimated bedbugs. Not like the ones in Kiev, those nasty spongers. These bedbugs were also good sized, but their bites weren't painful. Hunger reigned in Saratov, so much so that not only we but even our guards went hungry. There was nothing to eat. Of course, I must say we were given bread. But the bread had somehow shrunk; it was made with a large, an enormous, amount of water. One time I saw a tall, skinny guard, who was taking us for a walk down an iron staircase covered with dust from boots, spot a crumb of bread on the steps in front of us (we were schooled in spotting such things). And so, rather awkwardly—so that we wouldn't notice—he bent down as if he had dropped something and picked up that crumb of bread.

The bedbugs were not so much aristocratic bedbugs as bedbugs sublimated by hunger, and perhaps also by our blood, for our blood was no longer nutritious. The bedbugs' scent for blood wasn't in good working order since the chemical composition of our blood had evidently altered. Probably our blood was weak and dilute. Hunger made people hallucinate. Those bedbugs were interesting creatures. Their movements were full of dignity, slow. Not fat, but big, only somehow flattened out a little on top. At the borders of their world, which was deep in the walls, there was no longer any food to be found, and they fell into comas, semicomas.

In Kiev no one battled the bedbugs anymore. Evidently the prison officials had acknowledged there was nothing that could be done about them. They were so aggressive, bred so fast. They fucked like mad. Under good conditions they were obviously very passionate and multiplied like nobody's business. They were so aggressive that no one battled them. In Saratov, however, the prison authorities did battle with them. We were given some sort of acetylene lamps to be used for a little while in our cells to burn out their nests. Nothing did any good.

At that time I had already begun to suffer from insomnia. I would wake up before dawn, sometimes in the middle of the night, seized by anxiety for my family, and so in the morning I would see the bedbugs arise, ever so slowly. A certain slowness of movement is, as far as I have observed, part of their nature. But one time I did see a bedbug running fast—was it panic, or was it something else? So, bedbugs *aren't* turtles, they *can* run. I don't know, maybe that was an exception, a freak. In my entire life, that was the only bedbug I've ever seen tearing along, in a hurry.

All bedbugs have dignity. They advance in columns, one column after the other. Just like an army. In waves: one wave, then another. And here is a mystery that no one has ever fathomed. Every day the bedbugs would go up the wall to a certain point, quite high up but still a good way from the ceiling. They'd go up to this point, come to a halt, then go back down. Some of them would spend rather a long time there; then they'd all go back down. But some of them would spend an hour there. My cell was lit by a powerful bulb that burned all night. The bedbugs would stay at that point on the wall as if they were lost in philosophical revery. But there was clearly some kind of borderline there, some kind of taboo. They never went onto the ceiling. The Saratov bedbugs, never. What could it have been? Maybe some sense of microtemperature. There's a different microtemperature with every layer of air. We have no sense of it, although, because of my illness, I've started sensing microtemperatures. I tried to figure it out. Could there have been another coat of paint beneath the outer one that began right at that point? Another coat of paint that was, for them, repugnant? I don't know. But they always stopped at the same point. If it had been a taboo, there'd have been one who'd have transgressed it. There's always at least one in every society, human or animal. One freak, one rebel. I made daily observations. I woke up at night and would watch them for quite a long time, and I never saw one cross the line. I was intrigued, which made my sight even keener. The secret of the bedbugs. Just to think that no one will ever figure it out. Only God knows the secret of those bedbugs. And maybe that's some ontological proof of God's existence. For after all, there must be someone who knows their secret.

So the bedbugs gave us no peace, but we weren't very good to them either. We burned them alive. The meanness of man. His fundamental primitiveness. The jungle. Man does not kill only to eat. After all, they did us no harm. I don't even remember whether I could feel their bites or not. And I was very sensitive. In Kiev their bites and the smell of them had been a torture to me. The ones in Saratov had no smell, no bedbug stink. Strange bedbugs.

Another wave of fear for my family had come over me in the cell. As I've said, in prison even the least superstitious people look for signs. The least superstitious, the rationalists, the atheists, look for signs in everything. People also have the feeling—mistaken, of course—that they can interpret their own dreams. Despite Freud, I maintain that the majority of dreams are caprices of the imagination, like the caprices of clouds. Sometimes, however, in a dream you are aware that the dream has meaning. I don't say prophetic, but a dream with a meaning. Of course, you don't know what the meaning is, and here Freud is certainly right in part. But there are dreams that have meaning for you, and you know it when you wake up. The same holds true for events, for signs. In prison you have the feeling that certain things are signs. Usually they aren't. But in prison, everyone, truly everyone, believes, firmly believes, that certain things have a meaning, certain things are signs. Even the most skeptical people, those with the best defenses against superstition.

One sign became an obsession for me. Namely—as I told you—I was absolutely unable to recall Ola's face or Andrzej's, even though I would know those faces in the dark and knew them by heart. If I were a painter, I could have painted their portraits quite realistically without glancing once at them. But that disappeared as soon as I was arrested. *Effacé*. Wiped away. Trying doesn't help. I didn't consider this a sign from fate when I was in Zamarstynów. I didn't know how to explain it, but I consideed it rather a disturbance in memory caused by prison.

Later on, I was able to recall Andrzej's face, though the cause was a banal one. I already told you that when I was entering the prison in Kiev, a gang of young little *urks* walked past us. The one who ran over to us and even asked me for a cigarette was a very cheerful, good-looking boy, who resembled Andrzej. From then on Andrzej's face would appear to me. But Ola's, never. And so I took that as a sign, which I interpreted like this: since Andrzej's face was appearing to me now, that meant that Ola was still alive but Andrzej was not. And again I had to think that though Peiper was mad as a hatter, he might just have seen her.

31 THE HERETICAL MONK. SOLDIERS. A DIGRESSION ON THE EROTIC AND PERSONAL LIFE. THE DEVIL APPEARS. CONVERSION. ON JUDAISM AND CHRISTIANITY. HUNGER AND SICKNESS. A MEETING.

WAT: I'd like to go back a little and bring in a couple of people I'd forgotten and who had some significance. I was talking about the social circles in the large cell. One circle was nearly completely inaccessible: those were the officers; I think they were nearly all air force. They were very polite but kept their distance with everyone else. There was also a high NKVD official who had been in Lubyanka a long time. He had his own circle too. I think I heard people ask him—a constant question in those times—how many people are in the camps, the prisons?

There was also a group of very Russian people, a rather numerous group, it turned out; they all looked like Russian peasants, a little like Old Believers. One of them had very broad shoulders. He was relatively short, with a very large, full, but rather flat face, with ruddy cheeks, good-looking, a very black head of hair. That caught your eye because these newest prisoners hadn't had their heads shaved yet. The older prisoners usually had their heads shaved with automatic clippers every so often. So what you saw were scalps in one state of growth or another, but that prisoner had quite a full head of hair, true raven black hair. The face of a good, respectable person, but I wouldn't want to run into him in the woods. He could have a knife inside his jacket—a tough muzhik.

The whole group of them struck me as sectarians or former clergymen, and it flashed through my mind that this was the man Dunayevsky had told me about, who had been in prison with him for a time. The monk who was expelled from the monastery for theological heresy, but not an Old Believer. He had been very nice in the cell; he knew that Dunayevsky was a Jew and expounded his theory to him. According to Dunayevsky, who was something of an expert on this, there was a sect in the fourth or fifth century that had similar ideas. The theory held that the Second Coming can take place only at the moment when all the Jews, to a man, convert. That's the condition: to a man. But since

285

the Jews are a stiff-necked people and stubborn, to speed up the Kingdom of God, the Second Coming, the Parousia—for life had become absolutely impossible in Russia—all the Jews had to be slaughtered, to a man—to a man. According to Dunayevsky, the monk harbored no anti-Semitic sentiments. This conviction had an entirely different source; this wasn't political anti-Semitism. It flashed through my mind that this was he. And so I approached him the first chance I got. Not unfriendly at all, he smiled a lot, to everyone. I said, "Do you know Dunayevsky?"

"Hm," he said.

"Were you ever a monk?"

"Hm." I asked three or four more questions, and he always answered me with that "hm"! It was a very open "hm," no wriggling, just "hm." I could understand it to mean yes or no. I saw I would have no access to him and stopped bothering him. You had to be very delicate about those things in Soviet prisons. I knew that by then. You don't ask questions. You listen, but you don't ask.

As I was saying last time, I was heartsick with worry about my family. There was a lot of writing on the lavatory walls. I don't think names were used, but rather diminutives by which you could recognize people. Information: I've been here since such and such a date, and if you're here too, let me hear from you. Notes to wives, friends. That sort of thing, in a variety of styles, some flowery, some very simple, the simplest information. I saw one "if you're here, let me hear from you" written in Russian, in poor script, which meant that the woman who wrote it either had little education or was a foreigner. It was signed, Olya. I knew Ola's handwriting in Polish and this handwriting meant nothing to me, especially its childish scrawl. When I returned to the cell from the lavatory, I asked the little good-looking *urk* to make me a "telegraph." A search for thread, pieces were tied together, things were ripped up—he was very glad to do it. In Kiev the guards had been lenient about messages, but here they tore them down every couple of days. And so—threads, a matchbox, and, in the matchbox, a scrap of paper, which you could always find somewhere, a tiny note. What he did was throw the matchbox up at various angles, aiming for the shield over the window. How did they do that? The right muscle had to be tensed in a certain strange manner, a fantastic talent, fit for the circus. I set up a different sort of telegraph with the next cell. I began tapping. Russians don't do that often at all; it was a lost art under the Soviets. You also had to decide whether to use the Russian alphabet or the Polish, and I'd make mistakes with the Russian alphabet. Even if I sent the messages clearly, I'd botch up when receiving, and all sorts of nonsense would result. Naturally, I kept asking about Ola Wat, the wife of the Polish writer. And one message said that there was a prisoner nearby whose name might have been Wat but might also have been Wirt. In fact I think that was the wife of Wirt, the Russian writer. Heartsick, I thought to myself, Ola can withstand prison, but what's happened to Andrzej?

Come to think of it, I really have no idea what all this talk of mine amounts to. It's not an autobiography because, to take one example, I'm not dealing with the erotic, the sexual, things that are so important in my life and most people's lives. And besides, I don't think anyone has ever succeeded in speaking of that. Being candid about it leads to a certain degradation of the author himself, as shown by all those Frenchmen, that whole French school of Bataille who write about the sexual side of themselves. In these things it has to be all or nothing. Some Frenchmen even do write everything, but not only is this somehow nasty for the reader, but it's also clear that the author himself has slipped away in the course of writing. I think that the old great writers who made full confessions but in fictional form did the right thing. Very full confessions sometimes. If you read Tolstoy with a detective's eye, his confessions are more complete than those of the Frenchmen who lay themselves bare. Clearly, these matters require a certain modesty. I'm no puritan, but I think these things shouldn't be touched upon. But an autobiography without them? I was, I would say, a sensual person, and so obviously it's a shallow biography that leaves all that out. So are these memoirs? But memoirs require that you be not only a witness but a participant in history, a much greater one than I was. You have to be someone like Herzen. An actor in history. Confessions! But the entire aspect of personal life comes in there too.

Certain things are indispensable like our being a couple, no doubt a typical couple, but not for the literary world, especially the one in Warsaw where we were a legendary couple. And really right from the beginning we were so well matched—even during the furies of *amour passionnel* in which there are constant storms, we were so well matched that unconsciously I thought it a proof of fate, destiny. That was a great happiness in my life. In fact, I wrote a little about it in one poem, the only poem of that sort, the poem about the Siamese twins. It's interesting that the spiritual transformations and especially the religious experiences we had, without knowing anything about the other—me in Saratov and Ola on a state farm—were different but had taken absolutely the same direction and were strikingly similar. At that time, Ola was on the Krasny Skotovod State Farm. She was at the peak of her beauty then. Andrzej had a very subtle beauty about him, too. My relationship to communism was forever affected by seeing its boots destroying beauty, trampling beauty. It goes without saying that, for me, Ola and Andrzej are the incarnation of beauty, the pure beauty of the world. And so this was not only something personal but cosmological and historical as well. I had expected extermination, but not that trampling.

But let's go back to the others. Josek. I've already mentioned brushing up against old Steklov, who was shouting, "Stalin is a villain, a bandit." Josek provided details that he could not have invented. He said he knew Steklov's son well. And Josek told me Steklov's story. That little Josek was a gold mine of information about the people on top. Steklov, the editor of *Izvestiya* and so on; the worthy author of large books on Chernyshevsky, literature, politics; an associate of Lenin; Stalin was very fond of him. Steklov told stories that would make Stalin burst out laughing. An old SD, an old socialist. The fiftieth anniversary of Steklov's joining the party was supposed to be celebrated with great ceremony under the patronage of Stalin himself. Preparations were made, portraits in the newspapers. Everything was fine, and then the day before, or a few days before, bang, Steklov was locked up. His family was locked up too, his wife and son. And then in a strange act of mercy, Stalin not only released the wife and son but did not even have them made "disenfranchised citizens"; they were able to return to Moscow, where they were given part of the apartment they had previously occupied.

When she was released, Steklov's wife, of course, began running to see everyone she could for help. That was a very strange thing, but even during the worst periods of the terror, the wives were allowed to make a fuss. Later, they were often exiled, but if they weren't arrested, they were allowed to go around everywhere and even create scenes. The prosecutors would flee from those wives; they were afraid of them. One of life's mysteries. That was the arrangement, the setup. Brutality was not permitted against the wife of an arrested man, provided the wife was not under arrest herself. So Steklov's wife began making the rounds of the offices. She was told one thing and another, but after a time she received official written notice that Steklov had died.

There was another bit of business with Josek. I told you about the old German, the engineer, who was attracted to Russia because of German unemployment. He'd been tortured before he was brought to the cell; they'd made hamburger out of him too. On him it looked even worse because he had terrible varicose veins. A woman doctor came the very same day he was brought to the cell. I knew her from Lubyanka. An elegant woman in a gray English suit, very pretty as I recall, her eyes almost steely, a beautiful hairdo, fresh, young. A European. She would have been thought a good-looking, elegant, woman here in Paris. I jumped up and said she should have a look at what had been done to the engineer. "Let him show me," she said. The engineer lifted his pant legs, just the pant legs. And she said with almost a smile, a hint of a smile, "Ah, did you fall downstairs? How did you hurt yourself like that?" Such sangfroid. She said that she'd send him some salve and then left with a smile, at peace with herself. I mention this because later on I will be speaking of the Samaritan-like quality of Russian doctors, even in prison. That was something I encountered constantly. That woman doctor was the exception, the sole exception in my experience.

Anyway, the German had been in Russia many years, but he still couldn't express himself in Russian. Josek started talking German with him. But that caused some very serious misunderstandings. Yiddish has many Slavic words and a great many Hebrew words as well. Josek knew that Yiddish was somehow close to German and that German was the better language. Yiddish was the language of Jews. And so he thought that the serious, important words in Yiddish were German, whereas in fact they're Hebrew. They had long conversations, but they didn't understand each other. Josek used Hebrew words, but he didn't understand German, especially since that Prussian, who was probably a Berliner, was hard to understand. He said *yanz* instead of *ganz*. A dialogue of the deaf and dumb, but still they talked to each other; they talked at night. Josek would pepper him with questions, and the German would answer without having understood the question. I found that very amusing.

But Josek also treated the man like a father. Because every so often, every three or four days, the German would be taken from the cell and beaten and tortured. Then they'd carry him back to the cell. He was strong as a horse, that lanky German. Obviously, he had the constitution of a horse to be able to withstand all that. Unlike Taitz, he didn't sign anything—because it wasn't the truth. He didn't understand. How could he sign it if it wasn't the truth? It didn't enter his mind that he could make things easier for himself. An old, solid German who wasn't used to Slavic or Jewish deceit. They'd bring him in, and he'd lie on his bed in horrible pain. Josek would try to help him, stroke his head, wipe his face. He really does have a good heart, I thought; appearances are misleading. Later the German was pulled out again, and after one such interrogation he never reappeared in our cell. But a little while after that I was in the hospital, and I was near a man from the cell to which the German had been taken. And it turned out that Josek had concocted an entire story about the German from their conversations, a story that had not caused them to stop torturing the German. And so in this case appearances had not been deceiving.

We were starving. That was the most important fact in our life. Who knows, we might even have eaten bedbugs. We didn't, but we may have been close. Terrible hunger. What did they feed us? There was bread every day, but less of it now, not four hundred grams, maybe three hundred, two hundred fifty. That unnutritious bread sat like a stone in your stomach. There was a technique for eating bread. Of course by then I already knew various refined techniques. The Russians were very fond of crumbling a portion of their bread into boiling water. But I had already been taught how large each bite should be and more or less how long to keep it in the mouth before swallowing it. That's the most scientific way to eat bread. Of course, by then we all were skilled in eating bread, every last crumb. Everyone had a sense of the holiness of bread. Bread is holy.

I had known that, but not really. I learned it from our servant, our nurse, Anusia; and I never forgot how she yelled at me; she probably never had yelled at me like that before. She had given me a roll with something on it; I'd had enough and I threw it away. That was something you didn't do. I think that all peasants are like that. That was something you didn't do. From then on, that became a sort of involuntary, unthinking taboo: you don't throw bread away.

The holiness of bread, the absolute sacredness of bread. We ate that bread as if it were the Host. Even Josek, the degenerate, the product of atheism at its worst, ate his bread with a sense of the sacred. So in the morning, bread and boiled water. Then lunch and dinner were boiled water with a few cabbage leaves or something of that sort—but really just boiled water; it even tasted boiled. There were so few vegetables that they didn't even add any taste to it. The taste of boiled water.

But one day they gave us green tomatoes, two or three for each of us. A miracle, happiness. They gave us those green tomatoes twice a day for two or three days. And one time they gave us quite a lot of those green tomatoes. I came down with dysentery. None of my cell mates came down with it for some reason. I guess it must have been the beginning of November by then. There were some very cold days, but sometimes out in the air on our walks it felt almost like a warm Polish autumn. I ran a very high temperature for two days; it must have been over forty degrees. The woman doctor gave me some powders, which I took. A day passed, two, three. I was on the pot nearly all the time, making a terrible stench for my cell mates. Not only was I spreading infection, but I was fouling the air. We went to the latrine twice a day, but I had to spend all my time on the pot. By then I had wasted away, completely desiccated. Some people swell from hunger, but I was practically nothing but skin and bones.

I forgot the most important thing. I have to stop and go back because this is important; the order doesn't matter here. One night, I couldn't sleep because of the light bulb. I heard laughter, a flourish of laughter that kept approaching and receding. A vulgar laugh, actually. I didn't like opera, but my brothers and sisters did. And so I had seen *Faust* as a child and I knew Mephistopheles' laugh from it. It came in flourishes. Ha haha ha! Ha haha ha! It kept receding and approaching. It was then that I had a vision of the devil. I won't even try to reconstruct that night because I wouldn't succeed. But it was then that the breakthrough occurred. Evidently, there had been something missing. There had been some obstacle, some last partition, and then it broke with that laughter of the vulgar, the most vulgar devil of all, flourishes of vulgar laughter that kept approaching, then receding far away for a long time, a very long time. I saw the devil. Well, I saw a devil with hooves, the devil from the opera. I really did see him—it must have been a hallucination from hunger, but not only did I see him, but I could almost smell the brimstone. My mind was working at terribly high revolutions. It was the devil in history.

And I felt something else, that the majesty of God was spread over history, over all this, a God distant but real. I can't decipher it fully, I can't remember it all, but it was so actual, so sensual, as if the devil was in my cell, the ceiling of the cell was lifted away, and God was above it all. It was all straight from commonplace religious folk art. I don't know. I didn't see God, because God did not even actually show himself to Moses. God is blinding, but I did see that God—now I can say it—had a beard. The God of iconography. And a devil with hooves.

A strange night, very strange. I didn't sleep the entire night. And what was the laughter? It was a patrol boat. I suspected right away that there was a patrol boat out on the Volga that night that kept approaching and receding, and the laughter was its anti-aircraft alarm. And that I was aware of this meant that this was a vision of the devil in history. For that was history. The war had just broken out; Armageddon was approaching. And even there in Saratov, in the heart of Russia, on the Volga, an anti-aircraft alarm was sounding, and that was a manifestation of history.

It was then that I began to be a believer. Now I know that there was something bad about my conversion. I don't say it was a bad conversion; it may even have been a good one. But the devil works his way in guilefully everywhere, and there was something bad about it; it was a sublimation, but it was also something from the netherworld; that patrol boat also belonged to the world of hatred and fanaticism, and that other force, that lower force, was always with me after that. And it perverted the experience, no question of that. And so what I think ultimately formed me, and for the best, what I consider the high point of my life—my experiences in Ili—also had an undertone of deviltry, fanaticism, hatred. I know that now; back then, of course, I didn't. I didn't know anything; I didn't realize, didn't feel that there was more to it.

Everything was one that night. The main thing was the feeling of the oneness of the experience and my oneness with it. Before then I had felt mostly discord within myself, but that night I had such a feeling of monolithic unity, of a sort I was never to experience again in my life. As if I only became myself at that moment. That night, I truly was one, one and indivisible. It was a very long night. That night certainly transformed me and also the way I acted in prison. I have the impression that it was only after that night that I became human and was able to live in society with people. I had changed; I had truly changed. I changed my attitude toward my fellow prisoners, and I thought less about myself. Though I still thought constantly of Ola and Andrzej. I thought about them all the time, but that too had changed a lot because belief in the immortality of the soul had come to me with that experience. My relationship to my cell mates changed. I had learned to live with people, and it had come suddenly. Something had turned around and, for all my grief, I had peace.

The people in the cell said anti-aircraft alarms were being sounded in Saratov. Everyone was very upset. What's going to happen to us? They might have time to shoot us all before the Germans arrive. But then again they might not. What then? Everyone had his own plan. What did I picture for myself? I rather thought they'd finish me off. And what would I do if they didn't? I had minimized Nazism, as I told you. I didn't understand the threat. I thought, I'll start looking all over Russia for my family. How would I find them? I'd travel around, I'd go on foot, I'd search for them, I'd ask questions. And how would I live in starving Russia? I thought of being a palm reader. Russia is a very superstitious country, and people who can read coffee grounds do very well in Russia.

I had played around with palm reading when I was young. One time Roman Jasiński brought me to a very elegant, aristocratic ball. I was a big hit with the aristocrats and the landed gentry, and for some reason it occurred to me to read their palms. Anyway, I said some shameless things, and one of the young ladies' defenders, a very elegant light-cavalry officer, was offended. There was an exchange of calling cards, but actually he had liked my performance, and the next day he and I went out for vodka. And so sometimes I played at reading palms, but it really wasn't the palms, it was, rather, the faces I read, by intuition. And so I thought I'd go through Russia reading palms, walk across Russia until I found Ola and Andrzej.

So, back to the subject. I had dysentery. By then I was a Christian. I had a temperature of almost 106, but the hallucinations did not return, even during the fever.

MILOSZ: I'd like to ask you a question. Why did you say, "By then I was a Christian?" Why did your conversion take a Christian form?

WAT: What other form could it take? Judaism really is passé as a religion. Judaism did its part and ended in Christianity. There's Hasidism. Hasidism was an attempt to revive a Judaism that had become dry and utterly desiccated. Hasidism was an attempt to revive Judaism through gnosis, mysticism, influences completely alien to it. And besides, I had no grounding in Judaism. My father was a Hasid, but he didn't care if his children took after him; he probably didn't even want us to, because he knew that was impossible. My eldest brother studied Hebrew, the Bible; he might have even known the Gemara. But my other brother, the one who lives in Brussels, the one who's ten years older than I, knew less than I did. And so our home was actually atheistic. My brother in Brussels was in the PPS. When I was little, my sister was already studying set design. On the contrary, I saw Jews the way anti-Semites do: in gabardines, dirty, merchants, money. I actually had an anti-Semitic childhood. It was only during my student years that I began to feel solidarity with Jews. My father subscribed to *Hajnt* and the *Warsaw Courier*. He was a conservative in his political views.

It was a very strange family. But there are Jewish families like that. There were even converts in the family. My grandmother had an uncle, or a cousin, who was a canon in Vienna. Professor Luria from Lwów was related to my grandmother and his father had converted. It was a hotchpotch. One of my uncles ended up as a saint in Palestine long before the war. I remember him. He had a goatee; he was an ascetic who never left his books. When he came to see my father, he would lower his eyes at the sight of my mother. He took care not to touch her dress, not to brush against her dress. But his sisters went to Paris. Their grandfather was very rich: he had a foundry in Kuznice; he owned an estate.

And I'll tell you another strange thing. I came into the world dead, and the caretaker's wife forced me into life by smacking my behind. The caretaker's wife at the house at 5 Kupiecka Street. And her husband had saved my father's life. My father fell down a well out there in the country, and it was that caretaker who had saved him. And his wife had saved me. Those things happen.

I had not been initiated into religion and for the most part simply ignored it. Now, with the years, I rather attach significance to it. But back then I ignored it; I had a negative attitude toward religion, like all assimilated Jews. And I really am of the opinion that Judaism is a religion that must come to its end.

And besides that there were Christian influences. I was already a child Darwinist, an atheist, by the time I was seven or perhaps eight, but as I've told you, Anusia used to take me to church secretly for vespers, and that had its influence. Imagine a boy from what was still a Jewish home surrounded by all those candles, that music. So the inclinations were always there. A few people said that I would become a Catholic. There was a lousy woman writer, a terrible anti-Semite, Jewish by background, Zahorska (not Stefania, of course), who used to bring her novels to Gebethner's. They had published her before, but of course I wouldn't publish her after I took over. She wasn't discouraged; she kept coming, and even though I rejected her manuscripts, she kept insisting, "You'll see, you'll become a Catholic." And three years ago in Paris, Józef Wittlin said to me, "Do you remember, Aleksander, in Paris in 1929, we were walking by the Seine at night—I remember that conversation perfectly—I told you, you'll become a Catholic." And I was an atheist then; I had started moving toward communism. And so then why had he said that?

I read a lot. I read the theologians; I read the Church Fathers when I was young—I was very interested in that. I had read a great deal of the Church Fathers. I read all of St. Thomas's *Summa* when I was young, and in Latin besides. I've forgotten my Latin now, but I was good at Latin in high school, very good. And so there's nothing odd about its being well prepared in advance.

I was singing, irritating my cell mates. They demanded of the woman doctor that I be taken to the hospital. By then it was the fifth day or the sixth. My illness kept getting worse, but they weren't taking me to the hospital. On the seventh day I was so weak that I had to be held up by my arms to go to the latrine in the morning. I insisted that I had to go. It was at the far end of the corridor. The Georgian historian held me on one side and Josek on the other. I fell in the corridor coming back. No, that wasn't it! I fell and knocked my head on the stone floor in the latrine. And then it took four of them to carry me. I blacked out, lost consciousness. But then the guard said I'd be going to the hospital that day. And that was true. The guards were very good in Saratov, very human, at least the ones on our floor.

294

They put me in a Black Maria, one of the more comfortable ones. We drove across the Volga to another prison, which had a hospital. And in the Black Maria, whose rear slat was open quite wide to permit breathing, there was another person on the way to the hospital. Old Steklov. I introduced myself. He came to life when he found out I was from Warsaw, a writer from Warsaw. His eyes gleamed with good feeling and real interest. It was quite a long ride to that prison, but we finally arrived at the hospital, where they put us in the waiting room. Again, I have no sense of time, but the two of us sat on a bench talking with no guard for quite a long time. I mean, he talked. I asked him a few questions. He was calm now, serene. He had dysentery and was running a high fever too. When I had first seen him, he had seemed like a mad man, but now he was very calm, very refined. An intellectual, interested in literature, everything. He asked me a great many questions about Warsaw, the Poles, Żeromski (I don't know whether he knew him personally), and all sorts of other things as well. But he did know a great many Poles. I'm convinced that our fevers did not influence this conversation, that it was perfectly lucid. At least I was. And evidently he was too. My conversation with Steklov—well, only a small portion has survived in my memory, but what I do remember, I'm certain of. It was a very instructive conversation for me, very interesting, because most of his questions were about positivism and socialism in Poland. He spoke exquisite Russian, the most beautiful Russian, a Russian no one speaks in the Soviet Union now. With the intonation of a prewar intellectual; only certain émigrés have that same intonation.

32 TELL PEOPLE IN POLAND HOW OLD STEKLOV DIED. IN THE HOSPITAL. A SECOND TRUE HUMAN BEING— DUBIN. LEAVING PRISON.

WAT: I asked Steklov about what Josek had told me. I asked him if it was accurate. And he confirmed most of it. There probably were some differences, but minor ones. The basic things were true: he had been in Lubyanka for a very short time after his arrest and then was sent immediately to Omsk Central—you know, I always mix up Omsk and Tomsk, and so I wouldn't bet my life that it was Omsk Central or Tomsk Central—in any case, one of the famous centrals that basically were mausoleums for those who had been buried alive. They were all in solitary there, comfortable; every cell had its own toilet; they were fed well; they had books. A person could be in there ten years, and no one apart from the NKVD would ever know he was alive. Besides, even at Lubyanka there were rumors that people who had supposedly been executed were in fact in one of those centrals. There were even "gilded cages" like that in Lubyanka. Certain outstanding scientists were able to do work in their fields and were given whatever they wanted—food, clothing, everything. But that other central was actually extremely dismal, a tomb. Josek had been told by Steklov's family that he had died of a heart attack. But even those tombs had been disrupted by the war, and people began to be pulled out of them and sent to Moscow. At the very beginning of the war Steklov had been returned to Lubyanka and soon after had been sent on to Saratov.

At one point, just after the Revolution, Steklov had announced that he was writing a two- or three-volume study of Chernyshevsky. This work was looked on with such favor that he was given documents from the archives. Stalin had made a cult of Chernyshevsky, and so Steklov assumed that his work had been facilitated on orders from Stalin himself. Apparently Steklov had come close to finishing the work, and so it's somewhere in the NKVD archives.

You asked me how he and I could talk when we were both running high temperatures. But you know, a temperature can focus your attention and make the mind rapacious. And I also realized that I had a unique chance to get inside information on various things that had been gnawing at me for years, for example, the trials, the confessions, and so on. It was a clear-minded conversation, and, in fact, if it were reproduced on tape, it would certainly hold together and be logical, though there'd also be a certain feverishness about it. The look on his face was very different during that conversation; he had come very much back to life, though at times he would fade away. I was experiencing something different, and somehow it seemed to happen mostly when he was talking about Stalin. He spoke readily about Stalin.

Suddenly—despite all efforts and all my desire to listen—my attention, which is the basis of memory, began to flow away from me. I had the feeling of it flowing away to some sea, some sea within me. Far, far away, and I couldn't do anything to stop it. There'd be breaks, blank spots, gaps; then I'd come to and be listening to him again. I mostly listened and only spoke to ask questions.

Even though it was late autumn in Saratov, it was a warm day, something like autumn in Poland, sunny and bright. The two of us were just skin and bones; Steklov was swollen but desiccated. And we had that strange conversation on history, with me avid for the truth. Well, it was so bright in there, the room was so bathed in light, that I was able to observe him closely. A certain nobility, something aristocratic about his face. Very dry skin, wrinkles. I remember the wrinkles, but the general impression was of a smooth face. And though his skin drooped a bit, the face had a certain energy to it, so you weren't aware of that loose skin. His nose was quite prominent but did not dominate; the eyes dominated. Very dry eyes, the eyes of a deranged man, but they had a certain fire to them. How to put it—they had fire but no light. I don't know if you can say that. A certain dry fire. He spoke with incredible contempt about the heroes of the Revolution and Stalin: that lowlife Trotsky, that swine Ordzhonikidze. I don't know if he spoke about Lenin; that I don't recall. There was also hatred when he spoke of Stalin, a terrible hatred, a hatred all his own—one that was in fact keeping him alive. He gave the impression of being very sick, alive only because of that hatred.

My primary intention was to get him to shed some light on the trials, which remain a mystery no matter what. What was the purpose of those trials? Why precisely that sort? Why did the heroes of the Revolution confess? I asked Steklov that question: "Why did the heroes of the Revolution fall so low? Were they afraid of torture?" His answer: "Torture? Torture, for us? What for? All of us, all of us (this I recall nearly verbatim—a shudder went through me, a cold shudder went through my feverish body because of the way he said this), we were all up to our elbows in shit and blood. Each one of us heroes of the Revolution who'd been arrested knew that we could be presented with such a bill of immorality and degradation and villainy that dated back almost to the very start that nothing really mattered to us anymore. To confess or not to confess, that was no issue. Those people confessed because they were disgusted by their past."

Steklov's gaze was so heavy when he spoke of those things that I could feel the weight of it on me. That was the special feature of his eyes, not so much their dry fire as the incredible weight of his gaze. You felt it on your skin, especially when he was talking about the heroes of the Revolution. He used vulgar words but always spoke with splendid refinement.

What do I remember of what he said about Stalin? Not much. Perhaps the fever made me try so hard to remember and to remember so little. He told me about Yenukidze's fall. I checked that out later on in the literature. Steklov had a different version, a so-called unknown version, but one that I think was quite common in those times. Yenukidze was something of a master for Stalin, who listened to what he had to say for quite a long time; his opinion mattered to Stalin. Yenukidze was a gentleman, a bon vivant, a Georgian socialist, which was a very refined type. Ceretelli, the whole group of socialists, excellent Marxists, an entire school. They had great contempt for Stalin at the very beginning, and there was also that story of Stalin's robbing the train; he had a very ugly reputation. And so Stalin destroyed them, but clearly Yenukidze had been Stalin's hero as a young man, and Yenukidze must have so impressed him that Stalin spared him and he set great store by him.

But Yenukidze had a daughter who was a devotée in the cult of Stalin. By then, the father was very careful. A bon vivant, an old man, he wanted to die a natural death. He did nothing wrong. But he obviously did not conceal anything from his daughter, and he spoke ill of Stalin to her. And she went running to Stalin. That must have been very cutting for Stalin, and Yenukidze was locked up. Besides, there was a similar incident with Warski, which people talk about in Warsaw but which, of course, has never been in print. Stalin probably would have spared Warski, too. He was retired, old, out of things. He lived in the Kremlin, a favorite; he'd received honors. But he used to go for lunch with an old friend from his youth, Dzierżyński's widow. And she ran to Stalin and repeated what Warski had said about him. And so they took Warski away. So that was a rather common occurrence with those Passionarias, those devotées of the cult of Stalin. It's odd that looks played no role here, for there's no question that there was a sexual undercurrent to all that, but male good looks played no role in it; rather, it was power. Because Stalin was basically monstrous-looking: a low shaggy forehead, a short man with a pockmarked face and horrible eyes.

What else did Steklov say about Stalin and Stalin's court? That it wasn't a court but a clique, actually just a gang, that he chose mainly people who were extremely vulgar, common, and coarse. He spoke with disgust about those conversations around the table over vodka when important decisions were being made, the extreme vulgarity and cruelty of those people.

At one point, toward the end of our talk, Steklov said to me, "When you return (this I remember verbatim), when you return to Poland, you absolutely have to tell people how old Steklov died!"

To which I replied immediately, and sincerely, because that's what I thought, "I'll never return there!"

He grew angry at me. "Of course you'll return; you absolutely will!"

And then I realized that this old erratic egocentric thought that I had to return because now I had a mission to carry out: to tell people how old Steklov had died. Then they came for us, and that was the end of the conversation. They took him first, and he shouted it from the doorway again, "Tell people in Poland how old Steklov died!"

They took him; then they came for me. I was taken to a rather large hospital room entered directly from the corridor. Steklov was two or three doors down from me. They had excellent medicine for dysentery there, and after three days I was able to get out of bed and go to the bathroom myself. Conditions were rather free there—a soldier in front of each ward, but the corridor wasn't guarded and I could hear Steklov's voice from there. Once I heard him say, "Radi Boga" (for God's sake), but by then his voice sounded like a broken instrument. He was calling somebody, probably the nurse.

I stood in front of his door twice in one day, on my fifth or sixth day there. Once, in the morning, the guard—you could tell by his face he was gentle—let me stand there, but he said, "No talking allowed here."

But Steklov had noticed me and once again he said, "Tell people how old Nahamkes Steklov died!" I remember that he used his first name that time. For the first time. I made a gesture of friendship and he too placed his hand on his heart, a nice smile on his face. I stopped by his door again that evening. He'd changed terribly; his face had changed completely, like day and night. His eyelids were lowered, just narrow slits now, eyelids that I had observed closely in that waiting room and that were almost like fine Chinese porcelain, but now they were thick like tires, and his face wasn't so much a death's head as the head of Ramses, the mummy of Ramses. His jaw was already drooping, his breathing was heavy, he didn't say anything. He still shouted a few times about Stalin, his obsession. And the nurse in our ward, a very kind old woman—all those old nurses were very kind—would cross herself on the sly whenever Steklov said Stalin's name. It was obvious he was dying. I never saw him again.

I regained my health quickly. I felt comfortable in that ward, and I begged God to let me stay there as long as possible. You asked me, why Christianity? I want to return to that because I left out something important in my answer to that question. Specifically—ever since I began to live life consciously, even when I was an absolute atheist, not just an agnostic but a militant atheist, and even when I did not believe in Christ's historical existence, I also had no hesitation or doubt that humanity had created nothing more sublime and beautiful than the face of Christ. I say the face of Christ because I thought of Rozanov's *The Dark Face of Christ*. That really makes for a laughable contrast. Rozanov, raised in the Russian Orthodox religion, hates that face. And I, a Jew, the son of a Hasid, am drawn by the very figure and phenomenon of Christ. Not only that, I believed that if humanity had reached so high as to have invented this, that was a miracle in itself. An indirect proof of the existence of God and the divine. Because from where else could that image have come to man? And so I had always been prepared for Christianity by the face of Christ—for a long, long time. Even in the periods when I needed sacrilege.

I felt good in that hospital ward. It was very clean, like any decent hospital. A large, bright ward, relatively few beds, curtains on the windows. Maybe there were even some flowers—I don't remember—there probably weren't. There was a young Jew in the ward, from a small town in Poland, extremely dark haired. Definitely a communist. There were no political conversations there, but if he heard a word that could serve as a pretext for a political conversation, he would interrupt to defend the Soviet Union. Either out of fear or overzealousness, or perhaps he figured there was an informer in the ward and he wanted to be seen as a zealous defender of the system. Or maybe he had doubts himself. For example, the word "war" was enough for him to say, "In his wisdom, Stalin saw the war coming!" No one asked him how wise it was to make a pact with Germany; no one attacked Stalin.

By then I was a fanatic. That was after the night of my vision. I decided to employ Broniewski's method, but in my own way: to say nothing but no. I suffered terribly over my softness; I was tremendously guilty over that and thought that I had to redeem myself. My mind was medieval at that time. As I already told you, one time a junior investigator, Omarkhadzhev's assistant, said to me in Alma-Ata, "Wat, you know, you're a real Savonarola!" I had a medieval mind, a Crusader's hatred.

But to be fair, I have to say that deep down I didn't even hate the investigators I had later on, and Omarkhadzhev never. I felt no hatred; in fact the only one I hated personally was Stalin. This may not be as nice as it looks; it's actually a certain weakness of character. I was capable of hating persons, not just the idea of the system, but I wasn't capable of it face-to-face. When I found myself face-to-face with someone, my worst enemy, I didn't really feel anything, not the slightest trace of hatred. And that probably comes from weakness. I don't know. In any case, it's a small point. I had a tremendous hatred for Stalin, and apart from that I hated the system. A medieval mind—I had seen the devil, a devil with hooves. Before that crucial night, I had written a petition in Saratov to Comrade Stalin, which I probably began by paying him homage, and then I asked to be sent to the front. Our cell had word that people were being released from some prisons to be sent to the front, which really was infinitely better. Later that night I told myself, No, no, I won't have any part of it!

So, when the young man spoke about the wisdom of the pact, I answered him very pointedly. He was as frightened as a hedgehog, shamefaced, and he didn't say any more.

In the bed across from me was a man with a broad, handsome, fine, strange Jewish face, with absolutely transparent skin. No sign of any blood in it. He couldn't walk; he just lay there, one hand bandaged. The chief physician came to see him every day. Not only did he come to see him, but he'd bring him tomatoes, carrots, onions, and, occasionally, fish—in Saratov where the hunger was terrible. The patient was taciturn. The physician was constantly asking him how he was feeling and examined him with unusual care. He spoke quietly with him, sat with him a long time. The patient was Dubin, the leader of the Latvian Jews and a senator in independent Latvia; he had once received an invitation from Hoover, and that was the main charge in the accusation. Since he had been arrested, Dubin had eaten nothing *treif*. Meaning that for months on end he had eaten nothing but bread, no cooked food. In the hospital he had come to trust that doctor. And Dubin was a man with a university education.

Dubin's first conflict was this: when you're taken for interrogation, when you pass from the prison to the investigation section, there's a little table with a sign-in sheet; the guard signs in and the prisoner signs in. And so one time, at the very beginning, he was taken for interrogation late on a Friday evening. Dubin refused to sign in. There was a terrible scene, but he kept refusing. Socialist formalism, legalism, socialist law and order required that signature, and so he could not be let out; even the warden could not let Dubin out of that section. The investigator was furious; the warden was furious. They put him in a punishment cell. The next day they called him in again, thinking that he was going to refuse again. But by then it was late Saturday evening, and now he was free to sign. And so of course he did.

He ate only bread, that horrible prison bread. After a few months he had reached a state of complete emaciation. I think he had been force-fed at Lubyanka. He'd fought them too; he must have been strong at one time. They had dislocated his arm, or broken it; that's why it was bandaged. A fanatic? No, not in the least. A humanist, an educated man. And so I said to him, "Excuse me but I know that the Talmud is straightforward about saying that if someone is threatened by serious illness or has a weak heart, he has the right to eat on Yom Kippur. If someone is threatened by illness or danger he has the right to break the Sabbath."

"It's a right, not a duty," said Dubin, adding that not a hair would fall from his head without God's so wishing it. He had a family—a wife, children. A biblical Jew, he played an enormous role in my life. Later, in Ili, when the Soviets tried to force Poles to accept Soviet citizenship, there were only two whose memory inspired me, Dubin and Taitz.

And because of my religious state at that time, I felt much closer to Dubin.

I didn't tell Dubin that I had converted, not because I was concealing it, but how could I explain all that to him? Out of the question. He thought I was an atheist and tried to bring me back to Judaism. He was like a father to me. My father hadn't done that, but Dubin did and he did it like a father, a surrogate father. He said it was a question of human dignity, a duty. He asked me if I had said Kaddish for my father after he died. I told him that I hadn't. That made him terribly . . . not angry, because he was a gentle man, but he thought that not to say Kaddish for your father was a terrible thing, a crime against God and the memory of your father. He urged me to observe the Sabbath, to pray, saying this was an essential part of being human. A person is human when he prays. He admitted that the Jewish religion really did have too many injunctions from the past. He complied with them, but of course he realized that not everyone was capable of this. But there are certain elementary things: saying Kaddish for your father, praying on Yom Kippur, observing the Sabbath—anyone can do that. I listened with great attention. And despite my Crusader-like Christianity, I felt no disharmony between us, none.

I don't know what miracle it took for that doctor to obtain food for Dubin. I've already spoken of this, but I want to add here that even under Stalinism, which depraved everyone—especially anyone with any feel for politics, anyone who meddled in politics—the medical caste preserved the old traditions of the Russian doctors who did not become doctors as a career but from a sense of calling—the entire caste or at least the overwhelming majority of it. And this had been preserved in Stalin's Russia to a considerably greater degree than it had in noncommunist prewar Warsaw—with the exception of that one woman doctor who was more NKVD than a doctor.

We all came back to life. We were given kasha manna and other such delicacies. Not fish or tomatoes, though, but some vegetables. Where could you get them in Saratov? That doctor managed to. Because even where Soviet poverty was at its worst, a person who had some connections and a genuine desire could do a lot of good for people. That doctor was just that sort of person, and he did an incredible amount in that hospital. I left there with a little bag of sugar that was later to save my life. Moreover, he created a normal hospital atmosphere, not a prison one—the people in charge could do that. Of course, there was a guard at the door, but I seem to remember even the guards were kindhearted. It was all very human there. I tried to stay there as long as possible, but the doctor had to discharge me. I even asked him straight out, saying I was emaciated. I was already cured of the dysentery; he spread his hands, a gesture meaning there was nothing he could do, and I was discharged.

There were a few other people there. Aha! A funny story that was told by a concert organizer about a previous cell he had been in. One story had to do with the question of which category of people weren't being put in prison. (That was a subject for discussion in all the cells I had been in. There were certain universal subjects like that. What category of people are not being put in prison?) His cell mates had decided that in Russia the best thing to be was a gravedigger. But as luck would have it, they were joined a little while later by a gravedigger. I don't remember what he was in for—not burying someone deep enough or something like that.

He told another story that came from his time in prison in Central Asia; he had been in a long time. In one of the Central Asian capital cities there was a petty official, a party member but without any rank, who always adapted to the latest change of fashion. He had portraits in his house, including one of the party secretary of Uzbekistan—or maybe it was some other place. Naturally, he had portraits of Stalin, Lenin, and Marx, but he also had one of the party secretary. But when the party secretary was put in prison, the petty official immediately took down his portrait. He didn't know what to do with it, and so he put it in a trunk. A new party secretary arrived, and the petty official hung the new secretary's portrait at home. But someone denounced the petty official, saying that he had the old secretary's portrait in his trunk. Eternal Russia. And so he was arrested. But on the first day of interrogation, the investigator's entire fury was focused not on the petty official's having a portrait of the old secretary in his trunk but on his having a portrait of the new one on his wall. The new one was now in prison too and, as the freshest victim, was the most hated.

And so even though I say that I was a Crusader filled with hatred I have to add that things were not that simple. The hatred, that was the bad side of that crucial night, but the good side was an incredibly keen feeling—one that was on my skin, in my entire being, and in every nerve—for the sufferings of millions of families, terrible, irremedial suffering. Both through fate and through degradation. Millions upon millions of families. Quantity has enormous significance here; it turns into quality. Not only does it turn into quality, but all of society acquires an utterly new aspect, another meaning, if a certain quantity is exceeded. The old riddle of Sodom: God's question of how many just men there are. If there are ten, He'll forgive the city. That's the difference between the ethical Jewish mind and the logical Greek mind with its sophism: what constitutes a pile of sand, how many grains of sand? It's actually the same problem, but with all the ethics scoured away. And it's the same here, the same paradox. How many people are needed to save a city? But here there's some mystery connected with quantity, with numbers. Some secret we will probably never understand—that when a certain quantity is exceeded, all meaning is turned inside out. And, my God, the same thing happened with the Jewish ghetto, the destruction of the Jews by Nazism, Nazism in general. Quantity is a terrible thing here. It's not just that the more there is, the worse. Everything is different. It can't be compared to anything else even though there's no actual difference. There's no comparison. I felt this powerfully. Formerly, I had held Russia in contempt and had given myself airs, but now I felt a deep sympathy for the Russians. Again this is paradoxical, because in comparison with Poles they acted very badly when humiliated. I'm not speaking of the intellectuals, and especially the writers, but one has to compare the Polish people who did not allow themselves to be degraded and the Russian people who did.

Why do I think *Doctor Zhivago* is a great book? I know that Pasternak is a great poet, a distinguished poet, but I don't feel it; I read him and don't feel anything, with the exception of the poems in *Zhivago*, which move me greatly. But in general I have no feeling for him as a poet. As a novel *Zhivago* is a disaster. Its narcissism is hideous, ugly. Yet that pales beside the other things that Pasternak felt and rendered with a poet's heart and nerves: the image of Russia, the image of Russian bolshevism as nothing but suffering, the history of the nation's suffering, the entire society's. The book has that and that's why, in my opinion, it will remain great. It has things that are more important than the art of writing and the ugliness of egocentricity, though his egocentricity and narcissism are simply ugly, shameless. And so that was what I felt after that night; I was tormented by the suffering of all those people.

I had to return to the cell, to those people. I liked a couple of them. By then the professor was gone, the academician was gone, the German was gone. But the historian whom I liked a lot was still there. The people in the cell were gloomy, but mostly they were hungry. Terribly hungry. All it took was leaving the hospital to feel immediate hunger pangs. The little bag of lump sugar I saved up helped me through a bit.

Winter had just about begun. In the hospital I had heard there was some sort of amnesty for Poles, that some Poles had gotten out, some, but not all. I tried to figure out who was getting out; I kept searching for rational explanations. In the hospital someone had said that a Polish officer who had been in prison with him had gotten out. And so I thought, Evidently they're taking Polish officers. I'm neither an officer nor an enlisted man, and so that won't affect me.

But the historian said, "You'll probably get out too; there's no more reason to keep the Poles in."

I said it wouldn't happen.

He said, "It will, and just in case, memorize my sister's name in Alma-Ata. Tell her that we're dying of hunger here."

I wasn't summoned once for interrogation. I requested it but nothing happened. But then one day I was called in for questioning. A high-ranking officer, a dry, unpleasant man. He looked glumly at me; his voice was very unpleasant. Of course, he took down all my basic personal data. Then he said that in the cell I had compared Stalin to Hitler. I had. Now I realized that Josek had been eavesdropping. But I denied it. He continued questioning me. I denied everything or gave no answer. He was becoming upset, but I said, "I don't have to answer because I am a Polish citizen."

"Prove it." What an idiotic thing to say! How could I prove it? They had taken all my papers from me in Lwów and now I was supposed to prove it?

"You have the proof!" I told him.

He changed his tone, which had been dry till then, and said, "We'll see." That saved me because their system was in disarray.

As I found out later, Broniewski had been released right at the beginning of the war even though he had already been sentenced, a light sentence; I think it was five years in Alma-Ata, deportation at liberty. I saw him in Alma-Ata, sloshed to the gills. A year without alcohol, that was as much as he could stand. But he was released immediately after the amnesty. Maybe the embassy needed him and he was on some list. But to the Poles I was a commie Jew and so evidently my name didn't come up; I'd been forgotten.

I weighed myself a while after I got out. I weighed 45 or 46 kilograms. My normal weight is 82; I was 81, 82, before the arrest. Nearly half. I was at death's door. Later on I went to the baths in Dzhambul. I don't know why—maybe it was a regulation—but there was a mirror in the baths, a cracked mirror. I stood there and cried. A starving Hindu, folds of skin on a skeleton. A terrible state of emaciation. After all, I could barely walk when I left prison.

Josek's denunciation had saved me, because one day I was told to get ready and bring my things. The historian said farewell to me, certain that I was being released. I was not in the least convinced of that; I always take the dark view. But in fact they did bring to me to another cell where there were two Polish officers, one of them a captain in intelligence—it was Józef, whose last name I don't know; I'd been in the large cell with him in Saratov—and the other was a colonel in the Polish army, a Georgian by origin. There were a lot of Georgians in the Polish army after 1920. And that dark-haired *Komsomolets* was there too. He wasn't defending communism any more, not a peep out of him. I had my own reasons for not liking him, but the two officers didn't like him because they were anti-Semites. But Józef, who had talked with me a lot in Saratov and who knew a great deal about me, basically everything, greeted me very warmly, very affectionately.

By then we knew we were being released, though we still couldn't be absolutely certain of it. A last bit of malicious monkey business: they took us to the barber again; our hair had grown back to normal, but the barber shaved our heads with electric clippers. Then we waited and waited. Then they called us and gave us each I think it was two loaves of bread, about a kilogram of bread. As soon as the NKVD man had disappeared from view, we immediately cut up the bread, which was supposed to be for the road, and began eating it.

Then we were brought to a senior officer, who asked, "Where do you want to go, which place?" In the hospital someone had told me that my family had most probably been sent to Kazakhstan, because nearly all Polish families were in Kazakhstan, or to Siberia. The families were released after the amnesty, and most of them headed south, which was madness because the hunger was greater there. "Your wife must be somewhere in the south of Kazakhstan." But how could I find her? Kazakhstan is enormous! "It's extremely easy. Go to the NKVD in Alma-Ata. You'll be let into a large room, something like a waiting room, and most likely on the right-hand side you'll see a little window with a raised molding and a little wooden screen that opens and closes. Walk over to the window and knock. There'll be a man, or more likely a woman there. Give your wife's and son's personal data, and in fifteen minutes you'll have exact information about where they are."

I said, "Have you been there?"

"No, I haven't."

And so when that officer asked me where I wanted to go, I said Alma-Ata. His answer was, "Out of the question. That's the capital; you don't have the right to go there." Then, remembering the map, I chose Ushtob, which was further south. "Well, all right, you can go to Ushtob." I took a pass to Ushtob; then he clicked away on his abacus and paid me out a sum of money for the ticket and for food on the way, apart from the bread I had been given. He figured out how many days' travel it was to Ushtob—naturally, he took the smallest possible number.

Then we were taken back to the cell and the officer told me not to be crazy, that I was in no condition to go looking for my wife and that I should go with them to Buzuluk. Józef said, "I can get you set up there."

"No, first I have to find my wife," I said. "And besides I took the pass to Ushtob."

"I assure you that those passes don't have any meaning for us now; we can go wherever we want. You absolutely must come with us. I'll work through the army to help you find your wife."

I said no. Once again he tried to convince me, and I made a fatal mistake: stubborn as a mule, I kept saying I had to go to Alma-Ata.

Then we were let out. It must have been the beginning of December or the end of November, and terribly cold; I was freezing. We started walking. It was at night, a truly pitch black night in Saratov. It was a miracle we could even walk. The Georgian had scurvy and was all swollen, full of water. I was a skeleton, Józef was a skeleton, and the Georgian was in the middle; we all had our arms around each other. But we were happy.

We walked through the dark city of Saratov, happy people. Maybe not happy, but rejoicing at divine justice, retribution. It was finally collapsing, and they had to release us. Oh, that feeling that the empire was finished was a very common one, even among Russians. It was a miracle we got where we were going; we just followed our noses. It was quite a hike. We'd run into someone on the road every once in a while, but not very often.

We reached the train station, which was well lit. The station was already packed. There was a small crowd of people freezing in front of the station; they begged the guards by the station gate to let them in. The guards were Polish soldiers in Polish uniforms, two of them. There were also Russian soldiers there, but the Poles were in charge. Poles released from the camps were filling the cities and guarding train stations. Fantastic. They had Polish eagle emblems on their caps, insignia, everything. Naturally, they let us in immediately. I saw a striking image of suffering there. All of Russia was like that then—Solzhenitsyn has described it magnificently. A migration of nations. Of course, primarily those were people who had fled from the Ukraine and Byelorussia from the Germans, but there were also native Russians, people from the Saratov area. All of Russia was on the move, everyone, peasants, collective farmers, and especially people whose passports had been taken from them and who had only identification cards. An enormous percentage of the population. They had not been able to leave their district without an NKVD pass. But suddenly all that was overturned; the wave of war had destroyed even those barriers, and Russia was on the move.

33 SOVIET TRAIN STATIONS. A JOURNEY BY TRAIN. IN DZHAMBUL. ALMA-ATA. THE POLISH DELEGATION. A MYSTERIOUS SUBTENANT IN VICTOR SHKLOVSKY'S ROOM. MOSFILM'S SCRIPT-WRITING DEPARTMENT.

WAT: The train station in Saratov was absolutely mobbed. But first, a minor footnote about the railway system. I was told why the train stations in Russia are so far from the cities. It's simply because the cabmen had powerful unions in the era when the railways were being built. They were an enormous business, numerous and very diversified. The capitalists who were building the railways were richer but less numerous. And so the fierce competition between them ended with the cabmen's backers buying off the construction engineers, who were mostly Poles, and who had the tracks and stations built far from the cities— somewhere between six and eight kilometers. That way, everyone was happy. Russia has large trunk lines but very few, too few for such an enormous country, and so you're always changing trains. The Soviet authorities had introduced a truly hellish regulation, which caused me suffering more than once. When changing trains you had to have your ticket validated again at the window, and it always turned out that there were no seats for the next two, three, four days. Since there were no hotels, there was no choice but to camp out at the station. There were permanent camps during the war, entire families with their bundles waiting a day, two, three. When a train would stop at a station, there'd usually be a woman conductor standing by the door of the train car. A weak woman, and not a soldier in sight. And there was that wild mob of starving people who were sleeping and living at the train station. But those mobs did not dare board the train. One woman conductor but the great power of the NKVD, that implied threat, was behind her. I saw that again and again. Of course, there was one other method for getting on: bribes. But they didn't always work, and not everyone could afford them.

I'd like to bring up the cell and Dubin again. As I was saying, Dubin, in a severe voice—I mean, a very human, very understanding voice— ordered me to say Kaddish for my father. After I was out of prison, of course. That can be done only on a holy day and when there are ten Jews present, what's called a minyan. Ten Jews constitute a community that can pray together. And Kaddish can be said only along with the community. I felt absolutely no contradiction here despite my conversion, and I told Dubin I would do it the first chance I had. But strange things happen with such imperatives: I forgot all about it and kept my word only two years later.

And so I was at the station. And the scene? As I already said, pure Solzhenitsyn, meaning peasant men and women, whole families, middle-class people, workers, intellectuals, all on the miserable floor of the train station. Sometimes there were little groups entrenched in a circle around their bundles, because there were a great many *urks* prowling around, obvious *urks* just waiting for a chance. That night when I was walking through the dark at the periphery of the station, I came on a woman being raped. It was a very large station. A few tramps and a woman. They were simply raping her. No one paid it any attention, and no one would have come to her defense even if she had screamed.

A long night, a terribly long night. I shuffled around, barely able to stand on my feet. I probably couldn't have looked any more miserable or any weaker, but there were three of us and the other two were Polish officers; they found a good place for us. A family must have just left. One of us always stayed to guard the place while the other two walked around. We didn't walk so much to have a look at things as to listen for someone speaking Polish, and every once in a while we'd happen on a Pole. From one Pole, who probably had leftist or communist connections, I learned that Wanda Wasilewska, Ważyk, and Putrament were in Saratov giving informal talks. Now I can see that it never even entered my mind that I should go see them, even though there was no doubt that they'd have welcomed me with open arms and not even have demanded any show of communist loyalty from me. What's more, they could have been a great help in finding Ola and Andrzej's trail, which I was pursuing like a madman. It didn't even enter my mind. I heard the news and that was that. It didn't concern me.

People were lying on the ground. In the cell in Saratov I had had a vision of those great, enormous, expanses gigantic Russia with its millions of human tragedies, that immense tragic nation, millions of tragic families. And there it was before me in the flesh—tragic Russia. It didn't matter whether they were young or old, whether their faces were energetic or slack, sluggish, and weary; they all had a glazed look, not the slightest spark of rebellion against that terrible waiting. The breakthrough I had experienced in Saratov seemed to have reached to my very depths, but the layers of experience are very thin. I was not moved by this spectacle; I saw those people as human manure.

The two officers kept vigorously trying to persuade me to go with them to Buzuluk. "How can you travel in your condition?" But we had information that a train would leave the next day for Alma-Ata, and we even knew that there'd be a car or two of Polish exiles from somewhere in the north who were traveling south to Kazakhstan. And so of course there was no question of my not taking that train. The train did indeed arrive the next day. The two officers found one car or two with the Poles and helped cram me on. I didn't have any more bread of my own, but somehow they got hold of some, which they gave me for the road.

I found myself on a train, a heated cattle car of course, densely packed, incredibly dirty, much dirtier than the prison train that had taken me from Moscow to Saratov. I hadn't had any lice since Lubyanka. That car was covered with lice. As for the Poles, two were ethnic Poles; they looked like butchers, very tough, bristly faces. The rest were Polish Jews of various sorts. One family amazed me. They seemed to be exiles, but they had everything. A family—the father, the mother, three children, one unbearable little boy covered with lice. But they had fresh butter, canned food, canned Soviet crabmeat. Where had they gotten all that? I found out that there were some very good places where people were well off.

Once again I ate all my bread the first day and was terribly hungry. By then the hunger was mental. The sight of someone gnawing at a piece of bread would make me sick. Even later on when I was full, well-fed, fat, for several months I still couldn't look at a person eating anything, even a piece of dry bread. It would make my stomach turn; I'd feel faint. But there I was all skin and bones and horribly hungry. The two Poles were on some sort of plank bed; they knew I had nothing to eat and generously—but with a certain disgust because they could see I was a Jew—gave me something to eat twice, rather good-sized portions of bread and so on. Jews from Kraków helped me with the rest, sharing their meager supplies with me. It was quite a long trip. The mood was almost merry.

Everyone wanted to go south. Where? Everyone wanted to go to Tashkent. Why Tashkent? Because Tashkent was a "city of bread." That wasn't true. I was in Tashkent, and people were dying on the streets there. But that's the power of a title: *Tashkent, City of Bread.* Magic words. The book had been published in Russia, but it had been translated into Polish. The Poles didn't know about it, but all the Jews, even the ones who didn't read, had heard about it from others. *Tashkent,*

City of Bread. And so they rushed to Tashkent, where they were decimated by typhus.

No one had any shame about this, and I got used to it too: as soon as the train would stop anywhere—not even at a station, sometimes by a field—everyone would immediately squat down by the steps; there was no hole in the floor of that cattle car. Men and women, girls next to boys, eveyone squatting. They had to be very quick about it because we never knew when the train might suddenly pull away. It was the same at the stations.

At one station I found out that there was a train with Polish exiles four tracks from us. And so I jumped from our train and went as fast as I could. I worked my way under the trains and then went from car to car asking for Ola Wat, Ola Wat. No one knew anything about her. I told everyone to ask after her, to tell her I was well, but meanwhile I was in fear that my own train would leave. And my bundle was there, everything I had, which wasn't much—a few rags—but essential to keep on living. And so I went back under the trains; one was even just pulling away and I barely got clear in time.

I had to jump onto my car, which was closed now. The only place where there was any room—and that offered a little protection from the wind—was the upper platform, and there was a sentry there. I was on the bottom part, and now the train was going full speed. He shouted, "Get off or I'll shoot!"

"How can I get off?" I said.

He kept saying, "Get off or I'll shoot!" But he wasn't shooting. A strong wind and snow. I could barely stand on my feet; I was holding on for dear life. Fortunately, the train came to a stop. Again I didn't know whether it was just for a moment or longer, but I got off because the sentry was still shouting at me. I had barely run over to the next car when the train pulled away again. I climbed up on the platform, but there was no sentry on that one. I squatted down and rode for a couple of hours in the freezing cold until finally the train made a real stop at a station and I could get back on.

We had come to Dzhambul; that was already Asia. I don't know how many days it had taken—maybe a week. I don't think I spoke with anyone; I was in very low spirits, weak. In Dzhambul, it turned out that the train was going to Chimkent and then on to Tashkent instead of Alma-Ata. So, I got off in Dzhambul. Another station several kilometers from the city, but it was a large station with many services. A bread line, very long. But two Soviet officers, obviously back from the front, one with his arm in a sling, noticed me at the end of the line, walked over, and brought me to the head of the line. I must have looked very bad; in any case it was clear that I'd come out of prison or a camp. I got a loaf of bread, which I ate very quickly, immediately, and then looked around and began asking which way to the city. It was very far. I didn't know what to do. How could I walk there, weak as I was? I asked around. Maybe there'd be a train tomorrow, maybe the day after, maybe in three days. It was cold; I had to find shelter.

I was wondering what to do when Leopold Lewin came running over to me, wearing a quilted jacket. He had been released from a camp; he was ruddy, hale, and hearty. He threw his arms around me, and I was under his care from then on. He had been arrested the same night we had, because he had worked for the Jewish censor before the war. He had been in prison again since then; he'd been on death row for many weeks. He'd had a very hard time of it. But he had become fantastically fast on his feet in Russia. He was healthy, healthier than he'd been in Warsaw. He brought me some more bread, but better this time, almost white, a fragrant loaf of fresh bread.

He immediately brought me to a hostel for Soviet refugees at the station, run by an old, very respectable Jewish woman, a school-teacher type, a Litwak. It was only for Soviet citizens, but Lewin had a little talk with her and I was given a bed with clean sheets in a large, very clean room. Lewin said that I ought to stay in Dzhambul, that there was a Polish agency with a delegate, who was a doctor from Galicia and a bit of a writer himself, who could get me into a hospital. But for the time being I had to stay in that hostel because I had no strength.

There were refugees from Byelorussia and Odessa in the hostel. One of them caught my eye, a middle-class person around forty-five; he looked very glazed and sad. His features weren't especially Jewish. Very sad. I asked one of the others why that man was so depressed. His sadness was obvious, but he was also very calm. I was told that yesterday he had received word that his wife and three children had been evacuated from Odessa by ship and the ship had sunk. But he was so calm. A lesson in calmness, actually, in fatalism.

You could stay in the hostel only three days, and so first thing the next day Lewin brought me to the infirmary that was also at the station. An old Russian doctor. No, first I went to the baths to get deloused. There was a mirror in the baths. I couldn't bear the sight of my own body. My skin was hanging; I had the same amount of skin, and it was hanging off me. A terrible sight. I think I weighed 45 kilos then. The doctor examined me and, with Lewin there, said that I had two weeks at most to live and that he doubted greatly if I could be saved. For some reason, that didn't impress me all that much; two weeks seemed quite a lot of time to me. What mattered was getting to Alma-Ata.

Lewin said that I had go see the delegate with him. I agreed. But it was several kilometers: "How will I make it there?"

"I'll carry you; I'll hold you up."

And he really did; he held me in a way that was almost like carrying me. We walked to the end of the buildings and came out on a road. But the road was so bad that I lost one of the soles on my Polish boots, which had been beautifully resoled in Warsaw just before I fled. The mud seeped in through the sole and pulled out the nails. And so after a while I gave up; I said it was impossible and I turned back. And by chance the next train to Alma-Ata had just arrived. Lewin got me onto that train; it wasn't easy but he succeeded.

I got off at Alma-Ata, and again it was eight kilometers to the city. I don't remember now, but I think someone gave me a lift in. I knew that the main [Polish] delegation for all Kazakhstan was on Red Army Street in the city's most elegant hotel, to which all of Mosfilm's stars had been evacuated from Moscow. Alma-Ata is beautifully situated; the landscape is fantastic. It was winter; the poplars there are marvelous, especially the young ones; they're like a young girl's braids. Covered with ice, of course, so they looked as if they were strewn with diamonds. There was no snow on the street, but the mountains, the enormous mountains, the outer wall of the Pamirs, marvelous contours, were very close. It seemed that if you just walked a little way, you'd be up there in those snowy mountains. There's no snow that white anywhere else. It's not sugar white, it's pure whiteness. And that whiteness, the line and contours of that whiteness, silhouetted like a fine Chinese drawing against a beautiful Italian sky. Perhaps even a bit deeper shade of blue.

There were some Russian houses; the Soviet buildings in Turkestan were the worst, pseudo-mosque style—the opera house and so on. But you don't pay any attention to that, mostly because of the marvelous trees, Alma-Ata's poplars, which the city owes to a Pole, Governor General Kłopotowski, who had them planted there sometime in the seventeenth or eighteenth century. Especially in winter, those poplars are somehow truly evangelical, more beautiful than King Solomon's trees. Sunlit jewels. The moon comes out very early there. That day there was a silvery half-moon, very Islamic, a sign.

The houses on the little side streets are devastated by avalanches every so often. Boulders tumble down from the mountains, landslides. Later on, I lived on a street like that, full of rocks of various sizes. Some were enormous, like dolomites, most of them covered with moss. The

313

dominant color in those streets is a moss green. In spring, summer, fall, there's a rich moss green, with the lovely green of the poplars predominating, but in winter it's the crystals, the jewels.

Either someone gave me another lift or else I dragged myself to the delegation. It was very strange after all that suffering, prison, and misery. I entered the lobby, a large one, European scale; the hotel was almost up to Parisian standards. There were a lot of people in the lobby, mostly officers on leave, some of them wounded, but there were also beautiful young women in gorgeous clothes. Stars, starlets. And paupers—the Poles who gathered in front of the delegation, which was on the second floor. They were on the stairs waiting to be let in. They were let in by turn.

Someone recognized me at once, ran over, and said, "I'll introduce you to the delegate and then to Prince Sapieha." I was introduced to the delegate, Wiącek, a Warsaw-official type, a department director or section head, a very uninteresting man. I won't say much about the delegation—there's no time for that—but some things have to be said because false accounts have been made of them. The prince was extremely courteous; he invited me into his office and questioned me in detail: what my time in prison had been like, what prisons I'd been in, what I'd seen. He didn't press at all. And none of it was for use by intelligence. A great man, very courteous.

The man who had introduced me said, "I work only part time for the delegation; I speak good Russian and so I work as a translator here. But my real position is director of the Soviet canteen. You can come to the canteen. I'll get you some coupons right away."

"What about a place to stay?" I asked.

"You should be in a hospital; it won't be easy, but we have a Polish doctor from Łódź here, a very helpful person. He works in the hospitals. He's very well thought of; he'll try to accommodate you somehow. I'll give you his address; you should try to catch him today."

"But where will I spend the night?"

"With my brother-in-law, Doctor Turek, who lives at 40 Karakolska Street. I've already spoken with him. You should go find him; he works in a polyclinic on Angurska Street; it's fairly close to here. You can spend the night there. And tomorrow we'll see if we can get you right into the hospital."

I went to the polyclinic to look for that Polish doctor, but I had to wait four hours for him there. Evening comes early in Alma-Ata at that time of year, and I have never forgotten the impression it made. For me that city was a metropolis, the many-colored lights of the city, as in my childhood when there were light shows in honor of the tsar, for the tsar's name day, lamp lights of many colors—red, green—a distance away.

I walked to Karakolska Street, every step of the way laborious. I would sit down on the sidewalk when there was no place else to sit because I had to keep sitting down. Finally I arrived; it was already quite late, after nine. The doctor had found that I was suffering from a vitamin deficiency and could be saved, but I would need food. That wasn't reason enough for being admitted to the hospital, because the hospitals were overcrowded. The army was using them, constantly sending people in, and there were also the refugees, but he would do a urinalysis and move the decimal point one place over in my urea content, or whatever it was. And I should remember to howl when they poked my waist. I should come see him the next day, and he'd give me the address and urinalysis.

So there I was on Karakolska Street, in a sort of little Russian house with a very large sloping hallway, one well prepared for the winter, very warm as I entered. Domestic warmth, a pleasant atmosphere, the good smell of something being cooked came over me. The Tureks were living in a room where I was to live later on. They served me dinner; I was late, so I ate alone. The brother-in-law wasn't there yet. I said that I was very tired, and they said that I actually should go to the delegation; the delegate certainly wouldn't refuse to let me spend the night in the delegation.

It was eleven o'clock at night; there was a heavy frost and I froze as I walked. It was very far to the delegation, and it had become terribly icy. The streets were completely dark; I didn't know the way. It was a dark night and I kept falling. Walking and falling. One time I fell so hard that crystal bells rang in my head, beautiful bells, a beautiful ringing in my head. Echoes, reverberations, one after the other. I seemed to hear music for an hour. There was no pain. And the stars that night—I had never seen stars like that before. Immense flickering stars that spoke to you with the energy, with the force, that the Gnostics wrote about, the stars speaking directly to you. But it was dark all around, not a living soul in sight. And so I had the stars, the harmony of the spheres above my head, which had struck the icy pavement. I lay there, feeling good. It must have been a very short time though it seemed long to me. I didn't pass out; I felt no pain. But then some people came by, lifted me up; they showed me the way, then passed me on to other people who also helped me. Very dark streets, a few lamp lights, a few houses with lights on; the sidewalks were in good shape.

I must have been in five different people's hands before I reached the hotel on Red Army Street. I went into the lobby, which was warm; a wave of warmth swept over me at once. Many people in the lobby, mostly officers. All the places you could sit had clearly been taken a long time ago. They were spending the night in the lobby, and there was no place left to sit. But I didn't have the strength to stand. There was a statue of Lenin in the corner—you know, the usual statue, Lenin with his arm outstretched. I walked over to Lenin and I saw a place in back of him, a little hidden corner, and there was no one in it. A perfect place to curl up and go to sleep. So I lay down there. I slept wonderfully, a marvelous sleep. I probably never slept that well in my life. Exquisite sleep, but it lasted a very short time. At one point I woke up to find that a search was on, documents were being checked. I had no right to be in Alma-Ata. Lenin saved me.

I ate my fill again the next day because I was eating in two different canteens. I felt good and I went to the NKVD. I entered a very spacious lobby, a waiting room. There was a little window and it went up. I don't know how long it took, seven minutes, ten minutes at most, and I had my answer: since September your wife and son have been on the Krasny Skotovod State Farm, Zharma District, Semipalatinsk Province, and then had left for the south with the other Poles.

Where in the south?

That day, despite my exhaustion, I got a great deal done. The rubles I had been given in Saratov for traveling were gone, but Lewin had given me a few more. In Alma-Ata I learned that Józef Retinger was still in Kuibyshev or had been there. He and I had drunk a sea of vodka together at one time. So I sent him a telegram immediately, telling him to look for Ola and to send me money because I was out of prison. I also went to see that doctor, who truly was exceptionally helpful; he knew his way around Soviet life. He gave me the urinalysis with the falsified decimal point and a certificate of admission to the hospital, but he advised me to go there only the next day at such and such an hour because the woman doctor who would be on duty then was very understanding. No earlier, because they might check the analysis.

I went to the delegation where I was again given a warm welcome. The prince saw me again, and the delegate Wiącek too. I don't really know why they treated me so well. Perhaps that other man had spoken well of me, said that I was a known figure. And there were people with running sores, ulcers, people swollen with hunger standing for hours on the stairs, waiting to be seen. I was to spend the night there; they gave me a bench to lie on, apologizing for the discomfort. They could see that I was in terrible condition. I was to sleep in the room where they ate. They sat down to dinner, brought me food; I stayed lying

316

down. The prince had given me a marvelous Scottish blanket of the finest mohair to cover myself. They sat down to dinner. It felt like a Polish manor house, except for the caviar—caviar wasn't eaten in Polish manor houses. There was the chief bookkeeper, a Czech by background, and the queen of the manor, beautiful Jadzia, with whom everyone without exception was in love. Lisiewicz, a cavalry captain, was terribly in love with her; the delegate, Wiącek; the prince. She was a full-bodied, very Polish type of noblewoman, a very pure type, something from an early nineteenth-century miniature. A sweet voice. Wesely, the bookkeeper, played the mandolin during dinner. Excellent wine, cheeses, caviar, ham, sausage. They even brought some caviar to my bed—my bench, that is.

And those poor wretches from the camps were probably still waiting on the stairs because they had nowhere else to go. But I was enjoying myself. I felt like a Pole in a way I never had before, a patriot, almost a nationalist. Imperceptibly, I was becoming more of a nationalist all the time. A Jew, a Polish patriot, a Polish nationalist. I was turning into a National Democrat in that company. Man is weak; he rises, and then he falls immediately, then he rises again, and then he falls again immediately. I was becoming a National Democrat; it gave me tremendous pleasure to be at that court with Queen Jadwiga, admiring her from afar. I was completely asexual, and so I didn't look on her with lust. My libido had been extinguished. And, as I told you, I didn't see colors. I had of course been impressed by the lights of the city, but, apart from the dazzling moments when I saw a new landscape, everything was gray. I regained my sense of color only when my libido came back to life.

Dinner, then cards, bridge, and talk about who was related to whom by marriage, who knew whom, who had been promoted, and when, and in which ministry. No trace of September 1939 and all the rest. I liked that very much. I felt like a fish in water. The next morning I got up early and was brought to the canteen, where I had a good breakfast.

In the lobby I ran into Shklovsky who had been in Lwów a very short time, but he had sought out my friendship there because Mayakovsky had told him a lot about me. It was Shklovsky who had recognized me, not the other way around. He was very happy to see me in that nervous, excited way of his. He just looked at me, asking no questions. He didn't even want to hear anything, but he was glad that I was in Alma-Ata. Their whole group was there, and of course I would come see them and so forth. There was a certain amount of fraternization at that time.

I went back to the delegation to sleep until it was time to enter the hospital. But at the delegation Wiącek said to me; "Please forgive us. We're very sorry, but the delegate from Frunze has lost his accommodations, and we have to give him your place, and so you won't be able to spend the night here." I learned the real reason later on. I had been deloused several times in Dzhambul, and very thoroughly too, but apparently that Scottish blanket was crawling with lice after I'd slept with it.

On the third day I went to the hospital. It was just as the doctor had said. The woman doctor was on duty. She poked at my waist; I howled. She suspected something, her face clouded over, she was very angry. For a few minutes she didn't say anything, but in the end she gave me a bed. I was in that hospital a week, two weeks—at least two weeks, I think, which was against the rules. They should have dismissed me after a few days. There was a shortage of beds; critically ill people were being turned away.

I asked the physician-in-chief to get me on my feet because I had to go the Zharma district, to the Krasny Skotovod State Farm. I had written to the head of that farm at once. The doctor said, "You're out of your mind. You'll freeze to death in your condition." Finally, they had to release me. I still wanted to go to Zharma, but I hadn't received any reply from Zharma.

MILOSZ: Why did you want to go to Zharma when you knew they had already left there?

WAT: That's true, but there'd be a trail. I had to find someone who might know. How could I find them otherwise? I had spent a lot of money on postcards; I had written two hundred postcards to all the delegates. Then I also wrote one to Wanda Wasilewska—the only time I had anything to do with her after I got out of prison—and I asked her if by chance she knew where my wife was.

I found out that Broniewski was in the embassy in Kuibyshev, and I wrote to him. No answer. Finally, much later on, I got word from Broniewski: Your wife was seen in Chimkent—or some such place. Ola had gone to see the delegate, who gave her two hundred rubles; that was all Broniewski knew. Meanwhile, Ola had written Broniewski letters, but he probably hadn't read them, because he was drinking all the time.

I hadn't received a reply from Wanda yet; there'd been no reply from any of the delegates, so what could I do? Why lose time? I had to go to Zharma. But the weather was freezing; everyone tried to talk me out of it, saying I'd freeze to death, saying I wasn't used to the climate and I was in poor shape. But I'd gotten a lot of my strength back; I'd gained a lot of weight back in the hospital, where they'd fattened me up. I felt quite strong.

I left the hospital and went to the delegation again. Now they treated me rather ambiguously there; I could see that something had changed. Later on, it turned out that the man who had sent me to his brother-in-law and had introduced me to people and had given me coupons for his canteen was afraid that I'd be given a job at the delegation as a translator since I knew Russian, which meant that he'd lose that post. And probably someone had whispered to him that I was a communist.

I didn't know what to do. I would have liked to work at the delegation; I wasn't going to any collective farm. People told me that I might be sent to a collective farm. What could I do at a collective farm? There was no muscle on me; I'd die there. I ran into Shklovsky in the lobby again. He asked me how I was, what I was going to do now that I was out of the hospital.

I said, "I don't know. I have no right to be here. If they catch me, they'll deport me right away. I was thinking about working for the delegation, but there's no likelihood of that."

And he said, "You can stay with me, in my room." He took me to his hotel room and kept me there a week or even more, and he fed me too. Food was already becoming scarce in Alma-Ata. Shklovsky brought me jam, rice, cream of kasha. He fed me, but there was one condition: I couldn't leave the room. I had to take a leak five or six times a night, so he'd give me his fur coat (Shklovsky's much smaller than I, but the coat was a wonderful, big coat) and I'd hunch over and put up the collar so that people would think it was he.

There were get-togethers in his room. Paustovsky was there and Zoshchenko with his lovely young wife, who had a beautiful figure. Eisenstein used to come sometimes too, a fantastic person in a demonic sort of way. His eyes. When he looked at you, you knew you were being photographed. But he did that with his soul; it wasn't just physical. Strange eyes—I'd never seen anything like them. Marshak, the children's writer, came every once in a great while. But Zoshchenko was there all the time. And there was Shnaider, a marvelous man, a screen writer. He was in the final stages of tuberculosis. He'd also written some prose, which I read, very un-Russian prose, not a trace of any political tone or subtext. And there was Miss Shub, one of the founders of the avant-garde in film, Kinooka. That was the club.

I was asked a lot of questions during those get-togethers. It turned out that those people who were Mosfilm's screenwriting department not only did not know the Western poetry and literature of the few years before the war but had had absolutely no access to the films made in 1938, 1939. I had to tell them all the details, the plots, who worked on them, everything. They were tremendously interested. I also had a lot to tell them about writers, trends; there was a lot that was new. Conversations *à bâtons rompus*, very refined, civilized, on a very high level; they spoke excellently.

Once I was so callous as to ask them, "All right, fine, but what should one really think of socialist realism?" No one answered, there was silence.

Later on, I went with Shnaider to his room, which was next to mine, and then he said with a smile, "Well, you see, one talks about that at meetings, one writes about it, but it isn't mentioned in polite society." And that was so. There were no catchphrases, no slogans, no talk of communism. As far as politics was concerned, there was never a word on the subject from anyone. Throughout my friendship with Shklovsky, I never heard him defend or condemn. (But he did burst into tears a few times. He cried easily, but it was still real.)

When I was with Shnaider in his room, however, he'd say everything we now know about communism. He considered it Russia's disgrace, a terrible disgrace. He was not in the least afraid; he knew that he'd be dying soon. A noble, beautiful person, tubercular, with a beautiful but frivolous wife, a former actress. He was her second husband. He was very bitter toward her, but he loved her very much. He was dying and he knew it, and she would live on, frivolous as ever. I witnessed a person ebbing away, the twilight of a person. Night had come for him, and he knew that the day and the light and everything else were for others. His illness progressed during those two or three weeks; he lived another few months. He retained full consciousness; his analysis of the situation was superb; he was honest and calm in his judgment, but dying was terrible for him. He died bravely. He didn't cry, he didn't despair—a real man, but his heart was terribly heavy.

34 KAZAKH ARISTOCRATS. A NOBLE COURT IN ALMA-ATA. FRANK CONVERSATIONS WITH RUSSIAN WRITERS. THE DEATH OF MARINA TSVETAEVA. ON ZOSHCHENKO. REUNION WITH MY FAMILY.

WAT: A few days later Shklovsky informed me that I didn't have to hide in his room any more; I could move freely about and would have no problems. It turned out that he had spoken with the secretary of the Writers' Union about my situation and set up an appointment for me.

If he was not in the NKVD, the secretary was probably reporting to them at that time. A poet, in his early thirties, a handsome Kazakh. And handsome Kazakhs are something of a rarity. Quite rare, because the Kazakhs, who used to be known as the Kara-Kirgizi, were made up of fugitives and are a very mixed people. The secretary of the Writers' Union—I don't recall his name—was apparently not a bad poet. His mother had been a princess and the leader of her tribe in tsarist times. She had been widowed young, and as is often the case, she had become the dictator of the tribe. She was still alive and supposedly even had a certain position of honor and comfort, with servants. But he was a very zealous, genuine communist. At that time, he, like many others, was writing very nationalistic Kazakh epics—that was the order of the day. It was only after the war that accusations were brought against all those historians, poets, and writers who had revived the traditions of the Kazakh heroes fighting for their independence against the Russians, and most of them were imprisoned. I'm not sure if the secretary was put in prison or not.

A man with truly excellent manners, he had had a European education, which by then was already rather usual. In the mid-nineteenth century the aristocrats of those tribes began to send their sons to Petersburg to be educated; the Russian authorities would place those princelings in the corps of cadets and Petersburg schools. The first one was—what was his name?—a very interesting person who came to know Dostoevsky in Semipalatinsk. The correspondence between him and Dostoevsky has been preserved and is rather large. Dostoevsky was fascinated by him. All the people in those tribes possessed great subtlety and at the same time were capable of cruelty. As far as I'm concerned, the secretary treated me very well.

And I was also invited to the home of Auezov, who was something of a Kazakh Alexei Tolstoy. Auezov had a five- or six-room apartment, furnished in very European style. One room was crammed with books, the place of honor being given to the German classics—Goethe, Heine, in German. A piano. I recall that during our conversation, he quoted from Goethe, which was typical: "Jedes Existierende ist ein Analogen alles Existierenden" (Everything that exists is an analogy for all existence). That's quite a ways from Bolshevik indoctrination. Auezov was also very interested in Poland and spoke with enormous admiration about Gustaw Zieleński's poem "The Kirgiz," which he called the first poem about the Kazakhs. Zieliński had lived among the Kazakhs and he was still remembered, even something of a legend. Auezov mentioned another Pole who after the November Uprising had ended up there among the Kazakhs. He had lived with them in their tents—yurts—and wrote the first and most classic work on the Kazakh social and economic system. Auezov also told me that there were Kazakh songs about a Polish priest who had lived in Ust-Kaminogorsk. According to him, the Kazakhs had the highest opinion of the Polish exiles, an opinion that fell during this wave of exile. The earlier Polish exiles had done an enormous amount for the Kazakhs.

On the stairs in the lobby there were people swollen with hunger, always new ones; they kept coming from the camps. One day I ran into Rogoż there. We threw our arms around each other. He was completely swollen, covered with boils, lice, and rags. He was standing on the stairs too, but when he was let in and they found out that he had been the editor of *The Illustrated Weekly* (Tygodnik Ilustrowany) right before the war, he was given a job at once.

From late fall 1941 to spring 1942, Soviet-Polish relations were idyllic, at least in Alma-Ata. Only in the spring did they start to go bad. To accept Shklovsky's offer to work for Mosfilm was a problem: I'd have to have a residence permit. The Kazakh secretary told me that he had examined the case and said that since I had come out under the amnesty, I had not been absolved. Of course, this was just a formality; there wouldn't be many hearings, maybe one or two; I should institute a review of my case, which would, of course, end well, and I would receive a residence permit. Obviously, I refused immediately, without the slightest hesitation—that could have had horrible consequences.

All the same, I was tolerated, and the secretary and Shklovsky told me that for the time being I could stay in Alma-Ata. I'd be told when

322

my time was up. And so I began looking for a place to live. I'd gotten some money from the embassy again. I was constantly sending out postcards, but I still had no news of Ola. And I found a place to live; some Pole was moving on, and he turned over his room to me.

He lived with a night watchman, rather far away, between the train station and the city proper, behind a market. A very nice Russian, an old guy, exiled a long time ago with his family. He probably wasn't that old, but he gave the impression of being old. A night watchman, bottom-of-the-barrel poor, but somehow he managed. He was married to a Russian peasant woman; she looked old too—a wrinkled apple. I had a little corner to myself, meaning a plank bed. My hands hung down to the floor and my feet stuck out over the end; it was really just a bench. The family used that room during the day, and so I couldn't stay there very much; I'd just come for the night.

Besides, I wanted to eat; I never felt full. And so I would leave in the morning and go at once to the hotel where my writer friends were, and to the delegation. I'd eat in the canteen there. They weren't serving meals anymore, mostly just kasha with some oil, and there was always a little sugar. Then I'd go see my friends for a chat.

People got together every evening, and usually those conversations were broken off when bulletins from the front were broadcast. Everyone would go down to the lobby and listen intently to the bulletins. Without exception, everyone thought that it was a war to save the fatherland. And without exception they all believed that Hitler would be defeated in the end. There was gloom when the bulletins announced that such and such cities had been evacuated, daily depression, but at the same time they never lost faith in ultimate victory. Pasternak rendered all that very faithfully: everyone thought that when that wave of millions of hero-martyrs returned from the front, no Stalin could stop them. Russia would change totally, from the bottom up.

After the bulletins we usually went to Shnaider's room; he rarely got out of bed, and so our little meetings took place there. I'd go home after the meetings, quite early sometimes. Those trips back were tough. The city was still bearable even though I had no strength. Alma-Ata is at a very high altitude, and my legs were swollen, and my heart was failing.

I had to walk across the flea market, which played a certain role in my life, and so maybe I should describe it a little. An enormous square, perhaps as large as Red Square. By day it was Sodom and Gomorrah, a whirlwind of rags and people. Colorful. You could buy anything there. Nails, one rubber boot at a time, but there were also very substantial items—gold. They all held onto their goods for dear life. They slung them over their arms or held them in their hands, or the entire family would barricade them because *urks* cruised the market. And policemen too. It should be said that while in Russia the NKVD was a menace, the police were mostly undernourished and very anemic, like sleepy flies in the late autumn. They hung around the market. Incredible shouting in twenty languages, dialects. That was by day. But the nights were dark, pitch black. The stars lit nothing on that enormous square of horrible, sticky oozing mud and clay. An enormous square. Around it at a distance were a few huts with lights on, mostly very far away, and oil lamps that gave me no light either. You walked and you walked, and you wept because your feet would get stuck and sometimes you wouldn't have the strength to lift them up and you'd have to stop a while. It was very dark, the kind of darkness that creates a stillness. A strange phenomenon: despite the stillness you can hear cries—drunks singing, the cry of someone being murdered for all I know—and they seem right beside you, but they could be quite far away. That would go on the whole way. I had to cut across the square at an angle. Those trips back took a long time. Sometimes I told myself that I wouldn't go anywhere the next day. But how could I stay at the house, where there wasn't even a crust of dry bread, when I was ravenously hungry? I also told myself I'd go home during the day, but it was so good to be with my friends the writers, such warm, interesting, cordial people, that of course I always ended up going home late.

My friends. I don't remember who said what. And even if I do remember, I have to be careful; some of them have died and some are still alive, and so I'll speak in general terms. I've already mentioned that they all believed the war would be won and things would change. Eisenstein showed up two or three times, no more than that. One time when Eisenstein was there the conversation was about the coming changes. There was a sort of sardonic sneer on Eisenstein's face, that was all. I caught that sneer, or maybe I just imagined it.

They were interested in what I had to say. I gave them information about literature, art, film and also told about my experiences in prison. My friends there knew everything about the camps and the prisons, things a hundred times worse than what I'd been through, but evidently I had a certain way of seeing and speaking about my experience that was more interesting than what they already knew. I also spoke about my Christianity, but without any propaganda, preaching, or proselytizing. I didn't go into any details; I simply spoke about my Christianity. Those were not religious people, but they responded, Zoshchenko more than anyone else. I could feel him resonate.

He was there often with his lovely wife, a woman of very few words, and, besides, he had the least to say of anyone in the group, and when he did speak, he never once made anyone laugh or even smile. He never said anything funny. He may have been depressed because by then he had probably published *Before the Sunrise,* his attempt at applying Freud to himself to resolve his problems, a combination of Freudianism and Pavlovism. Childhood memories. Evidently he already had problems then; he was afraid. Besides, humorists are often very melancholy; they're sad people by and large. All the humorists I ever knew were sad people, and there was something else at work here too—the wisdom of silence, very rare among Slavic writers.

In any case, Zoshchenko never said anything comical. But one time he did say something striking. He asked me, "For example, do you believe at this very minute?" I remember that clearly: "at this very minute." I'm using my own words here, but more or less what he said was "All right, we're sitting in this room. Close your eyes and ask yourself if you believe in the divinity of Christ. Do you believe in the resurrection of the body, in the immortality of the soul, and so on?" I was a bit taken aback by that question, which was asked very seriously. That's why I said I felt him resonate, because I could see that this was a very fundamental question for him. I didn't close my eyes, but I tried to sound myself out. I really couldn't answer his question.

I told him that I didn't think it mattered if I believed at this very minute or not (after reflecting on it) but I assumed that once you had real faith, it was totally yours and you could not become a disbeliever, because you were in a place without any fundamental contradictions, where all the counterarguments were meaningless. That if you had been in that place once, you could find the path that led back to it. But it's like a fairy tale: the place is there but the path is lost.

Another very interesting point. One time the talk was about Freudianism, on which Zoshchenko was an expert. I remember an interesting remark Zoshchenko made, a very striking remark (which I later found in Berdyaev), about the Russian people's need to suffer. Zoshchenko pointed out that the rational and the irrational, the conscious and the unconscious, are intertwined in Russians in a way completely different from that in other peoples. And for that reason he thought that basically Freudianism could not provide the key to the Russian psyche.

I told them that I was a religious person, that I had been converted—in the most general terms; I didn't go into any details. By then I didn't feel like a jellyfish anymore. Beginning with the prison in Saratov, I had started to feel like my old self. Before Saratov, I had been like a mass of jelly. After Saratov, I could feel a strong, certain, firm consistency in myself. That means I was perfectly well aware that there are peaks; sometimes I'm at the peak and sometimes I'm on the bottom. I don't actually know when I'm at a peak and when I'm at the bottom, but I had a blind certainty about what the peak was and what the bottom was. And I could sense a voice inside me saying, Do this, don't do that. That lasted a very long time, nearly the entire time I was in Russia. I didn't want to see anything mystical in my conversion at Saratov, apart from the vision of the devil. For a long time, whenever I studied the mystics, I was very mistrustful of mystical conversions. But for me the prototype of the classical, pure conversion is Paul's epilepsy, meaning his conversion. Suddenly, not mystically, even though it's somatic, connected with epilepsy.

MILOSZ: But did you have a positive feeling about Paul's conversion, or were you suspicious of it?

WAT: No, I had a positive feeling about Paul's conversion. For me it wasn't a mystical conversion, even though I knew he's thought to have been an epileptic. All the mystical conversions, however—St. Teresa's, all those stigmata—all religious exaltation in general always grated on me. I found them suspicious and thought they had a somatic source in some form of hysteria. Someone in that group said something very wise to me—it must have been Shnaider, who was a very deep and wise man and a very irreligious one (to the very end; I saw him just before he died). It must have been a week before his death and he hadn't converted. It was then that he asked me, "Excuse me, but wasn't your conversion political?"

To a certain extent, I admitted, he was right, if politics means social history, the historical process. I didn't deny that. To my mind, that sort of conversion might not have been the most authentic, and maybe not the most deeply rooted, but it was more authentic than mystical conversion. I still operate on that assumption. For some reason, I can't stand people who convert out of exaltation, especially Frenchmen. I don't believe them. But the social aspect of history—maybe. There might be some confirmation of this in the religiosity of the Poles during Stalinism. Huge numbers of people in the churches. The churches packed with people who had not practiced their religion previously. Maybe it's the same thing.

There was also talk about certain things connected with Russian literature, certain secrets, peeks behind the scenes. I don't remember a lot of it, but I do recall clearly that Mandelstam's arrest was laid to Pavlenko. Pavlenko had been a Chekist at one time. Zoshchenko had also worked for them in his youth, in the criminal police. But Pavlenko had been a Chekist. Everyone knew that, but Mandelstam was a bit of a madman and had a strange belief and trust in Pavlenko. And apparently Pavlenko was one of the three or four people there when Mandelstam read his little poem about Stalin. In my reading, I never came across anything about Pavlenko's being the one who betrayed him. The same Pavlenko whom Broniewski and I went to, to complain about the Ukrainians, and who very kindheartedly told us that we should flee Lwów as quickly as possible, that it was dangerous territory for us.

Another story I remember, which I even noted down, concerned the death of Marina Tsvetaeva. Not long before the war her husband, Efros, and her daughter, Anya, were arrested right before her eyes. During the first weeks of the war all the Moscow writers were evacuated to Chistopol' on the Kama River—some were sent to the front as war correspondents. But Tsvetaeva stayed in Moscow. Finally, she received permission to be evacuated with her fourteen-year-old son. Pasternak came to help her pack her trunks. While tying up a bundle, he said, "In a pinch, a rope like this could do for a noose." She wasn't sent to Chistopol' where all the others were, but to Yelabuga, four hundred kilometers from Chistopol', also on the Kama. She was all alone there, surrounded by kolkhozniks, on a very poor kolkhoz. Her nerves couldn't take it. She traveled to Chistopol' to ask for permission to be there with everyone else. A committee of evacuees met on it. She was in one room—everything was very crowded there—and the committee was in the next room. Paustovsky was there, Shklovsky was there, and many others, including Piertsov, who was a friend of Shklovsky, a LEF theoretician, a well-known formalist, one of the most important of them. Piertsov said, "What do we need a White Guard poetess for? She hasn't written anything, nobody reads her, and all she wants is to come here." Only three voted to allow her to stay: Paustovsky, Shnaider, and I don't know who the third one was, maybe Shklovsky (even though Shklovsky was incredibly decent, he was also cowardly). Someone else at the meeting added, "White Guard whore!" And she could hear it all in the next room. She went back to Yelabuga and the next day hanged herself with the same piece of rope Pasternak had used to tie up her bundle. Tsvetaeva's son was on the second ship out when the writers were evacuated from Chistopol' to Alma-Ata. He joined the army and was killed immediately by a stray bullet at the front. There were a great many more stories like that, but I don't remember very much, of course.

My chief goal, my guiding star was still the same: to search for Ola and Andrzej. But now I did it like a calm person, a strong person, not a jellyfish. Physically, I was weak, but I had a strong character, a strong will, a clear head. I was still sending out postcards anywhere there was the slightest trace of information. I inundated the south with postcards since apparently that's where they'd gone. And then all of a sudden I received an answer, after a long time, from the Semipalatinsk Region delegate:

In reply to your letter of December 27, 1941, I can inform you that, according to our records, your wife is not here. According to our information, however, the Polish citizens who had resided in Ivanovka, on the Krasny Skotovod State Farm, left for the south after receiving their ID cards. You can receive further information from Miss Olga Krzemińska, presently residing in Tyurbok District, Sergeyevka Station, Village of Antonovka. Signed, Doctor Sarniecki, Embassy Delegate.

He had sent it on January 14, 1942, but I received it only at the end of February or the beginning of March—in any case it was already spring. I wrote a letter to that station, to Olga Krzemińska.

Ola was there. And she immediately sent me a telegram and a letter at the same time. And I sent her a letter immediately, but I won't go into that here. The world changed in my eyes; I began to see colors, to hear, to smell, to see women, to smell women.

The atmosphere among my friends the writers was sexually charged. And there were some love affairs. Not dolce vita—there was no trace of that. It was romantic in the Russian romantic style. But there were affairs. As for me, even though I was emaciated, a certain Miss Shub had designs on me, though none of that had any reality for me at that time.

Now, I had begun to see women. There were some beautiful actresses there. Now when I walked through Alma-Ata, it seemed like a garden to me. I was very happy.

Ola had written that she had saved a few of my things—she had very few things; she was baking bread for the road and would bring it to me; she had another half sack of flour. Later on, I learned that was all she had. She had no prospects, had received no help. She and Andrzej were working in the cotton fields and were near starvation.

I still had some of the money from the embassy left. There wasn't much chance of my finding work, but I assumed that in the end the embassy would give me some help. The editor of the *Teachers' Newspaper* and a Georgian who was working on Mayakovsky tried to talk me into writing my memories of Mayakovsky; I'd be paid well. I had a lot of memories of Mayakovsky and they were still fresh, but I was allergic to everything that had impelled me toward communism in my youth, Mayakovsky in particular, and so I refused not only to write about him but even to talk about him. And since I had not agreed to a review of my case, I was at loose ends in Alma-Ata; my only hope was the delegation. All the same, I of course telegrammed Ola and Andrzej at once to come there.

This took quite a long time. Their journey was full of strange adventures like waiting at night at little stations surrounded by bandits, nights with drunken tramps. And before that, she had to get a wagon to the station, pack a few utensils and rags in her bags, the bare necessities. For a long time they didn't want to spare her a horse and wagon. They were let off at some little crossing and spent nights with drunken tramps, thieves, bandits. Finally, the "stationmaster," whom Ola had bribed, managed to cram them onto a train that was pulling away and threw their bags in after them.

They were coming to join me, who slept on a bench with my arms dangling down. Where would I put them? The floor was a possibility, but then a new complication arose. On the day before their departure— I know because I was constantly receiving telegrams from them— the night watchman's son died of scarlet fever. When I returned to the night watchman's on the day before Ola and Andrzej were to arrive, the little boy's body was on the table. Scarlet fever is contagious.

I went to see Kaganowski, whom I'd known very well before the war in Warsaw and asked him just to take Andrzej. Kaganowski refused outright. And he had a very large room, though it's true he did have a family. I asked him if maybe one of the Yiddish writers from Poland or someone else could help me. He went out, asked around, and came back with a no.

But by then I had made contact with the Georgian woman who was the sister of the historian who had been my cell mate in Saratov. She'd already managed to send him a few packages in Saratov; he really was dying of hunger. She was very grateful to me and every so often invited me for a Georgian dinner. She was doing very well, a successful doctor. Unusually hospitable, as Georgians are. She had sent some other relatives to see me and hear me tell about Saratov Prison and their relative. Family feeling in Georgia is unlike anything known in Europe. And since I was their friend and had helped them, they would do anything for me. As soon as I told her about Andrzej, she said that they both could stay with her. Ola didn't have to, I said, but I would put Andrzej with her. It was late by then; I could barely drag myself home, but they could be arriving any minute.

And they arrived. Andrzej looked like a child from the Warsaw ghetto. He had the beginnings of tuberculosis, a corpse's skull. How old was Ola then? She was thirty-odd years old and looked like a sixty-year-old woman, completely ravaged. And her clothes! I can't forget the skirt she had on. She had fled Warsaw with two good fur coats, a pelisse and a fur. She had sold the pelisse—actually she swapped it for flour and lard. The fur coat was made of Persian-lamb paws, strips of fur and wadding. But her skirt was so riddled with holes that you could see her shirt through them. And the bags and odds and ends she was carrying—tin cans with holes in them, God knows what else. But she really did have a large loaf of bread. I was so vile! I knew there was no more flour; the preparations for the journey had taken so long that all the flour had been used up. There was only the bread. And I was so vile that despite their hunger, I devoured nearly the entire loaf. All by myself. I attacked the bread.

I brought Ola to see my friends; she was given a very warm welcome, the kind only Russians can give. By then there was very little to eat in Alma-Ata. You had to stand for a long time in line on the stairs for the canteen, and, as I said, all they served you was a plate of cream of kasha, with a light sprinkling of sugar, and sometimes some sunflower oil. But not always. At that time I was drinking Georgian wine with pleasure. All the writers drank. Excellent Tsynabari and a strawberry liqueur that was even better. I don't like fruit liqueur, but that one was exceptionally good. But that ran out. And when the strawberry wine ran out, the bread ran out; everything ran out. But the writers, especially the more eminent ones, had their own store and their own very modest rations.

Shklovsky immediately dashed to his room (I wasn't there; Ola was at the Shnaiders') and, without a word, brought her all his supplies, all the rice he'd stored up for his son. Shklovsky thought he could get him out of the army. Shklovsky packed Ola quite a few bags of rice, burst into tears (he cried very easily), and ran out of the room. He also brought Ola and Andrzej to a good doctor, who found that Andrzej's condition wasn't critical even though he did have tuberculosis. Andrzej was given food and medicine; they fattened him up.

I still had some money; I'd gotten another small sum from the embassy, a thousand rubles, five hundred, that was money back then. But I couldn't buy any food. True, there was a kolkhoz market that had onions, garlic, sausage, and meat. The apples were the best things there. (Alma-Ata means "father of the apples.") The apples there were large, hard, with subterranean juices under the skin. The best apples I ever ate, and later on, in the summer, they had the best melons, the sweetest, the best. But the prices were sky-high at that kolkhoz black market, and I couldn't afford to buy much at all there. Ola was still wearing that skirt, even to the meetings of our little club. They were all very well dressed—spoils from Poland and Latvia. The whole Mosfilm group, the writers and movie people—the women were dressed in grand style. And Ola was wearing that sieve of a skirt. At one point I told her we had to do something about it, and she went and bought some clothes.

It was idyllic, a time of happiness, but we had to think about the future too. And so what should we do? We could live a while on our own money, but I wasn't getting official bread rations because I wasn't registered. I couldn't sponge off my friends. Our money wouldn't last; we had to come up with something. But apparently something had come in from the embassy to Wiącek because he called me in and said he could employ me, but not in Alma-Ata. Even though there was a place in Alma-Ata; no one spoke good Russian there and they were in constant need of a translator. The one they had, Cygielstreich, did the job poorly; his Russian was awful. Wiącek said, "I'm asking you to go to Molotovobad as a delegate. Molotovobad is in Kirghizia, at the end of the famous Fergana Valley. Things were very good there even before the war. It's in the mountains, a beautiful spot. There's a delegate there, a Jew from Galicia, a dentist, but I don't trust him; he doesn't answer letters. I'll recall him and you'll take his place. There's great poverty among the Poles there. You'll be given one hundred thousand rubles, a prepaid ticket, all your expenses."

The salary was, as I remember, around four hundred rubles—not enough to live on. In my naïveté I asked, "Excuse me, but I don't have any money right now and the trip will take three, four, five days, and I'll have to get settled there. Could I get an advance on my salary?" Wiącek said, "Taking advances on salary isn't a good habit, but we'll make an exception and give you four hundred rubles right away. You can buy some things here and Meller will issue you some bread, bacon, fat, Bovril, and a little sugar so you'll have something for the trip."

We started getting ready; we had to leave in a couple of days. And that meant leaving our Russian friends who had been so tremendously warm to us. Paustovsky's wife came running with a large crock of rice and preserves and other such priceless gifts. Ola made something like a corset out of cloth quilted on both sides, which I wore on my bare chest; the hundred thousand rubles had been sewn inside, a fortune. The only way to keep the money from being stolen. By then we had a bit of baggage. Ola bought some clothes, a dress. We kept all our best things in one grip, and we had a few other bags, three or four.

We got on the train; the tickets were taken care of at once; the stationmasters had already been informed. A Pole from the delegation could have anything. With a little bribe, dirt cheap.

331

35 ISAAC BABEL. THE POLISH INTELLIGENTSIA.
THE TRIP TO MOLOTOVOBAD. ESCAPE. RETURN
TO ALMA-ATA VIA KOKAND AND TASHKENT.
RICH POLES.

WAT: Each time after we tape, I wake up in the middle of the night deluged by incidents, situations, and people I forgot to mention. Some of the incidents are significant and some aren't, but I can't bring in the ones that are the next day, because then that would start assuming impossible proportions, just from the technical point of view.

Still, I'd like to go back to Alma-Ata, because there are two points that seem quite important to me. One concerns the literary world, the Russian writers, and the other is connected to the Poles' situation. As for the literary world, I'd like to point out that their level of conversation and debate was much higher than, say, at the Skamandrites' café table. There were no jokes, but the level was much higher since nearly all those people were very well educated in philology. Because of me, Poland was discussed. As I mentioned earlier, Shklovsky especially had admired the architecture in Lwów, and he also admired Poland for having a feudal period and, above all, a period of chivalry, knighthood. The Russians thought that Poland lacked, however, what Russia had had from the tenth to the twelfth century: an authentic literature in the native language. I think there are something like twenty-five codices, monuments of language and literature, that have come down from those two centuries. That was the Novgorod and Kiev period, very important.

Babel was talked about quite a lot—things I've never seen in print. One of the Russians characterized Babel as a *nagly trus*, an audacious coward. He quivers and quakes, then suddenly, out of cowardice, he goes and says something, does something. That was the direct cause of his arrest, the reason for it. Maybe they would have eliminated him anyway, but the direct reason was that he wanted to write a collection of short stories about Chekists. He began to hobnob with Chekists and ask them questions, and that was the direct cause of his arrest.

And second, there was his attitude toward Stalin. He had a very odd idea—I don't know if this appears in anyone's recollections—specifically, how would Dostoevsky have described Stalin? Babel came to the conclusion that Dostoevsky would have written an apologia for Stalin, would have viewed him as the creator of some new, great Russia. And Babel planned to write a story in a Dostoevskian style—not using Stalin's name, of course, but with a character who would correspond to Stalin. Marshak told me about this. Babel's friends talked him out of it.

Another interesting detail about Babel. Three years ago during a conference of Russian specialists at Oxford, there was a lot of discussion about whether what Babel said in 1934—let's learn to write like Stalin, let's study Stalin's style—had been sarcasm or not. Obviously, there's no question that anyone could have allowed himself even the most veiled sarcasm at the first congress of the Writers' Union in 1934. (For example, Olesha—Olesha the drunkard—declared, and supposedly with passionate enthusiasm, that he'd been having enormous problems in writing and had stopped writing, but now, after that congress, he felt like a sixteen-year-old boy, the world was blossoming before his eyes and so forth.) Sarcasm was out of the question. My Russian friends considered Babel's admiration for Stalin sincere to a certain extent, ambiguous but sincere. And here I'd add that if ultimately Stendhal in some sense admired the legal code, then why shouldn't Babel, who strove to be laconic, admire Stalin's laconic style, which in any case deserves to be studied, very much so.

There was a large Polish patriotic demonstration just before our departure. A priest had arrived with the troops for a short stopover. "Oh God, Watch Over Poland" was sung. Everyone cried. We all cried. I was very moved. But my main point here is that there was a priest at the demonstration in Alma-Ata. I knew there was such a thing as the baptism of the heart and that it wasn't necessary to be baptized to be a Christian, a Catholic, but, in prison, I had thought that if I found a priest, I'd be baptized. The priest was there only a couple of weeks. I approached him. He was very polite, relatively young, and quite nondescript. Maybe he was an anti-Semite, maybe not; maybe he was a National Democrat, maybe not; maybe he was wise, maybe a fool. Neither one thing nor another. An army chaplain. I could see it was impossible. And probably my old hostility toward the clergy also came into play here. I always knew that if nine out of ten Poles were *naturaliter* anti-Semites, the sermons Poles had heard for at least a couple of centuries had also helped educate them in anti-Semitism. In any case, it was the work of the clergy to a great extent. And so I couldn't bring myself to it.

We had excellent seats on the train—thanks to some connections and some gifts; we'd gotten a compartment for the three of us. We left Alma-Ata, seeing an even greater panorama of the Ala Tau mountains, some very high peaks; Talgar is over five thousand meters high. Right outside of Alma-Ata, which is an oasis, there are mulberry trees and white acacias and fruit trees and little mountain streams, called *taras*, that flow constantly, and it's there that what's almost a desert starts—barren land, salt marshes, steppe, but a parched steppe with salty soil and all the vegetation that usually grows in salty soil.

We traveled two, three days, I don't remember how many, but toward the evening of the second day we had to change trains in Gorchakov. We got out and were on our way to the other train; it was nighttime, and, can you imagine, a Polish troop train was making a stop there. I was lucky to run into Gold's and Peterburski's musicians. "Where are you going?" I asked them.

"To Iran!" A complete surprise. I'd never even dreamed that anyone would be released, especially in wartime—I still thought, maybe after the war—but in wartime?

A soldier—some violinist or trombone player; I don't recall—who also knew me, said, "If you give our sergeant a liter of vodka, you can get on the train and go with us to Iran!" It was like being in Hell and being told that for a liter of vodka you could get out of Hell. All right, but I had 100,000 rubles with me that I had to deliver somewhere at the ends of the earth where I knew people were dying of starvation. So I told him that I couldn't. He answered, "It's no big deal; you can deposit the money with an officer at the border!" I played Hamlet for a moment, but it was my duty to go to Molotovobad with the money; they were waiting for it there. So I let a chance to get out of the country go by.

I arrived in Molotovobad, an out-of-the-way little place right where the Pamirs begin, near the Chinese border. We got off the train in the town of Kizylkiya, a small industrial town, a coal town, and from there we had to walk ten kilometers or so to Molotovobad with our bags. We passed no one on the road.

The trees were like something from a Chinese painting. You could see that the wind blew from various directions because the boughs and branches had been twisted into very emotional gestures—praying, beseeching, threatening. Exactly like hands. There were Uzbeks on small horses; I had never seen horses like that before, very beautiful faces. The Uzbeks were almost entirely in rags, but they had handsome faces, masculine profiles, the faces of real mountain people. Each of them wore a bright, colorful Eastern silk sash. They were dressed in rags but their sashes were always in perfect condition. Red silk, blue, green, turquoise.

We left Kizylkiya around five in the morning and dragged ourselves into Molotovobad around three in the afternoon. It was the most beautiful landscape I had ever seen in my life. Molotovobad is in the mountains, about fourteen hundred meters up. Fantastic configurations and very old. No straight lines; everything undulated. A stream ran through the middle of the city, a powerful stream but fairly shallow. The stream was a marvelous green, with many shades, especially in the sun. The streambed was basalt that went from a light to a very dark green.

It was already spring there. A symphony in violet everywhere you looked. The almond trees were already in bloom and they were a light violet. The almond blossoms, but especially the apricot trees, which were also between rose and violet in color. And the ground on the low hills was also covered with violet. An incredible symphony of colors and that roaring stream you could hear at a distance everywhere, that roaring green stream flowing down from those very high mountains. The mountain peaks were granite, black granite, white granite, sapphire granite. And then forests, but not green, violet. I may be wrong, but I didn't see any green on the hills, just incredible amounts of violet, in every possible shade.

A large Uzbek village; there were a few Tadzhiks there too. The Tadzhik women had braids in their hair, many braids; they're lovely until they're fifteen or sixteen years old—fantastically beautiful, those girls; even the ten-year-olds were very well formed. At one time this place was called Uchkurgan. In my time it was Molotovobad, but they may have gone back now to Uchkurgan again.

A lot of forests. There were supposed to be bears and badgers in those forests, golden eagles, all sorts of eagles, hawks, vultures. An enormous number of birds, birds of prey. But there were also very small birds like the kind you see in California.

The first thing we asked about was the canteen. Some Polish children took us there right away. A promise of things to come. In the canteen I presented my credentials as a Polish delegate; that still carried weight in Russia at the time, and so we were given permission to take a meal there. We were given three herrings, but we couldn't eat them because we were surrounded by a gang of starving Polish and Jewish children. Later, carrying our bundles, we passed the black market. There was nothing there, just some grain. There really was nothing to eat, not even on the black market.

This was the Fergana Valley that had been trumpeted as a valley of plenty. Before the war this enormous area, probably larger than

France, had been designated for the growing of cotton, nothing but cotton. The collective farmers had their own little plots, but they weren't allowed to grow wheat or rice, only vegetables. Everything was centered on cotton. Before the war, before 1941, it was possible to ship food in there, but after the war started, transportation collapsed and people were simply dying of starvation.

The Uzbeks are a very knightly race; they looked like impoverished knights and were magnificent horsemen. I found out that all of the young people had gone off to the mountains to avoid the draft, and some of them had taken weapons. They had gotten out their buried weapons and were preparing for an uprising. The Russians, the Jews, the fugitives, the refugees—everybody was expecting a bloodbath.

There was no communication among the authorities, the newcomers, and the natives. The natives lived a life apart. Their clay homesteads were surrounded by walls, like those in Morocco—they reminded me of films about Morocco I'd seen. The homes had interior courtyards completely hidden from sight. The married women wore veils made of horsehair.

There was a ruined mosque on the town square, but no services were held there; the mullah had been arrested. But the elders were still around, the elders of the tribe—sitting on cushions in the tea-houses. I dropped by the teahouse a few times myself. I was given a polite welcome, but nobody would strike up a conversation with me. I don't even know if they spoke Russian. In any case, they pretended they didn't. The gray-bearded elders sat on cushions and drank their tea. They were very thin from hunger, but they had enormous dignity; I never saw anything like that in all the time I was in Russia.

Finally we reached the house of the current delegate—a young Jew, extremely likable, married, with two children; the whole family very likable, well mannered, intelligent. He was the local power. He had power because he was the only dentist for fifty or one hundred miles. The party secretary, whom I met later, was a total brute, a Quasimodo. He suffered from canker sores and toothaches, and so he was dependent on that Polish dentist. And so of course they were doing very well; they gave us a very hospitable welcome, let us stay with them—they had two rooms—and fed us. I was in an awkward position, but he had no grudge against me because he considered his duties as a delegate a great burden. He was earning a lot of money, more than anybody else in the whole area.

That night I felt very relieved that I hadn't fled on the troop train because the very day after I arrived, one of the Poles died of starvation. A sixty-year-old man, a lawyer from Galicia, I think. He had literally starved to death. The Poles there were dragging themselves around; they could barely walk. One hundred thousand rubles—that was money even there, though there wasn't much you could buy with it. But you could still get some things. I immediately sent a telegram for material aid and food, but transportation had become exceptionally difficult.

The dentist took me to the chairman of the Soviet, an Uzbek or an Uigur, a good-natured man, but just a figurehead, and then to the party secretary. He was a Russian, though he didn't look like one. He was constantly gnashing his teeth. Always in a rage, he kept glancing at me with hatred.

After our first meeting I was supposed to be given lodgings, and a horse and cart. We had left our sacks in Kizylkiya, and we just had some baggage with us—and it had been hard to carry as it was; the sun had beat down on us the whole way. The sacks with all our pots and rags— all that had been left behind at the station in Kizylkiya. A day went by, two, three, four, and they still hadn't given me the horse and cart.

The party secretary said that he didn't like me and was going to kick me out of there. Meanwhile, my legs had swollen up, and I felt terrible. A Pole who had studied medicine for two or three years told me that my heart was in bad condition, that the altitude was bad for me, that I shouldn't be there. So I sent another telegram to Wiącek, saying I couldn't stay there. I received an answer saying that I was committed and had to stay there.

I wrote a letter to Shklovsky asking him to try and get me some sort of work. Shklovsky wrote me back a warm, cordial letter, but with one biting remark. I'd begun my letter with Molotovobad and described its beauty to him. Only after that did I move on to my own business, our hopeless situation, that I had to get away, I don't remember what else. He answered me very warmly, saying he'd try, but since I wouldn't get permission to stay in Alma-Ata, he didn't think much would come of his efforts. But I should come and they'd do what they could. And he wrote, "Your letter with the landscape . . ." That made me feel a little foolish, and from then on I remembered that when you have some business with someone, when you're asking someone a favor, you shouldn't write about landscapes.

And so we left there, but not in very good shape now. We had lost our connections. In the end, after two weeks or so, they gave us a horse and cart. The dentist and I parted on very good terms; we corresponded afterwards, and later—in 1944, I think—I found out that he'd been arrested and not released for the evacuation to Poland. I tried to find out what had happened to him, but I couldn't. And now I don't even remember his name.

And so, the trip. Once again I got off in Gorchakov. I no longer had any obligations, any money. There was a military post there; transports were leaving for Iran. I could escape, no two ways about it. First, I stopped a sergeant who looked like a nice person. He said, "What have you got to offer? If you had a fur coat . . . There was a Polish poet, Stern, here a short while ago with his wife. The major took a liking to her, and besides that she had a fur coat, and they left on the train. Does your wife have a fur coat?" My wife's fur coat was clearly in no shape to be of any use. Trying to come up with something, he said, "Go see the major!"

I went to see the major. The only document I had from the old days—Ola had kept hold of it—was my PEN Club card signed by Jan Parandowski. I went to the major, told him who I was, and showed him my PEN Club card.

"I know what the PEN Club is," he said. "An international communist organization."

I tried to explain who Parandowski was.

"I know who Parandowski is," he said, "but it's a communist organization."

So, I explained that it wasn't.

He listened closely to what I said, polite, intelligent. He accepted some of it and said, "All right, you can go for a physical. Come tomorrow at this time."

I also told him that I would die there because I was a writer and they wouldn't let me out for that reason. So many people had already lost their lives that this made no impression on him; my argument carried no weight. But I should go for a physical. I went into the physical wearing my underpants and they told me to take them off. They looked me over and decided I was unfit for military service. A bad break.

And so we traveled on. We still had some money, not much, just enough to get to Alma-Ata and buy food along the way. We got off at Kokand where—and these are very Russian paradoxes—right by the station people were making fried cakes on pieces of sheet metal over fire (they do something similar in Naples); they cook quickly and have wonderful fillings; you could eat all you wanted. That was all I saw in Kokand, because I didn't have the strength to walk around. We were taking a roundabout route, which was hard on us, but it was also the easiest way.

We also got off at Tashkent. Again I didn't have the strength to walk to the city, and I stayed at the station. People were lying on the benches at the station. The typhus epidemic had just ended, but people had

338

been dying and breathing their last on those same benches because there had been no room in the hospitals. We had a few bags and one small suitcase, relatively small, that contained our better and more valuable things. Two Jews from Łódź attached themselves to us. They were very sympathetic to us; they could see I had no strength—how could I get my ticket revalidated? The train pulling in was overcrowded already; the crowd was rushing toward it; the women supervisors [one per car] wouldn't let them on. One train to Alma-Ata left before we could get to it, and then the same thing happened again.

A day passed, and the next day at the station in Tashkent those same two Jews were fussing over us, wanting to help. They could help us get good spots rights by the track. They said, "Give us your bags; you run ahead with a few rubles for the conductor, and we'll toss you the bags." The train was pulling in; I could feel the bags by my foot. I had no great confidence in the two men from Łódź, one short, one tall. Well, the crowd surged forward, and I did too, dragging Ola and Andrzej, with only the suitcase in my hand. There were two or three bags, but when I looked back, they were suddenly gone. The small Jew grabbed at the other one and shouted, "Your bags are gone. He's a thief!!" The big one ran away with the small one after him. But we had to get on the train. I was right beside the conductor; I gave her a few rubles.

The bags and all our utensils were gone; we had two small suitcases left. That was all we had left in the world. Two small suitcases, one with the valuable items. Heartbroken and feeling like a complete ass, I took a seat, and, losing my wits the way you do when you're exhausted, I placed the precious suitcase under the seat to keep an eye on it. In the morning I looked around and it was gone. Now we had only the one small suitcase with a few things of Andrzej's in it, a few rags. Ola is very strong, stronger than I am. That didn't break Ola, but it broke me. When we were getting off at the station, I was seized by a pain in my stomach, and, for the first time in my life and the last, I shit my pants. That lifted my spirits a bit; it relieved me; I felt strong again, fearless. I washed up at the station. One benefit came from it all; by then we were so weak, my legs were swollen, and now there was nothing to carry.

First, I stopped by to see my friends, who gave us a very fond welcome. Ola and Andrzej stayed there while I went to the delegation, which was one floor up, expecting to be told when I tried to register that, sorry, I couldn't stay; relations had been broken off. But instead I was received with deep bows in the delegation. "Oh, sir, we thought that you were in such and such a place, in Frunze. Paweł Hertz was here, and we gave him a package, a very nice package, that came for you from the embassy. Moreover, 1,500 rubles came for you." Probably there had also been instructions to employ me right there in Alma-Ata. The delegate said, "Come see me tomorrow. We'll talk this over."

And so the question of making a living was resolved successfully: now I was working for the delegation. My job was school inspector; I was to set up schools for Polish children and also serve as an interpreter. It's not worth telling about—a lot of various adventures, various people, but it's all been described many times.

Relations with the Soviet authorities had deteriorated considerably by then. The petty harassments had started. The Soviet authorities weren't letting Jews into the Polish army. There was a Soviet officer on the board who wouldn't let the Byelorussians, Ukrainians, and Jews in Alma-Ata into the army. Not only Jews from the occupied territories, but Jews in general, which, as you can imagine, caused no protests from the Polish military authorities. And that made for a panic, because Jews would no longer be under the protection of the Polish posts. Which in fact happened, but at that time it was limited to Jews from the occupied territories, the Western Ukraine and Byelorussia. In this connection, there were some suicides and later on someone had to escape to avoid arrest. The doctor who had faked my urinalysis was arrested.

Meanwhile, the warehouses were bursting with goods. Trainloads of gifts from America and England had arrived, which saved a million people from death, not only Poles but plenty of Russians too! Countless trainloads of gifts. Naturally, they didn't arrive in full. A portion would disappear at the border, at the junctions. It went through a sieve of theft, many sieves. When the trains arrived in Alma-Ata, the stronger Poles were recruited as porters. Those strong Poles formed a powerful gang. But they had certain rules; they took only a certain percentage of the goods. There was more theft when the goods reached the warehouses. The delegation warehouseman, the watchman, everyone stole. Nevertheless, there was still a lot left for the citizens, but they stinted; they could have given out five times more. Because in the end, when the delegation was closed, there were still enormous warehouses packed with goods.

We dressed elegantly, the members of the delegation. I chose some used clothing, a wonderful suit, better than anything I'd had before, a beautiful tan material. I sold it later on, for food of course. I paraded around Alma-Ata in that wonderful suit. I found a winter coat for Ola, a used one, with a fox-fur collar: Maison Neuman, New York–Paris. It was sold later too for some grain. And so there was theft, an abundance of goods, warehouses, corruption—in a word, tremendous activity.

But it was all in jeopardy because [Polish-Soviet] relations were becoming more and more tense.

One time Wiącek was summoned by the chairman of the Provincial Executive Committee. By that time he'd come to trust me; evidently his suspicions about my communist past had been allayed. He always asked me to go with him. He didn't understand Russian, didn't speak Russian. He was very foolish, had no idea how to act. One day the chairman of the Provincial Executive Committee told Wiącek that he was being dismissed, that he had to quit. When I translated that for him, Wiącek went into a panic. He became utterly abject, pleaded. The chairman was a Kazakh, probably a figurehead but a very severe man. The Kazakh didn't understand a word of what Wiącek was saying; his Russian wasn't very good either. And so I had to invent something for Wiącek. I carried on quite a long conversation, playing the diplomat. The Kazakh also asked me to make notes. And I made notes on what Wiącek had supposedly said, a dry record that went on to Kuibyshev and was approved there—which led to some unpleasant consequences for me. Namely, orders came from Kuibyshev for me to travel as an arbitrator, judge, or inspector general, to Kirghizia, in the vicinity of Frunze, because the embassy had received complaints from the local citizens about the delegate there: primo, that he was stealing, and secondo, that he was a terrible anti-Semite. The delegate had been a figure in the National Democrat party. I mention this because this is the nasty sort of affair a person gets pulled into. It seemed that I had achieved an identity, become something, stopped being a jellyfish, but another nasty game was starting up.

I made a great mistake: I went to that town and I stayed with the delegate. I had been ordered to do this by the delegation, but I shouldn't have. I was received with open arms, given a beautiful room; the delegate's daughters waited on me hand and foot. The house was a peasant cottage that had evidently once belonged to Ukrainian exiles who had retained some of their wealth. A farmyard, whitewashed walls. An orchard, fragrant nights, and nightingales, nightingales, nightingales. It must have been May. They invited me to dinner, and I ate with them. Not a word was said about the case.

The school there was a large one, very well organized. It was both a school for the Polish children and an old people's home. On the whole, the settlement was quite well-to-do. There was a club or something of the sort there; an announcement was posted that I would be in such and such places at such and such times and would hear all who presented themselves. I had paper and took down depositions while sitting at a table under an oak tree. A judge under an oak tree. The delegate's assistant was there, a lawyer, a Jew from Galicia. The embassy had informed me that the delegate was an anti-Semite, that he discriminated against Jews when distributing goods, and so it was somewhat striking that he had a Jewish lawyer for an assistant. The lawyer kept the books and was also in charge of the warehouse.

I took depositions for a day, two days—there were a lot of Polish citizens there—three days. The three or four people who had sent the letter repeated their accusations, but in much milder form now. All the rest—and it was mostly Jews I called on—did not uphold the accusations. The Jewish lawyer said, "Excuse me, but those three are known speculators."

And the delegate said, "Yes, I did give the Jews less than the Poles, but not because they're Jews." He behaved with dignity, didn't say anything about being a philo-Semite, didn't pretend to be one, but he behaved like a National Democrat of the old school. He gave the Jews less, sometimes considerably less, because the Jews had come there mainly from settlements, and they were in quite bearable condition. Some even had some capital. That was confirmed. The Polish families, however, were mostly people who'd been in the camps or the widows of men who'd died in the camps.

I don't remember the details, but some anti-Semitic remarks he had made came to light. He shouldn't have made those distinctions; there was plenty of goods, all sorts, for him to give to both. The point was that he had offended people. But somehow the lawyer smoothed it all over. And so I wrote up a report, very objectively it seemed to me, which I reworked on the train and then sent to the embassy. My conclusion was that the accusations of abuses and discrimination against Jews had not proved true. But I assumed that he had expressed his anti-Semitism in remarks. I concluded that he should not be dismissed, just given a warning. I also recommended that the three instigators, who in fact turned out to be speculating on a large scale, lose supply privileges for three months—or maybe more; I don't remember now. King Solomon's court under an oak tree.

I ran into that lawyer in Krynica in 1947. He was very sick; he could barely walk. "Don't you recognize me?" he asked. I didn't recognize him. "I was the delegate's assistant. And you were a very fair judge."

I'm mixing up different times here; it's very hard to stay in sequence. I've spoken of Rogoż. I was very fond of him in Warsaw, though we didn't see each other often there. He was a person of great goodness. I came to know him better at one point in Zakopane. Wherever he went, children would come running up to him; he always had candy for the children. He was always taking care of children he barely knew. He was like a father. A man of ideal goodness, but he was also good company. At the time when I still drank vodka, I drank a lot of vodka with Wacek Gebethner and Rogoż.

The first time I saw Rogoż was on the steps of the hotel lobby in Alma-Ata in a ragged quilt jacket. He was covered with boils and abscesses. They took care of him there at the delegation, fed him. He worked in the delegation, but not for very long. He fell ill with typhus and ran a high temperature from the very start. There was a Doctor Polak at the delegation, a very good soul.

And so we took Rogoż to the hospital. We hired a Kazakh cab driver; he had two wonderful little horses, but the droshky was very narrow, so Rogoż sat between us and we were pressed up against him. The Kazakh was drunk and driving at a gallop. He didn't run anyone over—drunkard's luck. People scattered in fear. Since the seat was narrow, there was a danger of our falling off. We had to hold on for dear life, one foot on the running board. And he drove on. A Mongolian face, flat, with traces of syphilis on it. He turned around and said that if we gave him five rubles, ten, he'd show us what real speed was. And so there we were—Rogoż, Staszek Rogoż, the son of a beadle from Kraków, sick with spotted fever, and I from Warsaw, and that Doctor Polak from Łódź tearing along in a droshky with a Mongolian driver surrounded by the Altai mountains, their eternal snow, the Pamirs not far away, the sky almost like California's—tearing along, God only knows where. The strangeness of that life that had taken possession of us.

We reached the hospital, which was outside the city, among the orchards. The hospital attendants took Rogoż. The doctor and I were allowed into the waiting room, but they wouldn't allow us any further than that. Rogoż knew that he was dying; he talked about it the whole way there. He was very religious. He was in some sort of religious state, but his piety was noble, philosophical. Just before disappearing from sight, he turned around and made the sign of the cross. That was his farewell to us. He died a few days later. When I returned to Poland, I looked for his family to give them his death certificate, which I had kept with me. I couldn't find any of them.

36 THE JEWISH WAR. RICHES BEHIND CURTAINS. GREECE IN CENTRAL ASIA. DROHOJOWSKI. INTERROGATION. HUNTERS. STALINGRAD.

WAT: High-level Soviet-Polish relations had started to deteriorate very badly. Of course, as I was able to detect from various signs, that deterioration at the top was part of Stalin's plan. He was simply becoming more sure of himself; the front had been stabilized one way or the other. This was before Stalingrad, but the people, the Russian people—just the Russians and the Jews—were certain of ultimate victory. All the minorities, however, with the sole exception of the Jews—I stress this because I had contact with a great many different nationalities—were waiting for the Germans to arrive. That was true everywhere, even in Kazakhstan. But not the Jews.

This was also a Jewish war, not only a Russian one. In that sense the Jews' patriotism was incredibly dynamic. Aside from the masses of poor Jews who lived the same as they had in tsarist times and who had poured in from Lithuania, Byelorussia, and the Ukraine and filled all the little towns, settlements, and railroad stations, all the Jews who were active people, especially industrial engineers, performed miracles. They worked twenty hours a day, and the rapid transfer of industry into the depths of Russia, to Asia, was, to a tremendous extent, owing to Jewish organizational ability and dynamism.

Perhaps this has already been written about, but it also might be worth mentioning here that Stalin greatly encouraged the Jews to organize, to write to America. Nearly every Jewish family in Russia had an uncle, a cousin, a distant cousin in America; during the war they were encouraged to correspond with them, to track down those relatives, and, as you know, a committee was set up, headed by Mikhoels and Ehrenburg.

But Stalin's anti-Semitism made itself felt immediately after the war. I don't think that Stalin was an anti-Semite by nature; his anti-Semitism is very easy to explain. The Jews end the Seder with the words "'lshanna hab'a be Yerushalaim." For two thousand years or more the Jews had been ending the Seder by saying, "Next year we will meet in Jerusalem." That had become an abstraction and no source of any actual feel-

344

ing. The Zionists changed that. But in the mind of every Soviet Jew, without exception, from top to bottom, the true Jerusalem, the Jerusalem of the heart, the land of milk and honey, was America—and without question Stalin was aware of that. That was the source of his anti-Semitic tack, which was deliberate and, from his point of view, fully justified politically. And so relations with Poland had begun to deteriorate, and that was most likely part of the plan.

When I left prison in Saratov, Ważyk was the head of the local radio station, and Wanda Wasilewska was there too. And they were already thinking about forming Poland's future government. And as I've already mentioned, in Lubyanka they were already studying social relations in Poland, while Poland was occupied by the Germans. They were already thinking about means of influencing Polish society through the use of Polish writers. And so obviously it was necessary to break with the London government, with the Polish émigrés in London. That was done in stages, and done very coldly. But the Poles provided enormous pretexts.

What was going on in Alma-Ata? One fact is enough: suddenly, there was an influx of real riches, the greatest riches that could exist for Soviet citizens at that time. And not only the Poles, but the Polish Jews behaved arrogantly and treated Soviet people as subhuman. It was unintentional, and it was done even by very decent, refined, subtle people. I knew one extremely refined person, and when I saw him in the company of Soviet citizens, I sensed that for him any Soviet citizen whatsoever was subhuman. The English feel that way too, but they express it differently. I once spent a month in a pension with a worthy old English admiral who blushed when speaking with me. It took me a month to realize that every day he made an enormous effort to keep me from sensing his awareness of belonging to a higher race. The Poles and the Polish Jews did not have that gift for simulation; with them it hit you right in the eyes.

It was even worse in the army. The army had its points. First in Buzuluk and later on in Yangi-Yul, someone was always coming from the army or leaving for the army. Everyone advised me not to try to join the army. I found out that Broniewski was in the army, in the south, probably Ashkhabad, and had gotten someone in. I wrote him a letter saying, "Władek, get us in too, because we'll die here when the army leaves." I foresaw that the delegations and everything else would be eliminated. By then everything was bad. He answered, "You'd be very unhappy in the army. The atmosphere isn't good. You better not come!"

Relations at the top were deteriorating. The press was already saying that the Polish delegations engaged in espionage. Various arrangements for the Polish delegations and the consulates, which were made when Poland and the USSR became allies, took so long that by the time they reached us in Alma-Ata, the top wanted to wage war against us and destroy us. And so there were two sets of instructions in the works at the same time. The latest one was hostile, but still those other instructions from the top also had to be respected.

We were switched to the highest diplomatic corps rations, equal to that of a high party official, higher than that of the most important writers—as high as the highest party and state officials. The rations were issued in a completely disgraceful way, like a slap on the face. There was a *univermag*, a department store, on Red Army Street. People stood in line through the night in front of that *univermag* to get some rotten tomatoes in the morning, some tomato paste or rotten sweet potatoes that cattle wouldn't eat. And in very small quantities too. In back of the store, there was one scrawny policeman—no force was needed. You entered the warehouse through the back; they had everything there behind the curtains. Enormous quantities. First class Caucasian wines, hams, sausages, white French rolls, and sometimes caviar. Cheeses, butter. Everything, everything. So much that I didn't even have enough money to buy a full ration. Later on I received some additional money from the embassy.

We had already moved from Red Army Street by then and had found a room on a lovely boulder-strewn, moss-covered street with a Russian family, the Kolgomorovs. The grandmother was straight out of Pushkin—the nurse Pushkin's Tatyana opens her heart to. The grandmother was all kindness, all heart. She treated her tenants—we were the only ones at the time—like her own children. Her daughter was a wonderful woman, wise, tough, intelligent, fair, kind, human. She had all the best qualities of Russian women, the best Russian intellectual upbringing. She was a secretary at the Writers' Union in Alma-Ata. (I want to add that the Writers' Union in Alma-Ata was unusually liberal during the war. The unusually liberal atmosphere may have prevailed there because of the liberal attitude toward Kazakhs.) Her husband was in a camp. It was when we were living there that word came that he was alive but he did not have the right to correspond. He had been in since 1937.

Her son Yuri was a year older than Andrzej. It made me very happy that Andrzej became great friends with Yuri, who was an extremely well brought up boy. And a Komsomolets. It turns out that there were pure, very well brought up, intelligent boys even in the Komsomol. Yuri and Andrzej read like mad. There were some old books there, including a tattered copy of *The Count of Monte Cristo*. The boys would write each other letters from one room to another: "Dear Count," "Dear Marquis"—in Alma-Ata, during the war!

Ola would bring the food home from the *univermag*. I didn't go; the wife gets all the dirty work. It was terribly hard for me to walk there. I went a few times with Ola, but it was too much. It was difficult for me to walk in Alma-Ata; the altitude was too great for me. And it was summer then too, sweltering heat, a blazing sun, like the hottest days in Oakland. And the light was blinding as it was in Oakland. It blinded me; it hurt my eyes. Ola would go with Andrzej, or quite often with Yuri, because those were large amounts of food. First they went to the delegation, where the food was divided up, on certain set days of the week. Then we shared our rations again with the Kolgomorovs. Excellent flour, kasha. The grandmother was an excellent cook, and we set up housekeeping along with them.

There was a small cottage in the courtyard with a farmyard around it, and there was another house, a small one with a colonnade, the home of a Kazakh *akyn*, a folk poet who sang his poems while accompanying himself. There was an entire organization of *akyns* who were given support during the war. Homers. An organization of Homers. They held their own congresses. I never attended one, but Shklovsky told me some interesting things about a congress of *akyns*. They played an instrument that was supposedly a direct descendant of the Greek zither. I must tell you that in those parts of Central Asia, people have a genuine memory of Greece. It wasn't from the Renaissance. In fact, Europe got its memory of Greece from Central Asia; that part of Central Asia had always preserved the memory of Greece.

Relatively close to Alma-Ata, in Isykul, there were the ruins of a monastery from the time of the founding of the Jacobite sect, in a beautiful spot on the far side of a lake. And supposedly there were still Jacobites there even in Soviet times. But they must have been Monophysites, Mongolian Monophysites. Cities had flowered there at one point, before the invasion of the Mongols, the Huns. A few remained—Kokand, Samarkand—but in Alma-Ata province the desert had covered them with sand. But there were still some traces of them.

Aristotle was so popular that when I was in Molotovobad and went into a tea house, the only old man who spoke with me a little in Russian spoke about Aristotle. And about Alexander the Great. They're still heroes there, an unbroken line, not like in Europe. Of course, if I'd had more strength and energy, I'd have gathered some material on all that. I did gather a little, but my notes got lost somewhere along the way. There was a great deal of shamanism in their customs; the ones I recall were definitely shamanistic, pre-Islamic, but there were Greek elements too—from Greek Asia, that is.

My neighbor the *akyn* played his zither. I listened to him often. He didn't talk with me. He had a daughter, very good-looking, tall, well built. She talked with Ola, but not with me. The *akyn* didn't talk to me; he'd just smile at me. I'd greet him when we passed. The Soviet authorities had heaped the *akyns* with honors. This one lived very well, like a lord. He had a servant, a cook. And he wasn't even one of the great *akyns*.

One day Drohojowski arrived from Kuibyshev. He had come from the outside world, from London. He brought instructions to Kuibyshev, where he spent a short time. He'd been appointed ambassador to China by the Polish government in London. He was on his way to China. His plane stopped in Alma-Ata, where he spent two or three days. Did you ever see Drohojowski? A ladies' man, an elegant gentleman, a raconteur, a man of the world, a red count—he was a red count even before the war. He had carried out a radical agricultural reform on his own estate. He was dressed discreetly, his clothes beautifully tailored, excellent wool.

Drohojowski had arrived with two adjutants. I bring him in here because I just said that I was one of the most elegant men in Alma-Ata. One of his adjutants was wearing shorts. It was summertime. People ran after him and said, "Look, they ran short of material for pants." They found that very funny; they weren't scandalized but thought it was funny.

The delegation was no longer located in the hotel. It was now a distance away, on some other mossy, boulder-strewn street. Drohojowski questioned people closely about their thoughts on the situation. But he was careful about it; maybe microphones were being used by then, at least in Kuibyshev, and so he took people out for walks—it was a fine city for walking. He spent an entire afternoon walking with me, asking me what I thought.

I still believed—this was part of my madness dating back to Saratov—that this was the Apocalypse, Gog and Magog, that Russia would fall. That was still before Stalingrad. That was folly, because I had also seen proof that the panic at Lubyanka that had so impressed me—the documents tossed into trucks, meaning the backbone had been broken—had been mended. Everything was back in perfect order. All the documents were back in place. Then the wandering of nations was halted; it was simply no longer possible to travel without NKVD permission. And so that Russia of the train stations suddenly had to change; people had to settle down. In that place, at that time, there was no air of oppression. What you felt was iron order.

Drohojowski explained to me that I was mistaken, that Russia would be victorious. He hadn't the slightest doubt that Russia would win the war. He even told me certain confidential information he had from London about Russia's chances of victory.

The situation had grown much worse for us at that time. We kept on receiving rations up to the end, but three people from the delegation were arrested—Jan Wolski, Lisiewicz, and Meller. Meller was in charge of all the warehouses. We had to inform the embassy that people had been arrested. We sent three telegrams a day to Kuibyshev, but maybe none of them arrived.

The NKVD began issuing summonses. My last summons had been in Saratov, and I'd had no contact with the NKVD since then. But then the NKVD began summoning me. They called me in during the day. The corridor was clean; it wasn't a prison any more but an investigative agency, a ministry. The corridors resembled those in Lubyanka; evidently they'd been built on the Lubyanka model. Nearly identical, just smaller. I'd walk down those corridors with my heart in my throat, a trembling in my stomach. I'd come to the door and cross myself. And then I'd go in, hard as a rock, all the cowardice gone. I would tremble beforehand; I would tremble in the corridor, not literally but inwardly. I was quivering; I couldn't collect my thoughts. Fear, panic. But as soon as I pressed the latch and opened the door, I was a different man, with no trace of fear. That happened again and again. Always the same fear—not that I didn't have any fear afterward. The fear was always the same, and sometimes I had the impression that it might even have increased. In any case, it was more highly developed. Various waves of fear. Maybe they depended on my physiological state, but there was always fear. And then the door, the handle, the sign of the cross, and that was the end of it. It disappeared completely, not even the slightest trace. Magic.

A rather high-level official questioned me first about Drohojowski, what sort of espionage information he'd been gathering. No, that wasn't it—it was what information I had provided for him. I wasn't being accused of anything but that's what he asked me. I said that Drohojowski hadn't asked about anything. For a while I kept my answers cold but not pointed; that was the NKVD after all. On the contrary, I said, without going into details, Drohojowski had told me that a Russian victory was absolutely certain and so on. I didn't make up anything; I just mentioned the positive things he'd said. For example, he'd said that things were in fantastic order. He had even pointed to Alma-Ata: "Look how clean the city is. There's nothing to eat, but that's because it's wartime." He had replied with Soviet propaganda when I told him about that shocking warehouse and the people standing in line through the night.

On Red Army Street there were kiosks selling vodka every hundred meters. There was no bread, but vodka was always available everywhere. But at the NKVD I spoke of Drohojowski's positive remarks. I didn't make up anything; I spoke accurately. No, no, no. I stuck to my guns. They were very polite.

Then I was called in again. We went over the exact same ground. The investigator didn't write anything down; no record was kept. The tone may have changed a little. No, not even that.

The third time my investigator brought me to an office, another very nicely furnished one. At that time we were doing an inventory of the main warehouse. There had been thefts—there was that gang—and there were only the two of us. I took on the job. In the morning I'd been to the warehouse; I lived nearby. We'd closed the warehouse for a few days, and the caretaker and I counted shoes, underpants. And so I was brought to that office. There was a man sitting there, well dressed, aloof-looking. And a very dry voice. The one who'd brought me there reported that I refused to give any information and made up absurd stories. The man at the desk took a critical look at me and said, "Aren't you ashamed of yourself, you an intellectual, a writer. There's a war on and the future of the whole world, not just the Soviet Union, depends on it. All human history depends on it. It's hanging in the balance now; these are the key weeks, months. And what is Aleksander Wat doing? An intellectual, an educated man who speaks several languages, a poet, a novelist, a critic, and at the moment when all world history hangs in the balance, he's counting underpants!" As you see, he was no fool. But by then I was a clam when it came to the NKVD, and that didn't sway me. I listened to him with great pleasure as if I were listening to some intelligent person in the Café Ziemiańska. Inwardly, I acknowledged that he was right, but that didn't change the way I acted one iota. That was the enemy. *Timeo Danaos et dona ferentes* had been my motto since Saratov, my motto for Soviet Russia.

MILOSZ: What did he want from you? What did he want you to do?

WAT: They wanted to make me a professor of Western literature, and all the rest came clear in Ili. He wanted me to help him. For example, Drohojowski was an English spy; they had information. But I did not want to help Russia, which was making such sacrifices for Poland, for mankind, for history, Russia, which had shed so much blood and was in such a critical situation. They wanted accusations against Drohojowski. That was already after Stalingrad when the plans laid a long time before could gradually be carried out.

He emphasized that he wasn't concerned about the Polish government in London; he spoke of it with enormous scorn. But Drohojowski was an important agent, a specialist in China and the Far East, an important intelligence agent. They had very precise information on that. Drohojowski was stopping in Xinjiang on the way, but that wasn't true. It wasn't just a stopover; he was staying longer to set up an espionage post there. And, as you know, Xinjiang was an old Russian sphere of influence. They already had all the Mandarins in their pay. And Drohojowski was supposed to set up an anti-Soviet Intelligence Service post.

After the war Drohojowski was an ambassador for People's Poland, and I met him once in the Hotel Bristol when he was in the country for a short time. We were very glad to see each other, and I told him what had been said about him at the NKVD in Alma-Ata and the pressure that had been exerted on me by that Jew who was actually the NKVD minister in Alma-Ata, for Kazakhstan, during the war. I told Drohojowski everything in the greatest detail. He accepted it as completely normal and replied, "You know, now those things don't matter any more."

And so we were living in fear, under pressure. Now I want to go back a bit and say something about my friends, the Soviet writers. When I was already well established at the delegation, receptions were held every so often for Soviet intellectuals, especially actors; singers even performed. Practically no one came to the final reception. Orlova strayed in and wanted to leave immediately. Not Orlova the film star, but a great actress from Stanislavsky's theater—an older woman, but she still had great beauty and elegance. A prewar actress. She was unhappy when she saw that nobody else had come. Before, even officials, party people, used to come. She lived alone and evidently there hadn't been time to warn her. So she came, sat for a short while, blushing deeply, frantic. She sat for a respectable time and then she left. I saw that was a sign that relations with the Soviet intellectuals absolutely had to be broken off, that it was becoming dangerous for them.

When Tatyana Alekseevna, who's now Paustovsky's wife and at that time was married to Shnaider, the one with tuberculosis, visited Ola, Ola told her not to come by anymore and that she wouldn't be visiting her either because the arrests had started. One time, when it was no longer possible to keep up relations, Shklovsky came to see me at my apartment to say that their chief, the head of all Soviet cinematography, an important party official—Bolshakov, I think his name was— was in the hospital suffering from typhus, and they had no English sulfa tablets. By chance, did we have any at the delegation? We did. I told Wiącek, because they needed a rather large amount. Wiącek agreed and I gave the tablets to Shklovsky, which saved Bolshakov's life. Shklovsky was still being cordial and I was too; nothing had changed between us, but on the street I'd pretend not to see him.

One other person came, a charming man, Feyerman, who wrote books about hunting for children. He told me wonderful stories about the forests and hunting! It turned out that hunting, nature, was the only escape from Stalinism for decent people in the Soviet Union. Somehow or other that loophole was provided, encouraged, because folklore was involved. They'd bring back journalistic accounts of customs and conditions. There was support for that. They were given guns, ammunition, the necessary equipment, and they'd travel far, far, to Siberia, the north.

My relations with the Russian writers had been broken off. But every once in a while we'd run into each other in the lobby and say hello. Besides, it would have been foolish to pretend, considering the informers. Just a few words, but said so that others could hear.

Did anything else memorable happen? I said that in the evening people listened to the bulletins about the war. I remember Stalingrad, the communiqué about the decisive victory at Stalingrad, the German army encircled, Paulus's surrender. And you know, even Shnaider who did not believe in my prophecies but simply took my word that the Stalinist system would be overthrown and demolished, Shnaider who hated Stalin, had tears in his eyes, and he said that Stalin was "great, the savior of Russia!" That was true of everyone. Lenin had not been that popular; no one in Russia ever had the popularity that Stalin had in that brief period between Stalingrad and the end of war. I'm talking about Russians, not minorities. But probably this also applied in part to the minorities. Not the Ukrainians of course; that I know, because I was in contact with Ukrainians again in Ili, but among Russians and Jews there was love for Stalin. That was truly a period of love for Stalin. And suddenly all of Stalin's bestial features were smoothed over in people's minds, disappeared, just as my cowardice had disappeared; it was that same sort of magic. Stalingrad changed everything. Paustovsky worshiped Stalin then too. Everyone did, everyone, no exceptions. Shklovsky shed his customary tears. Everyone was there. It was hysteria, but the hysteria of people melting in patriotic emotion, incredibly fervent. I have to admit that I shared in it too. In spite of my hostility to that world, to Stalin. Obviously, I never worshiped Stalin for a single second. For me, Stalin remained what he had been. But Stalin, the defeat of the Germans! That was a staggering evening. We were all staggered.

37 WORKING WITH WESELY. SHNAIDER'S DEATH AND ZOSHCHENKO'S DECLINE. ELEGANCE AND THOMAS À KEMPIS IN CENTRAL ASIA. DEPARTURE FOR ILI. AMONG POLISH JEWS.

WAT: Things were calm for a time, a short time. And then I was summoned in again, this time to someone else entirely, one of those brutal NKVD men. An athletic type. He hinted that I would be beaten, but I must say that I was never beaten. One time they leaped around me, putting their fists in my face, but I was never struck. After taking down my personal data, he ordered me to remove my tie and shoelaces. He was treating me as if I were already under arrest, hinting or saying straight out—I don't remember now—that everything depended on the evidence I gave now: either I'd stay in there or I'd be let out. He gave me three small sheets of paper and said that he'd go out, leave me alone for an hour, and that during that time I should write about the anti-Soviet activities of my colleagues at the delegation. That was all; he didn't exert any pressure on me. He left, he locked the door, and I was alone with the paper.

I set to work at once and covered one sheet. In brief terms I wrote that my colleagues had always displayed utter loyalty toward the Soviet authorities and system, and that neither in word nor in deed had they overstepped the rules laid down for international diplomatic relations—more or less that sort of thing and without going into personal detail. That was one page's worth.

The key ground in the lock and the NKVD man was there. I grabbed the sheet of paper, balled it up, and swallowed it, suddenly realizing that everything was dangerous, even a sheet of paper like that one. He didn't say anything and slammed the door as he left. I sat there maybe two hours without my tie and shoelaces. He came back after two hours, a guard gave me my tie and shoelaces, and I left without anyone's bothering me.

I was on very good terms with the embassy. Parnicki worked in the embassy, and he saw to it that I received an allowance of five hundred rubles a month in addition to my salary, which wasn't large. He wrote me very sensitive letters and in general behaved extremely well, espe-

353

cially after he received the obituary I wrote for Rogoż. Rogoż had died in April and I wrote the obituary in May.

I thought I should use the obituary to cut myself off from the old Wat, from my past, in a way that would break all ties. I wrote in Catholic terms and spoke of my conversations with Rogoż in Alma-Ata, in the lobby of an elegant hotel at the foot of the Tian Shan, surrounded by movie stars. I said that we were eyewitnesses to a confusion of tongues, an apocalyptic shattering of cultures and civilizations that had wished to rule solely by the laws of human reason. We had spoken about daily bread, home, tradition, the simplest things, hallowed by centuries. We used the simplest words, catholic words, in the sense of universal, and we understood each other like two people witnessing a simple event who describe it to each other as it occurs. Then I described our trip with the droshky driver, how the Polish doctor and I had accompanied Rogoż to the infectious hospital. I wrote: "The drunken wagon driver with a flat, Mongol face who was pulled besotted out of a bar . . ." I mention this because later on, during the passport process, Colonel Omarkhadzhev shouted at me, "So you don't like Mongolian faces!" Actually, I had always liked Mongolian faces.

Alma-Ata had lost its most interesting element, meaning the Russians, the ones from Central Russia, Moscow. There were only Russians from Leningrad and some Ukrainians left. I've already said that my relations with the writers had become very loose, spotty, but by then they had all left, with the exception of Mikhail Yakovlevich Shnaider. His wife, now Paustovsky's wife, was with him for a while. I would visit them from time to time. He was very good about dying. He died with enormous dignity, but he didn't want to die; he was angry at having to die, acrimonious. He must have given his wife, Tatyana, a lot of trouble. It would be hard to imagine a greater contrast than the one between that incredibly juicy woman, that Russian beauty, an earth-mother type, you know, born to have children and pleasure, and him dying of tuberculosis, and angry and acrimonious. She left him. I don't know what went on between them. Someone there took care of him till the end.

Aha, there was another Russian there too, Zoshchenko. He was there quite a long time. But he and I never became any closer. We saw each other from time to time; he was terribly despondent. Evidently the machine had already been turned against him; maybe he was already being summoned in. He bore himself very badly; he was a rag of a man by that time. He was trying to return to favor; he was writing, but none of it was any good. He died in great poverty, forgotten by everyone. His wife probably left him, too, because only three men followed his coffin to the cemetery. One of them was a writer—I don't know who—and he made a speech at the cemetery. A very sad end. But he was already completely destroyed before then.

As I told you, I was very elegant in Alma-Ata, very stylish. I wore that stunning cheviot wool suit, olive gray with a light blue weave; it was used, but in excellent condition. A tie with smart, broad stripes, a thick Basque beret, and a pair of low English shoes, old but very good. Where did I get that taste for elegance from? In all my life I never had the taste for elegance I had then. Of course, it felt wonderful after prison and those rags, but that wasn't the reason. And it wasn't that I felt myself to be a representative or an ambassador of any sort. It was something less than that and something more. I felt that I was the embodiment of the West and Christianity. I walked around that barbarous land, that world of poverty and Eastern barbarity thousands of years old, and I was an embodiment, an image, an imago. The imago of the West, the entire past history of the West and Christianity.

I was eating my fill at that time. My mental hunger was gone by then, and I was able to look at people eating. My hunger was completely satisfied. There were hungry people around me. I would see hungry people in the line in front of the *univermag* on my way to get all those delicacies from in back. I saw them standing in line for twenty hours for rotten tomatoes.

I was a Christian. The only book I had was a copy of St. Thomas à Kempis. I got it at the delegation, and I knew that it was going to be my book, my Bible. I was constantly reading it. I not only read it, but I also used it as an oracle. I would close my eyes, open the book at random, put my finger on the page, and take whatever I touched as advice.

I did that again at the decisive moment when everything hung in the balance and I had to choose between accepting a Soviet passport and making some sort of life for us, or refusing it and condemning me and my family to death. I opened St. Thomas à Kempis and what I came on was: "It is hard for thee to kick against the pricks." And who was meant by that? Stalin or God? Both of them. It was difficult to interpret. But at that time I thought that God was more real than Stalin and took this to mean, do not lash out against "pricks" from God, against what God commanded me to do.

At that time, however, I had been inspired with the spirit of the Crusades, perhaps through Thomas à Kempis. I was reading Thomas à Kempis surrounded by poverty and hunger. Naturally, I was aware of that before then and afterward too, but at that time I was eating my full, eating well. Cheese, sausage, ham. And all around me were hungry people. And so what was that? Hypocrisy? I don't think so now; that wasn't hypocrisy. Was it the same attitude most Poles had toward the Russian people: we couldn't care less about those hostile sub-humans? I don't suppose it was that either. Perhaps there was a bit of hypocrisy and a bit of that other feeling, but they weren't fundamental. I think that my cheviot suit, the ham I was eating among the hungry and ragged, and my elegance were a desire to stand apart from all that, to keep myself outside that world where everything was turned into rags—clothes, faces, people. A process that turned things to rags—Stalinism generated a process that turned everything to rags. And that was also a reason for my elegance. At that time I examined my conscience scrupulously; every day I took very strict stock of my conscience, and even now I assume that if a man with a conscience went to India, he'd feel the same thing I did. Meaning that he was in the world of the doomed and that neither he nor anyone or anything could help them.

Four or five months later I was herded from the Second Section to the Third Section down those same streets where probably some of the same people had noticed me before as something from the West. I wasn't wearing my cheviot now; it had been sold for grain in Ili. I was in my old Warsaw clothes that I had worn in all those prisons, but I still had my good Basque beret. I was herded in broad daylight very ostentatiously from the Second Section to the Third, which was far away, at the very outskirts. I was in a group of thirty thieves, the worst kinds of *urks*, and young prostitutes. I was the only adult, the only old one. I walked stiff as a ramrod. I had never walked with pride like that before, my head held high. Poor Ola ran after us. We were driven at a quick pace, police in front and back. A policeman she knew in Ili had informed her that I was being transferred that day to the Third Section, where she also had spent a day and where the Poles were tortured terribly to force them to accept Soviet passports.

Ola had found out and came to Alma-Ata with a bag of various things and a blanket. She ran down the sidewalk after us and kept trying to give me the things, but the policeman kept driving her off. She followed me all the way to the gate, the large wooden gate of the Third Section, and then for the last time I saw a face without a face. Ola's face. People were tortured in there and she was afraid I'd be tortured too. And so four months later all that elegance appeared in a different light.

But, before all that—I don't recall if it was in December 1942 or January 1943—I received a summons. There was a gloomy-looking man at a desk, in civilian clothes but the policeman type. He said that we were to leave Alma-Ata within the next forty-eight hours; we could chose any district we liked, but it had to be in Alma-Ata province.

I was very sick at the time, and the doctors gave me certificates that I had swollen legs and that my heart was giving me a lot of trouble. On the whole, my health was ruined by the time I came out of Saratov. I had been eating plenty, but there were serious aftereffects from the severe vitamin deficiency. My teeth, for example. All my life, the one beautiful thing I had was my teeth. I had exceptional teeth, so much so that when I was fourteen or fifteen, Ważyk's sister, a dentist, was supposed to extract one of my teeth and broke into tears because she couldn't pull it out. And ever since that NKVD man struck me when we were arrested in Lwów, I had a loose tooth that I used to play with, turning it at a right angle. That went on from 1939 to 1950; it was only in 1950 that I let it be removed. That's how strong my teeth were. But in Alma-Ata all my teeth were loose; I had been destroyed by vitamin deficiency. Scurvy, vitamin deficiency, and malnutrition.

And so I had certificates from doctors, and those were Soviet doctors who had done a lot to save me. I refused to leave Alma-Ata, saying the only place I could go was Samarkand. Ola had a brother-in-law in Samarkand, who worked in the delegation there. And so I said if I'm given a pass for Samarkand, fine, and if not, I wasn't budging from Alma-Ata. I refused point-blank. The man at the desk answered that I could choose three locations in the province and that I had to be out of Alma-Ata within forty-eight hours. I kept citing my pseudo-diplomatic status and my poor health.

And every day at around two or three in the afternoon, an old policeman would come to our place, a fatherly guy in a rag-cotton uniform, around fifty or so, very nice, a kindly man, a Russian, and he'd ask if I was leaving tomorrow, when I was planning to leave. We'd have him for lunch every day and he prayed that I wouldn't leave because he was getting one good meal a day with us. We still had a good stock of supplies. That went on for ten days, but I knew it had to end.

I wasn't being summoned in; the policeman would just come and remind me that I had to leave the city within forty-eight hours. I dragged it out for ten or eleven days. In the meantime I was sending telegrams to Kuibyshev, but there was practically nothing happening there. I didn't expect any reply, and I didn't receive any.

And so there was the question of where to move. There were three possibilities, places where there were delegates with whom I was on good terms: Kaskalen, Talgar, and Ili. Both Kaskalen and Talgar were beautiful places, very beautiful, but they were high in the mountains. Around three-quarters of a mile high, with wonderful streams. It was always green there and the people were very nice. But they were out of the question for me; I knew I couldn't take it there, so I had to choose Ili, a place I knew because I had set up a school there at one point. A terrible place. Dirty sand, overgrown with some kind of dirty weeds, wretched little buildings, Kazakh huts made of clay and dung. A long village too, with three trees, and at the end, by the river, a very decent little building that was the library, club, and hospital for the men in the steamship trade.

At one time Ili had been a principal point in the shipping trade with China, with the province of Xinjiang; cargo was transshipped there. In my time there was no longer any traffic between Ili and Xinjiang; relations had been broken off. Once some of our people, Poles, friends of ours, committed a major break-in and found wool cloth, Parisian silk, famous perfumes, excellent chocolate. It turned out that in the midst of all that Russian poverty, there were still factories working to export to areas like Xinjiang where the Chinese authorities had been paid off.

But it was a terribly dreary place. Nothing but sand. A few wooden houses. It was a long way from the station to the village; then you had to cross a large marketplace where they sold rusty pieces of metal, keys, pots with holes in them. There was a photographer's booth, a watchmaker's booth, and a booth where vodka was sold. The population was Kazakh, Ukrainian, and a few Jews from the Ukraine who held positions in the local industrial enterprises; they were managers, bookkeepers. And there were also some bandits, exiles, but with faces like bandits. A dreary place, and a hungry one for the Poles. There were scarcely any Poles, just Jews, and Jews from Galicia at that. Shoemakers, tailors, lawyers, small merchants.

And it was there I was to begin a new cycle in my life. My three and a half years in Ili, interrupted by a few months in prison. Those years are like a world unto itself. I lived a Soviet life in Ili, the life of the Soviet underclass, the proletariat. I lived the life of the Soviet working masses for three and a half years.

It was truly a desert; Thomas à Kempis had come true word for word. It was the Middle Ages there. People lived on roots, sweet potatoes, poisonous plants; there was constant hunger. People lived surrounded by cows and camels. The lodgings were utterly biblical. A world of criminals. An epic time in my life, the one epic time in my life. Everyone has some short period of heroism in life; millions of people did during that war. And I had my time of heroism there. The main thing was—I can see that now—that the good and the bad seeds from that night in Saratov flowered there in Ili.

I was in a strange situation. A Jewish settlement. There were only two or three Polish families, who kept to themselves and didn't associate with the Jews. Those were small-town Jews. One of them, a man by the name of Moll, was an Orthodox Jew, a very good and very decent person, a merchant from Düsseldorf. When the Polish Jews were thrown out of Germany, he made his way to Poland, as far as Lwów, and then was exiled with his wife and little son. He was a German merchant, used to German customs, German business. He probably had some sort of clothing store there. He was quick at learning how to do business in the Soviet Union. He was brilliant at it, and he helped me a great deal later on. Always active, always vibrant, always with a hundred deals and projects in the works, he did very well for himself. A very good person. There were Hasids there, all from Orthodox families. A few families of lawyers from Galicia, rather religious too. With the exception of two families, those were all religious Jews.

And then I came. Everyone knew—and I never hid being a Jew—that first I was a representative of the majesty of the Polish Republic, because Wesely and I were London's only representatives in Kazakhstan, and, second, that I wore a brown Bakelite cross on a string around my neck. The delegation had distributed crosses.

Later on, when I had typhus, the brown faded and the Bakelite turned yellowish, like ivory. I still had that cross when I returned to Poland; then it got lost, but I did keep hold of an icon of the Virgin of Ostrobrama. I was very devout, and we took an oath to make a pilgrimage on foot to Wilno, to the Ostrobrama Virgin, when we returned to Poland. And when I was sick—in Ili I suffered constantly from typhus, dysentery, pneumonia—the icon of the Virgin of Ostrobrama was on the wall over my bed. And I have it to this day.

And so my situation was a very strange one. In fact, according to the letter and the spirit [of Jewish law] and to the customs that still prevailed in the Jewish ghettos in the twentieth century, I was subject to death by stoning. But I don't know what it was, perhaps a feeling for the majesty of the Polish Republic . . . a twofold feeling, each absolutely the same in intensity. One feeling was pedestrian, practical: fear. They wanted to be able to return to Poland. The other feeling was an incredibly ardent Polish patriotism.

The greatest Polish patriot in that settlement that numbered five hundred Jews was Kamer, a shoemaker from Radom, who had two sons, excellent shoemakers too. He was something out of a ballad, that Kamer. An old communist with an excellent political mind. His sons were old communists too; they had been through the Komsomol, been through prison. Kamer was a shoemaker, and so he was very well off. I started studying shoemaking with him, but I didn't have the strength for it. It turns out you need some strength in your hand even to make sandals. That was the only thing made there. The soles were pieces of car tires, and there was cloth on top; and when I started to learn, I had no strength left in my hands. Kamer was a passionate Polish patriot. His nostalgia for Poland, his longing for Radom, for Polish life, even with its anti-Semites, was so powerful and genuine that now when I think about it coolly, it's beyond my powers to imagine. But it was real.

And so perhaps those Jews granted me religious amnesty because I was a representative of the Polish government, the old Poland. I can't fathom why I was so well received right from the start. And it stayed that way to the end.

If it hadn't been for that, we would have died a hundred times; we didn't have the slightest business sense. The one time I tried to do some business, I ended up rather on the losing side. Neither Ola nor I was in the least suited to business. It's a terrible thing when a Jew has no skill in business. Trade and speculation were the only possible way of surviving those three and a half years; and so if it hadn't been for the kindness, the warmth that those people, those Orthodox Jews, showed to me, a *meches*, a converted Jew . . . They didn't know whether I had been baptized or not. I never talked about it. But I wore a cross. Later on, when we were in revolt [against accepting Soviet passports] and were under arrest together, it was so hot that I took off my shirt. And yet I was the leader of those pious Jews in prison, me, a Jew with a cross around his neck.

EPILOGUE: A SELECTION FROM THE MEMOIRS OF
PAULINA WAT

My husband, Aleksander Wat, did not have time to describe the dramatic campaign to force Poles to accept Soviet citizenship, so-called passportization.

That campaign was carried out by the NKVD in March 1943 in Kazakhstan and wherever there were groups of Poles who had been released from prisons, camps, and places of exile.

My husband attached great significance to this campaign that was yet another act of violence against Polish deportees. It gave us, unfree people, some leverage to do battle, a battle that Aleksander entered no longer a prisoner as he had been until recently, but a man who had been "freed"—Wat had more than two years in Soviet prisons behind him, with all the suffering that entailed. This was not only a battle against "passportization" but a protest against everything that had to be opposed.

Those few months of battle in Ili where Wat played the role of instigator in the revolt of the Polish population were, in Wat's judgment, events of large measure in his wartime odyssey.

At the beginning of March 1943, disturbing word began to arrive from the Poles scattered throughout Kazakhstan that they had been forced to accept Soviet passports. Those reports grew more and more alarming—NKVD pressure was increasingly brutal, and there were cases of suicide. To accept a Soviet passport meant to see an end to what was probably your last hope of returning to Poland.

The passport process imposed by the NKVD in this period coincided with the official founding of the Union of Polish Patriots; my husband assumed that this had occurred "with the coordinated agreement of the Union's leaders." He wrote:

Compulsory passportization took place in March 1943 at the same time as the Union of Patriots was granted legal status. Its emissaries immediately took over the offices vacated by the delegates as well as the enormous stores of American aid. Passportization and the granting of legal status to the Union of Patriots occurred at the same time and were part of the same plan: to turn a million or a million and a half Poles into Soviet subjects while giving them hope of returning to Poland. The Union of Polish Patriots was founded to turn those million and a half Poles into Soviet subjects. All the Poles in the Union of Patriots along with those great patriots' entire army and officers' staff did, after all, enter Poland as Soviet citizens.

Our attitude toward the Union of Patriots was one of extreme mistrust from the very beginning, and for good reason.

Having assured himself that the reports on passportization were entirely genuine, my husband began organizing the Poles in our settlement to resist. First in private conversation, then at meetings, he presented people with the situation, but chiefly he roused their violated sense of dignity and their awareness of what submission would mean in this case.

With sorrow my husband recalled that "to their own great detriment and to my renewed imprisonment, they followed me when I incited them to rebel against the NKVD's brutal imposition of Soviet passports."

Apart from a few so-called intelligentsia, mostly simple people lived in our settlement; by trade they were shoemakers, tailors, small businessmen, mainly Jews from Galicia. There were many Jewish communists who, as Aleksander Wat wrote, "often had not even been in Soviet prisons. They had fled the Germans and, arrested at the border, had been deported to settlements in North Kazakhstan from which they returned in relatively good condition."

The first general meeting my husband organized was held at the home of Kamer the shoemaker. The Kamers were a family of Jewish communists from Radom. They made a decent living as shoemakers there in Ili. Kamer was a wonderful person, strong; he carried himself beautifully. In Poland he had read Marx and Rosa Luxemburg; a communist, he had raised his two sons in that spirit. His sons had already managed to do time in Polish prisons. It was at the Kamers' that our meetings were held, and he was one of the most fired up to do battle.

The first meeting was very stormy. Though there were very few "patriots," meaning members of the Union of Polish Patriots, in Ili, some people thought it madness to oppose the mighty NKVD, which would only speed our ruin. But most people understood the moral values involved.

Wat was of course aware that it wasn't paper but power that counts with the Soviet authorities. "And it was nearly certain that whether or not they released us had nothing to do with our possessing, or not possessing, Soviet citizenship. That's what common sense said. But something stronger than that in us commanded us to act in one definite way and no other."

362

One day the NKVD commission that was to force us to accept Soviet citizenship arrived in Ili. Several people in uniform, wearing their decorations. They were led by Colonel Omarkhadzhev, a splendid-looking man, handsome in a distinctly Kazakh way, who concerned himself in particular with my husband, knowing that he had played the role of mutineer in the Ili area.

The NKVD people were quartered in one of the few wooden houses with porches, very luxurious for Ili, which were reserved for just such guests. The police, who had been brought into Ili for the purpose, began to go around to the Poles designated by the NKVD and bring them in for interrogation.

Wat's instructions were that all those who were summoned should go at once and take along a bag packed with the things a person needs most in a camp. Drawing on his own prison experience, he also instructed people not to enter into any conversations, for those would always be turned against them; to answer the question, Would they accept a Soviet passport? with a brief no; and to reply to the question, Why not? with "because we are Polish citizens," no more than that.

People began to be summoned. First astounded, then enraged by the unexpected mass resistance, the NKVD men became increasingly brutal. Things reached a point where a woman with a child in arms was beaten, and when her husband, who was present, appealed to the constitution, he was clubbed on the head and told, "Here's the constitution for you!"

My husband's turn came. A Kazakh policeman, armed with a revolver, a sword at his side, appeared at our home in the late evening. Aleksander was prepared. We had to say good-bye without knowing whether it would be forever.

Forced to a quick march at gunpoint, Aleksander was taken down a side path to a small wooden house. He was received politely. Smiling too sweetly, Colonel Omarkhadzhev let him know that he was aware of who Aleksander was—"Aren't you a writer?"—and also that he knew a little something about Aleksander's past and his role as the editor of *The Literary Monthly*. All of a sudden, Omarkhadzhev asked, "If I'm not mistaken, weren't you a communist?" "A communist?" answered Aleksander in surprise. "Perhaps. But that was so long ago that I can't remember it now." That set the tone at once, and then came the question that had been expected from the start: "Will you accept the passport?"

After Aleksander's terse reply, the NKVD men grew excited and began shouting and pounding the table with their fists. It appeared they were going to beat him. But they didn't. All this lasted quite some time until, tired themselves, they took aside the policeman who had brought Aleksander there and gave him instructions. The policeman then prodded Aleksander to a small room whose sole furnishings consisted of a small table and a rickety little chair that was missing one leg. The policeman ordered Aleksander to sit on the chair, not to lean against the table, and to keep quiet. Time passed slowly; it was late at night by then. As his tension eased, Aleksander was overcome by fatigue and sleepiness. But at the slightest movement of the wobbly chair, the Kazakh would dart over and, at a shout, remind Aleksander of the orders. The night hours passed in that struggle to keep his balance and to overcome his ever greater need for sleep.

But then at some point between the end of night and daybreak, wearied by his vigil and perhaps also by the monotony of his task, the policeman suddenly said in a tone of rebuke, "What a fool you are! What difference does the passport make to you? It's a piece of paper. There are Kazakh bards who have a good life here, and do you know why? Because they understood an important thing: 'Stalin makes the rules, and you have to obey them.' They understood that. They write songs about Stalin and they're rolling in clover. And you? They'll send you to a camp where weaklings like you drop dead in no time."

And so the policeman from the Tian Shan mountain area proved a philosopher. Now, having unburdened himself, the policeman became less strict and even allowed his prisoner to lean against the table and doze off for a while.

The NKVD renewed their attack in the early morning. In the end, they ordered Aleksander taken to jail. In the process, a comic incident caused the whole crew of them to burst out laughing. My husband automatically handed his sack to the policeman to carry. Enormously amused, the NKVD shouted, "Bourgeois to his bones!"

Kamer and his two sons were already in jail along with a dozen or so other Poles. Each of them was summoned in a few more times and then, after ten days, they were all transported to Alma-Ata, where they disappeared from sight.

I can't remember now exactly how many Poles there were in Ili, but it must have been around four hundred. People were still being summoned constantly, but the arrests had stopped. People were sent home after refusing the passport. We were well aware, however, that this wasn't the end of the matter. And, indeed, one day all those who had refused were arrested. I have a clear memory of the moment when they came for me and I had to say good-bye to my son, who was eleven years old at the time.

We were assembled in the marketplace in Ili that had been cleared for that purpose—about a hundred and thirty men and women, mostly Jews, including a group of timid old religious people, who bore the special brunt of the guards' anger en route. Close by, standing in a dense group, were the people who had accepted the passport. But we were all alike in misfortune. I looked over at my son, who was about to approach me, when one of the guards drove him away using the flat of his sword. All the same, Andrzej ran after me toward the train station, trying to hand me a small bag of food. Later on, he told me that not far from the station, the policeman had grabbed him again, dragged him to the police room at the train station, ordered him to crawl under a wooden bench and then began kicking him with his heavy hobnail boots, letting the blows fall where they might. An NKVD officer watched this "game" for quite a long time before confiscating Andrzej's bag of food and throwing him out the door.

Finally, the train left for Alma-Ata, where our fate would be decided. There, after a head count, we were force-marched to the city. They kept speeding up the pace, beating those who couldn't keep up, especially the old Jews. They beat them on the head, on the back, with whatever was at hand. And that was how we ran the more than eight kilometers to the center of the city. I suppose that they had purposely chosen a roundabout way to exhaust us. We were taken to a rather large building where the NKVD was headquartered, and there, without allowing us to sit and refusing us water, they ordered us to wait. After a time, a bizarre and frightening figure appeared: a dry-looking man of average height with a dark, narrow face and exceptionally long hands, in one of which he held a type of whip. He was wearing a dark brown apron clearly marked with blood stains. Walking around us at a quick, decisive pace, he stopped in front of one man, then another, and ordered them to follow him. We were duly impressed by the theatrics.

So we were standing in silence by the wall when we heard the screams of a man being beaten. A moment later the man in the bloody apron appeared in the room again and, seeming very rushed as he looked us over, he walked up to me and ordered me to follow him.

He led me into a rather good-sized room in whose center was a chair and a simple table; there were a few chairs in one corner. Having ordered me to sit on the chair in the center, he left the room. I was alone, tense, expecting the worst. This phase did not last long, for the door opened a few minutes later and a young man with a likable face, wearing a somewhat overlong coat and a peaked cap, appeared in the doorway. Taking a chair from by the window, he sat down near me and, looking me over with evident friendliness, said calmly, "And so, citizen, will you accept the passport now?" I could detect concern in his voice. Having fully regained my self-control by then, I told him that I would not accept a Soviet passport. "That's a pity," he said. "I feel sorry for you. You're still a young woman, you have a child, and you'll be an old woman after a few years in a camp. Your son will be taken to an orphanage, and who knows if you'll ever see him again. I sincerely advise you to accept the passport."

"That's impossible," I answered with a smile, feeling for a second that this was a friendly, social conversation.

My nice NKVD man's expression was clearly one of distress when the door swung open and several other NKVD men, led by Colonel Omarkhadzhev, entered the room. They grabbed chairs from the wall and sat in a circle around me, asking what progress had been made with me. They reacted instantaneously to the answer, cursing, shouting, hovering over me, but the colonel ordered them to calm down and said aggressively, "All right, tell me why you don't want to accept a Soviet passport. What's so disgraceful about that?"

"The reason is simple," I answered. "I'm a Pole, a Polish citizen. And I'm certain that you'd do the same in an identical situation. None of you would accept Polish citizenship; that would be tantamount to betraying your country."

Evidently that answer caught them off guard, for they were silent for a fraction of a second. Finally one of them burst out: "What a smart one this is! Her husband must have taught her that, the instigator. But one way or the other you'll either accept the passport or die in a camp."

"Take her away!" Omarkhadzhev shouted to the guard, no longer looking at me. Relieved, I got up and left the room.

Reginka, a girl from our settlement, was standing in a side corridor downstairs, accompanied by a guard. She wasn't more than seventeen years old. The NKVD's conversation with her had gone rather smoothly. They had not expended much energy in their effort to change her mind, only telling her again that a refusal could mean two years in a camp.

We were now both being guarded by a boy in army uniform with a nice, still somewhat childish, face. He tried to maintain a serious expression, but no sooner were we outside, a short distance from the NKVD building, than he quickened his pace, saying in a lowered voice, "I'll take you through the market. You can buy something to eat there." Then, looking away from us, he added, "Oh, it's going to be bad for you there. It's bad in the prison they're taking you to." I was very moved by this and replied that, after all, there would be other women there too, and if they could take it, so could we. The boy shook his head and lapsed into a deep silence.

In the bazaar, looking around carefully in every direction, he told us to be quick about it. Our purchases were small, very modest: two hard-boiled eggs and a piece of black bread. Then we found out that we still had delousing and the baths ahead of us before being taken to jail.

When we arrived, a gloomy-looking man in a dark apron ordered Reginka and me to strip naked. What? There? In that little courtyard that led to the baths and where a few soldiers were standing around, having probably arrived with a transport of prisoners? The man in charge of us hurried us to undress. Our instinct for self-preservation now at a low, we began laying our clothes at one side of the courtyard. When we were almost naked, one of the soldiers suddenly took off his coat and used it to screen me, saying, "Now no one can see you." I could hear compassion and shame in his voice. Shame at even having to play that role.

The guard led us into the building where those "institutions" were housed. We entered a darkish room painted brown, where a gloomy-looking man in a gray and not overly clean smock was waiting for us, armed with a large pair of scissors. Without saying a word, he began to search our hair for lice with his efficient fingers. Our heads would be shaved if even one were found, and there was never any shortage of lice. Fortunately, we escaped his scissors and left there with the feeling that something valuable had been saved. Then in the baths, with their slippery stone floor covered with gray suds and the rising smell of sweat and bad soap, we had to submit to the routine and plunge into the murky water of the pool. From there we proceeded directly to the gates of the prison.

The prison was called the Third Section. With its dark underground cells, the Third Section was a sort of transfer prison where bandits, thieves, and prostitutes were held before being sent to the camps. The building was set in a typical nineteenth-century Russian merchant's property. An ample courtyard with a latrine for the prisoners, two-story wooden buildings built in tsarist times, all surrounded by a tall fence of thick planks topped with three rows of barbed wire.

From the large cobblestone courtyard we were taken into a long corridor that had a few doors in it. One of the doors opened, and in the threshold I saw the likable NKVD man who had tried with such concern to persuade me to accept the passport. He walked over to me, and I could hear the entreaty in his voice as he said, "Take the passport." I looked at him in surprise, sensing that it was not only concern for my future that had him anxious. I am sure that he was ashamed of everything that I had to see and experience there.

After the formalities and a body search, he accompanied us to the cell door with the prison guard and then made his request once again.

367

The cell door was opened, the jailer gave me a light push, and then immediately I heard the key grind in the lock. I was in a prison cell. I had read so much about it, my husband had told me so much about it, but still my heart sank when I heard the key grind in the lock for the first time.

Half sunk in darkness, the cell seemed large. Directly across from where I stood was a small barred window on sidewalk level. On the straw mats by the wall were women, spectral women in frozen motion. Heads shaved, haggard, in rags, deathly pale; scratching their shins with dry scabby hands, they stared greedily at us. I leaned against the cell door and looked at them, my fear mixed with pity. That moment couldn't have lasted very long. A few women, distinctly different from the rest, got up from their places under the barred window. They looked big, their heads weren't shaved, and they gave the impression of great strength. The ones by the wall remained motionless, not daring to approach us, while the others sprang nimbly to their feet all at the same time, motioning us to come closer and sit down in the center of the cell. Then one of them, probably the cell leader, snatched away the parcels of food we'd bought at the bazaar. Divided in a flash, the food was eaten with greedy haste, the women watching us out of the corners of their eyes and exchanging cynical remarks about us. Stimulated and excited by that extra meal, as if by signal they all began tearing at us, ripping our clothes off. Then, seeing that we were offering no resistance, they ordered us to strip naked. They pulled some reeking, filthy rags and rotted shoes from the corners of the cell and, chuckling, having a good time, as if playing a game of ball, they began throwing those rags at us, hurrying us to put them on. All this happened at lightning speed.

My husband had already told me of the customs that prevail in a cell among criminals. In every cell there are always a few, the strongest ones, those whose exploits had won them the highest rank, who rule the cell.

When we had our new clothes on and were sitting waiting to see what would happen next, one of them walked over to Reginka. "I know what's going on," she said in an authoritative voice. "So tell me if you're going to take the passport." Frightened, and with little grasp of what was happening, Reginka seemed to seek support in my eyes and then answered that she would not accept the passport. They all attacked her at once, beating her, kicking her in the head, the back, the chest. Reginka was tossed back and forth like a ball. Panting, excited, agile, they seemed to be playing with her, shouting to urge each other on.

I was sitting right beside her and I knew my turn was next. Seeking refuge in prayer, I was overcome with a strange feeling. Instantly, everything became unreal and my fear vanished. A wave of exaltation lifted me from that strange, dark world. I felt protected and gave myself entirely to that sense of confidence and peace. I did not notice when they stopped beating Reginka and I smiled automatically as the women bent over me, asking the now-familiar question. They argued whether to put me under the blanket (people beaten under the blanket cannot breathe or make a single gesture in their own defense), but one of them decided they would deal with me where I was.

I truly did not feel the first blows. It was only a hard kick in the ribs under my left breast that tore a cry of pain from me. The rib was fractured, making every breath and movement painful for a long time after. Then they took a break, beaming with satisfaction, as after a job well done.

In the corner, right by the door, was a very large bucket where the prisoners relieved themselves between their morning and evening trips to the latrine, cramped doorless stalls in the prison yard. Our tormentors stacked a mass of rotted, stinking shoes by the bucket and ordered us to sit on them and lean against the filth-spattered wall. Then, as in a ceremonial procession, they walked over, mounted the bucket, and with squeals of almost sensual pleasure, they relieved themselves in front of our faces.

Finally, they informed us that if we did not accept Soviet passports, we would be beaten again and that the beatings would become more and more painful. Then, on the way back to their mats, they kicked and shoved any of their other cell mates who happened to be within range, and for no other reason than that.

And so this was the method chosen to force us to accept Soviet passports.

The cell grew quiet except for someone weeping softly, helplessly, on one of the mats. Suddenly the silence was broken by the cries of men being beaten. Cries and shouts for help. I could hear fists pounding on a cell door. Someone shouted in a heartrending voice that they were murdering his son. I recognized the voice as that of old Kamer the shoemaker, and to my horror I realized that my husband was also in one of those cells. The cries and the pounding on the door grew more intense, racing through the corridors of the prison.

I don't know how long that had been going on, growing more and more intense, when suddenly I heard a key grinding a lock closed and, looking up, I saw the fearful faces of two Polish women from our settlement. They stood motionless by the door, paralyzed by what was happening around them. In a moment they too would be beaten. With a feeling of doom, I extended my arms to them, but not a single word was able to pass my lips.

As the women approached from their position under the window, one of them noticed my gesture, ran over to me, and struck me in the face. Then the two stunned, half-unconscious Polish women were pulled from the door and made to sit down in the middle of the cell. The ritual was reenacted in the same order and at the same pace. Robbed of their clothing, redressed in rags, beaten, they went and sat by the bucket on the side of the cell facing us. The other women were back in their places, examining their new clothing, clearly fully satisfied with those possessions.

The walls of the prison seemed to vibrate and tremble with waves of human suffering. We kept hearing the cries of women being beaten, the footsteps of newly arrived groups of men prisoners, guards running, yelling to speed up the prisoners, then a sudden dead, tension-filled silence. No, I couldn't take that for very long; I was nearing the limits of my endurance.

The cell door opened again, and again I saw two women from our settlement at the door: an old sick woman and her daughter, a frail girl who was forever worried about her mother. They looked at us, a question in their frightened eyes. In a short while the cruel ritual was reenacted once again. A night of terror. No one slept that night.

Then the cells began to quiet down a little; no doubt the torturers were tired by then. But still every once in a while a brief cry would ring out. Close to dawn there was the sound of men moving down the corridors, the crash of bodies smashing against walls, screams. Violated, paralyzed by terror, we did not dare to speak even in a whisper.

Then it started to grow light. Now, the exhausted women were safely curled in deep nests of sleep. But soon they woke up, almost all at the same time, stretching, yawning, mumbling still half asleep.

The guard came in and ordered us to line up. He counted us, checked his count, and led us out. The corridors were empty, silent. In the prison yard the women went to the doorless stalls, which gave us a chance to be with each other a little. So recently proud of our decision and our readiness to make sacrifice, we now saw each other crushed by humiliation and the knowledge of our helplessness. So should we accept the passports? Should we give in?

Then latrine time was over and we were herded back toward our cells, but the guard singled out the Poles, saying that we were to go to the doctor.

After the morning meal—sliced chunks of bread and a mug of fairly bitter grain coffee—we were taken from the cell and then went one by

370

one into a bright room whitewashed with lime. After the dark spectral cell, I was stunned and dazzled by the beauty of those white walls, the muslin curtains on windows full of sunlight and sky, potted plants on the window sill.

The doctor was a thin, gray-haired, older woman with a fine, delicate face that seemed sprinkled with ash. While giving me a very superficial examination, she suddenly asked in a whisper if I spoke French and, without waiting for me to answer, said a few words in that language, her smile a smile of memory. I don't remember what she said, but I can still feel that moment; I can still see her suddenly speaking a language of the free world, which brought the past back to her for a moment. She smiled timidly at me as she touched my fractured rib, and she became my secret ally and, in the trust she showed in me, a friend.

On the way back to the cell, one of the women said to the guard that we wanted to see the warden. The guard expressed no surprise, and soon we were in one of the side corridors. I saw a group of our people, men and women, standing in front of a closed door. Their heads lowered, marked terribly by their beatings, bloodied, wearing stinking rags and rotted shoes, they stood in silence and took turns entering the room where the person in charge was: that likable NKVD man. When my turn came and I went in, he rose slightly on seeing me. Writing out my Soviet passport on a slip of shoddy yellow paper, he said lowering his voice, "So, you see, citizen, I was right."

A group of our people were already outside when I went out. We waited for the rest, looking at each other with sorrow and despair. The women were so changed that the sight of them brought tears to some of the men's eyes.

Finally, our group was complete. There must have been about a hundred and twenty of us. Stumbling on aching legs, in stinking shoes that were not our own and most of which were much too large, we set out on the way back, no hope left to us now. In rags, we felt like rags. Soviet citizens!

My husband was not in our group. It was only on the way back that I was told by people who had been arrested with him that, as the instigator of the Poles' rebellion, he had been separated from the rest of the prisoners as soon as they arrived in Alma-Ata.

Back in Ili, I found Andrzej, who had stayed with people we knew. He didn't ask me any questions, all the details being known there already.

Life had to go on, existence without Aleksander.

In Ili there was a policeman who was relatively young and who carefully concealed his sympathy for Poles because of the dangers that could entail. Promising to reward him, I appealed to him to inquire among his colleagues in Alma-Ata as to Aleksander's whereabouts. Late one evening a few days later, he came to inform me that my husband was in the Second Section in Alma-Ata but would be transferred to the Third Section. He would let me know when that happened.

The Third Section! So I decided to go to Alma-Ata and try to obtain permission to see my husband. I traveled there at once the next day and, at NKVD headquarters, I requested a meeting with Omarkhadzhev, who was charge of Aleksander's case. To my surprise, my request for an audience was granted very quickly, and three days later I found myself in Omarkhadzhev's light and spacious office that was decorated with a large portrait of Stalin. He gestured to a chair and then began slowly pacing the room without saying a word. Large, with a dark complexion and slanting eyes, he was strikingly handsome in a predatory Kazakh sort of way. He had played cat and mouse with the Poles during the passport campaign in Ili; suddenly shifting from brutal attack to deep reverie, he would retreat into his thoughts and, vacant, his gaze would soften. At such moments, it could seem that he might free his victim at any second.

Suddenly he stopped in front of me and said, "Such an educated, intelligent person, a poet, a writer; he could be a professor, lecture at the university in Moscow, and live like a cultured person, not in poverty in Ili. Why is he resisting? Why did he incite the others to revolt? You have to talk sense to him. Let him take the passport and everything'll change right away; you'll go to Moscow. He still doesn't know that the Polish embassy was expelled from Kuibyshev and that he can't count on its help anymore. Those who did not accept the passport have been sentenced to two years in a camp, and that includes two women officials from the delegation in Alma-Ata. He should stop resisting and accept the passport, because that's the ruling of the Soviet authorities and the Union of Polish Patriots."

So he had been willing to see me so that I would pass all that on to my husband and attempt to change his mind.

The audience was over. He waited for my answer. Naturally, I agreed to everything to be able to see my husband. When saying good-bye, he added in a soft voice, "It would be a waste. A camp means certain death for him." He ordered me to come in a week and report to the small window downstairs, where I would be issued a pass and told where my husband was.

The policeman in Ili did not forget the promise he had made me. He had been in touch with his colleagues in Alma-Ata, and on the third day after my visit to Omarkhadzhev, he informed me that in two weeks Aleksander would be transferred from the Second Section to the Third. I decided to be outside the Second Section on the morning of that day to see him, if only at a distance. And so I did.

I waited in front of the prison gate, thick, sharp-pointed boards topped with three rows of barbed wire. There were quite large chinks between the boards, probably made by people like me wanting to see someone they loved, if only for a split second. I had been standing there rather a long time when I suddenly caught sight of some prisoners approaching. When they came to a stop, they were ordered to sit on the paved yard. Their names were checked against a list. I could see Aleksander at a relatively short distance from me. His head, like those of the rest of the prisoners, had been shaved and he looked strange to me. He was very pale, haggard; his eyes seemed larger. He sat looking straight ahead, lost in thought.

Much later, when he was free, he told me that in the Second Section the superstitious Kazakh prison guards were visibly afraid of him. One of them asked him outright if he were a sorcerer and asked him not to cast a spell on them, the guards, because they weren't to blame.

After a short while, the prisoners were lined up, the gate was opened, and, surrounded by guards, they began coming out. Aleksander saw me right away and smiled. His smile gave me courage, heart. His fellow prisoners had already told him what had happened in the Third Section, that Poles had been beaten. I tried to move closer to him and hand him a little bundle of food, but the guards drove me off with threats. Later, when I renewed my attempts, they threatened me with prison. And so I ran behind at a distance, trying just not to lose him from sight, all the way to the prison gate of the Third Section.

Two days later I was at the little window in the NKVD building. I was issued a pass for the meeting Omarkhadzhev had promised me, but it would not take place for five days. And so, five more days. That Aleksander was still in prison meant he had not accepted the passport.

On the day before the meeting I traveled to Alma-Ata in a train that was so packed you couldn't breathe. I arrived in the early morning. There were a few hours until I was to see Aleksander, and to pass the time, I went for a slow walk through the streets of that beautiful city. I walked to a single-story house covered with ivy, its shutters, with small hearts carved in them, closed against the sun, its old wide porch so hard to navigate in the winter when its slant was slippery. When Aleksander worked for the delegation, we had lived for a few months with Mrs. Kolgomorov, the nicest of women, who had been waiting for years for her husband to return from a camp. But I could not go see her. In the current situation, I could have exposed her to trouble.

The time for the visit was approaching and I went back to the prison gate. I was allowed in, and after the food package I had brought with me was checked, I was taken to a small gallery where there was a small yellow table and two wooden chairs. The gallery led out to the prison corridor; a door on the left opened to the guards' room. One of the guards standing in the doorway ordered me to sit down. About fifteen minutes later Aleksander was brought in.

We were allowed to go up to each other. He put his arms around me and said softly, "Don't worry. Nothing bad will happen to me here. Keep that a secret." The guard walked over and ordered us to sit down. Looking at each other, we were both aware that this would be a brief moment of happiness before we again faced the unknown.

Aleksander was even more haggard now. The skin on his face had gone gray, but there were no marks of beatings, abuse, torture. He radiated peace, goodness, affection.

He could not say more about what he had whispered to me; the guard was standing nearby and clearly listening in. Aleksander told me that Omarkhadzhev came to see him often, had not resorted to any brutality, and only peered at him, invariably asking whether he had decided to accept the passport yet, each time increasing the severity of the consequences a refusal would entail.

I told him about my visit to Omarkhadzhev and the temptations he had dangled before me. That was all—I asked no questions. Later, when he was free, Aleksander told me that on that day with him in prison, I had given him the greatest proof of love by not trying to persuade him of anything, by leaving him his freedom of choice.

After the Poles returned to Ili, life went on unchanged, full of poverty, illness, and hunger.

I was not able to learn anything further about my husband. All I knew was that he was still in the Third Section. I made renewed attempts to see him, but Omarkhadzhev would no longer see me or speak with me. Three months had passed since my husband was imprisoned.

And then one afternoon Aleksander appeared in the doorway of our mud hut. He had a heavy beard, his hair had grown back but had turned very gray, and his complexion had the sallowness typical of prisoners. He radiated peace and happiness at being back with us. Aleksander had not accepted a Soviet passport, and right there in the doorway he showed me his old ID card, marked with the seal of the London government, that had been returned to him before he left the Third Section.

Aleksander told me that one night when he was in Zamarstynów Prison in Lwów, he had dreamed he was being followed, tracked, that in a moment his pursuers would overtake him, seize him, arrest him, and put him in prison. A nightmare. And so when he woke in that prison cell, still cringing in fear, he had almost sighed with relief.

He had felt the same when crossing the threshold of the cell in the Third Section. He knew what was in store for him there, knew how savagely the other Poles had been beaten for refusing to accept a Soviet passport. And so, standing by the cell door that had been slammed shut behind him and looking around, he had no trouble in spotting his future torturers, who, at the sight of him, began lazily rising from their spot under the barred window. The cell was underground and darker than it was light. He saw three half-naked giants coming toward him.

As I've already mentioned, my husband's appearance was quite unusual at this time, but that was not only because of his ascetic appearance, his eyes blazing with rebellion, his shaved head. It is difficult to describe the aura around a person who has the sense of freedom that comes from being true to himself, who is determined both within himself and in his actions. This Aleksander had achieved. He was the "arrow and the target" (as he wrote in his poem "Japanese Archery") at one and the same time and, when crossing that threshold, must surely have sighed to God, asking that he bless both the arrow and the target.

Valentin, the leader of the cell, stood a short distance from Aleksander. A tall, strong, handsome man, he looked Aleksander over with the patience of a predator that knows it has time because its prey has nowhere to run. That expectant hush was broken by Aleksander's voice, sounding unfamiliar even to him. And so when he spoke his first sentence, when he asked in a severe tone of voice whether Valentin believed in God, he too was surprised by the question, so unexpected there. The others were surprised too, but it was Valentin who shouted violently, "Why did you ask me that?" And then in a powerful resolute voice Aleksander said everything that followed irrevocably from his initial question: "I know that you're supposed to beat me, beat me until I accept a Soviet passport. So, if you believe in God, please beat me efficiently and competently so I don't suffer too long, so it doesn't take too long. Because I won't accept a Soviet passport."

How is one to explain what happened next? Quiet until then, suddenly everyone in the cell began talking at once, turning toward Valentin as if awaiting his decision. But Valentin said nothing and, staring at

375

Aleksander, seemed to be fighting his way free of some reality of his own or some long-forgotten dream. Suddenly shouting, kicking, and brutally shoving anyone in his way, he headed for his place under the window, where he shouted in a voice that brooked no opposition, "Anyone who touches a hair on this man's head will have to deal with me. Is that clear?"

What wave of memories had Aleksander's words triggered? What had those unexpected words stirred in Valentin? What was he rebelling against, siding with Aleksander in that rebellion?

Aleksander sat down where Valentin indicated, near him and his comrades. The other prisoners, some twenty or so teenagers, including the son of the vice chairman of the City Committee and the only son of the regional party secretary, went back to their places along the walls. The great majority of them were petty thieves, with crude, often syphilis-pocked faces. Most of them were the products of orphanages.

No sooner had Aleksander settled in his place than Valentin began speaking in a voice quivering with restrained fury. "A Soviet passport!" he shouted. "A Soviet passport, that's us, that's this hole in the Third Section, prisoners, camps, fear. Fear and terror! That's a Soviet passport. It's hatred for those steel claws at our throats that makes us turn to crime." Saying that, he jumped up and began pacing the cell, then pounded the door with his fist, shouting with fury, "I'll escape from here! I'll escape even though we're freer in here than out there. We can do anything in here. We can shout, curse the people in power and the father of nations, because we've got nothing left to lose and so much to gain."

He only lived to escape, making one plan after another. He spoke of escape constantly all the while Aleksander was in that cell, stubbornly returning to that thought that gave him no peace. He told about escaping from a camp in the north when he had hidden in a hole in the ice of a river. Ice was stacked around the hole. For weeks half-dead with hunger, he had hidden in the forests, the mountains, the steppes. And invariably he would end his reminiscences with a resolve to escape again.

Valentin's comrades began joining in his monologue, and they too were seething with hatred. Each of them wanted to tell the story of his own life, each one's fate so much like the other's.

Aleksander listened intently and, sensing that in him they had a witness to their fate, they were roused to greater confidences until finally they broke off, weary and breathless. And it was then that they asked my husband to tell them about himself and the free world of which he was a part.

376

Aleksander spoke wonderfully to them. And there in that gloomy cell, surrounded by rebellious prisoners filled with hate though well inclined to him, he transported them from their prison walls out into the great world. For all the time he was there, sometimes late into the night, he would tell them plot summaries of books and films, recite poems from memory. As he told me later, they would beg him to tell them one such story a day. *The Red and the Black*, for example, won their admiration. And they especially liked the stories of O. Henry, of which my husband must have translated fifty and which were, he said, perfectly suited for prison. O. Henry had, after all, started writing them in prison.

Valentin—whose specialty was holding up freight trains and who, as he said, detested "wet work" [bloodshed]—and his comrades, most of whom were in the same line as he, read a great deal. They knew Gorky, Tolstoy, Dostoevsky. They could recite Pushkin's poems by heart, and in the evening they would sing to a mournful melody Esenin's beautiful poem "Letter to My Mother," which Aleksander taught me after he came home.

From the very first my husband was aware of the danger his situation posed. Beatings would have to be staged so that he was not transferred to another cell. Valentin understood this as well and with great reluctance the next day he and his group created a terrible clamor; his shouts "Take out the bucket, Polak!" echoed through the corridors, down which, along with another prisoner, Aleksander carried out the bucket, bent double, head down, giving every sign of pain and anguish. Late that afternoon Omarkhadzhev appeared and peered intently at Aleksander, obviously searching for traces of a beating, and then put the question to him again.

Omarkhadzhev would come at least three times a week, and it seemed to Aleksander that his behavior differed every time. He was always menacing and tense, however, attacking his obstinate prisoner with raging hatred. But at the same time, he had grown interested in this madman who pursued certain death instead of the honors and pleasures offered him.

Later we both reflected on the hidden motive in Omarkhadzhev's procrastination, his not sending Aleksander to a camp as he constantly threatened, his delaying any decision about him. Could one of the Polish writers who were then in Moscow and collaborating with the Union of Polish Patriots have been an influence here without my husband's knowing it? More or less at that time Ważyk, in tandem with Putrament and Wanda Wasilewska, was doing informal radio programs in Saratov. Or could the legend of *The Literary Monthly* have tipped the scales in this event?

Aleksander had been in prison three months when, receiving an unchanged refusal, Omarkhadzhev informed him that now he would irrevocably be sent to a camp, most likely on the following day.

Returning to the cell, Aleksander told Valentin of this meeting with Omarkhadzhev and the decision that had been made about him. He had to assume that this would be their last night together. Just in case, Valentin took our address in Ili, for his resolve to escape was unshakable, as was his certainty that he would succeed. In that event, he would come to me and tell me of my husband's fate.

The next day my husband was told to get his things. Genuinely moved and grateful, he said good-bye to his rescuer and friend, Valentin, and to Valentin's comrades as well.

In the warden's office, Aleksander asked if he could be allowed to write a few words to his wife. Barely concealing his smile, the warden handed him a paper to sign, and said, "Why write her? You'll be seeing her soon." Then he handed Aleksander his ID, a sheet of printed paper with the words "Republic of Poland" at the top, stamped with a round seal at the bottom that read "PR Embassy Delegation, Alma-Ata." A so-called London passport.

Everything returned to normal, meaning to hopelessness, a procession of gray and hungry days. And then one day Valentin appeared at our house.

I remember that Aleksander was sitting on the cot, leaning against the whitewashed wall, a pencil stub in his hand as he intently made notes in a school notebook with lined paper. When we heard a light knock, I opened the low door padded with flour sacks and saw before me a tall, broad-shouldered man with a powerful, well-proportioned head and a very expressive, almost handsome face. In an even voice he asked if Aleksander Wat lived there. Bending to pass under the low doorway, he entered and, seeing my husband, shouted his name with joy. Bewildered, as if suddenly wakened from sleep, Aleksander looked at him for a moment and then, jumping off the bed, he ran over and kissed Valentin on both cheeks, shouting, "It's Valentin, Valentin." Stirred, I ran over and took his hand with a feeling of immense gratitude. Andrzej stood to one side and watched, fascinated. It was the first time he had ever seen a real bandit, a convict sentenced to hard labor.

Valentin looked very elegant. He was wearing a dark blue suit and gleaming black shoes, and one arm, heavily bandaged, was in a sling. Aleksander gazed at him with unconcealed astonishment.

After the first emotion had subsided, Valentin looked around the hut and hooked the lock on the door, asking if we lived alone and if we were expecting any visitors. On the way through the marketplace, he had spoken with Poles who pointed out which earthen hut was ours. Not wishing to arouse any interest, he told them he was back from the front, wounded, and on leave to see his family; on the way he was visiting Aleksander Wat, whom he knew from Alma-Ata, where he used to chauffeur off and on for the Polish delegation.

Having assured himself that our place was safe, his own spirits raised by our joy and gratitude, Valentin began unwinding his unusually long bandages, which fell to the mud floor. Then suddenly money began falling from the bandages; the more he unwound, the more money fell out. We watched in silence, frightened, thrilled. Then, turning to Andrzej, Valentin said in the calmest voice in the world, "Pick up the bills and stack them nicely, boy."

Fatigued by emotion and this uncommon sight, Aleksander sat down on the cot and we both watched Valentin's arm emerge healthy and whole from the bandages.

"So, ma'am," he said, thrusting a thick handful of money at me, "go to market now and buy anything you want. We're hungry, aren't we?" Then he took off his gleaming new shoes, complaining that they pinched his feet. He couldn't buy them himself; "his woman" had done it for him. Calm and in a fine mood, he sat down by Aleksander on the cot and began telling the story of his escape.

The preparations for escaping from the Second Section had taken several weeks. Everything had to be thought through, every detail. During the evening walk on the day he had selected, he had jumped the nine-foot wooden prison fence with the help of his fellow prisoners, and, as he fled, cried "Stop, thief," to confuse the few passersby there were. He had an excellent sense of the prison's location and the surrounding area and so could set off at a fast run.

While the jailers were summoning the other guards to help, while they organized themselves to give chase, and while the rest of the prisoners were being shoved into their cells, several valuable minutes passed, which the powerful, agile Valentin put to good use, racing further and further away, heading for a nearby forest.

Darkness fell at just the right time for him. Hearing the pursuit party, the dogs barking, gunfire, cries, he pressed on, plunging deeper and deeper into the increasingly dense forest. Suddenly, he spotted railroad tracks on which, as if conjured there by magic, a freight train was chugging slowly along. Valentin hopped on and lay down at once on the platform. Six or seven miles later, he jumped off and ran to a copse, then to a forest, where he hid several days and nights, with nothing to eat but the chunk of bread he'd brought with him and forest berries.

Aleksander had already told me of Valentin's other escapes from prisons and camps. Valentin had escaped many times and under much more difficult conditions. For the most part, the Second Section in Alma-Ata was child's play in comparison with his other escapes. After all, that was only a transfer prison. It's difficult to imagine how he held out during those other escapes. He was a strong man and had often succeeded in escaping to freedom even though in that Soviet world, he felt, as he said, freest in prison.

And so he had given them the slip again! One night, feeling that he was beyond the reach of any search party, he left his hiding place and went to a town on the outskirts of Alma-Ata where his woman lived. Criminals, *urks*, have their own women wherever they go throughout the whole expanse of Soviet territory. Feeling safe with those women, they rest up with them and prepare for their next adventure. It was his woman who had bought him the suit, the shoes, the splint, the bandages, and the military decoration for his lapel. It would have been dangerous, however, to prolong that convenient situation. So he decided to take the plunge and acquire the funds he needed to carry out his plans.

The woman and her *urk* friends gathered the information he required and then late one night, rested, well-fed, and wearing his suit, Valentin climbed into the second-floor home of a high-ranking NKVD official (everyone knows they have the most money, he said), thoroughly familiar, of course, with the exact layout of the apartment. It was summertime. He entered through an open window and, he assured us, it went off without the need for a "wet work," which he disliked and would do only in the extreme. The important official slept soundly, and his family was away in their dacha. Valentin took his money, his gold watch, and, in addition—and this made him happy as a child—his party card, the loss of which can cause NKVD people great trouble, sometimes even expulsion from the party.

Now Valentin wanted to go to Semipalatinsk, where his sister lived, a nurse married to an NKVD man who had already fabricated papers for him several times. Valentin was very fond of them and the feeling was mutual. He spoke of his sister with genuine emotion, glad that he would be seeing her soon. With his fake papers he would attempt to reach the front and surrender to the Germans the first chance he got. Later on, he would like to reach Poland and begin a new life as an honest man there. But he might have to do a few break-ins there too, for how else could he get the money to open a restaurant and begin an honest life?

We had no hesitation about giving him the address of Aleksander's sister, Seweryna Broniszówna. Valentin had his own code of morality, and we knew that he would be no danger to Seweryna.

At that point in his story Valentin remembered that he was hungry and asked me to go to the market.

I took Andrzej with me. The wonderful prospect of eating our fill did not lull my vigilance. At the market you could buy pieces of very fatty mutton, corn, eggs, flour, and dark, gummy bread. It was all very expensive and I was rarely able to afford such delicacies. And so I began going from one Kazakh to another, buying negligible quantities from each, trying to keep them from noticing that I was buying the same things from others at a distance from them. My heart was pounding with anxiety, but also with joy at the feast awaiting us all. On the way back, I thought about the menu; never a good cook, I was worried that the dinner might not be a success.

When we came back, Valentin and Aleksander were still in a lively discussion on the cot. I set to work making a wonderful hasty soup out of mutton, garlic, and noodles in a black cast-iron pot. We were alone because the Kazakhs with whom we lived were out working in the corn fields.

After dinner we had real tea with sugar and bread smeared with salted mutton fat. We were full and very lively. Valentin kept asking for more details about Warsaw, city of his future liberation. Suddenly he decided to go out and walk through Ili, probably wanting a sense of its geography. We were left alone, full for the first time in so long, which lifted our spirits. We were also aware of the singularity and the gravity of Valentin's fate, part of which was being played out there with us.

After about an hour, worried about Valentin, Aleksander sent me out to reconnoiter. I found Valentin at the outskirts of our little settlement. He was lying on the ground in the shade of an anemic bush, his hands behind his head. He was asleep and his face was peaceful. But as soon as I came a little closer, he jumped up, ready to flee or fight. Seeing me, he smiled calmly and said, "It's so nice to sleep under the open sky." He shook the dust off his new clothes, and we went back to the house together.

The day was drawing to its end. The settlement was deserted, but soon people would be coming home from work. Valentin suggested that we sit outside. And so we sat by the wall of the mud hut, on the cracked earth near the fence and the haystack. It was quiet, the only sound the plaintive neigh of a donkey. The sky became rose-colored; a breeze lifted a small cloud of dust. The people we lived with returned and, after greeting us politely, disappeared into their part of the house. In that swiftly gathering dusk, we all felt how fragile Valentin's life and freedom were. And ours too. We knew that we would have to part with him soon and were frightened by the abyss of time and space that in a moment would swallow him and in which his life would move toward its culmination.

Valentin was becoming more and more watchful, listening intently, glancing toward the railroad tracks that were on a high embankment at a good distance from us. The famous Turksib line that joined Novosibirsk with Tashkent ran through Ili. From time to time he would bring his eyes to a stop on us, an almost tender look in them. None of us spoke.

Suddenly, without saying a word, he sprang to his feet. Not realizing what was happening, we watched him jump the fence and dash off toward the tracks. It was only then that we heard the regular beat of the chugging freight train's wheels. A moment later we caught sight of Valentin against a fading, now dark blue sky where the first stars were gleaming. He was standing straight and tall on the platform, big, defiant, free, and with the lit end of his cigarette he made a sign of farewell to us against the sky. Spellbound, we watched until the train and Valentin had disappeared into the golden streak of the horizon. We never saw him again.

NAMES MENTIONED IN THE TEXT

Akhmatova, Anna A. (1899–1966). Russian poet.

Anders, Władysław (1892–1970). General, leader of the Second Corps of the Polish Army in Italy that took Monte Cassino. Died an émigré.

Anusia. See Anna Mikulak.

Aragon, Louis (1897–1982). French communist poet and novelist.

Asch, Sholem (Polish spelling: Szalom Asz (1880–1957). Well-known Yiddish novelist and playwright.

Auezov, Muchtar (1897–1961). Kazakh writer and scholar.

Azef, Evno F. (1869–1918). Agent provocateur of the tsarist Okhrana (secret political police) in the combat wing of the Socialist-Revolutionary Party (SR).

Babel, Isaac E. (1894–1941). Russian short-story writer and playwright. Best known for *Red Cavalry* and *Tales of Odessa*.

Bahr. Department director in the pre-war Polish Ministry of Internal Affairs.

Bakunin, Mikhail A. (1814–1876). Russian revolutionary, anarchist.

Balicki, Juliusz Ignacy (1911–1941). Actor and director.

Balicki, Stanisław Witold (b. 1909). Director, State Publishing Institute (PIW) in Poland.

Balmont, Konstantin D. (1867–1942). Russian Symbolist-Decadent poet. Tremendously popular before the Revolution.

Balzac, Honoré de (1799–1850). French writer.

Barbey d'Aurevilly, Jules Amédée (1808–1889). French writer and critic.

Barbusse, Henri (1873–1935). French writer; editor of *L'Humanité*. Extremely popular novelist. Joined Communist party in 1923. Died in Moscow.

Barcikowski, Wacław (b. 1887). Lawyer; held high state position in Polish People's Republic.

Barthou, Jean Louis (1862–1934). French politician, premier.

Bataille, Henry Felix (1872–1922). French playwright and poet.

Baudelaire, Charles (1821–1867). French poet.

Beck, Józef (1894–1944). Colonel, minister of foreign affairs in pre-war Poland. Major political figure. Died in Rumania.

Beckett, Samuel (b. 1906). Irish novelist, playwright, poet. Writes in French. Nobel Prize for literature, 1969.

Bedny, Demyan (orig. Yefim Pridvorov) (1883–1945). Russian poet.

Benedict, Ruth (1887–1948). American anthropologist and sociologist.

Berdyaev, Nikolay A. (1874–1948). Important figure in Russian philosophy. In Paris as an émigré after 1922.

Bergson, Henri (1859–1941). French philosopher. Nobel Prize for literature, 1927.

Beria, Lavrenty Pavlovich (1899–1953). Soviet minister of internal affairs, head of the secret police. Removed from office and executed after death of Stalin.

Berman, Jakub (1901–1984). Polish communist. Vice-premier of Polish People's Republic, removed from party in 1957.

Bierut, Bolesław (1892–1956). President of People's Poland, later premier and first secretary of Central Committee.

Blok, Alexander A. (1880–1921). Greatest Russian symbolist poet. His masterpiece "The Twelve" (1920) depicts Christ leading twelve Red Guards during the Revolution.

Bobrzyński, Michał (1849–1935). Polish historian and politician.

Boethius (ca. 475–525). Roman philosopher and statesman.

Bogatko, Marian (1906–1940). Bricklayer. Wanda Wasilewska's second husband.

Bolshakov, Ivan G. (b. 1902). Head of Soviet cinema.

Bondy, François (b. 1915). Swiss journalist and writer, former editor of *Preuves* (Paris).

Borejsza, Jerzy (1905–1952). Polish publicist, communist.

Borowski, Tadeusz (1922–1951). Poet and short-story writer. Author of *This Way for the Gas, Ladies and Gentlemen.*

Boy Żeleński, Tadeusz (1874–1941). Polish drama and literary critic, essayist, translator. Founder of famous Zielony Balonik (Little Green Balloon) cabaret in Kraków. Executed by Germans in Lwów.

Breiter, Emil (1886–1943). Polish lawyer and literary critic.

Brodsky, Joseph A. (b. 1940). Russian poet.

Broniewski, Władysław (Władzio, Władek) (1897–1962). Polish poet. Joined Piłsudski's Legions in 1915 and fought in Polish-Soviet war in 1919–1920; decorated for bravery. Author of revolutionary and patriotic poems. "Bagnet na broń" ("Fix Bayonets"), written 1939 during German invasion, widely known. (Milosz describes his poetry as "virile and concise.") Later, he wrote an ode to Stalin and was proclaimed "national poet."

Broniszówna, Seweryna (b. 1891). Actress. Aleksander Wat's sister.

Brucz, Stanisław (b. 1899). Polish journalist and translator.

Bryusov, Valery Y. (1873–1924). Russian poet, prose writer, literary critic. Important figure in Symbolist movement.

Buczkowski-Ruth, Marian (b. 1910). Polish writer.

Bukharin, Nikolai I. (1888–1938). Bolshevik theoretician and political figure. Leader of Comintern. Victim of Stalin's purges.

Buridan, Jean (ca. 1300–1358). French philosopher and physicist.

Capek, Karel (1890–1938). Czech novelist, playwright. Coined the word "robot" in his play *R.U.R.* (1921).

Cerctelli, Irakly (1882–1959). Georgian Social Democrat and Menshevik leader.

Chaliapin, Fyodor (1873–1938). Russian operatic basso.

Chekhov, Anton P. (1860–1904). Russian short-story writer and playwright.

Chernyshevsky, Nikolai G. (1828–1889). Russian revolutionary, novelist, and philosopher. His novel *What Is To Be Done* had great influence on Russian social thought and Soviet leaders.

Churchill, Sir Winston Leonard Spencer (1874–1965). British statesman, prime minister during World War II.

Chwat, Berek (d. 1863). Aleksander Wat's grand-uncle; perished in the January Uprising (the Polish rebellion against Russia in 1863).

Chwat, Ewa (1894–1931). Aleksander Wat's sister.

Chwat, Izrael. Wonder-working rabbi from Kozienice.

Chwat, Mendel Michał (1866–1939). Aleksander Wat's father.

Chwat, Rozalia (née Kronsilber) (1869–1939). Aleksander Wat's mother.

Clausewitz, Karl von (1780–1831). Prussian general, writer, and military theoretician.

Cygielstreich. Interpreter in the Polish delegation in Alma-Ata.

Czachowski, Kazimierz (1890–1948). Polish historian of literature and literary critic.

Czapiński, Kazimierz (1882–1942). Active in PPS, member of parliament. Perished in Auschwitz.

Dan, Aleksander. Writer from Lwów.

Daszewski, Władysław (Władek) (1902–1971). Polish painter, set designer.

de Broglie, Louis-Victor de (b. 1892). French physicist, Nobel laureate.

Deutscher, Isaac (1907–1967). Polish writer and historian; active in socialist movement.

Dirac, Paul Adrien (b. 1902). English physicist, professor, Nobel laureate.

Dix, Otto (1891–1969). German painter and graphic artist.

Dostoevsky, Fyodor M. (1821–1881). Russian writer.

Dovzhenko, Oleksandr (1894–1956). Ukrainian film director and painter.

Drobut. A worker. Wat's fellow prisoner in Zamarstynów.

Drohojowski, Count Jan. Polish diplomat.

Drzewiecki, Henryk (orig. H. Rosenbaum) (1901–1937). Polish literary critic and writer. Victim of Stalin's purges.

Dubin. Wat's fellow prisoner in Saratov.

Dunayevsky, Evgeny Y. Writer, linguist. Wat's fellow prisoner in Lubyanka.

Dzierżyński, Feliks (1877–1926). Pole; member of SDKPiL and Bolsheviks. Head of the Cheka.

Ehrenburg, Ilya G. (1891–1967). Russian novelist and journalist; talented writer. Apologist for Stalin; his novel *The Thaw* gave the name to the period following Stalin's death.

Eichmann, Adolf (1906–1962). Nazi war criminal.

Eisenstein, Sergei M. (1898–1948). Russian film director whose films include *Ivan the Terrible* (Parts I and II) and *Alexander Nevsky.*

Eluard, Paul (orig. Eugène Grindel) (1895–1952). French poet, associated with dadaism and surrealism. In Resistance during World War II; later identified with communists.

Engels, Friedrich (1820–1895). German philosopher. Active in the international socialist movement; collaborated with Karl Marx.

Epictetus (ca. 50–130). Roman philosopher.

Erlich, Henryk (1882–1942). Polish lawyer, leader of Bund. Put to death in Soviet Russia.

Erlich, Mieczysław Sławek (1901–1946). Polish communist.

Esenin, Sergei A. (1895–1925). Russian poet who remains extremely popular. Married to Isadora Duncan. Committed suicide.

Ezhov, Nikolai I. (1901–1938). Chief of the Soviet political police. Victim of Stalin's purges.

Feffer, Izak S. (1900–1952). Soviet Jewish writer, victim of Stalin's purges.

Feyerman. Russian author of children's books.

Fischer (or Schultz). Wat's fellow prisoner in Zamarstynów.

Flammarion, Camille (1842–1925). French astronomer.

Fumet, Stanislas (b. 1896). French Catholic essayist.

Gacki, Stefan Kordian. Polish poet, editor.

Gałczyński, Konstanty Ildefons (1905–1953). Popular Polish poet who mixed wild fantasy with accessible language.

Gary, Romain (orig. R. Kacer) (1914–1980). French writer; author of *The Roots of Heaven.*

Gebethner and Wolff. Book publishing company in Warsaw where Wat worked. Founded in 1857.

Gebethner, Jan. Co-founder of Gebethner and Wolff. Member of parliament.

Gebethner, Wacław (Wacek). Co-owner of Gebethner and Wolff.

Genet, Jean (1910–1986). French novelist and playwright. Author of *The Thief's Journal, Our Lady of the Flowers, The Blacks, The Balcony.*

Genghis Khan (1162–1227).

Genia. The Wats's maid.

Giedroyc, Jerzy (b. 1906). Polish editor of the influential émigré journal *Kultura*, published in Paris.

Giergielewicz, Mieczysław (b. 1901). Historian of literature; professor at the University of Pennsylvania.

Gobineau, Count Joseph de (1816–1882). French writer; theoretician of racism.

Goering, Hermann (1893–1946). Nazi leader; marshal of the German air force.

Goetel, Ferdynand (1890–1960). Polish writer. His novels won international acclaim in the twenties and thirties. In 1939, he came out in favor of Nazism and fascism.

Gogol, Nikolai V. (1809–1852). Russian novelist, playwright, short-story writer. Author of *Dead Souls, The Inspector General.*

Gold, Henry (1899–1977). Polish musician. Died an émigré.

Golikov, Filip I. (1900–1976). Russian general; marshal of the Soviet Union.

Gombrowicz, Witold (1905–1969). A leading twentieth-century Polish playwright and novelist. Author of *Ferdydurke, Pornografia, Cosmos.*

Gomułka, Władysław (1905–1982). Polish Communist political figure. First secretary, Central Committee.

Goncourt (brothers), Edmond de (1822–1896), and Jules de (1830–1870). French writers and diarists.

Gorky, Maxim (orig. Alexei Peshkov) (1868–1936). Important Russian novelist and playwright. Author of *My Universities, The Lower Depths.*

Górska, Halina (1898–1942). Polish writer. Killed by Germans.

Greene, Graham (b. 1904). English writer.

Grossman, Gregory (b. 1921). Professor of economics, University of California, Berkeley.

Grosz, George (1893–1959). German painter and graphic artist.

Grubiński, Wacław (1883–1973). Polish writer. Died in London.

Guicciardini, Francesco (1483–1540). Italian diplomat, political figure, and historian.

Hegel, Georg Wilhelm Friedrich (1770–1831). German philosopher.

Heine, Heinrich (1797–1856). German poet.

Hempel, Jan (1877–1937). Polish communist. Journalist. Victim of Stalin's purges.

Henry, O. (orig. William Sydney Porter) (1862–1910). American short-story writer.

Hertz, Paweł (b. 1918). Polish poet and essayist.

Herzen, Aleksandr I. (1812–1870). Russian thinker, writer, and revolutionary. Author of multivolume memoir, *My Past and Thought.*

Hindenburg, Paul von (1847–1934). German field marshal; president of German Reich (1925–1934).

Hölderlin, Friedrich (1770–1843). German poet.

Ibarruri, Dolores (known as La Pasionaria) (b. 1895). Spanish communist.

Jadwiga, Queen (1370–1399). Queen of Poland 1384–1399.

Januszajtis, Żegota Marian (1889–1973). Polish general. Member of Piłsudski's Legions.

—The general's brother. Wat's fellow prisoner in Lubyanka.

Jasieński, Bruno (1901–1939). Polish poet and novelist. Like Wat, he switched from futurism to communism. Lived in Moscow, a member of Soviet Writers' Union executive committee. Wrote one of first Socialist realist novels, *Man Changes His Skin* (1932). Died on way to a camp in Kolyma.

Jasiński, Roman (Romek) (b. 1900). Polish pianist and music critic.

Kaganowski, Efraim (1893–1958). Polish writer.

Kamenev, Lev. B (orig. L. B. Rosenfeld) (1883–1936). Bolshevik, diplomat, journalist. Victim of Stalin's purges.

Kaplan, Fania (d. 1918). Russian Socialist-revolutionary who made an attempt on Lenin's life.

Kasman, Leon (b. 1905). Polish communist. Editor of *Trybuna Ludu.* Member of parliament in Polish People's Republic.

Kiesewatter. Author of a book on Homer.

Kireevsky, Ivan V. (1806–1856). Russian journalist and literary critic, advocate of Slavophilism.

Kirsanov, Semyon I. (1906–1971). Russian poet. Influenced by Mayakovsky.

Khlebnikov, Velemir (1885–1922). Russian futurist poet.

Kleber, Kurt (1897–1959). German communist. Writer, editor of *Linkskurve.*

Kleist, Heinrich (1777–1811). German writer.

Kłopotowski. Governor-general in Alma-Ata.

Kmiciński. Wat's fellow prisoner in Zamarstynów.

Koestler, Arthur (1905–1983). English writer of Hungarian birth. Author of *Darkness at Noon.*

Kołakowski, Leszek (b. 1927). Polish historian of philosophy, philosopher, writer. Now an émigré in England.

Kolgomorov, Yuri. Friend of Andrzej Wat's in Alma-Ata.

Kolgomorov Family. Wats lived with them in Alma-Ata.

Konarzewski, Daniel (1871–1935). Polish general; vice-minister of defense.

Korneichuk, Oleksandr (1905–1972). Ukrainian playwright; socialist-realist. Member of Central Committee, third husband of Wanda Wasilewska.

Korsak, Władysław (1890–1949). Pre-war Polish vice-minister of internal affairs. Died an émigré.

Korzycki, Antoni (b. 1904). Pole; vice-premier in Józef Cyrankiewicz's government.

Kotarbiński, Tadeusz (b. 1886). Polish philosopher, logician.

Krahelska, Halina (1892–1945). Polish writer and journalist. Perished in Ravensbrück.

Kruczkowski, Leon (1900–1962). Polish novelist and playwright. Deputy minister of culture and chairman of Writers' Union in Polish People's Republic.

Krygier, Alfred (1887–1956). Member Polish Socialist party (PPS).

Kwiatkowski, Mieczysław (1889–1943). Polish communist.

Lagerlöf, Selma (1858–1940). Swedish novelist. Nobel Prize, 1909.

Langner, Władysław (1896–1972). General in the Polish army. Died an émigré.

Lec, Stanisław Jerzy (1909–1966). Polish poet and satirist. Two collections of his brilliant aphorisms, *Unkempt Thoughts* and *New Unkempt Thoughts,* have been translated into English.

Leibniz, Gottfried Wilhelm (1646–1716). German philosopher and mathematician.

Lenc-Lenczowski. Wat's fellow prisoner in Zamarstynów.

Leontiev, Konstantin N. (1831–1891). Russian novelist and conservative philosopher. Author of *The Egyptian Dove.*

Leszczyński, Julian (pseud. Leński) (1899–1939). Polish journalist; communist. Victim of Stalin's purges.

Lewin, Leopold (b. 1910). Polish poet; communist.

Lewis, Matthew Gregory (1775–1818). English poet and writer.

Liebknecht, Karl (1871–1919). German socialist; later, the founder of

German Communist party; leader of Spartacus uprising.

Lipper, Elinor (b. 1912). Swiss communist; author of the book *Eleven Years in Soviet Prison Camps* (London, 1951).

Lisiewicz, Captain. In Polish delegation in Alma-Ata.

Loria (Luria). A priest and canon in Vienna.

Loria (Luria), Isaac (1534–1572). Jewish mystic, Cabalist.

Loria (Luria), Stanisław (1883–1958). Polish physicist, professor.

Losky, Nikolai O. (1870–1965). Russian philosopher.

Ludwig, Emil (1881–1948). German writer.

Lunacharsky, Anatoly V. (1875–1933). Russian Marxist politician, critic, esthetician, dramatist. Commissar of education (1917–1929).

Luxemburg, Rosa (Polish spelling: Roza Luksemburg) (1871–1919). Polish-born founder of SDKPiL; theorist and activist in the Polish, German, and international workers' movement; co-founder of the German Communist party.

Machajski, Jan Wacław (1867–1926). Activist, theoretician of the Polish and Russian workers' movement.

Mackiewicz, Józef (1902–1985). Polish émigré writer.

Majteles. Wat's fellow prisoner in Zamarstynów.

Makarenko, Anton S. (1888–1939). Soviet pedagogue and writer.

Malinovsky, Roman V. (1876–1918). Russian; member of Duma (parliament), Bolshevik, provocateur, agent of the Okhrana (tsarist secret political police).

Malinowski, Bronisław (1884–1942). Polish-born anthropologist; author of *The Sexual Life of Savages*.

Mandelstam, Osip E. (1891–1938). Eminent twentieth-century Russian poet. Victim of Stalin terror.

Marinetti, Filippo Tommaso (1876–1944). Italian poet, founder and theoretician of futurism. Author of *First Futurist Manifesto* (1909).

Marr, Nikolai I. (1864–1934). Soviet linguist.

Marshak, Samuil Y. (1887–1964). Russian children's writer and translator.

Mayakovsky, Vladimir V. (1893–1930). Russian poet and playwright. An important twentieth-century figure, he was active in the Social-Democrat movement when young and served time in prison. Avant-garde poet who tried to serve the Revolution in his poetry. Author of plays *The Bedbug* and *The Bath-House*. Poems include "A Cloud in Trousers," "Vladimir Ilyich Lenin," "Brooklyn Bridge."

Meller. Warehouseman at the Polish delegation in Alma-Ata.

Merezhkovsky, Dmitri S. (1866–1941). Russian novelist, poet, religious and social thinker. Initiator of symbolist movement in Russia.

Meyerhold, Vsevolod E. (1874–1940). Russian actor and director. Victim of Stalin terror.

Michałowicz, Mieczysław (1876–1965). Polish doctor; member of Democratic party.

Michałowski, Czesław (1885–1939). Polish minister of justice. Murdered by NKVD.

Mickiewicz, Adam (1798–1855). Polish poet. His position as Poland's greatest poet and national bard is unchallenged, and *Pan Tadeusz*, his long novel in verse, is the national poem of Poland.

Miedziński, Bogusław (1891–1972). Polish colonel, journalist, member of parliament.

Mikhoels, Solomon M. (1890–1948). Russian actor, creator of Jewish State Theater in Moscow. Victim of Stalin's terror.

Mikulak, Anna (Anusia). Aleksander Wat's childhood nurse.

Miller, Jan Nepomucen (1890–1977). Polish literary critic.

Miller, Romuald (1882–1945). Polish architect.

Mirbeau, Octave (1850–1917). French playwright, novelist. Author of *Torture Garden* (published in English, 1899).

Młodożeniec, Stanisław (1895–1959). Polish poet.

Morand, Paul (1888–1976). French novelist and diplomat.

Morozov, Pavel (Pavlik) (1918–1932). Russian country boy who denounced his own father during collectivization. The father was executed and Morozov held up as an example to Soviet youth.

Nagler, Herminia (1890–1957). Polish prose writer. Wife of Leon Nagler. Died an émigré.

Nagler, Leon. Polish colonel. Deputy commander, State Police. Perished during Soviet occupation.

Nekrasov, Nikolai A. (1821–1878). A leading Russian poet in the second half of the nineteenth century. Best known for his descriptions of the hardships of peasant life.

Nicholas I (1796–1855). Russian tsar.

Nikolaev. Investigator at Lubyanka.

Novalis (orig. Baron Friedrich Leopold von Hardenberg) (1772–1801). German poet and prose writer.

Nowogródzki, Mojzesz (1903–?). Polish communist. Perished during German occupation.

Olesha, Yuri K. (1899–1960). Russian novelist, short-story writer and dramatist. Author of satirical novel *Envy* (1927).

Omarkhadzhev. NKVD colonel, investigator in Alma-Ata.

Ordzhonikidze, Grigory K. (1886–1937). Georgian Bolshevik; held high state position in the USSR.

Origen (185?–254?). Greek church father and theological writer.

Orlova, Vera M. (b. 1918). Russian actress.

Ossietzky, Karl von (1889–1938). German pacificist and journalist, editor of *Die Weltbühne*. Nobel Peace Prize.

Ovseenko-Antonov, Vladimir A. (1884–1938). Soviet ambassador in prewar Warsaw.

Panch, Petro (orig. Panchenko), (b. 1891). Ukrainian writer.

Parandowski, Jan (1895–1978). Polish novelist, essayist, translator. President of Polish PEN after 1933. Professor of classics at the university in Lublin.

Parnicki, Teodor (b. 1908). Polish novelist.

Pascal, Blaise (1623–1662). French mathematician and philosopher.

Pasternak, Boris L. (1890–1960). Russian poet and prose writer. Author of *Doctor Zhivago*. Nobel Prize, 1958.

Pasternak, Leon (1910–1969). Polish communist; poet, prose writer.

Paulus, Friedrich (1890–1957). German field marshal.

Paustovsky, Konstantin G. (1892–1968). Russian novelist, playwright. Best known in English for his multivolume autobiography *The Story of a Life*.

—His wife, Tatyana Alekseevna, née Valishevsky.

Pavlenko, Piotr A. (1899–1951). Russian writer.

Pavlov, Ivan P. (1849–1936). Russian physiologist. Nobel Prize.

Peiper, Tadeusz (1894–1969). Polish poet. Founder of the Kraków Vanguard, editor of *Zwrotnica* (*The Switch*).

Petersburski, Jerzy (b. 1895). Polish musician.

Piątek. A beadle's son. Wat's fellow prisoner in Zamarstynów.

Pieracki, Bronisław (1895–1934). Polish colonel; minister of internal affairs. Assassinated by Ukrainian nationalists.

Piertsov, Victor O. (b. 1898). Russian literary critic.

Pilnyak, Boris A. (orig. Vogau) (1894–1941). Russian novelist and short-story writer. Author of *The Naked Year* (1921), one of the better novels on the Russian Revolution, and *O.K.* (1933), describing his trip to America. Victim of Stalin's terror.

Piłsudska, Aleksandra (1882–1973). Second wife of Józef Piłsudski. Died an émigré.

Piłsudski, Józef Klemens (1867–1935). Born in Lithuania. Most important political figure in Poland between the wars. Fought for Polish independence and led victorious Polish army against Soviets in Polish-Soviet war of 1919–1920. Hero of the Battle of Warsaw. Twice ruler of Poland after Poland regained independence in 1918.

Piscator, Erwin (1893–1966). German director of plays.

Plekhanov, Georgy V. (1856–1918). Russian theoretician of Marxism; active in the Russian Social-Democrat movement.

Pogorzelski. Commissioner of state police in Warsaw.

Poincaré, Raymond (1860–1934). French political figure, minister, premier, president of the French Republic (1913–1920).

Polak, Doctor. From Łódź. In Alma-Ata.

Polewka, Adam (1903–1956). Polish communist, writer, journalist.

Priacel, Stefan (1904–1974). French journalist and writer of Polish origin.

Prus, Bolesław (orig. Aleksander Głowacki) (1847–1912). Important Polish novelist. Author of *The Doll*.

Prystor, Aleksander Błażej (1874–1941). Polish minister, premier. Perished in Soviet Russia.

Przyboś, Julian (1901–1970). Polish poet and essayist. Member of Kraków Vanguard.

Pugachev, Emelyan I. (ca. 1726–1775). Don Cossack; leader of peasant revolt.

Purman, Leon (1892–1933). Polish communist. Committed suicide in Moscow.

Purman. Leon's brother. A Trotskyite; later a member of PPS. Perished in a Soviet camp.

Pushkin, Alexander S. (1799–1837). Russian poet, playwright, novelist. He remains preeminent among Russian poets.

Putrament, Jerzy (1910–1986). Polish communist, writer, journalist.

Radek, Karol (orig. Sobelson) (1885–1939). Polish journalist and publicist. Active in the Polish, German, and Russian workers' movement; member of Comintern. Victim of Stalin's purges.

Rashi, Solomon ben Isaac of Troyes (1040–1105). Rabbi, renowned commentator on Bible and Talmud.

Reisner, Larisa M. (1897–1928). Russian writer, journalist, Bolshevik.

Remarque, Erich Maria (orig. Paul Remark) (1898–1970). German writer, author of *All Quiet on the Western Front*. Stripped of German citizenship in 1938, emigrated to United States in 1939.

Retinger, Józef Hieronim (pseud.: Jusuf) (1888–1960). Polish publicist and politician. Died an émigré.

Rilke, Rainer Maria (1875–1926). German poet.

Róg. A lawyer; Wat's fellow prisoner in Zamarstynów.

Rogoż, Stanisław (Staszek) (1898–1942). Polish literary critic; editor, *Tygodnik Ilustrowany* (*Illustrated Weekly*) in Warsaw.

Rolland, Romain (1866–1944). French novelist and playwright. Nobel Prize, 1915.

Rozanov, Vasily V. (1856–1919). Russian philosopher, essayist, critic. Author of *Solitaria* and *Fallen Leaves* (aphorisms) and *Dostoevsky and the Legend of the Grand Inquisitor*.

Rozenholtz, Arkady P. (1889–1938). Russian economist; Soviet commissar of foreign trade. Victim of Stalin's purges.

Rudnicki, Adolf (b. 1912). Polish novelist, short-story writer. Since World War II has devoted his work to the tragedy of the Jews.

Rzymowski, Wincenty (1883–1950). Polish journalist, translator. Minister of foreign affairs in Polish People's Republic.

Saint-Exupéry, Antoine de (1900–1944). French writer and aviator. Author of *Le Petit Prince*.

Saltykov-Shchedrin, Mikhail Y. (1826–1889). Russian satirical novelist and short-story writer.

Sapieha, Prince Eustachy (1881–1963). Polish minister of foreign affairs; member of parliament from Nonparty Bloc. Served in Polish Delegation in Alma-Ata. Died an émigré.

Sarniecki, Doctor. Delegate in the Polish embassy in the USSR.

Savinkov, Boris V. (1879–1924). Russian. Leader of the SR (Socialist-Revolutionary) party. Organized antitsarist terrorism. Lured back to USSR, where he was either killed or committed suicide.

Savonarola, Girolamo (1452–1498). Italian Dominican, preacher, religious-political reformer.

Schiller, Friedrich (1759–1805). German poet and playwright.

Schiller, Leon (orig. Leon Jerzy S. de Schildenfeld) (1887–1954). Leading Polish stage director.

Schopenhauer, Arthur (1788–1860). German philosopher.

Schwarc, Marek (1892–1958). Polish painter, sculptor.

Seifullin, Lidia N. (1889–1954). Russian writer.

Sempołowska, Stefania (1870–1944). Polish social activist and publicist.

Seneca (ca. 4 B.C.–A.D. 65). Roman philosopher and poet.

Shchedrin, N. See Saltykov-Shchedrin.

Shklovsky, Victor B. (1893–1984). Russian writer and literary critic.

Shnaider, Mikhail Y. Russian writer, screenwriter.

Shnaider, Tatyana A. Former Russian actress. Wife of Mikhail Shnaider; later married to Paustovsky.

Shostakovich, Dmitri D. (1906–1977). Russian composer.

Shub, Esfir I. (b. 1894). Russian film director.

Sienkiewicz, Henryk (1846–1916). Polish novelist and short-story writer. His historical novels—especially the trilogy *With Fire and Sword*, *The Deluge*, and *Pan Wołodyjowski*—are known by all Poles. Also author of *Quo Vadis?* Noble Prize, 1905.

Silone, Ignazio (orig. Secondo Tranquilli) (1900–1978). Italian novelist and social critic.

Sinyavsky, Andrei D. (pseudonym: Abram Tertz) (b. 1925). Russian novelist, short-story writer, literary critic, and historian. Author of *On Socialist Realism* and *The Trial Begins*. Key figure in the thaw. Now living in Paris.

Skuza, Wojciech (1908–1942). Polish poet and journalist. Perished in Soviet Russia.

Słonecki, Colonel. Wat's fellow prisoner in Zamarstynów.

Słonimski, Antoni (1895–1976). Polish poet, essayist, novelist, playwright. In Skamander group. Liberal humanist; important figure in Polish culture.

Słowacki, Juliusz (1809–1849). Major Polish Romantic poet.

Solovyov, Vladimir S. (1853–1900). Russian philosopher and poet.

Solzhenitsyn, Aleksandr I. (b. 1918). Russian writer. Nobel Prize, 1970. Forcibly exiled from USSR.

Spengler, Oswald (1880–1936). German philosopher. Author of *The Decline of the West.*

Stande, Stanisław Ryszard (1897–1939). Polish poet. Communist; victim of Stalin's purges.

Stanisław. Chauffeur at the Polish Consulate. Wat's fellow prisoner in Lubyanka.

Stawar, Andrzej (orig. Edward Janus) (1900–1961). Polish critic, journalist. Communist theoretician and activist.

Stefanowski, Antoni. Polish doctor.

Steklov, Yuri M. (orig. O. M. Nahamkes) (1873–1941). Russian Bolshevik; editor-in-chief of *Izvestiya.* Victim of Stalin's purges.

Stern, Anatol (1899–1968). Polish futurist poet.

Stirner, Max (orig. Kaspar Schmidt) (1806–1856). German philosopher.

Stróżecka, Golde Estera (1872–1938). Member of PPS; later, a communist.

Strug, Andrzej (orig. Tadeusz Gałecki) (1871–1937). Polish writer. Member of PPS; senator.

Struve, Gleb P. (1898–1985). Russian-born professor of Russian literature at University of California, Berkeley.

Stryjkowski, Julian (b. 1905). Polish novelist and short-story writer, specializing in Jewish themes.

Szemplińska, Elżbieta (b. 1919). Polish poet, communist.

—Her husband, Zygmunt Sobolewski.

Szenwald, Lucjan (1909–1944). Polish poet; in Polish communist army.

Taitz, Misha. Russian. Wat's fellow prisoner in Lubyanka.

Tarsis, Valery Y. (1907–1983). Russian émigré writer. Author of *Ward Number Seven.*

Tertz, Abram. See Sinyavsky, Andrei D.

Thomas à Kempis, Saint. (1380–1471). Catholic theologian; author of *The Imitation of Christ.*

Thorez, Maurice (1900–1964). French communist leader.

Togliatti, Palmiro (1893–1964). Italian communist leader and ideologue.

Tolstoy, Alexei N. (1883–1945). Russian novelist, playwright.

Tolstoy, Lev N. (1828–1910). Russian writer.

Tomsky, Mikhail P. (1880–1936). Russian Bolshevik; trade union leader. Victim of Stalin's purges.

Topf. A manufacturer from Erfurt.

Tretyakov, Sergei M. (1892–1939). Russian dramatist.

Trotsky, Leon D. (orig. Lev Bronstein) (1879–1940). One of the leaders of the Bolshevik Revolution, organizer of Red Army. Exiled from Russia. Writer, historian. He was assassinated in Mexico by a Soviet agent.

Tsvetaeva, Marina (1892–1941). Major twentieth-century Russian poet.

—Her husband, Efros.

—Her daughter, Anya.

—Her son.

Tucholsky, Kurt (1890–1935). German writer and publicist; editor of *Weltbühne*.

Tudor, Stepan (orig. Oleksyuk) (1892–1941). Ukrainian writer, editor.

Turek, Wiktor. A doctor in Alma-Ata.

Tuwim, Julian (1894–1953). One of the leading twentieth-century Polish poets, co-founder of Skamander.

Tychyna, Pavlo (1891–1967). Ukrainian poet.

Ulbricht, Walter (1893–1973). German communist. Vice-premier; later, chairman, State Council, East Germany.

Valentin. Russian bandit; Wat's fellow prisoner in Alma-Ata.

Vanya. Soviet sailor. Wat's fellow prisoner in Lubyanka.

Vettori, Francesco (1474–1539). Florentine historian and politician.

Vigilev, Boris D. (1883–1924). Russian Bolshevik.

Vogel, Debora. Jewish writer in Lwów.

Voznesensky, Andrei A. (b. 1933). Russian poet.

Wandurski, Witold (1891–1937). Polish poet and playwright. Communist. Victim of Stalin's purges.

Warski, Adolf (orig. Warszawski). Polish publicist. One of the leaders of the Communist party of Poland (KPP); member of parliament. Victim of Stalin's purges.

—His wife, Jadwiga (née Chrzanowski).

Wasilewska, Wanda (1905–1964). Polish writer. Later, Soviet political activist.

Wat, Andrzej. Aleksander Wat's son.

Wat, Ola (Paulina). Aleksander Wat's wife.

Ważyk, Adam (1905–1982). Polish poet and prose writer. His "Poem for Adults" important in post-Stalin thaw. Spent war in Soviet

Union and returned to Poland as officer in Polish Communist Army.

Weil, Simone (1909–1943). French philosopher and writer.

Wesely. Bookkeeper in the Polish delegation in Alma-Ata.

Wiącek (Więcek), Kazimierz. Polish government delegate in Alma-Ata.

Wieniawa-Długoszowski, Bolesław (1881–1942). Polish general, Marshal Piłsudski's adjutant. Polish ambassador to Rome. Died an émigré.

Wierzyński, Kazimierz (1894–1969). Polish poet in Skamander. Later, an émigré. His *Life and Death of Chopin* was published in the United States in 1949, a best-seller.

Wilde, Oscar (1854–1900). English writer.

Witkiewicz, Stanisław Ignacy (known as Witkacy) (1885–1939). Polish novelist, playwright, philosopher, painter. Key figure in twentieth-century Polish culture. He accompanied Malinowski to New Guinea and Australia. His novel *Insatiability* is available in English, as are some of his plays. He committed suicide when Soviets invaded Poland in September 1939.

Wittlin, Józef (1896–1976). Polish poet and prose writer.

Wodzińska, Maria (1819–1897). Polish pianist.

Wolff, Friedrich (1888–1953). German playwright.

Wolski, Jan (orig. Feldman). Polish doctor. Delegate of Polish government in Alma-Ata.

—His wife, Wacława.

Wygodzki, Stanisław (b. 1907). Polish poet and prose writer. Member of Communist party of Poland (KPP).

Wyspiański, Stanisław (1869–1907). Polish playwright, poet, painter. Leading figure of Young Poland movement.

Wyszyński, Stefan (1901–1980). Cardinal, archbishop, Primate of Poland.

Yagoda, Genrikh G. (1891–1938). Chief of the Soviet political police. Victim of Stalin's purges.

Yenukidze, Abel S. (1877–1937). Bolshevik; collaborated closely with Stalin. Victim of Stalin's purges.

—His daughter.

Yevtushenko, Evgeny A. (b. 1933). Russian poet.

Zabłudowski, Tadeusz. Polish communist.

Zahorska, Anna (pseudonym: Savitri) (1882–1942). Polish writer. Perished in Auschwitz.

Zahorska, Stefania (1889–1961). Polish art historian, writer.

Zarembina Szelburg, Ewa (1899–1986). Polish writer.

—Her husband, Józef.

Zarembińska (Zarębińska), Maria (d. 1947). Polish actress. Władysław

Broniewski's second wife.

Żarski, Tadeusz (1896–1934). Polish communist. Victim of Stalin's purges.

Zatorski. A Polish writer.

Żeleński, Tadeusz. See Boy.

Żeromski, Stefan (1864–1925). Polish novelist and short-story writer. He was called the "conscience of Polish literature." An outstanding figure of his time, still much read.

Zieliński, Gustaw (1809–1881). Polish poet.

Zinoviev, Grigory Y. (orig. Apfelbaum) (1883–1936). Russian Bolshevik; chairman of Comintern. Victim of Stalin's purges.

Zoshchenko, Mikhail M. (1895–1958). Well-known Russian humorist. In 1946, he was attacked along with Anna Akhmatova and expelled from Writers' Union. Gradually rehabilitated after Stalin's death.

INDEX

Akhmatova, Anna A., 200
Alekseevna, Tatyana, 351
Alexander the Great, 347
All That Is Most Important (Ola Wat),
 xxix
Alma-Ata: departure from, 356; food
 shortages in, 330; friends in, 324–327,
 329–330; influx of goods into, 345; in-
 terrogation in, 349, 353; journey to,
 310–313; literary world in, 332,
 351–352; prison in, 142, 182, 202,
 367–378; return to, 338–340; Rus-
 sians in, 345, 354
Ancestry, xvi
Anders, Władysław, 188, 191, 219, 236
Anti-Semitism, 86, 89–90; Polish charac-
 ter and, 235; of Stalin, 202, 344–345
Anusia. *See* Mikulak, Anna
Aragon, Louis, 20, 26
Aristotle, 347
Arrest(s): in Lwów, 97, 117–125; in Rus-
 sia, 91; in Warsaw, 60–65, 70, 118–
 122
Asch, Sholem, 57–58
Auezov, Muchtar, 322
Augustine, Saint, 13, 203, 209, 234
Auschwitz, xvi, 15, 240
Azef, Evno F., 6

Babel, Isaac E., 8, 279, 332–333
Bach, Johann Sebastian, 238, 239–241,
 242
Bahr, Councillor, 90
"Bakunin" (Broniewski), 35
Bakunin, Mikhail A., 35
Balicki, Juliusz Ignacy, 119
Belicki, Stanisław Witwold, 119
Balmont, Konstantin D., 23
Balzac, Honoré de, 223
Barbey d'Aurevilly, Jules Amedee, 15
Barbusse, Henri, xxv, 18
Barcikowski, Wacław, 88
Barthou, Jean Louis, 140
Bataille, Henry Felix, 287
Baudelaire, Charles, 206
Beck, Józef, 18

Bedny, Demyan, 106
Beckett, Samuel, 200
Before the Sunrise (Zoshchenko), 325
Benedict, Ruth, 147
Berdyaev, Nikolay, 211, 325
Bereza Kartuska concentration camp, 96
Bergholc, Stefan (pseud. for A. Wat), xix
Beria, Lavrenty Pavlovich, 259, 260
Berkeley, Calif., suffering in, 243
Berlin, decadence in, 29–30, 32
Berman, Jakub, 80, 257
Bielski, Count, 124
Bierut, Bolesław, 36, 59
Blok, Alexander A., 23, 45, 46, 200
Bobrzyński, Michał, 222
Boethius, 209
Bogatko, Marian, 108–109
Bolshakov, Ivan G., 352
Bolshevik(s): first encounter with, 43; old
 guard, 17; socialization of, 148
Bondy, François, 71
Boot in the Buttonhole (Jasieński), 7
Borejsza, Jerzy, 63, 88, 99, 112, 115, 196,
 224
Borowski, Tadeusz, 47
Boy Żeleński, Tadeusz, 225
Brecht, Bertolt, 20
Breiter, Emil, 19
Brodsky, Joseph, 199, 200
Broniewski, Władysław, xv, 26; alco-
 holism of, 14; in army, 345; arrest in
 Lwów, 119–120, 122; contact with
 Ola Wat, 318; as hero, 159–161; liber-
 alism of, 50; *Literary Monthly* and,
 19; in Lwów, 110; *New Culture (Nowa
 Kultura)* and, 6–7; patriotism of, 49;
 in prison, 67–68, 248, 276; prison re-
 union with Wat, 265–269; release of,
 305; standing as communist, 85–86;
 Wasilewska and, 109
Broniszówna, Seweryna, xvi, 381
Brucz, Stanisław, 6, 30
Brygidki Prison, 122
Bryusov, Valery Y., 23
Buczkowski-Ruth, Marian, 61
Bukharin, Nikolai I., 37, 73–74, 253

399

mination and, 69. *See also* Communism; Leninism; Stalinism
Matryona's House (Solzhenitsyn), 173, 199
Mayakovsky, Vladimir V., xi, xvii, 5–8, 23–25, 44–47, 56, 109, 163, 280, 317, 328; friendship with, 44–46; influence of, 23–25, 280; obituary, 56
Mediterranean Poems (Wat), xvii, xxiv
Me from One Side and Me from the Other Side of My Pug Iron Stove (Wat), xvii, 12, 24, 93, 98, 148
Meller, 331, 349
Merezhkovsky, Dmitri S., 23
Meyerhold, Vsevolod, 28
Michałowicz, Mieczysław, 88
Michałowski, Czesław, 22, 62, 76
Mickiewicz, Adam, 2, 11, 26, 141, 184, 202
Miedziński, Bogusław, 63
Mikhoels, Solomon, 344
Mikulak, Anna, xvi, 95, 116, 290, 294
Miller, Jan Nepomucen, 48, 88
Miller, Romuald, 88
Milosz, Czeslaw: on the Bauhaus, 25; on friendship with Wat, xix; on *Lucifer Unemployed*, 20; on Polish defeat, 123; on Red Army, 108; on Wat's illness, xix, xxi
Mirbeau, Octave, 182
Młodożeniec, Stanisław, xviii
Mokotów Prison, 76, 79–80
Molotov-Ribbentrop Pact, 96
Molotovobad, 331, 335
Mongolia, 114–115
Monk, The (Lewis), 182
Morand, Paul, 8
Morozov, Pavlik, 171
Moscow trials, 91–92
Mosfilm, 322
"My Soviet Passport" (Mayakovsky), 44
My Universities (Gorky), 145

Nagler, Herminia, 113
Nagler, Leon, 79
Nahamkes, O. M. *See* Steklov, Yuri
Naked Year (Pilnyak), 22
Napoleon Bonaparte, 205
National Assembly of the Western Ukraine, elections to, 105–106
National Democratic Party (ND), 90
Nationalist-Radical Camp (ONR), 53
Nazism, 4, 17, 85, 225–226, 292, 304
Nekrasov, Nikolai A., 189
New Economic Policy (NEP), 37
New LEF, 25

Nicholas I, 202
Nietzsche, Friedrich, 4, 5, 207
Nikolaev, 221, 223, 224, 225, 227, 233–234, 251
NKVD (Narodnyi Komissariat Vnutrennikh Del), xxix, 8, 31, 88, 101, 103, 104, 114–115, 120, 125, 145, 221; distribution network and, 188; interrogation by, 63, 353; Jews in, 201; passportization campaign and, 361–363; Soviet constitution and, 180; summons from, 349
Notre-Dame des Fleurs (Genet), 275
Novalis, 43
Nowa Kultura (New Culture), xix, 6
Nowogródzki, Mojzesz, 60, 65, 68–69, 79

Olesha, Yuri K., 333
Omarkhadzhev, Colonel, 114, 182, 300, 354, 363, 366, 372, 373, 374, 377
Omsk Central Prison, 251
One Day in the Life of Ivan Denisovich (Solzhenitsyn), 173
Oprichniks, 104
Order of Lenin, 180
Ordzhonikidze, Grigory K., 297
Origen, 238
Orlova, Vera M., 351
Orlovsky Central Prison, 251
Ossietzky, Karl von, 30
Ovseenko-Antonov, Vladimir A., 47

Panch, Petro (orig. Panchenko), 101, 107, 110, 111
Pan Tadeusz (Mickiewicz), 2
Paragraph, 58, 181, 258
Parandowski, Jan, 338
Parnicki, Teodor, 353
Pascal, Blaise, 22, 228
Passportization campaign, 361–378
Pasternak, Boris L., 40, 59, 195, 200, 253, 304, 323, 327
Pasternak, Leon, 118–119, 122
Paustovsky, Konstantin G., xix, 147, 280, 319, 320, 327, 331, 351, 352, 354
Pavlenko, Piotr A., 326–327
Pavlov, Ivan P., 148, 231
Pedagogical Poem (Makarenko), 170
Peiper, Tadeusz, 10, 118, 119, 270, 272, 284; arrest in Lwów, 122; in Lubyanka, 248; paranoia of, 276; reunion with, 265, 266
PEN Club, 115
People's Poland, 115, 338; dandyism in, 81; party hatred and, 194. *See also* Poland